Experimenting in Society

Issues and Examples
In Applied Social Psychology

John W. Reich
Arizona State University

Scott, Foresman and Company
Glenview, Illinois
Dallas, Texas
Oakland, New Jersey
Palo Alto, California
Tucker, Georgia
London, England

To My Father and Mother

Library of Congress Cataloging in Publication Data
Reich, John W., 1937-
    Experimenting in society.

    Includes bibliographies and index.
    1. Social psychology—Addresses, essays, lectures.
I. Title.
HM251.R424   302   81-5813
ISBN 0-673-15457-2   AACR2

ISBN 0-673-15457-2

1 2 3 4 5 6 - KPF - 86 85 84 83 82 81

Preface

Since their beginning, both social psychology and the broader science of psychology itself have had an enduring concern with the amelioration of individual and social problems. Psychology is a helping profession. Indeed, one statement in the charter of the parent national organization for psychologists, the American Psychological Association (APA), declares: "The purpose of the APA is to advance psychology as a science, as a profession, and as a means of promoting human welfare." The line between using a science to promote human welfare and the advocacy of certain social conditions is a thin one. But throughout the history of the field emphasis has been put on scientific analysis as a precondition. I believe the interest in experimenting in society represents a new conviction among psychologists in general and social psychologists in particular that their science is finally going to develop a strong connection between its pure science aspects and its concern with actual societal processes. Increasingly, psychologists are being called on to apply their scientific expertise to important social developments. This book is intended to communicate both the social psychological frame of mind, *per se,* and the power and range of its applications to ongoing social events.

Experimenting in Society is divided into two main sections. The first part is an introductory discursive review of the general nature of experimentation—the scientific approach applied to social life in naturally occurring settings; this includes coverage of some of the technical and ethical issues involved in experimenting in society. This part is followed by a series of actual research articles chosen to be representative of some of the central topics which have contributed to this new movement.

All research articles in this text are original rather than secondary. While this may necessitate slower and more careful reading, I have found that when students learn the purpose, method, and results of a given study, they tend to grasp the fundamental concepts of the research more thoroughly and retain them more effectively than when they read a secondary survey textbook treatment. Also, perhaps it is time for social scientists to begin training undergraduates in research techniques as physical scientists do.

A note on the criteria used for selection of the research articles: Perhaps the greatest achievement of social psychology has been the refinement of the principles of experimentation and the application of those principles to social behavior in natural contexts. The majority of articles presented here reflect that tradition. Further selectivity was exercised in order to create a text appropriate for undergraduates. Those articles with complicated methodology, data analysis or interpretation, or theoretical abstraction were excluded, along with those not focused on one of the four major topic areas of the book. Because this book is intended to introduce students to the possibilities of social experimentation, I sought nodal examples of the clearest and most succint form. The science of social psychology is sufficiently sophisticated such that teachers should feel comfortable training undergraduates in the fundamental skills that form the foundation of the approach. I chose the research examples to highlight that foundation.

This book is intended to be the center of any course concerned with experimenting in society. As such, it is appropriate for the following types of courses: (1) standard introductory social psychology courses; (2) courses in applied social psychology; and (3) undergraduate or graduate courses in research methodology.

Teaching and researching in psychology is a source of continuing stimulation and pleasure. To have the partnership of good students and colleagues doubles the satisfaction. I am particularly grateful to my social psychology colleagues, Drs. Sanford Braver, Robert Cialdini, Nancy Eisenberg-Berg, and Darwin Linder for their continuing intellectual and personal companionship. Ms. Sally Carney, our graduate training program secretary, deserves very special thanks for always keeping our efforts moving smoothly and efficiently. I'd also like to thank Dr. John P. Keating at the University of Washington, and Dr. Steven J. Sherman of Indiana University, for their comments and suggestions.

John W. Reich
Arizona State University

Contents

1

Introduction

The world of contemporary events has grown so complex, so dynamic and so unpredictable that it often seems as if the good old days of quiet and stability have receded permanently and will not return. People appear to be confused and unhappy with the way things are going. Although it is not at all clear that the actual events of those past days would be considered so pleasant now were they actually to return, the desire for a more stable, predictable, and orderly world is common and very understandable. It is hard to know why life has become so complex, but it does seem clear that one thing which might be contributing to our confusion is the lack of a fundamental understanding of the basic mechanisms of social arrangements, the processes whereby people group together, interact, and maintain a social order. Presumably there is some set of principles which, if fully understood, would reveal the operations of society and make them less confusing, and perhaps more controllable.

The science of psychology, particularly social psychology, has been concerned with analyzing scientifically human cognitive, emotional, and social processes for some time now. Recent developments have made it possible to gain better understanding of some of the social problems that plague us such as crime, pollution, and energy waste. Social action programs to solve those problems are themselves being analyzed scientifically (Cook & Campbell, 1979; Varela, 1971; Weick, 1969). A surprisingly powerful set of theories, methods, and facts about behavior has been developed from this new type of social science. While no one would claim more than modest success for these endeavors so far, it does appear that social psychologists and other social scientists may be on the right track, and that future generations of students can be encouraged to continue the pursuit. What can be called "social experimentation" or "experimenting in society" is now possible, and the prospects for the future are exciting indeed. *Experimenting in Society* is based on those developments.

There seems little question that in the historical developments leading up to this time, there was a tendency for psychologists to investigate questions of social behavior within the confines of rigidly controlled laboratory settings (Hendrick, 1977). Perhaps because of the prestige and power of physical scientists who are impressively successful at analysis and understanding of physical phenomena, psychologists have tended to concentrate their efforts at defining and characterizing social behavior and its effects in such ways as to make them amenable to analysis in the highly controlled (and hence "unnatural") world of the research laboratory.

A number of criticisms have been launched against the domination of the uses of laboratory settings for analyzing human behavior, particularly social behavior (Bickman & Henchy, 1972; McGuire, 1973; Ring, 1967). It is beyond our purview to consider those criticisms here. Perhaps the simplest way to refer to them would be to say that they concern the necessary falsification or distortion of naturally occurring, ongoing behavior in order to obtain laboratory purity, and the difficulty, if not impossibility, of adequately analyzing the myriad of simultaneously operating factors that go into the causation of even the simplest human behaviors (Deutsch, 1975; McGuire, 1973; Sherif, 1977).

The limitations of the strict laboratory approach have long been acknowledged within the fields of psychology and social psychology. In response, there is currently considerable pressure for the science to approach social phenomena in ways that retain their characteristics as naturally occurring phenomena (Helmreich, 1975). The goal of this new movement is to develop the ability to move back and forth between the laboratory and the real world and to understand the fundamentals of social behavior from both perspectives as much as possible. It is a difficult and elusive goal, perhaps more honored in name than in actuality, but it clearly is coming to be a major concern of contemporary social psychology. This book is intended to capture the essence of the trend by exploring its characteristics, its scientific and ethical implications, and then presenting a wide range of examples of such research as it is occurring.

It is only fairly recently in human history that people have come to apply the scientific approach to human behavior. The subsequent development that followed was to apply scientific principles to human *social* behavior, and it is this aspect of the evolution of social psychological research that is of concern here. Historically and in its current form, the growth of this science has ranged across many facets of human behavior and has been defined with many different rubrics. *Experimenting in Society* avoids committing itself to any one label, but it necessarily includes the issues and research studies in the fields of inquiry typically labeled *applied social psychology, field research,* and *action research,* and the more recent development called *evaluation research.*

The relationships among these areas have not yet been accurately represented in single texts or courses. The purpose of this book is to present some examples of the various ways of thinking and research methods involved in experimenting in society, and thus will help to give this area of interaction definition and shape. *Experimenting in Society* does not focus on any particular theory nor on any particular scientific method, but instead covers a large number of different topics and provides a sampling of the surprisingly wide range of activities which the new approach has made possible.

The book assembles research which to date has been available only in various and scattered sources. By having the research topics presented in one book and organized into cognate areas, the reader can obtain both an overview and an indepth acquaintance with social experimentation in its current form.

It has become apparent that this new approach to social psychology has developed along four parallel but interrelated tracks, some already well developed, some very new indeed. Each is discussed in some detail later, but the sections are listed here to demonstrate the range of topics which are covered.

I.   Analysis of the Individual (Chapter 6)
II. Analysis of Groups and Social Processes (Chapter 7)
III. Analysis of Social Problems (Chapter 8)
IV. Program Evaluation and Evaluation Research (Chapter 9)

Each of these areas has its own historical development and tradition of research concerns and methods; indeed, each topic very easily could be presented in a textbook-length work. However, there is a common thread or theme running through a substantial part of each of the sections, and it is this theme that is the concern of *Experimenting in Society:* The use of the scientific method to analyze social behavior in order to illuminate individual and social processes within the context of the natural environment outside of the controlled world of the research laboratory. To some extent, this area of interaction between science and society is a nebulous one, partly because the topic is so new. At the same time, there has been a continuing interest in such science since the formative years of social psychology, so the current development, nebulous as it may be, does have a clear historical development (Reich, 1981). We now can see the structure and orientation of this new approach well enough to be able to communicate it in a reasonably clear form. That is the purpose of this book. The opening chapters introduce the topic, present some detailed discussion of several examples, discuss the general structure of scientific experimenting in society, and then present a teaching aid in the form of how to read an actual experimental research report. This section is then followed by the actual research articles which have been chosen to represent the science. These articles cover both the more historically important studies, those which were original or initiating studies, as well as very recent studies demonstrating the current state of the art. Also, the studies vary from relatively traditional areas of social psychology up to the cutting edge of the newer developments in program evaluation and evaluation research. At this point it appears that the latter represents the direction of future developments in the science; the purpose of including evaluation research here is to insure that upcoming generations of students are aware of this form which will be a part of future social experimentation.

References

Bickman, L., & Henchy, T. Introduction: In L. Bickman & T. Henchy (Eds.), *Beyond the laboratory: Field research in social psychology.* New York: McGraw-Hill, 1972.
Cook, T. D., & Campbell, D. T. *Quasi-experimentation: Design and analysis issues for field settings.* Chicago: Rand McNally, 1979.

Deutsch, M. Introduction. In M. Deutsch & H. A. Hornstein (Eds.), *Applying social psychology: Implications for research, practice, and training.* Hillsdale, N.J.: Erlbaum, 1975.

Helmreich, R. Applied social psychology: The unfulfilled promise. *Personality and Social Psychology Bulletin,* 1975, *1,* 548-60.

Hendrick, C. Social psychology as an experimental science. In C. Hendrick, (Ed.), *Perspectives in social psychology.* Hillsdale, N.J.: Erlbaum, 1977.

McGuire, W.G. Some impending reorientations in social psychology: Some thoughts provoked by Kenneth Ring. *Journal of Experimental Social Psychology,* 1967, *3,* 124-39.

McGuire, W.G. The Yin and Yang of progress in social psychology: Seven koan. *Journal of Personality and Social Psychology,* 1973, *26,* 446-56.

Reich, J. W. An historical analysis of applied social psychology. In L. Bickman (Ed.), *Applied Social Psychology Annual.* Vol. 2. Beverly Hills, Calif.: Sage, 1981.

Ring, K. Experimental social psychology: Some sober questions about frivolous values. *Journal of Experimental Social Psychology,* 1967, *3,* 113-23.

Sherif, M. Crisis in social psychology: Some remarks towards breaking through the crisis. *Personality and Social Psychology Bulletin,* 1977, *3,* 368-82.

Varela, J. *Psychological solutions to social problems.* New York: Academic Press, 1971.

Weick, K. E. Social psychology in an era of social change. *American Psychologist,* 1969, *24,* 990-8.

2

Some Examples of Experimenting in Society

INTRODUCTION

You are the generation of students now enrolled in American universities who will be in middle age when the twenty-first century begins. All of you will be faced with problems and issues that cannot even be conceptualized now. No one today can train you specifically to know what to expect, yet you will be called upon by society to analyze those problems and issues and to make decisions about how to deal with them. The problem faced by teachers of today is how to prepare you to make optimum decisions for both your own benefit and the benefit of society.

One would hope that the facts, ideas, concepts, and theories scientists have developed concerning human behavior will be of some use in meeting the problems of that century. Unfortunately, the likelihood appears slim, given the rapidity with which new ideas and our understanding of them become outmoded as other concepts replace and alter them. It is possible, and it has been argued, that science does not progress as a continuous linear adding-up of one fact upon top of previous facts, but that it is a revolutionary process in which old facts and their related conceptualizations are overturned and give way to entirely new views (Kuhn, 1970). So it is not certain by any means that any facts or theories we develop now will be of much use in the next century.

One thing that does appear to endure and to have utility across time, however, is the pattern of thought and the way of approaching and analyzing issues known as science. While the problems which engage people may change, history shows us that certain fundamental ways of approaching those issues can be passed on; that way of behaving involves a number of steps which will be described here in some detail.

One way to investigate a question is to use the scientific method. Science is basically a way of thinking about things. It relies on close and sensitive observation, careful analysis of the elements of the observed phenomenon, and creative construction of ideas (hypotheses) about the essential elements of what is occurring in the phenomenon. Of course this is a very human activity, and is similar to the activities of artists, novelists, and poets. However, science takes an additional step beyond those followed by these other activities. It tests the validity of its own explanations by making additional observations. Assumptions and even facts are constantly tested by additional research.

This is the part of science that most people think of when they see someone in a white labcoat manipulating conditions and observing the impact of those manipulations. It is a dramatic picture. Looking over the history of human development, it appears that such manipulating has had a profound impact on the human race. Some argue that the impact has been positive, and some argue that it has been negative. But all would agree that the activity has become an integral part of human life and will continue to be so.

From the point of view of this book, it is the method or structure of the scientific approach that is the most powerful tool of contemporary social psychology that can be passed along to future generations. We will investigate this method with examples of scientific experimentation. By seeing firsthand how scientists approach phenomena involved in social behavior, you can learn not only the facts about social behavior that were generated by the studies, and which may or may not be of some use in the future, but also you can learn how the investigators viewed the phenomena of interest, how they analyzed them into their component parts, and how they determined how those parts are influenced by other events.

Basic Definitions

To match the aims of *Experimenting in Society* with the actual research of social psychology requires that some important conceptual distinctions be made. *Social psychology* has been defined as ". . . the scientific study of the experience and behavior of individuals in relation to social stimulus situations" (Sherif & Sherif, 1956, p. 4). As such it uniquely operates in the area representing the overlap of individual psychology and sociocultural variables, and combines the analytic and methodological strengths of sciences operating at both levels. We use the term *experimental social psychology* to distinguish the methodology used in this science from other techniques. Manipulation of variables, or analysis of situations where variables are changed naturally, is one of the hallmarks of the science of experimental social psychology, and has become a major aspect of the contemporary discipline.

The word "applied" is sometimes used to characterize the particular focus of social psychology as it has developed more recently. The term has a number of uses, but here it is used to mean broadened and deepened scientific understanding of social phenomena through analysis of them in real world, natural settings. The term can be distinguished from that of *action research* (Lewin, 1946) in which the aim is to directly alter conditions to resolve a social problem. Also, it can be distinguished from the term *field research,* which refers fairly specifically to research methodology used in this area and which is to be distinguished from strictly laboratory-based research; field research is experimentation and assessment performed in nonlaboratory settings (Campbell & Stanley, 1963; Cook & Campbell, 1979).

All of these involve research typical of experimentation in society, and no hard-and-fast distinctions will be drawn in this book. No single definition of social experimentation seems to be necessary, representing as it does a wide range of interests, approaches, and techniques, all of which are proving to be of value in helping people to understand what modern society is like and suggesting ways in which it might be improved.

THE NATURE OF EXPERIMENTING IN SOCIETY

It will help clarify things later on if we now go through some fairly extended treatment of several typical examples of experimental social psychological research. Two studies have been chosen: One deals with attitudes and cognitive processes (and thus involve what are called in this book *intraindividual process* variables) and the other deals with interpersonal variables in a helping context.

You will be going through the examples as if you actually were a participant (subject) in the studies. Do not be concerned so much with learning the actual results of the experiments or the techniques of data analysis used in them; just try to see the underlying patterns of logic and the conceptual analysis followed by the investigators to design, conduct, and interpret the experiments. The patterns can be generalized, are applicable in many types of situations, and should help you get used to seeing how researchers approach their subject of experimenting in society.

Attitude Processes

Imagine for a moment that the time is 1974 and that you are a suburban resident, a middle-class homeowner who has fairly typical attitudes about taxes, family, society, etc. You live in Pennsylvania, a state with no income tax; most homeowners oppose such a tax, but there is a movement to institute one, a movement you oppose. The country is in the last phases of the Vietnam war, and the social tensions that were rampant at the time still have lingering effects: Middle-class people such as yourself are upset and many blame hippies for being the cause of much of the trouble the country has faced.

You receive a telephone call. The caller states that he is representing a research institute and would like to send a worker to your house to discuss with you the issues of a state sales tax and a state income tax. Your opinion is then directly asked. You indicate that you are opposed to the income tax proposition. You then agree to the interview, and let someone come to your house to discuss it. In effect you have committed yourself publicly to a particular stand on the issue and to discuss it.

Soon your doorbell rings and a person, apparently a college student, is on your doorstep. Believe it or not, this person is a real mess: A hippie, army-jacketed, bearded, unwashed, not at all what you would expect from a national organization. Another set of people are approached not by a hippie, but by a very neat, clean, conventionally dressed person; more on that later. You allow this person into your home and for three to four minutes this person attacks the concepts of sales tax and praises the income tax proposal, and attempts to get you to approve of the idea and to support the establishment of such a tax in Pennsylvania. Somewhat in a rush because he has to see other people, he leaves hurriedly after finishing his talk.

Two days or so later, another person knocks at your door. The person is a college student conducting a public opinion poll for a national company. When you ask if the student is from the company that called earlier, the answer is no, but that the student had heard about the other company. The student then asks twenty-five questions about local, national, and international issues; among these is a question about a state income tax. What do you think your answer is?

What you have just read and imagined is a direct restatement of the field experiment by Cooper, Darley, and Henderson, 1974, entitled, "On the Effectiveness of Deviant- and Conventional-Appearing Communicators: A Field Experiment." According to the results of that experiment, you become more positive to the notion of an income tax if the campaigner who came to your door was the hippie than if he were the conventionally-dressed person, or if no one came at all (the control condition). Now that takes some explaining!

The experience you went through was actually an experiment, and it tested the reactions of three randomly selected samples of people: Those receiving contacts from a hippie-dressed person, a conventionally-dressed person, and a control group who received both contacts but no intervening campaigner contact. It was a *field experiment,* an experimental test of a theoretically based prediction, conducted in a natural, real world setting. The prediction was derived from the theory of cognitive dissonance proposed by Festinger (1957).

Experiments do not necessarily have to be conducted in laboratory settings and it can be argued that sometimes it is better if they are not. In this case, there was no scientist with a white laboratory coat noting reactions, there were no brass instruments (or these days, no electronic instruments), no lists of paired associates, or any of the other expected experimental trappings. Yet the study meets the major criteria of laboratory science: There was a random assignment of subjects to experimental conditions, proper control conditions, pre and post measures, and the experimenters who actually worked with the subjects did not know the hypotheses of the study. Yet it did not look like an experiment; you as a suburbanite had no idea it was one. That is especially important, for other research has shown that if people know they are in an experiment, they tend to alter their behavior somewhat and do not always react as they normally would.

The investigators in this study had to spend a good deal of time figuring out some ways to match three separate components of the inquiry process in order to determine the accuracy of their prediction from the theory and thus, by implication, the value of the theory itself for explaining behavior. (1) They had to derive from the overall theory itself a specific prediction about how the theoretical concepts would operate, in this case about how unforeseen negative consequences would influence attitude change. (2) They then had to determine how to arrange an experimental situation to elicit theoretically appropriate behavior from the residents, behavior which would match the requirements of the types of concepts subsumed by the theory. (3) Finally, the experimental arrangements had to blend into the normal daily living patterns of the residents and thus not lead to suspiciousness, faking, or desires to distort true feelings.

This particular experiment appears to have matched up all three components quite nicely. The results of it were clear and supported the predictions well. Of course there is no "perfect experiment," and perhaps you could develop some *rival plausible hypotheses* (Campbell & Stanley, 1963) about the outcome. For instance, seeing a hippie argue in favor of a tax is not a very common sight. One of the major characteristics of science is the constant challenging, retesting, and reformulating of theories and procedures and, of course, ideas. But for our purposes here, the study gives a good example of the tendency of social psychologists to incorporate theory testing into real world or naturalistic settings. This movement is replacing the predominance of pure laboratory methodology as the ultimate, if not the only, way to test theories about human behavior. We will have more to say about the characteristics of field research later; it does much more than just test theories.

In case you are wondering about the apparently peculiar outcome of the first study, the cognitive dissonance theory interpretation of it is fairly direct: The theoretical logic argues that subjects have initially committed themselves to undergoing the experience by answering yes to the request in the initial telephone conversation. There was little or no external pressure for them to say yes, they did so willingly and of their own choice. But for those who had the hippie come to their door, they found out that their own freely-chosen behavior had resulted in an unexpected and probably unpleasant experience, that of having a hippie come into their homes and try to convince them of something they oppose anyway. To resolve this unpleasant (dissonant) state of tension, the subjects must have concluded something along the line that the experience was not a bad one, that what they had chosen was a smart thing to do, and that (finally) the idea of having an income tax was not a bad idea. To admit that you willingly choose to subject yourself to an unpleasant experience is not congruent with most people's image of themselves, and they typically do not do it. The theory states that people bring their interpretations of events into line with their behavior toward those events and with their self-concepts; this showed up in this experiment as attitude change toward the advocated position. The study thus represents a good example of theory-testing research conducted in natural settings.

Helping Behavior

Now let us go through another example, this one showing that there is more to field research than just theory testing. Often the scientist has developed a methodology for analyzing behavior and wishes to test it in natural settings, more or less without guidance of a specific theory. This might be called *method-oriented research*.

For this example, imagine that you are driving down a city street in the South,

Tallahassee, Florida, to be exact. Pulled off the road is another motorist; the hood of his (or her) car is raised and he or she clearly needs help. Would you pull over to help?

This study by West, Whitney, and Schnedler, 1975 ("Helping a Motorist in Distress: The Effects of Sex, Race, and Neighborhood") is one of a large number of field experiments on helping behavior. Technically, this is defined as behavior in which subjects find themselves in a situation in which another person needs help but is not directly requesting it or putting pressure on the subjects to deliver it. The latter is in the category of *compliance* studies—examples of which are also included in this book. These studies in fact do have some theoretical substance, but generally, this area of research began as a methodological innovation in social psychology; it is treated as a methodological issue in this book. In these types of studies, the investigator either wants to find out what the impact of a manipulation is on subjects, or wants to use the manipulation to detect the influence of various types of variables. At any rate, such studies are more directed at methodological issues rather than theory development or testing, per se.

In the driving study, the investigators had manipulated the racial and sexual characteristics of the stranded motorist (black male or black female, white male or white female) as well as the predominant racial characteristics of the neighborhood (black or white) in which the incident occurred. Hidden observers noted the racial identity of any drivers who stopped to help. It should be obvious from this description that studies can be quite complicated in their execution in spite of the seeming simplicity of the actual experimental activity itself. When extended to natural settings, methodological studies often are expanded to include a larger range of variables in order to efficiently obtain data potentially useful for different aims. Helping is a very sensitive indicator and commonly is used in such a way.

The results of the study showed fairly complex patterns, more so than we need to go into here. Briefly, it was found that female victims were helped more often than male victims, while male drivers helped more often than females (92% of the helping was done by males). Black victims were helped more in black neighborhoods, and whites more in white neighborhoods. Finally, victims tended to be helped more by members of their own race than by members of another race.

THE INTERACTION OF COGNITIVE AND SOCIAL VARIABLES

The two experimental studies just reviewed each had a particular focus, the first on individual cognitive processes and the second on social or interpersonal behaviors. Both are quite typical of research topics in social psychology and both proved helpful to understanding behavior in natural social contexts. Some research has been successful at analyzing even more complex phenomena, those involved when the investigator attempts to link together into one research project both individual and social levels of analysis. It is true that individuals are surrounded by other people almost every minute of their lives, so research that can show how the two types of variables are intimately related to each other is very useful. This is especially true when the research is conducted in an ongoing social situation, in a natural context. The next study reviewed is such a study. Discussing it will have an additional advantage because the research focused on a significant social problem, crowding.

You are in a university library and wish to go to another floor. You go to the elevator, press the button, and wait for it to arrive. Four other people are also waiting; unbeknownst to you, they are confederates of the experimenter, and all four are following a very carefully prearranged pattern of entering the elevator and placing themselves in predetermined places. When the door opens, two enter before you and place themselves in the back of the elevator, arms spread, effectively filling in the back spaces. At the same time, a third person enters ahead of you and does one of two things depending on the experimental condition. The third confederate either stands directly in front of the panel of control buttons, such that you cannot go there, or else goes to the opposite front side so that you are induced to stand near the buttons. Finally, the fourth person moves in behind you and, by moving directly toward you, makes you move fully into the remaining space you have moved toward. As the door shuts, you either request the person in front of the buttons to strike the one for your floor (a few subjects reached across and did it themselves), or in the condition in which you end up in front of the buttons, you press the desired button yourself.

As the elevator door opens at your floor, one of the other students follows you out and introduces him or herself as an architecture student, conducting a survey of opinions about elevator design. You are then presented with a questionnaire, asking three questions: "How crowded did you feel?" "How unpleasant was the elevator?" and, "How constraining did the elevator seem?" What do you think you would answer to these questions?

According to the results of the study by Rodin, Solomon, and Metcalf, 1978, ("Role of Control in Mediating Perceptions of Density") you will respond more negatively to the elevator experience if you were on the side of the elevator away from the control buttons. Conversely, you will feel more positively about experiences when you have ready access to the control buttons and thus feel a sense of personal control over environmental events affecting you. Recent social psychological studies are beginning to indicate that a sense of control or personal efficacy is critically important in a number of human situations, especially social situations involving other people. Even a relatively simple situation such as having the control buttons near you makes a significant difference in your reactions to the elevator trip.

Looked at from another viewpoint, this is a study on a current social problem, the problem of crowding. Population pressures are increasing, with all the attendant problems that result: urban density, lack of privacy, personal inconvenience, and reduced effectiveness of social amenities. Research has shown that stress and tension are common accompaniments of crowded conditions. There are few if any serious proposals about how to change the problem other than lowering the birthrate, but in the meantime much more information on the ways in which people cope with crowded conditions and adapt to the resulting stress and tension clearly is needed. Social psychologists have attacked the problem with such manipulations as we have just seen. Both laboratory and field settings have been used for these analyses, and the study you have just read about is one such field experiment. The significance of the cognitive control variable in influencing perceptions of crowding is now a fairly well-established finding and is in agreement with studies on the control variable performed in other settings.

THE CENTRAL ROLE OF EXPERIMENTATION IN SOCIAL SCIENCE

It is clear from all that we have seen so far that social experimentation is at the heart of what social psychology is offering to society. At the same time, it seems equally clear that in a number of instances research has been largely directed toward social issues, problems, and processes outside the strict confines of the laboratory environment. Therefore, experimentation need not be defined only in terms of the laboratory. Several reasons are possible for an intimate connection between experimentation and the real world orientation.

On one hand, it is the general orientation of many psychologists to ameliorate social problems; certainly this was one of the fundamental tenets of Kurt Lewin, one of the intellectual leaders during the formative stages of social psychology. However, there is a general understanding among most social scientists that hypotheses must undergo the rigor of testing in natural settings before their validity is firmly established. This was strongly supported by Sherif (1963), also one of the founders of the field. The emphasis on testing is not limited to social scientists of course; physicists regarded the actual detonation of the atomic bomb in 1945 as the critical test of their hypotheses concerning atomic fission, and now are using rocket trips to test highly abstract Einsteinian hypotheses. Social psychological methodologists regard field tests of theoretical propositions as part of the more general issue of the establishment of external validity (Campbell & Stanley, 1963), which in turn involves test of the hypothesis in many different contexts with many different samples of people (Kerlinger, 1973; Carlsmith, Ellsworth, & Aronson, 1976). So although a theory or hypothesis need not be relevant or have social action implications to be acceptable to experimental social psychologists, its potential for generalization, and hence its overall value, is often felt to be tentative until it has been rigorously tested in a wide range of settings, including field settings.

THE CIALDINI FULL CYCLE MODEL

Science begins with observations of events as the fundamental step. This observation then leads to questions about these events, i.e., hypotheses. These hypotheses are then tested under controlled conditions (as much as possible), usually in laboratory settings. A successful prediction concerning the outcomes of the experimental test neatly increases the confidence one has in the explanations the scientist has formulated.

A more complete approach, however, goes an additional step. This involves taking the laboratory-tested hypothesis and reverting back to the original setting and devising more tests of the explanation again in that setting (Cialdini, 1980). Here the influences of the artificiality of the laboratory test can be assessed; a conceptualization that was initially adequate will withstand rigorous tests in the original setting as well as in the laboratory. In this model, observation of the phenomenon in the natural environment is performed both at the beginning of the explanation sequence, where it generates the basic phenomenon to be explained and the elementary concepts to do so, and again at the end of the explanation and analysis sequence, where the adequacy of the analysis is tested against the reality of the natural world. Thus, with an applied experimental social psychological science, we have the possibility of developing a successful full cycle approach (Cialdini, 1980).

Of course, not all phenomena are going to be amenable to laboratory tests in the first place; such phenomena as race riots, divorce, and wars will always be beyond laboratory control. Also, sometimes observation of events leads experimenters to develop a methodological approach itself rather than to an explanation of a substantive issue. An example in the physical sciences could be the development of the Geiger counter. In social psychology such techniques as the bystander intervention technique and compliance-directing manipulations are cases where a distinct applied experimental social psychological development has occurred without the presence of the formal full cycle approach. These certainly deserve our attention and will receive it in this book. But the full cycle model represents an ideal blending of pure and applied approaches and hopefully it will become more prevalent as social psychology matures.

References

Campbell, D. T., & Stanley, J. C. *Experimental and quasi-experimental designs for research.* Chicago: Rand McNally, 1963.

Carlsmith, J. M., Ellsworth, P. C., & Aronson, E. *Methods of research in social psychology.* Reading, Mass.: Addison-Wesley, 1976.

Cialdini, R. B. Full cycle social psychology. In L. Bickman (Ed.), *Applied Social Psychology Annual, Vol. I.* Beverly Hills, CA: Sage, 1980.

Cook, T. D., & Campbell, D. T. *Quasi-experimentation: Design and analysis issues for field settings.* Chicago: Rand McNally, 1979.

Cooper, J., Darley, J. M., & Henderson, J. E. On the effectiveness of deviant- and conventional-appearing communicators: A field experiment. *Journal of Personality and Social Psychology,* 1974, *29,* 752-7.

Festinger, L. *A theory of cognitive dissonance.* Stanford: Stanford University Press, 1957.

Kerlinger, F. N. *Foundations of behavioral research.* (2nd ed.) New York: Holt, Rinehart & Winston, 1973.

Kuhn, T. S. The structure of scientific revolutions. (2nd ed.) In O. Neurath, R. Carnap, & C. Morris (Eds.), *Foundations of the unity of science.* Chicago: University of Chicago Press, 1970.

Lewin, K. Action research and minority problems. *Journal of Social Issues,* 1946, *2,* 34-5.

Rodin, J., Solomon, S. K., & Metcalf, J. Role of control in mediating perceptions of density. *Journal of Personality and Social Psychology,* 1978, *36,* 988-99.

Sherif, M. Social psychology: Problems and trends in interdisciplinary relationships. In S. Koch (Ed.), *Psychology: A study of a science. Vol. 6.* New York: McGraw-Hill, 1963.

Sherif, M., & Sherif, C. W. *An outline of social psychology.* (Rev. ed.) New York: Harper, 1956.

West, S. G., Whitney, G., & Schnedler, R. Helping a motorist in distress: The effects of sex, race, and neighborhood. *Journal of Personality and Social Psychology,* 1975, *31,* 691-8.

3

The Nature of the Scientific Approach to Society

The previous chapter reviews some of the basic concepts of the social psychological approach. A definition of the field and some examples of both theoretical and methodological characteristics of research are presented. Experimentation is regarded as central to the social psychological approach. In this chapter a more detailed examination of scientific analysis itself is presented, concentrating on how it can be applied in experimentation in societal rather than laboratory contexts.

For convenience, the organization of this chapter will follow rather directly the organization of an actual experimental research project. The first section, *Asking the Research Question: Defining the Phenomenon* concerns the experimental question itself, the reason for the research. This *question-asking* phase is important: It is critical for a scientist that the issue (phenomenon) under investigation be appropriately defined and shaped into a reasonably approachable form. Also, in this section we shall outline and discuss briefly the types of research questions asked in the four major sections of research readings included in this book.

The second section of this chapter, *Formulating the Way to Answer the Question: The Experimental Design,* deals with the second phase of research, formulating the actual experimental procedure to be followed to get an answer to the research question. Although this topic can be very complicated and represents the methodological and technological heart of science, our treatment of it will be general and not overly technical. The actual research articles reprinted in the book will make clear the technical aspects of the methodologies involved in social experimentation.

The type of experimentation most representative of experimenting in society is categorized into four groups of readings. These cover a progression of topics: Intraindividual cognitive processes, interindividual social processes, research on social problems, and finally the most recently developed research area, the scientific evaluation of government and private social action programs and activities. All of these topics are major areas of research activity: All demonstrate the dynamic interaction of scientific thought and technology applied to significant questions about human social behavior. We have mentioned the four categories of research at this point because they derive directly from the question-asking phase of science.

The third section of this chapter, *Data Analysis to Answer Questions* will briefly examine the logic of interpreting data gained from a scientific investigation, concentrating on how data gained from research helps to determine the answer to the question posed in the research. Research is aimed at determining whether or not a proposed answer to the research question (in the form of a hypothesis) is correct or not. The data analysis and interpretation process is central to linking the obtained data pattern with that expected from the hypothesis. From there, the investigator seeks to join that answer with the knowledge already available about the phenomenon and attempts to interweave the total set of knowledge now available into a clearer framework of understanding of the phenomenon. How this is done will be discussed in this chapter and in the following research articles.

ASKING THE RESEARCH QUESTION: DEFINING THE PHENOMENON

We are surrounded by a dynamic, changing world, filled with events which are continually influencing us. Many of those events are physical, such as light, temperature, chemicals, foods, etc. Many are social, such as our family, friends, and strangers. We adapt to the onslaught of such constant stimulation so well that very commonly we are unaware of the impact that it has on us. Habits of adaptation are useful because they allow us to break free of the domination of too much stimulation and to operate at a habitual level during a large portion of our time.

Curiosity and Science

However, it occasionally happens that we have to stop our ongoing habits and pay more than usual attention to some particular event. Something catches our attention; we get stopped from doing what we were doing by some intrusion; we get upset by some social or political happening, or we hear something. Whatever the cause, in situations like these we tend to stop our ongoing activity and engage in what can be called *epistemic behavior* (Berlyne, 1960). Epistemic behavior is behavior which involves actions and responses such as questioning, gaining information, removing uncertainty, and changing the unknown to the known. This is fundamental behavior, not at all limited to human beings. When a dog sniffs the air or a cat peeks around a beanbag chair, you have another example of epistemic behavior.

This type of behavior is central to our purpose in this chapter and in this book, for it is at the core of the scientific approach. Science is a very human activity, and scientists are like everybody else: They get curious and they ask questions about things. It is true that in many ways they are more cautious and more systematic than the rest of us in asking their questions and getting their answers, but the basic core of their enterprise is very much like any normal human curiosity. We shall spell out in some detail how it is that scientists ask and answer questions about human social behavior. It is important early on to realize how pervasive and useful this type of behavior is.

Some simple examples might be helpful. Suppose that you find yourself wanting to know what time it is, so you decide to ask someone for that information. Analysis of that seemingly simple event will show that it actually is a very complex and abstract event. Concepts of time, awareness of how to use that knowledge, and knowledge of how other people might respond to your query are all involved. The interesting point is that given your knowledge of society and interpersonal relations, you *know how* to solve the problem of what time it is by simply asking someone.

A different type of question will also prove useful. It has become obvious recently (painfully so) that gasoline and energy prices have risen dramatically. One might want to understand this phenomenon. (Another question might be, "How am I going to pay for all this?" but that question is beyond the scope of this book.) Getting an answer to the question would not be too difficult, given the enormous publicity the issue has received lately, but what is of interest to us here is the pattern of thought, the epistemic behavior, one goes through when such a question arises. You know that there are certain ways to go about answering the question. For instance, you would *not* go to a grocery store clerk, a telephone repairman, or a policeman for an answer. However, you would go to an economist, to an oil company representative, or to your senator. These people might tell you that the increase in prices is due to a number of different factors including: a limitation on energy supplies, a political move to reduce consumption, or an international agreement by monopolistic forces to extract as much money as possible.

TESTING THE ACCURACY OF ANSWERS

So one way to get a question answered is to seek out an expert. But how does the expert get an answer? And how does the expert, or you, or anybody, know that the expert's answer is a good one? How do we find out if any answer is valid? In our few examples here, we have gone to the point where you receive your answer, but there is one additional step, a critical one, and that step is the one taken by scientists. It is the step that is the one truly characteristic hallmark of science as an enterprise. Whereas most people will somehow, somewhere get an answer that satisfies them and then call a halt to the questioning, scientists are difficult people to satisfy. In fact they are not comfortable with an answer and will not stop the questioning until they can *test* it. Science has been defined as nothing more than testing one's assertions. It takes whatever answer has been presented and then goes the additional step of finding out if it is accurate, under what conditions it holds true, and how many other answers also could be true. Science is a rigorous business, but fundamentally it is just another form of human curiosity, a form carried just a bit further than usual. We will analyze the various parts of scientific question-asking and answer-testing in some detail. The readings in the book provide actual examples of scientific behavior.

What we will discuss next is an analysis of the procedures and techniques characteristic of science when it is applied to social behavior. Although there are differences betweeen your decision to ask someone for the time of day and the economist's decision to track down the causes of increased energy prices, you both went through an initial process of (1) somehow having the question come to you, (2) delimiting the appropriate realm in which an answer might be found, and then (3) determining what maneuvers you might make to begin to get the answer. The differences need to be analyzed also.

The scientific enterprise begins with curiosity people have about their world. In social psychology the types of questions people ask tend to revolve around individuals and groups, and a good portion of the field consists of questions and answers about the social world plus the accumulated body of techniques of how to link questions and answers. More recently, social psychologists have been called on by others to answer questions about society. Governmental units, private foundations, and others call on social psychologists to answer questions about such highly complicated social phenomena as criminal justice, health care, pollution, population, and minority interests. The list continues to increase in length. Due to the growth of the science, these phenomena are being opened up for analysis. Just being able to ask the questions in such a way as to lead to scientifically based answers is encouraging. So a wide range of issues is going to be involved in our review.

RESEARCH TOPICS TO BE COVERED

The purpose of this book is to provide students with information and insights about the role of experimental science in social settings. This necessarily involves exposure to some rather technical material on the scientific approach itself, as well as some more conceptual and philosophical issues involved in such research. Perhaps the most effective device to explicate this type of science is through actual examples of the types of questions that have been asked and the ways in which answers to those questions have been achieved. To do this, representative examples of research are reprinted in the latter half of the book. There are four rather distinct and representative types of research questions which characterize experimentation in society, and all four are reprinted here. They are briefly characterized below.

Analysis of the Individual

A good deal of social psychological research has been concerned with analyzing the mental processes of the individual, particularly those that relate to social factors. The topic of attitude was one of the very first research topics in the field, and research on it set the pattern for decades of research, continuing on into the present time. Attitude represents an interesting melding of individual thought and emotional feeling processes, but its focus on thoughts and feelings about other people makes it uniquely suited as a social psychological topic. From that starting point, social psychologists have devoted their research effort to a wide range of individual intrapsychic processes. Included in this section of the readings are descriptions of research into attitude processes, attribution and cognitive control processes, and personality processes.

Analysis of Groups and Social Processes

Social psychology is also very concerned with social (interindividual) processes as well as intraindividual processes. Research on dyadic and group interaction variables began early in the field's history and continues today. Issues covered here have implications for society and the applications of research techniques and data to socially relevant concerns. How people feel attracted to each other, how they give and ask for help, and how they influence each other are relevant concerns and are represented in the selected research articles. Finally, larger scale research on intergroup relations in the form of how the individual's choices are influenced by social factors and the interaction patterns of competing and cooperating groups of youth are included.

Analysis of Social Problems

The direct application of scientific analysis to pressing social problems has been a continuing theme throughout the history of the social sciences. Much of the emphasis has come from researchers' desire to expand the range of their experimental tests of theories and concepts to settings outside the confines of laboratory experimentation. Part of this research has taken on the label of *field research,* since it concentrates on more purely scientific concerns of testing the validity of scientific constructs and hypotheses. Another type of this research historically has been more activist and concerned with social change and amelioration of social problems, and is typically called *action research.* With both types of research questions, the attention of the researcher is very much on developing a sensitivity in scientific methodology and concepts allow naturalistic functioning and change of factors which might influence social problems. Among the research examples included here are criminal justice issues, specifically shoplifting (with actual incidents created by the experimenters), pollution and littering control, studies on the effects crowding has on people's personal space, and techniques for studying and reducing energy use and conservation.

Evaluation Research

Perhaps the newest area of research activity for social scientists is what has come to be called *evaluation research.* Strong pressure has come from a number of political and social quarters for scientists to create accountability tests for social action programs, i.e., proof that the programs were having positive benefits on the recipients. This is similar to the bottom line criterion used by business to assure that the firm is meeting its goals. Previously, it appears that government and private social action programs were set up and allowed to continue relatively unimpeded. However, with the development of new evaluation research, programs are coming to be regarded as if they were experiments, manipulations of social variables with a determinate and measurable outcome. Since the scientific techniques of social psychologists and other social scientists are well suited to this task, evaluation research has recently become a major form of endeavor. In effect the initial issue of the question to be asked typically has been: "Does this program have a positive effect on the people who receive its treatments?" Another question is, "What aspects of this program are having a positive effect and which ones are not?" These are outcome and process questions which will be discussed in greater detail later in this chapter.

With these as the basic questions of interest, investigators then determine what variables can be measured, what experimental controls are necessary, what types of analyses are to be done, etc. These are more or less typical scientific questions. As we shall see, the breakthrough has been that they can be applied to large-scale, even nationwide social entities.

In actuality, evaluation questions are much more complicated than direct outcome and process questions, for sensitive administrative, political, financial, and even ethical issues are intimately involved in program evaluation. These issues have to be resolved somehow. For now, the general point to be made is that social psychologists are becoming deeply involved in applying their scientific skills to designing, evaluating, and altering programs which are aimed at reducing significant social problems. The readings included in this book are examples of such research work, and cover such topics as health and nutrition, prison living conditions and health, the impact of no fault divorce laws on divorce rates, the impact of welfare payments on family stability, and various legal issues, including the impact of antigun laws on homicide rates and driver education's impact on traffic fatalities.

FORMULATING THE WAY TO ANSWER THE QUESTION: THE EXPERIMENTAL DESIGN

To this point we have treated the question-formulation phase of social experimentation as rather discrete and unconnected to anything else. That is an overly simplified notion. In actuality, any form of human conceptual behavior, in this case question-asking, operates within a complex network of physical and verbal relationships. Concepts operate within an implicational network, not singly, and they influence each other. Thus while we may not know the answer to a question, we do operate in a realm of conceptual possibilities. We said earlier that if you wanted to know why energy prices were rising, you would not ask a policeman, or a grocery store clerk; you would ask someone who functioned in a realm of economic variables: Questions are not asked in an information vacuum. It is from this type of logical network that our scientific approach derives and moves toward some form of answer.

Operational Definitions

Formulating a potential answer to a question, an answer that can be tested, is a special process in science. The task is to refine the question from its generalized, common sense form to some way that it can be clearly, sharply, and unambiguously answered. Usually, the aim is to derive from the initial query a specific question that can receive a quantitative answer, or at least an unambiguous one. This process means that for each element in the question some corresponding event, variable, or factor has to be found that can be assessed and whose impact on the phenomenon can be clearly determined.

What we have just described is the process of forming an *operational definition.* This simply means that the investigator logically deduces that the concepts being analyzed (on both the cause and the effect sides of the equation) are observable and hence measurable in the form of a specific stimulus configuration or event. This is a tricky process in any case, but it is especially so in the case of social behavior and cultural phenomena such as those involved in program evaluation. Some details of this should be clarified.

In the case of program evaluation, for instance, the matter of measurement, or *operationalization,* as it is more technically labeled, is fairly clear because the investigator would be interested in rather obvious things. The major question would concern treatment, simply whether or not an individual was actually enrolled in the program and received the regimen provided by the program. Of course, how the recipients perceived that treatment or what they thought about it might be very important, but under the particular measure of treatment as participation this would be ignored. The other side of the assessment, the dependent variable side, would be something like successful conclusion of program. This would readily be measured as (1) was or was not returned to the program, (2) terminated drug usage, (3) was not rearrested for drunk driving, or (4) had had no more reported physical abuse of spouse. At this initial level, then, the investigator makes an attempt in the initial design of the evaluation to be sure to operationalize terms that are adequate to answer the experimental question but at the same time are as clear and unambiguous as possible.

The case of more intrapsychic variables so common in social psychology and other aspects of experimenting in society is more difficult. Such concepts as *attraction,* or *cognitive dissonance* or *attitude* are more difficult to define and measure. These types of terms are quite meaningful and communicate a lot about underlying mental processes. They also have a considerable amount of research supporting their use. However, oftentimes a good deal of spade work on concepts has to be done before actual measurement can begin. An example: The concept of attraction (as in subject A is attracted to subject B) could be measured as "A gazes into the eyes of B more than into the eyes of C," or "A chooses more often to sit near B than C," or "A marked '7' on a seven-point Like-Dislike scale when responding to B." All are reasonable and in fact things like them are traditional measures of the concept. But the measures themselves are quite different from each other, and the challenge for an investigator is to know precisely which definition of the concept is most adequate to answer the particular experimental question being investigated. Problems like this abound in the complex issue of applying the scientific approach to human social behavior.

The articles reprinted in this book have many types of sometimes complicated concepts under investigation; the experimental arrangements in those reports show clearly the value of appropriate choices of measurement for making clear how questions can be proposed and answered clearly.

Experimental Design

Following the process of delimiting the observed phenomenon and choosing the most appropriate concepts to be measured, the investigator's next task is to arrange the assessment techniques and measures into an organized set of procedures to follow to launch the investigation and answer the question. By convention, the set of operationalized constructs and procedures planned to obtain the data concerning them is called the *experimental design.* Although the term has many implications, we use it here to refer to the logical set of processes or factors that are to be investigated, and the specific details of how they are to be related to each other. We must discuss some other concepts before the term can be fully understood, however, and the next two sections of this chapter present material which will help. Right now, we can consider an experimental design to be more or less a road map, pointing out the major points of interest and how they relate to each other. Two characteristics of this map are of special interest to us here: (1) It guides the scientist's behavior in determining what experimental variables to measure and how to relate them to each other procedurally in obtaining the data, and (2) it precisely specifies how the form of the data is to develop and how the results of the study are to be statistically analyzed. Later sections of this chapter will show how important these characteristics are to the design.

Independent and Dependent Variables

Although we have not yet used the formal terminology, it should be clear by now that in our discussion of variables involved in explaining phenomena, we are using the familiar language of *independent* and *dependent variables.* As traditionally defined, the former is that which is chosen by the investigator as the possible cause of the effect under study. The investigator then "controls" the variable, usually by manipulating it in some fashion, and then systematically observes the resultant effect. The latter is called the dependent variable. However, the range and power of these traditional terms have been greatly expanded as a consequence of research developments in the movement toward experimenting in society, and so our views of them have now become more flexible. Our discussion here will review those more flexible uses.

For this review, we will use as examples parts of a social experiment on a topic in the area of criminal justice. It is a study on shoplifting by Bickman and Rosenbaum (1977). This is not a formal analysis of the study, only a selective use of various parts of it to demonstrate the logic behind some uses of the concepts of independent and dependent variables. The study is reprinted later in this book in Chapter 8.

Bickman and Rosenbaum carried out a set of two studies on shoplifting. In both studies, they actually created a genuine incident of shoplifting in a supermarket. In plain view of shoppers (the randomly selected subjects of the studies), a helper of the experimenters grabbed some items and placed them in her purse. Other supposed bystanders (actually also helpers of the experimenters) performed manipulations of the major independent variables by either suggesting to the subject that he or she should report the thief or that he or she should not. Then, as a manipulation of a second variable, that commentor either remained beside the observer subject or left the scene. The two independent variables manipulated were the theoretical concepts of behavior surveillance over an observer to a crime and the norm of social responsibility, in this case the obligation to report a criminal incident. Also assessed in the study but not manipulated formally was the age of the observer subject and whether or not he or she was a college student. The dependent variable of the studies was quite clear and unambiguous, whether or not the subject reported the crime. The particular theoretical and conceptual analysis of crime developed by the investigators need not concern us here; our purpose in discussing this particular project is to elucidate the logical structure of the scientific approach they followed. The results confirmed predictions: Those subjects encouraged to report the crime did so, and the surveillance condition by itself did not have an influence, as subjects tended to report the crime whether or not the bystander remained at the scene. A qualification of the latter finding is necessary, however, as we shall see shortly.

It is common in research in field settings to go to great lengths to create situations which are believable and realistic in order to increase the validity of the experiment. None of the subjects in this set of experiments indicated any suspicions about it, so it appears that the investigators were successful in creating a sensitive, uncontaminated assessment of the independent variables. Much of the research performed in the tradition of experimenting in society is similar in that the investigators often choose real world settings such as supermarkets, race tracks, downtown streets, and subways to test hypotheses about social behavior. This helps avoid the distorting of ongoing behavior inevitable in laboratory settings. It is interesting to note that Bickman and Rosenbaum actually performed both a laboratory and a field study and obtained highly comparable results. Note also that more than one variable was being experimentally investigated; a whole host of variables were tested in these studies, some of them external to the subjects, some internal such as attitudes, and all operating simultaneously.

So far, then, we have discussed and demonstrated an example of research on a social problem, crime, with a research technique in which the investigators deliberately manipulated independent variables. Now we will move to another aspect of how the impact of independent variables can be assessed in naturalistic settings.

In the Bickman and Rosenbaum study, note that the investigators did not systematically change people's ages and they did not deliberately make some subjects into students and some into nonstudents; these conditions (variables) existed naturally without manipulation. The experimenters kept careful records on the incidents and on the subjects' characteristics and, in effect, let the world of events fluctuate naturally to "manipulate" the independent variables. The data analysis was conducted after the fact, so to speak. Both experimenter-induced and naturally occurring variations in variables will operate anyway, and the alert investigator will be tuned to detecting them and assessing their impact systematically. These are traditionally called *classification variables.*

Another type of manipulation of independent variables also is not usually under the direct control of the experimenter. This occurs in evaluation research and program evaluation. The independent variable in such a setting is of course the occurrence of some social event or a program treatment given to or provided for people. The dependent variable in these settings would be such things as the peoples' reactions to the event or the outcome of the treatment program. Usually in these situations neither the independent nor the dependent variable is chosen by the investigator as a logical derivation from a theoretical or conceptual proposition, which is the ideal case for science. Generally things are very much more practical and the pure science approach has to take a secondary role.

Most commonly in evaluation research the investigator is brought in by program administrators to find what impact the program is having, what aspects of it are successful, which ones are not, and what types of changes are likely to be beneficial. It should be clear that a program can be considered to be like an experiment: There is an analysis of a phenomenon (e.g., high rates of drug abuse, high recidivism of juveniles from a detention center), and an attempt to change some types of factors that seem to be related to the problem. Sometimes the investigator, now in the role of a program analyst rather than a question asker per se, is brought in on the actual planning of the program, generally in a consultant capacity. In these fortunate cases the scientist is able to use his or her store of psychological and scientific knowledge in the actual development of the program and its evaluation. More commonly, however, the program already is operating and usually has been so for some time, so the investigator has to make do with the program ingredients as they have been mixed by other people who usually are not scientists themselves. The job then becomes one of finding out what and how program treatment factors (independent variables) are influencing the aims of the program, treated as dependent variables.

One consideration concerning dependent variable assessment arises specifically in the realm of evaluation research. When program directors seek to learn about the effectiveness of their program, there are two major categories of variables that might be of interest to them which can be assessed. The most obvious are *outcome measures,* those that characterize recipients of program treatment after the treatment is over. Technically, outcome measures are usually assessed in a before and after type of design: What were the characteristics of program recipients before they received program treatment, and how do they score on those same characteristics after the treatment? Before and after measures are able to detect any change, and whether it is positive or negative. If there is no change, or negative change, then the agency personnel have information that something about the program has to be altered. Outcome measures provide very valuable information to program personnel.

Outcome measures can be both objective and subjective. Objective measures would be quantitative scores such as the number of program recipients who do not have to return for further services, for instance, or the number of times they need to return for treatment relative to comparable recipients in comparable programs. Both are considered in terms of time and cost. Subjective measures would be such things as the attitude of recipients toward the program, their satisfaction with treatment and program personnel, and felt need for more treatment. Psychological research has shown a number of times that people's perceptions are as good a predictor of treatment effects as more objective measures are, so subjective information about program treatment effects provides a valuable source of variables for assessment. Of course, a complete assessment would get information from both types of sources.

One problem with outcome measures, however, is that they do not specifically guide program personnel in what ways to change the program if it is not found to be as effective as desired. If only outcome measures are used, then the black box approach is being followed: Something goes in, clients, and later comes out, and no one knows what is going on inside. Only the most rudimentary information is gained this way. However, by the addition of *process* measures, valuable additional information can be gained and the results more effectively used to change the program. Process measures vary from program to program, of course, but in general they are intended to assess the effects of the subparts or components of the program as they are actually implemented in treatment. They also can be either objective or subjective. In the case of objective measures, they would involve such things as how many contact hours of treatment the client received, work load of program personnel, and number of different activities for recipients. Usually all of these are correlated against later success and failure measures computed on the recipients themselves. Those which correlate with success are of course considered to be the more valuable aspects of program functioning. Subjective measures would be such things as recipients' perceptions of themselves, of program personnel, and their attitudes toward their activities. The same types of measures could be obtained from program personnel also, for the satisfaction of workers is often a significant factor in program success.

Needless to say, a whole range of measures can be taken in program evaluation. Programs are multifaceted enterprises, any one or combination of program characteristics could be having an impact, and knowledge about this would be of great value to program personnel seeking to improve their effectiveness. Just knowing that a program works or doesn't work is of some value, but using a multimeasure approach to the various types of independent and dependent variables is a much more powerful way to investigate program functioning. The use of scientific techniques for this purpose is one of the rapidly expanding applications of science in experimenting in society.

It is also important to note at this point that much more than formal social programs for helping people are amenable to analysis within this evaluation framework. The scientific approach is very flexible. Now that social scientists have developed their research tools to the point where this greater flexibility can actually be implemented, we can see that virtually any social phenomenon can be assessed from a scientific perspective. Even the impact of such common events as television shows, election campaigns and voting, and even natural disasters as hurricanes and earthquakes can be assessed. For instance, the current controversy over violence on television and its impact on people has been subjected to a number of experimental tests. Such questions as whether interpersonal aggressiveness in children increases as a function of number of hours per week of watching television have been asked and answers have been obtained (Kaplan & Singer, 1976). Also, the television show *Sesame Street,* generally considered to be of high educational value for children, has been studied for its impact (Cook, Appleton, Conner, Schaffer, Tamkin, & Weber, 1975). The list could go on.

Techniques of assessment used in such research have become highly sophisticated. It is now possible to obtain surprisingly stringent tests of the impact of variables in natural social settings even when the event was not carefully developed for scientific analysis in the first place. This gets us into the area of quasiexperimental designs (Cook & Campbell, 1979). This topic is far removed from our main point, but textbooks and even entire courses are now devoted to just such issues. All we shall note here is that this and other areas of scientific methodology are currently being developed to encompass a greater range of utilization and greater sophistication of technique.

To sum up what we have said so far, what we have seen about independent variables is that there are a number of ways that they vary and can be assessed, especially if the focus of investigation is beyond the confines of the laboratory and in the natural social world. Four major types of manipulations occur: (1) the investigator deliberately manipulates them, (2) the investigator does not directly manipulate them but takes systematic measures on classification characteristics such as age, social status, and ethnicity, (3) they are consciously manipulated not by the investigator but are deliberately manipulated by others, usually nonscientists, as in social action programs, and the investigator attempts to determine their effects by the best means available, and (4) they are recurrent in the course of ongoing social events such as television shows, political campaigns, economic changes, and natural disasters.

Dependent variables can be seen in a similar light. Generally they are chosen by the investigator, usually are quantitative, and are chosen to match the conceptual variables involved in the structure of the hypotheses of the study. Often, as in evaluation research, they are not as rigorously developed as would be desirable but have to be selected from the range of events available. Nevertheless, scientific methodology is now sufficiently refined that even under less than desirable circumstances very powerful assessments of them are possible.

DATA ANALYSIS TO ANSWER QUESTIONS

Analyzing the data of a study investigating relations between variables is a very technical and complex process. To delve into great detail on such issues as statistical inference and the computational structure of data analysis techniques would involve us in matters too specific for our purpose here. There is some advantage to be gained, however, by discussing in some detail how data analysis of a particular study cannot, and should not, be considered separately from the experimental design such as we have already discussed it. The conceptual analysis that led to the design of the experiment in the first place guides how the results will be analyzed and related back to the variables being investigated. The focus of our discussion therefore will be on that process, using some more data from the Bickman and Rosenbaum shoplifting study we have been analyzing.

Data Patterns

One can approach the results of a study in a bits and pieces approach, but it is more likely that the overall meaning of the results will be more obvious if one attempts to find a pattern occurring within them. The concept of *data pattern* is not a technical one. It is used here simply to refer to the ways in which the data obtained from the various experimental conditions of a study relate both to the overall question of the study and to each other as well. These interrelationships are often subtle and complicated. However, current statistical techniques are sensitive and powerful enough to determine the difference between random or unrelated results and those which are meaningfully related to each other. Our discussion now will focus on the detection and interpretation of those patterns.

Main Effects

In the earlier days of social psychological science, there was a tendency for experimenters to investigate the effect of a single specific factor or variable on a given behavior. This *single factor* research usually had only two conditions, an experimental group and a control group. Sometimes, two types of experimental groups were employed. Referring back to our examples of the Bickman and Rosenbaum study on shoplifting, we mentioned that they had directly manipulated two variables to see if they would influence shoplifting: (1) whether or not the observer of the shoplifting was encouraged or discouraged to report the incident, and (2) whether or not the person who did the encouraging continued to be present and observe the subject or left and was no longer observing the subject. Each variable had two aspects, hence created two cells of the experimental design.

Let us arbitrarily call the surveillance factor, Factor A, and look at the results. As you can see, there was only a slight difference between the two conditions;

Figure 1. Rates of reporting of an observed incident of shoplifting as a function of bystander's presence. (Data from Bickman, L., & Rosenbaum, D. 1977)

Factor A

A_1 (Surveillance)	A_2 (Nonsurveillance)
59%	44%

statistical tests showed it is not significant. At this point, it does not appear to make a difference in reporting rates if a bystander is or is not present; roughly half of the subjects report the crime. You probably could think of a half-dozen things that might have been operating during the mock shoplifting and could give some good account of this finding, but our purpose in discussing it is simply to point out how any given variable (such as surveillance and nonsurveillance) can be investigated in and of itself and considered independently of all other possible influences. Other things may or may not be operating, but if you want to study any single factor by itself then any other possible factors have to be considered as not operating—that is, as randomly distributed and not having an influence. Randomly distributed factors do not have systematic effects.

Multivariate Designs

More recently, psychology's scientific sophistication has expanded considerably, and now multivariate designs are very common; they are so common that single factor designs such as the one we have just presented are seldom seen in print any more. Multivariate designs allow the assessment of two or more factors operating simultaneously. Less reliance on assumptions of randomly distributed effects of other factors has to be necessary that way, and since the world itself is filled with multiple influences operating simultaneously, multivariate designs are much more meaningful and appropriate for valid assessment of the social environment.

Bickman and Rosenbaum in fact did include more variables; as pointed out earlier, they crossed the surveillance factor with another, simultaneous one: whether or not the bystander encouraged the subject to report the crime. Let us look at the results on the influence of this variable's impact. To do so, we shall momentarily ignore (by averaging) the impact of the surveillance condition. We will label this variable Factor B.

Figure 2.   Rates of reporting of an observed incident of shoplifting as a function of bystander encouragement. (Data from Bickman, L., & Rosenbaum, D. 1977)

Factor B

B_1 (Encourage Reporting)	B_2 (Discourage Reporting)
72%	32%

Here the differences in reporting between the two bystander behavior conditions are quite marked, and the statistical test shows them to be significantly different: There is more reporting when the bystander encourages it. We shall look at this a bit more closely later on.

In sum to this point, we have found that two separate factors were functioning in this study, but they had different affects on the reporting of shoplifting. We have discussed them as if they were tested in separate experiments, with the subjects run separately and the data analyzed separately. In fact, the study was run just once, on one set of subjects, with the subjects themselves categorized by two concurrent variables. Thus the very great efficiency and analytic power of multivariate designs is obvious: The simultaneous operation of several factors can be assessed with only one experiment. Furthermore, multivariate designs have the advantage of being more closely representative of the way the real world operates, we do not live in a single-variable world. In this study, it was very realistic for the bystander to say something about the shoplifting incident and then either remain or leave.

Our two examples of two-cell designs (A_1 and A_2 are two levels of A, B_1 and B_2 are two levels of B) have the danger of appearing too artificial if not simple; there are many ways to categorize variables. For instance, the bystander could have made any number of comments and each could be treated as a factor. In actuality, the number of levels of most variables can be expanded as much as seems necessary and desirable to match characteristics of events. So we should not assume that simple experiments are best: The complexity of the phenomenon under investigation is the most important determinant of how complex the experimental analysis should be.

Interactions

Now we come to the more common form of analysis, when more than one factor is being analyzed. The Bickman and Rosenbaum design will be employed again. We now must address the topic of *interactions,* the statistical term for the condition in which one factor's impact on the data is found to change systematically because of the impact of one or more simultaneously operating variables. We saw earlier in the results of Factors A and B that main effects had occurred with B but not A. The factors were tested alone to see how they caused differences in the data. The term *main effects* means that one cell is reliably different from another when both are within one variable, that is, when they are levels within that variable. But when two or more variables are cross-related within one design, then the differences could come either within one of the factors (as we saw with A and B earlier), or the differences could come in some cross-variable combination. So the term *interaction* means that the difference within one set of levels of a factor is itself different from the differences operating with another variable's levels. This is a very important finding for it means that we cannot pay much attention to interpretation of a main effect if an interaction is also operating in the data pattern: No single main effect conclusion is meaningful given that it would have to be qualified by another part of the set of main effect results from the other factor.

Figure 3. Rates of reporting of an observed incident of shoplifting as a function of bystander encouragement and surveillance. (Data from Bickman, L., & Rosenbaum, D., 1977)

		Factor B	
		B_1 (Encourage Reporting)	B_2 (Discourage Reporting)
Factor A	(Surveillance)	68%	50%
	(Nonsurveillance)	76%	14%

Adapted from "Crime Reporting as a Function of Bystander Encouragement, Surveillance, and Credibility" by Leonard Bickman and Dennis P. Rosenbaum. *Journal of Personality and Social Psychology,* 1977, Vol. 35, No. 8, pp. 577–586. Copyright © 1977 by The American Psychological Association, Inc. Reprinted by permission.

To be specific, the results actually obtained by Bickman and Rosenbaum are diagrammed above:

It is clear from this pattern that in order to adequately describe crime reporting in this circumstance not one but two separate related factors have to be taken into account. We now can see a very different social process going on in the reporting situation. Whereas we earlier concluded that bystander surveillance did not have an impact on reporting, we now see that it alters the influence of the encourage-discourage variable. So it does have an impact, but only when seen in context of the simultaneous operation of the other variable of bystander encouragement. Statistical tests show the overall pattern of four reporting rates to be reliable. We now know that the differences within one set of variables is itself different from the other as a total set of findings. Of course this means that we must be attentive and keep in mind two operating influences rather than one, so our job as scientists (data interpreters in this case) becomes more complex. Fortunately, we have our statistical tests as tools to tell us when we can have a simpler explanation and when we have a more complex one.

The overall point of this should be clear: The investigator of any phenomenon should be attentive to those potentially significant factors which might need to be accounted for in an explanation of the phenomenon under investigation. Experimental design technology is powerful enough to meet the requirements of most analyses of social behavior, and investigators have to be able to apply the appropriate concepts and techniques to unravel the complexities of that behavior.

In sum, then, we have seen in this chapter how the data patterns that result from a research study have to be interpreted carefully in light of the original aims of the study. Conversely, the investigator should have a clear view of the types of data patterns expected from the study. This is the delicate interactive process of derivation of a prediction (hypothesis), design of a study tuned to testing it adequately, and then responsive and sensitive conduct of the study. The data analysis method that will be used to assess the outcomes of the study should be determined in detail before the results are in. With the structure of the entire study clearly in mind, the investigator can expect the study to be a powerful source of information to guide his or her understanding of the phenomenon. It is the structure of this overall approach that has provided such a steady source of useful information as scientists go about their business of helping us understand the world in which we live.

References

Bickman, L., & Rosenbaum, D. P. Crime reporting as a function of bystander encouragement, surveillance, and credibility. *Journal of Personality and Social Psychology,* 1977, *35,* 577-86.

Berlyne, D. E. *Conflict, arousal, and curiosity.* New York: McGraw-Hill, 1963.

Cook, T. D., Appleton, H., Conner, R., Schaffer, A., Tamkin, G., & Weber, S. J. *"Sesame Street" revisited: A case study in evaluation research.* New York: Russell Sage Foundation, 1975.

Cook, T. D., & Campbell, D. T. *Quasi-experimentation: Design and analysis issues for field settings.* Chicago: Rand McNally, 1979.

Kaplan, R. M., & Singer, R. D. Television violence and viewer aggression: A reexamination of the evidence. *Journal of Social Issues,* 1976, *32,* 35-70.

4

The Implications and Ethics of Experimenting in Society

In today's complex and socially interwoven world, one person's actions invariably affect other people. Sometimes the effect is direct and intended, sometimes indirect and accidental. Some impact occurs rather immediately, some of it has longer-term consequences. It is important to know something about social impact; the costs of not knowing how we influence each other have become too high for us to allow them to remain unanalyzed.

Examples of impact and influence abound. Probably no U.S. military policy decision-makers, including a string of U.S. presidents, foresaw the ultimate impact of sending increasing numbers of "military advisers" to Vietnam. When the first oil was pumped out of a Pennsylvania field, nobody knew then that later global geopolitical developments would be irreversibly set in motion. When the first reliable vacuum tubes were invented, probably no one had any idea how much radio and television would come to dominate the lives of both individuals and society.

Our entire global society is now so tightly interconnected and has so many feedback loops built into it that it takes a great deal of cautious deliberation to feel even reasonably comfortable with decisions and actions. This holds true for everyone, scientists included.

Fully aware of this dilemma, social and physical scientists have tried to understand the role that their activities have, and might later have, on society. The issue is particularly critical for those scientists who do research on social variables and who conduct their investigations in society. We want to review in some detail the kinds of issues these scientists have faced and the conclusions they have drawn.

The voluminous published literature in this area is too much for us to cover here. What we shall do is review several of the more central concerns which have arisen from analyses of the issues when considered from the social psychological perspective. One issue in question is the power of research conducted in natural settings to enhance the development of the strength and the utility of the science of social psychology. Some have questioned the value of conducting scientific investigations in natural settings. They argue that the information gained from that endeavor is not necessarily superior to that gained in purer, more rigorously controlled laboratory settings and, even more, that social scientists may not be performing a valuable social role by attempting to alter social conditions through their scientific efforts. This issue goes to the very heart of experimenting in society and deserves our consideration. The second issue in question is how much responsibility societal agents have to use the results of scientific investigations to change society for the better. The focus of this latter issue is on the role of the interconnection between social science and social policy, especially actually putting research findings into practice. Following these topics, we shall then discuss an even more complex and sensitive issue, the ethics of doing research on and in the social environment.

AN EXPERIMENTING SOCIETY

In what has become one of the most influential papers in recent years, Donald Campbell (1969) articulates some of the logic of experimentation in society. The title, "Reforms as Experiments," indicates that changes in laws and social policy are, in effect, experiments even though the change agents responsible may not recognize them as such. Perhaps it is even more unfortunate that they do not take advantage of the situation. Campbell is asking—why should we have just an experimenting social science: Why not have an experimenting society?

Campbell explores the prospects of what happens when, and if, society's planners implement both the methods and the facts of social science research. When this happens, social psychologists and others engaged in analyzing social variables will be forced to trust their methods to give accurate and reliable facts. Campbell's major aim is to analyze scientific methodology itself, pointing out its strengths and weaknesses and, when possible, bolstering the methodology to make it as powerful and as useful as possible.

Within this framework, Campbell also explores the consequences of how social science knowledge itself can be combined with decision-making at the level of administrative and governmental policy. If the data and insights that social analysis and experimentation generate are valid, then the social system into which that knowledge is placed can have a determining influence on the consequences. Problems of effective use of that knowledge can arise and probably will. To explicate these problems, Campbell formulates the concepts of *the trapped administrator* and *the experimental administrator*.

HOW ARE SOCIAL EXPERIMENTATION
DATA TO BE USED?

It has been all too common, Campbell argues, that policy-making and policy-implementing agencies fall into traps when deciding to make changes. If a policy change is actually made, then powerful social, cultural, and political forces are set in motion. The act of making the policy change brings to bear a very common, and very natural, desire on the part of the policy makers to defend that decision and to prove that it works, and that their decision was the right one. If the change does work, then of course all the social disruption contingent upon it appears to have been wise. But what if the policy does not work? What if the social change created turns out to be marginally effective, ineffective or, in all too many cases, harmful? The administrators in charge of such programs might then want to deny responsibility for the decision, the implementation of it, or (and this is where social scientists become involved), the value of the data generated.

It is at this last point that the social scientist as evaluator has become embroiled in matters potentially beyond his or her control. The only ground a scientist has for defense is the logic and rigor of scientific analysis; this usually is effective in the realm of science. But in the public arena, nonscientists generally do not have grounds for evaluating the merits of scientific analysis; judgmental issues too readily become matters of values rather than fact.

Campbell's analysis of this situation brings a new light to the issue and, possibly, to society itself. If administrators thought of public policy changes as experiments, and themselves as experimenters who are searching for answers to problems as scientists do, then an entirely new cast would be put on the issue. Failure is very common in science and technology. Every scientist knows well how a carefully thought-out theory, a well-designed operation of experimentation, and carefully tested results, can all go awry. Failure is as common in science as success, if not more so. However, rather than defending their theories, operations, or data, scientists consider failure to be a learning experience, and use it constructively to improve their efforts.

If failure is common in the highly logical and rigorous world of science, think how much more likely it is in the rough-and-tumble world of social action. Unfortunately, it is very difficult for decision-makers in public policy matters to accept failure; a decision to make change seems to lead to a trap of permanent commitment. Changing a public policy is much more difficult than changing an experimental procedure; the lives of many people are often directly tied to the change. Scientists can tinker with their methods, they can fine-tune them to pick up precisely the effect they are seeking, and they can rerun the experiment. But in the social world and with policy matters, continual change simply is not feasible. On the other hand, relentless commitment to a failing program can lead to serious problems, ones often worse than the initial problem for which relief was being sought in the first place.

Campbell asks for a restructuring of the very role of government itself. If public policy makers could be induced to redefine their roles as those of experimenting administrators then an entirely new force for creative change would be possible. Reduced to its basics, Campbell's argument simply is that any change in social policy should be explicitly delimited in time, say five years, and any shortcomings, zero effects, or negative effects, would be considered as valuable information, and changes made accordingly. *Zero-based budgeting* and *management by behavioral objectives* are two current reflections of the tendency of policymakers to seek more planned and experimental ways to control social forces.

Regardless of the interventions of policy makers or scientists, it is obvious that society is constantly changing. We are now entering an era of even greater changes necessitated by the influence of such contemporary problems as overpopulation, energy, and poverty. It makes sense to assume that policy-induced changes would be less disruptive, and perhaps even beneficial, if logical control and experimentation were to be introduced into the decision-making process. In short, the manipulations are going to be made, and if they are not regulated by scientific data and feedback mechanisms, then they will be regulated by forces largely out of our control. An experimenting society is possible; the science for at least an initial approach along these lines is available, as the readings in this book give witness. If we remain trapped administrators, clutching at set ideas and rejecting information that contradicts those ideas, then we are likely to face a bleak future.

On the other hand, following a scientific model does not automatically guarantee immediate success and our imminent arrival at the promised land. But if we could make social progress just slightly comparable to the scientific progress that is apparent in our history, the future might appear more promising. If people would define themselves as both citizens *and* scientists, then the quest for a better future may be successful.

Some Cautions

Perhaps no professional group is more wary of uncritical acceptance of ideas and facts than scientists. Probably due to the very structure of the scientific enterprise itself, scientists as a group seldom are comfortable with a theory, hypothesis, or fact until it has been repeatedly tested for validity. To be convincing, this testing has to involve different investigators, all with their own particular biases: it has to involve different contexts and settings. In short, scientists withhold judgment on the validity of an explanation, and even on the reliability of an effect itself, until a great deal of investigation has been completed.

A similar degree of conservative hesitancy characterizes how psychologists regard their own impact at the level of social action or policy activity. Because they deal with intimate questions of value and with the potential for significant alteration of how people live their lives, psychologists have expressed consider-able uncertainty as to their own role in bringing about social change. It is clear that social scientists in general are coming to have a considerable impact on decision-making at all levels of society, and the doubts and hesitancies social psychologists feel about their influence are beginning to be aired publicly. From this concern has come some thoroughgoing investigations of just what it is the science is about, and some rather strong criticisms of it have been made by social psychologists themselves. A short review of some of the issues raised in this "family feud" will be very helpful to us as we read into the published research and consider its relevance for contemporary society.

One interesting distinction for psychologists to consider was raised by George Miller in his Presidential Address to the American Psychological Association in 1969. In his address, entitled "Psychology as a means of promoting human welfare" (Miller, 1969), he points out the very grave issues involved when psychologists start attempting to have an impact on society:

> ". . . . I believe that any broad and successful application of psychological knowledge to human problems will necessarily entail a change in our conception of ourselves and how we live and love and work together. Instead of inventing some new technique for modifying the environment, or some new product for society to adapt itself to however it can, we are proposing to tamper with the adaptive process itself" (p. 1066).

While Miller speaks of "giving psychology away" to society in order to help it, he discusses some of the difficulties involved in doing so. Of major concern is the difficult problem of being a scientist and a helper at the same time. It is his feeling that a clearer distinction between the two is necessary:

> ". . . Many psychologists, trained in an empiricist, experimental tradition, have tried to serve two masters at once. That is to say, they have tried to solve practical problems and simultaneously to collect data of scientific value on the effects of their interventions. Other fields, however, maintain a more equitable division of labor between scientist and engineer. Scientists are responsible for the validity of the principles; engineers accept them and try to use them to solve practical problems" (p. 1071).

There are some who would not agree with Miller's dichotomy. Streufert (1973) for instance, argues that there has not been a split, at least within the field of social psychology (Miller was addressing all psychologists) and, further, that both the scientific and the social action sides gain from combining the two. Needless to say, a number of other social psychologists would agree with that point of view. But from our perspective we can best regard this issue as unresolved, and perhaps unresolvable. It surely will receive more consideration in the future as psychologists become increasingly more active in extending their skills and interests to things outside their laboratories.

A rather more stern approach to field research is expressed by some social psychologists. It is argued that research in field settings can never be as powerful as that conducted in the laboratory. According to these critics, arguments that more realistic analyses of behavior can be obtained that way simply do not hold up to rigorous analysis.

For instance, Parke, Berkowitz, Leyens, West, and Sebastian (1977) have reviewed the research data on the effect of viewing violence on television on later violence in children. Certainly this is an important issue, and one for which the research methodology of social psychology should be highly useful and relevant. Much of that research was done in actual field settings, in this case in the homes of the children themselves. But Parke et al. argue that field research used in this way simply is inadequate:

". . . Social psychology will not necessarily advance by merely becoming more naturalistic. Nor is there much evidence that this has happened . . . Unfortunately, the field experimental approach is not well suited for testing subtle theoretical issues . . . Theoretical analyses of the operation of film violence, in short, have moved to a level of complexity that is difficult to test adequately in field contexts" (p. 168).

Similarly, McGuire (1973) argues against the wholesale application of straight experimental designs, such as those used in laboratory research, to applied problems or behavior in natural settings. Too often, he says, simple linear cause and effect reasoning which is common in laboratory research cannot match the complexities of events in their natural settings. Simply applying traditional methods will gain us nothing. He rather colorfully describes the dangers this way:

". . . in the field we put the question to nature in a world we never made, where the context factors cannot be so confounded by our stage management proclivities as they were in the laboratory. But in this natural world research, the basic problem remains that we are not really testing our hypotheses. Rather, just as in the laboratory experiment we were testing our stage-managing abilities, in the field study we are testing our ability as "finders," if I may use the term from real estate and merchandising. When our field test of the hypothesis does not come out correctly, we are probably going to assume not that the hypothesis is wrong but that we unwisely chose an inappropriate natural setting in which to test it, and so we shall try again to test it in some other setting in which the conditions are more relevant to the hypothesis. Increasing our own and our graduate students' critical skill will involve making us not better hypothesis testers or better stage managers but rather better finders of situations in which our hypotheses can be demonstrated as tautologically true" (1973, p. 449).

McGuire is not condemning field research, per se. He is warning that if we are ever to have a valid science of behavior, scientists will have to develop more creative insights into the multicausal complexity of behavior. Simple causal models cannot be adequate, regardless of whether we test them in the so-called false world of the laboratory or in the real world of naturalistic settings. A rush toward field experimentation simply because it is done in the field will be doomed to failure. McGuire's criteria for an adequate science of social behavior are stringent indeed, but they represent a challenge to improve on what has gone before.

There is no need to get involved in in-house arguments among social psychologists about what they can or cannot do with their science. But it should be clear that there is considerable ferment in the field about what is going to happen if and when social psychologists get drawn into using their scientific abilities in nonlaboratory settings either as data gatherers or as policy makers. Social scientists want to have a valid and useful science to offer society, but the path to it is a steep and thorny one. However, growth can and often does come from stress.

Another set of issues remains to be reviewed, a set perhaps more complex and perplexing than any so far considered. To some people, whether or not experimenting in society should be done at all is an unresolved question and needs discussion. The issues raised from this quarter involve ethical questions. Principles, values, and matters of moral concern have become major considerations as science has progressed in scope and power. Questions of ethics have become quite prominent as social scientists particularly have become more and more involved in the analysis of human affairs. These issues are of great concern to both the producers and consumers of experimentation in society.

THE ETHICS OF EXPERIMENTING IN SOCIETY

Should experiments be done on people? Do people have rights not to be observed? Does society gain when scientific information about behavior is gained? These questions are part of a broader concern in modern society with any kind of manipulation involving any living organisms. The question applies not only to social psychology but to all the social and life sciences. Of course these are not the type of questions to receive definite yes or no answers; a number of issues are intricately involved, issues which are extremely worthwhile to consider. Since the types of research represented by the articles in this book may be related to social planning and policy formation, some consideration of the ethical issues involved in this type of research is desirable.

The Central Issue of the Subject Rights

It is clear that science is, by its nature, an intrusive enterprise: Scientists do things to other things and then observe what happens. This is true for all branches of science, but of course certain sciences, such as astronomy, let nature do the manipulating. When the manipulating is done to rocks or to fluids, then few ethical questions are involved. There is some concern when scientists start doing things to, say, worms, and even more when they do things to rats, pigeons, and monkeys. When the manipulating is done to people, then very serious questions are raised.

The television show "Candid Camera" was a national pastime during its heyday. The producers of that show performed extraordinarily powerful manipulations on people, not all of which were completely harmless, or at least without stress. It was obvious to all concerned (with the possible exceptions of the naive subjects themselves) that the producers had no evil motives, and clearly had taken precautions to insure that no harm would come to the subjects. But the experiences generated for the show put many of the subjects under considerable pressure and even stress, although the discomfort was probably temporary. Apparently there has been no serious charges of unethical conduct leveled against the show.

Manipulations occur in other less contrived ways as well. Natural disasters influence people routinely, and people influence each other daily, not always in a positive manner. Once again, ethical matters are not generated by these types of events either. But when a particular scientist sets out to do something to people and to watch their reactions, then ethical questions become public concerns. It is within the context of the scientific enterprise that matters of ethics arise and must be considered.

Such writers as Shils (1959) and Kelman (1967) have written extensively on the dangers of allowing scientists the freedom to intervene in the lives of people in order to obtain data. Kelman specifically has analyzed the interaction between scientist and subject and found it to have an imbalance of power. The scientist is fully aware of what is occurring and thus has much more interpersonal power and influence than the subject, while the latter is naive and simply must place complete trust in what the scientist says. In some cases this power imbalance has been abused; scientific experimentation sometimes has rather serious consequences and within certain frameworks its effects are questionably, if not completely, unethical.

The dilemma for the scientist, and society itself, is to balance the value of obtaining scientific evidence about human (and animal) behavior with the inherent right of the person or organism to be left alone and not to have its behavior interrupted. The invasion of privacy is a common and natural event; you can be interrupted by friends, enemies, strangers, earthquakes, or even Candid Camera. However, in a strict interpretation, this is an irrelevant issue. Scientists, as agents of some social organization such as a government or a private foundation, cannot be given free reign to conduct any study imaginable under the protection of freedom of inquiry.

The scientist's view of this will become clear as we delve into some specific issues. Certainly there is a danger that social scientists can go too far with their intrusiveness, although there is not much evidence that as a group they have consistently violated individuals' rights by their investigations. On the other hand, there is evidence that they have taken considerable precautions to protect those rights. But in their quest for knowledge some questions have been raised by both scientists and nonscientists.

In 1963 Stanley Milgram published a study on obedience. Through verbal commands ranging from subtle to strong, he induced naive subjects to deliver supposed shocks to another person. At high levels of shock, the other person (a confederate) pleaded for the experiment to stop and ultimately ceased responding altogether, the apparent victim of a heart attack. The subjects were under pressure by the experimenter to continue giving shocks. The intent of the study was to determine if people would do so, and the results showed that 63% of them would.

This study received a good deal of national attention (including a dramatized television rendition of it). Most people found the results to be surprising, with almost everyone, including a sample of psychiatrists, predicting that almost no subjects would deliver shocks all the way. It is fair to say that most people learned something from this study and for that reason it was a worthwhile study.

However, a storm of controversy over the ethics of conducting the study soon arose. Baumrind (1964) for instance, publicly criticized Milgram in a leading psychological journal. Milgram (1964) replied to the criticisms. Neither side seems to have reached any conclusive victory on the ethical issues, which is typical of the entire topic of ethical matters in research. We use the Milgram study here only for the purpose of giving an example of how scientists can be called to account for their actions. In such cases, the value of the scientific enterprise itself is brought under review. This is not a trivial matter, for as scientists continue to refine their skills and continue their search for knowledge more such issues and controversies are likely to arise.

Some Empirical Data on the Public's Reactions

Interestingly enough, psychologists have treated ethical issues as amenable to empirical treatment, and several studies have investigated how the public responds to deceptive and unobtrusive research. For instance, Sullivan and Deiker (1973) selected a sample of 400 psychologists researchers and 357 undergraduate students and had them judge four experiments with design characteristics involving potentially controversial ethical issues. The consequences of the experimental manipulations (alteration of self-esteem, brief pain, induced stress) were described verbally to the subjects. The subjects then indicated if they would volunteer for the study knowing its impact, if they felt the deceit involved was unethical, how valuable the facts actually obtained from the study were, and a number of other questions. The results indicated that on eighteen of the twenty response categories, psychologists were significantly more strict in their ethical judgments concerning the studies than the students were. The investigators postulated that if the data represent what actually occurs in research laboratories, it would appear that psychologists would do a careful job of attending to ethical issues.

Wilson and Donnerstein (1976) focused a similar research methodology on field research. They chose eight experiments which used deceptive methodology in field settings and then had a random sample of people from all walks of life answer a set of questions about the experiments. The questions were designed to determine how upset the people were that the experiments had been done, how valuable the experiments were, and whether or not they were against the law, etc. Although there was a good deal of variability among the eight experiments, there was surprisingly high support for such research among the respondents. There was some feeling that the procedures might have harassed the subjects, but the studies were not seen as invading privacy or as unethical. Also, none of the cases was seen by the majority as not providing a scientific contribution, and trust in social scientists was maintained by majorities on each item.

On the other hand, Wilson and Donnerstein were led to provide a contradictory interpretation of the results that was also supported by the data. The majority responses on the items were favorable. But in many cases substantial minorities did not respond positively. One result showed that more than one in three subjects felt that it was not appropriate for scientists to deceive the public and that such research should be protested; a similarly large minority rated that their trust in social scientists was lowered by such manipulations. The investigators pointed out that even a minority of one person is sufficient to create a court case, so researchers who would ignore these results would risk seriously damaging public confidence in their science.

Ironically, another inquiry into ethical matters, conducted by Silverman,

(1975) presents yet another facet of the issue. His investigation, which was based on the cases used later by Wilson and Donnerstein, involved presenting descriptions of eight experiments to two professors of law, having them rate the cases for legal infractions of either civil or criminal law. The two disagreed with each other on almost all points of law. One said that there had been no invasions of privacy, no trespass violations, no grounds for harassment, and in general civil and criminal laws did not apply. The other lawyer said very nearly the exact opposite. Silverman pointed out that the two lawyers were in different branches of practice, the first one a practicing defense attorney, the other in medical jurisprudence, specializing in patients' rights. Silverman then sent the cases to a third lawyer, a judge of a criminal court. His opinions diverged from the first two. In general, then, it appears that the conflicts that the science of psychology had gone through in developing its approach to resolving the rights of subjects with the value of scientific knowledge are not limited to the field itself.

SCIENTISTS' RESPONSES TO ETHICAL ISSUES

For a number of years now scientists have devoted a good deal of attention to addressing the conflict between free inquiry and the necessity of protecting the rights of subjects. Psychologists have been very active in these matters, as we will see. At the current time, several different types of procedural and structural arrangements concerning ethics have become standardized to guide scientists in their research activities. As you read the individual research articles in this book, you will see examples of how these have been institutionalized into the research process.

The APA Statement on Ethics

The American Psychological Association, national parent body and accrediting organization for American psychologists, has long taken a strong stance on protection of the rights of subjects participating in experiments conducted by psychologists. The most recent statement on this is contained in the official publication of the organization, *Ethical Principles in the Conduct of Research with Human Participants* (1973). In fact, this handbook is a revision of a similar statement published in 1953: Ethical issues have been a concern of the field for some time.

This manual is the result of a continuing evaluation process going on within psychology; all facets of ethical performance in both research and clinical practice are spelled out in detail. Case histories are presented which illuminate the various types of ethical considerations to be put into practice. The document is a codified list of set principles to be followed in all phases of psychological research and practice. All members of the American Psychological Association are expected to maintain the highest standards of ethical practice, and can have their membership revoked if charges against their ethical conduct are proven to be well-founded.

Informed Consent and Voluntary Participation

Another solution to the problem of conducting research on people is the convention of *informed consent*. In this practice, now nearly universal in American psychological research, the potential subject is told that he or she has been selected to be in an experiment, and that his or her voluntary participation is sought. The experiment's procedures are described, along with the known risks and benefits. After the full range of information is presented to the subject and the experimenter has ascertained that the subject fully understands what the experiment will involve, then the experimenter asks the subject to sign a voluntary participation form giving the experimenter full permission to include him or her as a subject.

In field experimentation where the subject's behavior is natural and nothing out of the ordinary is involved, implementing the informed consent procedure could invalidate the data and render the experiment useless. As we have seen, the strength of field research is that subjects are not under the constraints of false or untypical stimulus conditions. While conducting field research it might be possible to inform the subjects and to request them to be the partner of the investigator in creating the data. But Kelman (1967) suggests that there is a very strong possibility that the subjects will not give natural, uncalculated responses, and thus will invalidate the data. Although there is still considerable controversy surrounding the issue of informed consent in unobtrusive research, there appears to be a consensus that as long as the subject is not in any way negatively influenced, and the behavior of interest to the investigator would be manifested by the subject naturally anyway, then informed consent is not necessary. Most investigators are strongly compelled by ethical considerations and refrain from even beginning experimentation if they can see any danger of harmful reactions occurring.

If naturally occurring events cause alterations in people's lives without the intervention of the experimenter (the rare so-called natural experiment) then investigators would feel no ethical qualms about assessing the effects of such an event without informed consent. They are bound only to assure that their assessment procedures do not add on any negative consequences. An example would be a natural disaster, such as a tornado, in which one side of the block is damaged while the other side of the block is not. An investigator would be able to define this as a stress experiment with experimental and control conditions. He or she could proceed as if an experiment without informed consent had been performed, but of course would have to insure that any approach made to the residents did not generate any additional stress.

Debriefing

In laboratory research, psychologists follow another standard ethical practice called debriefing. It is done after the experiment is concluded. This is simply an open, frank discussion with the subject on the nature of the experiment, what the investigator's purpose was, what the manipulations were intended to do, and how the results of the study can be applied to the larger questions behind the research. In addition, psychologists are especially sensitive to any unfavorable reactions the subjects might have had during the experiment and work with the person until they are eliminated. The guiding principle is that the subject should leave the laboratory at least in the same condition as when he or she arrived, or perhaps improved. The subject should never leave in a less positive state.

There is a body of research on precisely this issue, some of which shows that debriefing procedures do not return subjects back to their precise original state. However, other research data suggest that such a conclusion cannot be fully supported, so the issue is still unresolved. Investigators are sensitive to this issue and often refuse to conduct a study unless it is clear that the subjects will not be negatively influenced in some way.

A slightly different problem faces researchers conducting research in field settings, especially when the subjects never actually have contact with the experimenter. Littering studies are a good example of people being subjected to manipulations without knowing it. Generally, researchers do not feel compelled to interview subjects after the conclusion of such studies because it is sometimes impossible to find the subjects and because informing them that they were part of an experiment might be more upsetting than not informing them at all. Clearly some research does represent an invasion of privacy and violates the right to be left alone. The investigator has to consider fully if the research is worth that risk. But when subjects cannot be contacted individually before the experiment begins and therefore cannot be provided with informed consent, then perhaps it could be considered invasion of privacy to then inform them that they were in an experiment.

In general, most investigators do consider the debriefing phase to be an important one and they integrate it into their studies. But there are a number of types of studies in which it is either infeasible or not even advisable. Field research is beset with the difficult problem of trying to gather data unobtrusively and yet must insure that subjects are not negatively influenced by the procedures because that would require debriefing to remove those negative effects. Since the debriefing itself might have some unintended negative consequences it is often bypassed in field research.

Peer Review

As a final check on their ethical standards, psychologists, and in fact nearly all scientists in America, are accountable in some way to their peers to protect the rights of their subjects. One way in which this is monitored is during the peer review process. When a scientist files a research proposal with a supporting agency (which could be a local, state, or national agency), the proposal is formally evaluated by a panel of outside experts. They review the research for its appropriateness of design, adequacy of data analysis, and other characteristics. The full range of experimental issues is reviewed. Among these, and having high priority, is the adequacy of the experimenter's ethical concern for the subjects. The investigator is expected to have thoroughly considered all relevant factors of how the treatment might influence the subjects, both during the actual experiment itself and afterwards. Any potential negative effects have to be accounted for, procedures for handling them detailed, and alternatives for other experiments which might avoid any negative effects have to be considered and proven to be inapplicable. Should the investigator come up short on these criteria, the study is simply rejected.

For psychologists in universities, an additional criterion has to be met. Most university psychology departments have review committees that pass on any research done by the faculty members. Once again, ethical matters are thoroughly scrutinized by these reviewers before approval to perform the research is given. Similar committees are present in other university departments and medical schools too. In the overwhelming majority of cases, conflicts between the rights of the subjects and the value of obtaining research data have been resolved by researchers, so problems at this level are infrequent. But the tension between the needs and rights of the individual and the rights of scientists to conduct their inquiries is an everpresent dilemma. It deserves, and receives constant attention from concerned scientists.

These issues seem to have no clear resolution at this time in the history of the sciences. Perhaps there will be significant change in the future, change that either will restrict scientists more, or perhaps give them better direction. But as we go through the research examples reprinted in this book, ethical questions should be uppermost in your mind. These are basically nonreactive experiments. In general, the subjects as participants did not know that an experiment was in progress. As a student and as a citizen, it is important that you think about balancing the value of the information gained both for analyzing behavior scientifically and for use in societal improvement with the rights of individual subjects.

References

American Psychological Association. *Ethical principles in the conduct of research with human participants.* (2nd ed.). Washington, D.C., 1973.

Baumrind, D. Some thoughts on ethics of research: After reading Milgram's "Behavioral study of obedience." *American Psychologist,* 1964, *19,* 421-23.

Campbell, D. T. Reforms as experiments. *American Psychologist,* 1969, *24,* 409-29.

Kelman, H. Human use of human subjects: The problem of deception in social psychological experiments. *Psychological Bulletin,* 1967, *67,* 1-11.

McGuire, W. The Yin and Yang of progress in social psychology: Seven koan. *Journal of Personality and Social Psychology,* 1973, *26,* 446-56.

Milgram, S. Behavioral study of obedience. *Journal of Abnormal and Social Psychology,* 1963, *67,* 371-8.

Milgram, S. Issues in the study of obedience: A reply to Baumrind. *American Psychologist,* 1964, *19,* 848-52.

Miller, G. A. Psychology as a means of promoting human welfare. *American Psychologist,* 1969, *24,* 1063-75.

Parke, R. D., Berkowitz, L., Leyens, J. P., West, S. G., & Sebastian, R. J. Some effects of violent and nonviolent movies on the behavior of juvenile delinquents. In L. Berkowitz (Ed.), *Advances in experimental social psychology,* (Vol. 10). New York: Academic Press, 1977.

Shils, A. E. Social inquiry and the autonomy of the individual. In D. Lerner (Ed.), *The human meaning of the social sciences.* Cleveland: Meridian, 1959.

Silverman, I. Nonreactive methods and the law. *American Psychologist,* 1975, *30,* 764-9.

Streufert, S. How applied is applied social psychology: Editorial. *Journal of Applied Social Psychology,* 1973, *3,* 1-5.

Sullivan, D. S., and Deiker, T. E. Subject-experimenter perceptions of ethical issues in human research. *American Psychologist,* 1973, *28,* 587-91.

Wilson, D. W., & Donnerstein, E. Legal and ethical aspects of nonreactive social psychological research. *American Psychologist,* 1976, *31,* 765-73.

5

How To Read
An Original Source
Journal Article

Probably one of the most difficult tasks a student can attempt is to read and understand a scientific article which communicates technical material. An original source article is written in a specific style which has an internal structure and logic all its own. Such articles are not structured in ordinary discourse patterns and therefore are difficult to read if someone is not familiar with scientific writing. But once a student has gained an understanding of the structure of this type of communication, then a whole world of new information is readily available and the student is better equipped to join the open and exciting world of scientific discovery.

Scientific writing is clear and concise; it is an efficient communicator of information. Reading such material requires some skill. It is possible to provide a set of guidelines to reveal how articles are written and constructed which should make learning the pattern of scientific communication easier for nonscientists.

Scientists develop a sort of map in writing and reading articles; they set down a series of signposts, high and low trails and major crosspoints that lead them through the article down to the final destination: the conclusions of the investigation. The purpose of this chapter is to give you a generalized cognitive map to match up with the map followed by the writers of scientific articles—like the people who wrote the articles contained in this book. Technical issues, such as how to interpret statistical techniques and judgments of the merits of operational definitions will not be explained in detail here. It is not that these matters are not important issues in judging the merits of the contributions of an article, but rather that such issues can be pursued in advance coursework or left to the judgment of more professional readers. The aim here simply is to introduce you to scientific writing in its original form.

Perhaps the first major point to be made is the importance of the *sequence* of the material in a scientific article. There is a natural flow in such writing, and once you know what the sequence of highpoints is, then the side topics, ancillary points and subsidiary analyses will be seen as variations on the major theme and not be misleading. In ordinary conversation there is usually a central theme with subthoughts intertwined around it; this is true in scientific writing as well. What follows, therefore, is an outline of how articles are written and what you should look for as you read them.

THE TITLE

Although this may seem elementary, the title of a paper is quite important: Usually titles communicate a good deal of information. Many investigators know the difficulty of choosing an appropriate title. They worry that it will not say enough or will not get at the essence of the experiment, so the final title usually has been carefully chosen and is quite meaningful. Of course, articles vary in this; some are so vague or general that you only get a hint at the actual topic. Others are highly specific. For example, the Doob, et al. study is entitled "Effects of initial sales price on subsequent sales" (Chapter 6).

Most titles give the reader some information about both the independent and dependent variables involved in the study, so you should spend enough time thinking about the title to have a general feeling about what the investigator manipulated or assessed and what dependent variable-related behavior was of interest. When an article has some such clause as ". . . the effect of x on y" then you have been given sufficient information to know what is the focus of interest and the major variables under investigation.

THE ABSTRACT

The editors of scientific journals commonly require authors to develop an abstracted summary of their reports. The purpose of the abstract is to present in an extremely brief and condensed form the essence of the study. It should include the basic theoretical and conceptual material, the specific hypothesis of the study, the methodology, the results, and the conclusions to be drawn from the study. The reader is supposed to be able to develop a basic understanding of the study from the abstract, so the author is under considerable pressure to be as accurate and as brief as possible. The abstract can be invaluable to the student as well as the technically trained reader, for from it the reader can arrange a set of conceptual hooks upon which to hang the later technical details which constitute the body of the report itself.

THE INTRODUCTION SECTION

The introduction section, which is usually unlabeled, is the first major section of any research report. It is the author's attempt to spell out the conceptual foundations and rationale for the research to be reported; it details why the study was done. In the process of constructing the conceptual platform for the research that will follow, the author reviews any prior work which is relevant to the topic. The review touches on both prior theoretical and conceptual material which is relevant and deals with specific research results which already have been reported. The prior conceptual work and data are integrated into a statement about the topic of interest, and may involve such varied approaches as: a reinterpretation of previous research, an attempt to remedy procedural or conceptual flaws in prior research, the addition of a new variable previously unexplored, an integration of different theories not previously integrated, or even the analysis of variables never before investigated.

In this construction process, the report describes the careful analyses of the independent and dependent variables. The introduction also contains descriptions of those variables expected to have a measurable impact, the specific behaviors of interest to the investigator, and in the case of experimental social psychology, the behavioral processes expected to be influenced by the experimenter's manipulations of the independent variables.

Whatever the purpose of the study, you should be conscious of the *inverted pyramid* approach taken in most research report introduction sections: there is a broad coverage of the important conceptual empirical material, then a narrowing down to the specific question the investigator wishes to pursue. Commonly, at the end of the introductory section the investigator spells out the specific hypotheses or predictions of the study. The process of formulating and stating hypotheses is one of the more subtle but critical aspects of the scientific enterprise, for it is here that the investigator brings into sharpest focus the purpose of the research and its relationship to the conceptual material previously reviewed. An hypothesis follows logically and naturally from what has been stated previously and is designed to be the focal point for the actual data of the experiment itself. Therefore, the hypothesis is the best guidepost for the reader to keep in mind while going through the remainder of the research report.

THE METHOD SECTION

This section provides a complete report of the steps the investigator followed in conducting the study. In theory, this section should be so complete that someone reading it would be able to run the experiment in exactly the same way as the original investigator did, and thus get a measure of the stability (replicability) of the data. This is a rigorous demand, but scientific progress is critically dependent upon the development of standardized procedures and techniques which can be performed repeatedly in different settings by different experimenters. The methods section is central to this goal.

A standardized format for reporting methodological matters in such detail that they can be repeated by other experimenters has been developed over the years. This form will become obvious after you have read some of the articles in the next sections. The parts of the methodology section are divided into subsections.

The Subjects Subsection

In this subsection, the investigator spells out briefly but thoroughly the important characteristics of the people involved in the experiment. Such characteristics as the age, sex, and sometimes the race of the subjects are listed. Also, the experimental conditions (the cells of the experimental design) into which the subjects were assigned is sometimes mentioned. In general, this subsection includes the most important facts a reader would need to know to select and assign subjects to exactly replicate (repeat) the experiment.

The Procedure Subsection

The procedure subsection is the most detailed and densely written part because it involves a step-by-step review of exactly how the investigator conducted the experiment. This information is necessary for it tells the reader everything (within reason) that would be needed to conduct another experiment identical or nearly so to the one being reported.

The procedure subsection's format is chronological. It sequentially lists the steps of the experiment, how the independent variable manipulations occurred, how the experimental groups differed from the control groups, and how the dependent variable assessments were taken. Often any verbal instructions that were given to the subjects are reproduced exactly.

In reading the procedures subsection, you should be attentive to the conceptual issues presented in the introductory material, because at this point in the report the subtle interrelationship between theory and operationalization of the study's concepts becomes manifest. There should be a very close correspondence between the theoretical basis of a study and its procedures. Each of the experimental manipulations should be obvious to the reader. The reading here is slow and difficult. Referral back to the introductory material while reading the procedures section should create a clear and well-integrated understanding of the purpose and the empirical nature of the experiment.

THE RESULTS SECTION

This is the most technical section of a research paper and undoubtedly the most difficult for a beginning student to follow. However, it is in this section that the issues involved in the study begin to be resolved. The actual connections between the theoretical predictions of the study and the study's outcomes are described.

The reader of this section should focus on the trends in the results such as: the statistical reliability of patterns, tests of differences between group averages, and the reliability of correlation coefficients, among other outcomes. Quite often the major finding concerns how a group submitted to the experimental treatments differs from another group not submitted to them, the control group. Oftentimes graphs and figures are included to help clarify the results. The reader should also be attentive to differences between major analyses and ancillary analyses. Major analyses are those concerned with the major hypotheses of the study while ancillary analyses are the result of testing minor parts of the study such as tests of the subjects' perceptions of manipulations and preexisting group differences.

These less important parts usually are reported first, so that the smaller issues which might clutter up the report are discussed first and then set aside. This is followed by the major analyses. Along with the minor matters, the general orientation of this section is to build the reader's confidence in the overall pattern of data the investigator obtained.

The two most important parts of the results section are the reports of the patterns in the actual results themselves (group averages, frequencies, correlations, etc.), and the presentation of the findings of the statistical tests of significance of or the reliability of those obtained results. The information usually is presented in tables or graphs. The significance values indicate whether the pattern of results reported by the investigator was accidental (random, due to chance occurrences) or was so strong and clear that there is little likelihood that it was due to chance. If the significance tests values show that the pattern was not likely the result of chance, then the results were probably due to the experimenter's manipulations, the ones being tested in the first place. The heart of this determination revolves around a probability value (the so-called *p value,* a numerical score varying from .00 to 1.00) which simply indicates the probability that the pattern of the results was a random occurrence. The lower the *p value,* the more confidence you can have that the result was due to a real influence by the experimenter's variables. By convention, if the *p value* is .05, .04, .03, or less the researcher and the reader can feel confident that the pattern was not due to chance, but instead the experimenter's variables. By convention, the symbol $<$ means that the probability was smaller than the conventionally agreed upon value of .05, and the symbol $>$ means that the probability was greater than the value and hence more likely due to chance. So in reading the results section, you should keep in mind the importance of the stated *p values* and their size; those statistical tests that result in *p* values of .05 or smaller suggest that the reader can feel relatively confident that the obtained pattern of the data is meaningful.

THE DISCUSSION SECTION

The discussion section of a report is intended to provide a concise but clear interpretation of how the results of the study relate to the hypotheses. It also covers how the conceptual material in the introductory section has fared given the experimental manipulations. It is in this section that the investigator passes judgment on any prior research and the study being reported.

While relating the data of the experiment, the author is obligated to consider fully any alternative explanations of his or her data that might not have been tested in the experiment. How those alternative explanations themselves fare in the face of the evidence of the study has to be considered. Finally, any conceptual or methodological flaws that might render the data suspect also have to be considered and their potential threat to solid conclusions about the study have to receive full consideration. Usually, authors will attempt to develop a modified, more adequate view of the topic on the basis of the data gathered, and a relatively complete new picture of the area proposed. Also, any practical or applied implications of the study for real world living are commonly suggested, along with suggestions for how additional research might test those or other implications.

THE SUMMARY (CONCLUSIONS) SECTION

In some journals the author is required to present an extremely brief summarizing statement along the lines of an abstract (if an abstract is included this section usually is not presented). Conclusions sections do not present new material but make a statement about the purpose of the study, its results, and a statement or two concerning the overall implications of the study. Such sections are useful in consolidating the overall study in the reader's mind.

SOME HINTS ON HOW TO READ A SCIENTIFIC ARTICLE

Although students' learning habits vary widely and what works best for one student may not work well for another, a few general rules of thumb will apply to anyone unfamiliar with original scientific writing.

First, skim over the article once, reviewing the abstract and attempting to understand the general purpose of the study; the introductory material is especially useful for this. A brief scan of the methodology and results will lay out a picture of how the variables effected the behavior of the subjects, and a scan of the discussion will give the reader some general views of how the experiment related to the hypotheses. This first scan will give the reader a feel for why and how the investigation was conducted.

On a second reading concentrate on how the investigator lined up the introductory material to derive the hypotheses and predictions of the study. The material should cohere and the predictions should seem readily understandable. If you understand this conceptual material, then the method should be almost obvious and inevitable. How the concepts led to the experimental procedure should seem logical and the hypotheses should appear vulnerable to support or rejection by the methodology developed for testing them.

In the method section, follow the flow of events as they were arranged by the experimenter and as they impinged on the subject. The logical structure detailed in the introduction should help to clarify how the various experimental and control conditions relate to each other and to the hypothesis. The focus of reading here should be on how the behavior of the subject, elicited by the experimenter's stimulus arrangements, relates to the hypotheses of the study.

Given the above, then the results section material should be clear and fairly easy to read. Although the mathematical and statistical manipulations of the data may be unfamiliar, the trends in the data, especially if they involve intergroup differences or patterns of correlations, should be relatively easy to understand within the framework of the hypotheses of the study. The significance values (*ps*) only indicate which results patterns are reliable enough for the reader to place confidence in them.

The discussion section provides rather redundant information if you have understood the logic of the conceptual foundations of the study and how the data-acquisition and testing phases related to that foundation. The author's attempts at reviewing alternative explanations and practical implications should be useful in getting a concise but full picture of the entire study.

After a second more careful reading, think over the study and attempt to reproduce it mentally in the same sequential flow as the article described it. In their daily activities, professionals in a science commit to memory the major conclusions of important studies and use them readily in ordinary discourse. You can achieve the same ability by careful, deliberate reading; it is helpful to consolidate the material by restating the study in your own language.

Reading research can be an exciting, creative, and productive activity, one which you will find very useful. Thinking like a scientist is easier to develop after reading what scientists write.

6

Analysis of the Individual

From the earliest days of the social sciences, theorists and researchers have sought to understand the workings of the human mind. Since one main area of interest has been social processes and variables, the focus of their attention naturally has revolved around social factors as influences on mental processes and the social orientation of the mental processes themselves. William James, one of the early founders of the science of psychology, reflected this concern with his concept of the *social self,* that part of one's thoughts that reflects one's social bonds with other people. Later theorists such as James Mark Baldwin and Herbert Mead elaborated on this basic notion by conceptualizing the self as the internalized product of the reactions of other people to oneself; you think of yourself in concepts and ways that others have used to respond to you.

By the 1930s, when the quantitative and experimental approach had become firmly established in social psychology, concern with analyzing the internal psychological processes of individuals became a major activity of the field. The concept of attitude played a major role during that period and it continues to do so today. This concept represents an ideal combination of individual process variables with a social orientation: One has attitudes about other people and groups and about social values and institutions. Some of the readings in this first group of studies concern attitudes. The focus of the studies is on theories about how behavior is influenced by attitude processes as the person responds to events occurring naturally in the social environment. The research is quite successful in demonstrating the power of the scientific approach to analyze social behavior in its natural context.

Other aspects of mental processing also are of major interest in contemporary social psychology. What has come to be called *attribution theory* has provided a particularly broad and productive framework for research—studies from that tradition are included here. This approach is directly concerned with cognitive processes, particularly those focused on how the individual perceives causal relations and how one thing is perceived to influence another thing. This research also takes into account how things are perceived to cause the individual's own behavior and how one's behavior influences other things. This area includes research on *cognitive control processes,* processes whereby individuals do or do not attribute to themselves control over the events occurring in their lives. This research shows that knowledge of cognitive control processes can be used to help people, and the readings in this section reflect that type of application.

Personality research has a developmental history somewhat distinct from that of social psychology, but the two areas have developed along parallel and often interacting tracks. The concept of personality refers to stable and enduring characteristics of the person, including self-concept, disposition, and central values. When these involve social processes and interpersonal variables, then social psychologists become interested in analyzing them. The articles reprinted in the second part of this section demonstrate how useful it can be to combine personality and social variables in research on these complex facets of human behavior.

The particular research articles reprinted in this section are aimed at developing an understanding of social behavior's influence within the individual's own psychological process; the focus is on the individual. In the next section of the book, the research is aimed more at understanding genuinely social variables; that is situations in which more than one person is interacting, reacting, and judging with others.

ATTITUDE PROCESSES

The two articles in this section both apply one theory of attitude processes, dissonance theory (Festinger, 1957), to everyday behavior. The first study, by Knox and Inkster, analyzes the behavior of bettors at race tracks, and the second by Doob, Carlsmith, Freedman, Landauer, and Tom, analyzes people's small item purchasing behavior before and after a special introductory price campaign. These behaviors are not particularly complex or dramatic, but the fact that theory-based predictions about them can be rigorously tested in natural settings is very significant. The aim of science is explanation, and analyzing even simple behavior is an important aspect of social psychological science if it can elucidate behavior without the constraints of the artificial world of the laboratory.

By analyzing the cognitive processes which occur in decision-making, cognitive dissonance theory makes predictions concerning how people behave when a commitment-generating decision to some course of action has to be made, or has been made. The theory predicts that *cognitive balance* processes will operate; people will strive to keep their beliefs, attitudes, and cognitions aligned with each other and with their overt behavior. As one believes, so one behaves, and as one behaves, so one believes. Knox and Inkster's study, "Postdecision dissonance at post time," applies dissonance theory to a betting situation. The act of having made a bet generates an irrevocable commitment to that bet. In order to keep cognitions and behavior consistent, one's confidence that it was a good bet is increased. It would be dissonance provoking, not reducing, if one were to make a bet and then conclude that the horse were no good or the jockey incompetent, so the theory predicts that the confidence level of people who had already made a bet would be higher than those who had not yet bet. The results confirm the theoretical prediction. Another study in a different setting and with some changes in methodology also was conducted, and the prediction once again confirmed. The effect was found to be stable.

Additional research on a hypothesis is always recommended. It increases the range of generality of the phenomenon as well as increases one's confidence in it if it receives additional support in different settings and different techniques.

Doob, Carlsmith, Freedman, Landauer, and Tom ("Effect of initial price on subsequent sales") analyze the phenomenon of the low introductory price so common in marketing and product sales. Although at the common sense level this nearly universal practice appears to be a potent way of increasing sales, these investigators argue from cognitive dissonance theory that an unintended and in fact reverse effect might be generated by this practice. Their argument is that effort and attitudes are related, and that the more difficult or effortful a decision is, the more one will tend to like or support that decision. In the case of purchasing, to have purchased a product at a given price gives it a subjective value: The higher the price of the item, the more value it will have.

A prediction of the effect of a special low introductory price offer on sales from the viewpoint of dissonance theory is surprising but straightforward: Those customers who pay a higher initial price for a product will value it more than those who pay a lower price and, over time, will purchase it on a steady basis. If the price is later raised, those who paid a lower price initially and who do not value the product to the same degree will have less desire for it and will be less motivated to continue purchasing the product at a higher price.

In their studies on this prediction, the investigators effectively tested the hypothesis five times by checking sales records of the purchases of five different products over a long enough period of time to obtain good measures of sales patterns. Although the methods varied slightly, the general technique involved the introduction of a given product at several levels of price, one lower and one higher, and then later raising the price of the lower one up to the level of the higher one.

The data for all five sets of manipulations were consistent with each other and with the hypothesis: Those products introduced at a lower price and then raised had lower sales than those introduced at a higher price and maintained at that level. Dissonance theory's seemingly contradictory prediction received consistent support. One wonders what impact such impressive and surprising results might have on the marketplace if they were applied widely.

ATTRIBUTION AND COGNITIVE CONTROL PROCESSES

Social psychologists have expanded their notions about cognitive processes beyond attitude variables such as dissonance. One of the very recent developments in this area concerns the role of cognitive control processes. This refers to a person's interpretation of his or her ability to have an impact on environmental events. It has been shown that people tend to assume they have control when outcomes are positive and not to make that assumption when events are negative. The two studies reprinted here investigate control attributions in people who have been placed in special situations in which they have lost some control over their lives: A nursing home and the surgical ward of a hospital.

Langer and Rodin ("The effects of choice and enhanced personal responsibility for the aged: A field experiment in an institutional setting") chose as their research setting a home for the aged. All subjects were 65 years or older. "Being cared for" is central to the functioning of such a setting, but cognitive control theory would suggest that a sense of self-competence is valuable for positive feelings and loss of that sense might be related to unsatisfactory adjustment.

The investigators engineered a naturalistic manipulation of the control variable (the usual low and high conditions so common in research). To one group of residents they emphasized that they were being cared for and things would be done for them by the administrative personnel. To the other group they emphasized that the residents themselves should take responsibility and that how the home was run depended on their own initiative and responsibility.

In line with control theory predictions, the high control group was rated as having better adjustment than the low control group. In addition, the investigators conducted a long-term follow up study nineteen months later, and the same effect held. There was even a slight, though statistically nonsignificant, tendency for the high responsibility residents to have a lower mortality rate than the low responsibility group.

Although the manipulation of the control variable was rather simple, the results of this study, and others like it, are quite profound. Social psychological theory and research have societal implications for situations where people give over control to others, including those intending to help them. To be treated as if one were helpless is likely to lead one to behave that way, but to be treated as independent and capable of self-maintenance is likely to have more desirable short- and long-term consequences. This study makes a convincing case that social psychological theory is a valuable tool to help us plan for aiding people in the future.

Cognitive control theory also can be extended to analyze people's reactions to fear- and stress-provoking situations. Langer, Janis, and Wolfer ("Reduction of psychological stress in surgical patients") studied congitive control theory as it affected hospital patients facing surgery. Control was involved by helping the subjects (patients) alter their cognitive interpretation of the situation by selectively attending only to certain parts of the situation and concentrating on the positive benefits to be gained from the surgery. The logic is that suggestions about how to handle the stress one is going to feel could alter the actual stress response itself by providing a sense of personal control. Assessing pre- and postsurgery reactions is an excellent way to test the cognitive control prediction that subjects with such instructions would benefit from control-enhancing coping strategies.

The subjects read prepared statements concerning how people react to stress and how they themselves could learn to cut down their reactions by appropriate thoughts and controlling behaviors. Other conditions tested for other possible effects over and above those of the manipulations. Such things as anxiety, physiological measures of stress, and even how much medication was needed in the postsurgery phase were measured in the experiment. Pre- and postsurgery measures were taken and change effects were tested.

The results show that the coping instructions which manipulate attributional processes are effective. By helping the patients rethink the surgery situation along cognitive control lines, the investigators helped the patients gain control over their fear reactions and thus adapt to the stress.

From a study like this, we have a sound theory tested for analyzing human thought processes, but we also have a promising technique for helping people to help themselves in stressful circumstances. It should be clear that the areas of clinical and social psychology which formerly were considered distinct and separate have a common meeting ground in this area.

THE SELF AND SOCIAL INSTITUTIONS

It is a difficult task to determine how personality variables influence behavior. It demands attention to clear definition and measurement of the relevant personality constructs and careful analysis of how the surrounding societal variables might be related. Societal variables themselves can range from the presence of one person or a few people all the way up to the entire society. Sales found that there is a link between the belief and personality structure of people and large-scale social forces. His study's hypothesis is that the rates at which people join with a social organization such as a church can be predicted from the personality theory of authoritarianism and knowledge of societal stress such as economic recession.

The study by Zanna, Sheras, Cooper, and Shaw analyzes self-processes at a more personal level: the interaction of teachers and their students. Both studies are useful for their insights into how people respond to social forces both distant and close, and how these forces influence individual personality-based cognitive processes.

The study by Sales ("Economic threat as a determinant of conversion rates in authoritarian and nonauthoritarian churches") incorporates both individual and societal levels of analysis: It is a naturalistic study of how people respond to stress (in this case, the economic depression of the 1930s), and applies the personality variable of authoritarianism to both levels. Authoritarianism is conceptualized as a personality process closely related to perceptions of threat. Under threat, high authoritarian persons tend to become rigid, submissive to authority, more concerned with power relations, and desirous of structure and certainty in their lives.

Sales extends the general concept of authoritarianism to include social organizations, proposing specifically that churches can be ordered in terms of how they treat obedience matters, leadership, and tolerance of deviation. By analyzing their stated doctrines, he categorized churches and ranked them as relatively more to relatively less authoritarian. Given that analysis, he reasoned that there would be a relationship between membership and joining rates and the churches' authoritarian nature. He hypothesized that people would choose membership in more libertarian churches in economically good times and more authoritarian churches in economically stressful times. Sales gathered information on the rates of church conversions during the twenty year period from 1920 through 1939, which covers a wide range of economic conditions. In spite of some necessary approximations in the data, in two studies he shows that people do tend to convert and establish membership in authoritarian churches more in times of economic stress; the hypothesis was confirmed. Sales also refers to some laboratory based research which reaches essentially the same conclusion, so the data appear to be stable and valid. His support of field research with laboratory findings provides a solid foundation for confidence in his hypothesis.

Zanna, Sheras, Cooper, and Shaw ("Pygmalion and Galatea: The interactive effect of teacher and student expectancies") take a different approach to analyzing social variables in natural contexts. Whereas Sales assesses past events that he cannot change, Zanna and his colleagues actually manipulate interpersonal interaction in an institutional setting, schools. School experiences dominate our lives, especially in our formative years. Analyzing individual development which is subjected to institutional forces in the school is a fertile source of research hypotheses. In this case, the focus was on cognitive processes.

It has been known for some time that when teachers are led to expect high performances from students those students later tend to outperform and be rated as better than other students for whom teachers do not have such expectancies. This is called the *Pygmalion effect*. It appears as if the teachers' expectancies (attributions) somehow lead them to treat the students differently, although there is no direct evidence for such bias as a conscious or intentional factor.

By experimental instruction, the investigators gave teachers manipulated expectancies about their students. They also gave the students themselves expectations about their own performance, and thus were able to analyze the joint effect of these two cognitive attributional processes operating simultaneously.

The results show that each expectancy condition led to improved performance. However, when both conditions were operating simultaneously, significantly lower performance resulted. Apparently the expectations combined and created a pressure for excellent performance so high that a disappointment or frustration condition resulted. Teachers, students, parents, and school administrators should be aware of this subtle but potentially powerful influence which essentially is not under conscious or intentional control.

The effect need not be restricted to school settings only. Since people's expectancies for their own and other people's performance occur in almost any institutional setting, both theoretical and practical considerations dictate that experiments such as this be conducted to help us understand this important facet of social psychological phenomena.

SELF-ENHANCEMENT PROCESSES

In our final section on social psychological analyses of the individual, we come to a central and very important issue—how people regard themselves. Social psychologists use the concepts of self-esteem and self-based attributions to analyze how individuals make decisions and judgments and choose responses to the events in their lives. Of particular concern is how these decisions and responses are affected by the presence of others. The two studies reprinted in this section approach self processes from different angles. One, by Koocher, analyzes self-esteem attribution deriving from the acquisition of a sense of competence: Those people who acquired a particular skill, in this case swimming, develop a more positive and idealized image of themselves. The technique employed to study this is not an artificial experimenter-manipulated variable, but a very natural event, the teaching of swimming at a summer camp. The second study, by Cialdini and his associates, studies how self-esteem is closely tied to the images we project to others, even when those images do not involve our own behavior. They investigate BIRGing (basking in reflected glory), the process whereby people will go to sometimes extreme lengths to associate themselves with successful others even when their connection with them is weak or tenuous. They study the behavior of football fans after their favorite teams had won or lost football games. As in Koocher's research and all those collected in this book, they were able to use natural settings for their analyses and thus obtain very realistic yet rigorous tests of their explanations of human social behavior.

Koocher's study ("Swimming, competence, and personality change") approaches self-esteem enhancement through the investigation of people's feelings of successful attainment and competence. The subjects were young males who had less well-formed self-concepts than adults would. Therefore they were more likely to show the impact, if any, of competence-testing experiences. The hypothesis of the study is that being successful at an important task will raise self-esteem. The study was able to avoid the shortcomings of laboratory research on this effect by choosing a natural setting in an ego-involving behavior—swimming —which occurred naturally in the lives of the subjects.

The design of the study was simple: Self esteem ratings on a standard scale were assessed both before and after swimming competence was acquired. The basic data of interest was the discrepancy score between the *real self* (how you really are) and the *ideal self* (how you would like to be); this is a common measure of how positively one regards oneself. The data collected on each subject was grouped according to the characteristics of the subjects when the experiment began. The groups were those who already knew how to swim, those who did not know how to swim, and those who refused to learn.

The results show that subjects who initially could not swim but learned to do so developed more positive self-esteem than the controls, confirming the hypothesis. Parents, teachers, camp counselors, and others dealing with young children should be aware of the favorable impact that such experiences can have and should organize activities for children along these lines.

The traditional definition of the self is that it is the totality of the person's thoughts and attitudes about his or her possessions, appearance, and skills. The study by Cialdini, Borden, Thorne, Walker, Freeman, and Sloan ("Basking in reflected glory: Three (football) field studies") focuses on how the self concept is expanded to include the performance of individuals and groups which the person considers to be relevant to his or her own life. An important insight of these studies is that the self-definition process includes or excludes others on the basis of success or failure of those others. This is the BIRG effect (basking in reflected glory). The investigators hypothesized that this drive is so intense that people will attempt to BIRG even when the connection with the comparison other is totally unrelated to their own personal efforts.

The investigators used subtle and unobtrusive measures of self-esteem bolstering. In the first study, they found that college students tend to wear school-colors-related clothes more when their school wins a football game than when it loses a game. The wearing of clothes is an overt, public way of identifying oneself with a particular image one wishes to project. When the home team loses, not wearing colors-related clothing would be a way of maintaining self-esteem, and it was found that there was less colors-wearing after defeat. Of course, merely attending a school has no direct effect on its success or failure at football, so it is clear that the effect holds when the connection is a functionally irrelevant one.

The investigators also tested the effect with a completely different type of behavior, the use of the pronouns "we" and "they" as these correlate with winning and losing. Students were found to be more likely to use the term "we" ("we won") when the home team won and "they" ("they lost") when the home team lost. A third study involving actual manipulated personal success and failure experiences once again found the basic BIRGing effect. In sum, then, this is a very complete set of studies: There is a moving back and forth from initial naturalistic observation of football fandom to a more controlled experimental analysis. At all points the data matched the predictions well. The experimenters defined an effect, tested and supported predictions about it and, in doing so, illuminated a very common and powerful facet of human social behavior.

Attitude Processes

Postdecision Dissonance at Post Time[1]

Robert E. Knox   *University of British Columbia*
James A. Inkster

Abstract

Two experiments were conducted to investigate post-decisional dissonance reduction processes following a commitment to bet on a horse in the natural and uncontrived setting of a race track. In the 1st study, 69 $2 Win bettors rated the chance that the horse they had selected would win the forthcoming race and 72 other bettors provided ratings immediately after making a $2 Win bet. On the 7-point rating scale employed, prebet subjects gave a median rating of 3.48, which corresponded to a "fair chance of winning"; postbet subjects gave a median rating of 4.81, which corresponded to a "good chance of winning." This difference was significant beyond the .01 level. The general findings were replicated in a 2nd study in which harness-race patrons rated how confident they felt about their selected horse either just before or just after betting. Results from both studies provide support for Festinger's theory in a real life setting and

"Postdecision Dissonance at Post Time" by Robert E. Knox and James A. Inkster. *Journal of Personality and Social Psychology,* 1968, Vol. 8, No. 4, pp. 319–323. Copyright © 1968 by The American Psychological Association, Inc. Reprinted by permission.

indicate that dissonance-reducing processes may occur very rapidly following commitment to a decision.

In the last decade there have been numerous laboratory experiments conducted to test various implications of Festinger's (1957) theory of cognitive dissonance. In spite of sometimes serious methodological faults (cf. Chapanis & Chapanis, 1964), the laboratory evidence as a whole has tended to support Festinger's notions. Confidence in the theory, as Brehm and Cohen (1962) have previously suggested, can now be further strengthened by extending empirical tests from lifelike to real life situations. The present study investigates the effects of postdecision dissonance on bettors in their natural habitat, the race track.

Festinger (1957) had originally contended that due to the lingering cognitions about the favorable characteristics of the rejected alternative(s), dissonance was an inevitable consequence of a decision. Subsequently, however, Festinger (1964) accepted the qualification that in order for dissonance to occur, the decision must also have the effect of committing the person. A favorite technique for reducing postdecisional dissonance, according to the theory, is to change cognitions in such a manner as to increase the attractiveness of the chosen alternative relative to the unchosen alternative(s). At the race track a bettor becomes financially committed to his decision when he purchases a parimutuel ticket on a particular horse. Once this occurs, postdecisional processes should operate to reduce dissonance by increasing the attractiveness of the chosen horse relative to the unchosen horses in the race. These processes would be reflected by the bettor's expression of greater confidence in his having picked a winner after his bet had been made than before.

In order to test this notion, one need only go to a race track, acquire a prebet and postbet sample, and ask members of each how confident they are that they have selected the winning horse in the forthcoming race. The two samples should be independent since the same subjects in a before-after design could contravene the observed effects of dissonance reduction by carrying over consistent responses in the brief interval between pre- and postmeasurements. In essence, this was the approach employed in the two natural experiments reported here. More formally, the experimental hypothesis in both experiments was that bettors would be more confident of their selected horse just after betting $2 than just before betting.

EXPERIMENT I

Subjects

Subjects were 141 bettors at the Exhibition Park Race Track in Vancouver, British Columbia. Sixty-nine of these subjects, the prebet group, were interviewed less than 30 seconds *before* making a $2 Win bet. Seventy-two subjects, the postbet group, were interviewed a few seconds after making a $2 Win bet. Fifty-one subjects, interviewed before the forth and fifth races, were obtained in the exclusive Clubhouse section. Data from the remaining 90 bettors were collected prior to the second, third, sixth, and seventh races at various betting locations in the General Admission or grandstand area.

No formal rituals were performed to guarantee random sampling, but instead, every person approaching or leaving a $2 Win window at a time when the experimenters were not already engaged in an interview was contacted. Of those contacted, approximately 15% refused to cooperate further because they could not speak English, refused to talk to "race touts," never discussed their racing information with strangers, or because of some unexpressed other reason. The final sample consisted of white, Negro, and Oriental men and women ranging in estimated age from the early twenties to late sixties and ranging in style from ladies in fur to shabby old men. The final sample was felt to be reasonably representative of the Vancouver race track crowd.

Procedure

The two experimenters were stationed in the immediate vicinity of the "Sellers" window during the 25-minute betting interval between races. For any given race, one experimenter intercepted bettors as they approached a $2 Win window and the other experimenter intercepted different bettors as they left these windows. Prebet and postbet interview roles were alternated with each race between the two experimenters.

The introductory appeal to subjects and instructions for their ratings were as follows:

> *I beg your pardon. I am a member of a University of British Columbia research team studying risk-taking behavior. Are you about to place a $2 Win bet? [Have you just made a $2 Win bet?] Have we already talked to you today? I wonder if you would mind looking at this card and telling me what*

chance you think the horse you are going to bet on [have just bet on] has of winning this race. The scale goes from 1, a slight chance, to 7, an excellent chance. Just tell me the number from 1 to 7 that best describes the chance that you think your horse has of winning. Never mind now what the tote board or professional handicappers say; what chance do you think your horse has?

It was, of course, sometimes necessary to give some of the subjects further explanation of the task or to elaborate further on the cover story for the study.

The scale, reproduced here in Figure 1, was prepared on $8\frac{1}{2} \times 11$-inch posterboard. The subjects responded verbally with a number or, in some cases, with the corresponding descriptive word from the scale.

After each prebet rating the experimenter visually confirmed that his subject proceeded directly to a $2 Win window. In the few instances that subjects did wander elsewhere, their data were discarded. No effort was made to collect data in the 3 frantic minutes of betting just prior to post time.

Results

Since no stronger than ordinal properties may be safely assumed for the rating scale, nonparametric statistics were employed in the analysis. Several χ^2 approximations of the Kolmogorov-Smirnov test (Siegel, 1956) were first performed to test for distributional differences between the ratings collected by the two experimenters. For prebet ratings ($\chi^2 = .274$, $df = 2$, $p > .80$) and for the combined pre- and postbet ratings ($\chi^2 = 2.16$, $df = 2$, $p > .30$) the differences in the two distributions may be considered negligible according to these tests. Distributional differences on postbet ratings ($\chi^2 = 3.14$, $df = 2$, $p > .20$) were greater but still did not meet even the .20 probability level.[2] On the basis of these tests the two experimenters were assumed to have collected sufficiently compa-

Table 1 Division of Subjects with Respect to the Overall Median for the Prebet and Postbet Groups: Experiment 1

	Prebet group	Postbet group
Above the *Mdn*	25	45
Below the *Mdn*	44	27

rable ratings to justify pooling of their data for the subsequent test of the major hypothesis of the study.

The median for the 69 subjects in the prebet group was 3.48. In qualitative terms they gave their horse little better than a "fair" chance of winning its race. The median for the 72 subjects in the postbet group, on the other hand, was 4.81. They gave their horse close to a "good" chance in the race. The median test for the data summarized in Table 1 produced a χ^2 of 8.70, ($df = 1$), significant beyond the .01 level.

These results, in accord with our predictions from dissonance theory, might also have arisen, however, had a substantial number of bettors simply made last-minute switches from relative long shots to favorites in these races. Although this possibility was not pursued with the above sample of subjects, two follow-up inquiries on another day at the same race track indicated that the "switch to favorites" explanation was unlikely. The first of these inquiries involved 38 $2 bettors who were contacted prior to the first race and merely asked if they ever changed their mind about which horse to bet on in the last minute or so before actually reaching a Sellers window. Nine of the 38 indicated that they sometimes changed, but among the 9 occasional changers a clear tendency to switch to long shots rather than to favorites was reported. Additional evidence against a "switch to favorites" explanation was obtained from a sample of 46 bettors for whom the prebet procedure of Experiment I was repeated. Each of these bettors was then contacted by a second interviewer just as he was leaving the $2 Win window and asked if he had changed to a different horse since talking to the first interviewer. All 46 responded that they had not changed horses in midinterviews.

In order to investigate the robustness of the findings of Experiment I a second study was undertaken which was like the first study in its essentials but employed different experimenters, a different response scale, and a different population of subjects. It also provided for a test of the "switch to favorites" explanation among subjects in a postbet group.

Fig. 1. The Rating Scale Shown to Subjects in the Study.

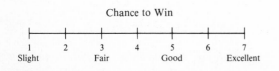

Chance to Win

1 2 3 4 5 6 7
Slight   Fair   Good   Excellent

EXPERIMENT II

Subjects and Procedure

Ninety-four subjects were interviewed at the Patterson Park Harness Raceway in Ladner, British Columbia. Forty-eight of these subjects, the prebet group, were interviewed prior to the first six races as they approached one of the track's four $2 Win windows. This contact was usually completed just a few seconds before the subject actually reached the window to make his bet, but occasionally, when the betting lines were long, up to ¾ minute elapsed between interview and bet. Forty-six subjects, the postbet group, were interviewed a few seconds after leaving one of the $2 Win windows. As in Experiment I, all persons approaching or leaving a $2 Win window at a time when the experimenters were not already engaged were contacted. Of those contacted, fewer than 10% refused to cooperate, thus producing a heterogeneous and, presumably, representative sample of $2 Win bettors.

The overall design was the same as in the first study. Two experimentors, different from those who interviewed bettors in Experiment I, were located in the immediate area of the Sellers windows. One of these experimenters would intercept bettors as they approached a $2 Win window and the other intercepted different bettors as they left a $2 Win window. The prebet and postbet interview roles were alternated between the two experimenters as in the first study.

After a brief introductory preamble, the experimenter established whether a bettor was about to make a $2 Win bet (or had just made such a bet) and whether he had been previously interviewed. The experimenters proceeded only with those $2 bettors who had not already provided data. These subjects were then asked to indicate on a 23-centimeter scale how confident they felt that they had picked the winning horse. The mimeographed response scales were labeled with the words "No confidence" at the extreme left and "Complete confidence" at the extreme right. Although no other labels were printed on the scale, the experimenters made explicit that mild confidence would fall in the middle of the scale and ". . . the more confident that a person felt, the further along he should put his mark on the scale." When subjects indicated understanding, they were handed a pencil and a mimeographed scale and directed to ". . . just draw a line across the point in the scale that best corresponds to your own confidence." All bettors in the postbet sample were also asked if they changed their mind about which horse to bet on while waiting in line or while on the way to the window.

Within the limits permitted by extremely crowded conditions, the prebet experimenter visually confirmed that subjects in his sample proceeded to a $2 Win window. Data collection was suspended during the last minute before post time.

Confidence scores for each subject were determined by laying a ruler along the 23-centimeter scale and measuring his response to the nearest millimeter.

Results

On the strength of insignificant Kolmogorov-Smirnov tests for distributional differences between ratings collected by the two experimenters, data from the two experimenters were combined to test the major hypothesis of the study. The median rating for the 48 subjects in the prebet group was 14.60, and for the postbet group it was 19.30. The median test for these data, summarized in Table 2, produced a χ^2 of 4.26 ($df = 1$), significant at less than the .05 level.

Since data in Experiment II might reasonably be assumed to satisfy interval scale assumptions, a t test between pre- and postbet means was also performed. The difference between the prebet mean of 14.73 and the postbet mean of 17.47 was also significant ($t = 2.31$, $p < .05$).

No subject in the postbet sample indicated that he had changed horses while waiting in line or, if there were no line, just before reaching the window.

DISCUSSION

These studies have examined the effects of real life postdecisional dissonance in the uncontrived setting of a race track. The data furnished by two relatively heterogeneous samples of bettors strongly support our hypothesis derived from Festinger's theory. The reaction of one bettor in Experiment I well illustrates the

Table 2 Division of Subjects with Respect to the Overall Median for the Prebet asnd Postbet Groups: Experiment II

	Prebet group	Postbet group
Above the *Mdn*	19	28
Below the *Mdn*	29	18

overall effect observed in the data. This particular bettor had been a subject in the prebet sample and had then proceeded to the pari-mutuel window to place his bet. Following that transaction, he approached the postbet experimenter and volunteered the following:

> *Are you working with that other fellow there? [indicating the prebet experimenter who was by then engaged in another interview] Well, I just told him that my horse had a fair chance of winning. Will you have him change that to a good chance? No, by God, make that an excellent chance.*

It might reasonably be conjectured that, at least until the finish of the race, this bettor felt more comfortable about his decision to wager on a horse with an excellent chance than he could have felt about a decision to wager on a horse with only a fair chance. In the human race, dissonance had won again.

The results also bear upon the issue of rapidity of onset of dissonance-reducing processes discussed by Festinger (1964). On the basis of an experiment by Davidson described in that work, Festinger argued that predecisional cognitive familiarity with the characteristics of alternatives facilitated the onset of dissonance reduction. It is reasonable to assume that most bettors in the present studies were informed, to some extent, about the virtues and liabilities of all the horses in a race before making a $2 commitment on one. Since never more than 30 seconds elapsed between the time of commitment at the window and confrontation with the rating task, the present results are consistent with the notion that the effects of dissonance reduction can, indeed, be observed very soon after a commitment is made to one alternative, providing that some information about the unchosen alternatives is already possessed. Furthermore, the exceedingly short time span here suggests that the cognitive reevaluation process could hardly have been very explicit or as deliberate as conscious rationalization.

Finally, these studies, like the earlier Ehrlich, Guttman, Schonbach, and Mills (1957) study which showed that recent new car buyers preferred to read automobile advertisements that were consonant with their purchase, demonstrate that meaningful tests of dissonance theory can be made in the context of real life situations. Insofar as real life studies are unaffected by contrived circumstances, improbable events, and credibility gaps, they may offer stronger and less contentious support for dissonance theory than their laboratory counterparts. It is also clear that such studies will help to define the range of applicability of the theory in natural settings.

Footnotes

[1]This study was supported by a grant from the Faculty of Graduate Studies, University of British Columbia. The cooperation of the British Columbia Jockey Club and the management of the Delta Raceways Limited is gratefully acknowledged. The authors also gratefully acknowledge the assistance of Herbert Lee, Ronald Douglas, and Warren Thorngate during the data-collection phases of these studies.

[2]The χ^2 approximation for Kolmogorov-Smirnov is designed for one-tailed tests, whereas the hypothesis tested here is nondirectional. However, since the differences were insignificant by a one-tailed test, they would necessarily be insignificant by the two-tailed test.

References

Brehm, J. W., & Cohen, A. R. *Explorations in cognitive dissonance.* New York: Wiley, 1962.

Chapanis, N. P., & Chapanis, A. Cognitive dissonance: Five years later. *Psychological Bulletin,* 1964, *61,* 1-22.

Ehrlich, D., Guttman, I., Schonbach, P., & Mills, J. Postdecision exposure to relevant information. *Journal of Abnormal and Social Psychology,* 1957, *54,* 98-102.

Festinger, L. *A theory of cognitive dissonance.* Stanford, Calif.: Stanford University Press, 1957.

Festinger, L. *Conflict, decision, and dissonance.* Stanford, Calif.: Stanford University Press, 1964.

Siegel, S. *Nonparametric statistics for the behavioral sciences.* New York: McGraw-Hill, 1956.

Effect of Initial Selling Price on Subsequent Sales[1]

Anthony N. Doob[2]   *Stanford University*
J. Merrill Carlsmith[3]
Jonathan L. Freedman
Thomas K. Landauer[4]
Soleng Tom, Jr.

Abstract

Five field experiments investigated the effect of initial selling price on subsequent sales of common household products. Matched pairs of discount houses sold the same product at either a discounted price or the regular price for a short period of time. The prices were then made the same for all stores. The results were consistent with the prediction from dissonance theory that subsequent sales would be higher where the initial price was high.

The "introductory low price offer" is a common technique used by marketers. A new product is offered at a low price for a short period of time, and the price is subsequently raised to its normal level. Since the goal naturally is to maximize final sales of the product, the assumption behind this technique is that it will accomplish this goal. An economic model based entirely on supply and demand would of course predict that the eventual sales would not be affected by the initial price. The lower price would be expected to attract many marginal buyers and produce greater sales; but as soon as the price is raised, these buyers should drop out of the market. The hope of the marketer, however, is that some of these marginal buyers will learn to like the product enough so that they will continue to purchase it even at the higher price.

"Effect of Initial Selling Price on Subsequent Sales" by Anthony N. Doob, J. Merrill Carlsmith, Jonathan L. Freedman, Thomas K. Landauer, and Soleng Tom, Jr. *Journal of Personality and Social Psychology,* 1969, Vol. 11, No. 4, pp. 345–350. Copyright © 1969 by The American Psychological Association, Inc. Reprinted by permission.

Unfortunately for the marketer, this may be a vain hope. There are various psychological reasons why we might expect the introductory low price to have an opposite effect from that which the marketers intend, such that the introductory low price would reduce rather than increase eventual sales. Since this technique is so widespread, it provides an unusual opportunity to investigate the applicability of social psychology in a natural setting, and to compare the marketer's predictions with that of social psychology.

The most interesting analysis of this situation is based on the theory of cognitive dissonance (Festinger, 1957). One of the clearest deductions from the theory is that the more effort in any form a person exerts to attain a goal, the more dissonance is aroused if the goal is less valuable than expected. The individual reduces this dissonance by increasing his liking for the goal, and therefore the greater the effort, the more he should like the goal. This prediction has received some substantiation in laboratory experimentation (e.g., Aronson & Mills, 1959; Gerard & Mathewson, 1966). Its applicability to the marketing situation is straightforward: the theory predicts that the higher the price a person initially pays for a product, the more he will come to like it. Presumably this greater liking will produce "brand loyalty" in the form of repeat purchases. Thus, when the initial price is high, a higher *proportion* of buyers should continue to purchase the product than when the initial price is low. Accordingly, although the introductory price will initially attract more customers, we may expect the sales curves for the two conditions to cross at some later point, and the higher brand loyalty induced by the dissonance involved in paying a high price to manifest itself in higher final sales in that condition.

Five experiments were performed to demonstrate that introducing a new brand of a product at a low price for a short time and then raising it to the normal selling price leads to lower sales in the long run than introducing the product at its normal selling price. The general design of all the experiments was to introduce the new brand at a low price in one set of stores and, after the price is raised to the normal selling price, compare sales with matched stores where the product was introduced at the normal selling price and held there throughout the course of the experiment.

All of the experiments that are to be reported here were done in a chain of discount houses. All sales figures have been multiplied by a constant in order to maintain confidentiality.

This chain of discount houses differs from most others in a number of important ways. They do not advertise much, and what advertising they do does not include prices on specific items. Price changes occur very seldom in these stores and are usually not advertised. In most cases, prices are lowered because an item is overstocked, and unless the customer remembers the regular selling price, he has no way of knowing that the price is lower than usual. Management in most of these stores is under direct control of the central office. When the manager receives orders from the central office, he has little or no power to change them.

The chain sells a large number of "house brands" at prices lower than the equivalent name brands. These house brands have the same registered trademark, and constitute a brand which customers can easily identify with the store. Generally, the quality of the house brand item is as high as the equivalent name brand, the differences usually being in characteristics which do not directly affect the usefulness of the item (e.g., mouthwash bottles are not as attractive as those of the name brand; the average grain size of powdered detergent is larger than that of the name brand which is chemically equivalent).

The products used in the studies reported here were house brands. All were being introduced into the stores at the time when the study was being run. The particular products used and the price differential were both determined by management.

EXPERIMENT I

Method

Twelve pairs of discount houses, matched on gross sales, were randomly assigned to one of two experimental conditions. In one store of each pair, the house brand of mouthwash was introduced at $.25 per quart bottle. The price was held at this level for 9 days (two weekends and the intervening days), and then the price was brought up to $.39 for all stores. In the other store, it was introduced at its normal selling price of $.39.

None of the managers had any reason to believe that the price of mouthwash at his store was not the same as in all other stores in the chain. No one was given any special instructions beyond the place in the store where the item was to be sold and its selling price. The location was essentially identical for all stores. In stores where mouthwash was introduced at the low price, the manager received a memo at the end of the first week instructing him to change the price to $.39 after that weekend.

Results

Sales were recorded by the sundries buyer as he replenished stock. At the end of each week these figures were sent to the central office and then relayed to the experimenters. Average sales for the 12 matched stores in each condition are shown in Figure 1. It is estimated that at least 2 weeks had to pass before customers would return to buy more mouthwash, and, therefore, one would not expect there to be any difference between the height of the curves until the third week. In fact, the curves cross at this point, and after this point, it is clear that the stores where the initial selling price was high were selling more mouthwash than stores where the initial price was low. This is true in spite of the fact that more mouthwash was sold

Fig. 1.   Mouthwash sales.

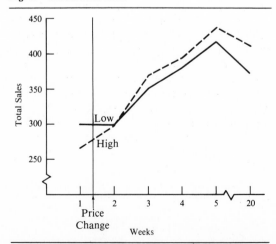

the first week in stores where the price was low. Unfortunately, for a variety of reasons, the authors were not able to collect continuous data. They were able, however, to check sales 19 weeks after the price change, and clearly the difference still existed. When sales for Weeks 3, 4, 5, and 20 are combined, sales of mouthwash were higher in the store where the initial selling price was high in 10 of the 12 pairs of stores ($p = .02$).

Sales in the two sets of stores during Weeks 3, 4, 5, and 20 (pooled) were also compared by use of a t test, resulting in a t of 2.11 ($df = 11$, $p < .10$). Thus, stores where the initial selling price was low sold less mouthwash than did stores where the initial selling price was the same as the final selling price.

REPLICATIONS

The same experiment was repeated four times, using different products. The procedures were very similar in all cases. In each experiment, the stores were rematched and randomly assigned independent of all other replications.

Experiment II: Toothpaste

Six pairs of stores were matched on the basis of sundries sales and randomly assigned to conditions in which the selling price for the first 3 weeks was either $.41 or $.49 for a "family size" tube of toothpaste. After 3 weeks, the price in all stores was set at $.49. The results are presented in Figure 2. When the sales for the last 4 weeks are combined as in the previous experiment, four of the six pairs show differences in

Fig. 2. Toothpaste sales.

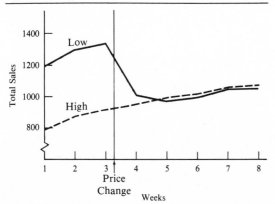

Fig. 3. Aluminum foil sales.

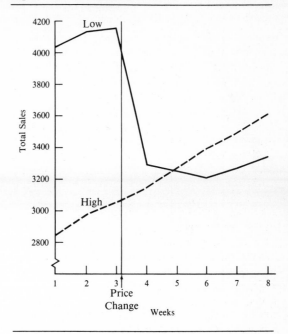

the predicted direction ($p = .34$). When the more sensitive t test is done on the data from these 4 weeks, the t is 2.26 ($df = 5$, $p < .10$).

Experiment III: Aluminum Foil

Seven pairs of stores were matched on the basis of grocery sales and randomly assigned to conditions in which the selling price for the first 3 weeks was either $.59 or $.64 for a 75-foot roll of foil. After 3 weeks, the price in all stores was set at $.64. The results are presented in Figure 3. For Weeks 5-8 combined, all seven pairs ($p = .01$) show differences in the predicted direction ($t = 5.09$, $df = 6$, $p < .005$).

Experiment IV: Light Bulbs

Eight pairs of stores were matched on the basis of hardware sales and randomly assigned to conditions in which selling price for the first week was either $.26 or $.32 for a package of light bulbs. After 1 week, the price was brought up to $.32 in all stores. The results are presented in Figure 4. For Weeks 3 and 4 combined, six of the eight pairs ($p = .15$) show differences in the predicted direction ($t = .837$, $df = 7$).

Fig. 4. Light bulb sales.

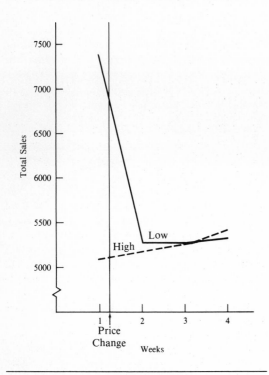

Although this difference is not significant, it might be noted in Figure 4 that there was the predicted reversal, even though initial sales were almost 50% higher at the low price.

Experiment V: Cookies

Eight pairs of stores were matched on the basis of grocery sales and randomly assigned to conditions in which the selling price for the first 2 weeks was $.24 or $.29 for a large bag of cookies. After 2 weeks, the price was at $.29 for all stores. The results are presented in Figure 5. For Weeks 4-6 combined, six of the eight pairs show differences in the predicted direction ($t = .625$, $df = 7$).

RESULTS

When the results of all five experiments are combined into one test of the hypothesis, a z of 3.63 ($p < .0002$) is obtained. Clearly, so far as this has been tested, the practice of introducing a product at a low price is not a good strategy for this chain of stores to use.

DISCUSSION

These studies indicate that introducing products at a lower than usual price is harmful to final sales. It was earlier argued that one possible reason for this is the lower proportion of buyers who return to a product when the initial price is lower than the normal price. Whether or not this causes eventual sales actually to be lower when the initial price is low is not critical to the argument. If, for example, there is an extremely large difference in initial sales, even a lower proportion of returning buyers may produce an advantage for the initial low price. Similarly, if the product has some special feature which would be expected to produce loyalty merely from exposure, it would be beneficial to maximize initial sales by the use of low introductory offers. In the experiments reported here, neither of these possibilities seems to have been present. For the range of prices studied, even a 50% increase in sales due to the lower price was not enough to overcome the

Fig. 5. Cookie sales.

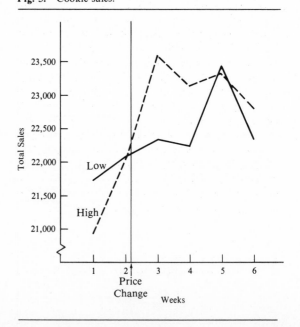

increased consumer loyalty engendered by the higher price. Because of the presence of other identical brands, differing only in price, exposure alone was not enough to produce loyalty.

Whether or not eventual sales are actually lower when the initial price is low is not critical to the argument. From a theoretical point of view, the only essential comparison is the relative proportion of repurchases in the two conditions. A stringent method of showing that this proportion is higher when the initial price is high is to demonstrate that the absolute volume of eventual sales is greater for the high-price condition, even though initial sales are lower. For the products and prices studied here, this was true.

There are at least two alternative explanations of this result. The first is that in the low-initial-price stores the market is glutted after the first few weeks, and it takes a long time for there to be any need to repurchase the product. This might be a partial explanation of the difference between the conditions, but seems implausible as a total explanation. For all the products except light bulbs the length of time that the sales curves were followed exceeded by a goodly margin the marketer's estimate of the normal time until repurchase. Indeed, with mouthwash, for which the repurchase period is about 2 weeks, the difference between conditions is still present 19 weeks after the price switch. Customers might have stocked up by buying more than their usual supply of a product, but pricing practices of this chain of stores makes this unlikely. These stores have rarely used low introductory price offers and they were not advertised as such for the products studied. Buyers therefore had no reason to believe that the "low price" was a special price and accordingly had little reason to stock up on the product. Thus, although one cannot entirely rule out this "glutting the market" explanation, it is not convincing.

A second and more interesting alternative is in terms of what might be called the customers' adaptation level regarding the particular product. When mouthwash is put on sale at $.25, customers who buy it at that price or notice what the price is may tend to think of the product in terms of $.25. They say to themselves that this is a $.25 bottle of mouthwash. When, in subsequent weeks, the price increases to $.39, these customers will tend to see it as overpriced, and are not inclined to buy it at this much higher price. Therefore, sales drop off considerably. In the $.39 steady condition, initial sales are lower, but there is no reason for them to drop off due to this effect. Therefore, introducing it at the ultimate price results in greater sales in the long run than does introducing it at the low price. This explanation fits the data as nicely as does the one in terms of cognitive dissonance. In many ways, they are quite similar and are difficult to distinguish experimentally.

It should be noted that the adaptation level and dissonance explanations are by no means mutually exclusive. It is entirely possible that both mechanisms are operating to some extent. In any case, the basic result stands—the introduction of a product at a low price tended to decrease subsequent sales, and this effect lasted for at least 20 weeks.

Footnotes

[1]This study was supported in part by National Science Foundation grants to Carlsmith and to Freedman. The authors are grateful to management and personnel of the discount chain for their cooperation in this research.

[2]Now at University of Toronto.

[3]Requests for reprints should be addressed to J. Merrill Carlsmith, Department of Psychology, Stanford University, Stanford, California 94305.

[4]Now at Bell Telephone Laboratories, Murray Hill, New Jersey.

References

Aronson, E., & Mills, J. The effect of severity of initiation on liking for a group. *Journal of Abnormal and Social Psychology,* 1959, *59,* 177-181.

Festinger, L. *A theory of cognitive dissonance.* Stanford, Calif.: Stanford University Press, 1957.

Gerard, H. B., & Mathewson, G. C. The effects of severity of initiation on liking for a group: A replication. *Journal of Experimental Social Psychology,* 1966, *2,* 278-287.

Attribution and Cognitive Control

The Effects of Choice and Enhanced Personal Responsibility for the Aged: A Field Experiment in an Institutional Setting

Ellen J. Langer   *Graduate Center, City University of New York*
Judith Rodin   *Yale University*

Abstract

A field experiment was conducted to assess the effects of enhanced personal responsibility and choice on a group of nursing home residents. It was expected that the debilitated condition of many of the aged residing in institutional settings is, at least in part, a result of living in a virtually decision-free environment and consequently is potentially reversible. Residents who were in the experimental group were given a communication emphasizing their responsibility for themselves, whereas the communication given to a second group stressed the staff's responsibility for them. In addition, to bolster the communication, the former group was given the freedom to make choices and the responsibility of caring for a plant rather than having decisions made and the plant taken care of for them by the staff, as was the case for the latter group. Questionnaire ratings and behavioral measures showed a significant improvement for the experimental group over the comparison group on alertness, active participation, and a general sense of well-being.

The transition from adulthood to old age is often perceived as a process of loss, physiologically and psychologically (Birren, 1958; Gould, 1972). However, it is as yet unclear just how much of this change is

biologically determined and how much is a function of the environment. The ability to sustain a sense of personal control in old age may be greatly influenced by societal factors, and this in turn may affect one's physical well-being.

Typically the life situation does change in old age. There is some loss of roles, norms, and reference groups, events that negatively influence one's perceived competence and feeling of responsibility (Bengston, 1973). Perception of these changes in addition to actual physical decrements may enhance a sense of aging and lower self-esteem (Lehr & Puschner, Note 1). In response to internal developmental changes, the aging individual may come to see himself in a position of lessened mastery relative to the rest of the world, as a passive object manipulated by the environment (Neugarten & Gutman, 1958). Questioning whether these factors can be counteracted, some studies have suggested that more successful aging—measured by decreased mortality, morbidity, and psychological disability—occurs when an individual feels a sense of usefulness and purpose (Bengston, 1973; Butler, 1967; Leaf, 1973; Lieberman, 1965).

The notion of competence is indeed central to much of human behavior. Adler (1930) has described the need to control one's personal environment as "an intrinsic necessity of life itself" (p. 398). deCharms (1968) has stated that "man's primary motivation propensity is to be effective in producing changes in his environment. Man strives to be a causal agent, to be the primary locus of causation for, or the origin of, his behavior; he strives for personal causation" (p. 269).

Several laboratory studies have demonstrated that reduced control over aversive outcomes increases physiological distress and anxiety (Geer, Davison, & Gatchel, 1970; Pervin, 1963) and even a nonveridical

"The Effects of Choice and Enhanced Personal Responsibility for the Aged: A Field Experiment in an Institutional Setting" by Ellen J. Langer and Judith Rodin. *Journal of Personality and Social Psychology,* 1976, Vol. 34, No. 2, 191–198. Copyright © 1976 by The American Psychological Association, Inc. Reprinted by permission.

perception of control over an impending event reduces the aversiveness of that event (Bowers, 1968; Glass & Singer, 1972; Kanfer & Seidner, 1973). Langer, Janis, and Wolfer (1975) found that by inducing the perception of control over stress in hospital patients by means of a communication that emphasized potential cognitive control, subjects requested fewer pain relievers and sedatives and were seen by nurses as evidencing less anxiety.

Choice is also a crucial variable in enhancing an induced sense of control. Stotland and Blumenthal (1964) studied the effects of choice on anxiety reduction. They told subjects that they were going to take a number of important ability tests. Half of the subjects were allowed to choose the order in which they wanted to take the tests, and half were told that the order was fixed. All subjects were informed that the order of the tests would have no bearing on their scores. They found that subjects not given the choice were more anxious, as measured by palmar sweating. In another study of the effects of choice, Corah and Boffa (1970) told their subjects that there were two conditions in the experiment, each of which would be signaled by a different light. In one condition they were given the choice of whether or not to press a button to escape from an aversive noise, and in the other one they were not given the option of escaping. They found that the choice instructions decreased the aversiveness of the threatening stimulus, apparently by increasing perceived control. Although using a very different paradigm, Langer (1975) also demonstrated the importance of choice. In that study it was found that the exercise of choice in a chance situation, where choice was objectively inconsequential, nevertheless had psychological consequences manifested in increased confidence and risk taking.

Lefcourt (1973) best summed up the essence of this research in a brief review article dealing with the perception of control in man and animals when he concluded that "the sense of control, the illusion that one can exercise personal choice, has a definite and a positive role in sustaining life" (p. 424). It is not surprising, then, that these important psychological factors should be linked to health and survival. In a series of retrospective studies, Schmale and his associates (Adamson & Schmale, 1965; Schmale, 1958; Schmale & Iker, 1966) found that ulcerative colitis, leukemia, cervical cancer, and heart disease were linked with a feeling of helplessness and loss of hope experienced by the patient prior to the onset of the disease. Seligman and his co-workers have systematically investigated the learning of helplessness and

related it to the clinical syndrome of depression (see Seligman, 1975). Even death is apparently related to control-relevant variables. McMahon and Rhudick (1964) found a relationship between depression or hopelessness and death. The most graphic description of this association comes from Bettelheim (1943), who in his analysis of the "Muselmanner," the walking corpses in the concentration camps, described them as:

> *Prisoners who came to believe the repeated statements of the guards—that there was no hope for them, that they would never leave the camp except as a corpse—who came to feel that their environment was one over which they could exercise no influence whatsoever. . . . Once his own life and the environment were viewed as totally beyond his ability to influence them, the only logical conclusion was to pay no attention to them whatsoever. Only then, all conscious awareness of stimuli coming from the outside was blocked out, and with it all response to anything but inner stimuli.*

Death swiftly followed and, according to Bettelheim,

> [*survival*] *depended on one's ability to arrange to preserve some areas of independent action, to keep control of some important aspects of one's life despite an environment that seemed overwhelming and total.*

Bettelheim's description reminds us of Richter's (1957) rats, who also "gave up hope" of controlling their environment and subsequently died.

The implications of these studies for research in the area of aging are clear. Objective helplessness as well as feelings of helplessness and hopelessness—both enhanced by the environment and by intrinsic changes that occur with increasing old age—may contribute to psychological withdrawal, physical disease, and death. In contrast, objective control and feelings of mastery may very well contribute to physical health and personal efficacy.

In a study conceived to explore the effects of dissonance, Ferrare (1962; cited in Seligman, 1975; Zimbardo & Ruch, 1975) presented data concerning the effects of the ability of geriatric patients to control their place of residence. Of 17 subjects who answered that they did not have any other alternative but to move to a specific old age home, 8 died after 4 weeks of residence and 16 after 10 weeks of residence. By comparison, among the residents who died during the initial period, only one person had answered that she had the freedom to choose other alternatives. All of these deaths were classified as unexpected because "not even insignificant disturbances had actually given warning of the impending disaster."

As Zimbardo (Zimbardo & Ruch, 1975) suggested, the implications of Ferrare's data are striking and merit further study of old age home settings. There is already evidence that perceived personal control in one's residential environment is important for younger and noninstitutional populations. Rodin (in press), using children as subjects, demonstrated that diminished feelings of control produced by chronic crowding at home led to fewer attempts to control self-reinforcement in the laboratory and to greater likelihood of giving up in the face of failure.

The present study attempted to assess directly the effects of enhanced personal responsibility and choice in a group of nursing home patients. In addition to examining previous results from the control-helplessness literature in a field setting, the present study extended the domain of this conception by considering new response variables. Specifically, if increased control has generalized beneficial effects, then physical and mental alertness, activity, general level of satisfaction, and sociability should all be affected. Also, the manipulation of the independent variables, assigning greater responsibility and decision freedom for relevant behavior, allowed subjects real choices that were not directed toward a single behavior or stimulus condition. This manipulation tested the ability of the subjects to generalize from specific choices enumerated for them to other aspects of their lives, and thus tested the generalizability of feelings of control over certain elements of the situation to more broadly based behavior and attitudes.

METHOD

Subjects

The study was conducted in a nursing home, which was rated by the state of Connecticut as being among the finest care units and offering quality medical, recreational, and residential facilities. The home was large and modern in design, appearing cheerful and comfortable as well as clean and efficient. Of the four floors in the home, two were selected for study because of similarity in the residents' physical and psychological health and prior socioeconomic status, as determined for evaluations made by the home's director, head nurses, and social worker. Residents were assigned to a particular floor and room simply on the

basis of availability, and on the average, residents on the two floors had been at the home about the same length of time. Rather than randomly assigning subjects to experimental treatment, a different floor was randomly selected for each treatment. Since there was not a great deal of communication between floors, this procedure was followed in order to decrease the likelihood that the treatment effects would be contaminated. There were 8 males and 39 females in the responsibility-induced condition (all fourth-floor residents) and 9 males and 35 females in the comparison group (all second-floor residents). Residents who were either completely bedridden or judged by the nursing home staff to be completely noncommunicative (11 on the experimental floor and 9 on the comparison floor) were omitted from the sample. Also omitted was one woman on each floor, one 40 years old and the other 26 years old, due to their age. Thus, 91 ambulatory adults, ranging in age from 65 to 90, served as subjects.

Procedure

To introduce the experimental treatment, the nursing home administrator, an outgoing and friendly 33-year-old male who interacts with the residents daily, called a meeting in the lounge of each floor. He delivered one of the following two communications at that time:

[Responsibility-induced group] *I brought you together today to give you some information about Arden House. I was surprised to learn that many of you don't know about the things that are available to you and more important, that many of you don't realize the influence you have over your own lives here. Take a minute to think of the decisions you can and should be making. For example, you have the responsibility of caring for yourselves, of deciding whether or not you want to make this a home you can be proud of and happy in. You should be deciding how you want your rooms to be arranged—whether you want it to be as it is or whether you want the staff to help you rearrange the furniture. You should be deciding how you want to spend your time, for example, whether you want to be visiting your friends who live on this floor or on other floors, whether you want to visit in your room or your friends' room, in the lounge, the dining room, etc., or whether you want to be watching television, listening to the radio, writing, reading, or planning social events. In other words, it's your life and you can make of it whatever you want.*

This brings me to another point. If you are unsatisfied with anything here, you have the influence to change it. It's your responsibility to make your complaints known, to tell us what you would like to change, to tell us what you would like. These are just a few of the things you could and should be deciding and thinking about now and from time to time everyday. You made these decisions before you came here and you can and should be making them now.

We're thinking of instituting some way for airing complaints, suggestions, etc. Let [nurse's name] know if you think this is a good idea and how you think we should go about doing it. In any case let her know what your complaints or suggestions are.

Also, I wanted to take this opportunity to give you each a present from the Arden House. [A box of small plants was passed around, and patients were given two decisions to make: first, whether or not they wanted a plant at all, and second, to choose which one they wanted. All residents did select a plant.] The plants are yours to keep and take care of as you'd like.

One last thing, I wanted to tell you that we're showing a movie two nights next week, Thursday and Friday. You should decide which night you'd like to go, if you choose to see it at all.

[Comparison group] *I brought you together today to give you some information about the Arden House. I was surprised to learn that many of you don't know about the things that are available to you; that many of you don't realize all you're allowed to do here. Take a minute to think of all the options that we've provided for you in order for your life to be fuller and more interesting. For example, you're permitted to visit people on the other floors and to use the lounge on this floor for visiting as well as the dining room or your own rooms. We want your rooms to be as nice as they can be, and we've tried to make them that way for you. We want you to be happy here. We feel that it's our responsibility to make this a home you can be proud of and happy in, and we want to do all we can to help you.*

This brings me to another point. If you have any complaints or suggestions about anything, let [nurse's name] know what they are. Let us know how we can best help you. You should feel that you have free access to anyone on the staff, and we will

do the best we can to provide individualized attention and time for you.

Also, I wanted to take this opportunity to give you each a present from the Arden House. [The nurse walked around with a box of plants and each patient was handed one.] The plants are yours to keep. The nurses will water and care for them for you.

One last thing, I wanted to tell you that we're showing a movie next week on Thursday or Friday. We'll let you know later which day you're scheduled to see it.

The major difference between the two communications was that on one floor, the emphasis was on the residents' responsibility for themselves, whereas on the other floor, the communication stressed the staff's responsibility for them. In addition, several other differences bolstered this treatment: Residents in the responsibility-induced group were asked to give their opinion of the means by which complaints were handled rather than just being told that any complaints would be handled by staff members; they were given the opportunity to select their own plant and to care for it themselves, rather than being given a plant to be taken care of by someone else; and they were given their choice of a movie night, rather than being assigned a particular night, as was typically the case in the old age home. However, there was no difference in the amount of attention paid to the two groups.

Three days after these communications had been delivered, the director visited all of the residents in their rooms or in the corridor and reiterated part of the previous message. To those in the responsibility-induced group he said, "Remember what I said last Thursday. We want you to be happy. Treat this like your own home and make all the decisions you used to make. How's your plant coming along?" To the residents of the comparison floor, he said the same thing omitting the statement about decision making.

Dependent Variables

Questionnaires.   Two types of questionnaires were designed to assess the effects of induced responsibility. Each was administered 1 week prior to and 3 weeks after the communication. The first was administered directly to the residents by a female research assistant who was unaware of the experimental hypotheses or of the specific experimental treatment. The questions dealt with how much control they felt over general events in their lives and how happy and active they felt. Questions were responded to along 8-point scales ranging from 0 (none) to 8 (total). After completing each interview, the research assistant rated the resident on an 8-point scale for alertness.

The second questionnaire was responded to by the nurses, who staffed the experimental and comparison floors and who were unaware of the experimental treatments. Nurses on two different shifts completed the questionnaires in order to obtain two ratings for each subject. There were nine 10-point scales that asked for ratings of how happy, alert, dependent, sociable, and active the residents were as well as questions about their eating and sleeping habits. There were also questions evaluating the proportion of weekly time the patient spent engaged in a variety of activities. These included reading, watching television, visiting other patients, visiting outside guests, watching the staff, talking to the staff, sitting alone doing nothing, and others.

Behavioral measures.   Since perceived personal control is enhanced by a sense of choice over relevant behaviors, the option to choose which night the experimental group wished to see the movie was expected to have measurable effects on active participation. Attendance records were kept by the occupational therapist, who was unaware that an experiment was being conducted.

Another measure of involvement was obtained by holding a competition in which all participants had to guess the number of jelly beans in a large jar. Each patient wishing to enter the contest simply wrote his or her name and estimate on a piece of paper and deposited it in a box that was next to the jar.[1]

Finally, an unobtrusive measure of activity was taken. The tenth night after the experimental treatment, the right wheels of the wheelchairs belonging to a randomly selected subsample of each patient group were covered with 2 inches (.05 m) of white adhesive tape. The following night, the tape was removed from the chairs and placed on index cards for later evaluation of amount of activity, as indicated by the amount of discoloration.

RESULTS

Questionnaires.   Before examining whether or not the experimental treatment was effective, the pretest ratings made by the subjects, the nurses, and the interviewer were compared for both groups. None of the differences approached significance, which indicates comparability between groups prior to the start of the investigation.

The means for responses to the various questionnaires are summarized in Table 1. Statistical tests compared the posttest minus pretest scores of the experimental and comparison groups.

In response to direct questions about how happy they currently were, residents in the responsibility-induced group reported significantly greater increases in happiness after the experimental treatment than did the comparison group, $t(43) = 1.96$ $p < .05$.[2] Although the comparison group heard a communication that had specifically stressed the home's commitment to making them happy, only 25% of them reported feeling happier by the time of the second interview, whereas 48% of the experimental group did so.

The responsibility-induced group reported themselves to be significantly more active on the second interview than the comparison group, $t(43) = 2.67, p < .01$. The interviewer's ratings of alertness also showed significantly greater increase for the experimental group, $t(43) = 2.40, p < .025$. However, the questions that were relevant to perceived control showed no significant changes for the experimental group. Since over 20% of the patients indicated that they were unable to understand what we meant by control, these questions were obviously not adequate to discriminate between groups.

The second questionnaire measured nurses' ratings of each patient. The correlation between the two nurses' ratings of the same patient was .68 and .61 ($ps < .005$) on the comparison and responsibility-induced floors, respectively.[3] For each patient, a score was calculated by averaging the two nurses' ratings for each question, summing across questions, and subtracting the total pretreatment score from the total posttreatment score.[4] This yielded a positive average total change score of 3.97 for the responsibility-induced group as compared with an average negative total change of –2.37 for the comparison group. The difference between these means is highly significant, $t(50 = 5.18, p < .005$. If one looks at the percentage of people who were judged improved rather than at the amount of judged improvement, the same pattern emerges: 93% of the experimental group (all but one subject) were considered improved, whereas only 21% (six subjects) of the comparison group showed this positive change ($\chi^2 = 19.23, p < .005$).

The nurses' evaluation of the proportion of time subjects spent engaged in various interactive and noninteractive activities was analyzed by comparing

Table 1   Mean Scores for Self-Report, Interviewer Ratings, and Nurses' Ratings for
Experimental and Comparison Groups

Questionnaire responses	Responsibility induced (n = 24)			Comparison (n = 28)			Comparison of change scores (p <)
	Pre	Post	Change: Post-Pre	Pre	Post	Change: Post-Pre	
Self-report							
Happy	5.16	5.44	.28	4.90	4.78	-.12	.05
Active	4.07	4.27	.20	3.90	2.62	-1.28	.01
Perceived Control							
Have	3.26	3.42	.16	3.62	4.03	.41	—
Want	3.85	3.80	-.05	4.40	4.57	.17	—
Interviewer rating							
Alertness	5.02	5.31	.29	5.75	5.38	-.37	.025
Nurses' ratings							
General improvement	41.67	45.64	3.97	42.69	40.32	-2.39	.005
Time spent							
Visiting patients	13.03	19.81	6.78	7.94	4.65	-3.30	.005
Visiting others	11.50	13.75	2.14	12.38	8.21	-4.16	.05
Talking to staff	8.21	16.43	8.21	9.11	10.71	1.61	.01
Watching staff	6.78	4.64	-2.14	6.96	11.60	4.64	.05

the average change scores (post-precommunication) for all of the nurses for both groups of subjects on each activity. Several significant differences were found. The experimental group showed increases in the proportion of time spent visiting with other patients (for the experimental group, $\overline{X}$ = 12.86 vs. -6.61 for the comparison group), $t(50) = 3.83, p < .005$; visiting people from outside of the nursing home (for the experimental group, $\overline{X}$ = 4.28 vs. -7.61 for the comparison group), $t(50) = 2.30, p < .05$; and talking to the staff (for the experimental group, $\overline{X}$ = 8.21 vs. 1.61 for the comparison group), $t(50) = 2.98, p < .05$.[5] In addition, they spent less time passively watching the staff (for the experimental group, $\overline{X}$ = -4.28 vs. 9.68 for the comparison group), $t(50) = 2.60, p < .05$. Thus, it appears that the treatment increased active, interpersonal activity but not passive activity such as watching television or reading.

Behavioral measures.   As in the case of the questionnaires, the behavioral measures showed a pattern of differences between groups that was generally consistent with the predicted effects of increased responsibility. The movie attendance was significantly higher in the responsibility-induced group than in the control group after the experimental treatment (z = 1.71, $p < .05$, one-tailed), although a similar attendance check taken one month before the communications revealed no group differences.[6]

In the jelly-bean-guessing contest, 10 subjects (21%) in the responsibility-induced group and only 1 subject (2%) from the comparison group participated (χ^2 = 7.72, $p < .01$). Finally, very little dirt was found on the tape taken from any of the patients' wheelchairs, and there was no significant difference between the two groups.

DISCUSSION

It appears that inducing a greater sense of personal responsibility in people who may have virtually relinquished decision making, either by choice or necessity, produces improvement. In the present investigation, patients in the comparison group were given a communication stressing the staff's desire to make them happy and were otherwise treated in the sympathetic manner characteristic of this high-quality nursing home. Despite the care provided for these people, 71% were rated as having become more debilitated over a period of time as short as 3 weeks. In contrast with this group, 93% of the people who were encouraged to make decisions for themselves, given decisions to make, and given responsibility for something outside of themselves, actually showed overall improvement. Based on their own judgments and by the judgments of the nurses with whom they interacted on a daily basis, they became more active and felt happier. Perhaps more important was the judged improvement in their mental alertness and increased behavioral involvement in many different kinds of activities.

The behavioral measures showed greater active participation and involvement for the experimental group. Whether this directly resulted from an increase in perceived choice and decision-making responsibility or from the increase in general activity and happiness occurring after the treatment cannot be assessed from the present results. It should also be clearly noted that although there were significant differences in active involvement, the overall level of participation in the activities that comprised the behavioral measures was low. Perhaps a much more powerful treatment would be one that is individually administered and repeated on several occasions. That so weak a manipulation had any effect suggests how important increased control is for these people, for whom decision making is virtually nonexistent.

The practical implications of this experimental demonstration are straightforward. Mechanisms can and should be established for changing situational factors that reduce real or perceived responsibility in the elderly. Furthermore, this study adds to the body of literature (Bengston, 1973; Butler, 1967; Leaf, 1973; Lieberman, 1965) suggesting that senility and diminished alertness are not an almost inevitable result of aging. In fact, it suggests that some of the negative consequences of aging may be retarded, reversed, or possibly prevented by returning to the aged the right to make decisions and a feeling of competence.

Reference Note

1. Lehr, K., & Puschner, I. *Studies in the awareness of aging.* Paper presented at the 6th International Congress on Gerontology, Copenhagen, 1963.

Footnotes

[1]We also intended to measure the number of complaints that patients voiced. Since one often does not complain after becoming psychologically helpless, complaints in this context were expected to be a positive indication of perceived personal control. This measure was discarded, however, since the nurses failed to keep a systematic written record.

[2]All of the statistics for the self-report data and the interviewers' ratings are based on 45 subjects (25 in the responsibility-induced group and 20 in the comparison group), since these were the only subjects available at the time of the interview.

[3]There was also significant agreement between the interviewer's and nurses' ratings of alertness ($r = .65$).

[4]Since one nurse on the day shift and one nurse on the night shift gave the ratings, responses to the questions regarding

sleeping and eating habits were not included in the total score. Also, in order to reduce rater bias, patients for whom there were ratings by a nurse on only one shift were excluded from this calculation. This left 24 residents from the experimental group and 28 from the comparison group.

[5]This statistic is based only on the responses of nurse on duty in the evening.

[6]Frequencies were transformed into arc sines and analyzed using the method that is essentially the same as that described by Langer and Abelson (1972).

References

Adamson, J., & Schmale, A. Object loss, giving up, and the onset of psychiatric disease. *Psychosomatic Medicine,* 1965, *27,* 557-576.

Adler, A. Individual psychology. In C. Murchinson (Ed.), *Psychologies of 1930.* Worcester, Mass.: Clark University Press, 1930.

Bengston, V. L. Self determination: A social and psychological perspective on helping the aged. *Geriatrics,* 1973.

Bettelheim, B. Individual and mass behavior in extreme situations. *Journal of Abnormal and Social Psychology,* 1943, *38,* 417-452.

Birren, J. Aging and psychological adjustment. *Review of Educational Research,* 1958, *28,* 475-490.

Bowers, K. Pain, anxiety, and perceived control. *Journal of Consulting and Clinical Psychology,* 1968, *32,* 596-602.

Butler, R. Aspects of survival and adaptation in human aging. *American Journal of Psychiatry,* 1967, *123,* 1233-1243.

Corah, N., & Boffa, J. Perceived control, self-observation, and response to aversive stimulation. *Journal of Personality and Social Psychology,* 1970, *16,* 1-4.

deCharms, R. *Personal causation.* New York: Academic Press, 1968.

Geer, J., Davison, G., & Gatchel, R. Reduction of stress in humans through nonveridical perceived control of aversive stimulation. *Journal of Personality and Social Psychology,* 1970, *16,* 731-738.

Glass, D., & Singer, J. *Urban stress.* New York: Academic Press, 1972.

Gould, R. The phases of adult life: A study in developmental psychology. *American Journal of Psychiatry,* 1972, *129,* 521-531.

Kanfer, R., & Seidner, M. Self-Control: Factors enhancing tolerance of noxious stimulation. *Journal of Personality and Social Psychology,* 1973, *25,* 381-389.

Langer, E. J. The illusion of control. *Journal of Personality and Social Psychology,* 1975, *32,* 311-328.

Langer, E. J., & Abelson, R. P. The semantics of asking a favor: How to succeed in getting help without really dying. *Journal of Personality and Social Psychology,* 1972, *24,* 26-32.

Langer, E. J., Janis, I. L., & Wolfer, J. A. Reduction of psychological stress in surgical patients. *Journal of Experimental Social Psychology,* 1975, *11,* 155-165.

Leaf, A. Threescore and forty. *Hospital Practice,* 1973, *34,* 70-71.

Lefcourt, H. The function of the illusion of control and freedom. *American Psychologist,* 1973, *28,* 417-425.

Lieberman, M. Psychological correlates of impending death: Some preliminary observations. *Journal of Gerontology,* 1965, *20,* 181-190.

McMahon, A., & Rhudick, P. Reminiscing, adaptational significance in the aged. *Archives of General Psychiatry,* 1964, *10,* 292-298.

Neugarten, B., & Gutman, D. Age-sex roles and personality in middle age: A thematic apperception study. *Psychological Monographs,* 1958, *72* (17, Whole No. 470).

Pervin L. The need to predict and control under conditions of threat. *Journal of Personality,* 1963, *31,* 570-585.

Richter, C. On the phenomenon of sudden death in animals and man. *Psychosomatic Medicine,* 1957, *19,* 191-198.

Rodin, J. Crowding, perceived choice, and response to controllable and uncontrollable outcomes. *Journal of Experimental Social Psychology,* in press.

Schmale, A. Relationships of separation and depression to disease. I.: A report on a hospitalized medical population. *Psychosomatic Medicine,* 1958, *20,* 259-277.

Schmale, A., & Iker, H. The psychological setting of uterine cervical cancer. *Annals of the New York Academy of Sciences,* 1966, *125,* 807-813.

Seligman, M. E. P. *Helplessness.* San Francisco: Freeman, 1975.

Stotland, E., & Blumenthal, A. The reduction of anxiety as a result of the expectation of making a choice. *Canadian Review of Psychology,* 1964, *18,* 139-145.

Zimbardo, P. G., & Ruch, F. L. *Psychology and life* (9th ed.). Glenview, Ill.: Scott, Foresman, 1975.

Requests for reprints should be sent to Ellen Langer, Social Personality Program, Graduate Center, City University of New York, 33 West 42nd Street, New York, New York 10036 or to Judith Rodin, Department of Psychology, Yale University, New Haven, Connecticut 06520.

The authors would like to express sincere thanks to Thomas Tolisano and the members of his staff at the Arden House in Hamden, Connecticut, for their thoughtful assistance in conducting this research.

Reduction of Psychological Stress in Surgical Patients[1]

Ellen J. Langer   *Yale University*
Irving L. Janis
John A. Wolfer

Abstract

This study assesses the effectiveness of two stress-reducing strategies in a field setting. The first strategy consists of a coping device which entails the cognitive reappraisal of anxiety-provoking events, calming self-talk, and cognitive control through selective attention. The second strategy consists of supplying information about the threatening event along with reassurances for the purpose of producing emotional inoculation.

Patients about to undergo major surgery were exposed to either the coping device, the preparatory information, both strategies, or neither. The prediction that the coping device would effectively reduce both pre- and postoperative stress was confirmed. An analysis of the nurses' ratings of preoperative stress showed a significant main effect for the coping device. There was also a significant main effect for the coping device on postoperative measures (number of pain relievers requested and proportion of patients requesting sedatives). The preparatory information, however, did not produce any significant effects on these postoperative measures.

"Reduction of Psychological Stress in Surgical Patients" by Ellen J. Langer, Irving L. Janis and John A. Wolfer. *Journal of Experimental Social Psychology* 11, 155-165 (1975). Copyright © 1975 by Academic Press, Inc. Reprinted by permission.

INTRODUCTION

Stress reactions have been shown to vary as a function of psychological variables that can be modified even though the nature of the threatening event remains constant. Laboratory research provides evidence that stress tolerance can be increased by perceived control over the aversive stimuli, (e.g. (Pervin, 1963)) the availability of a distractor (e.g. (Kanfer and Goldfoot, 1966)), and information about the threatening event (e.g. (Lazarus and Alfert, 1964)). The purpose of the present study was (1) to extend the applicability of some of these findings from the laboratory to a natural setting and (2) to compare and evaluate two strategies for reducing stress, one emphasizing cognitive control over aversive events and the other providing realistic information and reassurance. The two strategies, based on principles derived from laboratory research, were tested on hospital patients about to undergo major surgery.

Painful but harmless shocks and other such stressors employed in laboratory studies differ from naturally occurring stressful events such as surgery. The laboratory stressors are more specific and easily identifiable, more precisely localized in time, of shorter duration, and much less threatening for the person's future well-being or survival. Since the aversive stimuli that people are asked to cope with in the laboratory may be both qualitatively and quantitatively different from the stressful events they encounter in the real world, the present study was designed to test the generality of pertinent laboratory findings in a field setting.

The second purpose involved comparing the relative effectiveness of two strategies of stress reduction.

(1) Coping Device

The first of these strategies involves the cognitive reappraisal of anxiety-provoking events. Essentially, subjects are shown the degree to which attention to and cognitions about an aversive event determine the stress one experiences with regard to that event (cf. (Ellis, 1962; Meichenbaum, 1971)). They are taught to exercise cognitive control through selective attention, so as to distract themselves from negative aspects of the stressful events they encounter. This strategy is in keeping with experimental evidence on the effectiveness of distraction in reducing stress. For example, Kanfer and Goldfoot (1966), after instructing their subjects to keep their hands in ice water as long as

possible, found that those who were given an environmental distractor (such as viewing travel slides) were better able to tolerate the aversive event than those who were not distracted or those whose attention was directed toward the event.

Since a person about to undergo major surgery is not apt to be distracted for long by a totally unrelated event, the distraction in the present study consisted of the patient directing his attention to the more favorable aspects of his present situation whenever he anticipated or experienced discomfort, rather than by directing his attention away from the event entirely. This strategy has further advantages in that it makes the expected gains salient and is an active means of coping with stress under the patient's own control. The patient knows that he can initiate it at any time and in any situation.

The relationship between perceived control and pain tolerance has been explored in numerous laboratory studies. For example, Pervin (1963) showed that subjects are less anxious when they control the administration of shock than when the experimenter controls it, even though the amount of external stimulation is the same. Other investigators have also found that when subjects believe they have some control over impending aversive stimuli, the stimuli are rated as less aversive (e.g. (Bowers, 1968; Corah and Boffa, 1970; Geer, Davison, and Gatchel, 1970; Glass, Singer, and Friedman, 1969; Kanfer and Seidner, 1973)).

(2) Preparatory Information

The second stress-reducing strategy consists of supplying patients with information regarding the impending surgical experience for the purpose of producing emotional inoculation. On the basis of field and laboratory studies, Janis (1958, 1971) has suggested that successful emotional inoculation can be produced in persons facing severe stress by giving them preparatory communications containing accurate warnings about what to expect, together with pertinent reassurances. According to this conception, such preparatory communications are effective when they arouse a moderate level of anticipatory fear, which leads to constructive "work of worrying," i.e., mentally rehearsing the impending threats and developing realistic, self-delivered reassurances that prevent subsequent emotional shocks, severe disappointment in protective authorities, and feelings of helplessness when the threats materialize.

Evidence from a number of laboratory experiments indicates that preparatory communications can reduce the emotional impact of confrontations with stressful stimuli. Lazarus and Alfert (1964), for example, found much less fear manifested on physiological-arousal measures and on self-rating measures when young men, before they witnessed distressing scenes in a film depicting a primitive circumcision rite, were given preliminary information and reassurance that the procedure was harmless. When prior information about aversive stimulation is accompanied by reassurances, pain tolerance tends to increase (Staub and Kellett, 1972); whereas when such information is given without reassurances, pain tolerance tends to decrease (Kanfer and Goldfoot, 1966).

Many field investigations with hospitalized patients also suggest the potential value of preparatory communications (Chapman, 1969; Egbert, Battit, Welch and Bartlett, 1964; Elms and Leonard, 1966; Healy, 1968; Johnson, 1965; Johnson and Leventhal, 1973; Lindeman and Aernan, 1971; Moran, 1963; Pranulis, 1967). In most of these studies, however, it is not clear whether the effects are attributable to the information designed to induce emotional inoculation or to other types of information such as instructions about pain relieving exercises that could induce a sense of active control.

The present study sought to evaluate the effectiveness of a coping device, a somewhat new but familiar strategy, and to compare it with a preparatory information procedure which did not include explicit coping suggestions. It was predicted that the coping device would effectively reduce pre- and postoperative stress. However, since the preparatory information directed attention to the threatening event, an initial mild increase in stress was predicted, and hence its effectiveness would be seen only postoperatively. In order to be able to test these predictions and to assess the value of a treatment that combined both strategies, a control group and a coping-plus-information group were also included in the experimental design.

Methods

Subjects.   The experiment was carried out at the Yale-New Haven Hospital with 60 adult surgical patients. All the patients were about to undergo elective operations for which the prognoses were generally favorable. The operations included hysterectomies, hernia repairs, and cholecystectomies, as well as less serious major surgical procedures such as

transuretheral resections, tubal ligations, and D & Cs. Subjects were assigned to conditions on a stratified random basis, so that the experimental groups were equated on five relevant background factors: type of operation, seriousness of operation, sex, age, and religious affiliation.

Procedures.   The effectiveness of two different methods for relieving operative stress was investigated in a 2 × 2 factorial design. One variable consisted of presenting or not presenting a cognitive coping device; the other consisted of presenting or not presenting preparatory information that described the care and discomforts of the pre- and postoperative experience.

A short time after the patient was admitted to the hospital he was approached by a female investigator dressed in a laboratory coat, who introduced herself and stated that she was a psychologist studying preoperative stress. In order to allay fears that the patient might have been singled out because of special psychological problems the psychologist added that she was visiting all preoperative patients on his floor. After obtaining the patient's consent, the investigator conducted one of four standardized interviews.

(1) Coping device only.[2]   This condition involved presenting a prepared communication that included a standard explanation and examples of the coping strategy. The communication began with a standard introduction asserting that most people are somewhat anxious before an operation, but that people can often control their own emotions if they know how to. It was explained that it is rarely events themselves that cause stress, but rather the views people take of them and the attention they give to those views. To facilitate understanding, the coping device was introduced by way of an analogy. The patient was told to imagine playing an exciting football game and was asked if he thought he would have noticed receiving a minor cut. After he answered in the negative, he was told that if, on the other hand, he had been at home reading a boring newspaper and received a paper cut, he probably would have nursed it attentively. (Females were asked to imagine rushing to finish preparations for a dinner for 15 people and receiving a minor cut in the process.) Thus it was shown that the patient actually controlled the amount of stress experienced.

They were told that nothing is either all positive or all negative and that it is the wise person who finds alternative views of threatening situations and therefore prevents oneself from becoming stressed. Illustrative examples from everyday life of alternative ways of viewing seemingly negative events (e.g., losing one's job) were provided. Patients were then asked to generate examples from their own lives and present positive alternative views of the events. The communication then went on to relate the coping device to the hospital experience. If there are indeed at least two ways of interpreting every experience, then there must be a positive nonstress-provoking view of being in the hospital. Attention was called to the positive or compensatory aspects of undergoing surgery in a good hospital, focussing on the improvement in health, the extra care and attention the patient would receive, the probable weight loss (if appropriate), and the rare opportunity to relax, to take stock of oneself, to have a vacation from outside pressures, and the like. The suggestion was made that the patient rehearse these realistic positive aspects whenever he starts to feel upset about the unpleasant aspects of the surgical experience. He was assured that this approach was not equivalent to lying to oneself. The coping device did not encourage denial but rather encouraged maintaining an overall optimistic view by taking account of the favorable consequences and reinterpreting the unfavorable ones.

As a final check on his comprehension of the recommendation, the patient was given the following event to interpret: "Suppose that some emergencies have come up so that your operation has to be delayed for a few days. How would you view this positively?" If the patient did not give the expected type of response, he was given additional details and examples.

(2) Preparatory information only. This communication began with the same introduction, stating that most people are somewhat anxious before an operation, but added that it is often because they don't have enough information about what to expect. The same basic information was then given to all subjects in this condition. After asking the patient what he expected to happen in preparation for his operation, he was told about the nature of and reasons for such practices as skin preparation, elimination, preoperative medication, and anesthesia. The second half of the information was addressed to the postoperative experience. Again the patient was questioned about his expectations. He was informed that the surgery might be followed by gas pains, slight nausea, constipation, and difficulty in urinating. He was also alerted to the possibility that after the anesthetic had worn off he might experience some pain around the incision area as a result of the surgical procedure itself. All the information consisted of simple facts available in

standard nursing manuals concerning usual sources of discomfort and operative care. The probable pains and discomforts were made analogous to commonplace experiences rarely accompanied by stress. Additional statements of a reassuring nature called attention to the high quality of the hospital staff.

(3) Combination of preparatory information and coping device. After an introduction that combined the key statements used in each of the preceding two conditions, patients were given the preparatory communication concerning discomforts and operative care. Then they were given the explanation of the coping device. In an attempt to hold constant the amount of interaction with the psychologist, the combined condition was limited to approximately the same amount of time as the sessions in either condition alone. This was accomplished by using fewer examples (but still enough to ensure understanding) and a condensed discussion of each.

(4) Control. The purpose of this interview was to control for the possible effects on a surgical patient of the mere encounter with an interested psychologist. The interview was introduced in a similar way as the three experimental conditions, asserting that most people are somewhat anxious before an operation and that a patient's view of hospital routines may influence the stress he is undergoing. It was conducted in the same manner and lasted about the same amount of time as the other sessions. In order to avoid a discussion about fears concerning the present operation, the patients were asked relatively neutral questions relevant to the surgical experience, such as: Have you ever been in the hospital before? When did you first go to the doctor for this ailment? How long did you know you were going to have the operation before you came to the hospital? When did you last see your doctor? Could you tell me about the admitting procedure? All conversation was directed toward hospital routines; no questions were asked about the unpleasant aspects of the impending operation.

The sessions for each of the four treatments lasted approximately 20 minutes. All physicians, nurses, and others on the hospital staff were kept blind as to the patient's experimental treatment.

Dependent measures. Behavioral ratings and direct behavioral measures were used in order to evaluate the stress-reducing properties of the various communications. Immediate effects on the patients' emotional state were assessed by obtaining behavioral ratings from nurses on the surgical ward. Before the interview, the nurse who had admitted the patient to the hospital was asked to complete a short questionnaire evaluating the patient's level of stress in comparison with most major elective preoperative patients. The first asked for the patient's level of anxiety and provided anchors at (1) extremely anxious, (4) moderately anxious, and (7) not at all anxious. The second question asked the nurse: How well is the patient dealing with stress and discomforts? (1) not at all well, (4) moderately well, (7) extremely well. The nurse was told to answer the preinterview questionnaire on the basis of the impressions she had formed during the admitting procedure. Approximately 15 minutes after the experimenter's visit was completed, the same nurse was asked to revisit the patient and to complete the same questionnaire once again. The instructions stated that the nurse should ignore her previous ratings, since the patient may have changed in either direction.

In addition to the nurses' ratings, data on overt behavioral indicators of postoperative stress were also recorded. The total number of pain relievers and sedatives the patient requested, and his length of stay in the hospital were taken from the patient's record. In addition, physiological measures were obtained, blood pressure and pulse readings recorded by the nurses before and 15 minutes after the interview and again immediately before and about 1 hour after the operation.

RESULTS

Nurses' preoperative evaluations. Changes from immediately before to immediately after the psychologist's interview were assessed for each patient on the basis of the nurses' evaluations of the patients' level of anxiety and ability to cope with stress. Table 1, columns (a) and (b) present the mean change scores (after-before) for each experimental condition. A positive score reflects an improvement in successful coping. A separate analysis of variance was computed for each of the two measures. Both measures showed a significant main effect for the coping communication ("anxiety": $F(1,56) = 5.60$; $p < .05$; "ability to cope": $F(1,56) = 12.59$; $p < .01$). While the coping communication was expected to reduce stress, an initial mild increase in stress was anticipated for patients receiving only the preparatory information. A contrast describing this which set the two coping groups equal to each and superior to the control group, which, in turn, was superior to the information-only group, yielded reliable results for both ratings ("anxiety": $F(1,56) = 4.63$, $p < .05$; "ability to cope": $F(1,56) = 7.06$, $p < .05$).

Postoperative behavioral measures.[3] The four groups were compared on the basis of the mean number of pain relievers requested by patients during postoperative convalescence. The mean numbers of requests per patient were: 5.13 for the preparatory information and coping group; 3.36 for the coping group; 5.13 for the preparatory information group; and 9.27 for the control group. Patients in the preparatory information group were expected to make use of the information over time to reduce stress. Therefore, the control group, which was given neither the preparatory information nor the coping device, was expected to request more pain-relieving drugs than any of the other three groups. The comparison between the control group and the three experimental groups yielded an $F(1,55) = 4.44$; $p < .05$, although the main effects and interaction did not reach conven-

Table 1 Mean Changes in Nurses' Preoperative Ratings of Stress and Percentage of Patients Who Requested Drugs During Postoperative Convalescence

	Rated anxiety[a] (a)	Rated ability to cope[a] (b)	% req. pain relievers (c)	% req. sedatives (d)	% req. pain relievers and sedatives (e)
Coping; preparatory information	.53	.53	73	87	67
Coping; no preparatory information	.40	.67	64	72	50
No coping; preparatory information	−.20	−.13	80	87	73
No coping; no preparatory information	.13	0	93	100	93

[a] A positive change score indicates improvement, i.e., lower anxiety or higher ability to cope.
$n = 15/$group for preoperative measures; $n = 14$ or 15 for postoperative measures.[3]

tional levels of significance. Table 1, (column c) shows the percentage of patients in each group who requested pain relievers at least once. These data show essentially the same pattern as the data on mean number of requests. When the proportions are transformed into arc sines and analyzed, the analysis yields a significant main effect for the coping strategy ($Z = 1.75$; $p < .04$).[4]

The groups did not differ on mean number of sedatives requested. However, when we look at the percentage requesting sedatives at least once (Table 1, column d), we observe a pattern similar to that found for pain relievers. The main effect for the coping strategy and the interaction are significant at $p < .025$ ($Z = 2.02$, in both instances). The last column in Table 1 shows the proportion of patients in each group who requested both pain relievers and sedatives. Once again, the analysis yielded a significant main effect for the coping strategy ($Z = 2.24$; $p < .02$) and a significant interaction ($Z = 1.74$; $p < .05$).

While the groups were not reliably different with respect to the mean length of stay in the hospital, the results conform to the pattern found above; coping, 5.64 days; coping/preparatory information, 6.2 days; preparatory information, 7.2 days; and no coping/no information, 7.6 days.

Physiological measures; blood pressure and pulse rate.   A multivariate analysis of the systolic blood pressure, the diastolic blood pressure, and the pulse rate obtained before and after the experimenter's visit, and before and after the operation, failed to reveal any systematic variation in these measures. The measures did not differ among the groups, in contrast to the behavioral ratings and drug request measures that indicated differential stress among patients in the four conditions. Nor did the physiological measures differ within groups over time, although one might expect patients to be more stressed immediately prior to the operation than at earlier times. It is noteworthy that the changes in blood pressure and pulse do not correlate significantly with the behavioral measures of stress or with each other. The correlations of changes in pulse with changes in blood pressure ranged from $-.02$ to $.10$.

DISCUSSION

It is exceedingly difficult to carry out an experimental manipulation that consists largely of obtaining a certain category of responses from an interviewee, with the exacting control possible in a laboratory analogue. However, in as far as the present results corroborate previous experimental findings, they may be viewed as a meaningful extension of laboratory findings to a real world problem, operative stress. A coping device derived largely from laboratory studies on distraction and the perception of control, which entails the cognitive reappraisal of anxiety-provoking events, calming self-talk, and intentional cognitive control through selective attention, appears to be an effective means of reducing both pre- and postoperative stress. Unlike the control and information-only groups, those subjects taught this approach showed an immediate positive change as evidenced by the nurses' blind ratings of level of anxiety and ability to cope with discomfort. This relatively rapid decrease in anxiety and increase in coping ability in the groups given the coping communication may be partly attributed to the fact that although the immediate fears of these patients were recognized and discussed, the more concrete fears about the details of the pre- and postoperative procedures and about the pains and discomforts they might experience were not stimulated. Presumably, the patients' generally negative view of their physical condition, hospitalization, and the impending operation, were reinterpreted by directing their attention to the favorable aspects of their present situation.

In addition to being urged to focus their attention on positive features of the operation, the patients given the coping device, unlike those in the information-only and the control group, were explicitly told that they could exert more control than they might have realized. The coping device was portrayed as a mechanism for controlling one's emotions. This heightened perception of control may also have contributed to greater stress tolerance, by reducing the additional stress generated by feelings of helplessness that so often occur among hospitalized patients.

The patients who received the coping recommendation proved to be superior to those who did not on two postoperative measures of stress tolerance, pain relievers, and sedatives requested. There was a similar but nonsignificant trend for length of stay in the hospital. The data are consistent with the expectation that knowledge of the coping device helps surgical patients deal with potentially anxiety-provoking situations as they arise.

In the information-only group, on the other hand, very specific details of the pre- and postoperative procedure were discussed. This had the initial effect of making the impending operation more anxiety-arousing. While the negative effects of the communication apparently dissipated by the time the postoperative measures were taken, no evidence of a positive postoperative effect was found. When preparatory information is presented in a brief preoperative session, the patients may acquire more realistic conceptions of the postoperative discomforts to be expected and spontaneously develop some effective coping mechanisms. But they may still, so to speak, be tuned into the pains and discomforts. Focussing on expected suffering may be a less effective means, so far as tolerating temporary postoperative pains is concerned, than focussing on something else, and thereby not "noticing" the pain as much.

Although the behavioral measures based on the patients' requests for drugs indicate a differential level of stress for subjects in the four conditions, the blood pressure and pulse data show no systematic variation with condition or over time. Since the two physiological measures did not correlate with each other or with the behavioral measures of stress, they do not appear to be promising dependent variables for assessing the effects of preparatory communications on stress tolerance in surgical patients. Perhaps some other physiological measures, such as variability in heart rate (Porges, 1972), rather than changes in heart rate *per se,* will prove to be more valid for investigating changes under stress.

While it would seem beneficial to incorporate a procedure like that employed in the coping device condition into nurses' intake interviews with patients, it may also be important to return now to the laboratory to determine whether the positive effects of the coping device were a function of the increase in the perception of control over the stressful event, the distraction, or some combination of the two, so that an even more effective strategy may be developed.

Footnotes

[1] This research was conducted while the senior author was an N.I.M.H. predoctoral fellow (1F01 MH 5454-01) and was partially supported by Grant No. GS-30514X to Irving L. Janis, principal investigator, from the National Science Foundation. Requests for reprints should be sent to Ellen Langer, who is now at the Graduate Center, City University of New York, 33 West 42nd Street, New York, New York 10036.

[2] A more complete statement of the coping strategy can be found in Langer and Dweck, 1973.

[3] The data on pain relievers, sedatives, and length of stay are based on 59 cases, since the husband of one subject in the coping condition refused to sign the release for his wife to have a hysterectomy.

[4] See Langer and Abelson (1972) for a discussion of the use of the arcsine transformation in this context.

References

Bowers, K. Pain, anxiety, and perceived control. *Journal of Consulting and Clinical Psychology,* 1968, *32,* 596-602.

Chapman, J. S. Effects of different nursing approaches upon psychological and physiological responses. *Nursing Research Report,* 1969, *5,* 1-7.

Corah, N. L. & Boffa, J. Perceived control, self-observation and response to aversive behavior. *Journal of Personality and Social Psychology,* 1970, *16,* 1-4.

Egbert, L. D., Battit, E., Welch, C. E. & Bartlett, M. K. Reduction of postoperative pain by encouragement and instruction of patients. *New England Journal of Medicine,* 1961, *270,* 825-827.

Ellis, A. *Reason and emotion in psychotherapy.* New York: Lyle-Stuart, 1962.

Elms, R. R. & Leonard, R. C. Effects of nursing approaches during admission. *Nursing Research,* 1966, *15,* 39-48.

Geer, A. H., Davison, G. C., & Gatchel, R. I. Reduction of stress in humans through nonveridical perceived control of aversive stimulation. *Journal of Personality and Social Psychology,* 1970, *16,* 731-738.

Glass, D. C., Singer, J. E. & Friedman, J. Psychic cost of adaptation to an environment stressor. *Journal of Personality and Social Psychology,* 1969, *12,* 200-219.

Healy, K. M. Does preoperative instruction make a difference? *American Journal of Nursing,* 1968, *68,* 62-67.

Janis, I. L. *Psychological stress: Psychoanalytic and behavioral studies of surgical patients.* New York: Wiley, 1958.

Janis, I. L. *Stress and frustration.* New York: Harcourt Brace and Jovanovich, 1971.

Johnson, J. E. Effect of nurse-patient interaction on the patients' postoperative discomfort. Unpublished Master's thesis, Yale School of Nursing, 1965.

Johnson, J. E. & Leventhal, H. The effects of accurate expectations and behavioral instructions on reactions during a noxious medical examination, 1973. Mimeo prepublication report.

Kanfer, F. H. & Goldfoot, D. A. Self-control and tolerance of noxious stimulation. *Psychological Reports,* 1966, *18,* 79-85.

Kanfer, F. H. & Seidner, M. L. Self-control: Factors enhancing tolerance of noxious stimulation. *Journal of Personality and Social Psychology,* 1973, *25,* 381-389.

Langer, E. J. & Abelson, R. P. The semantics of asking a favor: How to succeed in getting help without really dying. *Journal of Personality and Social Psychology,* 1972, *24,* 26-32.

Langer, E. J. & Dweck, C. S. *Personal politics.* New Jersey: Prentice-Hall Inc., 1973.

Lazarus, R. S. & Alfert, E. Short-circuiting of threat by experimentally altering cognitive appraisal. *Journal of Abnormal and Social Psychology,* 1964, *69,* 195-205.

Lindemen, C. A. & Aernan, B. V. Nursing intervention with the presurgical patient: The effects of structured and unstructured preoperative teaching. *Nursing Research,* 1971, *20,* 319-334.

Meichenbaum, O. H. Cognitive factors in behavior modification: Modifying what clients say to themselves. Paper presented at the Fifth Annual Meeting of the Association for Advancement of Behavior Therapy, Washington, D.C., September, 1971.

Moran, P. A. An experimental study of pediatric admissions. Unpublished Master's thesis, Yale University School of Nursing, 1963.

Pervin, L. A. The need to predict and control under conditions of threat. *Journal of Personality,* 1963, *31,* 570-587.

Porges, S. Heart rate variability and deceleration as indexes of reaction time. *Journal of Experimental Psychology,* 1972, *92,* 103-110.

Pranulis, M. F. The patient and his role in a smooth anesthesia experience. Unpublished Master's thesis, Yale School of Nursing, 1967.

Staub, E. & Kellet, O. S. Increasing pain tolerance by information about aversive stimuli. *Journal of Personality and Social Psychology,* 1972, *21,* 198-203.

The Self and Social Institutions

Economic Threat as a Determinant of Conversion Rates in Authoritarian and Nonauthoritarian Churches

Stephen M. Sales[1]   *Carnegie-Mellon University*

Abstract

It has often been suggested that threat is an important contributor to individuals' levels of authoritarianism. A variety of findings seem congruent with this hypothesis; however, virtually all of these supportive data have been generated in laboratory experiments involving relatively peripheral aspects of the behavior of undergraduate students. The impact of these results is thus potentially limited to these somewhat artificial situations. The present investigation extends the validity of this hypothesis beyond such settings by indicating that economic bad times (exemplified both by the Great Depression and by recent conditions in the Seattle, Washington, area) increase the rate of conversions to authoritarian churches, while economic good times increase the rate of conversions to non-authoritarian churches. The implications of these data for Marx's description of religion as "the opiate of the people" are also discussed.

"Economic Threat as a Determinant of Conversion Rates in Authoritarian and Nonauthoritarian Churches" by Stephen M. Sales. *Journal of Personality and Social Psychology,* 1972, Vol. 23, No. 3, pp. 420–428. Copyright © 1972 by The American Psychological Association, Inc. Reprinted by permission.

In their highly influential book, *The authoritarian personality* (Adorno, Frenkel-Brunswik, Levinson, & Sanford, 1950), Adorno and his coauthors (1950) devoted some effort to determining the factors which caused some individuals to be authoritarian and others to be nonauthoritarian. Although their data regarding this issue seem somewhat suspect (Brown, 1965), the Berkeley group was nevertheless able to draw an apparently reasonable conclusion from their results. Specifically, they argued that the "threatening traumatic, [and] overwhelming discipline [p. 372]" to which some children are exposed causes them to have highly authoritarian personalities at maturity. Thus, Adorno et al. strongly implicated threat as a basic determinant of authoritarianism.

Rokeach (1960) reached the same conclusion. However, in contrast to Adorno and his collaborators,

Rokeach felt that threat in the environments of even mature subjects might influence these individuals' levels of authoritarianism. In Rokeach's terms, "The more threatening a situation is to a person, the more closed [i.e., authoritarian] his belief system will tend to become [p. 377]." This hypothesis is readily testable, and various investigations have offered supportive data. For instance, Rokeach reported several positive correlations between his dogmatism scale and anxiety, and Davids (1955) replicated this result for the California F Scale. More directly relevant to Rokeach's prediction, Sales and Friend (in press) reported that failure-induced threat tended to increase subjects' scores on a self-report index of authoritarianism, while success tended to decrease their scores on this index. Sales and Friend also found that their experimental conditions affected subjects' willingness to conform to an authority figure (a reasonable behavioral criterion of authoritarianism). Finally, Dittes (1961) indicated that threat caused individuals impulsively to reach closure on an ambiguous task, Zander and Havelin (1960) reported that threat led individuals to reject persons dissimilar to themselves, and Berkowitz and Knurek (1969) found that threat increased subjects' hostility toward members of experimentally created outgroups. All of the dependent variables used in these latter investigations are behaviors which are said to characterize authoritarian persons; all of them were increased (even in mature persons) by the presence of threat.

However, while the available data seem to indicate that threat is in fact an important contributor to high levels of authoritarianism, a methodological consideration clouds the issue. Virtually all of the investigations cited above were laboratory experiments performed on undergraduate psychology students. And, in most cases, the dependent variables involved were relatively peripheral to the ongoing lives of the subjects employed. It would clearly be unwise to reject these investigations on the basis of their methodological bias; there is no reason to believe that behavior in experimental settings is any less "real" than behavior in other settings, although it may be controlled by somewhat different variables. However, it would be useful to have evidence on the present question which involves important "real life" behaviors in a wide spectrum of subjects.

In a sense, two previous investigations may be interpreted as providing the desired evidence. However, both of these studies are unfortunately ambiguous regarding the issue under consideration. In the first of these studies, Hovland and Sears (1940) reported a correlation of -.67 between the number of lynchings (of Negroes) in 14 Southern states and the value per acre of the cotton crop. While the magnitude of the correlation has been disputed (e.g., by Mintz, 1946), students of this issue (e.g., Brown, 1954) have concluded that at least some relation does exist between economic prosperity and lynchings. Thus, the greater the economic threat in the predominantly rural South, the greater the number of attacks against members of an outgroup. Since hostility against members of an outgroup tends to characterize authoritarian individuals, one might interpret the Hovland and Sears finding as evidence for the hypothesis that threat increases authoritarianism. However, since frustration has been shown to increase nonauthoritarian aggression as well as attacks against members of an outgroup, the impact of the Hovland and Sears data for the present hypothesis is unclear. In the second relevant investigation, Rokeach (1960) directly examined the relationship between dogmatism and threat. In an ingenious use of historical data, Rokeach employed 12 Ecumenical Councils of the Catholic Church as his sampling points. For each of these Councils, Rokeach obtained ratings of *(a)* the threat to the Church in the situation which precipitated the Council and *(b)* the overall dogmatism of the Council's canons. The rank-order correlation between these two variables was .66. This result suggests that increased threat is indeed one cause of increased authoritarianism. However, since the Church is not an individual, since different persons participated in each of these Councils, and since the various Councils differed on many dimensions other than the threat inherent in the precipitating situation, Rokeach's data can be considered only suggestive.

The present investigation is an attempt to provide more direct evidence on the hypothesis that threat is one cause of increased authoritarianism. Specifically, this study examines patterns of joining authoritarian and nonauthoritarian organizations as a function of economic conditions. It is anticipated that during hard times authoritarian groups attract relatively large numbers of new members, while during good times nonauthoritarian groups become relatively more attractive.

Of necessity, the characterization of specific organizations as "authoritarian" or "nonauthoritarian" is subjective in nature. Since there exists no analogue of the California F Scale for formal organizations, one must rely upon potentially fallible judgments in classifying specific groups. However, there is a reasonable guide which might help one make this judgment. Specifically, the authors of *The authoritarian personality* (Adorno et al., 1950) named a variety of characteristics which they felt typified authoritarian persons. These included authoritarian submission (to the moral authorities of the ingroup), authoritarian aggression (against outgroups), superstition, overconcern with sexuality, ethnocentrism, and a preoccupation with strength and power. If one could observe *organizations* characterized by these factors, then one presumably would be fairly safe in terming these groups authoritarian organizations. Conversely, if one could observe organizations characterized by the lack of these patterns, one might be fairly safe in calling these groups nonauthoritarian organizations.

Church denominations appear to be a particularly useful choice for the present research, since one can apparently achieve a reasonable division of churches into more authoritarian and less authoritarian denominations.[2] This division is made possible by the fact that differences among religious denominations are often along lines quite similar to those named by Adorno and his coauthors. For instance, some churches demand absolute obedience either to the leadership of the church or to the Divine (authoritarian submission); others allow the parishioner more leeway in his decisions. Some churches condemn disbelievers and heretics (authoritarian aggression); others assume a more tolerant attitude. Some churches emphasize the mystical aspects of religion and apply a literal interpretation of scripture (superstition), while others stress a more intellectualized approach. Some churches exhibit strong concern about "sin" (including sexuality); others are much less exercised over this issue. Some churches believe that there is only "one true church," and that members of other denominations have been somehow misled (ethnocentrism); others feel that there are many equally acceptable forms of belief. Finally, some churches stress the unimaginable might (and potential punitiveness) of God, while others view the Divine more as a friend and helper. Furthermore, and equally important, these characteristics of churches seem to cohere into a "syndrome," just as their analogues at the individual level form a pattern. That is, denominations which demand obedience also condemn heretics, while denominations which apply an intellectual approach to religion also show relatively less concern over sinfulness.

Since this study is concerned with patterns of

joining authoritarian and nonauthoritarian organizations, its operational focus regarding churches is on conversion rates. Unfortunately, many denominations do not regularly publish data regarding converts. However, eight major churches that represent fairly clear positions on the authoritarianism dimension do report these figures yearly. On the basis of descriptive information provided by Williams (1969) and Mead (1965), one may reasonably classify four of these denominations (The Presbyterian Church in the United States of America, the Congregational Christian Church, the Northern Baptist Convention, and the Protestant Episcopal Church) as nonauthoritarian and four others (the Southern Baptist Convention, the Church of Jesus Christ of Latter-day Saints, the Seventh-day Adventist Church, and the Roman Catholic Church) as authoritarian.[3] These eight denominations serve as the basis for this investigation. In a sense, each of these denominations provides a separate test of the hypothesis under consideration; however, our primary interest is on the overall pattern of the data, not on findings specific to any of the churches.

STUDY I

Method

The period 1920-1939 was chosen for investigation in this study. Several considerations prompted this choice:

1. The period was recent enough that each of the eight churches gathered *(a)* relatively complete and *(b)* presumably relatively accurate data regarding conversions.

2. The period did not include any wars or major environmental threats other than economic ones. The "red scare" of 1919 had generally subsided by the summer of 1920; World War II did not begin until the fall of 1939, and its impact was not widely felt in America until 1940. Thus, no major noneconomic threats existed during this period which might cloud the anticipated relationship between economic conditions and conversions to the denominations studied here.

3. The period clearly incorporated extreme variations in economic conditions. The years from 1920 to 1929 were ones of great prosperity; those from 1930 to 1939 were ones of overwhelming depression. No other comparable period in the nation's history has included

such a variable economic picture. Indeed, no other period has involved any economic threat of the sort posed by the Great Depression. If economic factors were to have any effect upon religious conversions, they would surely do so during this period of great boom and great bust.

For each of the years during this time span, an estimate of American per capita disposable income (the average income following payment of all taxes) was obtained. Per capita disposable income was chosen because this variable seemed to present the clearest picture of economic threat or well-being in the nation as a whole. These estimates were achieved by dividing the United States Census Bureau's estimate of the population in each year into the Bureau's estimated disposable personal income for that year (Bureau of the Census, 1960). Clearly, these estimates are likely to be somewhat inaccurate. The census is taken only every 10 years, and it is known to be somewhat fallible. Thus, one would hardly be surprised if the Census Bureau's estimate of the American population for any specific year were as much as 3% or 4% in error. Similarly, the Bureau's estimate of disposable personal income is based on inaccurate sources, and it is likely to be even more in error than the estimate of the population. Thus, the yearly estimates of per capita disposable income used in this investigation are clearly open to some question. However, these estimates appear to be adequate for testing the present hypothesis. For instance, in the 20-year period under consideration, estimated per capita disposable income correlated .994 with the Census Bureau's (1960) estimate of per capita gross national product and −.960 with the Bureau's estimate of unemployment in the civilian labor force. Thus, the present estimates seem to be valid indicators of real economic conditions during the period involved. Furthermore, the inaccuracies inherent in these estimates seem not to be a serious problem for the present research purposes. Errors of measurement introduced by the estimating process are unlikely to be greater than a few percent, while the estimates of per capita disposable income vary from $682 to $364 within the period under consideration. Given this sort of real difference, small errors of estimation hardly seem to matter. And, in any event, all such errors are likely to be uncorrelated with rates of conversion. Their contribution would thus be to lower the correlations between economic conditions and the dependent variable used here.

For each of these 20 years, an estimated "conversion ratio" was obtained for the eight denominations under study. These ratios indicate the percentage of non-members of each church who converted to that church during any given year. All such ratios were achieved by estimating the number of non-X Americans (where X stands for a specific denomination) during a given year and then dividing this estimate into the number of individuals who actually converted to X during that year. The estimate of non-X individuals was obtained by subtracting the number of members reported for X in the *Yearbook of American Churches* from the Census Bureau's estimate of the total American population; the number of converts to X was obtained from material reported by the churches themselves.[4]

As with the estimates of per capita disposable income, these estimated conversion ratios are likely to involve some error. As indicated previously, the Census Bureau's estimate of the American population is somewhat inaccurate. Furthermore, the estimates of church membership are recognized (e.g., by Glock & Stark, 1965; Hudson, 1955) as highly suspect. (Among other considerations, most church denominations do not remove a member from their rolls merely for his failure regularly to attend church activities. For this reason, a given individual might join several different denominations over a period of years, and be active in none of them, but still be counted as a "member" by each.) Thus, the estimate of non-X Americans is surely erroneous for each of the eight denominations studied here during each of the 20 years in the period under consideration. However, as was the case for the estimates of disposable income, such errors of measurement are likely to have a conservative effect upon the present results. Furthermore, the value of the conversion ratio is little affected by small changes in the estimate of non-X Americans; reasonable error in these figures can thus have no particular impact upon the present results. The conversion ratios are, however, fairly sensitive to changes in the reported number of converts attracted. One may hope that these data, based on events which allow no ambiguity regarding whether an individual is or is not a convert during any particular year, are reasonably accurate.

These data have been subject to a relatively straightforward analysis. For each denomination, a product-moment correlation has been computed between *(a)* the yearly estimates of per capita disposable income and *(b)* the yearly estimated conversion ratios. Each year served as a separate sampling point for the calculation of these correlations; thus, *n* equals 20 for this analysis.

Results and Discussion

The findings of this investigation are presented in Tables 1 and 2. Table 1 lists the various correlations between per capita disposable income and conversion rates in the eight churches studied here; Table 2 summarizes the raw data on which these correlations are based. For ease of presentation of these raw data, the 20 years involved in this investigation have been combined into three general periods: economically "good" years (per capita disposable income between $625 and $700, $n = 7$); economically "moderate" years (per capita disposable income between $515 and $625, $n = 7$), and economically "bad" years (per capita disposable income between $350 and $515, $n = 6$).

As may be seen from Table 1, all of the correlations involving authoritarian denominations are negative, and three of the four are reliably different from zero.[5] All of the correlations involving nonauthoritarian denominations are positive; three of the four are significant, and the fourth (that for the Protestant Episcopal Church) barely fails to reach accepted levels of statistical significance. And, as indicated in Table 2, these correlations do not reflect only minor changes in patterns of conversions. For instance, the Presbyterian Church in the United States of America attracted about 30% fewer converts (per million non-Presbyte-

Table 1 Correlations Between Estimated per Capita Disposable Income and Estimated Conversion Ratios in Four Authoritarian and Four Nonauthoritarian Denominations

Denomination	r between estimated per capita disposable income and estimated conversion ratio
Authoritarian	
Church of Jesus Christ of Latter-day Saints	−.460***
Roman Catholic Church	−.456***
Seventh-day Adventist Church	−.867****
Southern Baptist Convention	−.193
Nonauthoritarian	
Congregational Christian Church	.503***
Northern Baptist Convention	.408**
Presbyterian Church in the United States of America	.533****
Protestant Episcopal Church	.312*

* $p < .10$.   *** $p < .025$.
** $p < .05$.   **** $p < .01$.

rians) during the 6 bad years than they did during the 7 good years, while the Seventh-day Adventist Church attracted about 68% more converts (per million non-Seventh-day Adventists) during the 6 bad years than they did during the 7 good years. These findings are clearly congruent with the prediction that individuals will be drawn to authoritarian organizations during hard times, but that they will gravitate to nonauthoritarian organizations when times are good. Stated more generally, these results are in accord with the hypothesis that threat is a contributor to an individual's level of authoritarianism, and they strongly support Sanford's (1966) speculation that "certain conditions in society, such as economic depression with declining confidence in the established order, seem more likely than others to foster authoritarianism in the society's members [p. 138]."

As with all cross-sectional investigations, the present findings are open to a variety of alternative explanations. Naturally, there is no likelihood that a shift in individuals' religious preferences brought about the Depression. Thus, the direction of causality is not in question. However, it is possible that some factor other than economic threat led to the observed changes in conversion patterns during the 20-year period studied here. The design of this study fortunately eliminates some possible extraneous variables from consideration. For instance, since conversion rates followed essentially the same pattern among all churches within the authoritarian and nonauthoritarian categories, it is clear that events specific to any single church (e.g., turnover in the national leadership; promulgation of new dogma) cannot account for the present data. Equally important, since churches with broad national representation (e.g., the Protestant Episcopal Church; the Roman Catholic Church) exhibited patterns similar to those of more locally based churches (e.g., the Church of Jesus Christ of Latter-day Saints; the Southern Baptist Convention), it is unlikely that region-specific factors could explain these findings.

Since members of authoritarian churches are generally lower in socioeconomic status than members of nonauthoritarian churches, the present results could possibly be explained without considering the relative authoritarianism of these denominations per se. That is, since the Depression increased the number of lower-class individuals in the American population, increased conversion rates to authoritarian churches during this period might indicate just that these newly lower-class persons tended to join denominations appropriate to their status. Similarly, since the 1920 boom period increased the number of middle-class and upper middle-class individuals in the population, increased conversion rates to nonauthoritarian churches during this period might only indicate that these newly wealthy persons tended to join denominations appropriate to their status. While this argument is reasonable, one aspect of the present data tends to negate it. One of the nonauthoritarian churches (the Northern Baptist Convention) is a lower middle-class denomination (American Baptist Convention, American Baptist Home Mission Society, 1961). If the present results indicated only that persons tend to join class-appropriate churches, then this denomination should yield a negative correlation between estimated per capita disposible income and conversion rates. The observed correlation, however, was .408 ($p < .05$). Furthermore, this correlation is significantly different ($p < .05$) from the parallel correlation for the more authoritarian Southern Baptist Convention, whose members are reasonably similar to those of the Northern Baptist Convention on economic factors. Naturally, this single datum does not rule out this potential alternative explanation: however, it does render this argument somewhat unlikely.

It is, however, quite possible that some condition specific to the period under consideration is the real cause of the present findings. One could test this contention by selecting another historical period and then determining whether or not the results reported here also obtained in this second period. Since no other period in American history has involved an economic threat similar to that posed by the Depression, one is at some loss in attempting to choose a period which might permit an appropriate replication of the present results. However, if one changes his frame of reference from the nation as a whole to specific regions within the nation, one can select historical periods which might prove adequate for purposes of replication. Study II attempts this tack.

STUDY II

Recent events within the Seattle, Washington, area seem to provide the conditions necessary for a replication of Study I. Although a large urban area, Seattle is primarily affected by factors specific to a single corporation. Furthermore, this corporation is involved in a highly labile industry (aerospace). Thus, at times during the past 10 years, Seattle's economy has exhibited considerable vigor, while at other times it has been relatively depressed. These fluctuations appear reasonably adequate for attempting to replicate the findings reported above.

Method

Data regarding economic conditions in the Seattle area have been taken from a periodical, *Area Trends in Employment and Unemployment,* published regularly by the United States Training and Employment

Table 2 Estimated Yearly Number of Converts (per Million Nonmembers) to Four Authoritarian and Four Nonauthoritarian Denominations as a Function of Economic Conditions

Denomination	Estimated per capita disposable income		
	High: $625–$700 (7 years)	Moderate: $515–$625 (7 years)	Low: $350–$515 (6 years)
Authoritarian			
Church of Jesus Christ of Latter-day Saints	55	59	62
Roman Catholic Church	314	376	378
Seventh-day Adventist Church	59	71	99
Southern Baptist Convention	1,720	1,874	1,820
Nonauthoritarian			
Congregational Christian Church	351	324	282
Northern Baptist Convention	568	512	480
Presbyterian Church in the United States of America	305	273	213
Protestant Episcopal Church	100	101	92

Service of the United States Department of Labor. These data suggest that 3 years from the most recent decade represented relatively good times in Seattle, in that unemployment during each of these years was significantly lower than it was during the preceding year; these good years were 1962, 1965, and 1966. Similarly, these data suggest that 4 years from this decade represented relatively bad times in Seattle, in that unemployment during each of these years was significantly higher than it was during the preceding year; these bad years were 1961, 1964, 1969, and 1970. Unemployment in Seattle during the relatively good years averaged about 4.0%; and the parallel figure for the relatively bad years was about 6.7%.

Not all of the denominations examined in this paper report conversion data separately for various geographic areas in the country. Thus, it is impossible to replicate all of the findings presented above. However, two of the churches studied here do annually list conversion data for various regions (including the Seattle area). Fortunately, one of these is an authoritarian denomination (the Roman Catholic Church), while one is a nonauthoritarian denomination (the United Presbyterian Church in the United States of America, a denomination formed by the merger of the Presbyterian Church in the United States of America and a much smaller Presbyterian group). Since only two churches are involved, the data which they provide will necessarily be suspect, for any trends could easily be a function of factors internal to either of these denominations. Further, the effects of year-to-year changes in the population of Seattle cannot be determined. (Indeed, the magnitude of these changes themselves can only be roughly estimated, since the census is taken only at 10-year invervals.) However, with these considerations in mind, it still would seem useful to determine whether or not the two groups did experience relatively different patterns of conversions in the Seattle area as a function of local economic conditions.

Results and Discussion

For the decade as a whole, one can easily calculate the proportions of each group's converts that were gained in the Seattle area. These calculations indicate that 1.23% of the Roman Catholic Church's converts during the period 1961-1970 were gained by the Seattle Archdiocese, while 1.79% of the United Presbyterian Church's converts during that period were attracted by the Seattle Presbytery. Knowing these overall percentages, one can then calculate the number of converts that each group would be expected to receive in Seattle during the relatively good and the relatively bad years considered separately. A comparison of these expected figures with the actual number of converts reported by these two churches indicates that the Seattle Presbytery of the United Presbyterian Church attracted 3.63% more converts than would be expected when times were good, but that it attracted 4.03% fewer converts than would be expected when times were bad. The Seattle Archdiocese of the Roman Catholic Church, on the other hand, attracted 4.34% fewer converts than would be expected during the good years, but it attracted .68% more converts than would be expected during the bad years. The chi-squares for these data are 26.07 for the United Presbyterian Church and 12.25 for the Roman Catholic Church; both are significant ($p < .001$). As with the data drawn from the period 1920-1939, these results for the Seattle area are open to alternative explanations. In particular, as indicated above, they may stem from denomination-specific conditions and not from the proposed relationship between threat and tendencies to join authoritarian organizations. However, these data do seem to replicate the findings reported earlier. This similarity of results suggests that these data represent real effects and are not a function of local conditions in either of the two periods studied here.

Observing that individuals are drawn to authoritarian denominations when times are hard and to nonauthoritarian denominations when times are good does not, however, necessarily support the argument made here. It is possible that some factor common to authoritarian churches (but not related to authoritarianism) functions to attract persons in times of stress, and that some factor common to nonauthoritarian churches (but not related to authoritarianism) tends to attract persons during good times. A factor of this sort would generate the findings reported here; however, data obtained through this mechanism would have no bearing on the contention that threat contributes to individuals' levels of authoritarianism.

This alternative argument cannot be refuted on the basis of the present data. Nor can it be refuted by observing specific similarities between authoritarian and nonauthoritarian churches, since there is an infinite number of potentially influential factors on which these churches could differ. However, this alternative explanation is drawn into some question by data presented elsewhere by Sales and Friend (in press). As noted previously, these research workers performed two laboratory experiments directed toward the general hypothesis studied here. Both of these investigations indicated that failure-induced threat led to increases in subjects' levels of authoritarianism, while success led to decreases in their levels of authoritarianism. Clearly, the data reported by Sales and Friend are unlikely to have been generated by any extraneous factor of the sort which could potentially have produced the present results; however, the parallelism between the data reported here and those obtained in the laboratory is clear. This parallelism suggests that both the experimental findings and the results presented above may indeed have been generated by a single cause, and that the findings reported here probably cannot be attributed to some extraneous difference between authoritarian and nonauthoritarian churches.

In a sense, a strong similarity exists between the hypothesis tested here and a contention which is almost a commonplace in writings about religion. This contention states that religious activity is a response to the frustrations of life, that religion makes bearable an otherwise threatening and frightening environment. In one form or another, this hypothesis has appeared in virtually every work on the psychological basis of religion; its best known forms are probably Reinhold Neibuhr's statement that "religion is a citadel of hope built on the edge of despair" and Marx's acerbic description of religion as the "opiate of the people."

While this hypothesis seems intuitively reasonable, very little data other than clinical observations have been marshaled in support of it. Indeed, most investigations directed toward this issue have yielded negative results (e.g., Argyle, 1958; Glock & Stark, 1965). The results of the present study seem to indicate the source of these nonsupportive findings. These data suggest that only certain churches become attractive in times of greatest stress and insecurity, while others appear to lose some of their appeal during these periods. Thus, it is apparently not religion as such that is the opiate of the people, but only some kinds of religion. When one combines all forms of religious activity, one may indeed conclude that "there is very little relation between religion and economic prosperity [Argyle, 1958, p. 139]." However, when one separates various churches into more authoritarian and less authoritarian denominations, the relation between religion and economic factors becomes fairly clear.

Footnotes

[1]The author is indebted to Garlie Forehand and Esther G. Sales for their helpful comments upon an earlier version of this paper.

Requests for reprints should be sent to Stephen M. Sales, Department of Psychology, Carnegie-Mellon University, Schenley Park, Pittsburgh, Pennsylvania 15213.

[2]Naturally, this classification in no way implies a relative superiority of either type of church. The taxonomy is meant to be descriptive, not evaluative.

[3]The appropriate categorization for the Protestant Episcopal Church is somewhat ambiguous (particularly because of the influence of the Anglo-Catholics), but the denomination does appear to be more on the nonauthoritarian end of the dimension studied here.

[4]Data from the Congregational Christian Church were taken from relevant numbers of the *Yearbook of the Congregational Christian Church;* those for the Protestant Episcopal Church were taken from *The Living Church Annual;* those for the Presbyterian Church in the U.S.A. were obtained from the *Minutes of the General Assembly of the Presbyterian Church in the United States of America;* and those from the Roman Catholic Church were taken from the *Official Catholic Directory.* Data for the other denominations were provided by church officials to whom the author is indebted.

For most of the denominations studied here, gathering data on converts posed no particular problem. However, several churches did present some difficulty in this regard. In the first place, the Seventh-day Adventist Church, the Northern Baptist Convention, and the Southern Baptist Convention do not report statistics on converts as such. Rather, they include all new members above some "age of accountability" in a single category ("baptisms"). The data for these denominations, thus, include many individuals who were born into the church and who therefore did not convert in the usual sense of the term. However, combining "real" converts with newly mature persons, born into the church, is likely to have a conservative impact upon the present results. Second, the data on conversions to the Roman Catholic Church are somewhat incomplete. During the 1920s, several Dioceses and Archdioceses (notably the Archdioceses of New York, Chicago, and St. Louis) failed to report any information concerning converts. Inclusion of their data during later years would, of course, artificially inflate any real difference which obtained for these churches between the 1920s and the 1930s. For this reason, we have only considered data gathered in the 94 Dioceses and Archdioceses (of 119) which reported information on converts throughout the period studied here.

[5]One-tailed significance tests have been employed throughout this report, since all hypotheses have been stated in advance.

References

Adorno, T. W., Frenkel-Brunswik, E., Levinson, D. J., & Sanford, R. N. *The authoritarian personality.* New York: Harper, 1950.

American Baptist Convention, American Baptist Home Mission Society. *Meet Mrs. Jones, typical American Baptist.* Valley Forge, Pa.: Judson Press, 1961.

Argyle, M. *Religious behaviour.* London: Routledge & Kegan Paul, 1958.

Berkowitz, L., & Knurek, D. A. Label-mediated hostility generalization. *Journal of Personality and Social Psychology,* 1969, *13,* 200-206.

Brown, R. W. Mass phenomena. In G. Lindzey (Ed.), *Handbook of social psychology.* Vol. 2. Cambridge, Mass.: Addison-Wesley, 1954.

Brown, R. W. *Social psychology.* New York: Free Press of Glencoe, 1965.

Bureau of the Census. *Historical statistics of the United States: Colonial times to 1957.* Washington, D.C.: United States Government Printing Office, 1960.

Davids, A. Some personality and intellectual correlates of intolerance of ambiguity. *Journal of Abnormal and Social Psychology,* 1955, *51,* 415-420.

Dittes, J. E. Impulsive closure as a reaction to failure-induced threat. *Journal of Abnormal and Social Psychology,* 1961, *63,* 562-569.

Glock, C. Y., & Stark, R. *Religion and society in tension.* Chicago: Rand McNally, 1965.

Hovland, C. I., & Sears, R. R. Minor studies of aggression: VI. Correlation of lynchings with economic indices. *Journal of Psychology,* 1940, *9,* 301-310.

Hudson, W. H. Are churches really booming? *Christian Century,* 1955, *77,* 1494-1496.

Mead, F. S. *Handbook of denominations in the United States.* (4th ed.) New York: Abingdon Press, 1965.

Mintz, A. A re-examination of correlations between lynchings and economic indices. *Journal of Abnormal and Social Psychology,* 1946, *41,* 154-160.

Rokeach, M. *The open and closed mind.* New York: Basic Books, 1960.

Sales, S. M., & Friend, K. E. Success and failure as determinants of level of authoritarianism. *Behavioral Science,* in press.

Sanford, R. N. *Self and society.* New York: Atherton Press, 1966.

Williams, J. P. *What Americans believe and how they worship.* (3rd ed.) New York: Harper & Row, 1969.

Zander, A., & Havelin, A. Social comparison and interpersonal attraction. *Human Relations,* 1960, *13,* 21-32.

Pygmalion and Galatea: The Interactive Effect of Teacher and Student Expectancies[1]

Mark P. Zanna   *Princeton University*
Peter L. Sheras
Joel Cooper
Charles Shaw   *Cheyney State College*

Abstract

An experiment was conducted to examine the effect of the manipulation of both teacher and student expectancies upon performance. Subjects were students from 6-8th grades participating in a summer enrichment program in Mathematics and English. Teachers were given positive expectancies about the potential of half of the students and no expectancies regarding the other half. In addition, half of the students in each of these groups were told that they would probably perform well in the program while half were given no such expectations. Each student's verbal and mathematics performance was measured by a standardized test before and at the end of the program. Results

"Pygmalion and Galatea: The Interactive Effect of Teacher and Student Expectancies" by Mark P. Zanna, Peter L. Sheras, Joel Cooper and Charles Shaw. *Journal of Experimental Social Psychology* 11, 279–287 (1975). Copyright © 1975 by Academic Press, Inc. Reprinted by permission.

showed an interaction between teacher and student expectancies such that, while each positive expectancy by itself yielded an improvement in academic performance, the two positive expectancies in combination did not.

People are affected by the expectations which others hold about them. Rosenthal and Fode (1963) were among the first to demonstrate the phenomenon as they showed that subjects in laboratory investigations tend to behave as experimenters expect them to behave. Rosenthal and Jacobson (1968) applied the notion of the self-fulfilling prophecy to the classroom. Noting that George Bernard Shaw's *Pygmalion* concerned itself with the effect of one person's expectations upon the thoughts and behaviors of others, Rosenthal and Jacobson called their work *Pygmalion in the Classroom*. Their study demonstrated that those children whose teachers expected them to "bloom" showed greater gains in reasoning and total I.Q. than those children whose teachers did not expect them to "bloom."

Rosenthal and Jacobson's study has not escaped criticism. Differences found between subtests of the intelligence scale as well as differences found for sex of student have been difficult to interpret. Moreover, the choice of the particular intelligence test used has been questioned (Snow, 1969), criticisms regarding the statistical analyses have been raised (Elashoff and Snow, 1971), and the administration procedures of the intelligence scale have also been questioned (Jensen, 1969). Nonetheless, the main results found by Rosenthal and Jacobson have withstood subsequent tests in a variety of situations and settings (e.g., Anderson and Rosenthal, 1968; Rosenthal and Evans, 1968). In addition, Meichenbaum, Bowers, and Ross (1969) reported self-fulfilling prophecies for academic and behavioral expectancies in a training school for female offenders while Word, Zanna, and Cooper (1974) found systematic expectancy effects in the behavior of job interviewers and interviewees in a simulated employment context.

But in all of the studies that have examined the effect of the authority person's expectation on an individual's performance, it has been assumed that either the individuals in question bring no expectations with them into the situation or that their expectations are merely a source of error variance. However, if we refer to the actual story of Pygmalion, an interesting and important consideration emerges.

In the original Greek myth upon which Shaw's play was based, Pygmalion was the sculptor of a statue which he called Galatea. By the intervention of the gods, Galatea was brought to life with all the characteristics and beauty envisioned by her creator. But Shaw's Galatea, Liza Doolittle, was not marble but human. When she first encountered her Pygmalion, Professor Higgins, she entered the situation with her own thoughts, desires, and expectations. The outcome of Shaw's story, then, must have been an interaction of the expectations of Pygmalion with those of Galatea.

The situation studied by Rosenthal and Jacobson appears to have been conceptualized along the lines of the original Greek myth when, in fact, Shaw's *Pygmalion* would have been more appropriate. The students under investigation have been treated like the original Galatea, i.e., devoid of any expectancies of their own. However, the thoughts, hopes, wishes, and expectations of the students in the interpersonal situation of the classroom were most probably not irrelevant to the phenomenon which Rosenthal and Jacobson investigated.

The present study seeks to investigate systematically the combined effect upon behavior of a target person's expectation in combination with the authority's expectation. Both student and teacher expectancies regarding success in a summer program for junior high students were systematically varied.

What is the likely result of a combination of expectations? Although there are many possibilities, the most pertinent previous research (Anderson and Rosenthal, 1968) suggests an intriguing hypothesis. In that study, a small group of mentally retarded boys served as subjects while participating in a summer day camp. Camp counselors were given positive expectancies concerning intellectual "blooming" for half of the subjects and no expectations for the other half. In addition, half of each expectancy group was selected for special tutoring on a one-to-one basis by a local high school student. The results of the experiment, as measured by changes in I.Q. scores over the course of the summer, indicated that subjects in the double treatment condition (i.e., those who were tutored and whose counselors expected greater intellectual performance) did not improve as much as the subjects in either of the single treatment conditions. It appeared that the combination of expectancies, one generated by being placed in the special tutorial program and one by experimental instruction, had a detrimental effect on performance, perhaps by placing the child under too much pressure to perform well. If the finding of Anderson and Rosenthal can be generalized to the present setting, we might predict an interaction between teacher and student expectancies on the performance of the students, such that each positive expectancy by itself yields improvements in academic performance but the two expectancies in combination result in less improvement, again perhaps by placing the student under too much pressure to perform well.

METHOD

Overview

In a 2×2 factorial design, both teacher and student expectancies were manipulated. Following Rosenthal and Jacobson (1968) teachers were informed that some of their students were projected to "bloom" (Teacher-Positive Expectancy condition) while no definite projection could be given for some of their students (Teacher-No Expectancy condition). In addition, some students were informed that they were projected to do well (Student-Positive Expectancy condition) while some students were not informed of anything concerning their potential (Student-No Expectancy condition). Both teachers and students were unaware that an experiment was in progress. The main dependent variable was change in English and Mathematics achievement, assessed before and at the end of the summer program.

Subjects and Program

The subjects were 54 students participating in a summer enrichment program in Mathematics and English. Subjects had just completed 6th, 7th, or 8th grade. Fifty-three subjects were black; one was white. Eighteen subjects were females. Most came from the same inner city junior high school in Trenton, New Jersey.

The program itself was designed either to correct deficiencies in or enrich students' understanding of English and Mathematics. Math classes were structured, using a workbook or a computer. In contrast, English classes were much more casual with little structured feedback, but with a great deal of informal student-teacher interaction. In neither class were formal grades administered. Each subject was enrolled in one Math and one English class. The program lasted 7 weeks.

Procedure

Subjects were brought from school to the psychology department of Princeton University in groups of 6-10 on the third day of the program. The testing was unannounced to the students. Upon arrival students were given two questionnaires, ostensibly designed to determine their academic potential. As each subject finished the questionnaires, he or she was taken individually to another room to be "interviewed." Interviews lasted approximately 2 minutes and were conducted by four black undergraduates. After the interview, subjects were brought back to the school.

Two days before the end of the program the students, again unannounced, were brought to Princeton and given standardized aptitude tests in Mathematics and English (Comprehensive Basic Skills tests).

Manipulation of Student Expectancies

During the 2 minute interview conducted as part of the initial testing session, subjects were asked to talk about why they were in the program and what they expected to get out of it. For half the students, those in the Student-No Expectancy condition, this is all that transpired. The other half of the students received, in addition, the following comment from the interviewer.

"One of the reasons we are asking you these questions is that we, too, are excited about this summer program. As you may know, the program has been changed a bit since last year and we expect it to be interesting, challenging, and enjoyable. Also, by looking at the scores on past tests you have taken, but mostly by looking at the first test you took today, we expect you to do very well academically this summer. This test indicates to us that you are really ready to start doing better in school work. Regardless of your past performance and experiences in school, this summer we have every reason to believe that your performance will be good."

This comment constituted the Student-Positive Expectancy manipulation.

Manipulation of Teacher Expectancies

Each teacher received a bogus printout from the director of the summer program at a regular staff meeting 4 days following the student testing day. The printout listed those students who were projected to do well (supposedly on the basis of their test scores) and those for whom there were "no projection." The cover sheet of the printout read as follows.

"Contained herein are the projections based upon the Princeton Academic Potential Inventory (PAPI) administered July 7, 1972. Projections are made on the basis of mode and pattern of responding on the inventory. Projections are not made in all cases; only when the data seem unequivocal. In these cases it seems evident that the student should perform well regardless of past record and/or experience. Students in this category (projected to do well) should begin to work at the level of their high academic potential. Those for whom no projection is made are not necessarily going to perform any worse; there is simply not enough information to make an accurate projection. Since the PAPI demands an accuracy confidence interval of .95 or better, some students who may perform well could be placed in the *no projection* category."

If a subject was assigned to the Teacher-Positive Expectancy condition, both his English and his Mathematics teachers were informed that he was expected to "bloom." If a subject was assigned to the Teacher-No Expectancy condition, both teachers were informed that no projection could be made.

This created a 2 × 2 factorial design with teachers' expectancies as one factor and students' expectancies as the other. Conditions were equated on the most recent aptitude scores so that no condition had an average aptitude score in Math or English significantly different from any other.[2] A control group consisting of subjects who did not attend the initial testing and interview session (and, therefore, did not receive any projection for themselves) and who were placed in the "no projection" group for teachers was also run.

Dependent Measures

Three weeks into the program, teachers were asked to grade the potential and performance of each student on 100-point scales. At the conclusion of the program, teachers were asked to make the same judgments and, in addition, to recall from memory those students in each class who had been projected to do well.

At the end of the program, each subject was administered a standardized reading and mathematics aptitude test (Comprehensive Basic Skills Test). Students had taken the same test (although a different form) in their school the previous March. The major dependent variable was the change in aptitude scores between the previous March and the end of the program.

RESULTS

A preliminary 2 (Teacher Expectancy) by 2 (Student Expectancy) by 2 (Subject Matter) analysis of variance was performed on each of the dependent variables. These analyses indicated that Subject Matter (i.e., English vs Mathematics) did not interact with the main independent variables; hence, data were collapsed across this dimension.

Teachers' Recollection of Potential "Bloomers"

Were teachers able to recall correctly which students had been projected to "bloom?" The mean number of teachers per condition who did recall that students were projected to bloom are reported in the first row of Table 1. Here it can be seen that although teachers were not perfect in their recollections after 7 weeks, students projected to do well more often [were] recalled as "bloomers" than students who were not so projected ($F(1,41) = 5.32$, $p < .05$).

Teachers' Evaluation of Potential and Performance

Teachers were also asked to evaluate their students' academic potential and performance, both midway through the program and at its completion on 100-point scales. Analysis of variance of the first set of evaluations, which are presented in the second and third rows of Table 1, indicated that the main effect for Teacher Expectancy was significant for both perceived potential ($F(1,38) = 8.53$, $p < .01$) and perceived performance ($F(1,38) = 5.53$, $p < .05$).[3] Students projected to "bloom" were judged as having more potential (overall means of 81.43 vs 65.84) and as having performed better (overall means of 62.90 vs 47.69) than students for whom teachers were not given such positive expectations. No other effect approached significance.

Analysis of variance of the final set of evaluations, which are presented in the fourth and fifth rows of Table 1, indicated that these initial Teacher Expectancy effects were greatly attenuated. Although students projected to "bloom" were rated more positively on potential (overall means of 87.45 vs 83.78) and on performance (overall means 70.56 vs 66.19) the main effects for Teacher Expectancy were trivial ($F < 1$ and $F = 1.40$ for perceived potential and perceived performance, respectively). In addition, no other effect approached significance on these ratings.

Table 1   Teacher Recollections and Evaluations

Dependent variables	Teacher-Positive Expectancy		Teacher-No Expectancy	
	Student-Positive Expectancy	Student-No Expectancy	Student-Positive Expectancy	Student-No Expectancy
Teachers' recall[a]	1.22	1.00	.54	.64
Midprogram potential	81.50	83.36	62.50	69.18
Midprogram performance	59.62	66.18	44.83	50.54
Postprogram potential	86.62	88.27	82.25	85.30
Postprogram performance	71.88	69.25	58.38	74.00
Initial academic performance	4.79	5.53	4.71	5.10
	(9)	(12)	(13)	(11)

Note. Cell *n*'s are in parentheses.

[a]Perfect recall scores would be 2.00 in the Teacher-Positive Expectancy conditions; 0.00 in the Teacher-No Expectancy conditions.

Academic Achievement

Mean change scores (postprogram minus preprogram) in academic achievement were first calculated. As mentioned previously, subject matter did not interact with either or both of the independent variables (each $F < 1$). In this analysis the three-way interaction was nearly zero, indicating that the pattern of change for Math was virtually identical with the pattern of change for English.

Because of straggling tails (Mosteller and Tukey, 1968) at both ends of two of the within-cell distributions, the mean change scores are not the most appropriate descriptions of these distributions. For this reason and because the estimates of the within-cell variance were significantly heterogeneous ($F_{max} = 6.31$; $p < .05$), the main analysis was conducted nonparametrically. The proportion of subjects whose average change in achievement fell above the overall median are presented in Table 2. The proportions were transformed to arcsines and a 2×2 analysis of variance was performed following the procedures of Langer and Abelson (1972). This analysis indicated that only the interaction between Teacher and Student Expectancies was significant ($F(1, \infty) = 8.34$, $p < .01$).

Planned comparisons between each condition and the baseline (i.e., the combination of the Teacher-No Expectancy / Student-No Expectancy and Control conditions) indicated that students improved to a greater extent when only their teachers held positive expectancies (.75 vs .30; $z = 2.56$; $p < .05$), when only they themselves held positive expectancies (.69 vs .30; $z = 2.25$; $p < .05$), but not when both their teachers and themselves held positive expectancies (.33 vs .30; $z < 1$). It should be noted that the first comparison effect was strongly replicated. The second comparison demonstrated what might be called a student expectancy effect, and the third comparison clearly indicated that the combination of expectancies did not result in any improvement whatsoever.[4]

DISCUSSION

The results of the present experiment provide support for the hypothesis that the combined effect of teacher expectancy and student expectancy results in an interaction in terms of performance. This interaction was supplemented by two other phenomena. First, it was found that in the absence of any particular teacher expectancy, students given a positive expectancy of their own performance did better than students with no such expectancy. One could label this result as a "student expectancy effect" suggesting that students will behave in ways consistent with the expectancies they have for their own performance. Such performances would fulfill their initial expectations. Second, it was found that in the absence of a positive student expectancy, students whose teachers were given posi-

Table 2   Proportion of Students above the Overall Median of Change in Academic Achievement

Student Expectancy	Teacher Expectancy		Control
	Positive	None	
Positive	.33	.69	
	(9)	(13)	.33
None	.75	.27	(9)
	(12)	(11)	

Note. Cell *n*'s are in parentheses.

tive expectancies of their performance did better than students whose teachers were given no such expectancy. This finding is consistent with that of Rosenthal and Jacobson (1968) and provides additional support for a "teacher expectancy effect."

While positive expectancies on the part of teachers produced increments in performance and while positive expectancies of students produced improved performance, the joint occurrence of the two expectancies was not positive. Our most provocative result, then, was the finding that when a positive teacher expectancy was combined with a positive student expectancy, no improvement resulted whatsoever. What might produce such an interaction? Following Rosenthal's (1969) interpretation of Anderson and Rosenthal's (1968) finding, we might suggest that the combination of two positive expectancies created too much pressure for students to handle. With students expecting superior performance and with teachers expecting superior performance, any evidence that performance was short of excellent may have caused frustration and/or anxiety and, consequently, depressed performance.

It is possible, however, to generate a different speculative explanation for the effect. As suggested by teachers during the debriefing session, students expecting to do well may not have been motivated to try as hard as usual. However, this may only be true to the extent that teacher's behaviors confirm or reinforce the student's initial expectations, as would be the case in the Teacher-Positive condition.

Since the present study does not clarify which underlying process might be responsible for the interaction between teacher and student expectancy and since determination of the process would seem to be important for understanding the potential of various educational programs, explication of the mechanism(s) involved is a key question for continuing research. A second and unequivocal implication of the present study is that the future consideration of expectancy effects (whether in classroom or laboratory) would be well advised to consider the expectations of not only the person in authority, but also the expectations of those under his control.

Footnotes

[1]This research was supported by a grant from U.S.P.H.S. #1-RO3-MH24463-01. The authors wish to thank Arthur Bergeron, Peter Buttenheim, Howard Hall, Tony Manutti, Victoria Mosley, Anthony Murray, David Tankel, and Jerry Wald for their assistance in the execution of this study.

[2]A 2 (Teacher Expectancy) $\times$ 2 (Student Expectancy) $\times$ 2 (Subject Matter) analysis of variance on the pretest scores revealed no significant effects (largest $F = 1,56$, for the Student Expectancy dimension). Overall, the Math aptitude mean was 5.14 (i.e., 5th grade, 1st mo.) with cell means varying from 4.79 to 5.54. Overall the English aptitude mean was 5.00 with cell means varying from 4.58 to 5.52. The pretest means averaged across Mathematics and English are presented by condition in the last row of Table 1.

[3]Variation in the within-cell degrees of freedom is due to the fact that some students in some conditions were not evaluated on specific dimensions by their teachers.

[4]A parametric analysis of mean change scores revealed the identical pattern of results. Analysis of variance did reveal that only the interaction between the two manipulated expectancies was significant ($F(1,49) = 4.32; p < .05$).

References

Anderson, D., & Rosenthal, R. Some effects of interpersonal expectancy and social interaction on institutionalized retarded children. *Proceedings, APA,* 1968, 479-480.

Elashoff, J., & Snow, R. E. *Pygmalion Reconsidered.* Worthington, Ohio: Charles A. Jones, 1971.

Jensen, A. R. How much can we boost I.Q. and scholastic achievement? *Harvard Educational Review,* 1969, *39,* 1-123.

Langer, E. J., & Abelson, R. P. The semantics of asking a favor: How to succeed in getting help without really dying. *Journal of Personality and Social Psychology,* 1972, *24,* 26-32.

Meichenbaum, D. H., Bowers, K. S., & Ross, R. R. A behavioral analysis of teacher expectancy effects. *Journal of Personality and Social Psychology,* 1969, *13,* 306-316.

Mosteller, F., & Tukey, J. W. Data analysis, including statistics *In* G. Lindzey and E. Aronson (Eds.), *The Handbook of Social Psychology.* Reading, Massachusetts: Addison-Wesley, 1968, Vol. 2, 80-203.

Rosenthal, R. Interpersonal expectations: effects of the experimenter's hypothesis *In* R. Rosenthal and R. Rosnow (Eds.), *Artifact in Behavioral Research.* New York: Academic Press, 1969.

Rosenthal, R., & Evans, J. Unpublished manuscript, Harvard University, 1968. Cited in R. Rosenthal. Teacher expectations. *In* G. S. Lesser (Ed.), *Psychology and the Educational Process.* Glenview, Illinois: Scott, Foresman, 1971.

Rosenthal, R., & Fode, K. L. Three experiments in experimenter bias. *Psychological Reports,* 1963, *12,* 491-511.

Rosenthal, R., & Jacobson, L. *Pygmalion in the Classroom.* New York: Holt, Rinehart and Winston, 1968.

Snow, R. E. Unfinished Pygmalion. *Contemporary Psychology,* 1969, *14,* 197-199.

Word, C. O., Zanna, M. P., & Cooper, J. The nonverbal mediation of self-fulfilling prophesies in interracial interaction. *Journal of Experimental Social Psychology,* 1974, *10,* 109-120.

Self-Enhancement Processes

Swimming, Competence, and Personality Change[1]

Gerald P. Koocher[2]   *University of Missouri, Columbia*

Abstract

This study was designed to show that increasing competence in one's environment leads to enhancement of self-esteem. Using pretest and posttest measures of the discrepancy between the ideal self and self-concept of 65 boys between 7 and 15 years old at a YMCA summer camp, it was found that success in learning to swim reduced the discrepancy significantly ($p < .05$). Subjects who did not learn to swim, and controls who could already swim and were matched to experimental subjects in age and socioeconomic status, did not experience significant changes in the ideal-self—self-concept discrepancies in either direction.

The self-concept has been a topic of study and conjecture since antiquity. Its development and functioning are central concerns of theorists and clinicians throughout psychology, and indeed, the last 2 decades have seen a resurgence of interest in personality theories pertaining to the self-concept. The present study was designed to investigate personality changes which may occur as a result of an individual's increasing competence in his environment. At various points, efficacy in dealing with one's environment has been thought to play a central role in determining the self-concept, but few investigators have attempted to experimentally examine the links which may be forged between development of competence in a specific area and its personality correlates. Using the self-concept paradigm, personality change was explored in the context of learning to swim.

The primary function of the present study was to test the general hypothesis that newly developed competence in a specific area, swimming in this case, would create changes in the self-concept of the individual concerned. It was also predicted that these changes would occur in a positive direction. These predictions might be made on the basis of theoretical constructs such as Allport's (1961) adequacy, Adler's (Kelly & Ansbacher, 1956) superiority, Woodworth's (1958) mastery, and White's (1959) effectance. There is, however, little research to provide empirical support for these theories that is not drawn from limited case studies or broad generalizations.

The selection of learning to swim as a specific case of competence development was not accidental. Aside from the almost universal recognition of swimming as a valuable skill, no great proficiency is necessary in order for a person to feel that he has succeeded in this area. Even momentary self-propulsion and unsupported control in the water can represent a quite significant mastery for many children. Simply daring to challenge the water in an attempt to gain control of oneself in the medium may carry powerful implications. In this learning situation the child needs no outside approval to tell him when he has succeeded.

In view of the preceding arguments and theoretical considerations, certain hypotheses were posited as follows: First, the self-ideal minus self-concept discrepancy decreases when the subject learns to swim. The amount of this decrease should be significantly greater than any changes which occur in the self-ideal minus self-concept discrepancy of a similar control subject over the same period of time. Second, the discrepancy reduction anticipated should result from a change of the self-concept in the direction of the self-ideal.

METHOD

Subjects

Sixty-five boys aged 7 to 15 years who were attending the summer program at a YMCA resident camp qualified as subjects. They had a mean age of 10.3

"Swimming, Competence, and Personality Change" by Gerald P. Koocher. *Journal of Personality and Social Psychology*, 1971, Vol. 18, No. 3, pp. 275–278. Copyright © 1971 by The American Psychological Association, Inc. Reprinted by permission.

years and a mean socioeconomic level of 3.0 on the Index of Social Position developed by Hollingshead and Redlich (1958, p. 394), which ranges from a high-status position of 1 to a low position of 5.

Measures

The instrument used as a measure of self-concept, self-ideal, and self-acceptance was a modification of the Index of Adjustment and Values (IAV) developed by Bills, Vance, and McLean (1951). The original IAV consists of 49 adjectives which the subject must mark in checklist fashion as descriptive of himself, his satisfaction with himself, and his ideal self in three columns, respectively. The present study used a form modified for use with school-age children (Bills, 1961), consisting of 35 adjectives, each of which was to be marked as describing the self "Most of the time," "About half the time," or "Hardly ever." In the second column, the subject expressed his feelings about the self as described in column 1 as, "Like it," "Neither like nor dislike it," or "Dislike it." Finally, in the third column, the subject described his ideal self on the same basis as the self. The IAV in this form was found to be easily within the capabilities of nearly all potential subjects.

Several studies have shown the IAV to have good reliability and validity. The most complete summary of these may be found in Wylie (1961, pp. 70-75). In her comprehensive critique of research on the self-concept, Wylie expressed skepticism regarding the construct validity of all instruments. She added, however, that Bills's work with the IAV "presents the most pertinent and convincing evidence on the question [p. 107]."

Procedure

All boys who had never attended this particular camp before took the IAV in groups upon arrival. The tests were administered by volunteer students not connected with the camp situation. The volunteers were given a set of guidelines for eliminating potential subjects from the study or assisting them if necessary. Subjects were disqualified if they could not complete the inventory without requesting definitions for more than three items, if their parents insisted on "helping" them, or if they appeared to rush through the IAV in a haphazard manner. On the other hand, many subjects could not pronounce some of the words properly, but recognized the word when it was spoken. In this case the subjects could have the words read aloud to them. Of 72 boys tested, 7 were eliminated from the study on the basis of these criteria, leaving the total *N* at the end of the study at 65.

The day after their arrival, all campers took a swimming test as part of the camp routine. The basic criterion for differentiating swimmers from nonswimmers was the ability of the boy to swim 25 yards unassisted. This judgment was made by members of the camp aquatic staff who were unfamiliar with the variables of the study or results of prior testing. All boys were encouraged to at least attempt the task, and were provided with assurance of assistance by at least two staff members who would accompany them each foot of the way. As a result campers were classified as P (passed the test), R (refused to attempt the test), or F (attempted, but failed). A sharp dichotomy was noted between those who attempted the task and those who refused. Although no one was forced to take the test, those who refused were unwilling to even venture an estimate as to what part of the distance they might be able to swim. All those who were rated as R or F were immediately qualified as subjects. A group of those who passed the test were selected as controls and approximately matched to the other subjects in age and socioeconomic status.

Since the basic period of camp operation was 2 weeks, a cutoff of 12 days was set. At the end of this period, the IAV was readministered to all subjects. Since the retest group contained boys of many ages and levels of swimming ability, there was no observable suspicion as to the purpose of the inventory.

It should be noted that an intensive learn to swim program was conducted by the camp aquatic staff during each 12-day period. All campers were encouraged to participate, and all subjects did attend swim instruction at least once.

RESULTS

For purposes of analysis the subjects were divided into three data groups: those who learned to swim during the 12-day period (Group A); those who had failed or refused originally and did not learn to swim during the observation period (Group B); and the control group, consisting of boys who passed the initial swimming test and spent the next 12 days improving their swimming skills (Group C). The total number of subjects was 65, divided as follows: Group A = 19, Group B = 16, and Group C = 30.

The discrepancy between the ideal self and the

Table 1   Intergroup Differences

Group	Status	n	M socioeconomic status	M age in years	M Self-ideal-self-concept discrepancy pretest	M Self-ideal-self-concept discrepancy posttest	t
A	Passed	0					
	Failed	16	3.26	9.82	8.26	3.37	2.17*
	Refused	3					
B	Passed	0					
	Failed	6	3.25	10.25	8.88	10.75	< 1
	Refused	10					
C	Passed	30	2.53	10.80	7.83	6.30	< 1
	Failed	0					
	Refused	0					

perceived self, as calculated by the column 1 score subtracted from the column 3 score on the IAV, was significantly lower in the Group A posttest, than in the pretest. The *t* of 2.17 is significant at the .05 level and in the direction predicted. These data are presented in Table 1. The discrepancies of Groups B and C did not change significantly between the pretest and posttest in either direction. In addition, the pretest and posttest scores were not significantly different from each other between the three groups per se. This is taken to show that those who learned to swim in the program did experience a decrease in self-ideal—self-concept discrepancy of significant proportions as a result of increases in self-concept. Subjects for whom swimming was already an area of competence, or who had failed to learn to swim (Groups B and C), maintained essentially the same self-ideal—self-concept discrepancy as they had from the outset.

Table 2 compares the net change (pretest to posttest) in the two experimental groups. This analysis yielded a *t* of 2.57, significant at the .02 level in the predicted direction. This comparison lends additional strength to the above results.

It should be noted that the subjects did not differ significantly in age or socioeconomic status. All members of Group C passed the initial swim test by definition. Of those who eventually learned to swim (Group A), only 16% had refused to attempt the test, while 84% tried but failed. Of those who did not learn to swim (Group B), 62% had initially refused the swimming test. These data are summarized in Table 3, and show a chi-square of 6.24, which is significant at the .02 level.

An item analysis was executed for all IAV pretest and posttest adjectives in order to determine which, if any, of these single items were significant discriminators between the three groups. Seventy 3×2 contingency tables were constructed, representing each of the 35 test items twice, once each for pretest and posttest conditions. Each item could have one of three possible self-ideal minus self-concept discrepancy scores. There might be no discrepancy, or a net difference of 1 or 2 points. Since few items showed any 2-point discrepancies, the contingency tables divide the item responses into discrepant or nondiscrepant columns, which were then divided into rows representing the three subject groups. Using a chi-square ($df = 2$), 12 items were found to be significant predictors of

Table 2   Net Change in Experimental Groups

Group	n	M change pretest to posttest	df	s^2
A	19	4.89	18	93
B	16	-1.88	15	-30

Note.—*t* = 2.57, *p* < .02.

Table 3   Failed versus Refused Comparison

Status	Learned to swim	Did not learn
Failed test	16	6
Refused test	3	10

Note.—χ^2 = 6.24, *p* < .02 (with Yates correction for continuity).

Table 4 Results of Item Analysis

Test item	Pretest *p*	Posttest *p*	High discrepancy group on this item
1. Agreeable	*ns*	.05	B
2. Alert	.05	*ns*	A
8. Cooperative	*ns*	.05	B
9. Dependable	*ns*	.05	B
11. Friendly	.05	.05	pre = A & B post = B
16. Helpful	*ns*	.05	B
18. Kind	*ns*	.01	B
19. Loyal	*ns*	.05	B
21. Obedient	*ns*	.05	B
23. Polite	*ns*	.05	B
32. Trustworthy	.05	.001	pre = B post = B
33. Understanding	*ns*	.05	B

Note.—The 23 items not listed were not significant for either the pretest or posttest conditions.
Levels of chi-square, *df* = 2.

one or more groups in the pretest, posttest, or both test conditions. These data are presented in Table 4.

DISCUSSION

The data support the hypotheses, indicating that the development of competence in an area heretofore marked by failure or avoidance results (at least in the case of swimming) in enhancement of the self-concept. These findings represent some behavioral support of White's (1959) theoretical approach to the study of the self-concept, which emphasizes the role played by gaining competence or the "experience of efficacy" in building self-esteem. Although well reasoned and illustrated with case studies, White's position lacks empirical support which the present study helps provide.

Diggory (1966) has suggested that people will tend to withdraw from situations in which they perceive their probability of success as low. The present findings are consistent with this view to the extent that boys who refused to take the swimming test (low estimate of probable success) were unlikely to learn to swim (possibly due to avoidance), as shown in Table 3.

Finally, it is important to note that the increased self-esteem attained in learning to swim, while significant, specific to the camp context, does not exert a generalized or long-lasting effect. This conclusion follows from the fact that the self-concepts of youngsters who already knew how to swim (i.e., had achieved that competence earlier) did not differ from those who could not swim at the beginning of camp. Coopersmith's (1967) conclusions also suggest that this should be the case. He found that external indicators of prestige do not have a pervasive effect or cross-situational transfer. When the child leaves camp and his new-found competence is less frequently demonstrated or praised, the gains specifically attributable to it may tend to fade. The self-concept changes found in the present case may be viewed as reflecting a somewhat momentary "aura" about mastery of swimming in the context of the camp experience.

Footnotes

[1]This report is based on a master's thesis submitted to the graduate faculty of the University of Missouri, Columbia. The author wishes to express his special thanks to his advisor, Fred McKinney, and the members of his committee, Irwin Nahinsky, William Chestnut, A. M. Shimkunas, and Daniel Hays for their support and advice.

The author acknowledges the cooperation of the 1969 staff at Camp Rotary and the generous assistance of the following people in the collection of data: Betty Andelman, Lois Andelman, Barbara Fleming, Janice Newman, Melvyn Berger, Brian Bixby, and Marion and David Koocher.

[2]Requests for reprints should be sent to the author, Department of Psychology, 209 McAlester Hall, University of Missouri, Columbia, Missouri 65201.

References

Allport, G. W. *Pattern and growth in personality.* New York: Holt, Rinehart & Winston, 1961.

Bills, R. E. *Manual for the Index of Adjustment and Values.* Unpublished manuscript, University of Alabama, College of Education, 1961.

Bills, R. E., Vance, E. L., & McLean, O. S. An index of adjustment and values. *Journal of Consulting Psychology,* 1951, *15,* 257-261.

Coopersmith, S. *The antecedents of self-esteem.* San Francisco: Freeman, 1967.

Diggory, J. C. *Self-evaluation: Concepts and studies.* New York: Wiley, 1966.

Hollingshead, A. B., & Redlich, F. C. *Social class and mental illness.* New York: Wiley, 1958.

Kelly, J. T., & Ansbacher, R. R. (Eds.) *The individual psychology of Alfred Adler.* New York: Basic Books, 1956.

White, R. W. Motivation reconsidered: The concept of competence. *Psychological Review,* 1959, *66,* 297-333.

Woodworth, R. S. *Dynamics of behavior.* New York: Holt, Rinehart & Winston, 1958.

Wylie, R. C. *The self-concept.* Lincoln: University of Nebraska Press, 1961.

Basking in Reflected Glory: Three (Football) Field Studies

Robert B. Cialdini   *Arizona State University*

Richard J. Borden   *Purdue University*

Avril Thorne   *Arizona State University*

Marcus Randall Walker   *Ohio State University*

Stephen Freeman

Lloyd Reynolds Sloan   *University of Notre Dame*

Abstract

The tendency to "bask in reflected glory" (BIRG) by publicly announcing one's associations with successful others was investigated in three field experiments. All three studies showed this effect to occur even though the person striving to bask in the glory of a successful source was not involved in the cause of the source's success. Experiment 1 demonstrated the BIRG phenomenon by showing a greater tendency for university students to wear school-identifying apparel after their school's football team had been victorious than non-victorious. Experiments 2 and 3 replicated this effect by showing that students used the pronoun *we* more when describing a victory than a nonvictory of their school's football team. A model was developed asserting that the BIRG response represents an attempt to enhance one's public image. Experiments 2 and 3 indicated, in support of this assertion, that the tendency to proclaim a connection with a positive source was strongest when one's public image was threatened.

It is a common and understandable tendency for people who have been successful in some positive way to make others aware of their connection with that accomplishment. However, there also appears to be a seemingly less rational but perhaps more interesting tendency for people to publicize a connection with *another person* who has been successful. This latter inclination might be called the tendency to bask in reflected glory (BIRG). That is, people appear to feel that they can share in the glory of a successful other with whom they are in some way associated; one manifestation of this feeling is the public trumpeting of the association. Such a phenomenon is not hard to understand when the one wishing to share in another's success has been instrumental to that success. However, the more intriguing form of the phenomenon occurs when the one who basks in the glory of another has done nothing to bring about the other's success. Here, a simple case of affiliation or membership is sufficient to stimulate a public announcement of the critical connection.

There does seem to be abundant anecdotal evidence that people try to make us cognizant of their connections with highly positive or successful others. The forms of these connections are varied. For example, they may imply similarity of residence, past or present: States and cities like to list the names of famous entertainers, statesmen, beauty contest winners, etc., who live or were born within their boundaries; the state of Indiana has even gone so far as to brag that more vice-presidents of the United States have come from Indiana than any other state. Other such connections involve ethnic or religious affiliation: Italians speak proudly of the ethnic background of Marconi, and Jews refer to Einstein's heritage. Still other connections reflect physical similarities: "Napoleon was short, too." Sexual identity may also give rise to the BIRG phenomenon: At a women's movement forum attended by one of the authors, there was a round of feminine applause when it was announced that Madame Curie was a woman and Lee Harvey Oswald was not. Finally, connections suitable for BIRGing may be as tenuous as an incidental contact: We all know people who delight in recounting the time they were in the same theater, airplane, or restroom with a famous movie star.

While there appears to be rich informal support of the sort described above for the existence of a BIRG phenomenon, there seem to be no experimental investigations of the effect. Thus, it was the purpose of this series of studies to examine this tendency to bask in the reflected glory of another or group of others. In so doing, it was hoped to (a) reliably demonstrate the existence of the phenomenon, (b) establish its generality over experimental contexts and measures, (c) determine a mediating process for its occurrence, and (d) discover some of its limiting conditions and thereby gain further information as to its nature.

One of the most obvious arenas for the working of BIRG effects in our society is the athletic arena. Fans of championship teams gloat over their team's accomplishments and proclaim their affiliation with buttons on their clothes, bumper stickers on their cars, and banners on their public buildings. Despite the fact that they have never caught a ball or thrown a block in support of their team's success, the tendency of such fans is to claim for themselves part of the team's glory; it is perhaps informative that the chant is always *"We're* number one," never "They're number one."

It was our view that a sports context would be ideal for a test of some of our notions concerning BIRG effects. Our expectation was that an individual would attempt to bask in the glory of an associated, successful source by publicly announcing his or her affiliation with the source and that this effect would obtain even when the affiliation was clearly irrelevant (i.e., noninstrumental) to the success of the source. In order to gather data relevant to the above hypothesis, an experiment was simultaneously conducted at seven universities with powerful intercollegiate football teams during part of the 1973 football season. It was predicted that students at these schools would be more likely to announce publicly their connection with their universities after the varsity football teams had been successful than after the teams had not been successful. We decided to measure students' tendency to announce their university affiliation by means of an examination of wearing apparel. The frequency with which students wore apparel that clearly identified the university that they attended was hoped to be a subtle yet sensitive measure of the willingness to declare publicly a university affiliation.

EXPERIMENT 1

Method

Procedure. From the third week of the 1973 collegiate football season through the last week of regular play, the apparel of students enrolled in sections of introductory psychology courses at seven large universities was covertly monitored. At each school, three types of data were recorded in the same classes every Monday during the season: (a) the number of students present in the class, (b) the number of students with apparel identifying the school of attendance, and (c) the number of students with apparel identifying a school other than the school of attendance. Data recorders at each place received the following definitions prior to data collection:

> *Apparel identifying the school of attendance is identified as apparel which unambiguously identifies your school through names, insignia, or emblems. Examples would be buttons, jackets, sweatshirts, tee shirts, etc., which display the school name, team nickname or mascot, or university insignia. Apparel which appears school-related solely through the use of colors would not qualify. Also excluded are utilitarian objects which announce a university affiliation such as briefcases, notebooks, or bookcovers. Apparel identifying a school other than the school of attendance are those which meet the same criteria for inclusion as above but which identify a school other than your own.*

The data recorders were not members of the classes they monitored.

Results

Over all schools and across all weeks, an average of 176.8 students were present in the monitored classes; an average of 8.4% of these students wore apparel identifying the university of attendance, while 2% of them wore apparel identifying a school other than the university of attendance. Because of huge differences among the schools in absolute amounts of these two kinds of apparel wearing and in order to make comparisons between the universities as well as between the types of apparel wearing, standardized indexes of relevant apparel wearing were considered necessary. The standard we decided on was the highest percentage of relevant apparel wearing that occurred on any Monday during the season; this standard was

Table 1   Indexes of Relevant Apparel Wearing at the Seven Monitored Universities

School	School-of-attendance apparel wearing		School-of-nonattendance apparel wearing	
	Wins	Nonwins	Wins	Nonwins
Arizona State	.63 (5)	.61 (1)	.58 (5)	.68 (1)
Louisiana State	.80 (5)	.33 (3)	.58 (5)	.51 (3)
Ohio State	.69 (4)	.30 (1)	.56 (4)	.94 (1)
Notre Dame	.67 (7)	.49 (1)	.62 (7)	.52 (1)
Michigan	.52 (5)	.83 (1)	.20 (5)	.00 (1)
Pittsburgh	.76 (4)	.27 (2)	.31 (4)	.50 (2)
Southern California	.36 (6)	.26 (1)	.17 (6)	.00 (1)
M	.63	.44	.43	.45

Note. Numbers in parentheses represent the number of games that fell into wins and nonwins categories for each school.

simply computed as the number of students wearing relevant apparel that day divided by the number of students in class that day. The percentages of apparel wearing on all other Mondays of the season were scored as proportions of the highest percentage. So, the Monday with the largest percentage of relevant apparel wearing was scored as 1.00, and any other Monday percentage was scored as a fraction (proportion) of that standard. This procedure was performed on the data from each school for the two relevant categories of apparel wearing: school-of-attendance apparel wearing and school-of-nonattendance apparel wearing. A mean proportion for each category was obtained for Mondays following a team's wins and nonwins; these are the mean proportions presented in Table 1. As can be seen from Table 1, these indexes showed a generally consistent tendency for students to wear school-of-attendance apparel more after victories than nonvictories; but this was not the case for school-of-nonattendance apparel. Because of the non-normality of the proportion data, the scores were converted to ranks, and Wilcoxon matched-pairs signed-ranks tests were performed using school as the unit of analysis.[1] Despite the conservativeness of such an approach (for this mode of analysis, *n* is only 7), the Wilcoxon *T* reflected a conventionally significant difference on the school-of-attendance measure ($T = 2$, $p < .05$, two-tailed). This result indicated, as predicted, that Mondays following football victories ranked significantly higher in school-of-attendance apparel wearing than Mondays following nonvictories.[2] The mean rank for victories was 3.2, while that for nonvictories was 4.9. A similar test for school-of-nonattendance apparel did not show any effect; the

victory and nonvictory mean ranks for this measure were 3.4 and 3.7, respectively. This latter result suggests that the obtained effect on the school-of-attendance measure is not attributable to a simple tendency to wear clothing of a certain type (e.g., athletic team jackets, sweat shirts, tee shirts, etc.) after an athletic team victory.

Discussion

In all, we found support for our expectations concerning the BIRG phenomenon. Students chose to display more apparel indicators of their academic affiliation after their university's varsity football team had recently been successful. It appears, then, from these data and from numerous anecdotal reports that people desire to make others aware of what seem to be their causally meaningless associations with positive sources.[3] Why? What do they intend to get from it? Perhaps, the answer has to do with Heider's balance formulation (1958). Heider discussed two types of perceived relations between things: sentiment relations, which imply a feeling state between stimuli, and unit relations, which merely imply that things are connected in some manner. It is the unit relationship that seems akin to the noninstrumental connection that people tend to publicize between themselves and a successful or otherwise positive source. The results of the present experiment could well be seen as consistent with balance theory. For example, if observers perceive a positive unit relationship (e.g., university affiliation) between a student and a successful football team and if observers generally evaluate successful teams positively, then in order to keep their cognitive systems in balance, the observers would have to evaluate the student positively as well. Hence, we might expect the student to want to make the unit connection evident to as many observers as possible, in this case, through the wearing of university-identifying clothing. The process whereby one publicly seeks to associate himself or herself with a successful other, then, may be reinforced by the tendency of observers to respond in a similar fashion to associated stimuli.

Indirect evidence that tends to support this hypothesis comes from research concerning the transmission of positive and negative information. Manis, Cornell, and Moore (1974) have shown that one who transmits information that the recipient favors is liked more by the recipient than one who transmits information that the recipient disfavors and that this liking occurred even though it was understood that the transmitters did not necessarily endorse the communicated information. Like the royal messengers of old Persia who were feted when they brought news of military victory but killed when they brought news of defeat, the transmitters in the Manis et al. (1974) study acquired the valence of the message with which they were simply paired. Moreover, there is evidence that people recognize this generalization effect and tend to take actions that connect them, in the eyes of observers, with positive rather than negative news. For example, Rosen and Tesser have repeatedly shown (e.g., Rosen & Tesser, 1970; Tesser, Rosen, & Batchelor, 1972; Tesser, Rosen, & Tesser, 1971) that people prefer to be connected with the communication of good news to another than with the communication of bad news. Investigating the basic effect, Johnson, Conlee, and Tesser (1974) found their subjects reluctant to communicate negative information not because they felt guilty about transmitting bad news but because they feared that they would be negatively evaluated by the recipient of such news; again, this was true even though all concerned knew that the communicators had in no way caused the bad news. Thus, it appears from these data that: first, individuals who are merely associated with a positive or negative stimulus (in this case, favorable or unfavorable information) will tend to share, in an observer's eyes, the affective quality of the stimulus; and second, at some level individuals seem to understand the workings of this phenomenon and make use of it in the ways they present themselves to others. We wish to interpret the results of Experiment 1 in terms of this formulation. Students at our seven monitored universities chose to

wear school-of-attendance apparel after football team victories in order to *display* their connection with the successful team and thereby to enhance their esteem in the eyes of observers to the connection. However, another explanation of our findings exists as well. Perhaps the tendency to wear university-related clothing following team wins had nothing to do with an attempt to proclaim the favorable connection to others but only reflected an increased positivity toward the university as a consequence of team success. That is, it is possible that a football victory caused students to like their school more, and this heightened attraction manifested itself in the tendency to wear school-identified apparel. To test these alternative explanations and to establish the generality of the tendency to BIRG in a different experimental situation than that of Experiment 1, a second experiment was conducted.

EXPERIMENT 2

The major distinction between the competing interpretations described above is the contention of the BIRG model that students wore school-of-attendance clothing after victories in order to publicize their university affiliations and hence increase their prestige in the view of *others*. The "heightened attraction" formulation makes no such claim: One is simply seen to like the school more following victories, and this, rather than the possibility of increased interpersonal prestige, is said to stimulate the wearing of relevant apparel. We decided to test these explanations by way of an examination of the pronoun usage of university students describing the outcome of one of their school's football contests. Earlier in this article we alluded to the tendency of athletic fans to crowd in front of television cameras, wave their index fingers high, and shout, *"We're number one!"* The choice of this pronoun seemed to us a very good measure of the tendency of BIRG. By employing the pronoun *we*, one is publicly able to associate oneself with another person or group of persons. Through the use of some other designation, for example, *they*, one is able to distance oneself from (i.e., to weaken the perceived association with) another person or persons. It was our feeling that in order to BIRG a successful football team, students would be more likely to describe the outcome of a team victory using the pronoun *we* than they would a team nonvictory. Thus, it was our expectation that this tendency to connect oneself with a positive source but distance oneself from a negative source would influence subjects to use the term, "We won," to describe a team win but use the third person (e.g., "They lost") to describe a team loss.[4] Further, in line with our BIRG model, it was expected that this differential use of language would be most pronounced when the subject's esteem in the eyes of an observer had been recently lowered. That is, if we are correct in proposing that one proclaims a connection with a positive source in an attempt to raise one's esteem in the view of others, then one should be most likely to declare such a connection when that esteem has recently been jeopardized. Thus, if we were to create experimentally in subjects a need to bolster esteem in the eyes of an observer, subjects should be most likely to announce publicly (through use of the pronoun *we*) a connection with a successful team and be least likely to publicize a connection with an unsuccessful team. On the other hand, subjects who have less need to elevate an observer's evaluation of themselves should show a lesser effect. The simple "heightened attraction" model would not make such a prediction, since one's prestige in the eyes of others is not a critical variable in that formulation.

Method

Subjects.   The subjects were 173 undergraduates at a large state university with a nationally ranked football team. Subjects were randomly selected from student listings in the university phone directory. The sample included approximately equal distributions of males and females.

Procedure.   During a 3-day period midway through the 1974 football season, subjects were contacted on the phone by one of 16 experimenters (eight males and eight females) indentified as an employee of a "Regional Survey Center" with headquarters in an out-of-state city. The caller explained that he (she) was conducting a survey of college students' knowledge of campus issues and was in town that day calling students at the subject's university. Subjects agreeing to participate (93%) were then asked a series of six factually oriented forced-choice questions about aspects of campus life (e.g., "What percent of students at your school are married? Would you say it's closer to 20% or 35%?"). Following the subject's sixth response, the caller administered the first manipulation. Half of the subjects were told that they had done well on the test, and half were told that they had done poorly. Specifically, subjects were told:

That completes the first part of the questions. The average student gets three out of six correct. You got [five; one] out of six correct. That means you [did really well; didn't do so well] compared to the average student.

Subjects were then told that there were a few more questions and that the first concerned students' knowledge of campus athletic events. At this point the second experimental manipulation occurred. Half of the subjects were asked to describe the outcome of a specific football game; their school's football team had won this game. The other half were asked to describe the outcome of a different game; this was a game that their team had lost. The question was phrased as follows:

In the [first; third] game of the season, your school's football team played the University of [Houston, Missouri]. Can you tell me the outcome of that game?

If a subject did not know the results of the game, a new subject was called. Otherwise the subject's verbatim description of the game outcome was recorded. At the end of the interview, all subjects were fully debriefed.

Independent variables.   Two factors were manipulated; a subject's personal outcome on the survey task (success or failure) and the affiliated football team's outcome in the game described (win or non-win). These factors combined to produce a 2×2 factorial design.

Dependent variables.   Subjects' tendency to use a *we* or *non-we* response in describing a team outcome constituted our dependent measure. Descriptions such as "We won," "We got beat," etc., were considered *we* responses. All other descriptions (e.g., "The score was 14-6, Missouri." "They lost.") were classified as *non-we* responses.

Predictions.   Two predictions were made. First, it was hypothesized that subjects would emit more *we* responses in describing a team victory than a team defeat. Second, it was expected that the effect of Hypothesis 1 would be greatest for subjects who had "failed" the survey test. The latter hypothesis was based on the assumption that subjects in the personal failure conditions would attempt to associate themselves publicly with a positive event or distance themselves from a negative event through language usage in order to bolster or salvage their damaged images in the eyes of the caller. Subjects in the personal success conditions were not expected to show a similar sized effect, as their prestige had already been ensured via their successful task performance. Evidence that public success and failure on an experimental task leads to differential tendencies for social approval has been offered by Schneider (1969). He manipulated success and failure and found failure subjects to present themselves more favorably to an observer who could provide an evaluation. Thus, if the BIRG phenomenon is indeed an attempt to gain social approval, we should see our failure subjects BIRG more than our success subjects.

Results

Of the 173 subjects, the data of 5 were discarded because they clearly reported the game results incorrectly. For example, the description "We won" was not counted if in fact the subject's team had lost the game in question. The percentages of *we* responses emitted in the four experimental conditions are presented in Table 2. The first prediction, that *we* usage would be greater in the descriptions of team victories than team defeats, was tested by comparing the team win conditions against the team nonwin conditions. A significant effect was obtained, $\chi^2 (1) = 4.20$, $p < .05$, confirming Hypothesis 1. The second prediction, that the tendency for *we* responses to attend victory rather than defeat descriptions would be strongest after a personal failure, was tested as an interaction of the two major independent variables. The resultant statistic, suggested by Langer and Abelson (1972) for testing interactions within a 2×2 contingency table, just missed conventional significance levels, $Z = 1.75$, $p < .08$, two-tailed. Tests of the simple main effects of the interaction strongly supported Hypothesis 2. The difference in *we* responding between the team success and team failure cells of the personal failure condition was highly significant, $\chi^2 (1) = 6.90$, $p < .01$. The comparable test

Table 2 Percentage of Subjects Using "We", Experiment 2

Team outcome	% Personal outcome		Mean %
	Success	Failure	
Win	24 (11/45)	40 (16/40)	32 (27/85)
Nonwin	22 (9/41)	14 (6/42)	18 (15/83)

within the personal success condition did not approach significance, $\chi^2 (1) = .07$, *ns*. There were no significant sex effects in the data.

DISCUSSION

The data of Experiment 2 seem clearly to support the general BIRG formulation. Subjects used the pronoun *we* to associate themselves more with a positive than a negative source, and this effect was most pronounced when their public prestige was in jeopardy. We interpret these results as evidence for our contention that people display even the most noninstrumental connections between themselves and the success of others so as to receive positive evaluations from the observers of those connections.

It should be evident that the observer's tendency to assign positivity to one who is associated with positive things is crucial to our hypothesizing about the BIRG phenomenon. It follows from our previously stated assumption that if a person understood that a given observer did not value the success of a specific source, that person would be less likely to try to BIRG that source to the observer. So, if one of our subjects knew that an observer abhorred successful college athletic programs, we would predict that there would be little likelihood of the subject attempting to make visible a connection with a winning football team. But this is a fairly obvious example; few people would predict otherwise. A more subtle and perhaps more informative demonstration might be obtained through a somewhat different manipulation of the observer's relationship to the connection. When an observer to a highly positive association can also lay claim to the association, the prestige of the connection is diffused and, consequently, reduced for anyone attempting to bask in its glory. It is when one's bond to a positive source is not shared by an audience that its prestige value is optimal. Thus, when everyone has a similar positive characteristic, there is no special prestige involved in possessing it, and the likelihood that any one person will boast about that quality should be reduced. For example, a resident of California is less likely to brag to fellow Californians about the favorable climate than to geographically distant others, especially those who cannot claim similarly pleasant weather. It is our hypothesis, then, that the tendency to BIRG a positive source should occur most often when one's connection with the source is stronger than the observer's.[5] A third study was conducted to test this contention.

EXPERIMENT 3

In Experiment 2, it was shown that a personal failure experience increased our subjects' tendency to associate themselves with a positive source and decreased their tendency to associate themselves with a negative source. We have argued that this result occurred because the failure experience lowered perceived prestige and motivated subjects to try to either bolster their images in the eyes of others or prevent them from being further degraded. Central to this argument is the assumption that one's simple, noninstrumental connections are seen to influence observers' personal evaluations. If so, it should be the case that in addition to their use as dependent measures, such connections could be used as effective independent variables. That is, it should be possible to influence subjects' behavior by publicly connecting them with either positive or negative events. In fact, if we are correct in our assumption, manipulating one's public connections with good or bad things should have the same effect as manipulating one's personal success or failure experiences. For example, just as Experiment 2 showed that subjects who failed a task increased the tendency to affiliate themselves with a winner and decreased the tendency to affiliate themselves with a loser in the eyes of an observer to their failure, it follows from our formulation that subjects who are merely publicly connected with a negative event should emit comparable BIRG responses in the presence of an observer to that connection. Experiment 3 was designed to test this possibility and represented a conceptual replication and extension of Experiment 2.

Method

Subjects.   The subjects were 170 undergraduates at a large state university with a powerful football team. The university was not the same as that of Experiment 2; however, subjects were selected for participation in a fashion identical to that of Experiment 2.

Procedure.   Following the completion of play for the university's football team, subjects were called on the phone by 1 of 18 experimenters (11 males and 7 females) identified as an employee of either the "university's Survey Center" located on campus or the "Regional Survey Center" located in an out-of-state city. Subjects were told that a survey was being conducted of "undergraduates' knowledge of university athletic events." Those agreeing to participate

(96%) were asked to describe the outcome of first one, then another of their football team's last games of the year. One of the games constituted an important victory, and the other an important nonvictory in the team's season. Half of the subjects were first requested to describe the nonvictory game and, having responded, to describe the victory game. The other subjects had the requests put to them in reverse order. The subjects' verbatim descriptions of the game results were recorded.

Independent variables.   Two factors were orthogonally varied: the strength of the subject's affiliation to the university team compared with that of the observer (same as observer's or stronger than observer's) and order of presentation of the games to be described (victory game description requested first or nonvictory game description requested first).

Dependent variables.   The dependent measure was the pattern of *we* and *non-we* usage employed by subjects to describe the combination of the victory and nonvictory games. Three combinations were possible. A subject could have used the same *we* or *non-we* term to describe both the victory and the nonvictory, could have used *we* to describe the nonvictory, and *non-we* to describe the victory, or finally, could have used *we* for a victory and *non-we* for a nonvictory.

Predictions.   It was predicted, first, that there would be an overall tendency for subjects to use *we* in their descriptions of a team victory and *non-we* in their descriptions of a team nonvictory. Such a finding would replicate the basic BIRG effect obtained in Studies 1 and 2. A second hypothesis was that the tendency to use *we* for victory and *non-we* for nonvictory descriptions would be greater in the nonvictory-description-requested-first conditions. Such a result would constitute a conceptual replication of the second finding of Experiment 2. On the basis of the BIRG model, we expected that the effect of publicly describing a negative event with which one is connected would be equivalent in nature to publicly failing on a task. Both operations were thought to reduce subjects perceptions of their prestige as seen by an observer and, hence, to increase the likelihood of subjects' attempts to ensure the positivity of subsequent evaluations. The third prediction was that Hypothesis 2 would hold most strongly when the observer was identified with an off-campus organization. This expectation was based on the belief that felt prestige to be gained from one's connections to a

Table 3 Percentage of Subjects Using Both "We" for Victory Descriptions and "Non-We" for Nonvictory Descriptions, Experiment 3

	Order of request[a]	
Strength of subject's connection to team relative to observer's	Victory description requested first	Nonvictory description requested first
Stronger than observer's	3 (1/39)	21 (10/47)
Same as observer's	11 4/36)	14 (7/48)
Mean %	7 (5/75)	18 (17/95)

[a]Numbers given are percentages.

source is greater and, thus more sought after, when one's connections to that source are stronger than an observer's. Confirmation of this prediction would appear as an interaction of the independent variables of the study.[6]

Results

As expected and consistent with the results of Experiments 1 and 2, the basic BIRG effect occurred in Experiment 3 to support our first hypothesis. That is, subjects used the term *we* nearly twice as often to describe a victory than a nonvictory (26% vs. 13.5%). This effect is further confirmed when the data are examined in terms of individual subjects' *we/non-we* usage patterns. The majority of subjects were constant in their pattern of responding to the two requests for descriptions; they consistently used either *we* or *non-we* to describe both game outcomes. Thus, there was a strong tendency for our subjects to be consistent in their verbal usage patterns for the two descriptions. However, in 23 instances subjects provided an inconsistent *we/non-we* pattern. In 22 of those instances, the pattern supported the BIRG model; the pronoun *we* was used for the victory description and a *non-we* term was used for the nonvictory description. Using McNemar's test for the significance of changes (Siegel, 1956, pp. 63-67) and correcting for continuity, the data are highly significant, $\chi^2 (1) = 17.39 \, p < .001$. The tests of Hypotheses 2 and 3 were conducted by considering the distribution (across the cells of our design) of the instances of *we/non-we* usage fitting the pattern predicted by the BIRG model. Table 3 presents these data.

Hypothesis 2 stated that more subjects would use *we* to describe the victory and *non-we* to describe the nonvictory when they were asked to describe the nonvictory first. As expected, subjects were signifi-

cantly more likely to so respond in the nonvictory-description-requested-first conditions, $\chi^2 (1) = 4.69, p < .05$. Hypothesis 3 stated that Hypothesis 2 would hold most clearly when the subjects were more strongly connected with the university team than was the observer. As predicted, Hypothesis 2 was supported to a greater extent when the observer was affiliated with an off-campus rather than a campus agency. However, this tendency did not quite reach conventional levels of significance, $Z = 1.72, p < .085$. As in Experiment 2, there were no significant effects for sex of subject.

GENERAL DISCUSSION

Overall, Experiments 1, 2, and 3 provided strong support for the BIRG formulation. All three experiments showed a significant tendency for students to strive to associate themselves publicly with their university's football team more after the team had been successful. A striking aspect of the phenomenon is that subjects sought to proclaim their affiliation with a successful source even when they in no way caused the source's success. This component of the effect suggests a mediator consistent with balance theory. It is our contention that people make known their noninstrumental connections with positive sources because they understand that observers to these connections tend to evaluate connected objects similarly. It appears that the tendency to BIRG is an attempt to secure esteem from those who can perceive the connection. Studies 2 and 3 provided support for such an interpretation. Both showed that experimental operations designed to threaten a subject's esteem in the eyes of an observer caused subjects to be more likely to try publicly to associate themselves with positive sources. Intriguingly, it was possible to increase the tendency to BIRG in these experiments either by initially causing the subject to experience personal failure in an observer's eyes or by initially causing the subject to be noninstrumentally connected with a negative event in an observer's eyes. These manipulations proved functionally equivalent in modifying subject pronoun usage. Thus, in support of our basic argument, being merely associated with someone else's success and failure had much the same effect as personal success and failure. Experiment 3 provided evidence in a different way as well that the desire for prestige is the mediator of the BIRG response. It demonstrated that when subjects' affiliation with a positive source was stronger than an observer's (and therefore carried a greater amount of prestige), they were most likely to BIRG that source in the presence of the observer.

These studies suggest a way to understand how the fortunes of affiliated sports teams can cause lavish displays of civic gratitude and pride in American cities, or "sports riots" in Europe, or murders in South America of players and referees whose actions had caused a home-team defeat. Through their simple connections with sports teams, the personal images of fans are at stake when their teams take the field. The team's victories and defeats are reacted to as personal successes and failures.

Throughout this article we have stressed an interpersonal mediator of the BIRG phenomenon— the perceived esteem of others. We do not wish, however, to preclude the possibility of the tendency to BIRG privately. That is, for wholly intrapersonal reasons, people may draw connections between themselves and positive sources. For example, one may well feel an enhancement of self-esteem that is unrelated to the assessments of others when one is associated with success or positivity. Such an effect could also be interpreted in terms of a tendency to respond similarly to associated objects. It might be that the results of our experiments are, in some degree at least, due to a desire to bolster or maintain one's self-concept. The tendency to employ appropriate apparel or language in a way that connects oneself to something good may involve an attempt to remind oneself of such connections and, thereby, positively affect self-esteem. The fact that in Experiment 2 we were able to influence the BIRG response simply by manipulating the characteristics of the observer suggests that the BIRG phenomenon is not mediated solely by intrapersonal phenomena. Nonetheless, it remains possible that the tendency to BIRG has its basis in a desire to affect self-image as well as social image. In fact, since there is evidence that how we

regard ourselves is influenced by how we perceive that others regard us (e.g., Harvey, Kelley, & Shapiro, 1957), these two mediators are not mutually exclusive.

Footnotes

[1]In any conversion of parametric data to ranks, the possibility exists that the ranked scores will not fully reflect the character of the parametric data. In order to examine such a possibility with respect to our results, a correlational analysis was performed on the standardized index scores and their derived rank scores. A highly similar relationship ($r = -.83$) between the two forms of scores was found; the negativity of this correlation is simply due to the fact that the better ranks of those of lower numerical value.

[2]It may be instructive to note that the single exception from this pattern in Table 1 occurred at the University of Michigan as a direct result of a 10-10 tie with Ohio State University in a game for the Big Ten Conference Championship. Most observers, especially the Michigan supporters, felt that the Michigan team had outplayed Ohio State that day and that the game demonstrated Michigan's superiority. However, that tie game constituted Michigan's only entry in our nonwin category, resulting in the only reversal in our data.

[3]It might be argued that some subjects felt that their presence in the stands on the day of a game *directly* contributed to their team's success. This seems an unlikely explanation for the obtained results, as an analysis of the data of Experiment 1 showed an equally strong BIRG effect for home and away games.

[4]It should be evident to the reader that the general statement of the BIRG formulation includes not only the tendency to bask in reflected glory but also the tendency to distance unattractive sources.

[5]We do not wish to suggest that the tendency to BIRG a positive source never takes place when the observer's association to a successful other is as strong as one's own but only that the prestige to be derived from a unique (vis-a-vis the observer) connection is relatively more desirable.

[6]The experimenters, undergraduate students in a laboratory social psychology course, were not fully aware of these predictions. In order to test the influence of conscious or unconscious experimenter bias on the results of this study, the experimenters were informed of the nature of Hypothesis 1. However, they were blind to the more subtle Hypotheses 2 and 3. If only Hypothesis 1 were confirmed, the data would likely have to be interpreted as potentially influenced by the experimenter bias artifact.

The investigation of such a possibility was deemed an important one, since in the prior experiments, experimenters had knowledge of the experimental hypothesis. In Experiment 1, some data recorders were unintentionally informed of the major hypothesis, while others were not. An analysis of the data from these two groups found only a minimal difference in the data patterns, with the uninformed group's data actually more favorable to prediction than the informed group. However, in Experiment 2, all experimenters had knowledge of the prediction.

References

Harvey, O. J., Kelley, H. H., & Shapiro, M. M. Reactions to unfavorable evaluations of self made by other persons. *Journal of Personality,* 1957, *25,* 393-411.

Heider, F. *The psychology of interpersonal relations.* New York: Wiley, 1958.

Johnson, R., Conlee, M., & Tesser, A. Effects of similarity of fate on bad news transmission: A reexamination. *Journal of Personality and Social Psychology,* 1974, *29,* 644-648.

Langer, E. J., & Abelson, R. P. The semantics of asking a favor: How to succeed in getting help without really dying. *Journal of Personality and Social Psychology,* 1972, *24,* 26-32.

Manis, M., Cornell, S. D., & Moore, J. C. Transmission of attitude-relevant information through a communication chain. *Journal of Personality and Social Psychology,* 1974, *30,* 81-94.

Rosen, S., & Tesser, A. On the reluctance to communicate undesirable information. The MUM effect. *Sociometry,* 1970, *33,* 253-263.

Schneider, D. J. Tactical self-presentation after success and failure. *Journal of Personality and Social Psychology,* 1969, *13,* 262-268.

Siegel, S. *Nonparametric statistics for the behavioral sciences.* New York: McGraw-Hill, 1956.

Tesser, A., Rosen, S., & Batchelor, T. On the reluctance to communicate bad news (the MUM effect): A role play extension. *Journal of Personality,* 1972, *40,* 88-103.

Tesser, A., Rosen, S., & Tesser, M. On the reluctance to communicate undesirable messages (the MUM effect): A field study. *Psychological Reports,* 1971, *29,* 651-654.

Requests for reprints should be sent to Robert B. Cialdini, Department of Psychology, Arizona State University, Tempe, Arizona 85281.

7

Analysis of Groups and Social Processes

Attitude and personality research dominated much of the field of social psychology in its earlier years and it retains a dominant position in the field today. However, another concept has been nearly as important in the field. The subject of *groups* became a distinct topic of concern in the 1930s, and over the era after World War II it became a major research concern. How people developed stable behavior patterns with others and how they developed status hierarchies, normative controls, leadership, and intergroup conflict, among other topics, became subjected to intensive investigation. The overwhelming majority of the studies on these topics was performed in controlled laboratory settings.

A melding of great significance occurred when group variables were found to be intimately related to individual psychological processes such as attitudes, prejudice, and cognitive and judgmental processes. The linkage of individual and social variables proved to be a useful way to conceptualize and study social behavior.

In their movement toward applied concerns, social psychologists have expanded the range of social psychological variables in group processes. Several of the representative aspects of research in this new approach tradition are reprinted in this section of *Experimenting in Society*.

What brings people together? What keeps them together? What leads them to break apart? Social psychologists have devoted considerable effort to studying these fundamental questions about social interaction. Among other topics, they have focused on the process of attraction. Basically, this involves the positive and negative feelings that people develop about each other. Some of the fundamental properties of attraction are analyzed in the research articles in the attraction subsection.

When investigators began to extend their research methodology into natural settings, their concepts about social interaction took on a *prosocial behavior orientation*. Prosocial behavior involves the supportive and helpful side of interaction, not the aggressive and destructive side. Helping behavior is a major type of prosocial behavior. The early research on this concerned the *bystander intervention* issue, whether or not people who passively observe someone needing help in an emergency provide or do not provide the needed help. This topic rapidly became a major focus of research, and it has become one of the larger areas of research in social psychology.

Closely related to helping research is what is now called compliance research. Although the line separating the two topics is thin, compliance is specifically defined as a situation in which one person directly asks another for a favor or for help. Compliance research goes directly to the heart of how people directly attempt to change the behavior of others. In research on helping, a direct influence attempt is not necessary, but the social norms for helping a needy other, whether or not help is solicited, are quite powerful and compelling. Both types of research have to be seen as closely allied in their concern with how people influence others.

Social psychologists have found that there are a number of other ways behavior can be influenced by others, and often these are not directly tied to strong social norms or direct manipulations of one person by another. These techniques are indirect yet effective. Such things as simply staring at another person or getting in his or her way are both powerful influences. These are also common forms of behavior and thus deserving of scientific analysis. Research on such processes is included in the indirect influence subsection.

Group influences on the behavior of an individual are a universal phenomenon. How the individual blends into a group, or does not, tells a lot about group and individual processes. Technically, a group is more than a collection of interacting individuals; it has a structure and a dynamic pattern of functioning separate from other forms of social processes. It also can be distinguished from the influence processes going on among individuals who do not know each other, the so-called *togetherness* situation. On the other hand, a togetherness situation, as a collection of people, is different in its impact from the presence of just one other person (such as is involved in many helping and compliance situations), so analyses of both group and togetherness variables are important sources of information about society. Several examples of these different types of influences are reprinted in the group influences set of readings.

ATTRACTION

Perhaps the fundamental process underlying social behavior (as opposed to individual behavior) is the basic process of attraction and rejection, the moving of people toward or away from each other. Understanding this concept has been an important goal for social psychologists. A number of basic psychological effects have been discovered in this quest. Much of the research has been conducted in carefully controlled laboratory settings. At the same time, some investigators have sought to extend those analyses to actual attraction phenomena in natural settings. Two such examples are reprinted here.

Although a number of complex psychological concepts have been developed to account for the phenomena involved in interpersonal attraction, the study by

Walster, Aronson, Abrahams, and Rottman finds that of the several factors they tested for influence on attraction, only one had predictive power of any consequence. It was physical attractiveness. Since their study was conducted at a college dance, their result reveals something about what it is that brings people together. The other attraction study points to an equally fundamental process. Byrne, Ervin, and Lamberth show that in addition to physical attractiveness, similarity in attitudes is strongly influential in determining individuals' attraction to each other. In combination, these studies show the close linkages between individual psychological processes and the forces that bring people together and make social life possible.

Human choice behavior is a complex process, one that has been subjected to a wide range of experimental approaches in psychological research over the years. Walster, Aronson, Abrahams, and Rottman ("Importance of physical attractiveness in dating behavior") apply complex theory about choice behavior and a related theory, level of aspiration theory, to a very simple but very interesting situation: getting a date with a person of the opposite sex. The study assesses such cognitive and personality processes as self-esteem, nervousness, intelligence, and achievement motivation.

The investigators arranged for a real computer dance for their college student subjects. This involved pairing off partners on the basis of a computer match of their personality and physical characteristics. This attempt to create a natural environment for the assessment of the variables was highly innovative. Though the subjects were involved in a natural event, the entire arrangement was carefully devised by the experimenters to assess which variables would be expected to be involved in dating choice. Interestingly, the study reveals that only one of the components had a significant influence: the physical attractiveness of the other person, male or female, regardless of other factors.

The consistent failure of other potential predictors of dating choice to show any significant effect, while only physical attractiveness did, creates a compelling picture of what was important to these college student subjects. The methodology of the study was entirely natural and the data appears to be valid. However, the study was conducted over fourteen years ago; one wonders if the same results would be obtained today given all of the seemingly major changes which have occurred with college generations since the 1960s.

In the study by Byrne, Ervin, and Lamberth ("Continuity between the experimental study of attraction and real-life computer dating") two distinctly different approaches to interpersonal attraction (dating choice) are tested. One involves physical attractiveness as we have just discussed with the Walster et al. study, and the other involves the variable of similarity. The latter variable has been the focus of research for a number of years, much of it by Byrne. To date, the research on it is conclusive in demonstrating that we feel more attracted to people who are similar to us in attitudes than those who are dissimilar. The *similarity - attraction* relation is a direct and linear one.

The investigators combine the effects of personality and attitudinal similarity and measures of physical attractiveness to determine the relative contributions of each. Research which links theories and concepts from different areas of investigation to focus on a phenomenon increases our understanding of that phenomenon. In addition, this study used a computer matching of potential daters, so a very rigorous assessment of the relevant variables was possible and very realistic. The investigators even assessed how closely the pair stood to each other during the study.

The results clearly show that physical attractiveness is a significant influence. In addition, both attitude and personality similarity have an impact, with greater similarity on each leading to greater attraction. Interpersonal attraction thus is a more complex process than just physical attraction. Nevertheless, because physical attributes have been shown so consistently to relate to attraction, social psychologists have a solid base for expanding their view of attraction phenomena. Similarity factors are important to people, so we now have a good deal of understanding of attraction, which is one of the central factors in initiating and maintaining human social interaction.

HELPING BEHAVIOR

Cooperation, giving, supporting, and helping relationships are vital parts of social life. Social philosophers have discussed these topics for generations, and social psychologists recently have been able to gain some experimental control over them by defining them behaviorally. Thus the title *helping behavior*. This framework has made helping behavior easier to test and the factors relating to it easier to analyze. Social psychologists have applied considerable methodological ingenuity to detecting what situations enhance or suppress helping behavior. The great majority of the studies have been conducted in natural settings where helping behavior occurs without the constraints of laboratory settings.

The first study reprinted here by Bryan and Test ("Models and helping: Naturalistic studies in aiding behavior") attempts to analyze helping as a consequence of behavioral modeling or imitation. This fundamental learning process means simply that organisms will reproduce closely the observed behavior of another. Modeling is considered a major socialization device, and the investigators apply the concept because it seems quite possible that helping behavior is acquired that way. A central factor in modeling is situational similarity; it is increasingly likely to occur the more similar a current situation is to a previously observed situation.

Therefore, the experimenters arranged a naturalistic situation which contained two central components: a person in need of help, and a modeling situation similar to the situation observed by the subject. This was readily arranged by the device of a stranded motorist, a woman standing beside her car with a flat tire, receiving help from a passing motorist. Both were confederates of the experimenters. Down the road was another female motorist, standing beside her car and similarly in need of help. The dependent variable of the studies using this technique is simply whether or not a passing motorist will stop to give aid.

As would be predicted from a modeling perspective, those subjects (motorists) who earlier observe a helping incident aid more than control subjects for whom no such prior observed incident is present. Other experiments have expanded the range of situations in which modeling has been tested (in the famous "coins in the kettle" experiment) and also have found the basic effect to hold.

Imitation is a broad-ranging and ever present phenomenon. Social psychologists use it as an analytic technique for detecting the influences of a wide range of factors in social behavior. Helping behavior is central to individual and social welfare, and the results of this study give us a valuable insight into the imitation processes that initiate and maintain it.

Gaertner and Bickman ("Effects of race on the elicitation of helping behavior: The wrong number technique") use helping behavior as a sensitive and yet nonreactive technique for assessing another aspect of societal processes, in this case, racial and gender influences on helping behavior. They discuss the problem of racism in a subtle way. Almost no one will directly state a prejudicial feeling in public, but someone might unknowingly reveal it if the situation is one in which public condemnation or image concerns are not operating. The helping situation is one such situation, so the investigators use it as a detection device to determine the prevalence (if any) of racist behavior.

In the now-famous wrong number technique, it appears to the randomly selected subjects that they have been called accidentally on the telephone by a person who needs help: his car has broken down on the parkway and he has used his last dime to call a garage for help. Since he has dialed a wrong number, the person receiving the "accidental" call is his last hope of receiving aid. The racial variable is manipulated simply by the black or white tone and dialect of the voice of the caller; The voices were pretested for validity. Race of the subjects themselves also is a major variable, and this is assessed through selective telephone calling within predominantly white or black residential areas.

Assuming that whites are subtly prejudiced against blacks, the investigators predicted that black callers would receive proportionally less help from white subjects than they would from black subjects. The results support the prediction although the different rates of helping are not great. Black subjects show a slight tendency to help the white subjects slightly more than they do the blacks, but this was not a statistically significant effect. Interestingly, the gender effect does not result in a very clear bias.

Given the careful detail the investigators devote to their assessment of the characteristics of the confederate callers and the subject sampling, the results of the experiment appear valid. The study's contribution is a solid one, both as an analysis of racism and as a technique for applied experimental research. The technique is applicable to naturalistically assessing sensitive and subtle social processes.

COMPLIANCE BEHAVIOR

Social psychologists have drawn a distinction between two forms of altruism, helping and compliance. Helping is seen as a more unsolicited form of interpersonal cooperation, whereas compliance is regarded as occurring when one person deliberately attempts to elicit cooperative behavior from another. A form of social pressure is involved. In that sense, manipulation of interpersonal processes occurs and that is in the spirit of experimentation. So social psychologists have devised a number of techniques to analyze compliance behavior; they investigate a wide range of situations and interpersonal variables relating to interpersonal situations. The research is closely related to applied social psychological concerns, especially in its inventive use of field settings and naturalistic manipulations to determine the conditions under which compliance is most likely to occur. The two studies reprinted in this section are two very different approaches to compliance. The first, by Freedman and Fraser, shows that compliance will result from very subtle pressures being placed on the subject, and the other, by Cialdini and his associates, shows that very great pressure also achieves high degrees of compliance. These revealing views of interpersonal relations have wide ramifications for understanding fundamental processes in human social behavior.

The foundation study in compliance research by Freedman and Fraser is reprinted here ("Compliance without pressure: The foot-in-the-door technique.") They use the everyday phrase "foot-in-the-door" to describe what was involved in the compliance situation they were investigating: the tendency for people to do something of considerable cost to themselves, a task they would ordinarily not do, if they have previously performed a smaller, easier, or lower-cost task. As the investigators note, a very common way to obtain compliance from others is to put a lot of pressure on them. But this sometimes backfires. However, very subtle or weak pressure can be effective also, particularly self-commitment pressure coming from getting the person to engage in a small, easy, or harmless task. Once that task is performed, the person will be more likely to agree to engage in a second (larger) task than control subjects who do not perform the first task.

To establish the basic effect in a natural setting, the investigators induced housewives to comply with a small first request, using a supposed telephone survey to ask a few questions about household product usage; a control group did not receive this first contact. Three days later, the same housewives received another phone call requesting what would amount to a major disruption of their homes for another survey, this time requiring a group of men coming into their homes and determining all of the household products in use and in storage. The control group received only the latter contact: The results show that only slightly more than 20% of the housewives agreed. Apparently it was considered a relatively unpleasant task (of course, the actual inspection never occurred). Over 50% of the housewives agreed to the larger request if they first had agreed to the smaller request. In effect, it appears as if the survey people had gotten their "foot-in-the-door" by first obtaining cooperation on a simple earlier task, then asking for the major task. Other experimental conditions and another study are included in the Freedman and Fraser article to test the stability of the effect, and it was found to be stable.

The authors conclude that something like a change in self-perception was responsible for the effect. If people agree to comply with a small request, they come to define themselves as people who agree to help others, and do so when given another opportunity, even though the second opportunity requires greater effort. The investigators also note that this explanation is only tentative and in need of further research. Nevertheless, the basic effect reliably occurs and represents an interesting insight into some of the dynamics of social relations.

In the experiment of Cialdini, Vincent, Lewis, Catalan, Wheeler, & Darby ("Reciprocal concessions procedure for inducing compliance: The door-in-the-face technique") compliance is obtained by a technique which is the procedural opposite of the Freedman and Fraser method. It involves making a very large first request, one so large as likely to be rejected, and then following that up with a smaller or average-size request. There is strong evidence in their experiments that this has an equally powerful influence in obtaining compliance.

Cialdini et al. reasoned that social interaction, particularly that involving requests for compliance, subtly involves what has been called a norm of reciprocity. This concept refers simply to the give-and-take of social interaction, indicating the general tendency of people to wish to maintain fairness and equity in relationships: One attempts to give and to get in fairly equal amounts.

Applied to the compliance situation, the norm of reciprocity could be brought into play when a requester requests something but then is rejected by the person asked. That person is then in the position of having generated essentially an inequitable situation. If the requester follows up with a second request, but one smaller, or simpler, or less troublesome for the subject, then the requester will be seen as one who has moderated his request, as one who has moved away from his own initial position to one closer to the subject. At that point, there is some subtle but very real pressure on the subject to yield to this second request. Thus this *rejection-then-moderation* approach should actually result in significant compliance with the second request. Note that the underlying cognitive processes in this technique differ considerably from the foot-in-the-door technique which appears best explained by a self-perception interpretation; the social norm of reciprocity seems better adapted to explain the door-in-the-face technique.

The investigators first conducted an experiment to find out if the effect genuinely occurs. The subjects were approached on a campus and asked to donate vast amounts of time to a charity in need; all rejected and then they were requested to volunteer for a less time-consuming task. A control group was either asked the second request only or presented both large and small requests simultaneously (the latter condition testing for a possible contrast in effect in which the mere size of the first request might make the second look so small as to be acceptable). The results showed that the two control conditions did not differ from each other, and both resulted in less compliance than the large-request-then-small-request condition, as predicted. Two follow-up examinations tested for the reliability of the basic effect while adding additional control conditions to test for alternative explanations. The effect continued to appear as predicted.

In general, these experiments demonstrate that techniques for gaining compliance in interpersonal interaction can rely on normative expectations and subtle understandings between people revolving around feelings of reciprocity. Since the studies were conducted in natural settings and employed very direct and clear manipulations of conceptually based variables, we can see that the full battery of scientific procedure has been used effectively to reveal an important new view of social processes.

INDIRECT SOCIAL INFLUENCE TECHNIQUES

Sometimes the behavioral variables that scientists wish to study are sensitive and a direct approach to studying them would not be successful because people are very conscious about how they appear to others in social settings and work to keep their image favorable. On the other hand, there are aspects of behavior that are equally difficult to study because people are not fully aware of the variables that are influencing their behavior. Social life is filled with both kinds of processes, and social psychologists have devoted considerable effort to discovering ways to analyze those processes with naturalistic yet experimental methods. In the research examples reprinted here, methods were found to study the relationship between social status variables and frustration and aggression, and the impact that nonverbal behavior (staring at someone) has on behavior. These topics are rather sensitive, and directly questioning people about them or trying to study them in laboratory settings can generate defenses against that sensitivity. Instead the techniques used were indirect yet the experimental manipulations were designed well enough to reveal interesting facets of how people respond in those sensitive situations.

Doob and Gross ("Status of frustrator as an inhibitor of horn-honking responses") seek to assess people's aggressive reactions to a frustrating event and to link that with the variable of social status. Both topics are the types of things that people might not wish to express directly, especially to a stranger such as a scientist. The setting was auto driving on city streets. The honking behavior of drivers who were blocked by a supposedly slow-reacting driver (in a wealthy or poor appearing car) is the focus of the study. Of course, horn-honking is itself not a particularly interesting form of human behavior, but it takes on considerable meaning when viewed as a manifestation of the more sensitive, and certainly more pervasive and important variable of interpersonal aggression. The investigators want to determine if high social status can inhibit the expression of aggression relative to low social status.

The investigators simply had their confederates hesitate a long time at red stop lights with either a luxury or poor car when one person, (the subject) was behind them. The dependent variable was how long it took the driver to honk, if at all, and whether the driver honked a second time. A second study described the conditions in a questionnaire format to see if the same pattern of results would occur.

The results show that there was less horn-honking aggression directed toward the high status driver than toward the poor driver. It appears that at least in this culture status acts as an inhibitor of aggressive behavior. Interestingly, the same results did not appear in the questionnaire study, but that may have been due to age differences in the samples. Given the importance of the topic of aggression, the findings are revealing for they indicate that methodological factors per se may play a significant role in shaping the understanding we have of social phenomena. This is likely to be especially true with sensitive topics.

What is called *nonverbal behavior* has become a research topic of significant interest to social psychologists because of its pervasiveness and because of its nonconscious, nonintentional nature. One such behavior, staring, is studied in field settings by Ellsworth, Carlsmith, and Henson ("The stare as a stimulus to flight in human subjects"). They develop a logical model of how staring has an impact on people. Based on an animal behavior model, they propose that staring leads to uncertainty and psychological discomfort resulting in a state of tension which the person seeks to remove; a desire to escape results, followed by flight.

This is the first study in this area, so the investigators sought to establish experimentally but unobtrusively the basic characteristics of the relationship between staring and subsequent flight.

The settings chosen for the experiments were city street corners. The subjects were drivers who had stopped at red lights and were forced to wait for the light to change. Experimenters' aides on motor bikes stopped beside the drivers and turned and stared impassively at them during the duration of the red light. Speed of leaving the intersection when the light turned green (observed by hidden aides) was the measure of flight, the dependent variable. The sex of driver, of experimenter, and the presence of passengers was recorded. It was found with a number of different experimental manipulations that drivers who had been stared at escaped from the intersection more rapidly than those not exposed to the stare.

Nonverbal behavior is a unique aspect of human social behavior, and discovering its basic properties is an important issue. This is the first study on this topic and more recent research has extended our understanding of the effect. For example, it is obvious that we often stare (gaze) at someone we love, so staring itself is not necessarily a threatening event. Further research is needed on context effects. From the perspective of this book, the study is a good demonstration of how research methodology can be developed to apply to very subtle and perhaps even unconscious behaviors in ways that almost completely avoid direct verbal interaction between the experimenter and the subject.

GROUP INFLUENCES

The concept of *group* is a broad one, commonly used to refer to social phenomena ranging all the way from collections of people interacting with each other to the technical definition of an organized body of people with well-defined norms, roles, leaders, followers, and purposes. In all uses of the term, social psychologists have focused their attention on the process whereby interaction with other people comes to influence the thoughts, feelings, and behaviors of people subjected to group influences. Group influences can in fact be distinguished from *togetherness* influences, which is a topic of interest in its own right. More generally, though, it is important to know how individuals are altered by the presence of others. The two studies in this subsection present very different approaches to group influences: Blascovich, Ginsburg, and Howe show how an individual's decision-making behavior, i.e., how risky a bet he is willing to place, is increased by the presence of other people. The next study, by the Sherifs and their colleagues, is concerned more directly with the process of group formation per se; how people informally become organized into groups and how those groups function and interact with other groups. In addition, this research also investigates intergroup conflict and how that conflict can be reduced. Both the Blascovich et al. and Sherif et al. studies ingeniously manipulate group influence variables in highly naturalistic settings while maintaining high degrees of experimental control; gambling casino and summer camp settings were chosen for the experimental settings.

Blascovich, Ginsburg, and Howe ("Blackjack and the risky shift, II: Monetary stakes") report a study on *risky shift* or *choice shift,* a phenomenon occurring when individuals make decisions which involve risk. In such situations, there is a tendency for peoples' decisions to be more risky or daring when they are in groups than when they make decisions alone. Although there is no single theory which can account for all the varied findings in this large and complex body of research, the effect is certainly an important one. If people do in fact make riskier decisions when in groups, then not only have we learned more about the effects of group variables on individual cognitive processes per se, but we may have a better approach to understanding major social phenomena such as how national leaders make decisions concerning war, how crowds influence speakers, and how business leaders make important economic decisions.

The original research on this effect involved only questionnaire methodology, and most experimental work on it has been performed in strictly controlled laboratory settings. From a naturalistic perspective, however, one of the most unique but representative events which matches the characteristics of the risky shift situation is gambling. Gamblers have the free choice of either playing relatively safe games or they can risk much or all of their resources. And they can play solitary games or they can play in larger groups. Blascovich and his colleagues chose the game of blackjack as a model of real world risk situations and in a series of studies demonstrated that the risky shift effect does occur in such settings.

The investigators arranged to have subjects gamble in a realistic casino setting and to gamble with their own money. The study was done in Reno, Nevada, and used as subjects conventioneers who would be gambling anyway. Real chips for real money were used, the cards were dealt by a real card dealer, and the room was arranged exactly as a casino would be.

In this situation, the risky shift effect would be revealed through riskier bets (higher amounts of money being wagered) when subjects were betting with others than when they were betting alone. The results show just that effect.

It is unusual for researchers to be able to link so closely naturally occurring phenomena with psychological theories and concepts. When this is done, we gain an opportunity for fruitful tests of theories and clarifications of natural events. The data of this study shows that the linkage can be very close indeed.

One of the classic experiments in social psychology is the Robbers Cave study by the Sherifs and their colleagues ("Intergroup Relations in *An Outline of Social Psychology"*). One of a series of field experiments on group formation, functioning, and actual intergroup conflict, this study formally tests theoretical models for the reduction of intergroup conflict. That conflict itself was experimentally arranged for in the structure of a two-week summer camp experience for eleven-year-old normal boys.

The experimenters had planned the camp experience to include activities which would quantitatively reveal the group structure variables as they occurred during group formation and underwent change as a function of intergroup conflict. The boys, carefully screened out to be normal and well adjusted, were split at random into two groups of initially unacquainted members. The experimenters had arranged a series of intergroup competitions of the *zero sum* type (if one team wins, the other loses) in order to lead toward intergroup competition, and thus bring about the conditions for testing the conflict reduction models. But it was found that the boys spontaneously sought competition with, and dominance over, outgroup members. Intense hostility arose naturally after the series of structured competitions such as baseball and tug-of-war began. This soon escalated into fights, name calling, and eventually organized destructive raids. Although the boys had been selected for normalcy, something very close to war became daily routine.

The phase of reducing intergroup conflict by various techniques then began. The one technique predicted by the experimenters to be successful, and found to be so, was the *superordinate goal* technique. This refers to the attainment of a desirable goal by group cooperation, the resources of neither group by itself being capable of attainment of the goal. By the end of the third stage of the experiment, the series of superordinate goal events had been so successful that the boys' own in-group boundaries had virtually dissolved; friendship clusters bridging former impenetrable group boundaries were widespread.

The superordinate goal concept is easy to translate into many different forms of intergroup hostility situations. Its power in reducing the intense intergroup hostility in this situation was impressive. It clearly deserves wider testing and use in social (if not international) relations. The series of studies on intergroup conflict by the Sherifs represent an excellent combination of theory, experiment, and sensitivity in naturalistic settings. Although groups, conflict, and superordinate goals are extremely complex social phenomena, the investigators were able to apply the criteria of scientific analysis to help illuminate the nature of these central social processes.

Attraction

Importance of Physical Attractiveness in Dating Behavior[1]

Elaine Walster   *University of Minnesota*
Vera Aronson
Darcy Abrahams
Leon Rottmann   *University of Nebraska*

Abstract

It was proposed that an individual would most often expect to date, would try to date, and would like a partner of approximately his own social desirability.

"Importance of Physical Attractiveness in Dating Behavior" by Elaine Hatfield (formerly Walster), Vera Aronson, Darcy Abrahams and Leon Rottmann. *Journal of Personality and Social Psychology,* 1966, Vol. 4, No. 5, pp. 508–516. Copyright © 1966 by The American Psychological Association, Inc. Reprinted by permission.

In brief, we attempted to apply level of aspiration theory to choice of social goals. A field study was conducted in which individuals were randomly paired with one another at a "Computer Dance." Level of aspiration hypotheses were not confirmed. Regardless of S's own attractiveness, by far the largest determinant of how much his partner was liked, how much he wanted to date the partner again, and how often he actually asked the partner out was simply how attractive the partner was. Personality measures such as the

MMPI, the Minnesota Counseling Inventory, and Berger's Scale of Self-Acceptance and intellectual measures such as the Minnesota Scholastic Aptitude Test, and high school percentile rank did not predict couple compatability. The only important determinant of S's liking for his date was the date's physical attractiveness.

In one of his delightful articles Goffman (1952) said that: "A proposal of marriage in our society tends to be a way in which a man sums up his social attributes and suggests to a woman that hers are not so much better as to preclude a merger or a partnership in these matters [p. 456]." Goffman's proposal suggests that one's romantic feelings and choices are affected both by the objective desirability of the romantic object and by one's perception of the possibility of attaining the affection of the other. Rosenfeld (1964) has demonstrated that an individual's choice of a *work partner* was affected by his assumptions about whether or not the partner would reciprocate his choice.

The following field experiment was conducted to see if one's romantic aspirations are influenced by the same factors that affect one's level of aspiration in other areas. (Level of aspiration theory is presented in Lewin, Dembo, Festinger, & Sears, 1944.) We wish to point out that this study concentrates on *realistic* social choices. In their discussion of *"ideal choices"* Lewin et al. conclude that an individual's ideal goals are usually based entirely on the desirability of the goal, with no consideration of the possibility of attaining this goal. Probably an individual's fantasy romantic choices are also based entirely on the desirability of the object. One's *realistic* level of aspiration, on the other hand, has been shown by Lewin et al. to depend both on the objective desirability of the goal and on one's perceived possibility of attaining that goal.

We propose that one's realistic romantic choices will be affected by the same practical considerations that affect other realistic goal setting. Lewin et al. note that since the attractiveness of a goal and the probability of attaining that goal are negatively correlated, the goal an individual can expect to attain is usually less attractive than the one he would desire to attain. In romantic choices, attractiveness and availability would also seem to be negatively correlated. The more abstractly desirable a potential romantic object is, the more competition there probably is for him (or her), and the less likely it is that a given individual will be able to attain his friendship. Thus, one's *realistic* social

choices should be less "socially desirable" than one's fantasy social choices. In addition, Lewin et al. note that one's realistic level of aspiration is affected by his perception of own skills. In the romantic area, we would expect that the individual's own social attractiveness would affect his level of aspiration. On the basis of the above reasoning, we would propose the following specific hypotheses:

1. Individuals who are themselves very socially desirable (physically attractive, personable, or possessing great material assets) will require that an appropriate partner possess more social desirability than will a less socially desirable individual.

2. If couples varying in social desirability meet in a social situation, those couples who are similar in social desirability will most often attempt to date one another.

3. In addition, we propose that an individual will not only *choose* a date of approximately his own social desirability, but also that after actual experience with potential dates of various desirabilities an individual will express the most *liking* for a partner of approximately his own desirability. This prediction is not directly derived from level of aspiration formulations. Lewin et al. predict only that an individual will choose a goal of intermediate attractiveness and difficulty; they do not propose that an individual will come to *like* goals of intermediate difficulty. We thought that unattainably desirable individuals might be derogated (although inappropriately difficult tasks are not) for the following reasons:

1. If a man chooses an inappropriately difficult task and then fails to attain it, all he suffers is defeat. The task cannot point out to him that he has been presumptuous in choosing a goal so far beyond his level of ability. We speculated, however, that an extremely desirable date can be counted on to make it clear to a somewhat undesirable individual that he is foolish to try to win her friendship and that he should not embarrass her by asking her out.

2. We thought that perhaps an extremely attractive date would not be as considerate of an unattractive date as with a date more average in appearance.

PROCEDURE

Subjects were 376 men and 376 women who purchased tickets to a Friday night dance held on the last day of "Welcome Week." (Welcome Week is a week of cultural, educational, and social events provided for incoming University of Minnesota freshmen.) The dance was advertised along with 87 other events in a handbook all incoming freshmen received. In fact, however, the dance was not a regular Welcome Week event and had been set up solely to test our hypotheses. The handbook advertisement describing a Computer Dance said: "Here's your chance to meet someone who has the same expressed interests as yourself." Freshmen were told that if they would give the computer some information about their interests and personalities, the computer would match them with a date. Tickets were $1.00 per person; both men and women purchased their own tickets. Long lines of subjects appeared to buy tickets on the opening day—only the first 376 male and 376 female students who appeared were accepted.

For experimental purposes, ticket sales and information distribution were set up in extremely bureaucratic style: The subject walked along a table in the foyer of the Student Union. First, a student sold him a ticket. He moved down the table, and a second student checked his identification card to make sure he was a student and told him to report to a large room two flights above. When the subject arrived at the upstairs room, a third student met him at the door and handed him a questionnaire with his student code number stamped on it and asked him to complete the questionnaire at an adjoining table. A fourth student directed him to a seat. (Proctors around the room answered the subject's questions and discouraged talking.)

Physical Attractiveness Rating

The four bureaucrats were actually college sophomores who had been hired to rate the physical attractiveness of the 752 freshmen who purchased tickets to the dance.[2]

We assumed that one's social desirability would include such attributes as physical attractiveness, personableness, and material resources and that these aspects would be positively correlated with one another. We chose physical attractiveness to be the indicator of the subject's social desirability since this trait was more quickly assessed under standard conditions.

As each subject passed, the four raters rapidly and individually evaluated the subject's physical attractiveness on an 8-point scale, going from 1 ("Extremely unattractive") to 8 ("Extremely attractive"). Obviously, these attractiveness ratings had to be made very quickly; usually the rater had less than 1 or 2 seconds to look at the subject before making his evaluation, and rarely did the rater get to hear the subject say more

than "OK" or "Thank you." The briefness of this contact was by design. Since we had chosen to use one aspect of social desirability as an index of total desirability, as far as possible, we wanted to be sure that the raters were assessing only that aspect. We did not want our ratings of attractiveness to be heavily influenced by the subject's personableness, intelligence, voice quality, etc.

Once the subjects were seated in the large upstairs room, they began filling out the questionnaire. The subject first answered several demographic questions concerning his age (nearly all were 18), height, race, and religious preference. The next measures were designed to assess how considerate the subject felt he would be of a fairly attractive date.

The remainder of the booklet contained material which we wanted to encourage the subjects to answer honestly. For this reason, a section prefacing the questions assured participants that their answers to the questions would not be used in selecting their date. We explained that we were including these questions only for research purposes and not for matching purposes. In addition, the subjects were reassured that their statements would be kept confidential and associated only with their ticket number, never their name. Four pages of questions followed this introduction. In the pages following this introduction, four variables were measured:

Subject's popularity (self-report). The subject was asked how popular he was with members of the opposite sex, how easy it was to get a date with someone he thought was exceptionally attractive, and how many dates he had had in the last 6 months.

Subject's nervousness. The subject was asked how nervous or awkward he felt about the idea of going on a blind date.

Measure of the subject's expectations in a computer date. The subject was asked how physically attractive, how personally attractive, and how considerate he expected his date to be.

Subject's self-esteem. Questions from a scale developed by Berger (1952) ended the questionnaire. The subject was asked how true 36 different statements were of himself. The subject was once again reassured that this information was confidential and would not be used in selecting his computer date. (A typical question is: "When I'm in a group, I usually don't say much for fear of saying the wrong things.") This test was scored so that a high score indicated high self-acceptance and high self-esteem.

From the University's state-wide testing service program at the University of Minnesota,[3] several additional measures were secured for the subject whenever possible. The subject's high school academic percentile rank, his Minnesota Scholastic Aptitude Test (MSAT) score, and his score on the MMPI or the Minnesota Counseling Inventory (MCI) were secured.

Two days after the subject completed his questionnaire, he was assigned to a date. Dates were randomly assigned to the subjects with one limitation: a man was never assigned to a date taller than himself. On the few occasions when the assigned female date would have been taller than the male, the IBM card next in the shuffled deck was selected as the partner. When subjects picked up their dates' name, the experimenter advised them to meet their dates at the dance. Many couples, however, met at the girl's home.

The dance was held in a large armory. In order to be admitted to the armory, the subjects had to turn in their numbered tickets at the door. In this way, we could check on whether or not a given couple had attended the dance. Of the 376 male and 376 female students who signed up for the dance and were assigned a partner, 44 couples did not attend.[4] The subjects generally arrived at the dance at 8:00 P.M. and danced or talked until the 10:30 P.M. intermission.

Assessing Subjects' Attitudes Toward One Another

Subjects' attitudes toward their dates were assessed during intermission. Several times during Welcome Week, we had advertised that couples should hold onto their ticket stubs until intermission, because these stubs would be collected during intermission and a $50 drawing would be held at that time. When the subjects bought their tickets, we reminded them that they would need to save their tickets for an intermission lottery. They were also told that during the dance they would have a chance to tell us how successful our matching techniques had been.

During the 10:30 P.M. intermission, the subjects were reminded that tickets for the lottery would be collected while they filled out a brief questionnaire assessing their dates and the dance. The purpose of the lottery was simply to insure that the subjects would retain their ticket stubs, which contained an identifying code number, and would report to an assigned classroom during intermission to evaluate their dates. Men were

to report to one of seven small rooms to rate their dates and to turn in their stubs; women were to remain in the large armory to evaluate their partners.

The forms on which the subjects rated their partner were anonymous except that the subjects were asked to record their ticket numbers in the right-hand corner. This number, of course, identified the subjects perfectly to us, while not requiring the subjects to sign their name to their evaluation. A crew of experimenters rounded up any subjects who had wandered to rest rooms, fire escapes, or adjoining buildings and asked them to turn in their ticket stubs and to complete the evaluation questionnaires.

In the eight rooms where the subjects were assembled to evaluate their dates, the experimenters[5] urged the subjects to take the questionnaire seriously and to answer all questions honestly. All but 5 of 332 couples attending the dance completed a questionnaire, either during intermission or in a subsequent contact 2 days later.

The intermission questionnaire asked the subject about the following things: *(a)* how much the subject liked his date, *(b)* how socially desirable the date seemed to be ("How physically attractive is your date?" "How personally attractive is your date?"), *(c)* how uncomfortable the subject was on this blind date, *(d)* how much the date seemed to like the subject, *(e)* how similar the date's values, attitudes, and beliefs seemed to the subject's own, *(f)* how much of an effort the subject made to insure that the date had a good time, and how much of an effort the date made on the subject's behalf, *(g)* whether or not the subject would like to date his partner again.

How often couples actually dated was determined in a follow-up study. All participants were contacted 4-6 months after the dance and asked whether or not they had tried to date their computer date after the dance. If the experimenter was unable to contact either the subject or the subject's date in 2 months of attempts, the couple was excluded from the sample. Only 10 couples could not be contacted.

RESULTS

Physical Attractiveness and Social Desirability

We assumed that we could use our ratings of physical attractiveness as a rough index of a person's social desirability. Is there any evidence that these outside ratings are related to the subject's own perception of his social desirability? When we look at the data, we see that there is. The more attractive an individual is, the more popular he says he is. The correlation between physical attractiveness and popularity for men is .31 and for women is .46. (Both of these *r*'s are significant at $p < .001$.)[6]

Hypothesis 1

Our first prediction was that a very socially desirable (attractive) subject would expect a "suitable" or "acceptable" date to possess more physical and personal charm and to be more considerate than would a less socially desirable subject.

We had two ways of testing whether or not attractive subjects did, in fact, have more rigorous requirements for an acceptable date than did less attractive individuals. Before the subject was assigned a date, he was asked how physically attractive, how personally attractive, and how considerate he expected his date to be. His answers to these three questions were summed, and an index of degree of the perfection he expected was computed. From the data, it appears that the more attractive the subject is, the more attractive, personable, and considerate he expects his date to be. The correlation between physical attractiveness and total expectations in a date is .18 for men and .23 for women.

A second way an individual's stringency of requirements could have been tested was by seeing whether or not the subject refused to go out with an "unsuitable" date. We wanted to eliminate the possibility that attractive and unattractive subjects would attend the dance with different frequencies, so we encouraged subjects to meet one another at the dance. However, it is possible that a few individuals were ingenious enough to get a preview of their dates before their public appearance together. We tried to determine whether or not attractive individuals rejected their partners *before* the dance more often than did unattractive ones.

It will be recalled that four raters rated each subject on an 8-point scale of attractiveness. We then separated subjects into three approximately equal-sized groups on the basis of these ratings. Men receiving an average rating of from 1.50 to 4.00 and women rated 1.50 to 4.75 were classified as *Ugly* individuals; men receiving an average rating of from 5.25 to 6.00 and women rated 5.00-5.75 were classified as *Average* individuals; and men rated 6.25-8.00 and women rated 6.00-8.00 were classified as *Attractive* individuals. We then contacted the 44 couples who did not attend the computer dance and interviewed them about their reasons for not attending. Attractive subjects did not reject their dates before the dance any more often than did unattractive subjects.

Behavioral Measures of Rejection

After men had arrived at the dance, or at their date's home, they met the partner who had been randomly assigned to them. Then during intermission, the subjects rated their liking for their dates. Since partners were randomly assigned, very attractive individuals should be assigned to just as attractive partners, on the average, as are average or ugly individuals. Thus, if during intermission, very handsome individuals rate their dates as less attractive, less personable, and less considerate than do less attractive men, this would indicate that attractive men are more harsh in their standards and ratings than are less attractive men. Also, if attractive individuals are more harsh in their standards they should, on the average, like their dates less, express less of a desire to date their partner again, and should actually try to date their computer partner less often than do less attractive individuals. When we look at the data, we see that this first hypothesis is confirmed.

The more attractive a man is, the less physically and personally attractive he thinks his date is ($F = 8.88$, *df* $= 1/318$, $p < .01$), the less he likes her ($F = 6.69$, $p < .01$), the less he would like to date her again ($F = 14.07$, $p < .001$), and the less often the date says he actually did ask her out again ($F = 3.15$, *ns*). Similarly, the more attractive a woman is, the less physically and personally attractive she thinks her date is ($F = 5.71$, *df* $= 1/318$, $p < .05$), the less she likes her date ($F = 2.23$, *ns*), and the less she would like to date him again ($F = 13.24$, $p < .001$).

Though it is clear that the more attractive subjects do appear to judge their dates more harshly than do unattractive subjects, we would like to note that this variable does *not* account for a very large portion of the total variance. For example, the relationships we have demonstrated between the subject's attractiveness and his expectations and evaluations of a date are strongly significant in five of the seven cases reported. However, correlations for the above variables range from only .07 to .20.

Hypothesis II proposed that an individual would most often choose to date a partner of approximately his own attractiveness. Hypothesis III stated that if individuals were to interact with partners of varying physical attractiveness, in a naturalistic setting, an individual would be better liked and would more often want to continue to date a partner similar to himself in attractiveness. Figure 1 depicts graphically the theoretical expectation that subjects will most often choose and most often like dates of approximately their own attractiveness.

Statistically, we test Hypotheses II and III by testing the significance of the interaction between date's attractiveness and subject's attractiveness in influencing the subject's *attempts* to date the partner, his *desire* to date the partner, and his liking for his date.

In Table 1, as in Figure 1, the subjects who supplied information to us were divided into three groups—Ugly subjects, Average subjects, and Attractive subjects. Unlike Figure 1, however, the actual attractiveness of the dates the subjects are rating is not allowed to vary continuously; for the sake of clarity, the dates were also divided into three attractiveness groups.

So that we could very precisely assess whether or not the interaction we predicted was significant, we also examined the data by dividing subjects and their dates into five attractiveness levels. When the 5×5 interaction is examined, however, the conclusions and Fs are identical to those we form on the basis of the less fine discriminations (3×3) reported in Table 1. For this reason, the smaller breakdown is presented.

Hypotheses II and III are not supported. The subject's attractiveness does not significantly interact with the date's attractiveness in determining his attempt to date her, his desire to date her, or his liking for her. In *no case* is there a significant interaction. If we look at the *actual* attempts of men to date their partners (Table 1:I), we find that men did not more

often ask out dates similar to themselves in attractiveness. (These data were secured in a follow-up study.) The only important determinant of whether or not the date was asked out again was how attractive the *date* was. The most attractive girls are most often asked out ($F = 12.02$, $df = 1/318$, $p < .001$). This is generally true *regardless of the attractiveness of the man* who is asking her out. There is *not* a significant tendency for subjects to try to date partners of approximately their own physical desirability. The interaction F which is necessary to demonstrate such a tendency is very small ($F = .07$).

Our hypothesis (III) that individuals would best *like* dates similar to themselves in attractiveness also fails to be supported by the data. During intermission, individuals indicated how much they liked their dates on a scale ranging from 2.5 ("Like extremely much") to –2.5 ("Dislike extremely much"). From Table 1, Sections II and III, it is apparent that by far the greatest determinant of how much liking an individual feels for his partner is simply how attractive the partner is. The more attractive the female date is, the better liked she is ($F = 59.26$, $df = 1/318$) and the more often the man says that he would like to date her ($F = 49.87$). Men do not overrate women at their own attractiveness level. (Interaction Fs for liking and desire to date $= 2.53$ and $.69$, respectively.) Very surprising to us was the fact that a *man's* physical attractiveness is also by far the largest determinant of how well *he* is liked. We had assumed that physical attractiveness would be a much less important determinant of liking for men than for women. However, it appears that it is just as important a determinant. The more attractive the man, the more his partner likes him ($F = 55.79$, $df = 1/318$) and the more often she says she wants to date him again ($F = 37.24$). As before, we see that women do not tend to overrate partners at their own attractiveness level. (Interaction Fs for liking and desire to date $= .07$ and $.08$, respectively.)

In order to get a better idea of the extent to which liking was related to the date's physical attractiveness, we examined the correlation between these two variables. The correlations between date's attractiveness and the partner's liking is almost as high as the reliability of the attractiveness ratings.

Our measure of physical attractiveness is not highly reliable. When rating the subject's physical attractiveness, raters saw the subject for only a few seconds as the subject moved along in a line. In addition, raters had to devise their own standards of attractiveness.

Fig. 1. Amount of Liking Predicted for Dates of Various Attractiveness by Ugly, Average, and Attractive Subjects.

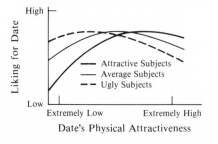

Attractive Subjects
Average Subjects
Ugly Subjects

Table 1 Various Measures of the Subjects' Liking for Their Dates and
Subjects' Desire to Date Their Partners

	Date's physical attractiveness		
	Ugly	Average	Attractive
I. % Ss actually asking date out			
According to ugly male Ss	.16	.21	.40
According to average male Ss	.12	.25	.22
According to attractive male Ss	.00	.26	.29
II. How much S says he liked his date			
According to ugly male Ss	.06[a]	.57	.90
According to average male Ss	−.10	.58	1.56
According to attractive male Ss	−.62	.16	.82
According to ugly female Ss	.03	.71	.96
According to average female Ss	−.10	.61	1.50
According to attractive female Ss	−.13	.21	.89
III. % Ss saying they wanted to date partner again			
According to ugly male Ss	.41	.53	.80
According to average male Ss	.30	.50	.78
According to attractive male Ss	.04	.37	.58
According to ugly female Ss	.53	.56	.92
According to average female Ss	.35	.69	.71
According to attractive female Ss	.27	.27	.68
IV. How many subsequent dates couples had			
Ugly male Ss	.09	1.23	.73
Average male Ss	.30	.94	.17
Attractive male Ss	.00	2.08	.53
V. Amount S thinks date likes him			
Guesses by ugly male Ss	.47[b]	.52	.43
Guesses by average male Ss	.55	.64	.65
Guesses by attractive male Ss	.77	.53	.58
Guesses by ugly female Ss	.41	.41	.35
Guesses by average female Ss	.38	.58	.55
Guesses by attractive female Ss	.63	.65	.61
VI. No. of Ss in each cell			
Ugly male Ss	(32)	(43)	(30)
Average male Ss	(43)	(36)	(41)
Attractive male Ss	(26)	(38)	(38)

[a]The higher the number, the more the subject says he liked his date.
[b]The higher the number, the more the subject thinks his date liked him.

Probably as a consequence of the preceding factors, the attractiveness ratings made by the four raters of the same individual intercorrelate .49-.58. In addition, there is a factor which may further reduce the reliability of our attractiveness measure from the time of the rating to the time of the dance. At the time of the rating, the subjects were in school clothes, casually dressed, while on the day of the dance they were dressed for a date. It is possible that this difference would have produced a change in the subject's relative attractiveness orderings. In spite of these limitations, the correlation between a *woman's* average physical attractiveness rating and her male partner's liking for her is .44; the correlation between her attractiveness and whether or not he wants to continue to date her is .39; and between her attractiveness and how much he actually does ask her out subsequently is .17. The correlations between a *man's* average physical attractiveness rating and his partner's liking for him and desire to date him are .36 and .31, respectively.

When we examine the relationship between the *individual's* own estimation of the date's physical attractiveness and his expression of liking for her, the correlations are still higher. The correlation between liking of the date and evaluation of the date's physical attractiveness is .78 for male subjects and .69 for female subjects.

It appears that the more attractive the date, the more he was liked, and the more the subject desired to date him regardless of how attracted the date was to the subject. The happy accommodation that we proposed between what an individual desires and what he can realistically hope to attain appears not to exist. The lack of symmetry between the individual's liking for his date and the date's liking for the individual is striking. The correlation between how much the man says he likes his partner and how much she likes him is virtually zero: $r = .03$. Nor is there a significant correlation between whether or not the subject wants to date his partner again and whether she wants to date him: $r = .07$. Clearly, a variable that we assumed would be very important—how much the date likes individual—does not appear to be an important determinant of the individual's ratings. Sheer physical attractiveness appears to be the overriding determinant of liking.

How can we account for the singular importance of physical attractiveness in determining the individual's liking for the other? There seem to be several plausible explanations:

1. Perhaps it could be argued that in the relationships we have discussed it is not really physical attractiveness that is so crucial, but one of the *correlates* of attractiveness. For example, we know from developmental studies of intelligent individuals (Terman, 1925, 1947, 1959) that intelligence, physical attractiveness, creativity, and certain personality traits are often positively correlated. Perhaps it is one of these correlated variables that is really important in determining liking.

    From the other evidence we have on this point and which we will present in the next paragraphs, it appears that "intelligence" and "personality" are *not* better predictors of liking than physical attractiveness.

Intelligence and Achievement Measures

Students' high school percentile ranks and MSAT scores are undoubtedly much more reliable measures than is our measure of physical attractiveness. Yet, these measures have only a very weak relationship to liking. The higher the male's high school percentile rank, the less his partner likes him ($r = -.18$) and the less she wants to date him again ($r = -.04$) ($N = 303$). Male's MSAT scores correlate .04 with both the woman's liking for him and her desire to date him ($N = 281$). The higher the female's high school percentile rank, the less her partner likes her ($r = -.07$) and the less he desires to date her again ($r = -.09$). His school rank is uncorrelated with his actual attempt to date her again ($r = .00$) ($N = 323$). Females' MSAT scores correlate $-.05$, $-.06$, and $-.06$ with these same variables ($N = 306$). It is clear then that intelligence is clearly not a variable of the same importance as physical attractiveness in determining liking. In no case did a subject's intellectual achievement or ability test scores have a significant relationship to the liking his date expressed for him.

Personality Measures

The subjects also completed several personality measures which could reasonably be expected to predict the liking one would engender in a social situation.[7]

MCI: Social relationships (SR). Low scorers are said to have good social skills, have acceptable manners, and be courteous, mature individuals (Berdie, Layton, Swanson, Hagenah, & Merwin, 1962).

MMPI: Masculinity-femininity (Mf). Low scorers are said to be more masculine in their values, attitudes, and interest, styles of expression and speech, and in their sexual relationships than high scorers (Dahlstrom & Welsh, 1962).

MMPI: Social introversion (Si). Low scorers are said to be more extroverted in their thinking, social participation, and emotional involvement.

Berger's Scale of Self-Acceptance (1952). When we look at the correlations between an individual's scores on these personality measures and the liking his date expresses for him, we see that these personality measures are not as good predictors of liking as is our crude measure of physical attractiveness. When we look at the data, we see that the low scoring individuals on the MCI (SR), on the

MMPI *(Mf)*, and on the MMPI *(Si)* or high scorers on Berger's Scale of Self-Acceptance are only slightly better liked by their dates than are high scoring individuals. Men's scores on these tests correlate −.11, −.12, −.10, and .14 with their dates' liking for them. Women's scores on these tests correlate only −.18, −.10, −.08, and .03 with their dates' liking. Our personality measures, then, like our intelligence measures, appear to be very inadequate predictors of liking.

It is, of course, possible that intelligence and personality determinants would have been more important had individuals had more time to get acquainted. It may be that 2½ hours is too short a time for individuals to discover much about their partners' intelligence or personality, while physical attractiveness is obvious from the start. It is not likely, however, that intelligence or personality variables are "really" underlying the correlations we obtained between attractiveness and romantic liking.

2. It may be that in this situation, individuals were not very affected by their dates' liking for them because the dates were so polite that it was impossible for the individual to know if he was accepted or rejected. Or, perhaps individuals were so eager to be liked that they did not want to correctly perceive the available cues.

The only available evidence for this position is ambiguous. The correlation between the partner's stated liking for the subject and the subject's perception of the partner's liking for him is .23 for male subjects and .36 for female subjects. The subject, thus, has some, though not a great deal of, ability in estimating how much his partner likes him. The reader may see subjects' guesses concerning how much their date likes them in Table 1:V. Possible answers to the question, "How much does your partner like you?" could range from (2.5) "Date likes me extremely much" to (−2.5) "Date dislikes me extremely much."

3. It may be that our findings are limited to large group situations, where young people are in very brief contact with one another. Perhaps if individuals had been exposed to one another for *long* periods of time, similarity of interests, beliefs, and reciprocal liking would come to be more important than physical appearance in determining liking. Finally, it might also be true that physical attractiveness loses some of its importance as individuals get to be *older* than the 18-year-olds interviewed in our study.

We should note that, even though further contact may have decreased the importance of physical attractiveness, whether or not the subject attempted to continue to date his partner depended on the partner's physical attractiveness. Similarly, though our findings may well be limited to the youthful population that we interviewed (average age: 18 years), it is also true that this is the age at which many individuals make their lifelong romantic choices.

4. Finally, it may be that if we had arranged more conventional single dates, the date's personality and conversational abilities would have been more important. It may have been that just getting to display a very attractive date compensated for any rejection on the date's part.

Footnotes

[1] This study was financed by the Student Activities Bureau, University of Minnesota.

[2] David Kushner, John B. Kelly, Susan Lampland, and Victoria Noser rated the attractiveness of all the subjects. These students were simply told to use their own judgment in rating the subjects and to be careful not to communicate their ratings to the other raters.

[3] We would like to thank Theda Hagenah and David Wark of the Student Counseling Bureau, University of Minnesota, for providing access to this information.

[4] By far the most common reason given by the subjects for not attending the dance was that the date was of a different religion than the subject and that their parents had objected to their dating.

[5] Darcy Abrahams, James Bell, Zita Brown, Eugene Gerard, Jenny Hoffman, Darwyn Linder, Perry Prestholdt, Bill Walster, and David Wark served as the experimenters. Male experimenters interviewed male subjects; female experimenters interviewed female subjects.

[6] With an N of 327, a correlation of .10 is significant at $p < .05$, a correlation of .15 at $p < .01$, and a correlation of .18 at $p < .001$.

[7] MCI scores were secured for 234 of the male subjects and 240 of the female subjects during freshman testing. In addition, the MMPI had been administered to a sample including 50 of the men and 41 of the women.

References

Berdie, R. F., Layton, W. L., Swanson, E. O., Hagenah, T., & Merwin, J. C. *Counseling and the use of tests.* Minneapolis: Student Counseling Bureau, 1962.

Berger, E. M. The relation between expressed acceptance of self and expressed acceptance of others. *Journal of Abnormal and Social Psychology,* 1952, *47*, 778-782.

Dahlstrom, W. G., & Welsh, G. S. *An MMPI handbook: A guide to use in practice and research.* Minneapolis: University of Minnesota Press, 1962.

Goffman, E. On cooling the mark out: Some aspect of adaptation to failure. *Psychiatry, 1952, 15,* 451-463.

Lewin, K., Dembo, T., Festinger, L., & Sears, P. Level of aspiration. In J. McV. Hunt (Ed.), *Personality and the behavior disorders.* Vol. 1. New York: Ronald Press, 1944. Pp. 333-378.

Rosenfeld, H. M. Social choice conceived as a level of aspiration. *Journal of Abnormal and Social Psychology, 1964, 68,* 491-499.

Terman, L. M. *Genetic studies of genius.* Vol. 1. Stanford: Stanford University Press, 1925.

Terman, L. M. *Genetic studies of genius.* Vol. 4. Stanford: Stanford University Press, 1947.

Terman, L. M. *Genetic studies of genius.* Vol. 5. Stanford: Stanford University Press, 1959.

Continuity Between the Experimental Study of Attraction and Real-Life Computer Dating[1]

Donn Byrne[2]   *Purdue University*
Charles R. Ervin   *University of Texas*
John Lamberth   *Purdue University*

Abstract

As a test of the nonlaboratory generalizability of attraction research, a computer dating field study was conducted. A 50-item questionnaire of attitudes and personality was administered to a 420-student pool, and 44 male-female pairs were selected on the basis of maximal or minimal similarity of responses. Each couple was introduced, given differential information about the basis for their matching, and asked to spend 30 minutes together at the Student Union on a "coke date." Afterward, they returned to the experimenter and were independently assessed on a series of measures. It was found that attraction was significantly related to similarity and to physical attractiveness. Physical attractiveness was also significantly related to ratings of desirability as a date, as a spouse, and to sexual attractiveness. Both similarity and attractiveness were related to the physical proximity of the two individuals while they were talking to the experimenter after the date. In a follow-up investigation at the end of the semester, similarity and physical attractiveness were found to predict accurate memory of the date's name, incidence of talking to one another in the interim since the coke date, and desire to date the other person in the future.

A familiar but never totally resolved problem with any experimental findings is the extent to which they may be generalized to the nonlaboratory situation. At least three viewpoints about the problem may be discerned. First, and perhaps most familiar, is instant generalization from the specific and often limited conditions of an experiment to any and all settings which are even remotely related. This tendency is most frequently seen at cocktail parties after the third martini and on television talk shows featuring those who popularize psychology. Second, and almost as familiar, is the notion that the laboratory is a necessary evil. It is seen as an adequate substitute for the real world, only to the extent that it reproduces the world. For example, Aronson and Carlsmith (1968) ask, "Why, then, do we bother with these pallid and contrived imitations of human interaction when there exist rather sophisticated techniques for studying the real thing [p. 4]?" They enumerate the advantages of experiments over field study, but emphasize that good experiments must be realistic in order to involve the subject and have an "impact" on him. Concern with experimental realism often is expressed in the context of positing qualitative differences between the laboratory and the outside world; it is assumed that in moving from simplicity to complexity, new and different principles are emergent. Third, and least familiar in personality and social psychology, is a view which is quite common in other fields. Laboratory research is seen not as a necessary evil but as an essential procedure which enables us to attain isolation and control of variables and thus makes possible the formulation of basic principles in a setting of reduced complexity. If experiments realistically reproduce the nonlaboratory complexities, they provide little advantage over the field study. Continuity is assumed between the laboratory and the outside world, and complexity is seen as quantitative and not qualitative. To move from a simple situation to a complex one requires detailed knowledge about the relevant variables and their interaction. Application and the attainment of a technology depend upon such an approach.

With respect to a specific psychological phenomenon, the problem of nonlaboratory generalization and application may be examined more concretely. The laboratory investigation of interpersonal attraction within a reinforcement paradigm (Byrne, 1969) has followed a strategy in which the effect of a variety of stimulus variables on a single response variable was the primary focus of interest. A model has evolved which treats all relevant stimuli as positive or negative reinforcers of differential magnitude. Attraction toward any stimulus object (including another person) is then found to be a positive linear function of the proportion of weighted positive reinforcements associated with that object. Attitude statements have been the most frequently employed reinforcing stimuli, but other stimulus elements have included personality variables (e.g., Griffitt, 1966), physical attractiveness (e.g., Byrne, London, & Reeves, 1968), economic variables (Byrne, Clore, & Worchel, 1966), race (e.g, Byrne & Ervin, 1969), behavioral preferences (Huffman, 1969), personal evaluations (e.g., Byrne & Rhamey, 1965), room temperature (Griffitt, 1970a), and sexual arousal (Picher, 1966).

Considering just one of those variables, attitude similarity-dissimilarity, why is it not reasonable to propose an immediate and direct parallel between laboratory and nonlaboratory responses? One reason is simple and quite obvious, but it seems often to be overlooked. Laboratory research is based on the isolation of variables so that one or a limited number of independent variables may be manipulated, while, if possible, all other stimulus variables are controlled. In the outside world, multiple uncontrolled stimuli are present. Thus, if all an experimental subject knows about a stranger is that he holds opinions similar to his own on six out of six political issues, the stranger will be liked (Byrne, Bond, & Diamond, 1969). We cannot, however, assume that any two interacting individuals who agree on these six issues will become fast friends because *(a)* they may never get around to discussing those six topics at all, and *(b)* even if these topics are discussed, six positive reinforcements may simply become an insignificant portion of a host of other positive and negative reinforcing elements in the interaction. A second barrier to immediate applicability of a laboratory finding lies in the nature of the response. It is good research strategy to limit the dependent variable (in this instance, the sum of two 7-point rating scales), but nonlaboratory responses may be as varied and uncontrolled as the stimuli. The relationship between that paper-and-pencil measure of attraction and other interpersonal responses is only beginning to be explored (e.g., Byrne, Baskett, & Hodges, 1969; Efran, 1969). The third barrier lies in the nature of the relationship investigated. For a number of quite practical reasons, the laboratory study of attraction is limited in its time span and hence might legitimately be labeled the study of first impressions. Whether the determinants of first impressions are precisely the same as the determinants of a prolonged friendship, of love, or of marital happiness is an empirical question and one requiring a great deal of research.

In view of these barriers to extralaboratory application of experimental findings, how may one begin the engineering enterprise? The present research suggests one attempt to seek a solution. Specifically, a limited dating situation is created in which the barriers to application are minimized. Independent variables identified in the laboratory (attitude similarity, personality similarity, and physical attractiveness) are varied in a real-life situation, and an attempt is made to make the variables salient and to minimize the occurrence of other stimulus events. Even though similarity has been the focus of much of the experimental work on attraction, the findings with respect to physical attractiveness have consistently demonstrated the powerful influence of appearance on responses to those of the opposite sex and even of the same sex. Both field studies (Megargee, 1956; Perrin, 1921; Taylor, 1956; Walster, Aronson, Abrahams, & Rottmann, 1966) and laboratory investigations (Byrne et al., 1968; McWhirter, 1969; Moss, 1969) have shown that those who are physically attractive elicit more positive responses than do those who are unattractive. The laboratory response measure was retained so that a common reference point was available, but additional response variables were also used in order to extend the generality and meaning of the attraction construct. Finally, in this experiment, the interaction was deliberately limited in time so that it remained close to a first-impression relationship. Given these deliberately limited conditions, it was proposed that the positive relationship between the proportion of weighted positive reinforcements and attraction is directly applicable to a nonlaboratory interaction. Specifically, it was hypothesized that in a computer dating situation *(a)* attraction is a joint function of similarity and physical attractiveness, and *(b)* the greater the extent to which the specific elements of similarity are made salient, the greater is the relationship between similarity and attraction.

The variety of ways in which similarity and attraction could be investigated in a field situation raises an interesting question of strategy. It should be kept in mind that there is no magic about the similarity effect. Similarity does not exude from the pores; rather, specific attitudes and other characteristics must be expressed overtly. It would be relatively simple to design a computer dating experiment in which no similarity effects would be found. For example, one could lie about the degree of similarity, and in a brief interaction, the subjects would not be likely to discover the deception. Another alternative would be to provide no information about similarity and then to forbid the subjects to talk during their date. Negative results in such studies would be of no importance as a test since they are beyond the boundary conditions of the theory. Another possible study would give no initial similarity information and then require an extended interaction period, but that has already been done. That is, people in the real world do this every day, and numerous correlational studies indicate that under such conditions, similarity is associated with attraction. The strategy of the present research was frankly to maximize the possibility of securing a precise similarity attraction effect in a real-life setting; in subsequent research, the limiting conditions of the effect may be determined.

METHOD

Attitude-Personality Questionnaire

In order to provide a relatively broad base on which to match couples for the dating process, a 50-item questionnaire was constructed utilizing five variables. In previous research, a significant similarity effect has been found for authoritarianism (Sheffield & Byrne, 1967), repression-sensitization (Byrne & Griffitt, 1969; Byrne, Griffitt, & Stefaniak, 1967), attitudes (Byrne, 1961, 1969), EPPS items,[3] and self-concept (Griffitt, 1966, 1970b). Each variable was represented by 10 items which were chosen to represent the least possible intercorrelations within dimensions; the rationale here was the desire to maximize the number of *independent* scale responses on which matching could be based.

Simulated Stranger Condition

In order to provide a base line for the similarity effect under controlled conditions, a simulated stranger condition was run in which the other person was represented only by his or her purported responses to the attitude-personality questionnaire. The study was described as an investigation of the effectiveness of the matching procedures of computer dating organizations. Subjects were told, "Instead of arranging an actual date, we are providing couples with information about one another and asking for their reactions." The simulated scales were prepared to provide either a .33 or .67 proportion of similar responses between stranger and subject. The subject was asked to read the responses of an opposite-sex stranger and then to make a series of evaluations on an expanded version of the Interpersonal Judgment Scale. This scale consists of ten 7-point scales. The measure of attraction within this experimental paradigm (Byrne, 1969) consists of the sum of two scales: liking and desirability as a work partner. This attraction index ranges from 2 to 14 and has a split-half reliability of .85. In addition, four buffer scales deal with evaluations of the other person's intelligence, knowledge of current events, morality, and adjustment. These variables are found to correlate positively with attraction, but they have somewhat different antecedents and are included in the analysis simply as supplemental information. Three new scales, added for the present study in order to explore various responses to the opposite sex, asked the subject to react to the other person as a potential date, as a marriage partner, and as to sexual attractiveness. Finally, a tenth scale was added in order to assess a stimulus variable, the physical attractiveness of the other person. In addition, the physical attractiveness of each subject was rated by the experimenter on the same 7-point scale on which the subjects rated one another.

Computer Dating Condition

Selection of dating couples.   The attitude-personality questionnaire was administered to a group of 420 introductory psychology students at the University of Texas, and each item was scored in a binary fashion. By means of a specially prepared program, the responses of each male were compared with those of each female; for any given couple, the number of possible matching responses could theoretically range from 0 to 50. The actual range was from 12 to 37. From these distributions of matches, male-female pairs were selected to represent either the greatest or the least number of matching responses. There was a further restriction that the male be as tall as or taller than the female. Of the resulting pairs, a few were eliminated because *(a)* one of the individuals was married, *(b)* the resulting pair was racially mixed, or *(c)* because of a failure to keep the experimental appointment. The remaining 88 subjects formed 24 high-similar pairs, whose proportion of similar responses ranged from .66 to .74, and 20 low-similar pairs, whose proportion of similar responses ranged from .24 to .40.

Levels of information saliency.   The experiment was run with one of the selected couples at a time. In the experimental room, they were introduced to one another and told:

> *In recent years, there has been a considerable amount of interest in the phenomenon of computer dating as a means for college students to meet one another. At the present time, we are attempting to learn as much as possible about the variables which influence the reactions of one individual to another.*

In order to create differential levels of saliency with respect to the matching elements, subjects in the salient condition were told:

> *Earlier this semester, one of the test forms you filled out was very much like those used by some of the computer dating organizations. In order to refresh your memory about this test and the*

> *answers you gave, we are going to ask you to spend a few minutes looking over the questions and your answers to them.*
>
> *The answers of several hundred students were placed on IBM cards and run through the computer to determine the number of matching answers among the 50 questions for all possible pairs of male and female students. According to the computer, the two of you gave the same answers on approximately 67% (33%) of those questions.*

In the nonsalient condition, they were told:

> *Imagine for the purposes of the experiment that you had applied to one of the computer dating organizations and filled out some of their information forms. Then, imagine that the two of you had been notified that, according to the computer, you match on approximately 67% (33%) of the factors considered important.*

All subjects were then told:

> *For our experiment, we would like to create a situation somewhat like that of a computer date. That is, you answered a series of questions, the computer indicated that you two gave the same responses on some of the questions, and now we would like for you to spend a short time together getting acquainted. Specifically, we are asking you to spend the next 30 minutes together on a "coke date" at the Student Union. Here is 50¢ to spend on whatever you would like. We hope that you will learn as much as possible about each other in the next half hour because we will be asking you a number of questions about one another when you return.*

Measures of attraction.   When they returned from the date to receive their final instructions, an unobtrusive measure of attraction was obtained: the physical distance between the two subjects while standing together in front of the experimenter's desk. The distance was noted on a simple ordinal scale ranging from 0 (touching one another) to 5 (standing at opposite corners of the desk). The subjects were then separated and asked to evaluate their date on the Interpersonal Judgment Scale.

Follow-up measures.   At the end of the semester (2-3 months after the date), it was possible to locate 74 of the 88 original subjects who were willing to answer five additional questions. Each was asked to write the name of his or her computer date and to indicate

Table 1 Mean Attraction Responses Toward Similar and Dissimilar Simulated Strangers with Two Different Titles for Experiment

Title of experiments	Proportion of similar responses	
	.33	.67
Evaluational processes	9.47	10.78
Computer dating	10.21	11.33
M	9.84	11.06

Note.—The mean attraction responses were 10.12 and 10.77 for the evaluational processes and computer dating experiments, respectively.

whether or not they had talked to one another since the experiment, dated since the experiment, and whether a date was desired or planned in the future. Finally, each was asked whether the evaluation of the date was influenced more by physical attractiveness or by attitudes.

RESULTS

Simulated Stranger Condition

The mean attraction responses of two simulated stranger conditions[4] which were run separately from the computer dating experiment are shown in Table 1. Analysis of variance indicated that the similarity variable yielded the only significant effect ($F = 4.00$, $df = 1/46$, p = approximately .05).

On the remaining items of the Interpersonal Judgment Scale, the only other significant similarity effect was on the intelligence rating ($F = 7.30$, $df = 1/46$, $p < .01$). Interestingly enough, there were several differences between the differently labeled experiments on the other Interpersonal Judgment Scale items. More positive responses were given in the "computer dating" experiment than in the "evaluational processes" experiment with respect to knowledge of current events ($F = 8.07$, $df = 1/46$, $p < .01$), adjustment ($F = 6.10$, $df = 1/46$, $p < .02$), and desirability as a marriage partner ($F = 6.57$, $df = 1/46$, $p < .02$). The sexual attractiveness item yielded a significant interaction effect ($F = 4.93$, $df = 1/46$, $p < .03$), with the dissimilar stranger rated as more sexually attractive in the computer dating experiment and the similar stranger as more sexually attractive in the evaluational processes experiment. While these latter findings are gratuitous, they suggest the importance of minor variations in the stimulus context and the sensitivity of the Interpersonal Judgment Scale items to such variations.

Predicting Attraction in the Computer Dating Condition

The mean attraction responses for male and female subjects at two levels of information saliency and two levels of response similarity are shown in Table 2. Analysis of variance indicated the only significant effect to be that of proportion of similar responses ($F = 13.67$, $df = 1/40$, $p < .001$). The attempt to make the matching stimuli differentially salient did not affect attraction, and there were no sex differences.

The other variable which was expected to influence attraction was the physical attractiveness of the date. It is interesting to note in the simulated stranger condition that while the manipulation of similarity influenced attraction, it had no effect on guesses as to the other person's physical attractiveness ($F < 1$). Thus, data in the computer dating condition indicating a relationship between attractiveness and attraction would seem to result from the effect of the former on the latter. Two measures of attractiveness were available: ratings by the experimenter when the subjects first arrived and by each subject of his or her own date following their interaction. The correlation between these two measures was significant; the correlation between the experimenter's ratings of male subjects and the females' ratings of their dates was .59 ($p < .01$) and between the experimenter's ratings of female subjects and the males' ratings of their dates was .39 ($p < .01$). As might be expected, the subject's own ratings proved to be better predictors than did the experimenter's ratings. In Table 3 are shown those correlations between physical attractiveness ratings and Interpersonal Judgment Scale responses which were consistent across sexes.

Table 2 Mean Attraction Responses of Males and Females with Similar and Dissimilar Dates at Two Levels of Saliency Concerning Matching Information

Level	Proportion of similar responses	
	Low	High
Male *Ss*		
Information		
Salient	10.00	11.91
Nonsalient	10.56	11.38
Female *Ss*		
Information		
Salient	10.73	11.82
Nonsalient	10.33	12.15

Table 3 Correlations Between Ratings of Physical Attractiveness of Date and Evaluations of Date

| Variable | Attractiveness of date Rated by *S*s | | Attractiveness of date Rated by *E* | |
	Male *S*s	Female *S*s	Male *S*s	Female *S*s
Attraction	.39**	.60**	.07	.32*
Dating	.66**	.57**	.21	.33*
Marriage	.56**	.55**	.18	.34*
Sex	.77**	.70**	.53**	.44**

* *p* < .05.
** *p* < .01.

Thus, the first hypothesis was clearly confirmed, but there was no support for the second hypothesis.

With respect to the prediction of attraction, it seems likely that a combination of the similarity and attractiveness variables would provide the optimal information. In Table 4 are shown the mean attraction responses toward attractive (ratings of 5-7) and unattractive (ratings of 1-4) dates at two levels of response similarity. For both sexes, each of the two independent variables was found to affect attraction.[5] The physical attractiveness variable was significant for both males ($F = 3.85$, $df = 1/39$, $p < .05$) and for females ($F = 10.44$, $df = 1/40$, $p < .01$). The most positive response in each instance was toward similar attractive dates, and the least positive response was toward dissimilar unattractive dates. An additional analysis indicated no relationship between an individual's own physical attractiveness (as rated by the date) and response to the other person's physical attractiveness.

Other Effects of Similarity and Attractiveness

On the additional items of the Interpersonal Judgment Scale, similarity was found to have a significant positive effect on ratings of the date's intelligence ($F = 4.37$, $df = 1/40$, $p < .05$), desirability as a date ($F = 8.92$, $df = 1/40$, $p < .01$), and desirability as a marriage partner ($F = 4.76$, $df = 1/40$, $p < .05$).

The simplest and least obtrusive measure of attraction was the proximity of the two individuals after the date, while receiving their final instructions from the experimenter. If physical distance can be considered as an alternative index of attraction, these two dependent variables should be correlated. For females, the correlation was $-.36$ ($p < .01$) and for males, $-.48$, ($p < .01$); in each instance the greater the liking for the

partner, the closer together they stood. Another way of evaluating the proximity variable is to determine whether it is influenced by the same independent variables as is the paper-and-pencil measure. For both sexes, physical separation was found to correlate $-.49$ ($p < .01$) with similarity. Thus, the more similar the couples, the closer they stood. Because similarity and proximity are necessarily identical for each member of a pair, it is not possible to determine whether the males, the females, or both are responsible for the similarity-proximity relationship. When the physical attractiveness measure was examined, however, there was indirect evidence that proximity in this situation was controlled more by the males than by the females. For females, there was no relationship between ratings of the male's appearance and physical separation ($r = -.06$). For males, the correlation was $-.34$ ($p < .05$).

In the follow-up investigation at the end of the semester, 74 of the 88 original subjects were available and willing to participate. For this analysis, each subject was placed in one of three categories with respect to the two stimulus variables of similarity and attractiveness. On the basis of the same divisions as were used in the analysis in Table 4, subjects were either in a high-similarity condition with a physically attractive date, a low-similarity condition with a physically unattractive date, or in a mixed condition of high-low or low-high. To maximize the possible effect, frequency analysis was used in comparing the two homogeneous groups ($N = 40$).[6] In response to the question about the date's name, the more positive the stimulus conditions at the time of the date, the more likely was the subject to remember correctly the date's name ($\chi^2 = 8.47$, $df = 1$, $p < .01$). With respect to talking to the other individual during the period since the experiment, the relationship was again significant ($\chi^2 = 4.95$, $df = 1$, $p < .05$). The same effect was found with regard to whether the individual would like or not

Table 4 Mean Attraction Responses of Males and Females with Similar and Dissimilar Dates Who Are Relatively Attractive and Unattractive

| Physical attractiveness of date | Proportion of similar responses | |
	Low	High
Male *S*s		
Attractive	10.55	12.00
Unattractive	9.89	10.43
Female *S*s		
Attractive	11.25	12.71
Unattractive	9.50	11.00

like to date the other person in the future ($\chi^2 = 5.38$, *df* = 1, *p* < .05). The only follow-up question which failed to show a significant effect for the experimental manipulation was that dealing with actual dating; even here, it might be noted that the only dates reported were by subjects in the high-similarity, high-attractiveness condition.

The only other question in the follow-up survey represented an attempt to find out whether the subjects could accurately verbalize the stimuli to which they had been found to respond. Of the 74 respondents, about one-third indicated that both attitudes and physical attractiveness determined their response to the partner, while about one-sixth of the subjects felt they had responded to neither variable. With the remaining half of the sample, an interesting sex difference emerged. Physical attractiveness was identified as the most important stimulus by 14 of the 18 males, while attitudes were seen as the most important stimulus by 16 of the 19 females ($\chi^2 = 14.30$, *df* = 1, *p* < .001). The present subjects seemed to have accepted Bertrand Russell's observation that "On the whole, women tend to love men for their character, while men tend to love women for their appearance." In contrast to these verbal sentiments, it might be noted that the date's physical attractiveness correlated .60 with attraction responses of female subjects and only .39 among male subjects. A further analysis compared the similarity-attraction effect and the attractiveness-attraction effect for those subjects who indicated one or the other stimulus variable as the more important. The similarity-attraction effect did not differ between the two groups ($z < 1$). It has been reported previously that awareness of similarity is not a necessary component of the similarity effect (Byrne & Griffitt, 1969). There was, however, a difference in the attractiveness effect. For the subjects identifying attractiveness as the major determinant, physical attractiveness correlated .63 (*p* < .01) with attraction responses; for the subjects identifying similarity as the major determinant, attractiveness correlated –.04 *(ns)* with attraction. The difference was a significant one (*z* = 2.16, *p* < .05).

CONCLUSIONS

Perhaps the most important aspect of the present findings is the evidence indicating the continuity between the laboratory study of attraction and its manifestation under field conditions. At least as operationalized in the present investigation, variables such as physical attractiveness and similarity of attitudes and personality characteristics are found to influence attraction in a highly predictable manner.

The findings with respect to the physical distance measure are important in two respects. First, they provide further evidence that voluntary proximity is a useful and unobtrusive measure of interpersonal attraction. Second, the construct validity and generality of the paper-and-pencil measure of attraction provided by the Interpersonal Judgment Scale is greatly enhanced. The significant relationship between two such different response measures is comforting to users of either one. In addition, the follow-up procedure provided evidence of the lasting effect of the experimental manipulations and of the relation of the attraction measures to such diverse responses as remembering the other person's name and engaging in conversation in the weeks after the termination of the experiment.

The failure to confirm the second hypothesis is somewhat puzzling. It is possible that present procedures, designed to vary the saliency of the elements of similarity, were inadequate and ineffective, that the actual behavioral cues to similarity and dissimilarity were sufficiently powerful to negate the effects of the experimental manipulation, or that the hypothesis was simply incorrect. There is no basis within the present experiment on which to decide among these alternatives.

In conclusion, it must be emphasized that striking continuity has been demonstrated across experiments using paper-and-pencil materials to simulate a stranger and to measure attraction (Byrne, 1961), more realistic audio and audiovisual presentations of the stimulus person (Byrne & Clore, 1966), elaborate dramatic confrontations in which a confederate portrays the stimulus person (Byrne & Griffitt, 1966), and a quasi-realistic experiment such as the present one, in which two genuine strangers interact and in which response measures include nonverbal behaviors. Such findings suggest that attempts to move back and forth between the controlled artificiality of the laboratory and the uncontrolled natural setting are both feasible and indicative of the potential applications of basic attraction research to a variety of interpersonal problems.

Footnotes

[1]This research was supported in part by Research Grant MH-11178-04 from the National Institute of Mental Health and in part by Research Grant GS-2752 from the National Science Foundation. The authors wish to thank James

Hilgren, Royal Masset, and Herman Mitchell for their help in conducting this experiment.

[2] Requests for reprints should be sent to Donn Byrne, Department of Psychology, Purdue University, Lafayette, Indiana 47907.

[3] Unpublished data collected by Donn Byrne and John Lamberth.

[4] Originally, the plan was to run the simulated stranger groups just after the computer dating groups. An unexpected finding was that almost all of the responses were positive and that the subjects were attired more attractively than is usual among undergraduates reporting for experimental sessions. From anecdotal olfactory evidence, even the perfume and shaving lotion level was noticeably elevated. In retrospect, it seemed clear that because the computer dating study was widely discussed and because this experiment was so labeled, the overwhelming majority of the 34 subjects were expecting to go on a date as part of their task. It then became necessary to rerun the simulated stranger groups at the end of the semester when the expectations of dates had diminished. The two levels of similarity were run under two different experimental titles, "Computer Dating" and "Evaluational Processes." The data reported in this paper are from these latter two experiments.

[5] The use of the term "independent variable" for physical attractiveness may be a source of confusion. In this experiment, there was obviously no manipulation of physical appearance, but attractiveness was conceptualized as one of the stimuli determining attraction. In other experiments, attractiveness has been successfully manipulated as an independent variable (e.g., Byrne et al., 1968; McWhirter, 1969; Moss, 1969). In the absence of any evidence that attraction determines perception of physical attractiveness (and some evidence to the contrary), it seems reasonable to consider attractiveness as an antecedent variable in studies such as the present one and that of Walster et al. (1966).

[6] When the 33 individuals who were heterogeneous with respect to similarity and attractiveness were included in the analysis, they fell midway between the similar-attractive and dissimilar-unattractive groups on each item. The probability levels were consequently reduced to the .02 level on remembering the date's name and to the .10 level on the talking and desire to date items.

References

Aronson, E., & Carlsmith, J. M. Experimentation in social psychology. In G. Lindzey & E. Aronson (Eds.), *The handbook of social psychology.* Vol. 2. (2nd ed.) Reading, Mass.: Addison-Wesley, 1968.

Byrne, D. Interpersonal attraction and attitude similarity. *Journal of Abnormal and Social Psychology,* 1961, *62,* 713-715.

Byrne, D. Attitudes and attraction. In L. Berkowitz (Ed.), *Advances in experimental social psychology.* Vol. 4. New York: Academic Press, 1969.

Byrne, D., Baskett, G. D., & Hodges, L. Behavioral indicators of interpersonal attraction. Paper presented at meeting of the Psychonomic Society, St.Louis, November 1969.

Byrne, D., Bond, M. H., & Diamond, M. J. Response to political candidates as a function of attitude similarity-dissimilarity. *Human Relations,* 1969, *22,* 251-262.

Byrne, D., & Clore, G. L., Jr. Predicting interpersonal attraction toward strangers presented in three different stimulus modes. *Psychonomic Science,* 1966, *4,* 239-240.

Byrne, D., Clore, G. L., Jr., & Worchel, P. Effect of economic similarity-dissimilarity on interpersonal attraction. *Journal of Personality and Social Psychology,* 1966, *4,* 220-224.

Byrne, D., & Ervin, C. R. Attraction toward a Negro stranger as a function of prejudice, attitude similarity, and the stranger's evaluation of the subject. *Human Relations,* 1969, *22,* 397-404.

Byrne, D., & Griffitt, W. Similarity versus liking: A clarification. *Psychonomic Science,* 1966, *6,* 295-296.

Byrne, D., & Griffitt, W. Similarity and awareness of similarity of personality characteristics as determinants of attraction. *Journal of Experimental Research in Personality,* 1969, *3,* 179-186.

Byrne, D., Griffitt, W., & Stefaniak, D. Attraction and similarity of personality characteristics. *Journal of Personality and Social Psychology,* 1967, *5,* 82-90.

Byrne, D., London, O., & Reeves, K. The effects of physical attractiveness, sex, and attitude similarity on interpersonal attraction. *Journal of Personality,* 1968, *36,* 259-271.

Byrne, D., & Rhamey, R. Magnitude of positive and negative reinforcements as a determinant of attraction. *Journal of Personality and Social Psychology,* 1965, *2,* 884-889.

Efran, M. G. Visual interaction and interpersonal attraction. Unpublished doctoral dissertation, University of Texas, 1969.

Griffitt, W. B. Interpersonal attraction as a function of self-concept and personality similarity-dissimilarity. *Journal of Personality and Social Psychology,* 1966, *4,* 581-584.

Griffitt, W. B. Environmental effects of interpersonal affective behavior: Ambient effective temperature and attraction. *Journal of Personality and Social Psychology,* 1970, *15,* 240-244. (a)

Griffitt, W. B. Personality similarity and self-concept as determinants of interpersonal attraction. *Journal of Social Psychology,* 1970, in press. (b)

Huffman, D. M. Interpersonal attraction as a function of behavioral similarity. Unpublished doctoral dissertation, University of Texas, 1969.

McWhirter, R. M., Jr. Interpersonal attraction in a dyad as a function of the physical attractiveness of its members. Unpublished doctoral dissertation, Texas Tech University, 1969.

Megargee, E. I. A study of the subjective aspects of group membership at Amherst. Unpublished manuscript, Amherst College, 1956.

Moss, M. K. Social desirability, physical attractiveness, and social choice. Unpublished doctoral dissertation, Kansas State University, 1969.

Perrin, F. A. C. Physical attractiveness and repulsiveness. *Journal of Experimental Psychology,* 1921, *4,* 203-217.

Picher, O. L. Attraction toward Negroes as a function of prejudice, emotional arousal, and the sex of the Negro. Unpublished doctoral dissertation, University of Texas, 1966.

Sheffield, J., & Byrne, D. Attitude similarity-dissimilarity, authoritarianism, and interpersonal attraction. *Journal of Social Psychology,* 1967, *71,* 117-123.

Taylor, M. J. Some objective criteria of social class membership. Unpublished manuscript, Amherst College, 1956.

Walster, E., Aronson, V., Abrahams, D., & Rottmann, L. Importance of physical attractiveness in dating behavior. *Journal of Personality and Social Psychology,* 1966, *4,* 508-516.

Helping Behavior

Models and Helping: Naturalistic Studies in Aiding Behavior[1]

James H. Bryan   *Northwestern University*
Mary Ann Test

Abstract

Four experiments concerned with helping behavior were conducted. Three were addressed to the effects of altruistic models upon helping, while one was concerned with the impact of the solicitor's race upon donations. Three investigations employed as a site parking lots of two large department stores in New Jersey, and indexed helping by contributions to the Salvation Army. A fourth experiment indexed helping by offers of aid by passing motorists to a woman with a disabled vehicle. Whether one employed motorists in California or shoppers in New Jersey, the results were quite consistent. The presence of a helping model significantly increased helping behavior. As race of the Salvation Army solicitor did affect the percentage of donors willing to contribute money, it was concluded that interpersonal attraction is a relevant variable affecting donations.

"Models and Helping: Naturalistic Studies in Aiding Behavior" by James H. Bryan and Mary Ann Test. *Journal of Personality and Social Psychology,* 1967, Vol. 6, No. 4, pp. 400-407. Copyright © 1967 by The American Psychological Association, Inc. Reprinted by permission.

Recently, concern has been evidenced regarding the determinants and correlates of altruistic behavior, those acts wherein individuals share or sacrifice a presumed positive reinforcer for no apparent social or material gain. Studies addressed to these behaviors have explored both individual differences in the tendency to be altruistic and the situational determinants of such responses. Gore and Rotter (1963) found that students at a southern Negro college were more likely to volunteer for a social protest movement if they perceived sources of reinforcement as internally rather than externally guided. Subjects high on internal control were more likely to volunteer as freedom riders, marchers, or petition signers than subjects who perceived others as primary agents of reinforcement. Experimental evidence has been generated supporting the often-made assumption that guilt may serve as a stimulus to altruistic activity. Darlington and Macker (1966) found that subjects led to believe that they had harmed another through incompetent performances on the experimental tasks (three paper-and-pencil tests) were more willing than control subjects to donate blood to a local hospital. Aronfreed and Paskal[2] and Midlarsky and Bryan (1967) found that children exposed to treatment conditions designed to produce empathy were more willing to donate M&M candies than subjects given control conditions, while Handlon and Gross (1959), Ugurel-Semin (1952), Wright (1942), and Midlarsky and Bryan have found sharing to be positively correlated with age among school-age children. Lastly, Berkowitz and Friedman (1967) have demonstrated that adolescents of the working class and the bureaucratic middle class are less affected in their helping behaviors by inter-personal attraction than adolescents of the entrepreneur middle class.

Three hypotheses have emerged regarding the situational determinants of self-sacrificing behaviors. One suggests that individuals behave in an altruistic fashion because of compliance to a norm of reciprocity. That is, individuals are aware of the social debts and credits established between them, and expect that ultimately the mutual exchange of goods and services will balance (Gouldner, 1960). Berkowitz and Daniels (1964) have suggested that individuals might show a generalization of such obligatory feelings and thus aid others who had not previously assisted them.

A second hypothesis was put forth by Berkowitz and his colleagues (Berkowitz, 1966; Berkowitz & Daniels, 1963; Berkowitz, Klanderman, & Harris, 1964; Daniels & Berkowitz, 1963) who have postulated the social responsibility norm. They have contended that dependency on others evokes helping responses even under conditions where the possibility of external rewards for the helper are remote. Using supervisor's ratings of an unknown and absent other to produce dependency, and a box-construction task as the dependent variable, considerable support has been generated for the suggestion that dependency increases helping.

A third major determinant of helping may be the presence of helping (or nonhelping) models. While attention to the effects of models has generally been directed toward antisocial behaviors (cf. Bandura & Walters, 1963; Freed, Chandler, Mouton, & Blake, 1955; Lefkowitz, Blake, & Mouton, 1955), some recent evidence suggests that observation of self-sacrificing models may lead to subsequent succorant behavior by children. For example, Rosenhan and White (1967) have demonstrated that children are more likely to donate highly valued gift certificates to residents of a fictitious orphanage if they have seen an adult do so. Hartup and Coates[3] found that nursery school children who have been exposed to a self-sacrificing peer were more likely to be altruistic than children not so exposed. Test and Bryan[4] found that female college students were more likely to render aid to another in computing arithmetic problems if they saw other people so doing.

The present series of experiments was designed to test the effects of models in natural settings on subject samples other than college or high school students, and in contexts other than a school room or university setting. The first three experiments reported are concerned with the impact of observing helping models upon subsequent helping behaviors, while the fourth is addressed to the influence of interpersonal attraction upon donation behavior.

EXPERIMENT I: LADY IN DISTRESS: A FLAT TIRE STUDY

Few studies have been concerned with the effects of models upon *adults,* and fewer still with the impact of *prosocial* models upon them (Wheeler, 1966). Those that have been concerned with such behaviors have invariably employed college students as subjects. For example, Rosenbaum and Blake (1955) and Rosenbaum (1956) have found that college students exposed to a model who volunteered, upon the personal request of the experimenter, to participate in an experiment would be more likely to consent than subjects not exposed to such a model or than subjects who observed a model refuse to cooperate. Pressures toward conformity in these experiments were great, however, as the request was made directly by the experimenter and in the presence of a large number of other students.

Test and Bryan found that the observation of helping models significantly increased the subsequent offers of aid by observers. However, in that study, subjects were given the task of solving arithmetic problems and then rating their difficulty, a task ordinarily requiring autonomous efforts. Furthermore, the experiment was conducted within a university setting, a context where independence of thought is often stressed. The effects of the model may have been simply to increase the subjects' faith that assisting others was allowed. While questionnaire data of the study did not support this interpretation, such effects could not be ruled out entirely. Thus, it is possible that the model impact was simply a propriety-defining activity which reduced the inhibitions associated with such helping behavior.

In general, then, investigations of modeling that employ adults as subjects and that demand self-sacrifice on the part of subjects are limited in number, exploit strong pressures toward conformity, and rely upon college students as subjects. The present experiment was designed to assess the impact of models upon subsequent spontaneous offers of help in other than a university setting.

Method

The standard condition consisted of an undergraduate female stationed by a 1964 Ford Mustang (control car) with a flat left-rear tire. An inflated tire was leaned upon the left side of the auto. The girl, the flat tire, and the inflated tire were conspicuous to the passing traffic.

In the model condition, a 1965 Oldsmobile was located approximately ¼ mile from the control car. The car was raised by jack under the left rear bumper, and a girl was watching a male changing the flat tire.

In the no-model condition, the model was absent; thus, only the control car was visible to the passing traffic.

The cars were located in a predominantly residential section in Los Angeles, California. They were placed in such a manner that no intersection separated the model from the control car. No turnoffs were thus available to the passing traffic. Further, opposite flows of traffic were divided by a separator such that the first U-turn available to the traffic going in the opposite direction of the control car would be after exposure to the model condition.

The experiment was conducted on two successive Saturdays between the hours of 1:45 and 5:50 P.M. Each treatment condition lasted for the time required for 1000 vehicles to pass the control car. While private automobiles and trucks, motorscooters, and motorcycles were tallied as vehicles, commercial trucks, taxis, and buses were not. Vehicle count was made by a fourth member of the experiment who stood approximately 100 feet from the control car hidden from the passing motorists. On the first Saturday, the model condition was run first and lasted from 1:45 to 3:15 P.M. In order to exploit changing traffic patterns and to keep the time intervals equal across treatment conditions, the control car was moved several blocks and placed on the opposite side of the street for the no-model condition. The time of the no-model treatment was 4:00 to 5:00 P.M. On the following Saturday, counterbalancing the order and the location of treatment conditions was accomplished. That is, the no-model condition was run initially and the control car was placed in the same location that it had been placed on the previous Saturday during the model condition. The time of the no-model condition was 2:00 to 3:30 P.M. For the model condition, the control car was placed in that locale where it had been previously during the no-model condition. The time of the model condition was 4:30 to 5:30 P.M.

Individuals who had stopped to offer help were told by the young lady that she had already phoned an auto club and that help was imminent. Those who nonetheless insisted on helping her were told the nature of the experiment.

Results

The dependent variable was the number of cars that stopped and from which at least one individual offered help to the stooge by the control car. Of the 4000 passing vehicles, 93 stopped. With the model car absent, 35 vehicles stopped; with the model present, 58 halted. The difference between the conditions was statistically significant ($\chi^2 = 5.53$, corrected for continuity, $df = 1$, $p < .02$, two-tailed). Virtually all offers of aid were from men rather than women drivers.

The time of day had little impact upon the offering of aid. Fifty vehicles stopped during the early part of the afternoon; 43 during the later hours. Likewise, differences in help offers were not great between successive Saturdays, as 45 offers of aid were made on the first Saturday, 48 on the second Saturday.

The results of the present study support the hypothesis that helping behaviors can be significantly increased through the observation of others' helpfulness. However, other plausible hypotheses exist which may account for the findings. It is possible to account for the differences in treatment effects by differences in sympathy arousal. That is, in the model condition, the motorist observed a woman who had had some difficulty. Such observations may have elicited sympathy and may have served as a reminder to the driver of his own social responsibilities.

Another explanation of the findings revolves around traffic slowdown. It is possible that the imposition of the model condition served to reduce traffic speed, thus making subsequent stopping to help a less hazardous undertaking. While the time taken for 1000 autos to pass the control car was virtually identical in the model and no-model condition and thus not supportive of such an explanation, the "slowdown" hypothesis cannot be eliminated. Assuming the model effect to be real, one might still argue that it was not a norm of helping that was facilitated by the model, but rather that inhibitions against picking up helpless young ladies were reduced. That is, within the model condition, the passing motorists may have observed a tempted other and thus felt less constrained themselves regarding similar efforts. Indeed, the insistence of some people to help in spite of the imminent arrival of other aiders suggested the operation of motives other than simply helping. Indeed, while the authors did not index the frequency of pick-up attempts, it was clear that a rather large number were evidenced.

Because of the number of alternative explanations, the evidence supporting the hypothesis that the observation of helpers per se will increase subsequent aiding is weak. Experiment II was designed to test further the prediction that the perception of another's altruistic activity would elicit similar behavior on the part of the observer.

EXPERIMENT II: COINS IN THE KETTLE

The investigation was conducted on December 14th between the hours of 10:00 A.M. and 5:00 P.M. The subjects were shoppers at a large department store in Princeton, New Jersey. Observations made on the previous day indicated that the shoppers were overwhelmingly Caucasian females.

A Salvation Army kettle was placed on the sidewalk in front of the main entrance to the store. Two females, both in experimenter's employ, alternatively manned the kettle for periods of 25 minutes. One solicitor was a Negro, the other a Caucasian. Each wore a Salvation Army cape and hat. Although allowed to ring the Salvation Army bell, they were not permitted to make any verbal plea or to maintain eye contact with the passing shoppers, except to thank any contributor for his donation.

The model condition (M) was produced as follows: Once every minute on the minute, a male dressed as a white-collar worker would approach the kettle from within the store and contribute 5 cents. As the model donated, he started a stopwatch and walked from the kettle toward a parking lot as if searching for someone. He then returned to the store. The following 20-second period constituted the duration of the treatment condition.

Following a subsequent lapse of 20 seconds, the next 20-second period defined the no-model condition (NM). Within any one minute, therefore, both M and NM treatments occurred. There were 365 occasions of each treatment.

It should be noted that it was possible that some subjects in the NM condition observed the contribu-

tion of the model or a donor affected by the model. If that hypothesis is correct, however, the effects of such incidents would be to reduce rather than enhance the differences between treatments.

Results

The dependent variable was the number of people who independently donated to the Salvation Army. People obviously acquainted, as for example, man and wife, were construed as one potential donating unit. In such conditions, if both members of a couple contributed, they were counted as a single donor.

Since there were no differences in model effects for the Negro or Caucasian solicitor, data obtained from each were combined. The total number of contributors under the NM condition was 43; under the M condition, 69. Assuming that the chance distribution of donations would be equal across the two conditions, a chi-square analysis was performed. The chi-square equaled 6.01 ($p < .01$).[5]

In spite of precautions concerning the elimination of correlated observations within a treatment condition, it was possible for subjects in any one observational period to influence one another. Such influence may have been mediated through acquaintances not eliminated by our procedures or the observations of others as well as the model donating. A more conservative analysis of the data, insuring independent observation, was therefore made. Instead of comparing treatments by analyzing the number of donors, the analysis used, as the dependent variable, the number of observation periods in which there was a contribution, that is, those periods in which more than one donation occurred were scored identically to those in which only a single contribution was received. Occasions of donations equaled 60 in the M treatment, 43 in the NM condition. The chi-square equaled 2.89 ($p < .05$).

The results of Experiment II further support the hypothesis that observation of altruistic activity will increase such behavior among observers. But the matter is not yet entirely clear, for when the observer saw the model donate he saw two things; first, the actual donation, and second, the polite and potentially reinforcing interaction that occurred between the donor and solicitor. Conceivably, the observation of an altruistic model, per se, who was not socially reinforced for his behavior, would have little or no effect on an observer. The third experiment was designed to examine this possibility.

EXPERIMENT III: COINS IN THE KETTLE II

The experiment was conducted at a Trenton, New Jersey, shopping center from the hours of 10:00 A.M. to 5:00 P.M. Again, the majority of the patrons were Caucasian females. It is likely, however, that these shoppers were of a lower socioeconomic status than those in the Princeton group.

Salvation Army kettles were placed before the main entrance of a large department store (Kettle 1) and a large food center (Kettle 2). The kettles were separated by more than 200 yards. During the first 120 observations (10:00 A.M. to 12:00 P.M.), two male college students, employed by the Salvation Army and wearing its uniform, manned the kettles. The site of the experiment was Kettle 1, except on those occasions where the worker took his "coffee break." At those times, data collection was centered at Kettle 2. An equal number of M and NM conditions were run at each site, although approximately two-thirds of the observational time was spent at Kettle 1. During the remaining 240 observational periods (1:00 P.M. to 5:00 P.M.) the same male worker and his spouse alternately manned Kettle 1. The wife was stationed by the kettle for 136 minutes, the male for 104 minutes. The experiment was conducted only at Kettle 1 during the afternoon period.

Solicitors were told to make no verbal appeals for donations or responses to the model upon his contribution. While they were not informed of the hypothesis underlying the experiment, they may well have deduced it. The model was the same as in Experiment II, and again was dressed as a white-collar worker.

The imposition of the treatment conditions were identical to those described in Experiment I with the following exceptions. Since the kettle was more visible at this site than at the previous one, 30-second rather than 20-second periods were used for each treatment. To simplify the procedures, no waiting periods between treatments occurred. Additionally, after donating, the model would return to the parking lot. There were a total of 360 occasions of each of the M and NM conditions.

Results

The criteria defining a donor were identical to those outlined in Experiment I. Under the M condition, 84 donors were tallied; under the NM treatment, 56. The chi-square value was 4.86 ($p < .025$).

Since it was possible that one donor might have seen a donor other than the model receive social approval from the solicitor, the more conservative comparison of the treatments as outlined in Experiment II was made. That is, treatments were compared by noting the number of observational periods in which any donation occurred. Therefore, those donors who may have been influenced by a contributor receiving the solicitor's thanks were excluded. Of the 360 observational periods under the M condition, there were 75 in which some donation was made. Of the 360 periods, 51 were marked by contributions. Chi-square yielded a value of 5.09 ($p < .025$).

EXPERIMENT IV: ETHNOCENTRISM AND DONATION BEHAVIOR

While Experiment III was conducted to eliminate the solicitor's explicit social approval as a mechanism underlying donation behavior, it is possible that the model's impact was due to the information communicated to the observer regarding the consequence of donations. Work by Bandura, Ross, and Ross (1963), for example, found that children observing a model rewarded for aggression would be more aggressive than children who had observed a model being punished for such behavior. Additionally, considerable data have been gathered within the university laboratory suggesting that interpersonal attraction may greatly influence the helping response. Berkowitz and Friedman (1967), Daniels and Berkowitz (1963), and Goranson and Berkowitz (1966) have suggested that positive affect increases the probability of low payoff helping behavior.

The present experiment was designed to assess the impact of the solicitor's race upon the donation behavior of shoppers. It was assumed that a Negro solicitor would be held in less esteem by Caucasian shoppers than a solicitor of their same race, and that such attitudes would affect contributions. While the applicability of the "consequence to the model" hypothesis in accounting for the model's effect was not tested directly, the study assesses the importance of interpersonal attraction in eliciting charitable behavior.

Method

The experiment was conducted on December 2 and 3 between the hours of 10 A.M. and 6 P.M. at the Trenton area site. The subjects were Caucasian shoppers at a large department store.[6] Three thousand seven hundred and three shoppers were observed; 2,154 females and 1,549 males. In order to reduce the possibility of including the same subject in the experiment on more than one occasion, tallies were made only of exiting shoppers.

Two Salvation Army kettles were placed at two store exits, their location being separated by approximately 75 yards. Two female solicitors, a Negro and a Caucasian, manned the kettles. Both were in their early twenties, wore the uniform of the Salvation Army, and were in the employ of the experimenter. Each was instructed to make no verbal appeals for donations and to avoid eye contact with the shoppers. After a period of 25 minutes, the girls rotated kettle assignments, and during the last 10 minutes of the hour were allowed to take a coffee break. Hence, during a single hour, each solicitor manned both kettles. Each solicitor manned each kettle on seven occasions per day. Thus, each solicitor was observed for a total of 28 observational periods; 14 on each day (seven on each kettle) over a period of two days.

Two observers, each assigned to a particular kettle, tallied the number and sex of the exiting shoppers and contributors during each of the 25-minute periods. In addition, records were kept of the amount of money donated within any period, although it was impossible on this measure to separate those donations made by incoming from outgoing customers.

Results

The dependent variable was the percentage of donors contributing to the kettle within an observational period. That is, observational periods were assigned a percentage donor score. Shoppers within an observational period were treated as a single group, with differences between groups on percentage donor score forming the critical comparisons. The total N of the study was then the 56 observational periods, rather than the 3,703 shoppers. Since the mean group size for the Negro solicitor was 70.32 and for the Caucasian 61.93 (standard deviations equal to 53.33 and 42.98, respectively), it was assumed that the percentage score was relatively stable.

The effects of race, kettle location, and day and their interactions were analyzed by analysis of variance.

As can be seen from Table 1, both the main effect of race and of day were significant. As predicted, the Negro solicitor elicited a statistically significant lower percentage of donors than did the Caucasian. For the Negro solicitor, the average percentage donor score

Table 1   Analysis of Variance of Percentage Donor Scores

	df	MS	F
Race (A)	1	38.778	4.84*
Day (B)	1	98.315	12.28**
Kettle (C)	1	.018	
A × B	1	1.511	
A × C	1	11.340	
B × C	1	1.031	
A × B × C	1	3.206	
Error	48	8.009	

* $p < .05$ (2-tailed).
** $p < .01$ (2-tailed).

for observational periods was 2.22 ($SD = 2.36$), while for the Caucasian solicitor the average percentage donor score was 3.89 ($SD = 3.60$). Additionally, Saturday shoppers were by and large less generous than Friday customers. The average percentage donor score of the group was 1.73 ($SD = 1.97$) for the Saturday shopper, and 4.38 for the Friday shopper ($SD = 3.52$).

A second dependent variable was the amount of money donated during each time period. No significant differences were found for race, day, or kettle location.

The present investigation does support, albeit equivocally, the notion that interpersonal attraction may affect donations even when the solicitors are not the eventual recipients of such contributions. While it is possible that race differences simply fail to remind observers of their social responsibilities, it is also feasible that the subjects wanted to avoid interpersonal contact with a minority group member. If this is true, then it is interesting to note that interpersonal attraction may play an important role even in those situations where personal anonymity is high and escape from unpleasant situations easy.

DISCUSSION

The results of the first three experiments clearly replicate those of Test and Bryan and extend the findings over a variety of subject populations, settings, and tasks. The results hold for college students, motorists, and shoppers; in the university laboratory, city streets, and shopping centers; and when helping is indexed by aiding others solve arithmetic problems, changing flat tires, or donating money to the Salvation Army. The findings then are quite consistent: the presence of helping models significantly increases subsequent altruistic behavior.

That generosity breeds generosity is interesting in light of the recent concern with helping behaviors in emergency contexts. Darley and Latané[7] and Latané and Darley[8] have found that subjects are less inclined to act quickly in emergency situations when in the presence of other potential helpers. Whether faced with a medical emergency (a simulated epileptic seizure) or a dangerous natural event (simulated fire), the rapidity with which students sought to aid was reduced by the presence of others. These findings have been interpreted in three ways: as reflecting the subjects' willingness to diffuse responsibility (others will aid); as reflecting their diffusion of blame (others didn't aid either); or as reflecting conformity to the nonpanicked stooges. It is clear that the results of the first three experiments in the present series do not follow that which might be predicted by the diffusion concepts. A giving model apparently does not lend credibility to the belief that others than the self will make the necessary sacrifices. The helping other did not strengthen the observer's willingness to diffuse his social obligations, but rather stimulated greater social responsibility. In light of these results, the delayed action exhibited by the subjects tested by Darley and Latané might be best attributable to conformity behavior. As they have suggested, subjects faced with a unique and stressful situation may have been either reassured by the presence of calm others or fearful of acting stupidly or cowardly. Additionally, it is possible that diffusion of responsibility is only associated with anxiety-inducing situations. The current data fail to indicate that such diffusion occurs in nonstressful situations which demand fulfillment of social obligations.

While it appears clear that the behavior of the motorists and shoppers was not dictated by a variety of situational and social pressures usually associated with the study of modeling in adults or experiment in academic settings (Orne, 1962), the mechanisms underlying the effects are not obvious. While the presence of the model in the flat-tire study may have reminded the motorists as to the social responsibility norm, a hypothesis does not appear reasonable in accounting for the results in the coins-in-the-kettle series. The bell-ringing Salvation Army worker, with kettle and self placed squarely in the pathway of the oncoming pedestrian, would seem to be reminder enough of one's obligation toward charity. A priori, it would not appear necessary to superimpose upon that scene the donating other for purposes of cognitive cueing (Wheeler, 1966).

One hypothesis to account for the model effect is that the observer is given more information regarding the consequences of such donation behavior. Experiment IV suggested that solicitor status or personal attraction might operate on donation behaviors even under conditions of personal anonymity and few social constraints. It is possible that the model serves to communicate to the potential donor relevant information concerning the consequences of his act. That is, the model may demonstrate that an approach to the solicitor does not involve an unwanted interpersonal interaction (e.g., lectures on religion).

A second hypothesis to account for the data pertains to the shame-provoking capacities of the model. It is reasonable to assume that most people feel that they are, by and large, benevolent and charitable. Furthermore, it is likely that such a self-image is rarely challenged: first because charitable acts are not frequently required; second, at least in the street scenes employed in the current series of studies, solicitations are made in the context of many nongiving others. That is, a multitude of negative models—of noncharitable others—surround the solicitations in the current series of studies. Indeed, the contexts are such that most people are not helping; many more cars pass than stop to offer aid to the lady in distress; and there are many more people who refuse to put coins in the kettle than those who do. However, the witnessing of a donor, an individual who not only recognizes his social responsibility but in fact acts upon it, may produce a greater challenge to the good-self image of the observer. Acts rather than thoughts may be required of the observer in order to maintain the self-image of benevolence and charity. If such is the case, then the model characteristics most effective in producing prosocial behavior by socialized adults would be those directed toward shame or guilt production (e.g., donations from the poor), rather than those reflecting potential reinforcement power (e.g., donations from the high status).

Whatever the mechanism underlying the model effect, it does appear quite clear that prosocial behavior can be elicited through the observation of benign others.

Footnotes

[1]While Mary Ann Test collaborated with the senior author on Experiment I, the remaining work is the latter's sole responsibility.

Thanks are due to Cheryl Dellhoussay, Betty Umann, Joe McNair, and Frank Siri who served as the experimenters and stooges for Experiment I, and to Edward Nystrom, Alice Anderson, Katherine Moore, and Irene Paramoure who served as the models, observers, and solicitors in studies II, III, and IV. Studies II, III, and IV were carried out while the author was affiliated with Educational Testing Service and were supported by the National Institute of Child Health and Human Development, under Research Grant 1 PO1 HD1762-01. The authors are especially grateful to the Salvation Army of Trenton, New Jersey, and specifically to George H. Gibb, whose cooperation made these experiments possible. Thanks are also due to Perry London, David Rosenhan, Ladd Wheeler, Lawrence Stricker, and Bruce K. Eckland for the many helpful comments upon various portions of the manuscript.

[2] J. Aronfreed & V. Paskal. Altruism, empathy and the conditioning of positive affect. Unpublished manuscript, 1965.

[3] W. W. Hartup & B. Coates. Imitation of peers as a function of reinforcement from the peer group and reward-ingness of the model. Unpublished manuscript, 1966.

[4] M. A. Test & J. H. Bryan. Dependency, models and reciprocity. Unpublished manuscript, 1966.

[5] All chi-square analyses were corrected for continuity and all tests of significance were one-tailed.

[6] As there were very few Negro donors ($N = 7$), analysis was confined to the behavior of Caucasian shoppers.

[7] J. Darley & B. Latané. Diffusion of responsibility in emergency situations. Unpublished manuscript, 1966.

[8] B. Latané & J. Darley. Group inhibition of bystander intervention in emergencies. Unpublished manuscript, 1966.

References

Bandura, A., Ross, D., & Ross, S. Vicarious reinforcement and imitative learning. *Journal of Abnormal and Social Psychology*, 1963, *66*, 601-607.

Bandura, A., & Walters, R. H. *Social learning and personality development.* New York: Holt, Rinehart & Winston, 1963.

Berkowitz, L. A laboratory investigation of social class and national differences in helping behavior. *International Journal of Psychology*, 1966, *1*, 231-240.

Berkowitz, L., & Daniels, L. Responsibility and dependency. *Journal of Abnormal and Social Psychology*, 1963, *66*, 429-436.

Berkowitz, L., & Daniels, L. Affecting the salience of the social responsibility norm: Effects of past help on the response to dependency relationships. *Journal of Abnormal and Social Psychology*, 1964, *68*, 275-281.

Berkowitz, L., & Friedman, P. Some social class differences in helping behavior. *Journal of Personality and Social Psychology*, 1967, *5*, 217-225.

Berkowitz, L., Klanderman, S. B., & Harris, R. Effects of experimenter awareness and sex of subject and experimenter on reactions to dependency relationships. *Sociometry*, 1964, *27*, 327-337.

Daniels, L., & Berkowitz, L. Liking and response to dependency relationships. *Human Relations*, 1963, *16*, 141-148.

Darlington, R. B., & Macker, C. E. Displacement of guilt-produced altruistic behavior. *Journal of Personality and Social Psychology*, 1966, *4*, 442-443.

Freed, A., Chandler, P., Mouton, J., & Blake, R. Stimulus and background factors in sign violation. *Journal of Personality*, 1955, *23*, 499.

Goranson, R., & Berkowitz, L. Reciprocity and responsibility reactions to prior help. *Journal of Personality and Social Psychology*, 1966, *3*, 227-232.

Gore, P. M., & Rotter, J. B. A personality correlate of social action. *Journal of Personality*, 1963, *31*, 58-64.

Gouldner, A. The norm of reciprocity: A preliminary statement. *American Sociological Review*, 1960, *25*, 161-178.

Handlon, B. J., & Gross, P. The development of sharing behavior. *Journal of Abnormal and Social Psychology*, 1959, *59*, 425-428.

Lefkowitz, M., Blake, R., & Mouton, J. Status factors in pedestrian violation of traffic signals. *Journal of Abnormal and Social Psychology*, 1955, *51*, 704-706.

Midlarsky, E., & Bryan, J. H. Training charity in children. *Journal of Personality and Social Psychology*, 1967, *5*, 408-415.

Orne, M. On the social psychology of the psychological experiment: With particular reference to demand characteristics and their implications. *American Psychologist*, 1962, *17*, 776-783.

Rosenbaum, M. The effect of stimulus and background factors on the volunteering response. *Journal of Abnormal and Social Psychology*, 1956, *53*, 118-121.

Rosenbaum, M., & Blake, R. Volunteering as a function of field structure. *Journal of Abnormal and Social Psychology*, 1955, *50*, 193-196.

Rosenhan, D., & White, G. M. Observation and rehearsal as determinants of prosocial behavior. *Journal of Personality and Social Psychology*, 1967, *5*, 424-431.

Ugurel-Semin, R. Moral behavior and moral judgment of children. *Journal of Abnormal and Social Psychology*, 1952, *47*, 463-474.

Wheeler, L. Toward a theory of behavioral contagion. *Psychological Review*, 1966, *73*, 179-192.

Wright, B. A. Altruism in children and perceived conduct of others. *Journal of Abnormal and Social Psychology*, 1942, *37*, 218-233.

Effects of Race on the Elicitation of Helping Behavior: The Wrong Number Technique[1]

Samuel Gaertner[2]   *University of Delaware*
Leonard Bickman   *Smith College*

Abstract

A nonreactive field research technique was used to indicate the extent to which racial attitudes affect helping behavior in the general adult population. Five hundred and forty black subjects and 569 white subjects received what was ostensibly a wrong number telephone call. The caller, clearly identifiable by his voice characteristics as being black or white, explained that he was attempting to reach his mechanic from a public phone booth located on the parkway because his car had broken down. The caller further claimed that he had no more change with which to make another phone call to the garage. The subject could help the caller by contacting his garage for him. The relative frequency with which black and white men were helped was used as an indication of racial discrimination. The results showed that black subjects extended relatively equivalent levels of assistance to blacks and to whites. However, white subjects helped black callers somewhat less frequently than white callers. In addition, ignoring the race of the subject and the caller, male subjects helped more often than female ones.

Racism is a major problem in American society; however, awareness of overt discrimination appears to come only after it has taken place. We rely on the publicizing of, for example, housing and job discrimination as an indication of racism. Public opinion polls and questionnaires have also been used to indicate the extent of discrimination. However, these methods are concerned primarily with verbal attitudes, which are quite susceptible to modification and distortion, par-

"Effects of Race on the Elicitation of Helping Behavior: The Wrong Number Technique" by Samuel Gaertner and Leonard Bickman. *Journal of Personality and Social Psychology,* 1971, Vol. 20, No. 2, pp. 218–222. Copyright © 1971 by The American Psychological Association, Inc. Reprinted by permission.

ticularly in the presence of an interviewer. Nevertheless, these polls may provide some basis on which to predict behavior of white citizens toward blacks and vice versa.

The experimental study of racial conflict has almost entirely been limited to the laboratory, where few attempts have been made to expand the sampling base so as to include the general public. The present study attempts to bridge the gap between experimental laboratory studies and public opinion polls.

Although the present research is mainly concerned with white racism, we sought also to discover whether there was any antiwhite discrimination by blacks. Marx (1969), in a study of black attitudes toward whites in 1964, found little evidence of the intolerance that whites show toward blacks. However, since 1964, many changes appear to have occurred in the black community. The riots and the voices of militant leaders lead one to assume that the attitudes of most blacks have changed. However, in reviewing the numerous surveys of black attitudes since 1964, Marx (1969) concluded that black attitudes have not changed. Marx feels that the mass media have given a distorted picture of how the majority of blacks feel toward whites. He concluded that "blacks remain perhaps the most tolerant group in American society [p. 224]."

Marx pointed out that there are alternative explanations for the data collected from public opinion polls. Blacks could have been lying to white poll takers, single males could have been undersampled, and the real militants may have refused to be interviewed. In other words, public opinion polls have many of the weaknesses of the more reactive social psychological experiments. One of the aims of the present study was to assess how blacks behave toward whites without the biases introduced by asking them directly.

Our approach to the study of racism was through the observation of helping behavior. Berkowitz and his colleagues (Berkowitz, 1966; Berkowitz & Daniels,

1964; Berkowitz, Klanderman, & Harris, 1964) have conducted a number of experiments in the general area of helping behavior. They have assumed the existence of a "social responsibility norm" in our society that accounts for one person's helping another when no tangible rewards can be gained. If antiblack sentiment is present, then we would expect that the social responsibility norm would be violated more frequently for a black man in need of help than for a white man in the same situation. Therefore, we have used the relative frequencies with which a black and a white man are helped as an indicator of discrimination.

To date, there have been three studies on helping behavior that have studied race. Piliavin, Rodin, and Piliavin (1969) found some tendency for more same-race helping in a face-to-face emergency situation. Bryan and Test (1967) found significant differences between the number of persons who contributed to a Salvation Army kettle, depending upon the race of the person who was soliciting. White persons in a shopping center tended not to contribute as often when the kettle was manned by a black woman. Wispé and Freshley (1970), however, failed to observe a race effect in the willingness of passersby to assist a black or white female whose bag of groceries had just broken in front of a supermarket. Wispé and Freshley suggested that the immediacy of the onset of the incident may have attenuated a race effect.

In summary, we predicted that whites would discriminate against blacks by not helping them as frequently as they help their fellow whites. In addition, based on the results of polls of blacks, we expected that blacks would not show any discrimination against whites, that is, that blacks would extend equivalent levels of assistance to black and white victims.

METHOD

Subjects

The subjects were 1,109 residents of Brooklyn, New York. Subjects were sampled from the 1968-1969 *Brooklyn Telephone Directory*. The 540 black subjects were selected from the directory on the basis of last name (e.g., Jones, Brown, and others common among blacks in New York City), and then on the basis of place of residence. In order to be classified as black, the subject had to live in an area that was almost totally inhabited by blacks, as indicated by the 1960 Census tracts. The 569 white subjects were drawn from

the telephone directory without regard to last name but using a similar geographic criterion.

A further check on the racial identification of the subject was made when the actual study was conducted. Based on the voice characteristics of the subject, the caller and his assistant, both of whom were unaware, prior to the call, of the subjects' racial classification, name, and area of residence, had to agree in their identification of the subject's racial classification in order for the subject to be included in the data analysis. Fewer than 1% of the subjects were rejected for failure to meet this criterion. No doubt, selecting subjects on the basis of the residential criterion results in a black sample that is lower socioeconomically than the white sample. Without the benefit of a follow-up interview, or the sampling of identifiably middle-class black subjects, it is impossible to disentangle the effects of race and social class when discussing differences in the helping behavior of the black and white subjects.

Procedure

The apparent race of the caller was manipulated by varying his speech characteristics. When the caller (victim) was to seem black, a black confederate employing a modified "southern Negro" dialect placed the call and identified himself as George Williams. Similarly, when the caller was to seem white, a white confederate using a recognizably white speech pattern (i.e., typical of whites in New York) called and similarly identified himself as George Williams. Grammatically, the messages of the black and white victims were identical; only the pronunciation of the words was varied. Seven black males and seven white males were used as callers.

To insure that both male and female subjects would be home to receive the calls, the study was conducted between the hours of 6:30 and 9:30 P.M. If anyone identified by voice characteristics as being under 18 years of age answered, the caller apologized for reaching the wrong number and hung up. When an adult (someone over 18) answered, the caller repeated the following:

Caller: Hello . . . Ralph's Garage? This is George Williams . . . listen, I'm stuck out here on the parkway . . . and I'm wondering if you'd be able to come out here and take a look at my car?

Subject's expected response: This isn't Ralph's Garage . . . you have the wrong number.

Caller: This isn't Ralph's Garage! Listen, I'm terribly sorry to have disturbed you, but listen . . . I'm stuck out here on the highway . . . and that was the last dime I had! I have bills in my pocket, but no more change to make another phone call . . . Now I'm *really* stuck out here. What am I going to do now?

Subject: . . . [Subject might volunteer to call the garage.]

Caller: Listen . . . do you think you could do me the favor of calling the garage and letting them know where I am . . . ? I'll give you the number. . . . They know me over there.

Prod A: Oh brother . . . listen, I'm stuck out here . . . Couldn't you PLEASE help me out by simply calling the garage for me [pleadingly]?

Prod B: Listen . . . If YOU were in my situation . . . wouldn't you want someone to help you?

If after Prod B the subject refused to place the call but did not hang up, he was relieved of any concern he may have had for the stranded motorist when the caller reported: "Oh, one second . . . here comes a police car . . . I think he will be able to give me a hand."

If the subject agreed to help, the victim gave him a telephone number to call. In fact, the subject's call was received by an assistant acting as the garage attendant. The assistant assured the subject that the victim would be helped immediately, and graciously thanked him for his helpfulness.

To identify which subjects actually helped, the following procedures were employed. First, black and white callers gave the subjects different telephone numbers to call. Second, each time a subject agreed to call, the caller changed his location on the parkway, rotating eight different locations. At the "garage," the subject was asked for the location of the stranded motorist. Finally, the time at which the call to the subject was completed, along with the time at which subject's call was received at the garage, was recorded.

Only if the subject actually called the garage was he credited with a helping response. If the subject refused to help after Prod B, or hung up after the caller stated "and that was the last dime . . ." a no-help response was scored. However, if the subject hung up prior to the word "dime," a *premature hang-up* response was recorded and was considered separately from the help, no-help response categories. In the case of a premature hang-up, the subject could not reasonably be expected to realize that the caller needed *his* assistance.

RESULTS

Perceived Characteristics of the Black and White Callers

College students listening to tape recordings of the callers' practice performances of the experimental dialogue judged the white callers as "white" 92% of the time ($n = 89$) and judged the black callers as "black" 97% of the time ($n = 97$).   In addition, the students perceived social and personality differences between the black and white callers. Although blacks were perceived to be of lower social class ($t = 2.57, p < .01$) and less education ($t = 1.97, p < .05$), both groups were judged as being lower-middle class and as having completed a high school education. Furthermore, blacks were perceived to be more good-natured ($t = 2.13, p < .05$), while, in general, both groups of callers were judged favorably on characteristics such as good-naturedness, friendliness, courteousness, reliability, truthfulness, and sincerity.

Effects of the Race of the Victim on Helping Behavior

The results (see Table 1) of this experiment show that white subjects helped the white victims 12% more frequently than they helped the black victims ($x^2 = 7.40, df = 1, p < .01$). Therefore, the results support

Table 1   Percentages of Black and White Subjects Helping Black and White Victims

	White subjects		Black subjects	
Item	White victim	Black victim	White victim	Black victim
% overall	65	53	67	60
n	251	236	247	239
	$x^2 = 7.40$****		$x^2 = 2.34$*	
% males	73	59	69	68
n	97	97	84	87
	$x^2 = 4.50$***		$x^2 = .05$	
% females	60	49	66	57
n	154	163	163	152
	$x^2 = 3.89$***		$x^2 = 3.12$**	

  * $p < .20$.
 ** $p < .10$.
*** $p < .05$.
**** $p < .01$.

the hypothesis. However, although this 12% difference is statistically significant, the magnitude of the effect is rather small.

Blacks, on the other hand, were not at all antiwhite. In fact, among black subjects, white victims were accorded help 6.6% more frequently than black victims. This 6.6% difference, however, is not statistically significant ($\chi^2 = 2.34$, $df = 1$, $p < .20$).

The relative extent to which the subjects' helping behavior appeared prowhite was not significantly greater for the white than the black subjects ($\chi^2 = .83$). Thus, although whites extended help less frequently to the black than to the white victims, whites did not favor whites to a greater extent than blacks favored whites.

The complexion of the findings changes somewhat when the subject's sex is considered. Table 1 reveals that among whites, both males and females helped the black victims less frequently than white victims. Black females similarly helped white victims somewhat more frequently than black victims ($\chi^2 = 3.12$, $df = 1$, $p < .10$). Black males, however, extended equivalent levels of assistance to the black and white victims.

Ignoring the subject's and the victim's race, the stranded motorists were assisted by 67% of the male subjects and by only 58% of the female subjects. The difference of 9% in the frequency with which males and females helped was statistically significant ($\chi^2 = 7.35$, $df = 1$, $p < .01$).

Premature Hang-Ups

A subject's response was categorized as a premature hang-up rather than help or no help if he hung up before the stranded motorist had the opportunity to state "and that was my last dime." The results show that neither the white nor the black subjects discriminated in terms of the premature hang-up. The white male and black female subjects, however, seemed to hang up prematurely somewhat more frequently on the black than on the white victims ($p < .10$). Overall, white subjects hung up prematurely more frequently than black subjects. That is, 14.2% of the white subjects, but only 9.4% of the black subjects, hung up prematurely ($\chi^2 = 6.07$, $df = 1$, $p < .02$). A sex difference also emerged in the rate of premature hang-ups. Fourteen percent of the females, compared to 5% of the males, hung up prematurely ($\chi^2 = 18.41$, $df = 1$, $p < .001$).

DISCUSSION

In this nonreactive study, it appears that among whites, the social responsibility norm was violated somewhat more frequently for black than for white victims. It should be stressed, however, that for 88% of the white subjects, the race of the victim did not seem to affect whether or not they helped. Therefore, the race of the victim (inferred from his dialect) has a small but detectable influence upon the helping behavior of white residents of New York City.

Black subjects, confirming the findings of public opinion polls, did not discriminate against whites. Somewhat surprising, but approached cautiously because of the low level of statistical significance, was the unpredicted finding that black females also tended to help white victims somewhat more frequently (9%, $p < .10$) than the black victims.

Comparing the wrong number technique with more traditional measures, some advantages of the technique can be noted: *(a)* The method is nonreactive; *(b)* it measures *overt* behavior, rather than belief or intention to behave; *(c)* it permits the investigator to expand the sampling base beyond the college student population; *(d)* large numbers of subjects may be tested in a relatively short period of time (i.e., each caller averaged 12 subjects per hour). Speed is especially important if we wish to gauge the immediate effects of current events or programs to reduce intergroup tension.

However, there are some disadvantages and limitations associated with the wrong number technique: *(a)* Although the sampling base is greatly expanded, the sample must be limited to those people with telephones whose phone numbers are listed in the public directory. However, the widespread use of telephone service tends to minimize this problem. Nevertheless, investigators interested in sampling black and white households must recognize that their sample of the black population will probably be less representative than their sample of whites, based solely upon economic factors. An examination of elementary school records in areas populated largely by blacks revealed that approximately 70% of the children's homes maintained private telephone service. Thus, nearly 30% of the black population may be inaccessible via telephone. *(b)* The investigator has no control over the subjects' behavior prior to the telephone call for help. The subject may have been doing something at home which might have interfered with or increased his willingness to help, and thus the relationship between race and helping may have been attenuated. However, this may be only an apparent disadvantage since the complexity of the situation was real, and thus the result might be more representative of how people actually behave in real-life situations. *(c)* A more serious disadvantage of the wrong number technique is its possible insensitivity to varying degrees of prejudice necessitated by the restrictive response categories (i.e., help-no help). Are all white subjects who help the black victim nonprejudiced? Most probably not. They are, however, nondiscriminators in this situation. This method may be relatively insensitive, but it need not be the sole instrument in a researcher's battery of measures. Also, it would be a mistake to view the wrong number situation solely as a one-item test with a yes-no response. Actually, the subject makes a number of responses in this situation which may be systematically recorded; for example, does he hang up immediately, does he volunteer to help without being asked, does he agree to help only after the victim pleads for help, does he help grudgingly or in friendly spirits, does he actually call the garage? A cursory view of this complex set of responses indicated, however, that only the help–no-help response yielded any meaningful differences.

Other studies using this technique are in progress. An investigation of whether the sex of the victim is important in determining the subject's response is being conducted. Will a black female get more help than a black male? In addition, the political affiliations of the subjects are being considered. Will members of different political parties with their different ideologies (conservative versus liberal party) behave in different ways?

The usefulness of this method is not limited to the study of intergroup attitudes. For example, the manner in which the victim asks for help is under investigation. Determination of whether help is more likely when the victim requests or demands help is being made. In addition, the relationship between the sex of the victim and the sex of the subject is being studied.

Footnotes

[1] This research was supported by the grants-in-aid program of the Society for the Psychological Study of Social Issues.

[2] Requests for reprints should be sent to Samuel L. Gaertner, Department of Psychology, 220 Wolf Hall, University of Delaware, Newark, Delaware 19711.

We would like to acknowledge the assistance of the following individuals who served for long hours and for many evenings without pay: Joey Butler, Fred Kleiman, Phyllis Klepper, Howard Leopold, Sunny Pecker, Jay Schissel, Robert Unger, Andrew Ursino. We want especially to thank Mark Kamzan for being our most dedicated and hard-working research assistant.

References

Berkowitz, L. A laboratory investigation of social class and national differences in helping behavior. *International Journal of Psychology,* 1966, *1,* 231-242.

Berkowitz, L., & Daniels, L. Affecting the salience of the social responsibility norm: Effects of past help on the response to dependency relationships. *Journal of Abnormal and Social Psychology,* 1964, *68,* 275-281.

Berkowitz, L., Klanderman, S., & Harris, R. Effects of experimenter awareness and sex of subject and experimenter on reactions to dependency relationships. *Sociometry,* 1964, *27,* 327-339.

Bryan, J. H., & Test, M. A. Models and helping: Naturalistic studies in aiding behavior. *Journal of Personality and Social Psychology,* 1967, *6,* 400-407.

Marx, G. *Protest and prejudice.* New York: Harper Torchbooks, 1969.

Piliavin, I. M., Rodin, J., & Piliavin, J. A. Good samaritanism: An underground phenomenon? *Journal of Personality and Social Psychology,* 1969, *13,* 289-299.

Wispé, L., & Freshley, H. B. Race, sex, and sympathetic helping behavior: The broken bag caper. *Journal of Personality and Social Psychology,* 1970, *17,* 59-65.

Compliance Behavior

Compliance Without Pressure: The Foot-in-the-Door Technique[1]

Jonathan L. Freedman   *Stanford University*
Scott C. Fraser[2]

Abstract

Two experiments were conducted to test the proposition that once someone has agreed to a small request he is more likely to comply with a larger request. The first study demonstrated this effect when the same person made both requests. The second study extended this to the situation in which different people made the two requests. Several experimental groups were run in an effort to explain these results, and possible explanations are discussed.

How can a person be induced to do something he would rather not do? This question is relevant to practically every phase of social life, from stopping at a traffic light to stopping smoking, from buying Brand X to buying savings bonds, from supporting the March of Dimes to supporting the Civil Rights Act.

One common way of attacking the problem is to exert as much pressure as possible on the reluctant individual in an effort to force him to comply. This technique has been the focus of a considerable amount of experimental research. Work on attitude change, conformity, imitation, and obedience has all tended to stress the importance of the degree of external pressure. The prestige of the communicator (Kelman & Hovland, 1953), degree of discrepancy of the communication (Hovland & Pritzker, 1957), size of the group disagreeing with the subject (Asch, 1951),

perceived power of the model (Bandura, Ross, & Ross, 1963), etc., are the kinds of variables that have been studied. This impressive body of work, added to the research on rewards and punishments in learning, has produced convincing evidence that greater external pressure generally leads to greater compliance with the wishes of the experimenter. The one exception appears to be situations involving the arousal of cognitive dissonance in which, once discrepant behavior has been elicited from the subject, the greater the pressure that was used to elicit the behavior, the less subsequent change occurs (Festinger & Carlsmith, 1959). But even in this situation one critical element is the amount of external pressure exerted.

Clearly, then, under most circumstances the more pressure that can be applied, the more likely it is that the individual will comply. There are, however, many times when for ethical, moral, or practical reasons it is difficult to apply much pressure when the goal is to produce compliance with a minimum of apparent pressure, as in the forced-compliance studies involving dissonance arousal. And even when a great deal of pressure is possible, it is still important to maximize the compliance it produces. Thus, factors other than external pressure are often quite critical in determining degree of compliance. What are these factors?

Although rigorous research on the problem is rather sparse, the fields of advertising, propaganda, politics, etc., are by no means devoid of techniques designed to produce compliance in the absence of external pressure (or to maximize the effectiveness of the pressure that is used, which is really the same problem). One assumption about compliance that has often been made either explicitly or implicitly is that once a person has been induced to comply with a small request he is more likely to comply with a larger demand. This is the principle that is commonly referred to as the foot-in-the-door or gradation technique and is reflected in the saying that if you "give them an inch, they'll take a mile." It was, for example, supposed to be one of the basic techniques upon which the Korean brainwashing tactics were based (Schein, Schneier, & Barker, 1961), and, in a somewhat different sense, one basis for Nazi propaganda during 1940 (Bruner, 1941). It also appears to be implicit in many advertising campaigns which attempt to induce the consumer to do anything relating to the product involved, even sending back a card saying he does not want the product.

The most relevant piece of experimental evidence comes from a study of conformity done by Deutsch and Gerard (1955). Some subjects were faced with incorrect group judgments first in a series in which the stimuli were not present during the actual judging and then in a series in which they were present, while the order of the memory and visual series was reversed for other subjects. For both groups the memory series produced more conformity, and when the memory series came first there was more total conformity to the group judgments. It seems likely that this order effect occurred because, as the authors suggest, once conformity is elicited at all it is more likely to occur in the future. Although this kind of conformity is probably somewhat different from compliance as described above, this finding certainly lends some support to the foot-in-the-door idea. The present research attempted to provide a rigorous, more direct test of this notion as it applies to compliance and to provide data relevant to several alternative ways of explaining the effect.

EXPERIMENT I

The basic paradigm was to ask some subjects (Performance condition) to comply first with a small request and then 3 days later with a larger, related request. Other subjects (One-Contact condition) were asked to comply only with the large request. The hypothesis was that more subjects in the Performance condition than in the One-Contact condition would comply with the larger request.

Two additional conditions were included in an attempt to specify the essential difference between these two major conditions. The Performance subjects were asked to perform a small favor, and, if they agreed, they did it. The question arises whether the act of agreeing itself is critical or whether actually

carrying it out was necessary. To assess this a third group of subjects (Agree-Only) was asked the first request, but, even if they agreed, they did not carry it out. Thus, they were identical to the Performance group except that they were not given the opportunity of performing the request.

Another difference between the two main conditions was that at the time of the larger request the subjects in the Performance condition were more familiar with the experimenter than were the other subjects. The Performance subjects had been contacted twice, heard his voice more, discovered that the questions were not dangerous, and so on. It is possible that this increased familiarity would serve to decrease the fear and suspicion of a strange voice on the phone and might accordingly increase the likelihood of the subjects agreeing to the larger request. To control for this a fourth condition was run (Familiarization) which attempted to give the subjects as much familiarity with the experimenter as in the Performance and Agree-Only conditions with the only difference being that no request was made.

The major prediction was that more subjects in the Performance condition would agree to the large request than in any of the other conditions, and that the One-Contact condition would produce the least compliance. Since the importance of agreement and familiarity was essentially unknown, the expectation was that the Agree-Only and Familiarization conditions would produce intermediate amounts of compliance.

METHOD

The prediction stated above was tested in a field experiment in which housewives were asked to allow a survey team of five or six men to come into their homes for 2 hours to classify the household products they used. This large request was made under four different conditions: after an initial contact in which the subject had been asked to answer a few questions about the kinds of soaps she used, and the questions were actually asked (Performance condition); after an identical contact in which the questions were not actually asked (Agree-Only condition); after an initial contact in which no request was made (Familiarization condition); or after no initial contact (One-Contact condition). The dependent measure was simply whether or not the subject agreed to the large request.

Procedure

The subjects were 156 Palo Alto, California, house-wives, 36 in each condition, who were selected at random from the telephone directory. An additional 12 subjects distributed about equally among the three two-contact conditions could not be reached for the second contact and are not included in the data analysis. Subjects were assigned randomly to the various conditions, except that the Familiarization condition was added to the design after the other three conditions had been completed. All contacts were by telephone by the same experimenter who identified himself as the same person each time. Calls were made only in the morning. For the three groups that were contacted twice, the first call was made on either Monday or Tuesday and the second always 3 days later. All large requests were made on either Thursday or Friday.

At the first contact, the experimenter introduced himself by name and said that he was from the California Consumers' Group. In the Performance condition he then proceeded:

> *We are calling you this morning to ask if you would answer a number of questions about what house-hold products you use so that we could have this information for our public service publication, "The Guide." Would you be willing to give us this information for our survey?*

If the subject agreed, she was asked a series of eight innocuous questions dealing with household soaps (e.g., "What brand of soap do you use in your kitchen sink?") She was then thanked for her cooperation, and the contact terminated.

Another condition (Agree-Only) was run to assess the importance of actually carrying out the request as opposed to merely agreeing to it. The only difference between this and the Performance condition was that, if the subject agreed to answer the questions, the experimenter thanked her, but said that he was just lining up respondents for the survey and would contact her if needed.

A third condition was included to check on the importance of the subject's greater familiarity with the experimenter in the two-contact conditions. In this condition the experimenter introduced himself, described the organization he worked for and the survey it was conducting, listed the questions he was asking, and then said that he was calling merely to acquaint the subject with the existence of his organization. In other words, these subjects were contacted, spent as much time on the phone with the experimenter as the Performance subjects did, heard all the questions, but neither agreed to answer them nor answered them.

In all of these two-contact conditions some subjects did not agree to the requests or even hung up before the requests were made. Every subject who answered the phone was included in the analysis of the results and was contacted for the second request regardless of her extent of cooperativeness during the first contact. In other words, no subject who could be contacted the appropriate number of times was discarded from any of the four conditions.

The large request was essentially identical for all subjects. The experimenter called, identified himself, and said either that his group was expanding its survey (in the case of the two-contact conditions) or that it was conducting a survey (in the One-Contact condition). In all four conditions he then continued:

> *The survey will involve five or six men from our staff coming into your home some morning for about 2 hours to enumerate and classify all the household products that you have. They will have to have full freedom in your house to go through the cupboards and storage places. Then all this information will be used in the writing of the reports for our public service publication, "The Guide."*

If the subject agreed to the request, she was thanked and told that at the present time the experimenter was merely collecting names of people who were willing to take part and that she would be contacted if it were decided to use her in the survey. If she did not agree, she was thanked for her time. This terminated the experiment.

RESULTS

Apparently even the small request was not considered trivial by some of the subjects. Only about two thirds of the subjects in the Performance and Agree-Only conditions agreed to answer the questions about household soaps. It might be noted that none of those who refused the first request later agreed to the large request, although as stated previously all subjects who were contacted for the small request are included in the data for those groups.

Our major prediction was that subjects who had agreed to and carried out a small request (Performance condition) would subsequently be more likely to comply with a larger request than would subjects who were asked only the larger request (One-Contact condition). As may be seen in Table 1, the results support the prediction. Over 50% of the subjects in the Performance condition agreed to the larger request, while less than 25% of the One-Contact condition agreed to it. Thus it appears that obtaining compliance with a small request does tend to increase subsequent compliance. The question is what aspect of the initial contact produces this effect.

One possibility is that the effect was produced merely by increased familiarity with the experimenter. The Familiarization control was included to assess the effect on compliance of two contacts with the same person. The group had as much contact with the experimenter as the Performance group, but no request was made during the first contact. As the table indicates, the Familiarization group did not differ appreciably in amount of compliance from the One-Contact group, but was different from the Performance group ($\chi^2 = 3.70$, $p < .07$). Thus, although increased familiarity may well lead to increased compliance, in the present situation the differences in amount of familiarity apparently were not great enough to produce any such increase; the effect that was obtained seems not to be due to this factor.

Another possibility is that the critical factor producing increased compliance is simply agreeing to the small request (i.e., carrying it out may not be necessary). The Agree-Only condition was identical to the Performance condition except that in the former the subjects were not asked the questions. The amount of compliance in this Agree-Only condition fell between the Performance and One-Contact conditions and was not significantly different from either of

them. This leaves the effect of merely agreeing somewhat ambiguous, but it suggests that the agreement alone may produce part of the effect.

Unfortunately, it must be admitted that neither of these control conditions is an entirely adequate test of the possibility it was designed to assess. Both conditions are in some way quite peculiar and may have made a very different and extraneous impression on the subject than did the Performance condition. In one case, a housewife is asked to answer some questions and then is not asked them; in the other, some man calls to tell her about some organization she has never heard of. Now, by themselves neither of these events might produce very much suspicion. But, several days later, the same man calls and asks a very large favor. At this point it is not at all unlikely that many subjects think they are being manipulated, or in any case that something strange is going on. Any such reaction on the part of the subjects would naturally tend to reduce the amount of compliance in these conditions.

Thus, although this first study demonstrates that an initial contact in which a request is made and carried out increases compliance with a second request, the question of why and how the initial request produces this effect remains unanswered. In an attempt to begin answering this question and to extend the results of the first study, a second experiment was conducted.

There seemed to be several quite plausible ways in which the increase in compliance might have been produced. The first was simply some kind of commitment to or involvement with the particular person making the request. This might work, for example, as follows: The subject has agreed to the first request and perceives that the experimenter therefore expects him also to agree to the second request. The subject thus feels obligated and does not want to disappoint the experimenter; he also feels that he needs a good reason for saying "no"—a better reason than he would need if he had never said "yes." This is just one line of causality—the particular process by which involvement with the experimenter operates might be quite different, but the basic idea would be similar. The commitment is to the particular person. This implies that the increase in compliance due to the first contact should occur primarily when both requests are made by the same person.

Another explanation in terms of involvement centers around the particular issue with which the requests are concerned. Once the subject has taken some action in connection with an area of concern, be it surveys, political activity, or highway safety, there is

Table 1 Percentage of Subjects Complying with Large Request in Experiment I

Condition	%
Performance	52.8
Agree-Only	33.3
Familiarization	27.8*
One-Contact	22.2**

Note.—$N = 36$ for each group. Significance levels represent differences from the Performance condition.
* $p < .07$.
** $p < .02$.

probably a tendency to become somewhat more concerned with the area. The subject begins thinking about it, considering its importance and relevance to him, and so on. This tends to make him more likely to agree to take further action in the same area when he is later asked to. To the extent that this is the critical factor, the initial contact should increase compliance only when both requests are related to the same issue or area of concern.

Another way of looking at the situation is that the subject needs a reason to say "no." In our society it is somewhat difficult to refuse a reasonable request, particularly when it is made by an organization that is not trying to make money. In order to refuse, many people feel that they need a reason—simply not wanting to do it is often not in itself sufficient. The person can say to the requester or simply to himself that he does not believe in giving to charities or tipping or working for political parties or answering questions or posting signs, or whatever he is asked to do. Once he has performed a particular task, however, this excuse is no longer valid for not agreeing to perform a similar task. Even if the first thing he did was trivial compared to the present request, he cannot say he never does this sort of thing, and thus one good reason for refusing is removed. This line of reasoning suggests that the similarity of the first and second requests in terms of the type of action required is an important factor. The more similar they are, the more the "matter of principle" argument is eliminated by agreeing to the first request, and the greater should be the increase in compliance.

There are probably many other mechanisms by which the initial request might produce an increase in compliance. The second experiment was designed in part to test the notions described above, but its major purpose was to demonstrate the effect unequivocally. To this latter end it eliminated one of the important problems with the first study which was that when the experimenter made the second request he was not blind as to which condition the subjects were in. In this study the second request was always made by someone other than the person who made the first request, and the second experimenter was blind as to what condition the subject was in. This eliminates the possibility that the experimenter exerted systematically different amounts of pressure in different experimental conditions. If the effect of the first study were replicated, it would also rule out the relatively uninteresting possibility that the effect is due primarily to greater familiarity or involvement with the particular person making the first request.

EXPERIMENT II

The basic paradigm was quite similar to that of the first study. Experimental subjects were asked to comply with a small request and were later asked a considerably larger request, while controls were asked only the larger request. The first request varied along two dimensions. Subjects were asked either to put up a small sign or to sign a petition, and the issue was either safe driving or keeping California beautiful. Thus, there were four first requests: a small sign for safe driving or for beauty, and a petition for the two issues. The second request for all subjects was to install in their front lawn a very large sign which said "Drive Carefully." The four experimental conditions may be defined in terms of the similarity of the small and large requests along the dimensions of issue and task. The two requests were similar in both issue and task for the small-sign, safe-driving group, similar only in issue for the safe-driving-petition group, similar only in task for the small "Keep California Beautiful" sign group, and similar in neither issue nor task for the "Keep California Beautiful" petition group.

The major expectation was that the three groups for which either the task or the issue were similar would show more compliance than the controls, and it was also felt that when both were similar there would probably be the most compliance. The fourth condition (Different Issue-Different Task) was included primarily to assess the effect simply of the initial contact which, although it was not identical to the second one on either issue or task, was in many ways quite similar (e.g., a young student asking for cooperation on a noncontroversial issue). There were no clear expectations as to how this condition would compare to the controls.

METHOD

The subjects were 114 women and 13 men living in Palo Alto, California. Of these, 9 women and 6 men could not be contacted for the second request and are not included in the data analysis. The remaining 112 subjects were divided about equally among the five conditions (see Table 2). All subjects were contacted between 1:30 and 4:30 on weekday afternoons.

Two experimenters, one male and one female, were employed, and a different one always made the second contact. Unlike the first study, the experimenters actually went to the homes of the subjects and interviewed them on a face-to-face basis. An effort was made to select subjects from blocks and neighborhoods that were as homogeneous as possible. On each block every third or fourth house was approached, and all subjects on that block were in one experimental condition. This was necessary because of the likelihood that neighbors would talk to each other about the contact. In addition, for every four subjects contacted, a fifth house was chosen as a control but was, of course, not contacted. Throughout this phase of the experiment, and in fact throughout the whole experiment, the two experimenters did not communicate to each other what conditions had been run on a given block nor what condition a particular house was in.

The small-sign, safe-driving group was told that the experimenter was from the Community Committee for Traffic Safety, that he was visiting a number of homes in an attempt to make the citizens more aware of the need to drive carefully all the time, and that he would like the subject to take a small sign and put it in a window or in the car so that it would serve as a reminder of the need to drive carefully. The sign was 3 inches square, said "Be a safe driver," was on thin paper without a gummed backing, and in general looked rather amateurish and unattractive. If the subject agreed, he was given the sign and thanked; if he disagreed, he was simply thanked for his time.

The three other experimental conditions were quite similar with appropriate changes. The other organization was identified as the Keep California Beautiful Committee and its sign said, appropriately enough, "Keep California Beautiful." Both signs were simply black block letters on a white background. The two petition groups were asked to sign a petition which was being sent to California's United States Senators. The petition advocated support for any legislation which would promote either safer driving or keeping California beautiful. The subject was shown a petition, typed on heavy bond paper, with at least 20 signatures already affixed. If she agreed, she signed and was thanked. If she did not agree, she was merely thanked.

The second contact was made about 2 weeks after the initial one. Each experimenter was armed with a list of houses which had been compiled by the other experimenter. This list contained all four experimental conditions and the controls, and, of course, there was no way for the second experimenter to know which condition the subject had been in. At this second contact, all subjects were asked the same thing: Would they put a large sign concerning safe driving in their front yard? The experimenter identified himself

as being from the Citizens for Safe Driving, a different group from the original safe-driving group (although it is likely that most subjects who had been in the safe-driving conditions did not notice the difference). The subject was shown a picture of a very large sign reading "Drive Carefully" placed in front of an attractive house. The picture was taken so that the sign obscured much of the front of the house and completely concealed the doorway. It was rather poorly lettered. The subject was told that: "Our men will come out and install it and later come and remove it. It makes just a small hole in your lawn, but if this is unacceptable to you we have a special mount which will make no hole." She was asked to put the sign up for a week or a week and a half. If the subject agreed, she was told that more names than necessary were being gathered and if her home were to be used she would be contacted in a few weeks. The experimenter recorded the subject's response and this ended the experiment.

RESULTS

First, it should be noted that there were no large differences among the experimental conditions in the percentages of subjects agreeing to the first request. Although somewhat more subjects agreed to post the "Keep California Beautiful" sign and somewhat fewer to sign the beauty petition, none of these differences approach significance.

The important figures are the number of subjects in each group who agreed to the large request. These are presented in Table 2. The figures for the four experimental groups include all subjects who were approached the first time, regardless of whether or not they agreed to the small request. As noted above, a few subjects were lost because they could not be reached for the second request, and, of course, these are not included in the table.

It is immediately apparent that the first request tended to increase the degree of compliance with the second request. Whereas fewer than 20% of the controls agreed to put the large sign on their lawn, over 55% of the experimental subjects agreed, with over 45% being the lowest degree of compliance for any experimental condition. As expected, those conditions in which the two requests were similar in terms of either issue or task produced significantly more compliance than did the controls (χ^2's range from 3.67, $p < .07$ to 15.01, $p < .001$). A somewhat unexpected result is that the fourth condition, in

Table 2 Percentage of Subjects Complying with Large Request in Experiment II

Issue[a]	Task[a]			
	Similar	N	Different	N
Similar	76.0**	25	47.8*	23
Different	47.6*	21	47.4*	19

One-Contact 16.7 ($N = 24$)

Note.—Significance levels represent differences from the One-Contact condition.

[a]Denotes relationship between first and second requests.

* $p < .08$.

** $p < .01$.

which the first request had relatively little in common with the second request, also produced more compliance than the controls ($\chi^2 = 3.40$, $p < .08$). In other words, regardless of whether or not the two requests are similar in either issue or task, simply having the first request tends to increase the likelihood that the subject will comply with a subsequent, larger request. And this holds even when the two requests are made by different people several weeks apart.

A second point of interest is a comparison among the four experimental conditions. As expected, the Same Issue-Same Task condition produced more compliance than any of the other two-contact conditions, but the difference is not significant (χ^2's range from 2.7 to 2.9). If only those subjects who agreed to the first request are considered, the same pattern holds.

DISCUSSION

To summarize the results, the first study indicated that carrying out a small request increased the likelihood that the subject would agree to a similar larger request made by the same person. The second study showed that this effect was quite strong even when a different person made the larger request, and the two requests were quite dissimilar. How may these results be explained?

Two possibilities were outlined previously. The matter-of-principle idea which centered on the particular type of action was not supported by the data, since the similarity of the tasks did not make an appreciable difference in degree of compliance. The notion of involvement, as described previously, also has difficulty accounting for some of the findings. The basic idea was that once someone has agreed to any action, no matter how small, he tends to feel more

involved than he did before. This involvement may center around the particular person making the first request or the particular issue. This is quite consistent with the results of the first study (with the exception of the two control groups which as discussed previously were rather ambiguous) and with the Similar-Issue groups in the second experiment. This idea of involvement does not, however, explain the increase in compliance found in the two groups in which the first and second request did not deal with the same issue.

It is possible that in addition to or instead of this process a more general and diffuse mechanism underlies the increase in compliance. What may occur is a change in the person's feelings about getting involved or about taking action. Once he has agreed to a request, his attitude may change. He may become, in his own eyes, the kind of person who does this sort of thing, who agrees to requests made by strangers, who takes action on things he believes in, who cooperates with good causes. The change in attitude could be toward any aspect of the situation or toward the whole business of saying "yes." The basic idea is that the change in attitude need not be toward any particular issue or person or activity, but may be toward activity or compliance in general. This would imply that an increase in compliance would not depend upon the two contacts being made by the same person, or concerning the same issue or involving the same kind of action. The similarity could be much more general, such as both concerning good causes, or requiring a similar kind of action, or being made by pleasant, attractive individuals.

It is not being suggested that this is the only mechanism operating here. The idea of involvement continues to be extremely plausible, and there are probably a number of other possibilities. Unfortunately, the present studies offer no additional data with which to support or refute any of the possible explanations of the effect. These explanations thus remain simply descriptions of mechanisms which might produce an increase in compliance after agreement with a first request. Hopefully, additional research will test these ideas more fully and perhaps also specify other manipulations which produce an increase in compliance without an increase in external pressure.

It should be pointed out that the present studies employed what is perhaps a very special type of situation. In all cases the requests were made by presumably nonprofit service organizations. The issues in the second study were deliberately noncontroversial, and it may be assumed that virtually all subjects initially sympathized with the objectives of safe driving and a beautiful California. This is in strong contrast to campaigns which are designed to sell a particular product, political candidate, or dogma. Whether the technique employed in this study would be successful in these other situations remains to be shown.

Footnotes

[1]The authors are grateful to Evelyn Bless for assisting in the running of the second experiment reported here. These studies were supported in part by Grant GS-196 from the National Science Foundation. The first study was conducted while the junior author was supported by an NSF undergraduate summer fellowship.

[2]Now at New York University.

References

Asch, S. E. Effects of group pressure upon the modification and distortion of judgments. In H. Guetzkow (Ed.), *Groups, leadership and men; research in human relations.* Pittsburgh: Carnegie Press, 1951. Pp. 177-190.

Bandura, A., Ross, D., & Ross, S. A. A comparative test of the status envy, social power, and secondary reinforcement theories of identificatory learning. *Journal of Abnormal and Social Psychology,* 1963, *67,* 527-534.

Bruner, J. The dimensions of propaganda: German short-wave broadcasts to America. *Journal of Abnormal and Social Psychology,* 1941, *36,* 311-337.

Deutsch, M., & Gerard, H. B. A study of normative and informational social influences upon individual judgment. *Journal of Abnormal and Social Psychology,* 1955, *51,* 629-636.

Festinger, L., & Carlsmith, J. Cognitive consequences of forced compliance. *Journal of Abnormal and Social Psychology,* 1959, *58,* 203-210.

Hovland, C. I., & Pritzker, H. A. Extent of opinion change as a function of amount of change advocated. *Journal of Abnormal and Social Psychology,* 1957, *54,* 257-261.

Kelman, H. C., & Hovland, C. I. "Reinstatement" of the communicator in delayed measurement of opinion change. *Journal of Abnormal and Social Psychology,* 1953, *48,* 327-335.

Schein, E. H., Schneier, I., & Barker, C. H. *Coercive pressure.* New York: Norton, 1961.

Reciprocal Concessions Procedure for Inducing Compliance: The Door-in-the-Face Technique

Robert B. Cialdini   *Arizona State University*
Joyce E. Vincent
Stephen K. Lewis
José Catalan
Diane Wheeler
Betty Lee Darby

Abstract

Three experiments were conducted to test the effectiveness of a rejection-then-moderation procedure for inducing compliance with a request for a favor. All three experiments included a condition in which a requester first asked for an extreme favor (which was refused to him) and then for a smaller favor. In each instance, this procedure produced more compliance with the smaller favor than a procedure in which the requester asked solely for the smaller favor. Additional control conditions in each experiment supported the hypothesis that the effect is mediated by a rule for reciprocation of concessions. Several advantages to the use of the rejection-then-moderation procedure for producing compliance are discussed.

"Reciprocal Concessions Procedure for Inducing Compliance: The Door-in-the-Face Technique" by Robert B. Cialdini, Joyce E. Vincent, Stephen K. Lewis, José Catalan, Diane Wheeler, and Betty Lee Darby. *Journal of Personality and Social Psychology,* 1975, Vol. 31, No. 2, pp. 206–215. Copyright © 1975 by The American Psychological Association, Inc. Reprinted by permission.

The foot-in-the-door technique has been investigated by Freedman and Fraser (1966) as a procedure for inducing compliance with a request for a favor. They demonstrated that obtaining a person's compliance with a small request substantially increases the likelihood of that person's compliance with a subsequent, larger request. Freedman and Fraser suggest that the mediator of the foot-in-the-door effect is a shift in the self-perception of the benefactor. After performing or agreeing to perform an initial favor, a person "may become, in his own eyes, the kind of person who does this sort of thing, who agrees to requests made by strangers, who takes action on things he believes in, who cooperates with good causes. . . . The basic idea is that the change in attitude need not be toward any particular person or activity, but may be toward activity or compliance in general." Thus, one effective way to obtain a favor is to begin by making a *minimal* first request which is sure to produce *compliance* and then to *advance* to a larger favor (the one which was desired from the outset). It may well be, however, that an equally effective method for getting a favor done involves the exact opposite procedure. What would be the result of making an *extreme* first request which is sure to be *rejected* and then asking for a more *moderate* second favor (the one which was desired from the outset)? There are two lines of evidence suggesting that such a technique would be efficacious in producing compliance with the second request.

The first sort of evidence comes from work investigating the concept of reciprocation. Gouldner (1960) maintains that a norm of reciprocity exists in all societies. Gouldner states the norm of reciprocity in its simple form as: "You should give benefits to those who give you benefits." (p. 170) There is considerable experimental evidence attesting to the workings of such a rule in our culture (e.g., Brehm & Cole, 1966; Goranson & Berkowitz, 1966; Pruitt, 1968; Regan, 1971; Wilke & Lanzetta, 1970). In each case, receipt of a favor has been shown to increase the likelihood that the favor will be returned, although not necessarily in kind. While Gouldner (1960) speaks of the norm of reciprocity almost exclusively in terms of the reciprocation of benefits and services, it seems likely that a norm for reciprocity governs other types of social exchange also. Specifically, we would like to postulate a reciprocal concessions corollary to the general norm of reciprocity: "You should make concessions to those who make concessions to you." Such a rule can be seen as having an important societal function. Very often in social interaction participants begin with require-

ments and demands which are unacceptable to one another. In order for the interaction to continue and hence for common goals to be achieved, compromise must be struck. *Mutual* concession is crucial. If there is no implicit prescription that retreat from an initial position by one participant should be reciprocated by the other participant, then it is unlikely that compromise attempts would be initiated and, consequently, that the interaction would continue. However, given a principle for reciprocation of concessions, an interaction participant could instigate compromise attempts with little fear of exploitation by his partner.

Evidence for the existence of a reciprocal concessions relationship in our society can be seen in numerous terms and phrases of the language: "give and take," "meeting the other fellow halfway," etc. Much more compelling, however, are the data which come from a number of studies of negotiation behavior. An experiment by Chertkoff and Conley (1967) demonstrated that the number of concessions a subject makes in a bargaining situation is significantly affected by the number of his opponent's concessions; more frequent concessions by the opponent elicited more frequent concessions from the subject. In a somewhat similar context, Komorita and Brenner (1968) had subjects bargain as buyers against opponent-sellers. In one condition, the opponent initially proposed what was a perfectly equitable selling price and refused to move from that price throughout the course of the negotiations; in other conditions, the opponent began with an extreme offer and then gradually retreated from that price as bargaining progressed. The consistent result was that the former condition elicited the least amount of yielding on the part of the subjects. Komorita and Brenner conclude that, "in a bargaining situation, if one party wishes to reach an agreement at a 'fair' price, clearly a strategy of making an initial offer at that level and remaining firm thereafter is not an effective means of reaching an agreement." (p. 18) Finally, an experiment by Benton, Kelley, and Liebling (1972) had subjects negotiate the allocation of funds with a preprogrammed opponent in a mixed-motive game. One condition of the experiment saw subjects faced with an opponent who repeatedly made an extreme demand during the first two minutes of the bargaining session and who then reduced this demand during the next two minutes. The number of subjects' own extreme demands was drastically reduced by this strategy. In contrast, another condition, in which the opponent remained intransigently extreme, produced almost no reduction in the number of extreme subject demands during this second two-minute period. In sum, it seems that the likelihood of a concession by one party is positively related to the occurrence of a concession by another party.

Let us now return to the original question, "How might we enhance the probability that another will comply with our request for a favor?" The analysis above suggests that if we were to begin by asking for an extreme favor which was sure to be refused by the other, and then we were to move to a smaller request, the other would feel a normative strain to match our concession with one of his own. Since the situation is such that the other's response to our request involves an essentially dichotomous choice—yes or no—the only available reciprocation route for him would be to move from his position of initial noncompliance to one of compliance. So, by means of an illusory retreat from our initial position, we should be able to obtain another's agreement to the request that we desired from the outset.

In line with the formulation we have proposed, two things are crucial to the success of such a procedure. First, our original request must be rejected by the target person; once this has occurred, the target will have taken a position and an apparent concession on our part will pressure him to meet us halfway and hence to yield to our smaller request. Second, the target must perceive that we have conceded in some way. Thus, the size of our second favor must be unambiguously smaller than that of the first; only then can the action of a reciprocal concessions norm come into play.

EXPERIMENT 1

In order to test the effectiveness of this procedure for inducing compliance, an experiment was conducted. It was expected that a person who followed a refused initial request with a smaller request would obtain more agreement to the smaller request than a person who made *only* the smaller request. Such a result could be explained, however, in a way quite apart from the theoretical account we have proposed. Rather than through the action of a reciprocal concessions mechanism, the superiority of the technique we have described could be seen as occurring through the action of a contrast effect. Exposure to an initial, large request could cause subjects to perceive a subsequent, smaller request as less demanding than would subjects who had never been exposed to the large request; consequently, the former type of subject might be expected to comply more with the critical request. It was necessary, therefore, to include in our experimental design a condition which differentiated these two theoretical explanations.

One point of departure for the two accounts lies in the requirement of the reciprocal concessions explanation for the target's refusal of and the requester's moderation of the initial, larger favor. The contrast effect explanation does not demand this sequence of refusal and moderation; rather, it requires only that the target person be previously exposed to the larger request. An experiment was performed, then, which included three conditions. In one condition, subjects were asked to perform a favor. In a second condition, subjects were asked to perform the critical favor after they had refused to perform a larger favor. In a final condition, subjects heard the larger favor described to them before they were asked to perform the critical one.

Method

Subjects.   Subjects were 72 people of both sexes who were moving along university walkways during daylight hours. Only those individuals who were walking alone were selected, and no subjects were selected during the 10-minute break period between classes.

Procedure.   A subject meeting the conditions above was approached by a student-experimenter[1] who initiated interaction by introducing him- or herself as being with the County Youth Counseling Program. At this point, the experimenter made (for the Youth Counseling Program) either an extreme request followed by a smaller request or made just the smaller request.

The extreme request asked subjects to perform as counselors to juvenile delinquents for a period of at least two years. Specifically, the experimenter said:

We're currently recruiting university students to work as voluntary, nonpaid counselors at the County Juvenile Detention Center. The position could require two hours of your time per week for a minimum of two years. You would be working more in the line of a Big Brother (Sister) to one of the boys (girls) at the detention home. Would you be interested in being considered for one of these positions?

The smaller request asked subjects to perform as chaperones for a group of juvenile delinquents on a two-hour trip to the zoo. Specifically, the experimenter said:

> We're recruiting university students to chaperone a group of boys (girls) from the County Juvenile Detention Center on a trip to the zoo. It would be voluntary, nonpaid, and would require about two hours of one afternoon or evening. Would you be interested in being considered for one of these positions?

Subjects were randomly assigned to one of three conditions.

Rejection-moderation condition. Subjects in this condition heard the experimenter first make the extreme request. After subjects refused the large request, the experimenter said, "Well, we also have another program you might be interested in then." At this point the experimenter made the smaller request.

Smaller request only control. Subjects in this condition were asked by the experimenter only to perform the smaller request.

Exposure control. In this condition the experimenter first described the extreme and then the smaller favor and requested that the subjects perform *either* one. Specifically, subjects in the exposure only control heard the experimenter give the standard introduction and then say:

> We're currently recruiting university students for two different programs. In the first, we're looking for voluntary, nonpaid counselors to work at the County Juvenile Detention Center. The position would require two hours of your time per week for a minimum of two years. You would be working more in the line of a Big Brother (Sister) to one of the boys (girls) at the detention center. In the other program, we're looking for university students to chaperone a group of boys (girls) from the detention center on a trip to the zoo. It would also be voluntary, nonpaid, and would require two hours of one afternoon or evening. Would you be interested in being considered for either of these two programs?

No subject during the course of the experiment ever agreed to perform the initial, large favor. However, when a subject agreed to the smaller request, the experimenter took his or her name and phone number. The experimenter promised to call if the subject was needed but explained that "there is a chance that you won't be called because of the large number of people who have already volunteered to help." At this point, the experimenter thanked the subject and moved on.

Predictions.   Two predictions derived from the reciprocal concessions model were made. First, it was expected that the subjects in the rejection-moderation condition would comply with the smaller request more than would subjects in the two control conditions. Second, it was predicted that the amount of compliance with the smaller request would not differ between the two controls.

Results

No subject in the present experiment agreed to perform the extreme favor. The percentage of subjects who complied with the smaller request in each of the treatment conditions can be seen in Table 1.

Planned orthogonal contrasts designed to test the two experimental predictions were performed on the data. The first contrast, comparing the compliance rates of the two control groups, found no difference, $\chi^2 = .50$, *ns*. The second contrast tested the combined control conditions against the rejection-moderation condition; this analysis produced a highly significant difference, $\chi^2 = 6.42$, $p = .011$. All tests in this and subsequent experiments are two-tailed.

Additional analyses investigating the extent to which the pattern of results above was affected by such factors as the sex of the subject and the identity of the experimenter provided no statistic which approached conventional levels of significance; the same pattern obtained for all three experimenters and for male and female subjects. In all, then, it seems that the only factor which enhanced the amount of agreement to the smaller request was the procedure of moving to the smaller request *after* the larger request had been refused.

Table 1   Percentage of Subjects Complying with the Smaller Request

Treatment	% Compliance
Rejection-moderation condition	50.0
Exposure control	25.0
Smaller request only control	16.7

Note. The *n* for each condition = 24.

Discussion

It is clear from the findings above that making an extreme initial request which is sure to be rejected and then moving to a smaller request significantly increases the probability of a target person's agreement to the second request. Moreover, this phenomenon does not seem mediated by a perceptual contrast effect; simply exposing the target to the extreme request beforehand does not affect compliance.

While the results of this first experiment lend some support to the reciprocal concessions explanation, they do not, of course, necessarily confirm the validity of the interpretation. If we are to gain confidence in such a model, additional predictions derivable from it must be proposed and demonstrated. To this end, it was decided to replicate and extend our findings in a second experiment.

EXPERIMENT 2

The reciprocal concessions formulation we have described suggests that a target person feels pressure to change from his initial position of noncompliance after it is seen that the requester has changed from his own initial position. It is not enough that the target has been asked to comply with a large then a smaller request, the target must perceive the request for the smaller favor as a concession *by the requester*. If this is in fact the case, a target person who is asked an extreme favor by one individual and a smaller favor by some other individual in a second interaction context should not experience a reciprocation-mediated tendency to agree to the smaller request. The second requester should not be perceived as conceding and thus, according to our model, the target should not be spurred to reciprocate via compliance. On the other hand, if, as in Experiment 1, the requests are made by the same person, compliance with the smaller request should be enhanced.

To test the importance of the perception of concession, an experiment was conducted which included three conditions. In one condition, subjects were asked to perform a favor by a single requester. In a second condition, subjects were asked by a single requester to perform the critical favor after they had refused to perform a larger favor for that requester. In the third condition, subjects were asked to perform the critical favor by one requester after they had refused to perform a larger favor for a different requester. An additional benefit of this third condition was that it afforded another test of the perceptual contrast explanation for the obtained effect and thus provided a conceptual replication of one aspect of Experiment 1.

Method

Subjects.   Subjects were 58 males who were selected for participation in a fashion identical to that of Experiment 1.

Procedure.   A subject meeting the conditions above was approached by two student-experimenters, one male and one female; we call them Experimenters A and B, respectively. Experimenter A initiated interaction by introducing both himself and Experimenter B to the subject. At this point, a second male experimenter (Experimenter C) who was apparently an acquaintance of Experimenter B, approached the group and engaged Experimenter B in conversation about an upcoming exam they both would be taking. This procedure uniformly distracted the subject's attention for a second, so Experimenter A waited for the subject to turn back to him. Here the three treatment conditions of the study differed.

Rejection-moderation condition. Subjects in this condition next heard Experimenter A ask for the extreme favor. The extreme favor was the same as that used in Experiment 1. After the subject had refused to comply, Experimenter A made the smaller request, which in this experiment asked subjects to chaperone a group of "low-income children" to the zoo. Specifically, he said:

> *Oh. Well. I'm also with the Campus Volunteer Service Organization in another program that has nothing to do with the Juvenile Detention Center. It involves helping to chaperone a group of low-income children on a trip to the zoo. We can't give you any money for it, but it would only involve about two hours of one afternoon or evening. Would you be willing to help us with this?*

Two requester control. The procedures of this condition were similar to those of the rejection-moderation condition except that, upon refusal of the extreme request, Experimenter A thanked the subject and walked away from the group with Experimenter B; this left Experimenter C alone with the subject. At this point, Experimenter C made the smaller request. He prefaced the request by saying,

Excuse me, I couldn't help overhearing you say that you would not be able to be a counselor to juvenile delinquents for two years. [If a subject had given a reason for refusing the extreme request, Experimenter C mentioned that he had overheard the stated reason as well.[2]] But maybe you can help me. My name is _____, and I'm with the Campus Volunteer Service Organization in a program that has nothing to do with the Juvenile Detention Center. [The remainder of the request was identical to that made in the rejection-moderation condition.]

Smaller request only control. The procedures of this condition were similar to those of the rejection-moderation condition except that the extreme request was not made. The events in this condition were as follows: Experimenters A and B approached the subject; Experimenter A introduced himself and Experimenter B; Experimenter C joined the group and engaged Experimenter B in conversation; Experimenter A made the smaller request. It should be noted that in this and both other conditions the roles of Experimenter A and Experimenter C were alternated between the two male experimenters of the study.

Predictions.   The predictions of the present experiment were similar to those of Experiment 1. It was expected, first, that the two control conditions would not differ from one another in amount of compliance with the smaller request. Second, it was thought that the rejection-moderation condition would produce more compliance with the smaller request than would the controls.

The experimenters in this instance were not aware of the nature of these predictions; in fact, they were led by the principal investigator to expect opposite results. As in Experiment 1, the experimenters were undergraduate research assistants. Because of evidence indicating that undergraduate experimenters have in the past produced results consistent with prediction via experimenter expectancy effects (Rosenthal, 1966) or conscious data fixing (Azrin, Holz, Ulrich, & Goldiamond, 1961), a test of such explanations for the obtained effect in Experiment 1 seemed in order. Hence, the experimenters of Experiment 2 were told that the principal investigator was predicting that the smaller request only control would produce the most compliance. This would supposedly be so because of an "irritation or reactance tendency in people who have been asked for favors twice in succession." If the pattern of results

nonetheless appeared as predicted by the reciprocal concession formulation, experimenter bias could no longer be offered as a possible explanation for the superiority of the rejection-moderation condition.

Results

Three subjects in Experiment 2 complied with the extreme request, two in the rejection-moderation condition and the other in the two requester control. These subjects were removed from the analysis and replaced by three other subjects.[3] The percentage of subjects who complied with the smaller request in each of the treatment conditions of Experiment 2 can be seen in Table 2.

Again, a priori orthogonal contrasts were used to test the experimental predictions. One contrast compared the amounts of compliance with the smaller request within the two control conditions; no conventionally significant difference occurred, $\chi^2 = 2.53, p = .111$. The other comparison, which tested the rejection-moderation condition against the combined control conditions, did produce a clearly significant difference at conventional levels, $\chi^2 = 6.85, p = .009$.

Discussion

It appears from the results of Experiment 2 that the target's perception of concession by the requester is a crucial factor in producing compliance with the smaller request. Only when the extreme and the smaller favors were asked by the same requester was compliance enhanced. This finding provides further evidence for a reciprocal concessions mediator of the rejection-then-moderation effect. It seems that our subjects increased the frequency of assent to the smaller request only in response to what could be interpreted as concession behavior on the part of the requester; such assent, then, would seem best viewed

Table 2   Percentage of Subjects Complying with the Smaller Request in Experiment 2

Treatment	% Compliance
Rejection-moderation condition	55.5
Two requester control	10.5
Smaller request only control	31.5

Note. The n for the rejection-moderation condition = 20; the n for each of the two control conditions = 19.

as reciprocal concession behavior.

It might be noted that compliance in the two requester control was inhibited relative to that in the small request only control. This finding replicates quite closely a result obtained by Snyder and Cunningham (1975) and fits very well with evidence suggesting that in most cases, people are quite consistent in their responses to requests for favors (Freedman & Fraser, 1966; Snyder & Cunningham, 1975). Unless there was a pressure to reciprocate a concession, 89.5% of the subjects in our experiment who said, "No" to an initial request said, "No" to a subsequent one.

EXPERIMENT 3

While the data of Experiments 1 and 2 are wholly consistent with the reciprocal concessions formulation, an alternative explanation for these results is applicable as well. It may have been that the heightened compliance in our rejection-moderation conditions was due to the fact that only in these conditions did one requester persist in making a second request after his first had been refused. Perhaps subjects in these conditions acquiesced to the critical, zoo trip request not because of pressure to reciprocate a concession but because they were dunned into accession by a tenacious requester or because they wanted to avoid the requester's perception of them as having a generally antisocial or unhelpful nature.

In order to test this type of explanation, a third experiment was performed. Included in Experiment 3 was a procedure in which subjects were asked to perform an initial favor and then were asked by the same requester to perform a second favor (the critical request) of *equivalent* size. Since the proposal of an equivalent second favor does not constitute a concession on the part of the requester, the reciprocal concessions model would predict no increased compliance with the critical request from this procedure. However, if the persistence of a single requester is the mediator of enhanced compliance, then such a procedure should produce heightened agreement to perform the critical request. A second function of Experiment 3 was to provide a conceptual replication of Experiment 2. As in Experiment 2, one group of subjects received two requests but should not have construed the second request as a concession on the part of the person who made it. In Experiment 2, the

perception of concession was avoided by having a second requester make the smaller, critical request; in Experiment 3, it was done by making the initial request equivalent in size to the critical one. For both procedures, the results should be similar—no enhancement of compliance.

Method

Subjects.   Subjects were 72 people of both sexes who were selected for participation in a fashion identical to that of Experiments 1 and 2.

Procedure.   A subject meeting the conditions above was approached by a student-experimenter in a fashion identical to that of Experiment 1.[4] Subjects were randomly assigned to one of three conditions.

Rejection-moderation condition. Subjects in this condition were treated identically to subjects in the comparable condition of Experiment 1; that is, after hearing and rejecting an extreme request (to perform as a counselor to a juvenile delinquent for a minimum of two years), a subject heard the same requester make a smaller request (to perform as a chaperone for a group of juvenile delinquents on a two-hour trip to the zoo).

Smaller request only control. Subjects in this condition were treated identically to subjects in the comparable condition of Experiment 1; that is, a subject heard the requester make only the smaller request to chaperone a group of juvenile delinquents on a trip to the zoo.

Equivalent request control. Subjects in this condition heard a requester initially request that they perform as chaperones for a group of juvenile delinquents on a two-hour trip to the city museum, after the subjects responded to this first request, the experimenter then requested that they chaperone a group of juvenile delinquents on a two-hour trip to the zoo.

Predictions.   As in the previous experiments, it was predicted on the basis of the reciprocal concessions model that, first, the two control conditions would not differ from one another in amount of compliance with the critical request (the zoo trip) and, second, that the rejection-moderation condition would produce more compliance with the critical request than would the controls.

Table 3 Percentage of Subjects Complying with the Smaller Request in Experiment 3

Treatment	% Compliance
Rejection-moderation condition	54.1
Equivalent request control	33.3
Smaller request only control	33.3

Note. The *n* for each condition = 24.

Results

No subject in Experiment 3 complied with the extreme request in the rejection-moderation condition. However, eight subjects complied with the initial request in the equivalent request control. The percentage of subjects who complied with the critical request in each of the treatment conditions of Experiment 3 can be seen in Table 3.

As before, two planned orthogonal comparisons were used to test the predictions. The first contrasted the two control conditions; no significant difference resulted, $\chi^2 = 0.0$, *ns*. The second tested the rejection-moderation condition against the combined controls; a marginally significant difference occurred, $\chi^2 = 2.88$, $p = .091$. Two features of the data from this experiment argue against the interpretation that a requester's persistence in making requests accounts for the superiority of the rejection-moderation condition. First, the equivalent request control, which involved successive requests from the same requester, produced exactly the same amount of compliance as the smaller request only control. Second, of the eight subjects who agreed to perform the critical request in the equivalent request control, only one had refused to perform the similar-sized initial request. Clearly, then, it is not the case that a persistent requester induces compliance to a second request solely through the act of making a second request. Indeed, in the equivalent request control, subjects were stoutly consistent in the nature of their responses to the two requests. Twenty-two of the 24 subjects in that group responded similarly to both requests.

GENERAL DISCUSSION

Taken together, the findings of Experiments 1, 2, and 3 seem to support the reciprocal concessions model. Each experiment indicated that proposing an extreme request which is rejected and then moving to a smaller request increases compliance with the smaller request. The results of Experiment 1 suggested that the target person's rejection of the initial, extreme request is crucial to the effectiveness of this technique. Through his refusal to perform the large favor, the target puts himself in a position from which virtually his only possible retreat is accession to the smaller request. Thus when the requester moves from his extreme proposal to a smaller one, the target must agree to the second proposal in order to relieve any felt pressure for reciprocation of concessions. As was shown in Experiment 1, if movement to a smaller request occurs without the target's initial rejection of the extreme request, compliance with the smaller request will not be significantly enhanced. Experiment 1 demonstrated further, as did Experiment 2, that merely exposing a target person to an extreme request does not increase the likelihood of his compliance with a subsequent smaller request; such results tend to disconfirm a perceptual contrast explanation of the phenomenon. Experiments 2 and 3 demonstrated the importance of concession. Simply presenting a target person with a smaller request after he had rejected a larger one or simply presenting a target person with a second request of equivalent size, does not increase agreement to the second request. Only when the proposal of the second favor can be considered a concession on the part of the requester is compliance increased.

Several aspects of the phenomenon we have investigated suggest that its use would be highly functional for someone in need of a favor. First, it is clear that the effect is quite a powerful one for inducing compliance. Averaging over all three studies and comparing against the small request only control conditions, we were able to double the likelihood of compliance through the use of the rejection-then-moderation procedure. The strength of this procedure is further evidenced when it is realized that it is working in a direction counter to any tendency for the target to be consistent in his responses to requests for favors. It should be remembered that Freedman and Fraser (1966) found such a tendency for consistency to be a potent one in their foot-in-the-door study, and we found a similar tendency in the two requester control of Experiment 2 and the equivalent request control of Experiment 3. Seemingly, then, the size of the effect is such that it overwhelmed a strong propensity in our subjects for constancy in their reactions to compliance requests.

Second, the technique does not limit a requester to the receipt of small favors. It is only necessary that the critical request be *smaller* than the initial one for a reciprocal concessions mechanism to come into play. Evidence that a requester can use this technique to gain assent to a substantial request can be seen in the data of Experiment 1. The smaller request in that study might well be seen, objectively, as an extreme one in itself; it asked subjects to be responsible for an unspecified number of juvenile delinquents of unspecified age in a public place for a period of two hours outdoors in winter.[5] Only 16.7% of our population was willing to agree to such a request when it was the only one made. Yet, the proposal of this request after the rejection of a still more extreme favor produced 50% compliance.

Another benefit of the rejection-then-moderation procedure is that its force seems to derive from the existence of a social norm. Thus, a requester wishing to use the procedure need have little reward or coercive power over his target to be effective. Thibaut and Kelley (1959) speak of a norm in any two-person interaction as a third agent exercising power over each member but whose "influence appeal is to a supraindividual value ('Do it for the group' or 'Do it because it's good') rather than to personal interests. . . ." (p. 129) A recognition of this kind of normative influence in concession making may help explain some of the bargaining literature on the subject, in addition to the data of the present study. For instance, Pruitt and Drews (1969) report with some surprise their subjects' failure to try to maximize their outcomes when faced with a bargaining opponent who made a large, constant concession on each game trial. Even though this sort of opponent was perceived as significantly weaker and less demanding than one who made constant but small concessions on each trial, no advantage was taken of the vulnerable opponent. Everytime an opponent made a standard concession, no matter what the size, a subject responded with a standard concession of his own. Pruitt and Drews admit to being mystified by the lack of "rationality" on the part of their subjects and describe "them as 'automatons' tuning out external stimuli and new ideas, and moving mechanically a standard distance from the position adopted on the first trial." (p. 57) Perhaps much of the mystery can be eliminated by assuming that the subjects were reacting to the pressures of a norm requiring that regular concessions be reciprocated.

A final advantage of a compliance induction procedure which uses concessions involves the feelings of the target person toward the outcome of the interaction. Benton, Kelley, and Liebling (1972) present evidence suggesting that not only will someone who applies such a procedure be quite effective in obtaining favorable payoffs for himself but that the person to whom it is applied will feel more responsible for and satisfied with the outcome. In an allocation of resources situation, subjects faced a bargaining opponent who intransigently demanded the maximum payoff for himself, intransigently demanded a moderately favorably payoff for himself, or retreated from the maximum payoff demand to the moderate payoff demand. In each condition, failure to reach an allocation agreement resulted in a loss of all money by both participants. It was found that the retreat strategy produced the highest average earning for the opponent. Moreover, not only did subjects concede the greatest payoffs to an opponent using this tactic, they felt significantly more responsible for and satisfied with the outcome than did the subjects faced with an intransigent opponent. The results of this study when coupled with those of our experiments suggest some intriguing implications. One who feels responsible for the terms of an agreement should be more likely to meet his commitments concerning that agreement. Thus, someone who uses concession to produce compliance with a request for a favor is likely to see the favor actually performed. Second, one who feels fairly satisfied with the outcome of an interaction with another person should be willing to enter into interaction with that person again. Thus, the target person of a rejection-then-moderation moderation procedure may well be vulnerable to subsequent requests by the same requester. In all, then, it appears that the rejection-then-moderation procedure can be an extremely valuable technique for the elicitation of compliance.

A note of caution should probably be interjected at this point lest we make too much of the potential implications of the present findings. It is the case that the rejection-then-moderation procedure has been shown to work under a fairly limited set of conditions. The extent to which the effect is generalizable to other contexts and situations remains to be seen. For example, we have tested the effectiveness of the procedure only in situations in which the interaction was face-to-face, the interactants were of the same sex, and the requests were prosocial in nature. Moreover, it would be well to remember that, while the present research appears to support a reciprocal concessions interpretation of the effect, it in no way ultimately confirms that interpretation. Other explanations may exist which account completely for the data of this study; and to the extent that they do exist, they should be tested in subsequent work.

Future research on the reciprocal concessions procedure might also profitably investigate the nature of the concept of concession. In the present studies, a concession by a requester was operationalized as moderation from a large request to a smaller one. Involved in such moderation, however, are two separate components: the target will no doubt perceive the move from the large to the smaller request as *more* desirable for himself but *less* desirable for the requester and his cause. While these two aspects of concession usually occur together, there is no good reason to assume that both are necessary for the enhancement of compliance. It may be the proposal of a more desirable arrangement for the target—rather than the proposal of a less desirable arrangement for the requester—that is the crucial, compliance-producing aspect of concession; or the opposite may be the case. Stated otherwise, a concession involves two normally correlated but conceptually separate features: the granting of a more favorable situation to one's interaction partner and the surrendering of a more favorable position for oneself. It remains for further investigation to determine whether the aspect of concession which induces compliance involves the granting of something, the surrendering of something, or both.

Footnotes

[1] The experimenters were three college age students, one female and two male. Experimenters approached only subjects of the same sex as themselves.

[2] A replication of Experiment 2 was subsequently performed by the authors. The only difference between the original and replicated versions was that in the replication Experimenter C's performance in the two requester control did not include a claim that he had overheard the target's conversation with Experimenter A. The data of the two versions of Experiment 2 were virtually identical.

[3] It was necessary to discard the data of the original three subjects because of the likelihood that their responses to the second request would be mediated by a foot-in-the-door effect rather than a reciprocal concessions effect; thus our results would have been artificially inflated in the direction of prediction.

[4] In the present experiment there were four experimenters, three female and one male. Experimenters approached only subjects of the same sex as themselves.

[5] Only Experiment 1 was conducted in the winter of the year. Experiments 2 and 3 were conducted in the spring or summer which may account for the somewhat higher compliance rates in the small request only controls of these experiments.

Reprint requests should be sent to Robert Cialdini, Department of Psychology, Arizona State University, Tempe, Arizona 85281.

References

Azrin, N. H., Holz, W., Ulrich, R., & Goldiamond, I. The control of the content of conversation through reinforcement. *Journal of the Experimental Analysis of Behavior,* 1961, *4,* 25-30.

Benton, A. A., Kelley, H. H., & Liebling, B. Effects of extremity of offers and concession rate on the outcomes of bargaining. *Journal of Personality and Social Psychology,* 1972, *24,* 73-83.

Brehm, J. W., & Cole, A. H. Effect of a favor which reduces freedom. *Journal of Personality and Social Psychology,* 1966, *3,* 420-426.

Chertkoff, J. M., & Conley, M. Opening offer and frequency of concession as bargaining strategies. *Journal of Personality and Social Psychology,* 1967, *7,* 185-193.

Freedman, J. L., & Fraser, S. Compliance without pressure: The foot-in-the-door technique. *Journal of Personality and Social Psychology,* 1966, *4,* 195-202.

Goranson, R. E., & Berkowitz, L. Reciprocity and responsibility reactions to prior help. *Journal of Personality and Social Psychology,* 1966, *3,* 227-232.

Gouldner, A. W. The norm of reciprocity: A preliminary statement. *American Sociological Review,* 1960, *25,* 161-178.

Komorita, S. S., & Brenner, A. R. Bargaining and concession making under bilateral monopoly. *Journal of Personality and Social Psychology,* 1968, *9,* 15-20.

Pruitt, D. G. Reciprocity and credit building in a laboratory dyad. *Journal of Personality and Social Psychology,* 1968, *8,* 143-147.

Pruitt, D. G., & Drews, J. L. The effect of time pressure, time elapsed, and the opponent's concession rate on behavior in negotiation. *Journal of Experimental Social Psychology,* 1969, *5,* 43-60.

Regan, D. T. Effects of a favor and liking on compliance. *Journal of Experimental Social Psychology,* 1971, *1,* 627-639.

Rosenthal, R. *Experimenter effects in behavioral research.* New York: Appleton-Century-Crofts, 1966.

Snyder, M., & Cunningham, M. R. To comply or not comply: Testing the self-perception explanation of the "foot-in-the-door" phenomenon. *Journal of Personality and Social Psychology,* 1975, *31,* 64-67.

Thibaut, J. W., & Kelley, H. H. *The social psychology of groups.* New York: Wiley, 1959.

Wilke, H., & Lanzetta, J. T. The obligation to help: The effects of amount of prior help on subsequent helping behavior. *Journal of Experimental Social Psychology,* 1970, *6,* 488-493.

Indirect Social Influence Techniques

Status of Frustrator as an Inhibitor of Horn-Honking Responses[1]

Anthony N. Doob   *Department of Psychology, University of Toronto*

Alan E. Gross   *Department of Psychology, University of Wisconsin*

A. INTRODUCTION

Subjects may consciously attempt to present themselves in a favorable manner, they may cooperate with the experimenter or interviewer, and their reactions may be affected by the measurement process itself. In reviewing a number of such problems, Webb *et al.* (6, pp. 13-27) point out that some of these sources of contamination can be avoided when field data are collected from people who are unaware that they are subjects participating in an experiment. Although field procedures can reduce demand and reactivity effects, experimental manipulations outside of the laboratory may gain realism at the expense of control. The study reported here is an attempt to investigate unobtrusively some effects of frustration in a naturalistic setting without sacrificing experimental control.

Modern automobile traffic frequently creates situations which closely resemble classical formulations of how frustration is instigated. One such instance occurs when one car blocks another at a signal-controlled intersection. Unlike many traffic frustrations, this situation provides a clearly identifiable frustrator and a fairly typical response for the blocked driver: sounding his horn. Horn honking may function instrumentally to remove the offending driver and emotionally to reduce tension. Both kinds of honks may be considered aggressive, especially if they are intended to make the frustrator uncomfortable by bombarding him with unpleasant stimuli.

One factor that is likely to affect aggressive responses is the status of the frustrator (2, 3). The higher a person's status, the more likely it is he will have power to exercise sanctions, and although it is

improbable that a high status driver would seek vengeance against a honker, fear of retaliation may generalize from other situations where aggression against superiors has been punished.

Aggression is not the only kind of social response that may be affected by status. High status may inhibit the initiation of any social response, even a simple informational signal. Although it is difficult in the present study to distinguish informational from aggressive motivation, it is hypothesized that a high status frustrator will generally inhibit horn honking.

B. METHOD

One of two automobiles, a new luxury model or an older car, was driven up to a signal controlled intersection and stopped. The driver was instructed to remain stopped after the signal had changed to green until 15 seconds had elapsed, or until the driver of the car immediately behind honked his horn twice. Subjects were the 82 drivers, 26 women and 56 men, whose progress was blocked by the experimental car. The experiment was run from 10:30 a.m. to 5:30 p.m. on a Sunday, in order to avoid heavy weekday traffic.

1. Status Manipulation

A black 1966 Chrysler Crown Imperial hardtop which had been washed and polished was selected as a high status car.[2] Two low status cars were used: a rusty 1954 Ford station wagon and an unobtrusive gray 1961 Rambler sedan. The Rambler was substituted at noon because it was felt that subjects might reasonably attribute the Ford's failure to move to mechanical breakdown. Responses to these two cars did not turn out to be different, and the data for the two low status cars were combined.

2. Location

Six intersections in Palo Alto and Menlo Park, California, were selected according to these criteria: *(a)* a red light sufficiently long to insure that a high proportion of potential subjects would come to a complete stop behind the experimental car before the signal changed to green, *(b)* relatively light traffic so that only one car, the subject's, was likely to pull up behind the experimental car, and *(c)* a narrow street so that it would be difficult for the subject to drive around the car blocking him. Approximately equal numbers of high and low status trials were run at each intersection.

3. Procedure

By timing the signal cycle, the driver of the experimental car usually managed to arrive at the intersection just as the light facing him was turning red. If at least one other car had come to a complete stop behind the experimental car before the signal had turned green, a trial was counted, and when the light changed, an observer started two stop watches and a tape recorder. Observers were usually stationed in a car parked close to the intersection, but when this was not feasible, they were concealed from view in the back seat of the experimental car. High and low status trials were run simultaneously at different intersections, and the two driver-observer teams switched cars periodically during the day. Drivers wore a plaid sport jacket and white shirt while driving the Chrysler, and an old khaki jacket while driving the older car.

a. *Dependent measures.* At the end of each trial, the observer noted whether the subject had honked once, twice, or not at all. Latency of each honk and estimated length of each honk were recorded and later double-checked against tape recordings.

b. *Subject characteristics.* Immediately after each trial, the observer took down the year, make, and

model of the subject's car. Sex and estimated age of driver, number of passengers, and number of cars behind the experimental car when the signal changed were also recorded.

C. RESULTS AND DISCUSSION

Eight subjects, all men, were eliminated from the analysis for the following reasons: four cars in the low status condition and one in the high status condition went around the experimental car; on one trial the driver of the experimental car left the intersection early; and two cars in the low status condition, instead of honking, hit the back bumper of the experimental car, and the driver did not wish to wait for a honk. This left 38 subjects in the low status condition and 36 in the high status condition.

Although the drivers of the experimental cars usually waited for 15 seconds, two of the lights used in the experiment were green for only 12 seconds; therefore 12 seconds was used as a cutoff for all data. There were no differences attributable to drivers or intersections.

The clearest way of looking at the results is in terms of the percentage in each condition that honked at least once in 12 seconds. In the low status condition 84 percent of the subjects honked at least once, whereas in the high status condition, only 50 percent of the subjects honked ($\chi^2 = 8.37$, $df = 1$, $p < .01$). Another way of looking at this finding is in terms of the latency of the first honk. When no honks are counted as a latency of 12 seconds, it can be seen in Table 1 that the average latency for the new car was longer for both sexes. ($F = 10.71$, $p < .01$).

Thus, it is quite clear that status had an inhibitory effect on honking even once. It could be argued that status would have even greater inhibitory effects on more aggressive honking. Although one honk can be considered a polite way of calling attention to the green light, it is possible that subjects felt that a second honk would be interpreted as aggression.[3]

Forty-seven percent of the subjects in the low status condition honked twice at the experimental car, as compared to 19 percent of the subjects in the high status condition ($\chi^2 = 5.26$, $df = 1$, $p < .05$). This difference should be interpreted cautiously because it is confounded with the main result that more people honk generally in the low status condition. Of those who overcame the inhibitions to honk at all, 56 percent in the low status condition and 39 percent in

Table 1 Field Experiment (Mean Latency of First Honk in Seconds)

Frustrator	Sex of driver	
	Male	Female
Low status	6.8 (23)	7.6 (15)
High status	8.5 (25)	10.9 (11)

Note: Numbers in parentheses indicate the number of subjects.

Table 2 Number of Drivers Honking Zero, One, and Two Times

	Honking in 12 seconds		
Frustrator	Never	Once	Twice
Low status	6	14	18
High status	18	11	7

Note: Overall $\chi^2 = 11.14$, $p < .01$.

the high status condition honked a second time, a difference which was not significant. First-honk latencies for honkers were about equal for the two conditions. The overall findings are presented in Table 2.

Sex of driver was the only other measure that was a good predictor of honking behavior. In both conditions men tended to honk faster than women ($F = 4.49$, $p < .05$). The interaction of status and sex did not approach significance ($F = 1.17$). These data are consistent with laboratory findings (1) that men tend to aggress more than women.

Most experiments designed to study the effects of frustration have been carried out in the laboratory or the classroom, and many of these have employed written materials (2, 5).

It is undoubtedly much easier to use questionnaires, and if they produce the same results as field experiments, then in the interest of economy, they would have great advantage over naturalistic experiments. However, over 30 years ago, LaPiere warned that reactions to such instruments "may indicate what the responder would actually do when confronted with the situation symbolized in the question, but there is no assurance that it will" (4, p. 236).

In order to investigate this relationship between actual and predicted behavior, an attempt was made to replicate the present study as a questionnaire experiment. Obviously, the most appropriate sample to use would be one comprised of motorists sampled in the same way that the original drivers were sampled. Because this was not practicable, a questionnaire experiment was administered in a junior college classroom.

Subjects were 57 students in an introductory psychology class. Two forms of the critical item were included as the first of three traffic situations on a one-page questionnaire: "You are stopped at a traffic light behind a black 1966 Chrysler (gray 1961 Rambler). The light turns green and for no apparent reason the driver does not go on. Would you honk at him?" If

subjects indicated that they would honk, they were then asked to indicate on a scale from one to 14 seconds how long they would wait before honking. Forms were alternated so that approximately equal numbers of subjects received the Chrysler and Rambler versions. Verbal instructions strongly emphasized that subjects were to answer according to what they actually thought they would do in such a situation. No personal information other than sex, age, and whether or not they were licensed to drive was required.

After the questionnaire had been collected, the class was informed that different kinds of cars had been used for the horn-honking item. The experimenter then asked subjects to raise their hands when they heard the name of the car that appeared in the first item of their questionnaire. All subjects were able to select the correct name from a list of four makes which was read.

One subject (a female in the high status condition) failed to mark the honk latency scale, and another subject in the same condition indicated that she would go around the blocking car. Both of these subjects were eliminated from the analysis, leaving 27 in the high status condition and 28 in the low status condition. The results were analyzed in the same manner as the latency data from the field experiment. Means for each condition broken down by sex are presented in Table 3. Males reported that they thought that they would honk considerably sooner at the Chrysler than at the Rambler, whereas this was slightly reversed for females (interaction of sex and status $F = 4.97$, $p < .05$). Eleven subjects, six males in the low status condition and five females in the high status condition indicated that they would not honk within 12 seconds.

It is clear that the behavior reported on the questionnaire is different from the behavior actually observed in the field. The age difference in the samples may account for this disparity. Median estimated age of subjects in the field was 38, compared to a median

Table 3 Questionnaire Experiment (Mean Latency of Honking in Seconds)

	Sex of subject	
Frustrator	Male	Female
Low status	9.1 (18)	8.2 (10)
High status	5.5 (13)	9.2 (14)

Note: Numbers in parentheses indicate the number of subjects.

age of 22 in the classroom. In order to check the possibility that younger males would indeed honk faster at the high status car, the field data were reanalyzed by age. The results for younger males, estimated ages 16 to 30, fit the general pattern of the field results and differed from the results of the classroom experiment. In the field, young males honked sooner at the Rambler than at the Chrysler ($t = 2.74$, $df = 11$, $p < .02$).

Unfortunately, because these two studies differed in both sample and method, it is impossible to conclude that the differences are due to differences in the method of collecting data. However, it is clear that questionnaire data obtained from this often used population of subjects do not always correspond to what goes on in the real world.

Footnotes

[1] We wish to thank Tina Fox and Mike Rosenberg, the observers in the field experiment, and Lorraine Soderstrum of Foothill College, Los Altos Hills, California, who made her class available for the questionnaire experiment. The first author was supported by a Public Health Service Predoctoral Fellowship.

[2] We have labeled this operation a "status manipulation" because a large expensive car is frequently associated with wealth, power, and other qualities which are commonly regarded as comprising high status. However, it could be argued that Chrysler is potentially inhibiting not because it is a status symbol, but because of some other less plausible attribute (e.g., physical size).

[3] Series of honks separated by intervals of less than one second were counted as a single honk.

References

1. Buss, A. H. Instrumentality of aggression, feedback, and frustration as determinants of physical aggression. *J. of Personal. & Soc. Psychol.* 1966, *3*, 153-162.
2. Cohen, A. R. Social norms, arbitrariness of frustration, and status of the agent in the frustration-aggression hypothesis. *J. Abn. & Soc. Psychol.*, 1955, *51*, 222-226.
3. Hokanson, J. E., & Burgess, M. The effects of status, type of frustration and aggression on vascular processes. *J. Abn. & Soc. Psychol.*, 1962, *65*, 232-237.
4. LaPiere, R. T. Attitudes vs. actions. *Social Forces*, 1934, *13*, 230-237.
5. Pastore, N. The role of arbitrariness in the frustration-aggression hypothesis. *J. Abn. & Soc. Psychol.*, 1952, *47*, 728-731.
6. Webb, E. J., Campbell, D. T., Schwartz, R. D., & Sechrest, L. Unobtrusive Measures: Nonreactive Research in the Social Sciences. Chicago, Ill.: Rand McNally, 1966.

Department of Psychology, University of Toronto, Toronto 5, Canada.

The Stare as a Stimulus to Flight in Human Subjects: A Series of Field Experiments[1]

Phoebe C. Ellsworth[2]   *Stanford University*
J. Merrill Carlsmith
Alexander Henson

Abstract

A series of field experiments were performed to test the hypothesis that avoidance behavior is elicited in human subjects by staring. In each experiment, the experimenter stared (experimental group) or did not stare (control group) at people stopped at a traffic light, and measured their speed across the intersection when the light changed. Experimenters rode a motor scooter (Experiment I) or stood on the street corner. Subjects were pedestrians (Experiment IV) or automobile drivers. Presence versus absence of staring, sex of experimenter, and sex of subject were varied. In all experiments, crossing time was significantly shorter in the stare conditions. Main effects and interactions for sex disappeared when four male and four female experimenters were used (Experiments III and IV).

"The Stare as a Stimulus to Flight in Human Subjects: A Series of Field Experiments" by Phoebe C. Ellsworth, J. Merrill Carlsmith, and Alexander Henson. *Journal of Personality and Social Psychology,* 1972, Vol. 21, No. 3, pp. 302–311. Copyright © 1972 by The American Psychological Association, Inc. Reprinted by permission.

Crossing time was significantly shorter when subjects were stared at than when they were confronted with an incongruous situation which did not involve staring (Experiment V). There was no correlation between staring time and crossing time.

One of the most frequently reported components of agonistic or threat displays in primates is a steady, direct gaze at the object of aggression. This type of gaze is characteristic of the aggressive behavior of chimpanzees (Van Lawick-Goodall, 1968), gorillas (Schaller, 1963), and a wide variety of monkeys (Van Hooff, 1967). Typically, it occurs as a prelude to attack or as a substitute for it, depending on the reaction of the other animal. This reaction is usually flight, a submissive display, a return gaze, or a combination of these elements. Aggressive staring is probably more common in the dominant animal in an encounter, although the subordinate may sometimes stare back temporarily. Gaze *aversion* is more characteristic of the subordinate animal, and seems to be an expression of submission (Altmann, 1967) or an indication of peaceful intent. There are also some nonaggressive situations in which one animal may stare at another, although, in adults, direct staring at the face seems to occur primarily in aggressive encounters. Tentatively, the evidence seems to indicate that staring is necessary, but probably not sufficient for a display to be communicative of aggression in nonhuman primates.

Several students of primate behavior have suggested that the fixed stare is also a form of threat in man (e.g., Schaller, 1963; Van Lawick-Goodall, 1968), and Van Hooff (1967) noted that staring is often a prelude to attack in man as well as in other primates. There is some evidence that a gaze fixated on the object is a component of the expression of anger in humans (Ekman, 1972); however, the fact that staring may precede attack does not necessarily imply that staring serves as a signal of aggressive intent in man. Research on eye contact has shown that in a situation in which they are being negatively evaluated, subjects avoid looking at a hostile interviewer (Exline & Winters, 1965a), thus showing behavior similar to primate submission, and also rate the situation and the interviewer more negatively when the interviewer makes frequent eye contacts than when eye contact is infrequent (Ellsworth & Carlsmith, 1968). In neither of these studies, however, was prolonged direct staring used as a variable. In most experimental studies of visual interaction in humans (e.g., Argyle & Dean,

1965; Exline, Gray, & Schuette, 1965; Exline & Winters, 1965a, 1965b), the visual behavior of the subjects has been the dependent variable. In experiments in which eye contact has served as the independent variable (Argyle, Lalljee, & Cook, 1968; Ellsworth & Carlsmith, 1968; Exline & Eldridge, 1967), staring has not been one of the variables of interest.

The work of Exline and others indicates that eye contact is associated with a variety of sentiments, such as affiliation and interest, which are not related to aggression, and that, in fact, "a higher percentage of eye contact between communicators is typically associated with more positive attitudes between the communicators [Mehrabian, 1969, p. 364]." It is possible, however, that staring has different consequences from mere looking. Typically, in a two-person interaction, the visual behavior of the participants is extremely interdependent, with the rate of change of gaze direction very highly correlated (Kendon, 1967). For the purposes of the current study, a stare was roughly defined as a gaze or look which persists regardless of the behavior of the other person. The impact of a stare may be mitigated if the starer responds to the other person by smiling or talking; maximal impact will be achieved if the starer simply continues to stare without making any facial or verbal response to changes in the other person's behavior. The starer's visual and facial behavior, not being responsive to the other person's behavior, creates a type of interaction which is different from those studied in the above-mentioned experiments.[3] A stare, in these terms, is more analogous to the "spatial invasions" studied by Felipe and Sommer (1966) than to "eye contact" as conceptualized by those who have studied visual interaction.

The current study, then, was designed to examine the effects of one particular form of human visual behavior: the stare. It was hypothesized that if a stare has negative or threatening cue properties for people, then it should tend to elicit attempts to withdraw or escape from the situation. If escape is temporarily impossible, tension may build up, so that when the opportunity to escape does arise, the response may be exaggerated and thus more readily observable. A series of experiments were carried out to study this hypothesis. In four of the five experiments, the subjects were drivers stopped at an intersection for a red light; in the fifth, they were pedestrians in the same situation. While the subject was waiting for the light to change, the experimenter stared at him. It was hypothesized that when the light changed to green, the subjects who had been stared at would cross the intersection ("escape") faster than a control group of subjects who were not stared at.

PILOT STUDY AND GENERAL OVERVIEW

A pilot study was carried out to determine the general efficacy of the procedure. The experimenter pulled up next to the target car on a motor scooter, stared at the driver of the car until the traffic light changed, and measured the time it took the car to cross the intersection. A control group was simply timed. The results of the pilot study were favorable to the hypothesis: drivers who were stared at crossed the intersection significantly faster than those who were not ($t = 2.17$, $p < .025$). In order to test the generality of the phenomenon, sex of experimenter and sex of subject were systematically varied in the four subsequent experiments. The first experiment was a simple replication of the pilot study. The use of the motor scooter in this experiment raised the possibility that any aggressive overtones in the situation might have been due to a certain motor-vehicle-oriented type of competition. Thus, a second experiment was run in which the experimenter simply stood on a street corner. In Experiment III, four male experimenters and four female experimenters were used in order to conduct a valid test of the effects of staring across dyads including all combinations of sex of experimenter and sex of subject. In Experiment IV, an attempt was made to extend the generality of the findings by using pedestrians as subjects. And finally, in Experiment V, a control group was added in which the experimenter engaged in an "incongruous," "inappropriate" behavior that did not involve eye contact with the subject.

Experiment I

Method   *Subjects.* Seventy-seven drivers, ranging in age from about 16 to 70, served as subjects. Of these, 36 were male, and all were Caucasian. Drivers making turns were not used as subjects, nor were drivers who initiated conversations with the experimenter. There were six subjects in this latter category, all of whom were in the stare condition.[4] Finally, two other potential subjects were eliminated because it was obvious that they did not notice the experimenter because their attention was occupied with a distracting store window display.

Setting. The experiment was carried out at a busy intersection on a four-lane street in the commercial center of a suburban town (population 56,000) near Stanford University. The results of the pilot study indicated that time of day was not a significant variable, so the subjects were run during both the morning and the afternoon at all hours except rush hours. Both the male and the female experimenters were college undergraduates.

Procedure. The situation was timed so that the experimenter, astride a rather dilapidated motor scooter, was always the first one to arrive at the red signal. The experimenter stopped at the signal in the inside lane, so as to be able to stare into the target car on the driver's side. Each experimenter had a list of the sequence of conditions in which the subjects were to be run, drawn up previously with the order of conditions determined by a table of random numbers. Every Caucasian subject who pulled up next to the experimenter at the light, and who proceeded straight across the intersection was included as a subject, precluding experimenter bias in the selection of subjects and their assignment of conditions. If the driver made a turn at the intersection, the next subject was run in the same condition.

In the stare condition, when the subject pulled up next to the scooter, the experimenter turned his/her head and stared directly at the subject's face. The eye-to-eye distance between the experimenter and the subject was between 4 and 5 feet. The experimenter never wore dark glasses and always delivered the stare manipulation with the naked eye. Subjects were run whether or not they were wearing dark glasses.[5] The experimenter maintained the same impassive, neutral expression throughout the staring period. The stoplight was visible in the experimenter's field of vision. As soon as it changed to green, the staring period ended and the crossing period began. The crossing period ended when the rear wheels of the subject's car crossed the nearer of the white lines on the far side of the intersection. The experimenter did not start driving until after the subject's crossing time had been measured. A two-handed stopwatch was used for measuring the staring time and the crossing time. (The stopwatch was kept in the experimenter's pocket throughout the timing, and was thus not visible to the subject.) As the experimenter began to stare, both hands were set in motion. One hand was stopped when the light changed (giving a measure of the staring time), and the other when the subject reached the other side of the intersection (giving a measure of total time). The crossing time was obtained by subtracting the staring time from the total time, and thus included the amount of time it took the driver to start as well as the actual time spent in crossing. The experimenter then turned the corner, pulled over to the side of the street, and wrote down the staring time, total time, and the subject's sex and estimated age (by decade).

The procedure in the no-stare control group was identical to that in the stare condition, except that the experimenter merely glanced at the subject to get the information on sex and age, and then looked away. When the light changed, the crossing time was recorded. The design thus was a $2 \times 2 \times 2$ factorial, varying presence versus absence of staring, sex of experimenter, and sex of subject. The results of Experiment I are discussed below along with the results of Experiment II.

Experiment II

Method.   In order to rule out possible "challenge" or "drag racing" effects which might potentially be expected to produce the predicted effect in Experiment I, where both the experimenter and the subject were equipped with motors and wheels, Experiment II was run without the scooter. The setting was switched to a one-way street parallel to the street in Experiment I and a block away from it. The experimenter stood on the corner of the sidewalk and, in the stare condition, began staring as soon as a car pulled up in the nearer lane and stopped for a red light. Eighty-eight Caucasian subjects were run, covering approximately the same age range as in Experiment I. Forty-seven of the subjects were male. Three additional drivers were not used as subjects because they did not notice the experimenter. The male experimenter was the same as in Experiment I, and the female was a graduate student. The eye-to-eye distance was between 4 and 6 feet. The assignment of subjects to conditions and the recording of staring times and crossing times were carried out in exactly the same manner as in

Experiment I, and the other precautions used in the experiment were also maintained. The street corner was not a popular hitchhiking location, and, in fact, neither of the experimenters ever found any other person waiting there. In addition, hitchhikers in this town almost always signal their intent with either a thumb or a painted sign or both, whereas the experimenters simply stood there. It is conceivable that some drivers believed the experimenters to be hitchhikers, though none gave any indication that this was the case.

The design was a $2 \times 2 \times 2$ factorial with the same variables as in Experiment I.

Results of Experiments I and II

The basic hypothesis was strongly supported in both experiments. Subjects who were stared at crossed the intersection significantly faster than subjects in the no-stare condition. In Experiment I, the mean crossing time was 5.3 seconds in the stare condition and 6.5 seconds in the no-stare condition; in Experiment II, the means were 5.5 seconds and 6.7 seconds, respectively. In both experiments, the variance was greater in the no-stare than in the stare condition, but according to Hartley's test (Winer, 1962, p. 93), the assumption of homogeneity of variance was not violated. Tables 1 and 2 show the eight means for each experiment. Tables 3 and 4 show the analyses of variance, calculated with an unweighted-means analysis (Winer, 1962, p. 222). In both experiments, the main effect for staring is highly significant ($p < .001$). The fact that the effect occurred in both experiments indicates that the increased speed was primarily an avoidance reaction rather than a response to a perceived racing challenge.

There was also a significant main effect for sex of experimenter in both experiments, with subjects crossing the intersection faster in the presence of a

Table 1 Mean Crossing Times in Experiment I (Scooter)

	Stare				No stare			
Male experimenter		Female experimenter		Male experimenter		Female experimenter	
Male subject	Female subject	Male subject	Female subject	Male subject	Female subject	Male subject	Female subject
5.2 (8)	5.9 (13)	4.8 (10)	5.3 (9)	8.0 (6)	6.5 (13)	6.1 (12)	5.9 (6)
5.6 (21)		5.0 (19)		6.9 (19)		6.1 (18)	
5.3 (40)				6.5 (37)			

Note.—$N = 77$; numbers in parentheses indicate cell *ns*.

Table 2   Mean Crossing Times in Experiment II (Street Corner)

	Stare				No stare		
Male experimenter		Female experimenter		Male experimenter		Female experimenter	
Male subject	Female subject	Male subject	Female subject	Male subject	Female subject	Male subject	Female subject
5.9 (10)	6.3 (11)	4.9 (12)	4.8 (10)	6.7 (13)	7.5 (9)	6.1 (12)	6.8 (11)
6.1 (21)		4.8 (22)		7.0 (22)		6.4 (23)	
5.5 (43)				6.7 (45)			

Note.—$N = 88$; numbers in parentheses indicate cell *ns*.

female experimenter (Experiment I: $p < .01$; Experiment II: $p < .001$). In Experiment I, there was also a significant interaction between staring and sex of subject, such that males crossed the intersection faster than females in the stare condition and slower in the no-stare condition ($p < .01$). This interaction was not significant in Experiment II, where there was a slight but significant main effect for sex of subject, with males crossing faster than females in all conditions ($p < .05$).

Since the duration of the stare could not be held constant (as it depended on how soon the target car arrived at the intersection before the light changed), the actual starting time varied from 3.4 seconds to 27.5 seconds in Experiment I and from 3.0 seconds to 19.5 seconds in Experiment II (the traffic light in Experiment II had a shorter period than in Experiment I). In neither experiment, however, was the staring time correlated significantly with the crossing time (Experiment I: $r = .09$; Experiment II: $r = .06$). Thus, it would seem that once a person recognizes that he is being stared at, the tendency to escape is immediately elicited at, or nearly at, full strength, rather than becoming stronger as the disturbing stimulus continues. Inspection of scatter plots of the

data suggested no evidence of nonrectilinear correlations.

The estimated age of the subjects was slightly correlated with crossing time in Experiment I ($r = .21$, $p < .05$). This correlation, however, was almost entirely due to the behavior of the subjects in the no-stare condition; age and crossing time were not significantly correlated in the stare condition. Thus, it seems highly unlikely that being stared at accentuates a competitive urge in peers. In Experiment II, there was no significant correlation between age and crossing time.

In neither experiment was there any difference in crossing time related to the presence of passengers in the car. Cars with passengers were not very common, and were fairly evenly distributed among the eight cells in both experiments.

Experiment III

Method.   The main effects and interaction for the sex variables in Experiments I and II were unexpected and difficult to interpret. In addition, it seemed unwise to draw any conclusions on the basis of the sex of experimenter variable, since there was only one

Table 3   Analysis of Variance for Experiment I (Scooter)

Source	df	MS	F
Stare (A)	1	31.93	24.75**
Sex of experimenter (B)	1	12.79	9.91*
Sex of subject (C)	1	.26	.20
A × B	1	2.38	1.84
A × C	1	9.79	7.59*
B × C	1	1.06	.82
A × B × C	1	2.29	1.78
Within error	69	1.29	

*$p < .01$.
**$p < .001$.

Table 4   Analysis of Variance for Experiment II (Corner)

Source	df	MS	F
Stare (A)	1	36.31	44.28**
Sex of experimenter (B)	1	20.00	24.39**
Sex of subject (C)	1	4.16	5.20*
A × B	1	1.96	2.39
A × C	1	1.41	1.71
B × C	1	.33	.40
A × B × C	1	.23	.28
Within error	80	.82	

*$p < .05$.
**$p < .001$.

Table 5 Mean Crossing Times in Experiment III (Eight Experimenters, Driver Subjects)

Stare				No stare			
Male experimenter		Female experimenter		Male experimenter		Female experimenter	
Male subject	Female subject	Male subject	Female subject	Male subject	Female subject	Male subject	Female subject
5.6 (20)	5.8 (12)	5.5 (21)	5.6 (11)	6.3 (22)	6.5 (10)	6.0 (17)	7.0 (15)
5.7 (32)		5.5 (32)		6.3 (32)		6.5 (32)	
5.6 (64)				6.4 (64)			

Note.—$N = 128$; numbers in parentheses indicate cell *ns*.

experimenter of each sex in each experiment, and the results could easily have been due to other characteristics of the individual experimenters. In order to elucidate the problems raised by the significant sex effects, Experiment III was run with four male experimenters and four female experimenters. Because the street used in Experiment II had been switched to two-way, the setting was moved to another one-way street in the same town, about 10 blocks away. The method was the same as in Experiment II, except that an observer, unaware of the condition for each subject, recorded the crossing times from a position on the other side of the street from the experimenter. This procedure precluded the accurate recording of staring times, but given the near-zero correlations between staring time and crossing time in Experiments I and II, it seemed more valuable to eliminate the possibility of measurement bias arising from the experimenter's knowledge of the subject's condition than to gather additional data on the staring

Table 6 Analysis of Variance for Experiment III (Eight Experimenters, Driver Subjects)

Source	df	MS	F
Stare (A)	1	5.78	30.42*
Sex of subjects (B)	1	.97	
Experimenter (C)	7	.63	
Sex of experimenter (D)	1	.11	
A × B	1	.66	
A × C	7	.19	
A × D	1	.19	
B × C	7	.38	
B × D	1	.16	
A × B × C	7	.21	
A × B × D	1	.39	
Within error	96	.32	

*$p < .005$.

time–crossing time relationship. The observer could not tell whether the experimenter was staring or not. A total of 128 subjects were run, of whom 80 were male. Each experimenter ran 16 subjects. None of the experimenters had run subjects in Experiment I or Experiment II, and all were college freshmen. The eye-to-eye distance between the experimenter and the subject was the same as in Experiment II, and the selection of subjects and their assignment to conditions were carried out in the same manner as in the other two experiments, except that non-Caucasian subjects were also run.

The design of the experiment was thus a $2 \times 2 \times 2$ factorial, varying stare versus no stare, sex of subject, and sex of experimenter. In addition, we can analyze the effect of the eight experimenters.

Results. The results are presented in Table 5, and an unweighted-means analysis of variance is shown in Table 6. The results are analyzed as a $2 \times 2 \times 8$ factorial, with experimenters contributing the eight levels in order to show the appropriate error terms for the F tests. Sex of experimenter, with one degree of freedom, is shown as a part of each mean square involving experimenters. It is apparent once again that staring reduces the amount of time taken to cross the intersection. When subjects are stared at, they take an average of 5.6 seconds to cross the intersection; when not stared at, they average 6.4 seconds. Viewing experiments as a random factor in the analysis, the appropriate F test for this effect uses the Stare × Experimenter interaction as an error term ($F = 30.42$, $df = 1/7$, $p < .005$).

Table 6 also indicates that the troublesome effects attributable to sex which appeared in the first two experiments have disappeared. There are no main effects of either sex of experimenter or sex of subject which approach significance, nor are there any interactions which appear to approach significance.

Evidently, the effects observed in the first two experiments were due to idiosyncratic characteristics of the particular experimenters used. It is of some interest to note that in this experiment there was no effect due to the experimenters, nor did that variable interact with anything else. This gives us some confidence in the extent to which we can generalize about this phenomenon across various individuals who may be staring.

Experiment IV

Method.   In the three experiments reported so far, the subjects were always automobile drivers. Although the "drag-race challenge" hypothesis was ruled out by depriving the experimenters of their wheels, the possibility remains that drivers may be motivated to demonstrate the power of their cars, the speed of their reactions, or other less obvious qualities when supplied with an attentive spectator. In order to rule out car-specific hypotheses altogether, Experiment IV was conducted with pedestrians as subjects, on the assumption that fast walking is not considered indicative of prowess or bravado. The street corner was the same as in Experiment I. The experimenter stood on the corner of the sidewalk, and in the stare condition began staring as soon as a pedestrian came up to the crosswalk and faced the red light. Each experimenter had a supply of 16 jelly beans in his/her pocket, 8 each of two different colors. One color signified the stare condition, the other, the no-stare condition. When a potential subject arrived at the crosswalk, the experimenter removed 1 of the jelly beans, noted its color, and ate it. In this manner, a quasi-random assignment of subjects to conditions was achieved without the experimenter attracting the attention of the subject and other bystanders by consulting a list. As in Experiment II, the timing was

done by an observer on the other side of the street who was unable to tell whether the experimenter was staring or not. Since the first person to reach the corner was always the subject, the observer had no difficulty determining which pedestrian to time. The crossing time was defined as the interval between the onset of the green light and the moment when the subject stepped up onto the curb after crossing the street. The eight experimenters were the same as in Experiment III, and the eye-to-eye distance between the experimenter and the subject varied from 3½ to 4½ feet. The staring manipulation may have been somewhat more salient to the subjects in this experiment than in the car studies, since occasionally a third person would come up and block the experimenter's line of regard, forcing him to shift his position in order to reestablish a clear view. Each experimenter ran 16 subjects, for a total of 128, of whom 73 were male.

The design of this experiment is essentially the same as Experiment III. A $2 \times 2 \times 2$ factorial design, varying stare versus no stare, sex of subject, and sex of experimenter comprised the basic design. Again, the analysis treats the design as a $2 \times 2 \times 8$ design, with one degree of freedom corresponding to sex of experimenters pulled out from the experimenter and experimenter interaction sum of squares in each case.

Results.   Again, the results suggest a strong effect due to the staring of the experimenter. Table 7 shows the mean crossing time for all groups. The means are not comparable to earlier experiments, since the subjects in this experiment had to walk across the intersection. Subjects who were stared at crossed the intersection in an average of 11.1 seconds; control subjects required 12.2 seconds. This difference is reflected in the analysis of variance by an F ratio of 29.91 ($df = 1/7$, $p < .005$). Once again, there is no strong evidence of any main effect or interaction

Table 7   Mean Crossing Time for Experiment IV (Eight Experimenters, Pedestrian Subjects)

Stare				No stare			
Male experimenter		Female experimenter		Male experimenter		Female experimenter	
Male subject	Female subject	Male subject	Female subject	Male subject	Female subject	Male subject	Female subject
11.1 (23)	10.9 (10)	11.6 (16)	10.9 (17)	12.1 (17)	11.0 (14)	12.8 (17)	12.9 (14)
11.0 (33)		11.2 (33)		11.6 (31)		12.9 (31)	
11.1 (66)				12.2 (62)			

Note.—$N = 128$; numbers in parentheses indicate cell *ns*.

Table 8 Analysis of Variance for Experiment IV (Eight Experimenters, Pedestrian Subjects)

Source	df	MS	F
Stare (A)	1	10.17	29.91*
Sex of subject (B)	1	2.52	
Experimenter (C)	7	2.91	
Sex of experimenter (D)	1	3.79	
A × B	1	.01	
A × C	7	.34	
A × D	1	1.36	
B × C	7	1.19	
B × D	1	.37	
A × B × C	7	.62	
A × B × D	1	.65	
Within error	96	1.00	

*$p < .005$.

involving sex of experimenter or sex of subject. Again, staring leads to flight, as defined by speed of departure from the presence of the starer when the situation permits. This phenomenon is independent of any characteristics observable in our sample of eight starers.

Experiment V

Although the results of the first four experiments supported the notion that a direct fixed stare elicits avoidance in a variety of situations, the interpretation of the situation in terms of the interpersonal, communicative aspects of the stare was not the only possible approach to an explanation of the effect. The behavior of the starer was unusual and incongruous, and it was impossible to rule out an interpretation based on the hypothesis that people are motivated to withdraw from all situations in which other people are behaving incongruously or inappropriately. According to this hypothesis, staring would simply be one example of incongruous behavior, and the fact that it happened to be a form of behavior included within the framework of nonverbal communication research would be irrelevant in terms of its motivating properties in the experimental situation reported here.

Method.   In order to test this hypothesis, it was first necessary to devise an adequate operational definition of incongruity. The authors wished to avoid using an incongruous behavior that would "load" the experiment one way or the other, either by using a situation with threatening overtones (e.g., a male experimenter standing on the corner cracking a whip),

or by using a situation with sexual overtones (e.g., a female sunbathing on the sidewalk). In order to provide a fair test, it was important to select a behavior in which incongruity was the only salient and reliable stimulus property. In order to find such a behavior, an informal questionnaire containing a list of 20 possible "incongruous" behaviors that could be applied in the experimental paradigm was presented to 30 undergraduates taking the introductory psychology course. The students were asked to rate the situations on a number of scales and to provide their own adjectival label for each situation. On the basis of the results of this pretest and other informal questioning, an operational definition of perceived incongruity was devised.

Procedure.   The experimenter sat on the sidewalk with a hammer, on a street corner a block away from that used in Experiment III, and began to tap and pick at the sidewalk in front of her whenever a car pulled up in the nearer lane and stopped for a red light. She did not look at the driver of the car or acknowledge his presence in any way, but simply went on with her activity, calmly and quietly. Two additional conditions were run: a replication of the stare condition used in Experiments II-III and a replication of the no-stare condition. During these two conditions, the experimenter hid the hammer behind a telephone pole so that it was not visible to the subject. The experimenter was the same female graduate student as in Experiment II, and the drivers were timed across the intersection by a high school student who was hired for the occasion and who was unaware of the hypothesis. The timer stood on the sidewalk across the street from the experimenter and a little to the rear of the car, as in Experiment III. Thirty subjects were run, 10 in each condition. The distance between the experimenter and the subject was the same as in Experiments II and III, as was the method by which the subjects were selected and assigned to conditions.

Results.   The hypothesis that incongruity is the relevant stimulus to flight in this situation was not confirmed. The mean crossing times were 4.0 seconds in the stare condition, 5.7 in the no-stare condition, and 5.5 in the incongruity condition. A one-way analysis of variance was performed on the data, yielding a significant effect for treatments ($F = 5.97$, $p < .01$). A comparison between the stare condition and the average of the other two (Winer, 1962, p. 67) indicated that the stare condition was clearly different from the other conditions and that there was very little difference between the incongruity and the no-stare condition ($F = 11.68$, $p < .005$). Thus, the construct of incongruity, in itself, seems insufficient to explain the results of the series of experiments reported here.

The variance was smallest in the stare condition, intermediate in the no-stare condition, and largest in the incongruity condition, but these variances did not differ among themselves sufficiently to violate the assumption of homogeneity. In this and the other experiments reported here, the consistently low variances in the stare conditions are probably due to a floor effect. The differences among the variances, however, provide some slight additional evidence that the effect of staring is not the same as the effect of any incongruous situation which does not involve staring. In the incongruous situation, the variability was slightly increased over that in the no-stare control group, while staring seems to have a more unifying effect on subjects' behavior.

DISCUSSION

Staring Time and Crossing Time

The fact that the staring time was not correlated with the subjects' speed across the intersection in Experiments I and II is quite important, since it indicates that the full avoidance response is elicited by the perception that one is being stared at. The duration of the gaze necessary for it to be perceived as a stare and therefore to produce the avoidance response is very short; in these experiments, subjects who were stared at for less than 5 seconds drove off just as fast as those who were stared at for 18 seconds or more. Psychologically, the actual amount of time spent gazing is probably less relevant to the perceiver's reaction than certain behavioral criteria, the most important of which is the starer's failure to react to the other person's glance. The expected reaction on the part of the starer would seem to be either gaze aversion (analogous to a primate appeasement signal), or a mitigating change in facial expression, such as a smile (also a signal in the absence of hostile intent), or some verbal clarification of the situation; if none of these occurs immediately, the gaze is capable of eliciting the avoidance response, even in the absence of other hostile signals (such as a frown). This temporal relationship was clearly apparent in the behavior of the subjects in the experiments reported here. As soon as they had stopped at the light, most of them would begin to look around and would almost immediately notice the starer. Within a second or two, they would avert their own gaze and begin to indulge in a variety of apparently nervous behaviors, such as fumbling with their clothing or radio, revving up the engines of their cars, glancing frequently at the traffic light, or initiating animated conversation with their passengers.[6] If there was a long time interval before the light changed, the subjects tended to glance furtively back at the experimenter, averting their gaze as soon as their eyes met his. It should be remembered that the six drivers who attempted to converse with the experimenter in Experiment I (and thus were not used as subjects) were all in the stare condition. In the no-stare condition, the subject's eyes occasionally met the experimenter's while the experimenter was glancing over to make a note of the subject's age and sex. In these cases the experimenter immediately looked away, the subjects sat quietly waiting for the light to change, then crossed the intersection at speeds no different from those of the subjects who did not see the experimenter glance at them.

The Staring Effect

The studies reported here demonstrate that staring at humans can elicit the same sort of responses that are common in primates; that is, staring can act like a primate threat display. Furthermore, this effect was obtained by 11 different experimenters in three different situations. However, the fact that avoidance is a predictable response in these situations does not necessarily imply that staring functions as an unequivocal signal of aggressive intent in man as it does in many other primates. Nor does it necessarily imply that staring automatically triggers a response (attack or flight or their surrogates) appropriate to an agonistic encounter. In most primate groups, both the role relationships and the individual's "rules" of behavior for expressing aggressive, nonaggressive, or submissive intent are relatively clear-cut, so that the question of what a behavior means or what response is appropriate in a given situation comes up much less frequently than it does in human interactions. In the experiments reported here, it is quite possible that the subjects became tense for lack of an appropriate response for the situation. Thus, there are two possible explanations for the results, the degree of overlap between them depending on the generality of the perception of staring as a form of threat. The first is that staring is generally perceived as a signal of hostile intent, as in primates, and elicits avoidance (or, in some circumstances, counterattack). The second is that gazing at a person's face is an extremely salient stimulus with interpersonal implications which cannot be ignored. The stare, in effect, is a demand for a response, and in a situation where there is no appropriate response, tension will be evoked, and the subject will be motivated to escape the situation.

A situation in which there is no apparent response often involves incongruous behavior, or, in Sommer's terms (Felipe & Sommer, 1966), norm violation. The incongruous or norm-violating properties of the staring situation, however, are insufficient to account for the avoidance response; in Experiment V, it was demonstrated that avoidance is not a necessary response to incongruous behavior. Although there was no apparent appropriate response in the incongruous condition, neither was there any demand for a response from the subject; he could remain uninvolved. If it is assumed that staring is a salient stimulus which forcibly involves the subject in an interpersonal encounter and demands a response, the fact that there is no appropriate response becomes very important to the subject, arousing tension and eliciting avoidance at the earliest possible moment. The invasions of personal space studied by Felipe and Sommer (1966) have properties similar to those postulated here for staring; in addition to violating a norm, the experimenter's behavior was of a kind that precluded subjective noninvolvement.

This interpretation of the stare in human interactions, as well as the alternative hypothesis that staring is typically perceived as a threat, should be tested in the laboratory. The questions which this line of research next suggest are: *(a)* Do subjects perceive a stare as an indication of hostile intent in the absence of other aggressive cues? *(b)* When appropriate responses are available, does the stare evoke these responses, or does it still evoke withdrawal? *(c)* Under what circumstances does staring elicit avoidance behavior, and under what circumstances is it perceived as a threat?

Footnotes

[1] Elizabeth Hastorf served as the female experimenter in Experiment I. In Experiments III and IV, the experimenters were Barbara Alperin, Jim Austin, John Mower, Judy Payne, Steve Savery, John Weeks, Kathy Weinberger, and Judy Whitney. Their assistance is gratefully acknowledged.

[2] Requests for reprints should be sent to Phoebe C. Ellsworth, who is now at the Department of Psychology, Yale University, New Haven, Connecticut 06510.

[3] This distinction is clearer in principle than in fact. In several of the experiments cited here, the experimenter maintained a steady gaze toward the subject, so as to be able to speak justifiably of "eye contact." The representativeness of this procedure has been questioned on the grounds of its similarity to staring as defined here (Duncan, 1969; Ellsworth & Carlsmith, 1968).

[4] Because of the possibility that the elimination of these subjects might have biased the results in favor of the predicted outcome (e.g., if the conversationalists were genial, slow-moving people), the data were reanalyzed, with the six slowest subjects in the stare condition eliminated. This procedure did not alter the significance level of the results ($t = 3.64$, $p < .001$).

[5] At the suggestion of Michael Argyle, a follow-up study was run to determine whether staring had differential effects on subjects with and without dark glasses. There were no differences in crossing time between the two groups.

[6] Incidentally, the variety of these behaviors coupled with the low variance in the stare condition provides some evidence against the possible alternative explanation that subjects in the stare condition were more attentive to the traffic light, and thus more likely to start moving as soon as it changed. No comparative data were collected on this question since it was impossible to observe the subjects' gaze direction in the no-stare condition.

References

Altmann, S. A. The structure of primate communication. In S. A. Altmann (Ed.), *Social communication among primates.* Chicago: University of Chicago Press, 1967.

Argyle, M., & Dean, J. Eye contact, distance and affiliation. *Sociometry,* 1965, *28,* 289-304.

Argyle, M., Lalljee, M., & Cook, M. The effects of visibility on interaction in a dyad. *Human Relations,* 1968, *21,* 3-17.

Duncan, S., Jr. Nonverbal communication. *Psychological Bulletin,* 1969, *22,* 118-137.

Ekman, P. Universals and cultural differences in facial expressions of emotion. *Nebraska Symposium on Motivation,* 1972, in press.

Ellsworth, P. C., & Carlsmith, J. M. The effects of eye contact and verbal content on affective responses to a dyadic interaction. *Journal of Personality and Social Psychology,* 1968, *10,* 15-20.

Exline, R. V., & Eldridge, C. Effects of two patterns of a speaker's visual behavior upon the perception of the authenticity of his verbal message. Paper presented at the meeting of the Eastern Psychological Association, Boston, April 1967.

Exline, R. V., Gray, D., & Schuette, D. Visual behavior in a dyad as affected by interview content and sex of respondent. *Journal of Personality and Social Psychology,* 1965, *1,* 201-209.

Exline, R. V., & Winters, L. C., Affective relations and mutual glances in dyads. In S. Tomkins & C. Izard (Eds.), *Affect, cognition, and personality.* New York: Springer, 1965. (a)

Exline, R. V., & Winters, L. C. The effects of cognitive difficulty and cognitive style upon eye-to-eye contact in interviews. Paper presented at the annual meeting of the American Psychological Association, Chicago, September 1965. (b)

Felipe, N. J., & Sommer, R. Invasions of personal space. *Social Problems,* 1966, *14,* 206-214.

Kendon, A. Some functions of gaze-direction in social interaction. *Acta Psychologica,* 1967, *26,* 22-63.

Mehrabian, A. Significance of posture and position in the communication of attitude and status relationships. *Psychological Bulletin,* 1969, *71,* 359-372.

Schaller, G. B. *The mountain gorilla: Ecology and behavior.* Chicago: University of Chicago Press, 1963.

Van Hooff, J. A. R. A. M. The facial displays of the Catarrhine monkey and apes. In D. Morris (Ed.), *Primate ethology.* Chicago: Aldine, 1967.

Van Lawick-Goodall, J. A preliminary report on expressive movements and communication in the Gombe Stream chimpanzees. In P. C. Jay (Ed.), *Primates: Studies in adaptation and variability.* New York: Holt, Rinehart & Winston, 1968.

Winer, B. J. *Statistical principles in experimental design.* New York: McGraw-Hill, 1962.

Group Influences

Blackjack and the Risky Shift, II: Monetary Stakes

Jim Blascovich   *Marquette University*

Gerald P. Ginsburg   *University of Nevada, Reno*

René C. Howe

Abstract

Group influence on risk taking was studied in a realistic casino setting, using blackjack as the criterion risk task and amount bet as the risk measure. State trial judges from around the nation volunteered to serve as participants and bet their own money. The results clearly reveal a shift to risk and replicate findings from prior blackjack studies which had used college students as subjects and gaming chips of no real monetary value. Specifically, a modest increase in risk levels over time was found for individuals before they entered into group play; and a strong increase in risk levels was obtained during subsequent group play. These findings were accounted for by Blascovich and Ginsburg's two-process model.

"Blackjack and the Risky Shift, II: Monetary Stakes" by Jim Blascovich, Gerald P. Ginsburg, and René C. Howe. *Journal of Experimental Social Psychology* 11, 224–232 (1975). Copyright © 1975 by Academic Press, Inc. Reprinted by permission.

Choice shifts, especially those involving risk, have been the subject of many social psychological investigations. It has been suggested that most investigations of choice shifts involving risk have relied upon a single instrument of questionable validity, the Choice Dilemmas Questionnaire, and that consequently our understanding of choice shifts must be recognized as tentative (Blascovich, Veach, & Ginsburg, 1973; Cartwright, 1971). A series of risky-shift studies (Blascovich, 1972; Blascovich & Ginsburg, 1974; Blascovich, Veach, & Ginsburg, 1973) used a conceptually and methodologically more adequate risk task, blackjack, and generated findings which counter some of the conclusions of recent reviews (Dion, Baron, & Miller, 1970; Pruitt, 1971a,b). For example, the blackjack investigations strongly implied that a social comparison rather than relevant arguments position is more tenable as an explanation of risky shifts.

The blackjack investigations have clearly demonstrated both an individual increase in risk taking which levels off over time and an additional group effect. In addition, while outcomes, wins or losses, differentially affect the level of risk taking (amount bet), they do not affect either the size or the directions of group produced shifts. The major findings of Blascovich *et al.* have been replicated by an independent investigator, using the blackjack task.[1]

Blascovich suggested (1972) and refined (1974) a pluralistic explanation of choice shifts involving risk. It is pluralistic because both an intraindividual and an interindividual process are postulated. The intraindividual process involves a type of a familiarization with the risk task and is reflected in the increases in risk taking (bets) by individuals over blackjack hands (Blascovich, 1972; Blascovich & Ginsburg, 1974; Blascovich, Veach, & Ginsburg, 1973). It should be pointed out that the type of familiarization specified in this theory is *not* of the type described by Bateson (1966) who suggested that a person develops enough self-justifying reasons to enable himself to make a riskier decision. Rather, the familiarization process suggested by Blascovich *et al.* involves the individual becoming acquainted or "familiar" with the risk task. This may involve "seeing how the cards are falling," and implies that the individual must experience outcomes in order to establish subjective probabilities of alternative outcomes. That an individual will gradually increase his level of risk taking may be due, at least in part, to the tendency of individuals to overestimate the probability of successful outcomes. This is a type of gambler's fallacy. It also has been called an optimism effect (Kidd and Morgan, 1969) and has been demonstrated in decision-making studies (Kidd, 1970), subjective probability studies (deFinetti, 1970) and gambling studies (Hochauer, 1970). Clearly, a tendency of individuals to overestimate the probability of successful outcomes could lead to a gradual increase in risk taking, especially on a risk task such as blackjack in which the probabilities of winning and losing are about equal.

In addition to the intraindividual process, an interindividual process has been specified, since increases in risk taking level off during continued individual play, but take a large jump during group play. Moreover, since both groups with discussion and groups without discussion, produced equally large increases (Blascovich, 1972; Blascovich, Veach, & Ginsburg, 1973), Blascovich *et al.* (1973) concluded that the interindividual process is likely to involve some type of social comparison process rather than a relevant arguments process.

In a recent study using blackjack, Blascovich and Ginsburg (1974) manipulated betting norms by use of confederates. Subjects played the usual first session (20 hands) of blackjack as individuals. In the second session (20 hands) subjects played side by side in three-man groups. Two of the players were confederates of the experimenters, and they sat on either side of the naive subject at the blackjack table. They bet according to prearranged plans. There were three experimental conditions: in the first, the confederates consistently bet higher than the previously established average individual bet[2]; in the second, confederates bet about the same as this average; and in the third, the confederates consistently bet lower than this average. The results indicated that when the risk levels of other group members are higher than one's individual risk-taking preference, one will conform by increasing his risk-taking level; when the risk levels of other group members is the same as one's individual preference, one will maintain approximately his individual level of risk taking; and when the risk levels of other group members is lower than one's individual preference, one will conform by decreasing his level of risk taking. In addition, while individuals shifted their risk-taking preferences in the direction of the group norm, the risk taking levels of most subjects in the group situation were between their initial individual preference and the group norm.

Thus, Blascovich and Ginsburg (1974) specified a social comparison process similar to that of Levinger and Schneider (1969) as the interindividual component in their model. According to this notion, individual risk-taking decisions represent a compromise between ideal individual risk preferences and an assumed group standard. If through information exchange the individual discovers that his assumption about the group standard is higher or lower than he had initially assumed it to be, his risk-taking behavior will shift accordingly. In addition to enabling Blascovich and Ginsburg to specify the type of social comparison process involved in choice shifts involving risk, the results of the norm formation study also imply that a social facilitation process is an unlikely explanation of choice shifts involving risk.

A few other "gambling" tasks have been used in the study of risky shifts (Pruitt & Teger, 1969; Zajonc *et al.,* 1969), but their results have been somewhat contradictory. In addition, it is doubtful whether those tasks can really be classified as realistic gambling tasks (Blascovich, 1972).

On the other hand, McCauley *et al.* (1973), in an interesting field study of the risky-shift phenomenon using thoroughbred race track betting as the criterion risk task, found a conservative shift in the group setting. Although this finding must be tempered by a consideration of recent criticisms of its statistical analysis (Abelson, 1973a,b), the study did involve a realistic gambling task. Furthermore, the subjects did use real money, part of which was their own. Thus, the McCauley *et al.* study apparently does not fit the demonstrated pattern of the blackjack studies: a strong risk taking increase under group conditions, unless deliberately manipulated downward, which appears to involve a social comparison process.

To pursue the matter further, there is a difference between the previous blackjack studies and regular gambling in the casinos and other field situations which concerns the stakes involved. In our previous blackjack studies, subjects were given $5.00 worth of gaming chips and were asked to play as if they had bought them with their own money. Thus, a kind of role playing was involved. Was there something at stake for the experimental subjects? Blascovich (1972) argues that what was at stake for subjects in these experiments was usually some aspect of pride or skill. He bases this argument on responses to post-experimental interview questions designed to determine what, if anything, was at stake during the experimental blackjack game. In one study, Blascovich (1972) asked subjects during the post-experimental interview if there had been anything at stake during the blackjack game. Of those responding without any probing that there had been (40 out of 46), 90% (36 out of 40) stated it was pride, skill, face, or winning. This suggests that riskiness is positively associated by individuals with ability or skill, with being able to look upon oneself as successful, as has been hypothesized and demonstrated by Jellison and his colleagues (Jellison and Davis, 1973; Jellison and Riskind, 1970; Jellison, Riskind, and Broll, 1972). Thus, monetary stakes do not appear to be necessary in the blackjack game in order for experimental subjects to engage in risk-taking behavior.

Nevertheless, it did remain to be determined whether the major findings of the previous blackjack studies, including the demonstration of a risky shift, would hold up when subjects actually gambled with their own money. The conservative shift found in McCauley's race track field study, even though tempered by the statistical problems mentioned above, has to be taken seriously since subjects, at least in part of that study, used their own money and used real money throughout the study. Accordingly, an experiment incorporating the essential procedures of the previous blackjack studies but which required subjects to risk their own money was designed. The

design employed a control condition in which subjects played two sessions of blackjack as individuals, and an experimental condition in which subjects played one session of blackjack as individuals and a second session in three-person groups. Based on the previous work discussed above, three experimental hypotheses were tested.

Hypothesis I. An increase in level of risk taking occurs when individuals engage in risk-taking behavior over time, but this increase levels off.

Hypothesis II. An additional increase in level of risk taking occurs when individuals engage in risk taking in a second group session following an initial individual session, but not when they continue in a second individual session.

Hypothesis III. Group shifts to risk are unaffected by outcomes in a gambling situation.

METHOD

Subjects

Thirty-two volunteer males were recruited from the National College of State Trial Judges at the University of Nevada, Reno. All subjects were state trial judges attending the College in the summer of 1973. All of them know how to play blackjack, and none was a judge in Nevada.

Setting

The research was conducted in several rooms including individual waiting rooms, an observation room and the casino itself. The casino was the main setting for the research and was furnished realistically, including a casino blackjack table, stools, and slot machines. For the blackjack game there was a regulation deck of playing cards, gaming chips and a professional blackjack dealer. Also, as in real casinos, there was a one-way mirror through which observers could record events in the casino.

Observations

Observers recorded the amount each player bet ($.05–$1.00) before each hand of blackjack. This constituted the risk measure. Outcomes were also recorded for each hand, primarily in terms of wins and losses. The systematic record of hand-by-hand play provided objective measures of risk taking and outcomes.

Bets were chosen as the primary dependent measure for several reasons. First, they represent a straightforward quantification of risk taking since the odds for winning or losing blackjack hands remain about the same across hands. Second, they lend themselves easily to parametric statistical analysis without transformation and without the use of difference scores. Third, since bets are placed before the cards in a hand are dealt, they are independent of the ensuing hand. Fourth, they are easy to record. Fifth, there is probably no other unambiguous dependent measure of risk taking in the blackjack task. While assessing how one plays his hand in terms of "hitting" and "sticking" might be construed as a risk-taking measure, it is not likely to be independent of the bet placed before the hand was dealt and is probably more a measure of rationality than risk taking. Furthermore, hitting and sticking are ambiguous with respect to risk: a decision to stick at 16 could as easily be considered a risky decision as a conservative one. Sixth, bets are similar across many gambling tasks and, hence, their generalizability is probably greater than other aspects of blackjack which may be construed as measures of risk taking.

Procedures

Each player participated in two sessions of blackjack. For the first session of blackjack all subjects were run under identical procedures, although players in the group condition had already been assigned to three-man groups which were to be formed in the second session. Upon arrival, subjects were immediately seated in individual waiting rooms. Each subject was given individual instructions concerning the game. He was told that he should buy $5.00 worth of gaming chips and was informed that the limits per hand were $.05–$1.00. The subject was then taken to the casino where he played 20 hands of blackjack individually against the house. He then cashed in his chips and returned to his individual waiting room. The procedure for the second session of blackjack depended upon whether the subject was in the control condition, individual-individual (I-I), or in the experimental condition, individual-group (I-G).

After a 10 min. waiting period, subjects in the I-I condition were again instructed as above, brought back to the casino and played another 20 hands.

Afterwards the subject was interviewed and debriefed. In the I-G condition, after all three subjects had played individually and after an additional 10 min. waiting period, they were given the following instructions as a group:

Now you are going to be taken as a group to the casino where you will again play blackjack. You should again initially buy $5.00 worth of gaming chips. The stakes, rules, and limits are the same as when you played before, only now you will all be playing at the same time.

The group then was taken to the casino where they played 20 hands of blackjack side-by-side. After they had completed playing, subjects were interviewed and debriefed.

During both sessions, subjects were permitted to buy additional chips if they so chose. Only one subject did so in the last half of the group session. For the initial purchase in both sessions, subjects were given 14 quarter chips, 10 dime chips, and 10 nickel chips. Thus, all subjects started with the same denominations. All players cashed in their chips at the end of each session.

RESULTS

The major analysis was a $2 \times 2 \times 4$ split-plot factorial analysis of variance (Kirk, 1968) with repeated measures on the last two factors. The two levels of Treatment A represented the types of group influence in the second session of blackjack: a_1—no group influence and a_2—group influence. Treatment B was the session factor. The two levels of Treatment B were: b_1—first session and b_2—second session. The four levels Treatment C, a blocks factor, were c_1—first quarter (first five hands), c_2—second quarter (second five hands), c_3—third quarter (third five hands), and c_4—fourth quarter (fourth five hands). Thirty-two individuals were randomly assigned to either the group or no-group condition so that eight individuals were in the no-group condition and eight three-man groups were in the group condition. The data for the analysis consisted of mean bets. A mean was calculated for each block of five hands within a session separately for each individual in the no-group condition and for each group of three persons in the group condition. The overall means are represented graphically in Fig. 1.

Fig. 1. Overall Mean Bets by Quarter within Session. ⊙—⊙ Individual-Individual (a_1); ●—● Individual-Group (a_2).

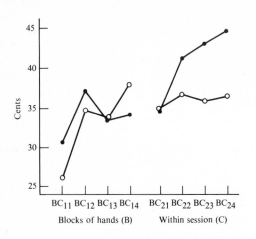

The main effects of sessions *(B)* and quarters *(C)* were significant ($F(1,14) = 7.73, p < .05$, and $F(3,42) = 5.56, p < .01$, respectively). Additional *a priori* analyses based on Hypotheses I and II above revealed an increase in betting during the first or individual sessions of both the control (a_1) and experimental (a_2) conditions (pertinent $t(7) = 2.70, p_1 < .025$ and $t(7) = 5.84, p_1 < .0005$). However, while there was the predicted significant increase in betting during the second (group) session of the experimental condition (a_2) (pertinent $t(7) = 5.20, p_1 < .0025$) no increase in betting was found during the second session (individual) of the control condition (a_1) (pertinent $t(7) = .89$, *n.s.*). In addition, there was a significant difference between the last quarter of the first (individual) session and the last quarter of the second (group) session for the experimental condition (a_2) ($t(7) = 2.90, p_1 < .025$), but not in the control condition (a_1) ($t(7) = .20$, *n.s.*).

A second analysis was performed on a subset of the data to determine if Hypothesis III was supported. The data consisted of mean bets following wins for individuals in both sessions of the experimental condition (a_2), and also of mean bets following losses for these same individuals. Significant upward or risky shifts were found following both wins ($t(7) = 2.15, p_1 < .05$) and losses ($t(7) = 2.75, p_1 < .025$).

DISCUSSION

The results of this study supported all three experimental hypotheses. An initial increase in risk taking occurred during the first or individual session for both the control and experimental groups. However, for the control condition this increase leveled off so that there was no increase in risk taking from the last quarter of the first individual session to the last quarter of the second individual session. For the experimental condition there was a significant increase in risk taking from the last quarter of the first (individual) session to the last quarter of the second (group) session. Thus, a group shift to increased risk taking did occur which cannot be explained by individual increases in risk taking over time.

As in previous studies (e.g., Blascovich, Veach, & Ginsburg, 1973) outcomes did not differentially affect the group shift to risk. The immediate effect of a positive outcome, a win, is an increase in the amount bet both for individuals playing alone and in groups. However, even when one takes outcomes into account, a group shift to risk still occurs whether one considers only the bets following wins or only the bets following losses. This result adds weight to the contention that the group shift to risk is a strong effect.

One of the key features of the present study was that participants used their own money throughout the blackjack game. Therefore, one can conclude that the risky-shift phenomenon is viable in realistic gambling situations. Another key feature of the present study was the use of state trial judges as participants. The demonstration of an unambiguous upward shift in risk under the group condition extends the generalizability of the risky shift phenomenon far beyond the point allowed by the typical subject population of purportedly acquiescent college students. It also is interesting to note that the trial judges and the college students reacted in the same fashion in the risk episodes.

Finally, the results of the present study are easily accounted for by the two-process explanation of shifts to risk described above and lend added weight to it. In that explanation, it was pointed out that both an intraindividual and an interindividual process must be posited to explain shifts to risk which occur when persons move from an individual risk taking situation to a group risk taking situation. The intraindividual process involves a type of familiarization with the task and is reflected in the increases in risk taking by individuals over blackjack hands. However, an intraindividual process alone cannot explain the obtained risky shifts, since additional increases in risk taking due to group influence are also evident. This interindividual or group effect is explained by a type of social comparison process as specified by Levinger and Schneider (1969) and incorporated into the pluralistic model discussed above.

While the present study did not experimentally test the social comparison hypothesis, it did replicate the major results of previous blackjack studies and serves to further validate the blackjack task and paradigm since subjects in the present study risked their own money. Those previous blackjack studies described above, especially Blascovich and Ginsburg (1974), have demonstrated that a social comparison rather than a relevant arguments or a social facilitation explanation is the most tenable explanation of choice shifts involving risk.

Footnotes

[1]Personal communication from Robert Lowman, Ph.D., Department of Psychology, University of Wisconsin—Milwaukee, Milwaukee, Wisconsin 53201. An article based on this replication has been submitted for publication.

[2]The previously established, individual, first session bet was approximately thirty cents. This was ascertained from all previous blackjack, risky shift studies.

References

Abelson, R. P. Comment on "Group shift to caution at the race track." *Journal of Experimental Social Psychology,* 1973, *9,* 517-521.

Abelson, R. P. The statistician as viper: reply to McCauley and Stitt. *Journal of Experimental Social Psychology,* 1973, *9,* 526-527.

Bateson, N. Familiarization, group discussion, and risk-taking. *Journal of Experimental Social Psychology,* 1966, *2,* 119-129.

Blascovich, J. Group factors on risk taking: A conceptual analysis and experimental manipulation. Doctoral Dissertation, University of Nevada, Reno, 1972. Xerox University Microfilms, Order No. 72 311, 712.

Blascovich, J., & Ginsburg, G. P. Emergent norms and choice shifts. *Sociometry,* 1974, in press.

Blascovich, J., Veach, T. L., & Ginsburg, G. P. Blackjack and the risky shift. *Sociometry,* 1973, *36,* 42-55.

Cartwright, D. Risk taking by individuals and groups: An assessment of research employing choice dilemmas. *Journal of Personality and Social Psychology,* 1971, *20,* 361-378.

DeFinetti, B. Logical foundations and measurement of subjective probability. *Acta Psychologica,* 1970, *34,* 129-145.

Dion, K. L., Baron, R. S., & Miller, N. Why do groups make riskier decisions than individuals? *In* Berkowitz, (Ed.), *Advances in Experimental Social Psychology,* Vol. 4, New York, Academic Press, 1970.

Hochauer, B. Decision-making in roulette. *Acta Psychologica,* 1970, *34,* 357-366.

Jellison, J. M., & Davis, D. Relationship between perceived ability and attitude extremity. *Journal of Personality and Social Psychology,* 1973, *27,* 430-436.

Jellison, J. M., & Riskind, J. A social comparison of abilities interpretation of risk-taking behavior. *Journal of Personality and Social Psychology,* 1971, *20,* 361-378.

Jellison, J. M., Riskind, J., & Broll, L. Attribution of ability to others on skill and chance tasks as a function of level of risk. *Journal of Personality and Social Psychology,* 1972, *22,* 135-138.

Kidd, J. B. The utilization of subjective probabilities in production planning. *Acta Psychologica,* 1970, *34,* 338-347.

Kidd, J. B., & Morgan, J. R. A predictive information system for management. *Operational Research Quarterly,* 1969, *20,* 149-170.

Kirk, R. E. *Experimental design: Procedures for the behavioral sciences.* Belmont, California: Brooks/Cole Publishers, 1969.

Levinger, G., & Schneider, D. J. Test of "risk as value" hypothesis. *Journal of Personality and Social Psychology,* 1969, *22,* 165-169.

McCauley, C., Stitt, C. L., Woods, K., & Lipton, D. Group shift to caution at the race track. *Journal of Experimental Social Psychology,* 1973, *9,* 80-86.

Pruitt, D. G. Choice shifts in group discussion: An introductory review. *Journal of Personality and Social Psychology,* 1971, *20,* 339-360.

Pruitt, D. G. Conclusions: Toward an understanding of choice shifts in group discussion. *Journal of Personality and Social Psychology,* 1971, *20,* 495-510.

Pruitt, D. G., & Teger, A. I. The risky shift in group betting. *Journal of Experimental Social Psychology,* 1969, *5,* 115-126.

Zajonc, R. B., Wolosin, R. J., Wolosin, M. A., & Sherman, S. J. Group risk taking in a two choice situation: Replication, extension and a model. *Journal of Experimental Social Psychology,* 1969, *5,* 127-140.

Production of Intergroup Conflict and Its Reduction— Robbers Cave Experiment

In the summer of 1954, the third experiment on group relations was carried out under the direction of M. Sherif. The general plan of the study followed the 1949 and 1953 experiments.

The crucial problem of the 1954 experiment was the *reduction* of intergroup friction and conflict. It was carried out in three successive stages:

I. *The stage of in-group formation.* In order to study intergroup relations, there have to be groups with definite structures and norms of their own.

II. *The stage of intergroup friction and conflict.* Before tackling the main problem, namely, that of changing unfavorable intergroup attitudes toward friendship and cooperation, it was necessary first to produce unmistakable manifestations of intergroup conflict.

III. *The stage of reduction of intergroup friction.* This stage is the crucial one and constitutes the really new step beyond the previous experiments in this series.

The study was carried out in Robbers Cave State Park, about 150 miles southeast of Oklahoma City. The 200-acre camp site is wooded, hilly, and completely surrounded by the state park. The camp site and surrounding areas afforded ample facilities for separate housing for the groups, varied activities, and lifelike problem situations.

Subjects were 22 boys of about 11 years of age. They all came from established, middle socioeconomic class, stable, Protestant families. None came from broken homes. None was a problem case in school, home, or neighborhood. They were all in the upper half of their class in scholastic standing and had above average IQ's. They were all healthy, socially well-adjusted boys.

Since the subjects came from a homogeneous socioeconomic, religious, and ethnic background, the results cannot be explained on the basis of social background differences. Neither can they be explained on the basis of failure, excessive frustration, maladjustment suffered in their life histories, or scholastic retardation or intellectual ineptitude. Since the subjects were not acquainted with one another prior to the experiment, groups were not formed around previously existing personal relationships.

The subjects were divided into two bunches prior to the experiment. These two bunches were matched in as many respects as possible (physical size, athletic ability, swimming, cooking, musical proficiency, and so on). The two bunches of boys were taken to the experimental site in separate buses and at different times. Until the last days of Stage I (group formation), the two groups carried on in-group activities unaware of each other's presence and activities in the camp.

The nature of goals introduced in each experimental stage was specified. In the first stage, goals required coordinated activity conducive to division of labor and hence to status and role differentiation. In the second stage, goals were conducive to friction between groups. In the third stage, goals were conducive to interdependent and cooperative activity between groups.

No special techniques by adults to manipulate interaction were used. There were no lectures, exhortations, emotional appeals, or discussions led by adults. Rather, carefully designed problem situations were introduced. When the group members reached a decision and took a course of action, they were given an effective hand by staff members in carrying it out.

STAGE I: FORMATION OF IN-GROUPS

The predictions concerning group formation and the conditions of interaction conducive to it were formulated in the following hypotheses:

1. A definite group structure consisting of differentiated status positions and reciprocal roles will be produced when a number of individuals (without previously established interpersonal relations) interact with one another under conditions (a) which situationally embody goals that have common appeal value to the individuals and (b) which require interdependent activities for their attainment.
2. When individuals interact under conditions stated in hypothesis 1, concomitant with the formation of group structure, norms regulating their behavior in relations with one another and activities commonly engaged in will be standardized.

These two hypotheses were verified in the Robbers Cave experiment. The change from togetherness situations to more and more stabilized groups took place during interaction in a series of problem situations over a week's period. Each of the problem situations had common goals which could not be ignored by the individuals and which required coordinated efforts for their attainment.

The emergence of differentiated statuses was ascertained in daily observations and independent status ratings made twice a day by staff members. The criterion for formation of group structures was stabilization of statuses occupied by members for two consecutive days, as revealed in high agreement between independent ratings of different observers. At the end of a week this criterion was satisfied. Each group had adopted a name, "Rattlers" and "Eagles" respectively. Each had appropriated a bunkhouse, hide-out, and swimming place as its own. The boys put the names of their groups on flags and T-shirts. The Eagles had named their swimming place ("Moccasin Creek"). The Rattlers appropriated the baseball field, which was closer to their area and which they had cleared for the coming competitive events when informed that another group was in the vicinity.

The sort of conditions which were introduced during this stage can be illustrated by representative problem situations. One was introduced by putting canoes near the bunkhouse of each group. When the group members discovered them, they wanted to take them to their special swimming place over rough terrain some distance away. The problem was discussed immediately and a plan carried out with the enthusiastic collaboration of group members.

Another typical problem situation was making available to the subjects the ingredients of a meal in unprepared form (e.g., meat, watermelon, Kool-Aid)

at a time when they were hungry. Turning these ingredients into a meal required preparation, division into portions, and serving, in which participation of all was necessary.

STAGE II: PRODUCTION OF INTERGROUP FRICTION

The formation of negative intergroup attitudes and stereotypes was planned in order to create the problem of reducing them. The main hypotheses for this stage were:

1. In the course of competition and frustrating relations between two groups, unfavorable stereotypes will come into use in relation to the out-group and its members and will be standardized in time, placing the out-group at a certain social distance.
2. The course of relations between two groups which are in a state of competition will tend to produce an increase in in-group solidarity.
3. Functional relations between groups which are of consequence to the groups in question will tend to bring about changes in the pattern of relations within in-groups involved.

To test these predictions, a series of competitive events and reciprocally frustrating situations was planned. As in the previous experiment, prizes were to be awarded to the group that accumulated the higher score in a tournament. There was great enthusiasm over this tournament in both groups. When the boys learned of the presence of another group during the last days of Stage I, each group to a man expressed intense desires to compete with that other group with a great confidence in themselves, and issued a challenge to the other group. Thus it appeared to the subjects that the tournament was the consequence of their own challenges. This strong tendency to want to compete with another group stemmed from their experiences and activities in the general culture.

In this experiment it proved unnecessary to introduce planned situations which were mutually frustrating. A series of mutually frustrating situations arose when the Eagles were defeated in a tug-of-war contest toward the end of the first day of the tournament. The Eagles burned the Rattlers' flag, which had been left on the backstop of the athletic field. The following morning the Rattlers arrived first at the athletic field and discovered their burned emblem. This seemed an outrage which must have been the vengeful deed of the Eagles. They drew up a strategy to destroy the Eagle flag if the Eagles admitted the misdeed.

So when the Eagles arrived at the field and admitted they had burned the flag, the Rattlers immediately went into action according to plan. The Eagles' flag was seized; the Eagles responded with some violence and in turn seized the remaining Rattler flag. Through all, the groups were scuffling and shouting derogatory names.

During the rest of this experimental stage, name-calling, physical encounters, and "raids" followed one another. After the skirmishes over the flags, the Rattlers staged a "raid" on the Eagle cabin, causing quite a bit of inconvenience and frustration to the Eagles. This raid was later reciprocated by the Eagles, who left the Rattlers' cabin in confusion. However, this was a mild affair compared to the Rattlers' retaliation some days later, which took place after the Rattlers lost the tournament.

In the competitive events, the success of one group meant the failure of the other. In the reciprocally frustrating engagements that flared up, unfavorable invectives were hurled across group lines. Physical encounters intensified intergroup hostility. Within six days the intergroup conflict produced such an unfavorable image of the out-group, with accompanying derogatory stereotypes, that each group was dead set against having any more to do with the other. Thus there arose extreme social distance between the two groups.

Estimation of Time by Groups on the Verge of Victory and Defeat

Each engagement in the competitive series implied considerable effort and zeal, which were reflected in characteristic psychological reactions and contributed to the building up of unfavorable attitudes toward the out-group. One of the noteworthy incidents is exemplified in the second tug-of-war. The Rattlers had won the first tug-of-war. The Eagles had retaliated by burning the Rattler flag, which initiated the series of conflict situations.

Before the Eagles came to the second tug-of-war on the next day, they devised a strategy to win. After the pulling started, on a prearranged signal the Eagles all sat down on the ground and dug in their feet. The confident Rattlers were on their feet pulling strenuously, but they were becoming exhausted and rapidly lost ground. After seven minutes, the Rattlers adopted the enemy strategy and dug in too.

Greatly exhausted during their initial pull in a standing position, the Rattlers were being pulled gradually across the line. At the fortieth minute of the contest, a time limit of an additional 15 minutes was announced. At the end of this time, the Rattlers had not yet been pulled completely over the line. The contest was declared a tie, to the indignation of the Eagles and the relief and satisfaction of the weary Rattlers.

The Rattlers, thus relieved of certain defeat had the contest lasted longer, were accusing the Eagles of employing "dirty" strategy and telling each other that the contest had appeared to them as if it would never end. The Eagles, on the other hand, were remarking to each other that the precious time flew too fast on the verge of their victory.

On the following day the participant observers of each group asked the members of their respective groups individually, "How long did the tug-of-war last after both groups sat down and dug in?" The actual duration was 48 minutes. The Eagle estimates ranged from 20 to 45 minutes. The Rattler estimates ranged from 1 hour to 3½ hours. Thus there was no overlapping at all between the estimates of time made by the two groups. Deliberately, the question was worded without specifying a time unit. The Eagles all gave their judgments in minute units. The Rattlers gave theirs in hour units.

Impact of Intergroup Events on In-Group Relations

The nature of in-group relations is essential in understanding intergroup relations. The reverse is equally true; for an adequate understanding of in-group relations, the understanding of relations between groups is also essential. A striking illustration was the downfall of Craig from the leadership status in the Eagle group as intergroup competition and conflict developed during Stage II. Craig rose to leadership during Stage I, when more peaceful activities were engaged in. But with the advent of Stage II, which required leadership that could stand in the front line in contests and engagements against an adversary, Craig did not live up to expectations. For example, he deserted the rope during the first tug-of-war when it became evident that the Eagles were losing. Several days later, he kept himself at a safe distance when the Eagles attempted a retaliatory raid on the Rattlers. Therefore, Mason, a high-status

Eagle, rose steadily and took over leadership in the group with his exemplary daring and front-line action in various contests and conflicts with the Rattlers.

In various events, defeats caused temporary confusion, bickering, and blaming each other within both groups. On the whole, however, the cumulative effect of intergroup friction was to intensify in-group solidarity. Temporary dissension within the group was followed typically by renewed efforts at in-group coordination, planning new tactics or engaging in acts directed against the out-group, and the like.

The change of leadership in the Eagles, reciprocal bickering, and maneuvering for positions within groups were family affairs. The Eagles were like members of a family or good friends who join hands immediately against an outside intrusion.

One of the telling indications of increased in-group solidarity was exhibited in both groups at Carlton Lake, a public beach a few miles from the camp. At the end of Stage II, each group was taken there separately. This was a test situation. The public beach was crowded with people and full of other distractions. However, each group behaved there as if the boys were by themselves; they were altogether preoccupied with their own business and their own fun.

These are examples of the general finding that intergroup relations, both in conflict and in the period of friendship between groups which followed, had significant consequences for the properties of interaction and the relations of members within the group structures involved.

Summary of Observational Findings in Stage II

The recurrent observations during Stage II indicate that intergroup friction which is consequential in the scheme of group activities (1) brings about unfavorable attitudes and stereotypes in relation to the out-group, (2) increases in-group solidarity, and (3) changes the pattern of relations within groups when such changes become necessary for effective dealings in intergroup relations. These results substantiate further the findings concerning intergroup friction in the 1949 experiment.[1]

Checking Observational Findings with Other Methods

At the end of Stage II, sociometric choices, ratings of stereotypes of the in-group and the out-group, and judgments of performance by in-group and out-group

were obtained in order to check the validity of observational findings.

Sociometric choices.   Sociometric questions were asked informally of every member of each group individually. Two of the criterion questions concerned friendship preferences. They were worded to specify choices from the *entire camp* and not just from one's in-group. The other two criterion questions concerned initiative in the group, i.e., choosing who gets things started and who gets things done.

The friendship choices were overwhelmingly toward in-group members. Sociograms constructed on the basis of weighted scores (4 for the first choices, 3 for second, 2 for third, and 1 for the rest) for the four criteria reveal clearly the unique hierarchical group structures formed among the Rattlers and Eagles (see Figs. 1 and 2).

Stereotyped images of in-group and out-group. Ratings of fellow group members and members of the out-group were obtained on a number of adjectives, of which six were critical. These critical terms were chosen from those actually used by subjects in referring to their own group or to the out-group during the height of intergroup friction. Three were favorable terms *(brave, tough, friendly)* and three were unfavorable *(sneaky, smart alecks, stinkers).* The rating technique was essentially like Avigdor's, ranging from "all of them are . . ." or "none of them are . . ." (see pp. 300-301).

As predicted from observational data, ratings of fellow group members were almost exclusively favorable (100 percent by Rattlers and 94.3 percent by Eagles). In contrast, ratings of the out-group after the intense intergroup friction were predominantly unfavorable. The ratings made by Rattlers of Eagle members were 53 percent unfavorable and 34.9 percent favorable. The ratings made by the Eagles of the Rattlers were 76.9 percent unfavorable and only 15.4 percent favorable. (Other ratings fell in the category "some of them are . . .") These significant differences between favorable and unfavorable designations of the in-group and out-group confirmed observational findings. They will be discussed further in giving results of Stage III, where shifts in these ratings brought about by changed intergroup relations constitute important substantiating evidence.

Judgments of performance by in-group and out-group.   It was predicted that an individual group member would have formed attitudes toward his own

Fig. 1.   Rattlers—End of Stage II, In-Group Structure.

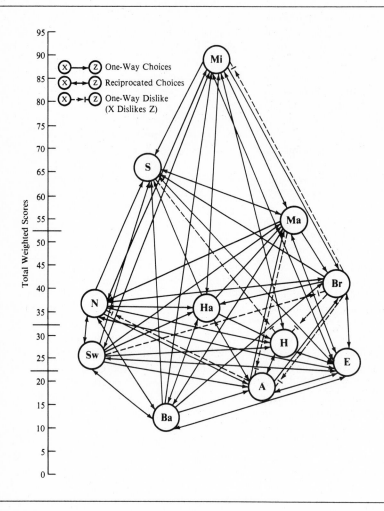

group and the out-group which would influence significantly his appraisal of the activities of other individuals in the respective groups. This hypothesis was made on the basis of observations that the individual members tend to depreciate the achievements of the adversary and magnify the achievements of their fellows. This unit illustrates how precise methods derived from the laboratory can be utilized as an integral aspect of field study in lifelike conditions.

The task was introduced as a contest between the two groups, with a $5 reward to the winning group. Since social distance between the groups was so great that neither wanted to be in a situation with the other, this prize and the news that the staff had made wagers

on the outcome of the event were inducements to take part. Once in the situation, members of each group participated with considerable zeal.

The contest was to be as follows: Each group was to collect beans which were scattered in two marked-off areas, one for each group, and then the number supposedly collected by each individual was to be judged. As far as subjects were concerned, both excellence in performance and accuracy in judgment were required to win the reward. The time for collecting beans was one minute. The beans were put in sacks with necks bound by a rubber hose so that they could not be counted.

After the collection the two groups went to a large

Fig. 2. Eagles—End of Stage II, In-Group Structure.

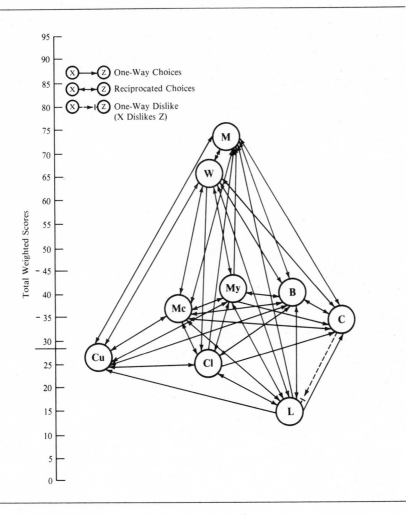

hall where, according to announcement, the performance of each person (viz., beans collected) was projected by an opaque projector and judged by every other person. As each individual's supposed performance was projected, he stood up to insure proper identification.

Actually the same number of beans was projected each time for 5 seconds. Pretests with different subjects had shown that this number (35) could not be counted in 5 seconds but that subjects felt they could just about count if they tried a little harder. Thus, the number and timing reduced possible objections that exposure was too brief, but prevented accurate counting. Subjects did not suspect that the same

number was projected each time. When the performance attributed to the Rattler leader was projected, admiring whistles were heard from his group.

The results of this unit were in numerical form, indicating the average amount of overestimation or underestimation of the number presented (35 in every case) as the performance by fellow group members or by members of the out-group. Thus the Rattlers tended to overestimate performance by fellow group members, the mean discrepancy between judgment and number projected being 3.40. In contrast, Rattlers tended to underestimate performance by Eagles with a mean discrepancy of –.29. Members of the Eagle group overestimated their own performance considerably more, the mean discrepancy being 11.80. In contrast, the Eagles' estimates of Rattler performance diverged from the actual number presented by only 4.56.

These differences between judgments of performance attributed to in-group members and of performance attributed to members of the out-group were highly significant and in the expected direction. It was concluded that the differing attitudes formed by individuals toward their own group and toward an antagonistic group affected their judgments. These results confirm the overall behavioral trends through reactions made in quantitative form by single individuals.

STAGE III: REDUCTION OF INTERGROUP CONFLICT AND STEREOTYPES

By the end of Stage II, each group saw the out-group as the "villain" and placed itself on the side of the angels, justifying its deeds and unfavorable stereotypes toward the out-group. Solidarity and cooperativeness within the in-groups did not lead to cooperativeness and solidarity between groups.

Choice of Measure for Reducing Intergroup Friction

Various measures have been proposed for reducing the intergroup frictions that prevail today. A few of these are listed here with brief notes explaining why they were or were not included among the experimental conditions in Stage III:

1. Disseminating favorable *information* in regard to the out-group was not chosen as the experimental measure. Information not related to the goals currently in focus in the activities of the groups in question is relatively ineffective.

2. In small groups like those in this study, it is possible to devise sufficiently attractive rewards to make individual achievement supreme. This may reduce tension between small groups by splitting the memberships on the basis of *"every man for himself."* Such a solution, however, has little relevance for actual intergroup tensions. In real life, social distance and intergroup conflict are in terms of membership in groups and of group alignments.

3. The resolution of conflict through leaders alone was not utilized. Group leaders, even when meeting apart from their groups around a conference table, cannot be taken independently of the dominant trends and prevailing intergroup attitudes of the membership in their respective groups. If the leader is too much out of step with these, he will cease to be followed. It is more realistic, therefore, to study the influence of leadership within the framework of prevailing trends and attitudes of the groups involved. This will give us leads concerning the conditions under which leadership can be effective in reducing intergroup tensions.

4. The "common enemy" approach is effective in pulling two or more groups together against another group. This was utilized in the 1949 experiment and yielded effective results. But bringing some groups together against others means larger conflicts, even though it may patch up frictions among a few groups temporarily.

5. Another measure advanced, both in theoretical and practical works, centers around social contacts among members of groups who stand at given social distances on occasions which are pleasant in themselves. This measure was tried out in the first phase of Stage III of this study.

6. In the second phase of Stage III, the measure that was effectively used was the introduction of superordinate goals which necessitated cooperative interaction between the groups.

Phase 1: Social contacts in reducing intergroup conflict. Before getting to the introduction of superordinate goals, contact in social situations was arranged. In this series of contact situations during the first two days of Stage III, both groups were left free in close physical proximity to interact with one another in situations which are pleasant in themselves. The staff members appeared to be out of supervision range on these occasions, as much as possible.

There were seven different contact situations, including eating together in the same dining hall, watching a movie together, and shooting firecrackers in the same area. These contact situations had no effect in reducing intergroup friction. If anything, they were utilized by members of both groups as opportunities for further name-calling and conflict. For example, they used mealtimes in the same place for "garbage fights," throwing mashed potatoes, leftovers, bottle caps, and the like accompanied by the exchange of derogatory names.

Thus, in line with our hypothesis to this effect, *contact between groups does not in itself produce a decrease in an existing state of intergroup tension.*

Because of its implications for learning theories and for practitioners in the intergroup relations area, special note should be made of the fact that these activities, carried out by the two groups in close physical proximity, were satisfying in themselves.

Phase 2: Interaction between groups toward superordinate goals.   Following the social contact situations, a series of superordinate goals was introduced which afforded challenging problem situations for both groups. These superordinate goals necessitated intergroup interaction toward common ends in problem situations which were real to the members of both groups. The goals were selected so that they would become focal to members in both groups; therefore, they could not be ignored or postponed easily. The attainment of superordinate goals could not be achieved through the energy and resources of one group alone but required the combined efforts and resources of both groups. This is why they are called *superordinate goals.*

The first of the two hypotheses tested during this period was:

1. When groups in a state of friction are brought into contact under conditions embodying superordinate goals, which are compelling but which cannot be achieved by the efforts of one group alone, they will tend to cooperate toward the common goal.

However, it is too much to expect that a state of friction, unfavorable stereotypes, and mutual social distance developed in a series of encounters over a period will be eliminated in a single episode of cooperation toward a common end. Therefore, the second hypothesis was:

2. Cooperation between groups necessitated by a series of situations embodying superordinate goals will have a cumulative effect in the direction of reduction of existing tension between groups.

Accordingly, during the following six days, a series of problem situations embodying such goals was introduced. The situations were varied in nature and required varied kinds of consideration, planning, and execution on the part of the subjects. But no matter how varied they were, all had an essential feature in common: they all involved goals that became focal for both groups under the given circumstances. These goals were urgent to the subjects; they had to be attended to. Psychological selectivity favored them. Yet their attainment clearly depended on communication, planning, and joint action by both groups. Thus the problem situations created a state of interdependence. The goal was highly desired by both groups, yet it could not be attained by the efforts and energies of one group alone.

All of the superordinate goals and problem situations introduced cannot be described here. Three of them are summarized below.

1. Both groups were warned several hours in advance that there was trouble in the water-supply system. Water came from a tank on top of a hill about a mile away. The tank was supplied with water pumped from a reservoir approximately two miles' walking distance from the camp. The terrain between camp and tank and reservoir was mountainous, rough, thickly wooded, and bushy. Both groups had had first-hand acquaintance with these places during Stage I, when each went on separate overnight camp-outs in the area. They had filled their canteens from a large faucet on the tank. So the water-supply system was real in the subjects' experience.

The problem situation was created by turning off a valve at the water tank and stuffing the open faucet on the tank with pieces of sacking. Several hours after a first warning, the water in the pipes leading to the camp was all drained through use. Therefore both groups were summoned to a central place at which the main pipe line in the camp divided into smaller lines supplying various points throughout the camp area. After demonstrating that the main pipe line and accessories were bone dry, the camp administration declared its inability to cope with the water situation within a reasonable time. It was explained that the defect might be leakage somewhere along the length of pipe line, at the pump by the reservoir, or in the supply tank. In order to make the outcome credible, it was stated that in the past vandals had been known to tamper with the supply system. Therefore, to solve the problem several parts of the system had to be attended to and about 20-25 men were required to discover the difficulty that day. By this time the Eagles were getting thirsty; the Rattlers still had a little water in their canteens.

Both groups promptly volunteered to tackle the situation. The details that volunteered for various segments of the water system were made up of either all Rattlers or all Eagles.

The announced plan was for all details to meet at the water tank after inspecting the pipe line and pump. In a little over an hour, all details congregated by the large tank. Since they were thirsty and hot, the first object of attention was the faucet on the tank. No water came out of the faucet. The members of the two groups took over the procedure. They tried to ascertain whether there was water in the tank.

When the faucet had been stopped up by the staff earlier in the day, the ladder, which leaned against the tank for climbing atop it, had been laid aside in the weeds about 30 feet away. Now the ladder was discovered by the boys. Almost to a man, Eagles and Rattlers were on top of the tank to look through the opening there and see if there was water in the tank. In short order, they came to the conclusion that the tank was practically full. Then the majority of both Eagles and Rattlers rushed again to the faucet. They discovered now that the faucet was stopped up with pieces of sack. Immediately they tackled the task of removing it. They pooled their available implements (mostly knives) and took turns at the work. Members of each group were mindful of and receptive to suggestions from members of the other group. There was common rejoicing at even the appearance of a few drops of water as efforts proceeded. This work lasted over half an hour. Then a Rattler suggested getting help from staff members. When the task was completed with staff help and the valve leading to the camp was turned on, there were expressions of satisfaction from all with the accomplishment, in which members of both groups had had an active and effective part.

This first cooperative action toward a common goal did not eliminate the stabilized intergroup friction. An hour later at supper, there was once again an exchange of invectives across group lines.

2. Another in the series of superordinate goals was the problem of acquiring the use of a much-desired feature-length movie. Both groups were called together and the possibility of procuring either *Treasure Island* or *Kidnapped* from the neighboring town was put to both groups. It was announced that the camp administration could put up half of the money to secure one film. (Since this was toward the end of the camp period, one group could not have provided the remaining sum alone without being destitute for the rest of the period.)

Following this announcement, suggestions poured in from both groups on a division of the needed sum. They made computations and agreed on a figure for each group to contribute. Then they computed the amount each member would have to

pay to secure the desired film. Both groups decided together on the film to be selected.

After supper that evening the film chosen *(Treasure Island)* was shown. Both groups felt that they had chosen it and had a part in getting it. As a test situation, five rows of benches were placed in the hall with an aisle between them. Both groups were called to the hall at the same time. Despite the cooperative efforts they had carried out in getting the film, the seats chosen by individual members to watch it followed group lines on the whole.

3. The most striking episodes of intergroup activities toward superordinate goals took place during a camp-out at Cedar Lake, an out-of-the-way spot in the hills about 60 miles from the camp. Previously, both groups were asked separately to name the activities they would like to enjoy during the last days of camp. Overnight camping was high on the list of both groups.

Cedar Lake had an attractive camping and picnic area overlooking a clear-water lake surrounded by hills. Since it was far off the main roads, there were no people, shops, or refreshment stands within miles. It afforded an ideal place for controlling experimental conditions for the introduction of superordinate goals.

Each group was taken in a separate truck to Cedar Lake early on the morning of the fifth day of this stage. Both groups were enthusiastic over the prospect of the overnight camp; but they stated a preference to enjoy the overnight camping by themselves, and not with the other group. Both groups, on their own initiative, loaded their respective trucks for an early start. When the trucks arrived in midmorning, each group went first to the swimming area, which is separated from the picnic area by a wooded valley. In the meantime, plans for the problem situations to be introduced were prepared in the picnic area.

Near lunch time, both groups returned to the picnic area. After the early breakfast, the trip, and the swim they were getting quite hungry by this time. At the picnic area there were separate tables and facilities and also a centrally located table on which eating and cooking utensils, mustard, and pickles had been placed. The groups rushed to this central table. The only means of transportation visible at the time was an old truck parked nearby.

A staff member announced in a voice audible to everyone that he was leaving to get food from a store some miles away. The groups were now standing about 15 yards apart. They watched the truck that was going to bring food. The truck made all kinds of noises, but simply would not start, as planned.

Several Rattlers suggested giving it a push so that it would start. This suggestion was not followed since the truck was parked facing uphill (as planned). The tug-of-war rope was lying piled up in plain sight. One Rattler suggested, "Let's get 'our' tug-of-war rope and have a tug-of-war against the truck." There was a little discussion of this idea and its practicality. Someone said: "Twenty of us can pull it for sure." Members in both groups voiced approval of this plan. Therefore they got into action. There was a little discussion concerning how to operate. This problem was settled by feeding the rope through the front bumper so that there were 2 lines for the pull. On the whole, the Rattlers pulled one line and the Eagles pulled the other.

It took considerable effort to pull the truck. Several tries were necessary. During these efforts, a rhythmic chant of "Heave, heave" arose to accent the times of greatest effort. This rhythmic chant of "Heave, heave" had been used earlier by the Eagles during the tug-of-war contests in the period of intergroup competition and friction. Now it was being used in a cooperative activity involving both groups. When, after some strenuous efforts, the truck moved and started there was jubilation over the common success.

While the truck went for food, the question arose of taking turns in the preparation of meals or of joint preparation by both groups. The Eagles, with some dissensions, decided to prepare their own meals separately. Preparing food in their own areas implied two sets of activities: dividing food for each group; preparing it in their respective areas. A few days earlier, both groups would have insisted upon separate facilities and independent activities even though this implied more work for each.

Now, however, when the truck returned with the food, the groups did not bother to divide the food into two parts for meals in their respective areas. They simply started preparing it together. In this instance actual cooperation in preparing a meal proceeded without discussion and even in a direction contrary to the prior decision of one group. That evening at Cedar Lake the meal was also prepared jointly.

The truck pull was repeated in the afternoon when the truck "stalled" again before going to get supper provisions. This time both groups knew what to do, and carried out the plan with the same success. But on this second occasion the two lines of rope were not pulled separately by the two groups. Members from both groups intermingled on both lines of the rope. Henceforth group lines were blurred on such cooperative occasions.

The Same Tool in the Service of Friction and Harmony

It will be remembered that the tug-of-war rope was used in the service of intense competition during Stage II. At the end of that stage the Rattlers used the same rope in activities within their own group. They had spent several days chopping at a dead tree at their hide-out. When the trunk was chopped through, the tree did not fall down. The fall was prevented by surrounding trees. As it stood, the tree was a hazard. It might have fallen down at an inopportune moment. Therefore the Rattlers used the tug-of-war rope to pull the trunk to a safe position. They rejoiced in loud tones over their victory in tug-of-war "against the tree."

As we have seen at the Cedar Lake campout, the Rattlers introduced "their" tug-of-war rope against the truck in a cooperative intergroup effort to get food for all. Here we see how the same weapon used in intergroup friction can be put into use for intergroup harmony.

Summary of Observations in Stage III

Only a few high points of the observations during this stage have been summarized. On the basis of the observational data, it was concluded: (a) When the groups in a state of friction interacted under conditions created by introducing superordinate goals, they did cooperate toward the common goal. (b) A series of such joint activities toward common, superordinate goals had the cumulative effect of reducing the prevailing friction between groups and unfavorable stereotypes toward the out-group.

In the closing hours of the experiment, the two groups decided together on their own initiative to put on a joint program at a campfire, entertaining each other with skits and songs. Also on their own initiative both groups requested that they leave the experimental site together in one bus. Thus, these two groups, which formed separately, met for the first time as rivals, engaged in sharp conflict which culminated in mutual antagonism and social distance, now appeared as friendly copartners.

Checking Observed Reduction of Intergroup Friction

The validity of observational findings was tested through other techniques at the close of this stage. These techniques were used specifically to check observations that repeated cooperation involving both groups toward superordinate goals resulted in (1) increased friendliness toward the out-group and its members and (2) reduction of the unfavorable stereotypes toward the out-group found at the close of intergroup friction.

Sociometric choices.   The sociometric questions given informally at the end of Stage II were repeated. The answers to the most general criterion which concerned friendship choices in the entire camp and an item tapping rejections (disliked individuals) provide clear verification of the changed attitudes toward members of the out-group. The change was from exclusive preference for the in-group and hostility toward the out-group toward increased preference for the out-group and reduced hostility toward its members.

Friendship choices were still largely for in-group members. However, when the choices for out-group members at the end of Stage III are compared with those after intergroup friction (Stage II), a substantial and significant change is seen. These comparisons are shown in graphic form in Figure 3. The Rattlers' choices of Eagles increased from 6.4 to 36.4 percent of their total friendship choices. In the Eagle group, the proportion of choices for Rattlers shifted from 7.5 to 23.2 percent. These shifts are statistically significant.

Along with the increased tendency to choose out-group members as friends, there was a significant reduction in rejections of members of the out-group as persons disliked. At the close of intergroup friction (Stage II), 75 percent of the Rattlers' rejections were of Eagles. By the end of Stage III, only 15 percent were of Eagles. Similarly, 95 percent of Eagle rejections were of Rattlers at the end of Stage II, but this percentage fell to 47.1 percent at the end of Stage III.

These findings confirm the observations that the result of a series of situations embodying superordinate goals was increasingly friendly associations and attitudes pertaining to members of the out-group accompanied by reduced hostility.

Fig. 3.   Comparison of Friendship Choices by Rattlers and Eagles Following Intergroup Friction and Intergroup Cooperation.

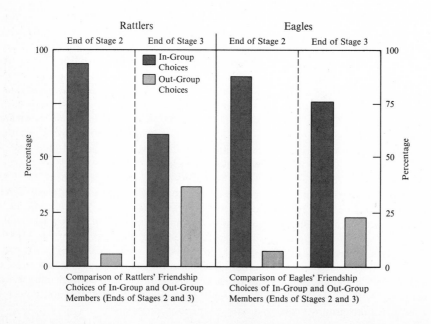

Fig. 4. (Top) Stereotpye Ratings of In-Group and Out-Group Members
Following Intergroup Cooperation (Stage III), Six Characteristics
Combined. (Bottom) Comparison of Stereotype Ratings of Out-Groups
Following Intergroup Friction (Stage II) and Intergroup Cooperation (Stage III).

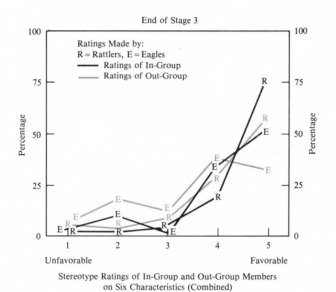

Stereotype Ratings of In-Group and Out-Group Members
on Six Characteristics (Combined)

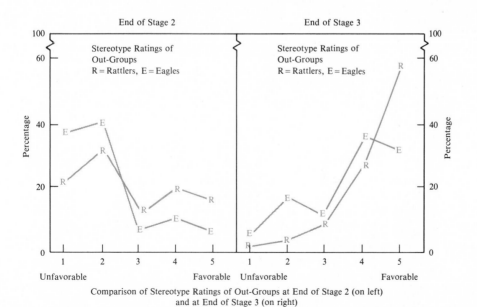

Comparison of Stereotype Ratings of Out-Groups at End of Stage 2 (on left)
and at End of Stage 3 (on right)

Stereotyped images of in-group and out-group. Observations during the last several days of Stage III revealed a sharp decrease in the standardized name-calling and derogation of the out-group which was common during intergroup friction and the contact situations without superordinate goals early in Stage III. In addition there was less blatant glorification of the in-group and bragging about its accomplishments.

To check these observations, the rating technique employed at the end of Stage II was repeated at the end of Stage III. It is noteworthy that when these ratings were repeated, several boys remarked that they were glad to do them again because they had "changed their minds" since the last ratings.

The significant changes in ratings are revealed in the graphs in Figure 4. The lower graphs show the marked shift from predominantly *unfavorable* ratings at the end of Stage II to predominantly *favorable* ratings at the end of Stage III. The upper graph demonstrates that, by the end of Stage III, ratings of members of the in-group and members of the out-group were both largely favorable. There were no significant differences between ratings of the in-group and ratings of the out-group following the period of cooperative activities toward superordinate goals involving both groups.

This resemblance between ratings of in-group and out-group members following intergroup cooperation did not come about simply because ratings of the in-group were lower than they had been following intergroup friction. In line with the observation of less blatant glorification and bragging about the in-group, the frequency of favorable ratings of in-group members was somewhat less than after Stage II. However, this change was not significant statistically. The increased similarity between ratings of in-group and out-group resulted chiefly from the large and significant changes in ratings of the out-group in a favorable direction.

Therefore the overall conclusions concerning the images of in-group and out-group following intergroup cooperation were:

1. Characteristics attributed to in-group members were still highly favorable, with a slight decrease in tendency toward extremely favorable ratings.
2. Images of the out-group changed from highly unfavorable stereotypes following intergroup friction to a predominantly favorable image following intergroup cooperation.
3. As a result, the ratings of members of the in-group and members of the out-group did not differ significantly after intergroup cooperation (Stage III).

These shifts in the images of the out-group and stereotypes of them are attributable to the changed conditions as these altered the properties of intergroup interaction. Because the subjects were chosen from homogeneous backgrounds, the formation of negative stereotypes in Stage II and their change to a positive image of the out-group cannot be attributed to perceived differences or similarities stemming from ethnic, religious, or socioeconomic affiliations. All of the subjects were normal, well-adjusted boys with secure and relatively high positions among age-mates and in their families. Therefore the image of the out-group formed in intergroup friction and its change cannot be attributed to any unusual personal predispositions which the subjects brought to the experimental situations.

The enthusiastic participation in intergroup competition during Stage II reflects the strong emphasis on such activities in the larger sociocultural setting. However, the rise of intergroup hostility, the persistent name-calling, and its crystallization as negative stereotypes violated another important value from this setting: "good sportsmanship" on the part of those participating as equals in competitive activities. Even though opportunity was allowed for the reduction of intergroup friction and hostility and for crossing the established social distances by bringing the groups together in situations which were rewarding to each group, friction and the maintenance of a derogatory image of the out-group did not decrease until the groups interacted repeatedly in a series of situations embodying superordinate goals.

Footnote
[1] In the 1953 study, this stage was not completed. In a frustration episode, the subjects attributed the plan to the camp administration. Since testing the hypothesis required that the source of frustration be attributed to the experimental out-group, the 1953 study was terminated at this point.

8

Analysis of Social Problems

One of the stereotypes people believe about the scientific approach is that it is a dispassionate search for truth and rejects practical concerns such as providing solutions to social problems. The phrase "Science for science's sake" describes that idea about science. Yet there is little evidence to support the notion that scientists are not concerned with practical matters or the relevance of their discoveries to the world of daily living. Even when they are thinking abstractly or at a purely theoretical level, scientists usually still have active concern with how their work meshes with the real world of people and things.

Social psychologists have become interested in linking their theoretical research work with concepts and theories of individual and social psychological processes as these occur in the natural environment. Social problem analysis is one topic that has yielded to scientific analysis. Several examples of that type of research are reprinted in this section.

One complication for social psychology scientists when they conduct experiments on social problems is simply the problem's occurrence. The occurrence is likely to be seriously altered or even suppressed if someone like a social scientist is on the scene making observations; shoplifting and pollution-causing behavior are good examples of topics of study where this *reactivity effect* may occur. So social psychologists resolve this dilemma by creative and ingenious field experiments. In some cases they actually create the problems under carefully controlled but highly naturalistic-appearing conditions. The research articles reprinted in this section represent some of the more exciting and promising examples of the application of field experimental methodology to significant social problems present in contemporary society.

The first social issue addressed in this section is shoplifting. The two studies investigate the conditions under which observers to a staged shoplifting incident do or do not report it to responsible authorities. Shoplifting is a major economic problem in contemporary society, and scientific analyses of it offer at least some chance of planning an effective approach to reducing it.

The next social problem treated is that of pollution and littering control. Both continue to impose major expenses on governments and agencies involved in environmental protection. Massive amounts of publicity have had little effect in eliminating these problems; some research shows that when people are exposed to antilittering media messages, they do not even read them or remember them. A number of social psychological investigations of the problem have been reported, some of which have used experimental manipulations in natural environments where littering is occurring. The procedures used in these studies obtain very significant reductions in the amount littered or in the amount of material saved and recycled. Promising results have been found, and it appears that attempts to implement these findings in social planning are in order.

Another social problem is crowding and feelings of territoriality that people have for the space around them. Social living is becoming increasingly complex, and just negotiating in physical space with other people has become a major problem. The research presented here finds that people can adapt to crowding better if they have knowledge of the situation and a sense of personal control in it. There is reason to hope that this type of information can be applied to help us adapt more successfully to the uncertainties in a society that appears to be moving inevitably toward more and more interdependence.

The last topic to be covered concerns one of the most urgent social problems facing modern society today—energy usage and conservation. Social psychologists have approached this problem from an individualistic perspective, defining the issue as one of changing the attitudes and behaviors of individuals toward using energy. In the research articles in this section, significant reduction of energy use is achieved by experimental manipulations focused on providing people with information about their use and with financial inducements to reduce use. Both techniques could be easily implemented in larger scale social projects should society commit itself to such an undertaking. This type of research offers very interesting possibilities for significant social change based on sound scientific principles.

SHOPLIFTING

Shoplifting is a major social problem of large proportions. To experimentally study it is difficult, most obviously because of the way it occurs; people do not steal in the carefully controlled world of the scientist's laboratory. Gelfand, Hartmann, Walder, and Page ("Who reports shoplifters: A field-experimental study it is difficult, most obviously because of the way it occurs; people do not Their study demonstrates the technical complexity but also the usefulness of an experimental approach to social problems.

The investigators approach the issue from the perspective of the *bystander intervention* model. That model initially was applied to studying helping behavior to determine the conditions under which people observing someone in need would come to that other's aid. Applied to shoplifting, the focus is on studying people who observe an incident of shoplifting as bystanders and then either do or do not intervene by notifying authorities about the incident.

The investigators arranged for a shoplifting event to occur right in front of customer-subjects. They arranged for a confederate dressed either in a standard manner or as a hippie to shoplift in full sight of a store customer. After the incident, they noted whether the customer reported the incident and the customer's personal characteristics. The dress of the shoplifter manipulated the similarity variable. The prediction was that people would be less likely to report a similar (normally-dressed) other.

The results showed, surprisingly, that only 28% of the subjects actually observed the incident, in spite of great efforts to make it observable. The reporting rate within that sample was 28%, a rather high figure according to professional estimates. The conventional or hippie dress did not have a significant influence. A number of personal characteristics of the subjects did relate to the frequency of reporting behavior. For instance, shoppers from rural backgrounds were more likely to report than those from urban backgrounds.

Since this was the first experimental study on shoplifting, followup studies seemed desirable. The study reprinted next, by Bickman and Rosenbaum ("Crime reporting as a function of bystander encouragement, surveillance, and credibility") delves more deeply into factors which influence reporting of shoplifting. The main advancement in their studies is the presence of another person with the subject during the shoplifting; the verbal comments and suggestions of this additional person were manipulated during staged shoplifting events and their effects on the subjects were studied.

Bickman and Rosenbaum theorize that other people can influence our behavior because they help define what the nature of the stimulus situation is; they thus serve an informing and defining function. In addition, other people's comments and actual behavior also define what is appropriate as responses, and in this way act as behavioral norm definers for us. Their studies involve both of these aspects of interpersonal interaction.

To test these notions, the other person with the subject during the shoplifting either stated that the responsibility for reporting it was theirs or it was the responsibility of store personnel. The presence or absence of the other person was manipulated, which altered social norm pressures by the presence or absence of social surveillance. Also, as in the Gelfand et al. study, subjects' characteristics and attitudinal variables were recorded.

The results show that what the other person says has a very powerful effect; when she encouraged reporting, 72% of the subjects did, but when she discouraged it, only 32% did. The presence or absence of the other person has a different influence, depending on what she says. Some of the subject characteristics and attitude variables also were influential.

People interested in increasing the rates of shoplifting reporting should note the potential value of these experiments. One major implication might be to rearrange store environments to increase observability. Another would be to enhance the operation of personal norms of responsibility in interaction among customers. These are difficult goals, but these studies have provided some useful information on the power of such influences.

POLLUTION AND LITTERING CONTROL

As society becomes more and more complex, the consequences that people have to face because of that complexity become more and more intrusive. Often events far removed from the life of an individual still have consequences for that individual which have to be faced. The required use of auto emission control devices is a ready example of the increased personal cost people have to pay to help protect the environment. The study by Mazis ("Antipollution measures and psychological reactance theory: A field experiment") studies the impact of antipollution measures on a common behavior, clothes detergent use. He applies a social psychological theory, reactance theory, in his analysis of the impact of the laws forbidding the sale or use of phosphate detergents.

Reactance is a theory of attitude processes, and concerns people's reactions to threats to their behavioral and decisional freedom. If one's perceived freedom to respond in a preferred way is threatened by some outside force, one will attempt to restore the threatened freedom by engaging in the behavior or changing his or her attitude toward the desirability of the forbidden object by increasing liking for it.

At the time of the law change which banned phosphate detergents, few brands were phosphate free, so shoppers found themselves with drastically reduced choice of legal detergents. The study of the effects of the restriction took place in Florida. The change was in force only in one city (Miami) and not in another (Tampa), so Mazis was presented with a natural manipulation of the reactance variable, low and high freedom. From reactance theory he predicted that shoppers in Miami would either consider nonphosphate detergents to be less desirable, or those with phosphate to be more desirable, relative to Tampa shoppers. Using several different measures, he was able to confirm his prediction.

Using the theory, it can be seen that environmental protection laws may have unintended consequences. Behaviors that are threatened by laws may actually increase in frequency or intensity because of the external pressure not to engage in them. Of course, this is not to suggest that such laws should not be passed; it is just that social changes may have unintended consequences if people's freedom to choose is threatened.

Behavior changing techniques also can be designed to increase behavior rather than limit it. It is possible that policies rewarding nonpolluting behavior (as opposed to punishing polluting behavior) can be effective. The study of Witmer and Geller ("Facilitating paper recycling: Effects of prompts, raffles, and contests") considers a social action program which encouraged and rewarded nonpolluting behaviors. The focus was on the saving and recycling of waste paper, the other side of the pollution issue.

The investigators arranged circumstances to reward people for saving and recycling waste paper rather than throwing it away and littering the environment. An operant conditioning technology was employed.

They used obvious rewarding events, matched to the natural social context, as reinforcement contingencies. Contests, raffles, and posted signs supporting recycling were presented in college dormitories. Weight of paper returned was determined and monetary rewards were made contingent upon the amount returned. In general, the contest and raffle conditions had dramatic influence;

both increased the amount of paper collected by at least ten times the amount obtained in the posted sign condition. However, after the contingencies were removed, the investigators continued to monitor how much paper was recycled, and there was a serious dropoff of amount recycled. This shows that the students were strongly influenced by the contingencies themselves and had not fundamentally altered their attitudes toward a permanent concern with recycling. The investigators detected that the students in the contest condition were using their earned money to support weekend beer parties.

The dropoff in recycling without contingencies indicates that the behavior is a difficult one to maintain. Nationwide, it is apparent that agencies concerned with reducing littering have not been very successful. Restructuring societal arrangements to reinforce recycling on a permanent and reliable basis might be more effective if contingencies could be arranged to remain effective. We might obtain greater success if business interests and other sources of influence became involved.

CROWDING

Another seemingly inevitable consequence of modern society is crowding. Increasing urbanization and the rate of population growth have had serious impact on individuals because of the sheer number of people present in one's life. A good deal of research has shown that crowding has negative effects on people, effects largely related to anxiety and stress. Although the exact nature of the crowding and stress relationship is not yet understood, social psychologists devote research to determining how crowding affects the individual and some possible cognitive processes that might enhance coping strategies. Some of that research has been conducted in such a way as to maximize the naturalness of the manipulations. The investigations are conducted in nonlaboratory settings. Two such types of research are included here.

Fisher and Byrne ("Too close for comfort: Sex differences in response to invasions of personal space") approach crowding's impact from the perspective of the individual, relating it to *personal space,* that area a person identifies with and regards as a boundary marker within which things are regarded as belonging to oneself. How people choose to mark off physical space that is important to them, and especially how they react when others approach or enter that space, has proven to be a sensitive indicator of interpersonal relations. It even reveals subtle differences between the sexes, as this study demonstrates.

Previous research has shown that males prefer to interact with someone who is directly in front of them, while females prefer to interact with others who are beside or adjacent to them. That research dealt only with friendship relations, however, and had not considered invasions—the incursion of a stranger within a person's personal space boundaries. That research did not assess emotional reactions to invasions either. Using a university library setting for their research, Fisher and Byrne had male and female confederates sit either directly across a library study table or one seat apart from male and female college students, whose reactions to that invasion were later obtained with a questionnaire.

The results show, as predicted, that males are more aroused by the across-table invasion than females: They feel more negative, dislike the library environment more, and feel more crowded when the stranger sits opposite them. Females feel these same reactions when the stranger sits adjacent to them rather than opposite them. A second study supports these results by demonstrating that females place coats, books, and other objects as personal space markers in such a way as to defend against invasions from side to adjacent positions, whereas males arranged defense markers against across and face-to-face seats.

In discussing their results, the investigators consider the possibility that socialization experiences might be responsible for these effects. Face-to-face positioning is chosen in competitive interaction situations, and males are trained to be more sensitive to competitive interaction than females. Conversely, females are trained to be more sensitive to unexpected closeness, as would be found in adjacent-seating invasion by a stranger. The relevance of Fisher and Byrne's results for this interpretation has not been directly tested yet, so further work on crowding and developmental processes clearly is needed.

Psychologists have been able to demonstrate that one way people can be helped to adapt to stressful situations is by giving them ways to gain a sense of control over the situation. They are more comfortable if they have been given a way in which they can interpret the situation and perceive that their reactions to the stressing situation as under their own control.

Langer and Saegert ("Crowding and cognitive control") define crowding as an event that overloads the person's information handling capacity and reduces the person's sense of control. If the person is able to restore a sense of control by realizing that any stress reactions he or she might feel in a crowded situation are due to the crowd itself, then the stress reactions can be reduced and adaptation enhanced. Crowding thus is defined as having two stress-inducing characteristics: information overload and behavioral restraint. When crowded one has to process a great deal of information simultaneously, part due to the task one plans to perform anyway, and part from all the input coming from other people. Behavioral restraint is involved because one's goal attainment is blocked by the numerous interferences of the actions of others.

To develop a naturalistic yet sensitive measure of the components of crowding, Langer and Saegert refer back to research in other branches of psychology. That research shows that arousal will enhance performance of simple or well-learned tasks but will hinder it on complex or poorly-learned tasks. So by varying the nature of task demands, investigators can assess the impact of crowding and at the same time assess the effectiveness of cognitive manipulations enhancing the subject's sense of control. To do this, the investigators chose the research setting of a grocery store where shopper-subjects are naturally exposed to high and low density crowd conditions (at busy and quiet times), and the investigators could assess the effects of task complexity and cognitive control instructions.

For task complexity, the subjects were paid three dollars to select the most economical grocery items from a set list of fifty. Performance could be scored as right or wrong, so a genuine behavioral measure of performance adequacy was possible. Cognitive control information was manipulated by telling half of the subjects what would happen to them if they began to feel stressed. They were told that it would be due to the crowded conditions, that busy times often make people feel tense, and that if they began to feel anxious, it was due to the crowding. The other half of the subjects, the control sample, was not given such control information.

The results show very clear differences between the crowded and uncrowded groups, with crowded subjects more negative on all measures. The differences between the information and no information group were equally significant, with information subjects outperforming the others. Even in the uncrowded condition, those subjects who had been given the cognitive control information outperformed those who had not been given the information.

The overall picture from this study gives clear support to cognitive control as a powerful way to ameliorate the negative effects of crowding. "Knowledge is power" is a phrase often used in other contexts, and it appears particularly appropriate for this study.

ENERGY AND CONSERVATION

Energy consumption and waste have become critical social problems recently. Increased demand and rising costs have made people conscious of the impact of energy use on their economic welfare. Governments are attempting to reduce consumption, so information and conservation campaigns are widespread. However, although consumers may be aware of the problem, finding ways for them to alter their actual energy use is a complex and difficult matter. Using energy is such a natural everyday occurrence that changing that behavior is not as easy as one would hope.

Psychologists approach the problem as one of changing individual behavior, and that involves not only giving feedback information to consumers but also directing people in ways to change their energy use behavior. One of the two studies reprinted here, by Becker and Seligman, approaches this two-component issue through the use of direct energy use information. The other study, by Walker, attempts to solve the problem of getting information to individuals about their own personal energy use. Given modern living and working arrangements, it is difficult for the individual to know how much energy he or she is using. Walker develops and tests one technique for individualizing information and finds that, given information and reinforcement contingencies, reduced use could be achieved. Both studies are based on sound psychological principles and offer considerable promise for helping to solve the energy problems we now face.

Becker and Seligman ("Reducing air conditioning waste by signalling it is cool outside") note the irony in single-dwelling residential air conditioning patterns. Users of air conditioning are instructed to keep their doors and windows shut while operating their unit; this makes the system more effective. However, at the same time this shuts out information about outside temperatures; in the early morning and late evening these can be cooler than inside temperatures and running the unit during these times is wasteful. Making that temperature information available to users might prove effective in reducing usage. However, another problem is that some way has to be developed for that information to be used easily and effectively. Walker and Seligman developed a technology for both.

The investigators selected four samples of similar single-family dwellings. One set of residents was provided with information about their usage only, another set was provided with an instrument that signalled when the outside temperature was lower than their thermostat setting, another set was provided with both, and the final set was given neither. The signalling device involved a thermometer indicating outside temperature and comparing it to the interior thermostat setting; it turned on a blinking blue light when the outside temperature was lower and could be turned off only by turning off the air conditioner.

The results show that the signal light resulted in a significant reduction of use, 15.7%. The information only condition did not have a significant effect. It seems clear from the data that homeowners are willing to experiment with their energy usage and that, given proper information, they can be successful at reducing their use. From a psychological perspective, approaches to reducing energy use should focus on the individual and should be related to that individual's motivational and behavioral tendencies.

The Becker and Seligman study was conducted on single-family dwellings. However, a great number of residents live in apartment complexes; these master-metered buildings do not have individual unit meters, so people do not have information feedback on their use patterns. This may be a major source of energy waste; energy consumption is 35% higher than in individually-metered apartments. However, in the study by Walker reprinted here ("Energy demand behavior in a master-metered apartment complex: An experimental analysis") an alternative approach was developed and tested for its effectiveness.

Other studies had attempted to use monetary incentives to encourage subgroups of apartments to reduce consumption, but in the long run they had proved unsuccessful. Walker changes the approach to one in which individuals were monitored by energy project observers and, if they met preset reduction criteria, they received cash awards. In effect, the project was run as a rebate contest, with individuals randomly chosen to be eligible for any given week. Those eligible had their apartment checked by project personnel to see if they met the contest criteria: a raised thermostat setting for air conditioning in the summer and a lowered setting for heating in the winter, plus closed doors and windows unless the thermostat was off. Perhaps the Becker and Seligman manipulation would have been of even greater effectiveness in this situation. Since the individual apartments were not metered, reduced use had to be measured on the basis of the entire complex's records.

The results show a significant contest effect. More individual apartments met the contest criteria after the introduction of the contest than before it, and use was reduced. For one measure, the experimental complex reduced its consumption by 8.6% compared to the control complex and also showed reduced use relative to its own baseline observation period. A followup five week observation period without the reward contingencies was recorded and showed that the residents were continuing to reduce their usage and thus were still making efforts at conservation.

Given the simplicity of the technique and the evidence of its effectiveness, its use beyond this rather limited experimental application seems warranted. According to the investigator's calculations, apartment managers who implement such a program would save enough money to cover the cost of paying the cash awards and the personnel to administer the program and still have money left over as profit. Remember that these calculations are based on energy costs long since outstripped by the increases in energy prices since the study was conducted, so now it would make even more sense to implement such changes. Given the significant results obtained here, and the critical nature of the energy problem facing society, making an attempt to institute similar projects in other settings seems eminently worthwhile.

Shoplifting

Who Reports Shoplifters: a Field-Experimental Study[1]

Donna M. Gelfand[2]   *University of Utah*
Donald P. Hartmann
Patrice Walder
Brent Page

Abstract

This field study investigated bystander and shoplifter characteristics differentially related to bystander rates of observing and of reporting shoplifting. Simulated shoplifting incidents were staged in two large drug-variety stores, one in an upper-income, suburban area, the second in a lower-income central-city location. The dress of the girl shoplifter was varied (hippie, youth-culture dress or conventional, conservative clothing). Observers recorded gender and estimated age of observers, as well as their duration and directness of observation of shoplifter, and attempts to report the shoplifter to store personnel. Despite the use of attention-attracting procedures, only about 28% of the shoppers tested were judged to have noticed the shoplifting. Of these observers, approximately 28% reported the shoplifter. Although those interviewed rated the conventionally dressed shoplifter as more likable than the hippie shoplifter, the shoplifter's appearance was not related to bystanders' rates of reporting her. Reporting the female shoplifter was more frequent for male customers and for persons raised in rural rather than large city environments. It is argued that rather than being due to overstimulatory or depersonalizing effects of city life, differential rates of intervention for country-reared and city-reared persons are attributable to social learning history differences.

"Who Reports Shoplifters? A Field-Experimental Study" by Donna M. Gelfand, Donald P. Hartmann, Patrice Walder, and Brent Page. *Journal of Personality and Social Psychology,* 1973, Vol. 25, No. 2, pp. 276–285. Copyright © 1973 by The American Psychological Association, Inc. Reprinted by permission.

A recent upsurge in research in social responsibility has been spurred by widespread public concern over an apparent decrease in the willingness of bystanders to intervene to aid victims of accidents and criminal attacks. Investigators have studied bystander reactions to a variety of simulated social crisis situations including medical emergencies (Darley & Latané, 1968; Latané & Rodin, 1969; Piliavin, Rodin, & Piliavin, 1969), minor inconveniences such as automobile breakdowns (Bryan & Test, 1967) or collapsing grocery bags (Wispé & Freshley, 1971), and petty crimes such as vandalism of abandoned vehicles (Zimbardo, 1969). A major aim of these studies has been to identify conditions under which witnesses will intervene on behalf of the victim. When the victim is an individual and is present, the aiding rates are relatively high. For example, Piliavin et al. (1969) found that in 95% of their trials, aid was offered to a subway rider who had apparently suffered a collapse, while Wispé and Freshly reported that 67% of their bystander subjects gave some assistance to a shopper whose grocery bag had burst. And a remarkable 100% of subjects tested alone reported an epileptic seizure victim in an adjacent room (Latané & Darley, 1968). Even children aid in emergencies; Staub (1971) found that when they were given tacit permission to do so, between 50% and 90% of the children he tested entered a nearby room to offer help to a person who had apparently fallen and hurt herself.

Many crimes and emergencies, however, have corporate rather than individual victims. In most cases of retail theft and check forgery, for example, the victims are business firms owned and operated by corporations, and no single person can be easily identified as victimized by the crime. In such instances, the absence of individual, personal appeals by the victim might be expected to decrease rates of bystander intervention. This argument seems likely especially since personal acquaintance with the victim is correlated with the speed with which the bystander goes to his assistance (Latané & Darley, 1970b). These same investigators also found a very low rate (20%) of bystander reporting of the theft of a case of beer. This negligible intervention rate may have been due to the nature of the victim, a large discount beverage store.

The present study aimed to determine conditions under which bystanders would take action in the interests of a chain drug-variety firm which was the apparent victim of a shoplifter. In a field experiment, blatant shoplifting was enacted in an attempt to discover shoplifter and bystander characteristics which would affect detection and reporting of shoplifting activities.

Shoplifting was chosen as the enacted activity because of its growing importance as a social problem. Retail merchants claim the loss of nearly 50% of their potential profits due to shoplifting (Domfeld, 1967), and shoplifting rates continue to rise alarmingly. According to Federal Bureau of Investigation estimates, shoplifting incidence tripled in the decade beginning in 1959 ("Rising wave of shoplifting", *U.S. News and World Report,* 1970). And a recent observational study conducted by Saul Astor in four large department stores located in eastern cities revealed that 1 out of each 15 shoppers scrutinized stole at least one item ("One of fifteen shoplifters, study discloses," *The New York Times,* 1970). Store security forces are hard pressed to detect and prosecute shoplifters, and other shoppers do not often report shoplifters to store personnel. Is the failure of bystanders to report shoplifting due to a failure to notice the activity or to the failure, having noticed, to report? The present study sheds some light on this question.

Presumably, shoplifter characteristics (e.g., wearing of hippie, youth-culture garb or tidy, conventional clothing) play a role in determining bystander observation and reporting rates. The research literature on similarity and liking (Collins & Raven, 1969) would indicate that a shoplifter of one's own social group would be found more appealing and consequently would be less likely to be reported than an individual from another subculture. Moreover, the shoplifter from a different social group might be observed more closely because of his foreign appearance. So it was expected that the hippie-clad shoplifter would be liked less, observed more, and reported more than would the same experimental accomplice dressed in a more conventional fashion.

Observation and reporting rates may also be related to bystander characteristics such as sex, age, and socioeconomic status. Latané and Darley (1970b) have reasoned that men may be more likely than women to intervene when the action is direct, involves skill, knowledge, physical strength, and contains an element of danger. Examples of such situations include breaking up a fist fight, extinguishing a fire, or halting a runaway horse. On the other hand, many reportorial or detour interventions require merely reporting the emergency to the proper authorities, for example, reporting a robbery to police or a fire to a nearby fire station. Such reportorial interventions should be equally often undertaken by men and women. Several previous bystander intervention studies have demonstrated that women are less likely to help than are men, especially if the helping necessitates physical effort (Piliavin, Rodin, & Piliavin, 1969; Wispé & Freshley, 1971), so the present study sampled both men and women shoppers to assess possible sex differences in reporting shoplifting. The subjects' accuracy of observation, reaction to the shoplifter, and attitudes toward shoplifting were assessed by means of interviews. And bystander age and socioeconomic status were also assessed from interviews and estimated from observations in an effort to investigate their relationships to the dependent variables.

Another shopper characteristic that might relate to intervention is his childhood place of residence—rural, small town, or urban. In contrast to those who live in cities, rural citizens are much more dependent upon one another to give help in a variety of crisis situations such as natural disasters and medical emergencies. Since specialized help in the form of police protection, fire fighting, and emergency medical treatment is not likely to be speedily available to the country dweller, he must call upon his neighbors for immediate aid. The atypical neighbor who refuses to help quickly becomes an object of scandal and social ostracism. So the farmer rushes his seriously ill neighbor to the hospital regardless of the degree of acquaintance between them. And he can confidently expect his neighbor to do the same for him. He does not necessarily change his behavior patterns if he moves to the city. His early training predisposes him to take action to help others.

The same may not be true for the city-reared person who has come to expect that ambulance emergency teams respond to medical crises and that the police and private security forces control crime. Consequently, the country-reared person takes action more readily in social crises than the city-reared individual. It should be noted that the argument presented here runs counter to the more familiar view that city living is accompanied by anomie, feelings of alienation, depersonalization, and an overload of sensory stimulation (viz., Milgram, 1970; Simmel, 1950; Wirth, 1938). If these negative effects do result from the city environment, then all city inhabitants should suffer this city syndrome equally, regardless of their places of origin. If anything, the adverse effects of city life should be accentuated for those who have grown up in a rural locale and who are unaccustomed to the overstimulation of the city. But if, on the other hand, patterns of helping are differentially learned by city and by country children, the size of the community in which a person is reared should be related to his intervention behavior, while the site of the emergency situation should be of secondary importance. In the present study, shoppers were interviewed and questioned about their childhood homes in an effort to test the differential predictions stemming from the overstimulation theory and the social learning theory. The overstimulation theory would lead us to predict that all shoppers tested in a city should be affected similarly by the city syndrome. In contrast, the social learning view would predict that a person's place of origin should be related to his helping behavior.

METHOD

Subjects

One hundred and eighty men and 156 women shoppers in two Salt Lake City chain drugstores served as unsolicited subjects. The experiments took place on weekdays between the hours of 3:30 and 10:00 P.M. and weekends between noon and 4:00 P.M. during the 8-month period of October, 1970, to May, 1971. In order to be selected as a subject, the shopper had to be an adult, be unaccompanied, be out of the visual range of a sales clerk, and be in a position to observe the shoplifting model easily. In addition, no other customers could be within approximately 30 feet and in the same aisle as the subject. Subjects' median age was about 44 years and the sample of 56 subjects interviewed ranged in age from 16 to 75 years. The majority of those interviewed were married (70%), were of the Mormon faith (80%), and had at least a high school education (75%).

Design

Systematically varied were *(a)* the location of the store in which the study took place (upper-income suburban versus lower-income, central-city location) and *(b)* the appearance of the female model (dressed in hippie versus conventional clothing). Each experimental condition was crossed with three age groups of subjects: adults under 30 years, adults between 30 and 60 years, and adults over 60 years. Each cell was also subdivided into men and women subjects. The hour and day of the week of the shoplifting incident were approximately balanced across treatment conditions. The two major dependent variables were subjects' rate of observing the shoplifter and rate of reporting the shoplifter to store personnel.

Procedure

The apparent shoplifter was a pleasant-appearing, 21-year-old college coed whose actions were directed by means of radio communication with two observers concealed behind a one-way observation window which ran the length of the store and about 15 feet above floor level. When a lone shopper approached, the shoplifter, who carried a miniature radio receiver in her purse and wore a concealed earphone, was instructed by an observer to begin her shoplifting performance. She first attempted to attract the customer's attention by either dropping some small article, rattling a package, or reaching for an item located very close to the shopper. When notified by the observer that the shopper was watching her, the shoplifter blatantly removed several items of merchandise and stuffed them into her handbag. The total value of the merchandise did not exceed $5 and included a variety of small items such as cosmetics (lipsticks, perfume bottles, shampoo containers), stationery supplies (pens, pencils, tablets, ink bottles), sewing supplies (thread, ribbons, boxes of pins, needles, and buttons), hardware (electric cords, plugs, switches, small repair tools), automotive supplies (spark plugs, small cans of oil, oil additives), and housewares (can openers, cooking implements, small utensils). After placing the items in her handbag, the shoplifter hurried to the front of the store and out the door without paying the cashier.

The action of both shoplifter and customer were videotaped through the observation window by means of a Sony DV 2400 portable videocamera equipped with a 16-64 millimeter zoom lens and a Sony DV-2400 videorecorder.

After the conclusion of the shoplifting incident and as each subject left the check-out stand, he was approached by a 20-year-old undergraduate interviewer dressed neatly in sports slacks, dress shirt, and tie. The interviewer identified himself as a researcher from the University of Utah, showed a plastic identification card verifying his claim, and asked the subject whether he would answer some questions. He was told that his replies would be recorded anonymously and that he need not answer any questions he did not wish to. The subjects who indicated willingness to be interviewed but who were in a hurry were interviewed by telephone as soon as possible after the shoplifting incident. Of eight subjects who expressed agreement to a telephone interview, four were successfully contacted and interviewed. All interviews

were tape-recorded on a transistorized Webcor cassette recorder Model T 140.

The interview consisted of a series of questions designed to assess the subject's *(a)* awareness of and reactions to the shoplifting incident, *(b)* rationale for reacting as he did toward our shoplifter (reporting or not reporting her), *(c)* attitudes toward shoplifting in general and factors which would dispose him toward reporting a shoplifter to store personnel, and *(d)* personal history including his age, marital status, occupation, residence, education, and whether he was reared in a rural, small town, or urban environment.

At the close of the interview, the subject was informed that the shoplifting incident he had witnessed was staged, and he was given a printed handout that thanked him for his cooperation and briefly explained the study and its purposes. Subjects who refused to be interviewed were also given the explanatory handout.

Independent Variables

Store location.   Equal numbers of shoppers were sampled in one drug-variety store located in a high-income suburban area and in a second branch of the same retail chain located in a lower-income central-city area. Our intention in choosing sites in these two different neighborhoods was to obtain samples of subjects who differed correspondingly in socioeconomic status.

Sex of subject.   We aimed to have equal numbers of male and female subjects in each treatment condition, but our sample finally included 47 men and 42 women who were judged to have witnessed the shoplifting.

Age of subject.   The subjects' ages were determined by interview and by judging ages from the videotapes for subjects who refused to be interviewed. Three age categories were used: adults under 30 years (32 subjects), those 30 to 60 years (33 subjects), and those over 60 years (24 subjects).

Shoplifter appearance.   For one-half of the subjects tested, the young woman shoplifter was dressed conventionally in a navy-blue medium-length coat with matching handbag and medium high-heeled shoes. She was well groomed with neatly combed hair.

The remaining subjects observed the same young lady dressed as a dishevelled, hippie shoplifter who wore worn bell-bottomed blue jeans with bleached spots, an old blue workshirt, and an army jacket. She carried a brown leather handbag and wore a leather headband over long, disarranged hair.

Performance Measures

Observation.   Since it was crucial to the data analysis to know whether or not each subject actually noticed the shoplifter, the two concealed observers rated each subject's reaction to the shoplifter on a 4-point scale as follows: The subject was in a position making it impossible to see shoplifting (e.g., facing in opposite direction, or view obscured by a merchandise display) (1). The subject could possibly see shoplifting but was not looking directly at shoplifter (2). The subject was looking directly at thief as she was shoplifting, but his observation was brief and involved no second or third glances (3). The subject looked directly at shoplifter and glanced at her one or more additional times after the initial shoplifting incident (4).

Reporting.   In order to assess reporting, the observers watched each subject until he had passed through the check-out stand and left the store. If the subject spoke to the cashier or any other store employee, one of the research team waited until the customer had left and then asked that employee whether the customer had reported the shoplifting. All sales personnel were aware that the study was in progress and had been instructed to employ their typical procedures in dealing with reported shoplifters. They asked the shopper for a description of the shoplifter and her location, told him they would take care of the matter, and thanked him for his information. If the shoplifter was still inside the store at the time, an employee would accost her and accompany her to the manager's office, ostensibly to report her criminal activity. In this manner, we attempted to maintain the credibility of our shoplifter until after the observing shopper had been interviewed. This procedure was intended to prevent the subjects' awareness that the theft was staged from affecting their responses to the interview questions.

In fact, only one subject reported having suspected that the shoplifting was staged. Six more subjects said that the interview itself led them to question the shoplifter's genuineness, but most of the people interviewed expressed surprise upon learning that the shoplifting was only an experimental manipulation.

RESULTS

The data for this study came from videotaped observations made of the bystanders at the time of the staged shoplifting incident and from interviews conducted with them as they prepared to leave the store. The former data source includes the 4-point observation rating and gender and age estimates for shoppers who were not interviewed.[3] A random sample of 25 videotaped subjects was independently rated to determine the reliability of the age and observational rating. In both cases, the percentage of agreement with the independent rater was excellent (96%). All interview tapes were also independently rated by two raters on 26 questionnaire responses. The interrater percentage agreement ranged from 80% to 100%, with a median value of 97%.

Observation Rate

Despite our attempts to make the shoplifting incident as obvious as possible while maintaining its credibility, the observing rate was nonetheless surprisingly low. If we include subjects rated 4 ($n = 70$), those rated 3 unless they denied observing during the interview ($n = 15$), and a number of those rated 2 based upon the proportion of 2s who were interviewed and admitted observing the incident ($n = 9$), the total number of customers who observed is 94. Thus, only 28% of the exposed shoppers observed the staged incident despite our precision-cueing, multiple-staging and attention-attracting procedures.[4] The number of subjects observing and not observing in each of the Sex $\times$ Age $\times$ Condition $\times$ Store cells is shown in Table 1. As can be seen from this table, the observing rate varied substantially among cells with a high of 83% for young upper-socioeconomic-status females who observed the conservatively dressed shoplifter to a low of 12% for middle-aged, lower-socioeconomic-status females who observed the shoplifter in hippie dress. In general, higher-socioeconomic-status shoppers were more observant than were lower-socioeconomic-status shoppers (30% versus 24%), and younger customers more observant than middle-aged and older customers (36% versus 22% and 27%, respectively). Furthermore, as

Table 1 Number and Percentage of Observing Subjects

| | Male | | | Female | | |
Age	Young	Middle	Old	Young	Middle	Old
Low-SES store						
Hippie	4 (27%)	7 (41%)	3 (30%)	4 (44%)	2 (12%)	3 (33%)
Conventional	4 (29%)	6 (18%)	3 (16%)	3 (33%)	4 (14%)	3 (20%)
High-SES store						
Hippie	3 (27%)	5 (36%)	3 (30%)	5 (31%)	2 (25%)	3 (60%)
Conventional	4 (40%)	3 (17%)	2 (22%)	5 (83%)	4 (22%)	4 (23%)

Note. SES = socioeconomic status. The $n = 89$ in this table includes all subjects rated 4, those rated 3 unless they denied observing to the interviewer, and only those rated 2 who were interviewed and admitted observing.

predicted, the shoplifter was more likely to be observed when attired in her hippie garb than when conservatively dressed (31% versus 23%).[5]

Reporting Rate

Twenty-eight (28%) of those customers who observed the staged shoplifting reported it to store employees. This rate was actually surprisingly high in view of the very low report rate we had expected from discussions with our retail security consultants prior to beginning the research. The number and percentage of observing subjects who reported in each cell of our design is summarized in Table 2. As can be seen from this table, the rate varied from a high of 67% for high-socioeconomic-status middle-aged males who observed the straight shoplifter to 0% which occurred in seven of the remaining cells (six of them containing women subjects only).

The most frequently given reason for reporting the thief (25%) was that stealing was immoral. Of the customers who failed to report, 57% justified their behavior with one of the following reasons: The shoplifter left too quickly, no clerk was readily available, or the store was too crowded. Surprisingly, 19% of the nonreporters indicated during the interview that they would always report.

Sex. Sex was a significant source of variation in rate of shoplifter reporting ($\chi^2 = 3.97$, $df = 1$, $p < .05$, and $\phi = .21$) with male shoppers reporting twice as frequently as female shoppers (38% versus 19%).[6] Low reporting rates were particularly characteristic of female customers who were either old (8%) or who shopped in the store located in the lower-socioeconomic-status neighborhood (5%). As is noted in a later section, the lower rates of reporting for women is consistent with their generally more permissive attitudes toward shoplifting.

Age. The customer's age was of borderline significance as a main effect ($\chi^2 = 4.88$, $df = 2$, $p < .10$, and $C = .23$). Middle-aged shoppers were almost three times more likely to report our clumsy shoplifter than were older shoppers and almost twice as likely to report than were young shoppers. Report rates were 25% for young, 42% for middle-aged, and 16% for old bystanders.

Socioeconomic status.[7] The socioeconomic-status variable was marginally related to reporting rate ($\chi^2 = 2.57$, $df = 1$, $p = .11$, and $\phi = .17$ with higher rates of reporting for customers of the store located in the higher-socioeconomic-status neighborhood (37% versus 22%). This finding is somewhat surprising in view of the greater liking for the shoplifter expressed by these shoppers as compared to the lower-socioeconomic-status shoppers ($t = 2.24$, $df = 32$, $p < .05$).

Residency. Shoppers were asked during the interview to classify their place of primary residency during childhood as large city (population greater than 100,000), small town (population less than 100,000), or rural. The shoplifter reporting rates for these residences are, respectively, 30%, 63%, and 75%. Because of the small number of shoppers raised in rural environments, the small-town and rural shoppers were combined for statistical analysis. The resulting 2×2 table yielded a $\chi^2 = 5.14$, $p < .05$ and $\phi = -.35$.

Hippie versus conventional dress. Surprisingly, the hippie versus conventional shoplifter condition failed to contribute to either main or interaction effects on report rate despite the fact that there was a clear difference in attitude expressed by the shoppers toward the shoplifter in the two conditions. On the 5-point scale of favorableness—unfavorableness of description, the conservatively dressed shoplifter was rated as slightly positive ($M = 3.9$), whereas the shoplifter dressed in hippie apparel was rated slightly below the neutral point ($M = 2.6$). This difference, which is highly significant ($t = 3.55$, $df = 32$, $p < .002$), confirms the prediction regarding greater bystander liking for the neatly dressed shoplifter. Differences between the two shoplifting conditions are particularly striking for males ($t = 3.125$, $df = 19$, $p < .01$) and for low-socioeconomic-status subjects ($t = 4.64$, $df = 13$, $p < .001$). Essentially, men and people of lower-socioeconomic-status negatively valued the hippie costume.

The interview data also revealed that, as predicted, subjects were able to describe the hippie shoplifter in greater detail than the conventionally dressed thief. When the number of shoplifter clothing items correctly described by the bystander is divided into three categories (one or less items, two items, three or more items), analysis of these scores by shoplifter appearance yielded an $\chi^2 = 5.65$, $df = 2$, $p < .10$.

Additional Questionnaire Data[8]

Of those bystanders interviewed, 28% indicated that they would *always* report shoplifting that they had observed. This rate is identical to the actual rate of reporting found in our research. Men were more than twice as likely as women to state that they would report all offenders (37% of men versus 15% of

women), whereas women's rate of reporting was much more likely to be determined by various characteristics of the shoplifter (12% of women versus 3% of men). In keeping with the more stern approach reported by males, they also were much more likely to recommend punitive consequences such as jail sentences for convicted offenders than were women (20% versus 7%).

Among the various characteristics that shoppers mentioned would promote reporting were the following: child rather than adult status (21% versus 2%), well dressed rather than shabbily dressed (25% versus 2%), and healthy rather than handicapped (38% versus 0%). Customers, not surprisingly, also reported that they would be more likely to report the theft of more expensive items (18% versus 0% for cheap items). Neither the sex nor the attractiveness of the shoplifter was related to verbalized willingness to report, and neither, surprisingly, was hair length.

Among those factors spontaneously mentioned by shoppers that would increase their hesitancy to report, uncertainty as to whether an offense had occurred was mentioned by 10% of the respondents and personal characteristics of the shoplifter by another 7%. Women (19% versus 3% for men) and older shoppers (50% versus 2% for younger- and middle-aged subjects) were particularly likely to mention uncertainty about the offense as a reason for not reporting, while high-socioeconomic-status subjects were more likely to mention characteristics of the shoplifter (14% versus 0% for low-socioeconomic-status subjects). When questioned about legal reasons that might decrease reporting, 16% of the subjects indicated that time spent in court might deter them, while 18% suggested that the possibility of a countersuit might make them hesitant to report. Another 7% offered both reasons.

Table 2 Number and Percentage of Observing Subjects Who Reported

Age	Male			Female		
	Young	Middle	Old	Young	Middle	Old
Low-SES store						
Hippie	1 (25%)	3 (43%)	1 (33%)	0 (0%)	0 (0%)	0 (0%)
Conventional	1 (25%)	2 (33%)	1 (33%)	0 (0%)	1 (25%)	0 (0%)
High-SES store						
Hippie	1 (33%)	3 (60%)	1 (33%)	1 (20%)	1 (25%)	0 (0%)
Conventional	2 (50%)	2 (67%)	0 (0%)	2 (40%)	2 (50%)	1 (25%)

Note. SES = socioeconomic status.

DISCUSSION

As compared with bystander intervention rates in many other social crisis situations, bystanders both observe shoplifting less (roughly 26% of those tested) and, having observed, are less likely to take action (roughly 30% of those who observed). The initial failure in observation is probably due to shoppers' almost total absorption in their task and to the lower attention-attracting nature of shoplifting than of the staged actions employed in other intervention studies. Stuffing several articles of merchandise into a bag simply does not command the same degree of attention as garbled cries, crashing groceries, and falling bodies. Thus many potential interveners were lost in this first phase of the intervention process, noticing that something is wrong (Latané & Darley, 1970a).

The low reporting rates by those who have observed the shoplifting are less easily explained. Of course, the corporate victim of the crime is less visible and arouses less sympathy than does the on-the-scene individual sufferer. This argument is supported by several of our subjects' comments to the effect that they believed the stores' security force would be using the one-way observation windows for scanning the area for shoplifters anyway, so shoppers' assistance would not be needed. A diffusion of responsibility effect (Latané & Darley, 1970a, 1970b) is evident in our informants' expressed beliefs that other people, specifically store employees, would and should assume responsibility for surveillance and action. So our shoppers frequently decided not to take action because they failed to feel personal responsibility to do so, Phase 3 in Latané and Darley's model of the intervention process. The corporate victim of the shoplifting is removed, impersonal, and is regarded as thoroughly capable of self-defense.

There is also nothing analogous to good-Samaritan laws (which compel passersby to aid accident victims) to spur observers of shoplifters to take action. On the contrary, legal considerations are more likely to impede than to facilitate reporting. Forty-one percent of the shoppers we interviewed mentioned possibility of either a countersuit by the person they accused or court appearance demands as reasons they would hesitate to report a shoplifter. So the costs of making a mistake resulting in a false or unprovable accusation are considered to be relatively great, most probably severe enough to inhibit reporting. Moreover, the costs are not confined to the bystander. His reporting will probably result in the apprehension, and perhaps the arrest, trial, fining, or incarceration of the person he accuses. The potential harm to the person whom he accuses might well help deter him from reporting.

In contrast, the potential rewards are minimal. Corporations are not known in any way to reward customers who report shoplifters; they offer neither monetary rewards, generous expressions of thanks, nor any other symbolic representation of gratitude. The individual is sustained in his reporting only by the somewhat comforting conviction that stealing is immoral and that he is playing a role in bringing a criminal to justice. And as the literature on guilt, equity, and justice demonstrates, it is frequently easier to derogate the victim or to minimize the transgression than it is to take action that may prove to be inconvenient, dangerous, and time-consuming (Lerner, 1970; Walster, Berscheid, & Walster, 1970). An objective cost-benefit analysis argues powerfully against the bystander's reporting the activities of an observed shoplifter. If retailers wish customers to aid in apprehending shoplifters, they must work both to promote greater vigilance and to redress this cost-benefit imbalance.

Similarity to and liking for the shoplifter apparently play no role in observers' willingness to take action against the shoplifter. Neither do the attention-attracting qualities of the thief's costume. While the shoppers apparently noticed and remembered the hippie shoplifter's clothing more and found her less likable than she was as a conservatively dressed shoplifter, they were no more willing to report her in her youth-culture guise. Counteracting the greater liking of the neatly dressed shoplifter was the frequently expressed opinion that shoplifting is immoral and illegal and should always be reported, if only for the shoplifter's own good. One of the women shoppers who did turn our accomplice in to store personnel explained that the shoplifter looked like such a nice girl that she should be apprehended in order to save her from a life of crime. It may also be the case that observers considered the blue-jean-clad shoplifter less wealthy than the conservatively dressed culprit. So, although they liked her less, they may have been more reluctant to turn in an apparently impoverished girl, as they also indicated to be the case in their interview answers.

Several bystander characteristics are differentially related to shoplifting-reporting rates. Male shoppers were not only more likely to report the female shoplifter, but they also held more punitive attitudes toward shoplifting as revealed in their interview responses. These findings are consistent with the data reported by other investigators (e.g., Wispé & Freshley, 1971) and may reflect the operation of cultural expectations that men are both more punitive and better able to deal with certain emergency situations than are women.

Other bystander characteristics marginally correlated with reporting were age, socioeconomic status, and place of residence during childhood. Better educated, upper-middle-class people were more likely to report than were those of lower-middle-class status. Our data fail to provide any hints concerning which variables mediated by social class affect bystander intervention rates. Perhaps differences in intelligence or education favoring higher socioeconomic-status subjects enable them to generate more adequately various methods of intervention and assess their consequences; or, perhaps the differences in reporting rates reflect different norms of social responsibility correlated with social class. The choice among these and other alternatives awaits further research. The middle-aged were more often reporters than were either younger or older shoppers, a result that parallels Sorokin's (1950) discovery that more middle-aged people (70%) tend to be among the "good neighbors" than either the young or the old. The younger shoppers matched the shoplifter more closely in age, possibly a report-inhibiting correspondence, while the aged persons showed a low incidence of both reporting and agreeing to be interviewed. The shoppers over 60 years of age may have failed to report because they were less sure of what it was that they had witnessed. One elderly lady told the interviewer that she had noticed the experimental accomplice taking articles out of her handbag and putting them on the display racks. And 50% of the older subjects interviewed offered uncertainty about the offense as a reason for observers' not reporting. Consequently, we were losing the elderly potential reporters at Step 2 of Latané and Darley's intervention model, deciding that the event is an emergency.

The results of this experiment lend support to Latané and Darley's (1970b) analysis of the intervention process as involving a sequence of five separate decisions, namely *(a)* that an event is occurring, *(b)* that the event is an emergency, *(c)* that the bystander should take personal responsibility for helping, *(d)* that he chooses the appropriate manner of giving help, and *(e)* that he implements the intervention. As we have pointed out previously, potential interveners in the shoplifting situation were lost at Stages 1, 2, and 3. Some were also lost as regards reporting at Stages 4 and 5. Some shoppers decided upon a mode of intervention but failed to implement it. These persons stated that the absence of nearby sales clerks in this self-service store deterred them from reporting our accomplice although they had decided that reporting was in order. One ingenious man, rather than reporting our shoplifter, accosted her and falsely claimed that he was the store security officer and that he would be forced to detain her if she did not put back all the merchandise she had stolen. His Stage 4 decision differed from that of most of the other subjects. Like Latané and Darley, we have no evidence that the five decisions are made in the sequence given above, but we did find that the failure to intervene can be attributed to any one of the choice points outlined in the Latané and Darley model.

The more populous was the observer's childhood place of residence, the less likely was he to report the shoplifting offense. Our findings in this regard again resemble Sorokin's (1950) finding that a majority (74%) of the individuals who were described as "good neighbors" were rural residents as children. And, although they deemphasize the importance of the finding, Darley and Latané (1968) also discovered a reliable negative correlation between size of the community in which an individual grew up and his speed in reporting a medical emergency.

Presumably, the country dweller's early training in responsibility for taking action in emergencies accounts for his high intervention rates. In contrast, the city-reared person is more accustomed to letting specialized authorities take the appropriate action. The concordance of our results with those obtained by others as regards the relationship between childhood residence and help-giving indicates the need for further investigation of the factors associated with country life that produce helpful citizens. If we can isolate these factors and build them into our city social environments, we might become able to move freely about American cities on foot, confident in the truth of the assertion that there is safety in numbers.

Footnotes

[1]This research was supported by Department of Justice Grant NI 70-065-PG-14, with funds provided by the Omnibus Crime Control and Safe Streets Act of 1968 to the National Institute of Law Enforcement and Criminal Justice. We wish to thank the employees of Skaggs Drug Centers for their cooperation, Bret Huish for serving as interviewer, and

Irwin Altman for reading the manuscript and offering helpful suggestions.

[2]Requests for reprints should be sent to Donna M. Gelfand, Department of Psychology, University of Utah, Salt Lake City, Utah 84112.

[3]Interviews were requested only of shoppers given observation ratings of 2 or above ($n = 112$). Those observers who complied with our request ($n = 56$) included a disproportionate number of customers who had reported the shoplifting activity (47%). Due to the potential confounding of the interview data by reporting rate, conclusions obtained from the interview should be considered highly tentative.

[4]A more conservative estimate of reporting rate (24%) is obtained by including all 4s in the observers category ($n = 70$), a number of 3s based on the proportion of 3s admitting having observed during the interview ($n = 5$), and those 2s who admitted observing during the interview ($n = 4$).

[5]If the observing subjects in each two-factor cell of the design are further divided by observational rating (2, 3, or 4), the proportion of "certain" observers (those rated 4s), varies from a high of 88.2% for young subjects observing the straight shoplifter to 41.2% for older subjects who viewed the hippie shoplifter. Because subjects rated 4 were more likely to report than those with lower ratings (38% versus 5%), reporting Rate × Condition comparisons might have been confounded by differences in the proportion of subjects rated 4 across conditions. As a check against this possible course of confounding, the statistical analyses reported below were also performed on the data from shoppers classified as "observers" by means of the conservative criterion (see Footnote 3). The two sets of statistical tests were highly similar with a slight trend for the reported tests to have *larger* probability levels.

[6]Since the only shoplifter presented was female, it is impossible to assess a potential interaction between sex of reporter and sex of shoplifter. Consequently, all conclusions regarding reporting rates in this study must be confined to the reporting of a woman shoplifter.

[7]The median years of school for shoppers who made their purchases in the store located in the lower-socioeconomic-status neighborhood was 12, whereas the median for subjects who shopped in the higher-socioeconomic-status neighborhood store was 12 plus (some college). When all subjects were divided into three educational levels (less than 12 years, 12 years, and more than 12 years), an analysis of these data by store location yielded an $\chi^2 = 7.23$, $df = 2$, $p < .05$, and $C = .34$. Occupational status, as obtained from the interviews was classified by means of Duncan's (1961) Population Decile Scale. A median test performed on these data yielded an $\chi^2 = 6.29$, df = 1, $p < .02$, and $\phi = .42$. The median occupational level for the lower-socioeconomic-status group was 6.75 and for the higher group was 8.8. Consequently, it seems that although the store location variable roughly distinguished two socioeconomic status levels, the separation between the levels was not great and both levels were essentially middle class.

[8]Due to the relatively small *ns* upon which these questionnaire responses are based, they were not subjected to statistical analyses. The results simply represent interesting trends in the data.

References

Bryan, J. H., & Test, M. A. Models and helping: Naturalistic studies in aiding behavior. *Journal of Personality and Social Psychology*, 1967, *6*, 400-407.

Collins, B. E., & Raven, B. H. Group structure: Attraction, coalitions, communication, and power. In G. Lindzey & E. Aronson (Eds.), *The handbook of social psychology*. Vol. 4. (2nd ed.) London: Addison-Wesley, 1969.

Darley, J., & Latané, B. Bystander intervention in emergencies: Diffusion of responsibility. *Journal of Personality and Social Psychology*, 1968, *8*, 377-383.

Domfeld, G. R. The shoplifter. *F.B.I. Law Enforcement Bulletin*, 1967, *36*, 2-5.

Duncan, O. D. A socioeconomic index for all occupations. In A. J. Reiss (Ed.), *Occupations and social status*. Glencoe, Ill.: Free Press, 1961.

Latané, B., & Darley, J. Group inhibition of bystander intervention in emergencies. *Journal of Personality and Social Psychology*, 1968, *10*, 215-221.

Latané, B., & Darley, J. Situational determinants of bystander intervention in emergencies. In J. Macaulay & L. Berkowitz (Eds.), *Altruism and helping behavior*. New York: Academic Press, 1970. (a)

Latané, B., & Darley, J. *The unresponsive bystander: Why doesn't he help?* New York: Appleton-Century-Crofts, 1970. (b)

Latané, B., & Rodin, J. A lady in distress: Inhibiting effects of friends and strangers on bystander intervention. *Journal of Experimental Social Psychology*, 1969, *5*, 189-202.

Lerner, M. J. The desire for justice and reactions to victims. In J. Macaulay & L. Berkowitz (Eds.), *Altruism and helping behavior*. New York: Academic Press, 1970.

Milgram, S. The experience of living in cities. *Science*, 1970, *167*, 1461-1468.

One of Fifteen Shoplifts, Study Discloses. *New York Times*, December 2, 1970, C45.

Piliavin, I. M., Rodin, J., & Piliavin, J. A. Good Samaritanism: An underground phenomenon? *Journal of Personality and Social Psychology*, 1969, *13*, 289-299.

Rising Wave of Shoplifting. *U.S. News and World Report*, March 2, 1970, 56.

Simmel, G. The metropolis and mental life. In K. Wolff (Ed.), *The sociology of Georg Simmel*. New York: MacMillan, 1950.

Sorokin, P. A. *Altruistic love*. Boston: Beacon Press, 1950.

Staub, E. Helping a person in distress: The influence of implicit and explicit "rules" of conduct on children and adults. *Journal of Personality and Social Psychology*, 1971, *17*, 137-144.

Walster, E., Berscheid, E., & Walster, G. W. The exploited:

Justice or justification? In J. Macaulay & L. Berkowitz (Eds.), *Altruism and helping behavior.* New York: Academic Press, 1970.

Wirth, L. Urbanism as a way of life. *American Journal of Sociology,* 1938, *44,* 1-24.

Wispé, L. G., & Freshley, H. B. Race, sex, and sympathetic helping behavior: The broken bag caper. *Journal of Personality and Social Psychology,* 1971, *17,* 59-65.

Zimbardo, P. G. The human choice: Individuation, reason, and order versus deindividuation, impulse, and chaos. *Nebraska Symposium on Motivation,* 1969, *17,* 237-307.

Crime Reporting as a Function of Bystander Encouragement, Surveillance, and Credibility

Leonard Bickman   *Loyola University of Chicago*
Dennis P. Rosenbaum

Abstract

Two studies were designed to examine the relationship between verbal-social influence and bystander intervention in a crime situation. The first study was conducted in a supermarket where the subject witnessed a shoplifting while waiting in the checkout line. A confederate either encouraged reporting, discouraged reporting, or made no comment. She then remained in line behind the subject or left the scene. The results indicated that a few verbal comments designed to assist the subject in answering the questions posited in Latané and Darley's model had a strong effect on rate of crime reporting. The ineffectiveness of the confederate's surveillance and the interaction between verbal influence and preexperimental variables suggested that internal processes, rather than mere compliance, were activated. The second study, conducted in the laboratory, not only confirmed the effectiveness of a few verbal comments, but demonstrated that the influence agent need not witness the crime in order to be influential.

"Crime Reporting as a Function of Bystander Encouragement, Surveillance, and Credibility," by Leonard Bickman and Dennis P. Rosenbaum. *Journal of Personality and Social Psychology,* 1977, Vol. 35, No. 8, pp. 577–586. Copyright © 1977 by The American Psychological Association, Inc. Reprinted by permission.

A husband and wife were watching television when suddenly they heard a loud noise outside. The wife said that it sounded like a woman's scream and the husband rushed to the back porch to check. Hearing no further noises, he decided that it was probably "some teenagers playing around," and suggested to his wife that they dismiss the thought that someone was in trouble. This event would not have been noteworthy except that the following day, the local newspaper reported an attempted rape in the alley behind the couple's apartment (Lavrakas, Note 1). In his book concerning the murder of Kitty Genovese, Rosenthal (1964) noted that only after seeking the advice of a friend in another part of the city did one man finally call the police. Both of these incidents suggest that bystander crime reporting is affected by the verbal behavior of nonwitnesses as well as witnesses. Many programs designed by police and other groups use verbal behavior in an attempt to increase crime reporting (Bickman, Lavrakas, Green, Walker, Edwards, Borkowski, Dubow, & Weurth, 1977). The present research seeks to examine how the verbal behavior of others affects a subject's reporting of a crime.

Previous research on bystander intervention has, to a large extent, focused on Latané and Darley's (1970) proposition that "felt responsibility" by individual group members is a major determinant of intervention (Allen, 1971; Bickman, 1971; Darley & Latané, 1968;

Latané & Darley, 1969; Latané & Rodin, 1969; Korte, 1969; Piliavin & Piliavin, 1972; Piliavin, Rodin, & Piliavin, 1969; Ross, 1971; Ross & Braband, 1973; Schwartz & Clausen, 1970; Tilker, 1970). Much of this research has been directed at varying the number or type of others present rather than their verbal behavior. Staub (1972a) has noted that others may influence intervention in a number of ways. They may define not only the situation but also the appropriate reaction. This defining process may be accomplished by either observing the actions of others present or by their verbal behavior. While the observation of others' actions has been extensively studied in modeling experiments, only two previous experiments have manipulated the verbal behavior of others (Bickman, 1972; Staub, 1972b). Both of these experiments were concerned with the verbal definition of an emergency situation and not the definition of appropriate action on the part of bystanders.

In the context of Latané and Darley's (1970) decision model of intervention, the present research assessed the impact of verbal communication between bystanders on crime reporting and perceptions of responsibility for reporting. According to Latané and Darley's model, a bystander will report a crime only after he has noticed the event, interpreted the event as a crime, taken personal responsibility to act, and decided how to report the crime. Oftentimes, this sequence of decisions must be made very quickly in an ambiguous situation. Our major supposition was that a second bystander could influence the subject in making these decisions and consequently affect the subject's tendency to intervene simply by employing a few verbal comments designed to answer the questions posited in the model, that is, questions the subject is assumed to be asking himself.

A situation was designed wherein a confederate attempted to influence subjects to notice an incident and interpret it as a crime and (combining stages three and four of the model) either encouraged the subjects to assume responsibility by reporting the crime or discouraged reporting. Assuming that encouraging or discouraging comments successfully provided subjects with a sense of personal responsibility and an appropriate course of action, these remarks should influence reporting behavior in the intended directions. The reporting behavior of uninfluenced control subjects provided the necessary baseline.

Furthermore, assuming that mere verbal communication between two strangers would influence rate of

intervention, an attempt was made to understand the nature of this influence process. Most social influence theorists distinguish between public compliance and private acceptance. Kelman (1961) delineated three distinct processes of social influence: compliance, identification, and internalization. *Compliance* is said to occur when an individual accepts influence from another person because he expects a positive reaction from the influencing agent. Influence via *identification* derives from a satisfying relationship with the influencing agent—an outcome that is unlikely when the agent is a total stranger. *Internalization* occurs when a person accepts influence because the induced behavior is useful for problem solving or because it is congruent with his own values or beliefs. Only internalization should result in private acceptance.

French and Raven (1959) also distinguished between compliance and private acceptance. They contended that compliance occurs only in the presence of the influencing agent. If influence occurs regardless of the presence or absence of surveillance by the influencing agent, then the behavior is assumed to be privately accepted. Based on this reasoning, surveillance by the influencing confederate was varied in this first experiment to shed more light on the type of influence being exerted. If the subjects conform to the agent's requests because they find the agent's comments congruent with their values or beliefs or because of the information value contained in these comments, then surveillance should have no effect on intervention. That is, private acceptance of the verbal message is assumed to be operating. If, however, the subjects comply because they are concerned with how the influencing agent will react to their behavior, then the influence attempt should be more effective under surveillance than under nonsurveillance.

Shoplifting was chosen as the crime to be staged for several reasons. First, it is relatively easy to stage in a field setting. Second, there is little or no danger that the "criminal" will be physically assaulted by some naive witness. Third, shoplifting carries considerable significance as a social problem. A 1972 national survey (Holiday Shoplifting Heads for a Record, 1973) estimated that shoplifting accounted for an estimated $845 million, or 2.6% of all total sales in retail stores. Not only has this crime affected the profits of these companies, but it has also resulted in each United States family paying an estimated hidden tax of $150 a year, as a result of stolen merchandise.

EXPERIMENT 1

Method

Subjects.   Over a 6-week period, 109 shoppers in an eastern city supermarket were selected from a population comprised of morning and afternoon weekday shoppers. Most of the subjects (83%) were female, married (62%), and had at least some college education (79%). Seventy-two percent were under 40 years old, and a sizable number were students (29%). The selection criteria were as follows: A person had to be an unaccompanied adult who appeared to be between the ages of 20 and 65 and who entered the checkout line behind the "shoplifter." Moreover, the subject was required to have observed the theft. This observation criterion was satisfied if the person later reported the crime, admitted to having seen the crime, or was rated by observers as having seen it (with 88% agreement, observers rated a subject as having noticed the incident if he or she maintained a direct gaze at the thief throughout the event). Of the shoppers exposed to the staged crime, 78% satisfied the observation criterion. Rate of observation did not differ significantly across experimental conditions. Furthermore, males and females were evenly distributed within the design.

Design.   The experiment was a 2 × 2 factorial design with one control group. Two levels of influence (encourage-discourage) were crossed with two levels of surveillance by the confederate (present-absent) after the influence attempt had taken place. In the control condition, the confederate simply got in line behind the subject and made no comments. Twenty-two subjects were expected in each of five conditions, but due to a clerical error, the encourage-absent conditions had only 21 subjects.

Procedure.   Two young female college students, attractive and conventionally dressed, posed as shoplifters. The apparent thief wheeled a shopping cart with 11 or 12 grocery items into an open lane leading to a cashier, with the exception of the express line.

When a shopper who met the criteria for being a subject moved into the checkout line behind the shoplifter, the shoplifter unloaded the cart and placed a large open purse between her groceries and the subject. When the thief judged that the subject was looking at her, she reached out and grabbed several items on the checkout display and shoved them into her purse.

The social influence and surveillance manipulations were carried out by a 35-year-old woman wearing a coat and hat and pushing a full cart of groceries. As the confederate-bystander, she immediately followed the subject into the line. At the start of the theft, subjects received one of the following influence statements from the confederate-bystander:

1. *Discourage reporting*—"Say, look at her. She's shoplifting. She put that into her purse. But it's the store's problem. They have security people here."
2. *Encourage reporting*—"Say, look at her. She's shoplifting. She put that into her purse. We saw it. We should report it. It's our responsibility."

After the confederate-bystander finished making one of the above comments, her surveillance of the subject was varied in the following manner:

3. *Surveillance*—The confederate-bystander remained in line and tried not to have any further conversation with the subject.
4. *Nonsurveillance*—The confederate-bystander said, "Where did my son go? I'd better go find him." She then left, calling "Billy," and headed down the nearest aisle where she remained out of sight until an interview with the subject was completed.

Finally, some subjects received only the following contact with the confederate-bystander:

5. *Control condition*—The confederate entered the line behind the subject, observed the suspicious events without saying a word, and remained in the checkout line.

Posttheft interview and measures.   If the subject reported to the cashier, the cashier motioned to a nearby interviewer. The interviewer approached the subject, displayed a badge identifying himself as a security officer, and then listened to the subject tell of the theft. The subject was then asked a number of questions.

If the crime was not reported, the interviewer approached the subject immediately after the groceries were purchased and said, "Excuse me, I'm with the store security. We're taking a survey and I'd like to ask you a few questions. Have you seen anybody who looked as if they might be shoplifting or putting some merchandise into their purse?" If the subject either reported the crime or acknowledged having seen it, the interviewer asked a series of questions pertaining to the incident and attitudes toward shoplifting (see measures below). Of the apparent witnesses who answered negatively, further prodding revealed that every individual who satisfied the criteria for inclusion as a subject admitted to having witnessed something suspicious. Thus, these people received the same interview as the other subjects. However, individuals who further denied having witnessed a shoplifting were asked only those questions which did not allude to the crime incident.

All shoppers exposed to the staged incident were thoroughly debriefed. The importance of finding solutions to the problem of shoplifting was stressed. The few subjects ($n = 6$) who expressed any concern about having participated were questioned more extensively.

Measures.   As a check on the verbal influence manipulation, subjects were asked: (a) if the customer behind them (i.e., the confederate-bystander) had noticed the incident, (b) what, if anything, the confederate had said, and (c) whether or not they felt that the confederate had made an influence attempt.

Subjects were also asked how much personal responsibility they felt for reporting the crime and how much responsibility should rest with customers in general. Judgments were requested concerning whether or not shoplifting constitutes a serious crime and how severely shoplifters should be punished. Finally, demographic information was secured on the variables of age, sex, education, place of residence, marital status, and the size of the town in which they spent their childhood.

Results

Manipulation checks.   Overall, 92% of the subjects in the experimental conditions indicated that the customer behind them had seen the theft. About 43% were able to recall precisely what the confederate-bystander said, while 36% were partially accurate in their recall.

Only 21% of the subjects felt that the confederate-bystander had tried to influence them. The encourage- and discourage-reporting conditions did not differ in perceived influence, $\chi^2 (1) = .02$, *ns.* However, there was a marginally significant tendency for subjects in the surveillance condition to report a stronger influence attempt, $\chi^2 (1) = 3.22, p < .10$.

Reporting.   The results strongly confirmed the major hypothesis that mere verbal communication

between two strangers would be sufficient to influence rate of crime reporting. As Table 1 indicates, 72% of the subjects who were encouraged to report did so, while only 32% of those who were discouraged from reporting actually reported, $\chi^2 (1) = 14.13, p < .001$. Moreover, a larger number of shoppers intervened in the encourage-reporting condition than in the control group, $\chi^2 (1) = 5.98, p < .02$, although the latter did not differ significantly from the discourage-reporting condition, $\chi^2 (1) = .53$, *ns.*

The absence of a main effect for surveillance, $\chi^2 (1) = 1.93$, *ns,* is consistent with the hypothesis that reporting behavior is the result of having activated internal processes rather than a mere act of compliance to external pressure. However, an unexpected interaction between surveillance and verbal influence, $z = 2.05, p < .04$, suggested that the presence or absence of the influencing agent was not altogether inconsequential.[1] A closer look revealed that comments discouraging reporting were much more effective when the confederate-bystander left than when she stayed. The surveillance by the influencing agent may have engendered some reactance in subjects, especially those who were discouraged from reporting the incident.

Preexperimental variables.   Significant differences in crime reporting were found between students and nonstudents and between younger and older subjects. Only 31% of the students reported the shoplifting, while 59% of the nonstudents did so, $\chi^2 (1) = 6.81, p < .01$. Similarly, 26% of the subjects below the median age of 31 reported the incident, and 65% of those people 31 or older intervened, $\chi^2 (1) = 12.50, p < .001$. Student status and age overlapped to such an extent that neither maintained a significant relationship to reporting when the other was held constant. However, a marginally significant interaction between these two variables was characterized by a noticeable difference in reporting between younger students (20%) and older students (50%), $z = 1.88, p < .06$.

Perhaps the strongest evidence for the activation of internalized norms or attitudes was the significant interactions that emerged between the verbal influence manipulation and these preexperimental variables. As one example, Table 2 displays the percentage of students and nonstudents who responded favorably to (i.e., consistent with) the influence attempt by the confederate-bystander. The interaction indicates that comments encouraging reporting were more effective with nonstudents than students, while just the

Table 1 Number of Subjects Reporting the Shoplifting in Experiment 1

Condition	Level of influence		
	Encourage reporting	Discourage reporting	Control
Surveillance	15 (68)	11 (50)	
			9 (41)
Nonsurveillance	16 (76)	3 (14)	

Note. Percentages are listed in parentheses.

opposite was true for discouraging comments, $z = 2.12$, $p < .03$. Age and verbal influence yielded virtually the same interaction pattern, with younger subjects responding like students and older subjects responding like nonstudents, $z = 2.92$, $p < .004$. These data suggest that preexperimental attitudes were activated by the verbal influence manipulation.

Attitudes. The preexperimental groups expressed different attitudes about shoplifting. Nonstudents, for example, were more likely than students to consider shoplifting a serious crime, $\chi^2 (1) = 7.84$, $p < .01$; to believe that shoplifters should be severely punished, $\chi^2 (1) = 7.67$, $p < .01$; and to feel greater personal responsibility for reporting shoplifting, $\chi^2 (1) = 6.08$, $p < .01$. However, with the exception of personal responsibility, these measures did not bear any direct relationship to reporting behavior. Hence, these attitude variables do not explain the impact of the preexperimental groups on crime reporting.[2]

Responsibility. The prediction that perceptions of responsibility would mediate the relationship between verbal influence and reporting behavior was not supported. Attributions of responsibility to oneself for reporting the crime did not differ across conditions, nor did perception of others' responsibility to intervene. However, interveners felt more personally responsible for intervening than noninterveners, $\chi^2 (1) = 19.28$, $p < .001$, and were also more likely to believe that customers in general should be responsible for intervening, $\chi^2 (1) = 8.64$, $p < .01$.

Additional demographic variables. Interveners and noninterveners did not differ in amount of education, sex, place of residence, marital status, or size of town in which they spent their childhood.

Discussion

Experiment 1 demonstrated that a few encouraging or discouraging comments by an unknown witness can strongly affect a bystander's willingness to report a criminal incident. The strength of this finding stands in contrast to the negligible effects of attitudes toward the thief (Bickman & Green, 1975; Gelfand, Hartman, Walder, & Page, 1973), relevant authorities (Bickman, 1976), and nonpersonal sources of influence (Bickman, 1975; Bickman & Green, 1977) on crime reporting.

There was little evidence that self-attribution of responsibility served as the mediating link between verbal influence and reporting behavior. However, the results do suggest that internal processes had some impact on the subject's decision to report or not report the crime. First, because surveillance by the influencing agent had no main effect on reporting, the "mere compliance" explanation of verbal influence was rendered implausible. The extent to which researchers can place their confidence in null hypothesis results has become a salient issue (e.g., Greenwald, 1975). The present findings should carry some credence in that the effectiveness of the surveillance manipulation and the sensitivity of the reporting measure were demonstrated in this experiment.

Finally, the interactions between preexperimental differences and the verbal influence attempt leads to the conclusion that people are more willing to accept a verbal influence attempt that is consistent with their prior attitudes or internalized norms than an influence attempt that is counterattitudinal.

Table 2 Number of Students and Nonstudents "Complying" With the Influence Attempt in Experiment 1

Subjects	Level of influence	
	Encourage reporting	Discourage reporting
Students	7 (64)	13 (87)
Nonstudents	23 (79)	17 (59)

Note. Percentages are listed in parentheses.

EXPERIMENT 2

Experiment 1 demonstrated that a few verbal comments communicated from one bystander to another, when carrying information that defines the observed event as a crime and suggests the appropriate course of actions, can have a strong influence on the recipient's tendency to report the suspicious event to the proper authorities. Given the available data, the effectiveness of this verbal influence manipulation was best explained in terms of information working to activate internalized norms or attitudes about reporting shoplifting.

This second experiment was conducted to assess the stability of this finding and to seek a more complete understanding of the influence process. Consequently, an attempt was made to replicate the verbal influence effect in a laboratory setting where more control was possible. Thus, comments either encouraging or discouraging reporting should be effective once again. Furthermore, the credibility of the influence agent was varied (i.e., a confederate-bystander witnessed or did not witness a suspicious event) to determine if witnessing the incident is a necessary precondition to influencing the reporting behavior of another bystander. This use of the term credibility is unlike the usual manipulation of credibility which implies personal trustworthiness. *Credibility* here refers to the amount of evidence on which the communication is based. If a personal norm is activated via the encouraging or discouraging information, reporting behavior should be little affected by whether or not the influence agent witnessed the crime. However, if the subject needs a witness to confirm the validity of her interpretation, credibility should affect the subject's reaction.

Bystanders can either define a suspicious event as a crime or decide that no crime occurred. In Experiment 1, the confederate attempted to inhibit reporting by discouraging the subject from reporting the crime without affecting the interpretation of the event. In the second experiment, the confederate attempted to influence the subject's perception of the event by defining it as not a crime. It is predicted that, as compared with the conditions where the confederate expresses the appropriate course of action, subjects exposed to this interpretation manipulation will be less likely to define the event as a crime. Clearly, if people do not interpret the event as a crime, they will not report it.

Method

Subjects and confederates.   Subjects were 108 female undergraduates at an all female college who were promised either course credit in introductory psychology or $1.00 in return for their participation in an observational study of consumer behavior. Two female undergraduates acted as confederates.

Design.   Subjects were randomly assigned to six conditions (18 in each cell) in a 2×3 (Credibility $\times$ Verbal Influence) factorial design. In half of the conditions, the confederate witnessed the crime, while in the other half, she pretended to have contact lens problems during the theft. The confederate either encouraged reporting, discouraged reporting, or simply interpreted the event as not being a case of shoplifting.

Procedure.   The experimenter met the confederate and the subject in a hallway and escorted them to a small cubicle where they were told they were to observe a live telecast from a supermarket in town (transmitted via TV cable). Both subject and confederate were asked to record the reactions of shoppers to a display located near one of the checkout lines. They were told that two observers were required in the event that one of them was unsure of, or missed, any particular behavior. They were encouraged to collaborate frequently and converse as often as necessary. The subject was unaware that she was about to observe a videotape in which a confederate, posing as a customer, shoplifted two packages of film from the display.

The subject, who was always seated nearest a phone, was instructed to call the store to ask them to turn on the camera. The number actually dialed by the subject was that of a phone in the experimenter's cubicle. When the phone rang, the experimenter answered it and placed it near a tape recorder which presented the voice of a supposed store employee: "Hello, Stop & Shop" (the subject asked her to turn on the camera). "Oh, sure, I'll be glad to do it. The picture should be on in a minute. Have fun. Bye." The experimenter then waited approximately 1 minute before turning on the videotape.

The confederate pretended to collect data as if she were an actual subject. She was blind to the experimental condition until a few moments prior to the theft, at which time she surreptitiously looked at a slip of paper revealing the condition. (The shoplifting occurred 9.5 minutes after the start of the tape.)

In the three witness conditions, the confederate waited until the shoplifter had put the first of two shoplifted items into her purse before speaking. In the witness/noncrime-interpretation condition, she said, "Oh, no! She's not shoplifting. I'm sure she'll pay for it. She probably told the clerk she put it in her purse." However, in the witness/encourage-reporting condition, she said, "She's shoplifting! (pause) We should call the store and tell them. It's really our responsibility." In the event that the subject requested the confederate to call, the confederate said, "But the phone's right next to you." In the witness/discourage-reporting condition, she said, "She's shoplifting! (pause) But it's not our responsibility. The store must have security people to take care of it."

In the three not-witness conditions, just before the shoplifting occurred, the confederate said, "Darn it, there goes my contact again. Tell me if I miss anything." She then looked down and away from the TV monitor, placed both hands over her eyes, and pretended to fix her contact lenses. The confederate waited until the subject mentioned the shoplifting (all subjects informed the confederate of the incident) before talking. In the not-witness/noncrime-interpretation condition, she said, "I didn't see it, but she couldn't be shoplifting," and then continued the same dialogue as in the noncrime/witness condition. In the not-witness/encourage-reporting and not-witness/discourage-reporting conditions, the dialogues were identical to the corresponding witness conditions, except for the inclusion of the following introductory remark: "I didn't see it, but if you saw her shoplift . . ."

If the subject actually called, a tape recording of the "manager's secretary" went as follows: Hello, Stop & Shop." (Subject then reports incident) "Oh, well, thank you for letting us know. We'll look into it. Thanks again for calling. Bye."

At the end of the 14.5 minutes observation period, the experimenter "unexpectedly" met the subject and the confederate in the hallway. If the subject mentioned the shoplifting, the experimenter responded as though she were surprised. As soon as the experimenter expressed an interest in discussing their observations separately, the confederate promptly volunteered to wait.

Postexperiment interview. In private, the experimenter questioned the subject regarding: (a) her recall of the events and the confederate's remarks, (b) her suspiciousness of the reality of the theft, (c) how certain she was that the observed incident was in fact a shoplifting (interpretation), (d) how responsible she felt for reporting the incident, (e) whether she thought there were security personnel in the supermarket, and (f) what she thought of the confederate on several evaluative dimensions. Finally, the subject was thoroughly debriefed and the experimenter pointed out the potential social importance of research on crime reporting.

Results

Manipulation checks. The witness manipulation was very effective, as 96% of the subjects in the witness condition reported that the confederate saw the theft compared to only 13% in the not-witness condition, $\chi^2(1) = 67.30$, $p < .001$.

Overall, 74% of the subjects in the influence conditions were precisely able to recall what the confederate had said to them after the theft. However, subjects in the encourage-reporting and noncrime-interpretation conditions recalled the confederate's remarks more accurately than subjects who were discouraged from reporting the incident, $\chi^2 (2) = 10.88$, $p < .01$.

With regard to their interpretations of the suspicious event, as predicted, subjects in the encourage- and discourage-reporting conditions were equally certain that a shoplifting had occurred while subjects in the noncrime-interpretation condition expressed much less certainty in this interpretation, $\chi^2 (1) = 15.55$, $p < .001$, and were less likely to mention the shoplifting when they met the experimenter in the hallway, $\chi^2 (1) = 5.23$, $p < .05$. Thus, there was evidence that subjects' definitions of the situation and their definitions of the appropriate responses were differentially affected by the verbal influence manipulations.

Suspicion. Five participating students expressed concern that the shoplifting had been staged and, consequently, replacement data were secured from five additional students. This suspiciousness was not concentrated within any particular condition.

Reporting. The number of subjects reporting the shoplifting in each cell of this 2×3 factorial design is displayed in Table 3. As hypothesized, the confederate's verbal statements had a very dramatic main effect

Table 3 Number of Subjects Reporting the Shoplifting in Experiment 2

| Condition | Level of influence | | |
	Encourage reporting	Discourage reporting	Noncrime interpretation
Witness	53	3	1
	(72)	(17)	(6)
Not witness	13	0	4
	(72)	(0)	(22)

Note. Percentages are listed in parentheses.

on crime reporting, $\chi^2 (2) = 41.81$, $p < .001$. That is, while 72% called when encouraged to report, only 14% called when told the incident was not a crime and only 8% called when discouraged from reporting. Thus, interpreting the event as a noncrime produced a similar level of intervention to the discouraging manipulation.

However, the credibility of the influence agent had no main effect on reporting behavior, $\chi^2 = 0$. In other words, whether or not the confederate had personally witnessed the shoplifting had no noticeable impact on her ability to influence the naive observer.

Responsibility.   Similar to the first experiment, the verbal influence manipulation did not have any direct effect on subjects' perceptions of responsibility for reporting. However, as in the first experiment, as compared to subjects who did not report the crime, subjects who reported the shoplifting felt more personal responsibility for reporting, $\chi^2 (1) = 27.71$, $p < .001$, and felt that, in general, people should be more responsible for reporting such crimes, $\chi^2 (1) = 14.16$, $p < .001$.

Discussion

Clearly, verbal comments from another bystander can help one decide whether or not a particular incident was, in fact, a crime. But more importantly, beyond providing an interpretation of the suspicious event, a few verbal comments can suggest the appropriate course of action, and thus have a strong impact on one's tendency to report the crime to the proper authorities. Hence, this laboratory experiment provided a strong replication of the verbal influence finding noted in the previous field experiment. The optimistic note here is that, even when the influence agent has not witnessed the crime, a bystander can be

easily encouraged to report a shoplifting incident through verbal-social influence. In the first experiment, subjects who were encouraged to report the shoplifting did so more often than single control group witnesses. Although no comparable alone control group was included in the laboratory study, a previous study (Bickman, 1976), using the same audio and video tapes, with subjects from the same student population, and conducted during the same academic year, found that 31% of the control subjects reported the crime. This figure is significantly less than the 72% reporting found in the encourage-reporting condition, $\chi^2 (1) = 4.18$, $p < .05$. This finding stands in contrast to the bulk of research on bystander intervention which demonstrates the inhibitory effect of other bystanders. Previous research has shown that by varying the characteristics of the second bystander, the level of helping behavior in this social setting can, at best, equal that of a single witness (e.g., Bickman, 1971; Darley, Teger, & Lewis, 1973; Ross, 1971).

The preferred explanation of verbal-social influence in terms of norm activation has received only indirect support from the present investigations, and thus has yet to be adequately tested. Although the confederate succeeded in influencing crime reporting regardless of her credibility, this finding, by itself, is clearly insufficient to demonstrate the operation of personal or social norms.

Several unexpected findings are particularly germane to the normative explanation of verbal influence. The first experiment demonstrated that students and nonstudents, as well as younger and older subjects, were differentially receptive to encouraging and discouraging comments. In sum, the effectiveness of verbal influence may be limited to those individuals who are in basic agreement with the personal and social norms to which the communication appeals. For these people, the increased saliency of the norms may serve as the catalyst for positive action. For those who enter the situation with a different set of norms or attitudes, the verbal influence attempt may engender psychological reactance (Brehm, 1972) and reduce the probability of reporting. The present data are suggestive, but more research is needed to confirm these suspicions about the interaction of internalized norms or attitudes and normative verbal influence. In any event, one can reasonably conclude that situation-specific norms, as with Schwartz's (1973) personal norms, hold more promise for predicting behavior than the more general norms.

Explaining the effectiveness of the verbal influence manipulation remains problematical. Although Schwartz

(1970) and others have argued that the self-ascription of responsibility is a necessary condition for norms to affect behavior, subjects' perceptions of responsibility for reporting the crime did not mediate the relationship between verbal influence and reporting behavior in either of the present studies. However, postdecisionally, reporters expressed more felt responsibility for reporting than nonreporters.

Perhaps the strong impact of a few verbal statements is best understood not by focusing on the extent to which norms of helping and responsibility are activated, but rather by noting that the influence agent firmly suggested what would be the appropriate reaction to the situation. The confederate-bystander defined the appropriate response as either reporting or not reporting the crime. Darley et al. (1973) have pointed out that when bystanders can see each others' responses, definition processes rather than diffusion of responsibility play the dominant role. Although Darley et al. discussed only the definition of the situation, the results of the present research suggest that the definition of the appropriate reaction might be even more important in determining intervention. In this respect, most subjects in the present research were willing to accept the judgments of another bystander.

Footnotes

[1]Interactions were analyzed using the arc sine transformation suggested by Langer and Abelson (1972).

[2]However, in another study, (Bickman & Bowman, Note 2), certain predecisional attitudes were found to affect the reporting of a shoplifting. In addition, data collected independently of any staged crime have shown that students generally do not perceive shoplifting to be a serious crime (Molitor & Carlson, 1969).

Reference Notes

1. Lavrakas, P. J. Personal communication, January 1, 1977.
2. Bickman, L., & Bowman, H. *Rewards, anonymity and the reporting of a crime.* Unpublished manuscript, 1974. (Available from L. Bickman, Psychology Department, Loyola University of Chicago).

References

Allen, H. Bystander intervention and helping behavior on the subway. In L. Bickman & T. Henchy (Eds.), *Beyond the Laboratory: Field Research in Social Psychology.* New York: McGraw-Hill, 1971.

Bickman, L. The effect of another bystander's ability to help on bystander intervention in an emergency. *Journal of Experimental Social Psychology,* 1971, *7,* 367-379.

Bickman, L. Social influence and diffusion of responsibility in an emergency. *Journal of Experimental Social Psychology,* 1972, *8,* 438-445.

Bickman, L. Bystander intervention in a crime: The effect of a mass media campaign. *Journal of Applied Social Psychology,* 1975, *5,* 296-302.

Bickman, L. Attitude toward an authority and the reporting of a crime. *Sociometry,* 1976, *39,* 76-82.

Bickman, L., & Green, S. Is revenge sweet? The effect of attitude toward a thief on crime reporting. *Criminal Justice and Behavior,* 1975, *2,* 101-112.

Bickman, L., & Green, S. Situational cues and crime reporting: Do signs make a difference? *Journal of Applied Social Psychology,* 1977, *7,* 1-18.

Bickman, L., Lavrakas, P. J., Green, S. K., Walker, N. N., Edwards, J., Borkowski, S., Dubow, S. S., & Weurth, J. *Citizen crime reporting projects: A phase I national evaluation program summary report.* Washington, D.C.: U.S. Government Printing Office, 1977.

Brehm, J. *Reponses to loss of freedom: A theory of psychological reactance.* Morristown, N.J.: General Learning Press, 1972.

Darley, J., & Latané, B. Bystander intervention in emergencies: Diffusion of responsibility. *Journal of Personality and Social Psychology,* 1968, *8,* 377-383.

Darley, J., Teger, A. I., & Lewis, L. D. Do groups always inhibit individuals: Responses to potential emergencies. *Journal of Personality and Social Psychology,* 1973, *26,* 395-399.

French, J. R. P., Jr., & Raven, B. The basis of social power. In D. Cartwright (Ed.), *Studies in social power.* Ann Arbor: University of Michigan, 1959.

Gelfand, D. M., Hartman, D. P., Walder, P., & Page, B. Who reports shoplifters? A field-experimental study. *Journal of Personality and Social Psychology,* 1973, *25,* 276-285.

Greenwald, A. G. Consequences of prejudice against the null hypothesis. *Psychological Bulletin,* 1975, *82,* 1-20.

Holiday shoplifting heads for a record. *U.S. News and World Report,* December 10, 1973, p. 47.

Kelman, H. C. Processes of opinion change. *Public Opinion Quarterly,* 1961, *25,* 57-78.

Korte, C. Group effects on help giving in an emergency. *Proceedings of the 77th Annual Convention of the American Psychological Association,* 1969, *4,* 383-384.

Langer, E. J., & Abelson, R. P. The semantics of asking for a favor: How to succeed in getting help without really dying. *Journal of Personality and Social Psychology,* 1972, *5,* 26-32.

Latané, B., & Darley, J. M. Bystander "apathy." *American Scientist,* 1969, *57,* 244-268.

Latané, B., & Darley, J. M. *The unresponsive bystander: Why doesn't he help?* New York: Appleton-Century-Crofts, 1970.

Latané, B., & Rodin, J. A lady in distress: Inhibiting effects of friends and strangers on bystander intervention. *Journal of Personality and Social Psychology,* 1969, *5,* 189-202.

Molitor, J. T., & Carlson, D. College bookstore pilferage. *The College Store Journal,* April/May, 1969.

Piliavin, I., Rodin, J., & Piliavin, J. A. Good samaritanism: An underground phenomenon? *Journal of Personality and Social Psychology,* 1969, *13,* 289-299.

Piliavin, J. A., & Piliavin, I. Effect of blood on reactions to a victim. *Journal of Personality and Social Psychology,* 1972, *23,* 353-361.

Rosenthal, A. M. *Thirty-eight witnesses.* New York: McGraw-Hill, 1964.

Ross, A. S. Effects of increased responsibility on bystander intervention: The presence of children. *Journal of Personality and Social Psychology,* 1971, *19,* 306-310.

Ross, A. S., & Braband, J. Effect of increased responsibility on bystander intervention II: The cue value of a blind person. *Journal of Personality and Social Psychology,* 1973, *25,* 254-258.

Schwartz, S. Moral decision making and behavior. In S. Macauley & L. Berkowitz (Eds.), *Altruism and helping behavior.* New York: Academic Press, 1970.

Schwartz, S. Normative explanations of helping behavior: A critique, proposal, and empirical test. *Journal of Experimental and Social Psychology,* 1973, *9,* 349-364.

Schwartz, S., & Clausen, G. T. Responsibility, norms, and helping in an emergency. *Journal of Personality and Social Psychology,* 1970, *16,* 299-310.

Staub, E. Instigation to goodness: The role of social norms and interpersonal influence. *Journal of Social Issues,* 1972, *28,* 131-150. (a)

Staub, E. *Interpersonal influences on helping in an emergency.* Paper presented at the Meeting of the Eastern Psychological Association, Boston, April, 1972. (b)

Tilker, H. A. Socially responsible behavior as a function of observer responsibility and victim feedback. *Journal of Personality and Social Psychology,* 1970, *14,* 95-100.

This research was supported by National Science Foundation Grant GS-35250 to the first author. The authors wish to thank the Stop & Shop Company for its cooperation.

Requests for reprints should be sent to Leonard Bickman, Applied Social Psychology Program, Loyola University of Chicago, 6525 North Sheridan Road, Chicago, Illinois 60626.

Pollution and Littering Control

Antipollution Measures and Psychological Reactance Theory: A Field Experiment

Michael B. Mazis   *College of Business Administration, University of Florida*

Abstract

A field experiment was conducted to determine if hypotheses derived from psychological reactance theory could explain response to the implementation of an antiphosphate ordinance. Deprived housewives expressed more positive attitudes toward the eliminated alternative than did control subjects thereby supporting reactance theory predictions. Within the experimental group, subjects were divided into two groups based on their degree of choice deprivation. As predicted, subjects forced to switch from their preferred detergent brand expressed less favorable attitudes about the effectiveness of no-phosphate versus phosphate detergent than subjects who could maintain brand continuity. Reduced attractiveness of forced alternative rather than enhancement of forbidden alternative was the principal mode of response resulting from psychological reactance.

"Antipollution Measures and Psychological Reactance Theory: A Field Experiment" by Michael B. Mazis. *Journal of Personality and Social Psychology,* 1975, Vol. 31, No. 4, pp. 654–660. Copyright © 1975 by The American Psychological Association, Inc. Reprinted by permission.

Psychological reactance theory asserts that when a person believes himself free to engage in a given behavior and his freedom is eliminated or threatened with elimination, the individual experiences psychological reactance, a motivational state directed toward reestablishment of the threatened or eliminated freedom (Brehm, 1966). One major determinant of reactance, external pressure applied through social influence or persuasive communications, has been studied extensively. Laboratory experiments have typically manipulated social influence by having confederates restrict subjects' freedom of choice through freedom threatening statements (Brehm & Sensenig, 1966; Worchel & Brehm, 1971).

Recent research exploring the influence of persuasive communications has focused on factors attenuating reactance effects. Conformity pressures (Grabitz-Gniech, 1971; Pallack & Heller, 1971), the involvement of peers in eliminating alternatives (Worchel & Brehm, 1971), and individual difference variables, including manipulated felt competence (Wicklund & Brehm, 1968), feelings of inadequacy (Grabitz-Gniech, 1971), and locus of control (Biondo & MacDonald, 1971) have been found to influence reactivity.

While the loss of options may be a major determinant of psychological reactance also, it has not been fully explored in reactance research. Grabitz-Gniech (1971) and Brehm, Stires, Sensenig, and Shaban (1966) examined the effect of reducing the choice of records and paintings, respectively, among college students in laboratory experiments. While statistically significant reactance effects were found, both experiments failed to present an ego-involving situation in which subjects lost an important freedom. The possibility of demand characteristics producing a reactive response must be considered. Perhaps a more appropriate laboratory for experimentation is the marketplace where consumers' freedom of choice has been frequently restricted through governmental action such as requiring safety devices on automobiles; recalling soups, cranberries, tuna, drugs, and automobiles; and restricting the use of energy. Unfortunately, the only field study (Weiner & Brehm, 1966) examining reactance effects was debilitated by the failure to apply unobtrusive pressure to subjects, thereby negating a major advantage of field experimentation.

The elimination of free choice by authority sources has been explored in reactance research, but the only authority source studied has been the psychological experimenter (Hammock & Brehm, 1966). For research involving authority sources to have generalizability, particularly for social issues, a wider sampling of authority sources is needed. For example, Davis and Eichhorn (1963) have studied the issue of compliance and noncompliance with physicians' regimens. The current experiment is directed toward determining if responses to the imposition of a "socially beneficial" governmental action (antiphosphate ordinance) might be predicted from psychological reactance theory.

Obviously, not all individuals react against all restrictions of free choice. It remains for research to specify which subjects and under which restrictions psychological reactance is manifested when options are eliminated or curtailed by authority sources.

The principal consequence of reactivity needs to be specified more precisely also. The present study explores two major manifestations of reactivity, enhanced attractiveness of restricted alternatives and reduced desirability of alternatives forced upon subjects. Most reactance studies have failed to separate these two effects.

The present investigation concerns response to an event affecting many households throughout the United States—imposition of an antiphosphate law. On January 1, 1972, Dade County (Miami), Florida, began prohibiting the sale, possession, or use of laundry detergents and other cleaning products containing phosphates. Since only a small number of popular brands were available in no-phosphate formulations, shoppers found their choice of laundry detergent drastically diminished. These dramatic changes in the number of choice alternatives provided an opportunity to examine psychological reactance theory predictions in a field setting.

According to reactance theory, Miami households would be motivationally aroused due to the phosphate restrictions and feel an increased desire to have the forbidden detergent as contrasted with households in a control city (Tampa) whose freedom of choice was unrestricted. The reactance aroused in Miami subjects should result in higher effectiveness attributed to phosphate detergents as compared with Tampa subjects and more negative attitudes toward governmental regulation of environmental matters which should influence the product evaluations of Miami consumers.

Since Miami households could be classified into three major subgroups, additional reactance theory predictions may be made. The first group consisted of housewives who were able to continue purchasing products labeled by their favorite brand names, but which were now being sold without phosphates; these households are referred to as "nonswitchers." Since one leading detergent manufacturer quickly began distributing no-phosphate reformulations of all its existing laundry detergent brands, users could continue to purchase their regular brands after the antiphosphate law went into effect.

Several other detergent manufacturers did not begin distribution of no-phosphate reformulations for several months and therefore users were forced to switch brands after the phosphate restrictions went into effect. These consumers, who were forced to switch from their regular brands, are referred to as "switchers."

Based on their dissimilar motivational states, it is anticipated that (a) switchers would express more negative attitudes about the effectiveness of no-phosphate products and/or more positive attitudes about the effectiveness of phosphate products than would nonswitchers and (b) switchers would have a more negative attitude toward the antiphosphate law than would nonswitchers.

Switchers should feel a greater restriction of their freedom of choice than should nonswitchers as a result of being unable to purchase a laundry detergent sold under their favorite brand label. It must be remembered that both switchers and nonswitchers were using a totally new product; however, in one case consumers were using a product with a "new" label or brand name, while in the other they were able to use a reformulated product being sold under their favorite brand name.

The third group of Miami households are those who defied the antiphosphate ordinance by smuggling detergent into Miami from surrounding counties or who accumulated large amounts of phosphate detergent before the January enforcement date. Since these smugglers and hoarders may have had very favorable attitudes toward phosphate detergents before the enactment of the no-phosphate restrictions, no predictions can be made concerning their attitudes about the effectiveness of phosphate brands based on reactance theory. Their predisposition toward phosphate brands may have been instrumental in their being categorized as "violators." On the other hand, switchers and non-switchers were placed into those categories as a result of detergent manufacturers' decisions about whether to produce no-phosphate reformulations of detergent brands.[1]

METHOD

An instrument was designed to determine attitudes about laundry detergents and related products, opinions about laws regulating the use of phosphates, and demographic characteristics. Seventy-six interviews were completed by four female interviewers in Miami and 45 completed questionnaires were returned by the two female interviewers in Tampa. Nine questionnaires were discarded as a result of incomplete responses. Interviews were conducted from a period from 7 to 9 weeks after the antiphosphate statute became effective.

Since only limited funding was available to defer the cost of interviewing, sample selection in both Tampa and Miami emphasized subject homogeneity to restrict the impact of extraneous variables. To enhance the similarity between Tampa and Miami samples, all respondents interviewed were: (a) English-speaking Caucasian women; (b) with family incomes of $7,500 to $15,000 per year; (c) who had at least one child under 16 years of age living at home; (d) who resided in single-family dwellings; and (e) who used primarily phosphate detergent brands during the preceding 6 months. Comparisons between Tampa and Miami samples revealed no significant income, age, or educational differences.

Two middle-income census tracts were chosen in both cities and blocks were randomly selected within tracts. Two sampling points were randomly designated within each block and interviewing commenced from each point in a clockwise direction until two respondents were found who met the criteria enumerated above.

RESULTS

Miami versus Tampa

At the beginning of each interview, subjects were asked to rate the effectiveness of the phosphate laundry detergent they had used most during the previous 6 months. Seven brand characteristics were evaluated on an 11-point scale labeled "absolutely perfect" and "poor" at the end points. Salient characteristics were determined through a free association procedure similar to that used by Fishbein (1967).

Reactance theory predictions are supported by the data in Tables 1 and 2. On all seven characteristics, Miami subjects gave higher mean effectiveness ratings to phosphate brands than did Tampa subjects.

Table 1 Means and Standard Deviations for Effectiveness Ratings of Phosphate Detergents

Characteristic	Miami (n = 76)		Tampa (n = 45)	
	M	SD	M	SD
Whiteness	8.68	1.87	8.27	1.56
Freshness	8.77	2.08	7.87	1.51
Cleans in cold water	8.52	2.15	7.47	1.83
Brightness	8.31	2.09	7.84	1.80
Stain removal	8.00	2.43	6.96	2.05
Pours easily	9.45	2.05	9.07	1.77
Gentleness	8.81	1.80	8.71	1.51

Note. Based on an 11-point scale with 11 labeled "absolutely perfect" and 1 labeled "poor."

Table 2 Analysis of Variance for Effectiveness Ratings of Phosphate Detergents

Source	MS	F
Groups: Miami vs. Tampa	77.74	5.42*
Error (Groups)	14.34	
Trials: Characteristics	35.06	20.07**
Groups × Trials	3.97	2.27*
Error (Trials)	1.75	

* $p < .05$.
** $p < .001$.

The two way Groups × Trials analysis of variance (Veldman, 1967, pp. 247-257) in Table 2 provides statistical support for the proposition that Miami housewives were in a reactive motivational state. Overall, Miami subjects rated phosphate detergents as being more efficacious than did Tampa subjects ($F = 5.42$, $p < .05$).

The significant interaction between cities and characteristics ($F = 2.27$, $p < .05$) shows that the reactivity of Miami housewives was not manifested uniformly across all characteristics. Also, there was a significant main effect for characteristics indicating that subjects did discriminate among various detergent attributes by not rating detergent brands as being equally effective on all characteristics ($F = 20.07$, $p < .001$).

Miami subjects expressed a less optimistic view about the success of governmental action in solving water pollution problems and toward the usefulness of phosphate content regulation than did Tampa subjects (see Table 3).

Tampa residents stated a stronger degree of agreement with the statement, "The government should play an important role in protecting our water from pollution," than did Miami subjects ($t = 3.62$, $p < .01$). In addition, Tampa housewives had greater expectations about the usefulness of laws restricting the sale of detergents containing phosphates than did Miami respondents ($t = 2.72$, $p < .01$), thereby sustaining the view that Miami housewives were experiencing psychological reactance.

Switchers versus Nonswitchers

Brand ratings. According to psychological reactance theory, the amount of freedom eliminated directly influences psychological reactance. Since switchers were experiencing more psychological choice deprivation, they should provide lower mean effectiveness ratings to no-phosphate brands than should nonswitchers.

The data in Table 4 shows that of the 76 Miami households responding (9 of which had incomplete data), the 44 switchers provided lower average effectiveness ratings across all seven detergent attri-

Table 3 Attitude Toward Government and Antiphosphate Laws

Variable	Miami		Tampa		
	M	SD	M	SD	t
The government should play an important role in protecting our water from pollution.	2.39	.90	1.64	1.20	3.62*
Legal restrictions should be imposed against the sale of detergents containing phosphates.	2.76	.93	2.20	1.17	2.72*

Note. Responses on Likert-type scale with "1" indicating strong agreement and "5" indicating strong disagreement.
* $p < .01$.

Table 4 Means and Standard Deviations for Effectiveness Ratings of Detergents

| | No-phosphate detergents | | | | Phosphate detergents | | | | Difference scores | | | |
| | Switchers | | Nonswitchers | | Switchers | | Nonswitchers | | Switchers | | Nonswitchers | |
Characteristic	M	SD	M	SD	M	SD	M	SD	M	SD	M	SD
Whiteness	7.07	1.60	7.87	1.72	8.59	1.63	8.61	1.51	1.52	.79	.74	1.70
Freshness	7.11	1.70	7.85	1.85	8.75	1.61	8.78	1.41	1.63	1.17	.91	1.88
Cleans in cold water	6.36	2.12	7.61	2.37	8.72	1.93	8.43	1.42	2.36	1.43	.83	2.43
Brightness	6.30	2.00	7.43	2.13	8.41	1.78	8.17	1.61	2.27	1.51	.74	2.26
Stain removal	6.14	2.53	7.41	1.96	7.79	2.00	8.13	1.95	1.66	1.27	.70	2.01
Pours easily	8.45	2.01	9.17	2.37	9.30	1.41	9.78	1.89	.84	1.05	.61	1.62
Gentleness	7.23	1.92	8.04	2.08	8.93	1.70	8.74	1.21	1.70	1.23	.70	2.01

Note. Based on an 11-point scale labeled "absolutely perfect" and "poor" at end points.

butes than did the 23 nonswitchers. The Groups × Trials analysis of variance in Table 5 reveals significantly lower attractiveness estimates for no-phosphate products by switchers than by nonswitchers ($F = 4.48$, $p < .05$).

The greater degree of psychological reactance being experienced by switchers may take the form of increased attractiveness of the restricted alternative (phosphate detergent), as well as decreased attractiveness of the alternative forced upon subjects (no-phosphate detergent). Similar ratings of phosphate detergent effectiveness between Tampa and Miami subjects are shown in the middle sections of Tables 4 and 5 ($F = .00$, $p < .99$). These nonsignificant findings are explored in the final section of this article.

In a within-subjects experimental design, the "total reactance effect" (Hammock & Brehm, 1966) can be examined by analyzing difference scores generated by subtracting each subject's rating of no-phosphate detergent from her rating of phosphate detergent for each characteristic. In this way both hypotheses derived from reactance theory (enhancement of forbidden alternative and derogation of forced

alternative) can be tested simultaneously. The last sections of Tables 4 and 5 indicate that switchers felt there was a substantial difference in efficacy between phosphate and no-phosphate formulations whereas nonswitchers felt that no-phosphate brands were only slightly less effective than phosphate variations ($F = 7.51$, $p < .01$).

Attitudes toward detergent use. In addition to rating phosphate and no-phosphate detergents on seven characteristics, subjects evaluated the potency and cost of alternative formulations. As a result of being in a reactive motivational state, subjects who were forced to switch from their favorite brands would be expected to express more negative attitudes about the amount of detergent and extra ingredients required for each washload and about the cost of washing clothes when using no-phosphate detergent than would nonswitchers.

Table 6 indicates that while nearly a third of switchers felt they had been using more no-phosphate detergent, $\chi^2 (2) = 9.45$, $p < .01$, and additional ingredients (e.g., bleach or fabric softener), $\chi^2 (2) =$

Table 5 Analysis of Variance for Effectiveness Ratings of Detergents

| | No-phosphate detergents | | | Phosphate detergents | | | Difference scores | | |
Source	df	MS	F	df	MS	F	df	MS	F
Groups:									
Switchers vs. nonswitchers	1	99.06	4.48*	1	.05	.00	1	99.27	7.51**
Error	65	22.09		65	12.88		65	13.21	
Trials: Characteristics	6	35.32	25.29***	6	15.33	13.92***	6	8.31	5.20***
Groups × Trials	6	.94	.67	6	1.32	1.20	6	3.22	2.02
Error	390	1.40		390	1.10		390	1.60	

* $p < .05$.
** $p < .01$.
*** $p < .001$.

4.15, $p < .05$, with each washload than they did with phosphate detergent, less than 10% of nonswitchers felt this was the case. There is a similar disparity about perceptions of the relative cost of using phosphate and no-phosphate products. Over 71% of switchers believed that no-phosphate brands were more expensive to use than products containing phosphates, but only 30% of nonswitchers expressed negative feelings about the cost of using their reformulated no-phosphate brands, $\chi^2 (1) = 9.58$, $p < .001$.

DISCUSSION

While student subjects in laboratory experiments have often behaved as predicted by psychological reactance theory, the current study provides strong support for the theory's predictions among housewives in a field setting. As predicted, Miami subjects rated phosphate detergents as being more effective than did Tampa subjects. Hypotheses derived from psychological reactance theory concerning Miami versus Tampa subjects' attitudes toward government's role in protecting the public from water pollution and in imposing legal restrictions against the sale of products containing phosphates were sustained as well.

Since adaptation effects (Helson, 1964) may have contributed to the enhanced attractiveness of phosphate detergent as a result of expanded use of the less effective no-phosphate brands, the most compelling evidence supporting a reactance theory interpretation is found in the attitudinal differences of switchers and nonswitchers. Analysis of effectiveness ratings revealed that there were no significant mean differences in the evaluation of alternative brands of no-phosphate detergent. As a result, the differential

attitudes expressed by switchers and nonswitchers can be attributed to psychological reactance rather than to physical differences in the brands used.

This research does make several contributions to the psychological reactance literature. First, it demonstrates that psychological reactance is not solely a laboratory phenomena. Housewives did feel more psychological choice deprivation when they were forced to switch from their favorite phosphate brands to unfamiliar brands of no-phosphate laundry detergent.

Second, greater insight into the consequences of reactance were obtained. Negative attitudes about the effectiveness of the alternative forced upon housewives rather than enhancement of the eliminated alternative was found.

Since most subjects expressed satisfaction with their laundry detergents, psychological reactance would be less likely to take the form of increased desirability of the eliminated alternative as compared with decreased attractiveness of the forced alternative due to ceiling effects. The mean rating for control group (Tampa) subjects was 8.02 on an 11-point scale. While the circumstances surrounding this experiment may be unique, it is possible that reactance often takes the form of a reduction in the attractiveness of the forced alternative since people are satisfied with the products they use as a result of dissonance reduction. More valuable than such speculation would be further research on this topic.

Third, public policy implications of psychological reactance research have been made apparent. From a societal perspective, the most appropriate laboratory for psychological reactance research might be the consumer market. While governmental agencies and legislators issue administrative decisions and enact

Table 6 Attitude Toward Detergent Use

Group	Amount of detergent used[a]			Amount of extra ingredients used[b]		Cost of no-phosphate detergent[c]	
	More	Less	Same	More	Same or Less[d]	More	Same or Less[d]
Switchers	14 (32%)	4 (10%)	26 (58%)	14 (32%)	30 (68%)	31 (71%)	13 (29%)
Nonswitchers	1 (4%)	5 (28%)	17 (68%)	2 (8%)	21 (92%)	7 (30%)	16 (70%)

[a] $\chi^2 (2) = 9.45$, $p < .01$.
[b] $\chi^2 (1) = 4.15$, $p < .05$.
[c] $\chi^2 (1) = 9.58$, $p < .001$.
[d] Categories combined to provide sufficient expected value per cell.

ordinances which restrict freedom of choice, consumer assessment after restriction is rarely undertaken. Too much restriction may result in extensive noncompliance. However, additional research is needed to assess the degree of consumer reactivity as a result of: (a) the issue, (b) the proportion of choice alternatives remaining and number of substitutes available, (c) the authority sources (e.g., federal vs. local and state government; legislative vs. executive decisions) used to eliminate freedom of choice, and (d) the permanence of a reactive motivational state.

Footnote

[1]No subjects classified as nonswitchers switched to another manufacturer's brand after enactment of the antiphosphate ordinance.

References

Biondo, J., & MacDonald, A. P. Internal—external locus of control and response to influence attempts. *Journal of Personality*, 1971, *39*, 407-419.

Brehm, J. W. (Ed.), *A Theory of Psychological Reactance.* New York: Academic Press, 1966.

Brehm, J. W., & Sensenig, J. Social influence as a function of attempted and implied usurpation of choice. *Journal of Personality and Social Psychology*, 1966, *4*, 703-707.

Brehm, J. W., Stires, L. K., Sensenig, J., & Shaban, J. The attractiveness of an eliminated choice alternative. *Journal of Experimental Social Psychology*, 1966, *2*, 301-313.

Davis, M., & Eichhorn, R. Compliance with medical regimens: A panel study. *Journal of Health and Human Behavior*, 1963, *4*, 240-249.

Fishbein, M. A behavior theory approach to the relations between beliefs about an object and the attitude toward the object. In M. Fishbein (Ed.), *Readings in attitude theory and measurement.* New York: Wiley, 1967.

Grabitz-Gniech, G. Some restrictive conditions for the occurrence of psychological reactance. *Journal of Personality and Social Psychology*, 1971, *19*, 188-196.

Hammock, T., & Brehm, J. W. The attractiveness of choice alternatives when freedom to choose is eliminated by a social agent. *Journal of Personality*, 1966, *34*, 546-554.

Helson, H. *Adaptation-level theory.* New York: Harper & Row, 1964.

Pallack, M. S., & Heller, J. F. Interactive effects of commitment to future interaction and threat to attitudinal freedom. *Journal of Personality and Social Psychology*, 1970, *14*, 39-45.

Veldman, D. J. *Fortran programming for the behavioral sciences.* New York: Holt, Rinehart & Winston, 1967.

Weiner, J., & Brehm, J. Buying behavior as a function of verbal and monetary inducements. In J. W. Brehm (Ed.), *A theory of psychological reactance.* New York: Academic Press, 1966.

Wicklund, R. A., & Brehm, J. W. Attitude change as a function of felt competence and threat to attitudinal freedom. *Journal of Experimental Social Psychology*, 1968, *4*, 64-75.

Worchel, S., & Brehm, J. W. Direct and implied social restoration of freedom. *Journal of Personality and Social Psychology*, 1971, *18*, 294-304.

This study was supported by a grant from the College of Business Administration, University of Florida.

The author thanks Robert B. Settle for aiding conceptualization of the study and Dennis C. Leslie for assisting in data analysis.

Requests for reprints should be addressed to Michael B. Mazis, College of Business Administration, University of Florida, Gainesville, Florida 32611.

Facilitating Paper Recycling: Effects of Prompts, Raffles, and Contests[1]

Jill F. Witmer   *Virginia Polytechnic Institute and State University*
E. Scott Geller

Abstract

The effects of prompts and reinforcement to promote paper recycling were compared in six university dormitories. For a Prompt condition, residents were urged to recycle paper for ecological reasons via flyers distributed to each room. For a Raffle contingency, residents were given one raffle ticket for every pound of paper brought to a collection center. For a Contest contingency, two dorms were paired and the dorm whose residents delivered the most paper won $15 for its treasury. Contingency awareness was strengthened via a flyer placed under the door of each resident's room. Flyers alone had little effect in increasing paper-recycling behaviors, but the raffle (substantially) and the contest (somewhat) increased the amount of paper brought to a dorm's recycling center. Students whose rooms were closest to the collection center showed the greatest participation. Removal of the reinforcement contingencies resulted in a return to baseline levels.

DESCRIPTORS: contingencies, group and individual; priming, prompt, ecology, recycling programs, community settings, community-based treatment, university students.

Ecological imbalance from the accumulation of waste materials has grown slowly and undesirable consequences remain remote for most people (Pirages, 1973). Even simple programs for handling environmental problems rarely get widespread support. For example, voluntary recycling programs have been set

up in many communities, but even the most effective projects reduce solid waste by less than 1% (Hall and Ackoff, 1972). In 1973, 130 million tons of refuse were collected in the United States ("U.S. Finds A Rich Resource: The Nation's Trash Pile", 1974). Although much of this material could have been reused, recycling requires a "reverse-distribution process", whereby the consumer becomes the first rather than the last link in the distribution process (Margulies, 1970). The present study was designed to study applications of behavior technology to initiate a paper-recycling process. Since paper makes up about 50% of environmental litter (Finnie, 1973), paper-recycling programs both reuse waste paper and reduce litter.

In an earlier application of reinforcement contingencies to promote paper recycling, residents of university dormitories were given a lottery coupon for delivering at least one sheet of paper to a collection room during a raffle contingency (Geller, Chaffee, and Ingram, 1975). For a contest condition, two dormitories were paired and the dormitory residents who collected the most paper in a week won $15 for their treasury. The amount of paper collected during the raffle and contest contingencies was equivalent and markedly greater than that collected during baseline conditions.

Given apparent widespread concern for ecology among college students, prompting alone might significantly increase paper recycling. Geller *et al.* (1975) announced each contingency by means of posters displayed on the bulletin boards of each dorm floor. Thus, results of low participation in that study may have been due to ineffective prompting; perhaps few residents attended to bulletin-board announcements and, therefore, most were not aware of the recycling program. Hence, the low participation was possibly due to a lack of contingency awareness, rather than a lack of contingency effectiveness. A more comprehensive prompting procedure was implemented in the present study by delivering written announcements of the recycling program to every dormitory room.

In addition to comparing paper-recycling behaviors following prompting with those due to a procedure combining both prompting and reinforcement techniques, the present research also compared the behavior effects of two reinforcement methods: an individual contingency that provided a raffle coupon for each pound of paper delivered and a group contingency that provided $15 for the treasury of one of two dorms whose residents collected the most paper in a week. In the raffle condition of the Geller *et al.* study, a raffle ticket was given for each paper delivery, regardless of the amount of paper delivered. This resulted in individuals making numerous, repeated deliveries each day with small amounts of paper. The raffle contingency of the present study emphasized the quantity of paper delivered by offering the dorm resident one raffle coupon per pound of paper delivered. Thus, greater amounts of delivered paper but fewer deliveries were expected in the present study than were observed in the prior program. The present research examined proximity effects by recording the room numbers of residents making paper deliveries and comparing distances to the collection site.

METHOD

Subjects and Setting

The residents of four male and two female dormitories on the campus of Virginia Polytechnic Institute and State University served as subjects. A room on the first floor of each dorm had been designated as a paper collection center by the Campus Committee for Ecological Rebalance (REBAL). REBAL collected the paper every two weeks and sold it to a paper mill for $15 a ton.

REBAL had promoted paper recycling in all campus dormitories for more than 16 months before the start of this study by maintaining one 76 by 86 cm recycling poster on the bulletin board of each dorm floor. The posters indicated the location of the collection room and the times that the room would be open (*i.e.,* 5:30 to 7:30 p.m. Monday through Friday).

Contingencies

All dorms began the experiment with a two-week Baseline condition. For the next three weeks, two

dorms received a Prompt condition, two received a Raffle contingency, and two received a Contest contingency. During the last three weeks, the prompting and reinforcement procedures designed to facilitate paper deliveries were removed from all six dorms in a Follow-up condition equivalent to Baseline. The dorms were paired as follows: (a) one male and one female dorm, each having a capacity of 333 students, received the Prompt condition; (b) one male and one female dorm, each having a capacity of 180 students, received the Raffle contingency;[2] (c) one R.O.T.C. male dorm and one civilian male dorm, each having a capacity of 333 students, received the Contest contingency. All dorms were filled approximately to capacity.

For the Baseline and Follow-up recordings the situation was exactly as it had been, except that a REBAL poster appeared on the collection-room door and a data recorder sat in the collection room from 5:30 to 7:30 p.m. Monday through Friday, recording the amount of paper delivered by each person. In addition, the data recorders kept track of the amount of paper brought to the collection room and left in front of the door at times other than the prescribed collection period (*i.e.,* from 7:30 p.m. on a given day until 5:30 p.m. the next day).

On three consecutive Sundays, following two weeks of Baseline recording, identically designed flyers describing the appropriate contingency for the week were distributed under the door of each dorm room. The message for the Prompt condition read:[3]

RECYCLE PAPER
YOU CAN HELP TO:
  PRESERVE OUR NATURAL RESOURCES
  PROTECT THE ENVIRONMENT
  SAVE TREES
  ALLEVIATE THE PAPER SHORTAGE
  BRING ALL RECYCLABLE PAPER
    (INCLUDING THIS SHEET)
  TO COLLECTION ROOM ON FIRST FLOOR
    MONDAY—FRIDAY
    5:30—7:30 p.m.

During the raffle contingency the written message was:

RAFFLE
WIN PRIZES EACH WEEK!!
1 COUPON PER POUND OF PAPER
BRING ALL RECYCLABLE PAPER
(INCLUDING THIS SHEET)

TO COLLECTION ROOM ON FIRST FLOOR
MONDAY—FRIDAY
5:30—7:30 p.m.
A LIST OF PRIZES AND RULES IS
POSTED ON COLLECTION ROOM DOOR

The Raffle rules explained that residents would receive one coupon for every pound of recyclable paper brought to the collection room on weekdays from 5:30 to 7:30 p.m. The 10 prizes raffled off each week had been donated by 24 local merchants and ranged in value from $3 to $20. The prizes were grouped so that each week's total value was approximately $80.[4]

For the contest flyers the message was:

CONTEST
BETWEEN BRODIE HALL
AND VAWTER HALL
THE DORM THAT BRINGS IN
THE MOST RECYCLABLE PAPER
EACH WEEK
WILL WIN $15.00
BRING ALL RECYCLABLE PAPER
(INCLUDING THIS SHEET)
TO COLLECTION ROOM ON FIRST FLOOR
MONDAY—FRIDAY
5:30—7:30 p.m.
DETAILS ARE POSTED ON
COLLECTION ROOM DOOR

The contest rules, an expansion of the information given in the flyer, were posted on the collection room door of the two dorms involved.[5]

Personnel and Procedure

The data recorders were undergraduate students fulfilling a requirement in a behavior modification course taught by the second author. Advanced undergraduate psychology majors were collection-center managers and supervised the data recorders' daily procedures as partial fulfillment of an undergraduate research course. All paper was weighed at the end of the 2-hr. period by both individuals. To ensure reliability of measurement, weekly weighings were taken by the authors. The discrepancy between the daily and weekly totals ranged from zero to six pounds, with the largest discrepancy being .08% of the total weekly poundage.

When arriving at the collection room at 5:30 p.m., the collection-center manager and data recorder immediately weighed any extraneous paper (*i.e.,* any paper that had been left at the collection site since the previous collection period) and recorded the results. The data recorder collected all paper brought to the room, obtained the room number of each person delivering paper, and kept the day's paper separate from other paper in the room. For the Raffle condition, the data recorder weighed each student's paper in his presence and then gave the participant one raffle coupon for each pound of paper delivered. One half of each raffle ticket, containing the name and room number of the resident, was deposited in a raffle box; the other half of the coupon was retained by the resident.

RESULTS

Pounds of Paper

Figure 1 depicts the amounts of paper delivered daily to each collection room from 5:30 to 7:30 p.m. The largest amount of paper delivered on any day was 488 pounds by the female dorm during the Raffle; this dorm's largest Baseline value was 86 pounds. The largest poundage for males in the Raffle condition was 193 pounds, as contrasted with this dorm's largest Baseline quantity of 18 pounds. In the Contest contingency, the male civilians delivered a high of 482 pounds on the ninth day of Contest, whereas the high for the R.O.T.C. dorm was only 71 pounds, delivered on the eleventh day of Contest. The contest dorms had almost identical Baseline levels, the civilian dorm reaching a high of 23 pounds and the R.O.T.C. dorm reaching a high of 15 pounds. The Prompt condition appeared to have relatively little influence; the quantity of paper delivered increased from a Baseline high of 20 pounds to only 21 pounds on the ninth day of prompting for females and from a high of three pounds in Baseline to a peak of 15 pounds during prompting for males.

The three-week follow-up period resulted in an immediate and marked drop in pounds of paper delivered during the critical hours by residents of the female raffle dorm (*i.e.,* from 488 pounds on the last day of Raffle to 31 pounds for the first day of Follow-up). For the male raffle dorm, daily pounds of paper delivered from 5:30 to 7:30 p.m. decreased at a more gradual rate, increasing from a daily high of 52 pounds in the third week of Raffle to 80 pounds on the first day to Follow-up, and then dropping to zero pounds by the third day of Follow-up.

Fig. 1. Pounds of Recyclable Paper Delivered Daily to Each Dorm Collection Room.

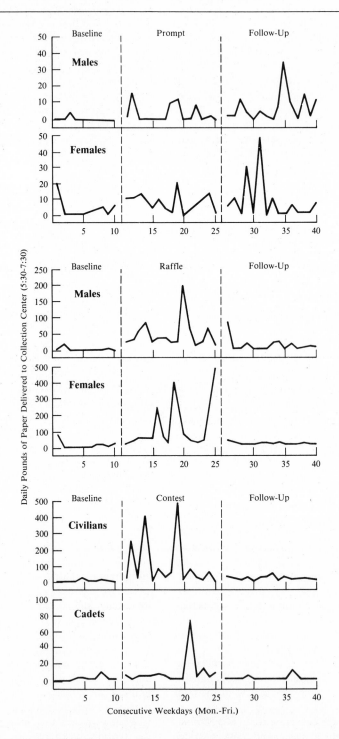

After the Contest weeks, paper delivered from 5:30 to 7:30 p.m. decreased for both contest dorms (*i.e.,* for civilians the poundage changed from a high of 60 pounds in the third Contest week to 30 pounds on the first day of Follow-up week, and for the cadets from 71 pounds to one pound). The amount of paper delivered during the critical hours in the two prompt dorms increased slightly during Follow-up, reaching a daily high of 50 pounds for females and 35 pounds for males.

Some relatively consistent sex differences can be observed in the results from the two pairs of male/female dorms. For the dorm-pair given the Prompt treatment, females delivered more paper than males in all but one week of the study. Similarly, for the raffle dorm-pair, females were consistently higher during Baseline and Raffle, although males delivered more paper than females during Follow-up.

During the Contest contingency, there were pronounced between-dorm differences in amounts of paper delivered. The civilians delivered more paper than the cadets during all three weeks of the contest, although the weekly totals for the civilian residents decreased over the three contest weeks (*i.e.,* Week 1 = 742 pounds, Week 2 = 637, Week 3 = 144). It is noteworthy that several civilians verbalized to the data recorder that they were determined to win each contest in order to help finance weekend dorm parties. Indeed, the males described the parties that took place after each contest and each party was attended by an estimated 100 dorm residents. Such parties are not permitted in the military-style R.O.T.C. dorm.

The total quantities of paper delivered during the critical hours was 147 pounds for the Prompt condition, 2459 pounds for the Raffle contingency, and 1633 pounds for the Contest contingency. Extraneous paper (*i.e.,* paper delivered at times other than between 5:30 and 7:30 p.m.) totalled 193 pounds for the Prompt condition, four pounds for the Raffle contingency, and 293 pounds for the Contest contingency. Thus, the Raffle and Contest conditions promoted delivery of markedly greater amounts of paper during the critical collection hours than did the Prompt condition.

Participation

A paper delivery was defined as a dorm resident delivering at least one 21.6 by 28 cm sheet of paper to the collection room between 5:30 and 7:30 p.m. Monday through Friday. For each dorm, the average number of deliveries was lower during Baseline than during the contingency of the next three weeks. In the Prompt dorms, the males had peaks of one delivery during the third day of Baseline and three deliveries in the first day of Prompt; females had peaks of two deliveries on the eighth and tenth days of Baseline and five deliveries on three occasions in the third week of Prompt. Both raffle dorms showed marked increases in participation as a result of the Raffle contingency; males increased from a daily high of five deliveries on the seventh day of Baseline to eight on two occasions during Raffle, and the number of female deliveries increased from four to 10 across the same period. For the contest dorms, the civilians showed a substantial increase in participation during the Contest (*i.e.,* from a peak of three on the ninth day of Baseline to a peak of 18 on the fourth day of Contest). In the R.O.T.C. dorm, however, participation for these same weeks decreased from three to four deliveries.

A weekly proportion of resident participation was found by dividing the number of individuals from a given dorm who made paper deliveries by the total number of residents in that dorm. The highest proportion of participation occurred for the Raffle condition, reaching peaks of 0.144 during the second Raffle week for females and during the third Raffle week for males. The highest participation proportions for the Prompt dorms were 0.054 in the third week of prompting for females and 0.018 in the first week of prompting for males. Percent participation by the cadets exceeded the civilians only during Baseline (*i.e.,* weekly highs of 0.022 *versus* 0.018); during the Contest, participation in the civilian dorm increased to a weekly high of 0.099 for the second contest, compared with the highest proportion of 0.039 for the cadets during the first contest.

Proximity

The room numbers of the agents of the paper deliveries were an indication of the distance travelled to reach the collection site. For this analysis of proximity effects, divisions were determined by floor, and proportion of participants per dorm floor was determined for each condition.[6] During Baseline, the majority of participants in every dorm were first-floor residents. In addition, for each dorm the relative number of first-floor participants decreased as a function of each treatment condition and remained below the Baseline proportions during Follow-up. An increase in participants from dorm floors other than the first floor was particularly apparent during the Raffle contingency for females and during the Contest contingency for civilians. As a result, a chi square test for homogeneity was significant in both of these cases ($ps < 0.02$). Figure 1 shows that the residents of these particular dorms consistently collected the largest quantities of weekly paper during treatment. It is noteworthy that for all but one dorm (*i.e.*, prompt/male) the participation distributions during Follow-up were more similar to the Baseline distributions than were the distributions during treatment conditions.[7]

DISCUSSION

The positive reinforcement contingencies (*i.e.*, the raffle and contest) prominently increased quantities of paper delivered to dormitory collection rooms above Baseline levels and above the levels observed subsequent to distributions of flyers urging paper-recycling behaviors for the improvement of ecology (*i.e.*, the Prompt condition). However, the percentage of dormitory residents who participated in the recycling program was disappointingly low (*i.e.*, less than 15%). Since every resident was informed of the reinforcement contingency by means of a flyer delivered to his or her room, it is reasonable to assume that most dorm residents were aware of the treatment condition. Thus, low participation in the paper drive was not due to a lack of contingency awareness as speculated by Geller *et al.* (1975), but rather to a lack of contingency effectiveness.

For the Raffle contingency, virtually all paper was delivered to the collection room between 5:30 and 7:30 p.m. when the coupon reinforcers were available, indicating that the Raffle was the motivating factor for those few individuals who did make paper deliveries. As expected, the contingency of giving one coupon per pound of paper resulted in a greater volume of paper per visit, and virtually eliminated the repeated visits observed by Geller *et al.* (1975). A substantially greater amount of paper was collected during the raffle of the present study than during the raffle of the previous study. However, the percentage of resident participation during raffle contingencies was similar for both studies, indicating that the larger paper quantities in the present study were due to greater individual effort. The increased numbers of prizes per raffle in the present study (*i.e.*, 10 *versus* four) probably influenced the differences.

The Contest contingency produced results directly opposite to the investigators' hypothesis that a group contingency would be more effective in an R.O.T.C. dorm, whose residents frequently act as a unit, than in a civilian dorm with no obvious group structure or unity. Perhaps the Contest contingency was more effective in the civilian dorm because certain residents of this dorm specified a method for spending the contest winnings that implied a common group reward. Specifically, the money from each contest was used to procure beer for weekend parties in the dorm. Such parties are not permitted in the R.O.T.C. dorm and, therefore, the between-dorm comparisons were biased by the fact that the $15 was translated into a group reinforcer for the civilians but not for the cadets. Perhaps the decreasing amounts of paper collected by the civilians over the three contest weeks was due to an increasing realization that the cadets were not providing competition.

Prompting alone was clearly the least effective intervention technique. Although most dorm residents should have become aware of a worthwhile ecology program through the prompting procedure, few individuals took the trouble to participate. Whereas there was some increase in both participation and amount of paper delivered during prompting, the changes were not substantial. Hence, the present study indicates that community ecology programs should at least offer individuals the possibility of receiving a tangible reward in return for their ecology-improving behaviors.

The relative convenience of the desired behavior is certainly an important factor determining the efficacy of ecology-promoting procedures. For example, prompting procedures alone were sufficient to augment the probability of an ecology-improving response when the response merely required the selection of drinks in returnable rather than throwaway containers (Geller, Farris, and Post, 1973; Geller, Wylie, and Farris, 1971) or the disposal of a handbill in a convenient location (Geller, 1973, 1975; Geller, Witmer, and Orebaugh, *in press*). In the present study, prompting not only had little influence on the relatively inconvenient behavior patterns of carrying recyclable paper to a collection room, but the probability of making paper deliveries was usually highest when the response was most convenient (*i.e.*, when the resident's room and the collection room were on the same floor).[8]

In conclusion, the procedures and results of the present investigation illustrate practical and effective procedures for promoting a reverse-distribution process that could be easily refined for community-wide application. For example, community collection centers could offer raffle coupons for particular quantities of recyclable commodities; and, as a result of the present study (and that by Geller *et al.,* 1975), the authors predict that community merchants would donate raffle prizes in return for the "good will" and publicity accompanying their support of a community ecology project. In addition, recycling contests between civic and/or church groups could be organized, and prize money could be procured from the sale of collected paper or aluminum to recycling plants. However, voluntary programs such as these are by no means sufficient. Mandatory programs such as municipal ordinances requiring the separate collection of paper and incentives for industry to use recycled paper are possible long-range solutions to the recycling problem. Whatever programs are implemented, individual cooperation is important and projects such as those presented here could help to initiate and maintain the appropriate behaviors. Although the market for recycled paper is at present low, aluminum is in great demand for recycling and the procedures outlined here are easily generalizable to that and other commodities.[9]

Footnotes

[1]This research served as partial fulfillment for the first author's Master of Arts degree from Radford College, Radford, Virginia. The authors are indebted to the following individuals whose cooperation made this study possible: (a) the dormitory managers for their assistance in data collection throughout the project—William Beatty, Gregory Burmeister, Deloris Jones, Richard Martin, Thomas Murray, and Paul Outten; (b) the VPI&SU Committee for Ecological Rebalance, especially Dana Donatucci, for providing supplies (including prize money) and transporting the dormitory paper to a centralized, recycling center; and (c) the merchants of Blacksburg, Virginia for donating commodities and services as raffle prizes. The comments of John D. Cone on an earlier documentation of this research are gratefully acknowledged. Reprints may be obtained from E. Scott Geller, Department of Psychology, Virginia Polytechnic Institute and State University, Blacksburg, Virginia 24061.

[2]A coin was flipped to determine which dorm-pair would receive the raffle contingency (the pair with 333 students per dorm or the pair with 180 students per dorm) and which would receive only a prompt.

[3]Illustrations of the actual flyers will be furnished on request to E. Scott Geller.

[4]An illustration of the raffle announcement that listed the prizes is available from the second author on request.

[5]An illustration of the poster that described the contest rules is available from E. Scott Geller on request.

[6]Preliminary analyses divided each dorm floor into specific sections based on relative walking distance from the collection room, but no consistent floor variations were observed.

[7]A table of the proximity data is available on request to the second author.

[8]Since residents with rooms on the same floor as the collection room were more likely to pass by the collection room with a REBAL poster on its door, the observed proximity effects may have been due in part to systematic prompting differences among dorm residents.

[9]By the end of the present study, the return for recyclable paper had dropped from $15 to $12.50 per ton, and at the time of preparing the revision of this manuscript there was no market for recyclable paper in Southwest Virginia.

References

Cash in trash? maybe. *Forbes,* January 15, 1970, p. 20.

Finnie, W. C. Field experiments in litter control. *Environment and Behavior,* 1973, *5,* 123-144.

Geller, E. S. Increasing desired waste disposals with instructions. *Man-Environment Systems,* 1975, *5,* 125-128.

Geller, E. S. Prompting anti-litter behavior. *Proceedings of the 81st Annual Convention of the American Psychological Association,* 1973, *8,* 901-902 (Summary).

Geller, E. S. Chaffee, J. L., and Ingram, R. E. Promoting paper-recycling on a university campus. *Journal of Environmental Systems,* 1975, *5,* 39-57.

Geller, E. S., Farris, J. C., and Post, D. S. Prompting a consumer behavior for pollution control. *Journal of Applied Behavior Analysis,* 1973, *6,* 367-376.

Geller, E. S., Witmer, J. F., and Orebaugh, A. L. Instructions as a determinant of paper-disposal behaviors. *Environment and Behavior, (in press).*

Geller, E. S., Wylie, R. C., and Farris, J. C. An attempt at applying prompting and reinforcement toward pollution control. *Proceedings of the 79th Annual Convention of the American Psychological Association,* 1971, *6,* 701-702 (Summary).

Hall, J. R. and Ackoff, R. L. A systems approach to the problems of solid waste and litter. *Journal of Environmental Systems,* 1972, *2,* 351-364.

Margulies, W. P. Steel and paper industries look at recycling as an answer to pollution. *Advertising Age,* 1970, *41,* 63.

Pirages, D. C. Behavioral technology and institutional transformation. In H. Wheeler (Ed.), *Beyond the punitive society.* San Francisco: W. H. Freeman and Company, 1973. Pp. 57-70.

U.S. finds a rich resource: The nation's trash pile. *U.S. News and World Report,* May 13, 1974, p. 24.

Crowding

Too Close for Comfort: Sex Differences in Response to Invasions of Personal Space

Jeffrey David Fisher   *Purdue University*
Donn Byrne

Abstract

It was hypothesized that females respond more negatively than males to side-by-side invasions of personal space, while males respond more negatively than females to face-to-face invasions. In an experimental field study, 62 males and 63 females were "invaded" by a male or female confederate in one of three spatial positions. Regardless of the invader's sex, a consistent pattern of interactions were observed such that affect ($p < .02$), attraction ($p = .05$), environmental perceptions ($p < .004$), and attributions of intent ($p < .005$) were negative for males when a stranger sat across from them and negative for females when a stranger sat adjacent to them. In an observational field study of 66 students, solitary males in a library were observed to erect barriers against face-to-face invasions, and females were found to erect barriers against adjacent invasions ($p < .02$).

Personal space has been defined by Sommer (1966) as an invisible boundary surrounding each individual, a territory into which others may not trespass. Dosey and Meisels (1966) have interpreted personal space as a buffer zone which serves as a protection against perceived threats. The size of this buffer zone is found to vary as a function of such variables as culture

(Baxter, 1970), personality (Leipold, 1963), and age (Willis, 1966).

An examination of sex differences in spatial behavior indicates that females have smaller zones of personal space and hence can tolerate closer interpersonal contacts than males (Baxter, 1970; Hartnett, Bailey, & Gibson, 1970; Liebman, 1970; Willis, 1966; Fisher, Note 1). When opposite-sex pairs are mutually attracted, it is not surprising to find that for both sexes the magnitude of such buffer zones decreases considerably (Allgeier & Byrne, 1973; Byrne, Ervin, & Lamberth, 1970). One striking difference between the sexes is with respect to spatial positioning; research on attraction indicates that males prefer to position themselves *across from* liked others, while females prefer to position themselves *adjacent to* liked others (Byrne, Baskett, & Hodges, 1971; Norum, Russo, & Sommer, 1967; Sommer, 1959). Such findings raise the possibility that sex differences in response to invasions of personal space might depend in part on whether a potential intruder occupies a face-to-face or side-by-side position. A logical synthesis of research on spatial invasion and research on attraction suggests that for each sex the position and distance configuration most appropriate for one who is liked may be least appropriate for a stranger; there is, moreover, suggestive evidence that the positioning effects found in attraction research have complementary parallels in research on spatial invasions. Horowitz, Duff, and Stratton (1964) reported that female strangers approach others more closely frontally than on the sides, while male strangers approach others more closely on the sides than frontally. In a library setting, Patterson, Mullins, and Romano (1971) observed more physical blocking by females than by males when the invader sat in an adjacent seat; however, there was more blocking by males than females when the confederate sat in a face-to-face position. A definitive examination of sex differences has consistently been obscured, however, by methodological deficiencies. For example, experimenters have used subjects of only one sex (e.g., Felipe & Sommer, 1966) and/or invaders of only one sex (e.g., Patterson et al., 1971). In the first study to be reported here, male and female confederates initiate spatial invasions of male and female subjects in both adjacent and across positions. It is proposed that females respond more negatively than males when spatial invasion is from the side, while males respond more negatively than females when the invasion is face-to-face; it is further proposed that these negative reactions are greater in response to an opposite-sex invader than to an invader of the same sex.

Previous research on spatial invasions has characteristically emphasized the observed defensive and avoidant behavioral reactions of the "victim" (e.g., Garfinkel, 1964; Mehrabian & Diamond, 1971; Quick & Crano, Note 2). Such studies have thus provided indirect and inferential evidence as to the emotional impact of personal space intrusions, but there has been no direct measure of affective responses to spatial violations. The first of the present investigations involves an attempt to determine the affective consequences of spatial invasions. A Sex of Subject × Sex of Invader × Spatial Position interaction is predicted such that the affective result of an invasion is more negative when the invader is of the opposite sex and such that females express more negative affect than males when the invader is adjacent, while males express more negative affect than females when the invader is face-to-face. In addition, the subsequent judgmental effects of affective arousal are examined. The reinforcement-affect model of evaluative responses (Byrne, 1971) specifies that evaluation of stimulus objects is a function of associated affect. In terms of the model, it is predicted that negative affect evoked by spatial invasions is inversely related to evaluative judgments of the invader and of the environmental surroundings. A final aspect of this first investigation deals with the proposal of Byrne, Fisher, Lamberth, and Mitchell (1974) that negative feelings not only influence the evaluation of an associated stimulus, but that people also tend to justify such feelings by vindicatively attributing appropriate positive and negative characteristics to the stimulus object. Thus, it is hypothesized that negative affective responses evoked by spatial invasions are associated with attributions of negative intent to the invader.

STUDY 1

Method

Subjects. Subjects were 125 Purdue University students (62 males and 63 females) who were studying in the University Library. The prerequisite for inclusion in the study was that a potential subject be sitting alone, studying at a rectangular table which had three seats on each side. The experiment was conducted during weekday mornings and afternoons.

Design. A 2 × 3 (Sex of Subject × Sex of Invader × Spatial Relationship of Subject and Invader) between-subjects design was employed in which male and female participants who met the criteria were randomly assigned to the remaining experimental conditions. The three spatial relationships between subject and invader were patterned after those used by Felipe and Sommer (1966): invader adjacent to the subject, invader one seat away from the subject on the same side of the table, and invader directly across the table from the subject. Five male experimenters and five male invaders plus five female experimenters and five female invaders took part in the experiment, and each was blind with respect to the experimental hypotheses. The sex of the experimenter was counterbalanced for each of the experimental cells.

Procedure. After a subject was selected, the invader walked over to the book stacks near the subject's table, looked for and selected a book, and sat down in a given spatial relationship to the subject. After taking notes from the book for 5 minutes, the invader pretended to have concluded his work, returned the book to the shelf, and left the area. Three minutes later the experimenter arrived and introduced himself as a student conducting a study for an introductory psychology class. The experimenter indicated that he had noticed that someone had been sitting at the subject's table and that he wondered if the subject could give his impressions of that person by rating him on a series of forms. The experimenter said that he was also interested in the student's perception of the library environment and that some additional forms were included for this purpose. All potential subjects agreed to participate, and each was given a folder containing the dependent measures. After the scales were completed, the experimenter debriefed the subject as to the purpose of the experiment; postexperimental interviews revealed that almost none of the subjects expressed any suspicions with respect to the role of the invader.

Dependent measures.   A feelings scale previously established as a self-report measure of affect by Byrne and Clore (1970), Griffitt (1970), and Griffitt and Veitch (1971) was used as an indicator of affect. This scale consists of six evaluative bipolar adjective pairs arranged as 7-point scales. Responses to these adjectives (e.g., happy–sad, pleasant–unpleasant) are summed to yield a measure of affect along a positive–negative dimension ranging from 6 (most negative) to 42 (most positive).

Attraction toward the invader was measured by means of the Interpersonal Judgment Scale (Byrne, 1971). This scale consists of six 7-point Likert scales and has been used extensively in attraction research. The first four items are buffers, and the last two items (personal feelings and feeling about working with the person) are summed to yield a measure of attraction ranging from 2 (most negative) to 14 (most positive).

Environmental perceptions were measured on two scales. The Judgments of Environmental Quality Scale consists of twelve 7-point bipolar adjectives which tap a single aesthetic quality dimension as indicated by a principal-components analysis (Fisher, Note 1). These items (e.g., lively–unlively, depressing–cheerful) are summed to constitute an index of perceived positiveness of environmental quality ranging from 12 (least pleasing) to 84 (most pleasing). The Personal Space Evaluation Scale measures perceived crowdedness. Of nine 7-point bipolar adjective items, five are buffers while the four remaining items (e.g., crowded–uncrowded, large–small) tap a single crowdedness dimension as indicated by a principal-components analysis (Fisher, Note 1). These items are summed to yield an index ranging from 4 (least crowded) to 28 (most crowded).

The subject's perception of the invader's motivation at the time he sat at the subject's table was measured by means of three 7-point bipolar adjective items (e.g., honest–dishonest, good–bad). These items are summed to yield a measure of positiveness of perceived invader intent ranging from 3 (most negative) to 21 (most positive).

Results

A $2 \times 2 \times 3$ unweighted means analysis of variance (Winer, 1971) was computed for each of the dependent measures.

Affect.   Analysis of the feelings scale revealed only a Sex of Subject $\times$ Spatial Relationship interaction, $F(2, 124) = 4.56$, $p < .02$. For this interaction, the Duncan multiple-range procedure indicated that females expressed more negative feelings than males when the invader sat adjacent to them; males expressed more negative feelings when the invader sat across from them than when the invader was in an adjacent seat (Table 1).

Attraction.   For interpersonal attraction, there was both a main effect for sex of the invader, $F(1, 124) = 14.38$, $p < .0005$, with females evoking more positive responses than males and a Sex of Subject $\times$ Spatial Relationships interaction, $F(2, 124) = 3.07$, $p = .05$. As shown in Table 2, the interaction was such that female subjects tended to like the invader less than did male subjects in both the adjacent and one-seat-away positions ($p < .10$); males liked the invader less in the across position than in the adjacent position.

Perceptions of environment.   On the Judgments of Environmental Quality Scale, a main effect was found for spatial relationship, $F(2, 124) = 24.57$, $p < .0001$, Sex of Subject $\times$ Spatial Relationship interaction was found, $F(2, 124) = 7.08$, $p < .002$. As shown in Table 3, the environment was perceived more positively when the invader sat one seat away than when he or she sat either in the adjacent or across positions. The interaction indicates that females perceived the library environment more negatively than did males when the invader sat adjacent; males perceived the environment more negatively when the invader sat across than when he sat adjacent, while female perceptions were the reverse for the two positions.

For the measure of crowdedness, both a main effect for spatial relationship, $F(2, 124) = 24.57$, $p < .0001$, and a Sex of Subject $\times$ Spatial Relationship interaction, $F(2, 124) = 5.93$, $p < .004$, were observed.

Table 1   Positiveness of Affective State

Sex of subject	Spatial relationship between subject and invader		
	Adjacent	One seat away	Across
Male	29.15$_b$	27.80$_{ab}$	23.57$_a$
Female	23.46$_a$	27.40$_{ab}$	26.79$_{ab}$

Note. Means with common subscripts do not differ at the .05 level as indicated by the Duncan multiple-range procedure.

Table 2 Attraction Toward the Invader

Sex of subject	Spatial relationship between subject and invader		
	Adjacent	One seat away	Across
Male	10.99$_b$	10.20$_{ab}$	9.14$_a$
Female	9.87$_{ab}$	9.16$_a$	10.14$_{ab}$

Note. Means with common subscripts do not differ at the .05 level as indicated by the Duncan multiple-range procedure.

Table 4 Perceived Crowdedness

Sex of subject	Spatial relationship between subject and invader		
	Adjacent	One seat away	Across
Male	11.48$_b$	8.50$_b$	17.04$_a$
Female	16.60$_a$	8.39$_b$	14.76$_a$

Note. Means with common subscripts do not differ at the .05 level as indicated by the Duncan multiple-range procedure.

As may be seen in Table 4, the main effect serves as a manipulation check with respect to the distance between subject and invader, and it is apparent that perceptions of crowdedness tended to reflect actual differences in seating distance. The interaction indicates that females felt more crowded than males when the invader sat adjacent, while males felt more crowded when the invader sat across rather than in an adjacent position. When the invader was one seat away, neither males nor females indicated feelings of crowdedness, presumably because negative feelings are not aroused by this seating distance.

Attributions. With respect to the perception of the invader's motivation in selecting a seat, only a Sex of Subject × Spatial Relationship interaction was found, $F(2, 124) = 5.75$, $p < .005$. Table 5 indicates that females attributed more negative motives than did males when the invader sat adjacent to them, whereas males attributed more negative motives when the invader sat across from them than when he was in an adjacent position.

Intercorrelations of dependent variables. The hypothesized effects of invasions of personal space on affect, attraction, environmental perceptions, and attribution processes indicate that such variables are expected to covary. As indicated indirectly by the experimental results reported above and as may be

seen directly in Table 6, this expectation was confirmed.

Discussion

Under the conditions of the present investigation, a consistent pattern of interactions of sex of subject by the invader—subject spatial relationship was repeatedly observed. Regardless of the invader's sex, males felt affectively more negative and made more negative evaluative and attributional responses than did females when the invader sat across from them; the opposite pattern of responses for males and females occurred when the invader sat adjacent to the subject. Thus, as expected, sex differences in response to invasions of personal space were found to be a function of the positional characteristics of the situation. It may be seen that the particular position and distance favored by each sex when interacting with a friend will evoke negative feelings when occupied by an invading stranger. It is possible that the sex–position effect may prove helpful in explaining previous studies of density effects in which sex differences were observed (e.g., Freedman, Levy, Buchanan, & Price, 1972; Stokols, Rall, Pinner, & Schopler, 1973). In such studies, males and females could have perceived themselves to be differentially

Table 3 Perceived Positiveness of Aesthetic Quality of Environment

Sex of subject	Spatial relationship between subject and invader		
	Adjacent	One seat away	Across
Male	83.53$_c$	81.10$_c$	67.88$_{ab}$
Female	66.29$_a$	80.20$_c$	76.62$_{bc}$

Note. Means with common subscripts do not differ at the .05 level as indicated by the Duncan multiple-range procedure.

Table 5 Positiveness of Motivation Attributed to Invader

Sex of subject	Spatial relationship between subject and invader		
	Adjacent	One seat away	Across
Male	16.19$_b$	15.05$_{ab}$	13.08$_a$
Female	13.23$_a$	16.00$_b$	15.25$_{ab}$

Note. Means with common subscripts do not differ at the .05 level as indicated by the Duncan multiple-range procedure.

Table 6 Intercorrelations of Dependent Variables

Variable	Attraction toward invader	Positiveness of aesthetic quality of environment	Perceived crowdedness of environment	Positiveness of motives attributed to invader
Positiveness of affective state	.43	.65	−.52	.50
Attraction toward invader		.30	−.23	.37
Positiveness of aesthetic quality of environment			−.55	.38
Perceived crowdedness of environment				−.46

Note. Each correlation is significant at $p < .01$.

crowded as a function of the seating arrangements employed, even though there was an objectively constant level of density.

The failure to find any effect for sex of the invader was at first surprising, but in retrospect the explanation may lie in the asocial quality of a library setting. Considering the work orientation which is appropriate to the studying process, the primary impact of a stranger coming to sit at one's table would be that of a fellow worker whose sexual identification is not particularly relevant. This interpretation suggests that in a more social context, such as a party, the sex of the stranger would assume significance.

Despite the consistency of the present results, some doubts as to their meaning might be raised by the use of pencil-and-paper measuring devices. It is conceivable that these various intercorrelated scales are simply tapping verbal evaluative responses and that such responses are unrelated to overt interpersonal behavior. A second type of doubt raised by experiments of this sort is that subtle demand characteristics are somehow influencing the results, even though the confederates and experimenters were blind to the hypothesized effects. One way to resolve such doubts is to seek parallel observational evidence of related behavior in a nonmanipulative field setting. It was assumed that sex differences in response to spatial invasions by strangers should be reflected in sex-specific defensive activity which would serve as a protection against possible invasions. It has been reported that students sitting alone tend to use books, coats, sweaters, etc., to mark off territory and to erect barriers against interpersonal intrusions. It was hypothesized that females erect barriers between themselves and adjacent seats, while males erect barriers between themselves and face-to-face seats.

STUDY 2

Method

Subjects. Each student (33 males and 33 females) who was sitting alone at a table in the Purdue University Library at the time of the observation was included. When the study was conducted, only about 5% of the tables in the library were occupied by more than one individual.

Procedure. An observer, who was blind to the purpose of the task, recorded for each subject whether the individual was male or female and where that person's books and personal effects were placed. Specifically, each placement was noted as being between the subject and an adjacent seat, between the subject and the seat across the table, or in both positions.

Results

The frequency with which male and female students exhibited adjacent, across, or both barrier positions is shown in Table 7. A 2×3 chi-square analysis indicated

Table 7 Barrier Placement by Solitary Males and Females

Sex of subject	Barrier position		
	Adjacent	Both	Across
Males	9	9	15
Females	17	10	6

significant sex differences in that males erected barriers in the across position more often, while females erected adjacent barriers more often ($\chi^2(2) = 6.37$, $p < .05$. When subjects who use both barrier positions are eliminated from the analysis, the difference between the sexes is even more evident, ($\chi^2(2) = 6.30$, $p < .02$.

Discussion

It was found, then, that the spontaneous defensive behavior of males and females studying in a university library is congruent with their differential responses to spatial invasions. Both in assessed verbal reactions to experimental manipulations and in naturally occurring physical acts, males and females yield sex-specific spatial positioning effects.

CONCLUSIONS

A totally convincing theoretical interpretation of the observed sex differences is not readily available. One possible explanation lies in the socialization process, with males being taught to be relatively competitive and females to be relatively affiliative (Maccoby, 1966). Past research (e.g., Norum et al., 1967; Sommer, 1965) has indicated that individuals generally sit face-to-face in competitive situations and adjacent in cooperative and affiliative situations. Thus, it is possible that a stranger who sits in an across position could be seen by males as presenting a threatening competitive challenge. Analogously, adjacent seating by a stranger could be seen by females as an unwarranted demand for affiliation. This rationale would be strengthened if it could be shown that regardless of sex, individual differences in competitiveness and in affiliative tendencies were related to spatial positioning behavior.

The relationship between the affective responses to the personal space invasions and the subjects' subsequent evaluations and attributions provides additional support for the generality of the reinforcement-affect model of evaluative responses (Clore & Byrne, 1974). In terms of that model, the differential affect induced by the invasion mediated the subsequent responses to all associated stimulus objects. Subjects who experienced negative affect as a result of the stranger's presence were less attracted to the invader, found the environment aesthetically more unpleasant, felt more crowded, and perceived the motivation of the invader as more malign when compared with subjects in whom negative affect was not aroused. Individuals were also observed to engage in spontaneous defensive maneuvers which could serve to prevent the occurrence of such unpleasant invasions. In addition, it was found that individuals tend to justify their feelings and evaluations by attributing intrinsic qualities to the stimulus object which are consonant with their feelings.

The present findings also indicate that a subject variable such as sex may act in conjunction with objective physical conditions such as position–distance to determine environment perception. These interactive effects are consistent with the proposals of Stokols (1972) and of Fisher and Byrne (Note 3) that the exclusive use of objective physical conditions to predict behavioral response to environmental stimuli is inadequate; it is the multiply-determined psychological reaction to the environment which is the mediator of behavioral responses. In addition, these findings suggest that when a situation-specific stress is introduced, preexisting environmental inadequacies may be magnified for those in the situation.

From the viewpoint of the interpersonal aspects of environmental design, it appears that male and female differences should be taken into account in arranging spatial configurations in settings such as physicians' waiting rooms or on public conveyances in which strangers are brought together. It appears that males would feel more comfortable than females with adjacent seating, while females would feel more comfortable than males with face-to-face seating. Perhaps the optimal solution is to make each type of arrangement available, assuming that members of each sex are aware of their own reactions. In addition to the possible psychological and behavioral consequences of spatial design, the male–female differences reported here conceivably are a source of miscommunication and misunderstanding between the sexes. A female who wants to befriend an unknown male may be surprised to find that a nonthreatening (to her) eyeball-to-eyeball approach causes consternation and alarm. In the same way, a male who attempts to ingratiate himself with an unknown female by sitting down beside her in a nonthreatening (to him) position may be surprised to find that he elicits a "Miss Muffet" reaction. Subsequent research will be directed at some of these problems of differential sensitivity with respect to the reactions of self and others to spatial positioning and with respect to the competitive and affiliative meaning of such positioning.

Reference Notes

1. Fisher, J. D. *Attitude similarity as a determinant of perceived crowdedness and perceived environmental quality: Support for an interactive model for prediction of the behavioral effects of density and other environmental stimuli.* Unpublished master's thesis, Purdue University, 1973.
2. Quick, A., & Crano, W. D. *Effects of sex, distance, and conversation in the invasion of personal space.* Paper presented at the meeting of the Midwestern Psychological Association, Chicago, May 1973.
3. Fisher, J. D., & Byrne, D. *Spatial and environmental quality evaluative judgments as a function of affective state of the individual.* Paper presented at the meeting of the Psychonomic Society, St. Louis, November 1972.

References

Allgeier, A. R., & Byrne, D. Attraction toward the opposite sex as a determinant of physical proximity. *Journal of Social Psychology*, 1973, *90*, 213-219.

Baxter, J. Interpersonal spacing in natural settings. *Sociometry*, 1970, *33*, 444-456.

Byrne, D. *The attraction paradigm.* New York: Academic Press, 1971.

Byrne, D., Baskett, G. D., & Hodges, L. Behavioral indicators of interpersonal attraction. *Journal of Applied Social Psychology*, 1971, *1*, 137-149.

Byrne, D., & Clore, G. L. A reinforcement model of evaluative responses. *Personality: An International Journal*, 1970, *1*, 103-128.

Byrne, D., Ervin, C. R., & Lamberth, J. Continuity between the experimental study of attraction and real life computer dating. *Journal of Personality and Social Psychology*, 1970, *16*, 157-165.

Byrne, D., Fisher, J. D. Lamberth, J., & Mitchell, H. E. Evaluations of erotica: Facts or feelings? *Journal of Personality and Social Psychology*, 1974, *29*, 111-116.

Clore, G. L., & Byrne, D. A reinforcement-affect model of attraction. In T. L. Huston (Ed.), *Foundations of interpersonal attraction.* New York: Academic Press, 1974.

Dosey, M., & Meisels, M. Personal space and self protection. *Journal of Personality and Social Psychology*, 1969, *11*, 93-97.

Felipe, N. J., & Sommer, R. Invasions of personal space. *Social Problems*, 1966, *14*, 206-214.

Freedman, J. L., Levy, A.S., Buchanan, R. W., & Price, J. Crowding and human aggressiveness. *Journal of Experimental Social Psychology*, 1972, *8*, 528-548.

Garfinkel, H. Studies of the routine grounds of everyday activities. *Social Problems*, 1964, *11*, 225-250.

Griffitt, W. Environmental effects on interpersonal affective behavior: Ambient effective temperature and attraction. *Journal of Personality and Social Psychology*, 1970, *15*, 240-244.

Griffitt, W., & Veitch, R. Hot and crowded: Influences of population density and temperature on interpersonal affective behavior. *Journal of Personality and Social Psychology*, 1971, *17*, 92-98.

Hartnett, J. J., Bailey, K. G., & Gibson, F. W. Personal space as influenced by sex and type of movement. *Journal of Psychology*, 1970, *76*, 139-144.

Horowitz, M., Duff, D., & Stratton, L. Body-buffer zone. *Archives of General Psychiatry*, 1964, *146*, 24-35.

Leipold, W. D. Psychological distance in a dyadic interview. Unpublished doctoral dissertation, University of North Dakota, 1963.

Liebman, M. The effects of sex and race norms on personal space. *Environment and Behavior*, 1970, *2*, 208-246.

Maccoby, E. (Ed.) *The development of sex differences.* Stanford, Calif.: Stanford University Press, 1966.

Mehrabian, A., & Diamond, S. G. Effects of furniture arrangement, props, and personality on social interaction. *Journal of Personality and Social Psychology*, 1971, *20*, 18-30.

Norum, G. A., Russo, N. J., & Sommer, R. Seating patterns and group task. *Psychology in the Schools*, 1967, *4*, 276-280.

Patterson, M. L., Mullens, S., & Romano, J. Compensatory reactions to spatial intrusion. *Sociometry*, 1971, *34*, 114-126.

Sommer, R. Studies in personal space. *Sociometry*, 1959, *22*, 247-260.

Sommer, R. Further studies in small group ecology. *Sociometry*, 1965, *28*, 337-348.

Sommer, R. The ecology of privacy. *Library Quarterly*, 1966, *36*, 234-248.

Stokols, D. A social psychological model of human crowding phenomena. *Journal of the American Institute of Planners*, 1972, *38*, 72-84.

Stokols, D., Rall, M., Pinner, B., & Schopler, J. Physical, social, and personal determinants of the perception of crowding. *Environment and Behavior*, 1973, *5*, 87-115.

Willis, F. N. Initial speaking distance as a function of the speaker's relationship. *Psychonomic Science*, 1966, *5*, 221-222.

Winer, B. J. *Statistical principles in experimental design.* (2nd ed.). New York: McGraw-Hill, 1971.

This research was supported in part by National Science Foundation Grant GS-40329 to Donn Byrne, principal investigator. The cooperation and assistance of the staff of the Purdue University Library and the statistical assistance of Marv Rytting are gratefully acknowledged. Portions of this article were presented at the meeting of the Midwestern Psychological Association, Chicago, May 1974.

Jeffrey Fisher is now at the Department of Psychology, University of Connecticut, Storrs, Connecticut.

Requests for reprints should be sent to Donn Byrne, Department of Psychological Sciences, Purdue University, West Lafayette, Indiana 47907.

Crowding and Cognitive Control

Ellen J. Langer   *Graduate School and University Center*
Susan Saegert   *of the City University of New York*

Abstract

This study was designed to test the effects of high densities in a field setting on complex cognitive and behavioral tasks and on affective responses. We also hypothesized that by providing subjects with increased cognitive control of the situation by giving them information about the effects of crowding, the aversive effects of the high-density situation would be ameliorated. We predicted that not only would subjects feel more comfortable, behave more effectively, experience less interference from others, and feel less crowded when provided with such information, but they would also perform complex cognitive tasks more effectively. Subjects were recruited in New York City supermarkets during crowded and uncrowded times and given a grocery list; their task was to select the most economical product for each item. Task performance and questionnaire measures of emotional reactions were taken. Results strongly confirmed the predictions. The provision of information also improved performance and emotional reactions not only in the crowded conditions but in the uncrowded ones as well.

"Crowding and Cognitive Control" by Ellen J. Langer and Susan Saegert. *Journal of Personality and Social Psychology,* 1977, Vol. 35, No. 3, pp. 175–182. Copyright © 1977 by The American Psychological Association, Inc. Reprinted by permission.

Several early studies of crowding seem to indicate that the experience of high densities has little or no effect on people in these situations (Freedman, Klevansky, & Ehrlich, 1971). These findings are surprising in light of the extremely severe negative social and physiological consequences of high densities that have been observed for animal populations (cf. Calhoun, 1962; Christian, 1970; Davis, 1971). Working on the idea that crowding would be stressful and therefore arousing, investigators focused on measures of task performance, expecting that such arousal would be reflected in improved performance on simple tasks and less successful performance on complex ones. However, these task effects failed to occur (Freedman et al., 1971; Stokols, Rall, Pinner, & Schopler, 1973). Epstein and Karlin (1975) have demonstrated the expected improvement in simple task performance as a function of crowding, but decrements in complex task performance were still not obtained. Sherrod (1974) also failed to find poststress effects of high-density experiences on a proofreading task, although poststress reduction in tolerance for frustration was observed. Indeed, on the basis of his own program of research, Freedman (1975) has been led to conclude as follows:

> *It has been shown that population density bears little or no relationship to any kind of pathology among humans. While conditions of high density, either in a neighborhood or within one's own dwelling, obviously have substantial effects on how one lives, they do not appear to have generally negative consequences. Under more controlled circumstances, research demonstrates that people can function quite well even when very crowded and isolated for considerable periods of time. Indeed, at least within the limits used in these studies, increasing the density has, if anything, positive effects—reducing hostility and stress. Density has also been shown to have no effects on performance on a wide variety of tasks, thus making it seem highly unlikely that it produces stress in the usual sense of the word. (p. 89)*

However, recently Paulus, Annis, Seta, Schkade, and Mathews (1976) have found decrements on complex tasks as a function of density, with group size having a more reliable negative effect than room size.

Other investigators, not focusing on task performance, have found various effects of high densities that suggest the occurrence of arousal. Saegert (1974) and Aiello, Epstein, and Karlin (1975) have reported increased palmar sweating and increased electrodermal activity for groups of subjects in higher density conditions. In fact, in both of these studies, a subject's levels of physiological arousal seems to continue to increase over time as a function of density, rather than showing a pattern that would indicate adaptation to the high-density situation. Griffitt and Veitch (1971) and Sundstrom (1975) have presented data showing that subjects in higher density environments feel more crowded, less comfortable, and less positively oriented to becoming acquainted with other people.

Field studies of high-density environments have linked increased blood pressure (D'Atri, 1975) and greater frequency of illness (McCain, Cox, & Paulus, 1976) in prisoners to crowding. Bickman et al. (1973) found less willingness to help in higher density student dormitories, a finding that has recently been replicated and extended to other aspects of social relationships in a low-income housing project (McCarthy & Saegert, Note 1).

In a study of subjects' reactions to crowding in an urban train station, Saegert, Mackintosh, and West (1975) found increased feelings of anxiety and inadequacy to the tasks at hand and decreased positive feelings toward other people in the high-density condition. In this study, a variety of task effects were also obtained. Subjects in the crowded train station could perform fewer of the kinds of tasks usually required in such an environment (e.g., finding out when trains were leaving, finding the rest rooms, etc.). In a second study conducted in a department store, those authors found that crowded subjects showed no postcrowding decrement on a task requiring memory for descriptions which they themselves had written during a high-density experience. However, these same crowded subjects *did* manifest significantly less incidental learning of the environment. Maps of the environment drawn by subjects who had experienced crowding were much less complete and accurate than those drawn by subjects who had been in the same environment in low-density conditions.

Clearly, the studies of crowding and task performance described above differ in many ways. Freedman and his colleagues' work involved small groups of interacting subjects in a laboratory setting; Aiello et al.

(1975) employed a similar setting but did not encourage interaction. Saegert et al. (1975) used field settings which hundreds of people passed through in the course of one experimental session. The tasks employed in these studies also differed; whereas paper-and-pencil tasks were typical of laboratory settings, measures employed in the field setting were usually related to transactions with the environment. It could be argued that the failure to find task effects in the paper-and-pencil measures occurred because involvement in such tasks is itself a coping device allowing subjects to tune out effectively their awareness of the density conditions. However, none of the field studies actually demonstrated decrements on a cognitively complex task performed in the high-density situation.

In addition, Freedman (1975) has argued that crowding intensifies ongoing emotional responses in the situation. That is, if one feels positive and is crowded, one will feel more positive, and likewise, if one feels negative, crowding will increase the negativity. However, this approach to crowding has certain limitations. On the one hand, it seems to overlook the functional consequences of high densities for people who are trying to go about their business in such environments. Furthermore, as Sundstrom (1975) demonstrated, whereas high density may decrease certain responses, for example, comfort and the intimacy of affiliative behavior, it has no intensifying effects upon reactions to other sources of irritation.

The present investigation was intended to speak to the effects of high density on the performance of complex tasks and to reevaluate the emotional concomitants of high-density situations. Saegert (1973, in press) argued that a more accurate understanding of the dynamics of high-density situations can be achieved by focusing on two components of such experiences: attentional overload and behavioral constraint.

OVERLOAD

When large numbers of people occupy a rather restricted space while engaging in individual tasks, the amount and complexity of situationally relevant information can lead to attentional overload. This hypotheses has been suggested by Milgram (1970) as an important determinant of urbanites' behavior; its implications for high-density situations generally have been discussed by Saegert (in press) and generalized to other conditions of environmental stress (Cohen, in press). The emotional and cognitive effects of such overload seem to be more serious when the subject is engaged in tasks requiring an understanding of and movement through the environment. Proximity to many other people engaged in at least partially unpredictable activities makes it difficult for the subject (a) to form a clear image of the environment at any particular time, (b) to predict its state in the future, and thus (c) to coordinate behaviors with others. Cognitively complex tasks requiring processing of environmental information, evaluation of alternatives, much decision making, and performance of consequent behaviors would be expected to produce more negative affect and lower task performance in higher density situations. A number of studies support these hypotheses but leave some questions unanswered (cf. Baum, Harpin, & Valins, 1975; Baum & Koman, 1976; Baum, Reiss, & O'Hara, 1974; Saegert et al., 1975; Valins & Baum, 1973).

The overload perspective emphasizes the cognitive involvement of the subject in experiences of crowding. Density per se is not seen as the primary determinant of task performance, affect, and social behavior, but rather as a physical condition that can give rise to attentional overload when a subject is engaged in active transactions with, or scanning of, the environment. The increased information in environments occupied by large numbers of people coupled with decreased behavioral freedom is seen as leading to a loss of both behavioral and cognitive control, conditions which can exacerbate the negative consequences of crowding even further. Thus the negative effects of high density are viewed not as direct consequences inevitably linked to this environmental condition, but rather as the outcome of interference with rather common types of exchanges with the environment. We assume that under many circumstances, people try to obtain relevant information from the environment, physically move about on the bases of such information, and coordinate their behaviors with others. High-density situations can add to the complexity and difficulty of accomplishing these activities.

COGNITIVE INTERVENTION

While it is difficult to decrease the density or increase a person's behavioral control in naturally occurring crowded situations, the overload perspective suggests the possibility of reducing the negative consequences of crowding through cognitive means. There has been recent evidence showing that when behavioral control is limited, individuals may still reduce the experienced aversiveness of a stressful situation through cognitive control. This may be accomplished (a) through a belief in control even when instrumental responding is unavailable (e.g., Bowers, 1968; Corah & Boffa, 1970; Glass & Singer, 1972); (b) through cognitive reappraisal of a threatening event (e.g, Ellis, 1962; Langer, Janis, & Wolfer, 1975; Meichenbaum, Note 2); or (c) by having information about physiological symptoms that allows for the exploration and validation of experience (e.g., Calvert-Boyanowsky & Leventhal, 1975; Ross, Rodin & Zimbardo, 1969; Staub & Kellet, 1972; Storms & Nisbett, 1970).

The following study was designed to test the proposition that the previously described aversiveness of a high-density situation that limits behavioral control could be attenuated by increasing the subject's cognitive control through the use of the last of the above-mentioned strategies, the presentation of information that explains and validates arousal. Indeed, a link between the research on crowding and the control literature has already been made by Rodin (1976), who showed that long-term crowding experiences can lead to a decreased desire to exert control. In the present study, a situation was chosen that required complex person–environment transactions; further, the environment that was selected was one that regularly becomes extremely crowded and in which such complex transactions are normally necessary. It should be emphasized that whereas most previous research has assessed the effects of density on tasks in which the behavior of others could not interfere, the present study clearly employed a task susceptible to behavioral interference. Subjects, recruited outside of a supermarket at crowded and uncrowded times, were given a long shopping list and told to choose the most economical product for each item. They were allowed 30 minutes to make as many selections as possible, then measures of their reactions to the situation were taken. Half of the crowded and half of the uncrowded subjects were given the information that many people feel somewhat anxious and aroused when supermarkets become crowded. Our predictions were that this information would increase both positive affect and task performance and that this would be especially true in crowded conditions. These predictions are particularly interesting, since the task employed, making the most economical decisions, involved complex calculations. Most studies of cognitive reduction of stress responses (e.g., Calvert-Boyanowsky & Leventhal, 1975; Ross et al., 1969) have indicated that attributions can affect physiological processes, comfort, and poststress task performance. None, however, has shown that complex task performance, usually reduced by stress, can be affected in this way.

METHOD

Subjects

Eighty women between the ages of 25 and 45 served as subjects in this study, 20 in each of the four conditions. Subjects were recruited, 1 at a time, outside of the two New York City grocery stores in which the study was conducted. Of the two experimenters, one carried out 64 experimental sessions and the other 16. Both experimenters ran an equal number of subjects in each of the four conditions. Within the crowded and uncrowded conditions, subjects were randomly assigned to one of the two information groups according to a predetermined schedule.

Subjects were approached by the experimenter and asked if they had time to spare to participate in a study of how people used their local grocery stores. They were offered $3 and were informed that the study involved choosing but not actually buying products to match a shopping list.

Procedure

The study employed a 2 × 2 factorial design, testing the effects of crowding and information. Crowding was varied by selecting subjects as they entered the grocery store at a time when it was either quite crowded or rather uncrowded. Experimenters recorded the number of people entering and leaving the store and the number on checkout lines to provide an objective estimate of density. In the two crowded conditions, these measures indicated more than twice as many people were using the store than in the uncrowded conditions, $F(1,76) = 45.00, p < .001; F(1,76) = 29.69, p < .001; F(1,76) = 46.65, p < .001$, respectively. There were no differences either between the two crowded or the two uncrowded conditions.

All subjects were given the following instructions after they agreed to participate:

Here is a shopping list. What we want you to do is to note which brand and size of each item you would buy so that it would cost you the least money. We want you to go through the list being as economical as possible. So, for example, if we asked you to buy a half gallon of milk, it might be cheaper to buy two quarts or it might be cheaper to buy a half gallon. Here is a pad with a shopping list.

You will have thirty minutes to choose the brands and quantities you would buy, for as many items as you can decide on in this amount of time. Again, please try to make the most economical decisions possible and try to complete as many items as you can, even though the list is too long to complete all of the items in thirty minutes.

The shopping list the subjects received, identical in all cases, asked for varying quantities of 50 familiar household items which were located throughout the store. Spaces were provided for writing down the brand, size, quantity, and total price of each item selected. The list was arranged so that if the subject simply began at the beginning and went through item after item, a great deal of movement would be required. Of course, subjects could organize the order in which they selected items to require fewer traverses of the store.

Information

Half of the subjects in both the crowded and uncrowded conditions were then given the following information: "While you are carrying out this task, the store may become crowded. We know from previous research that crowding sometimes causes people to feel aroused and sometimes anxious. We just wanted you to know this so that if you feel aroused or anxious you will know why." The remaining subjects were not given any information regarding the effects of crowding. Prior to entering the store, each subject was told the time and given a location where the experimenter would meet her 30 minutes later. Questions were answered and the task description was briefly reiterated.

When the time was up, the experimenter met the subject, collected the shopping list, and led the subject out of the store. At this time the subject was given a 7-item questionnaire entitled "Supermarket Survey Questionnaire" to complete. The subject was then paid and the purpose of the study was partially explained. Complete debriefing was not possible because experimenters were not informed of the hypotheses. It was, of course, impossible for them to be blind to the subject's condition, but in order to limit as much as possible the effects of experimenter bias, the two experimenters were told that they were a part of a larger study comparing shopper's behavior and attitudes in urban and suburban settings. After all subjects were run, the study was thoroughly explained to the experimenters.

Dependent Measures

The behavioral measures included the number of items that the subject completed and the number incorrect, that is, the uneconomical choices made. The postexperimental questionnaire given to the subjects was made up of questions concerning (a) satisfaction with the grocery store; (b) difficulty in finding products; (c) feelings of comfort in the store; (d) other customers getting in the subject's way; (e) difficulty in deciding on products; (f) crowdedness of the store; and (g) information about habitual shopping patterns. The first six questions were answered on 9-point rating scales. The last item was used only to confirm the comparability of the groups.

RESULTS

High Density

Our predictions about the effects of high-density situations were strongly confirmed. Crowding interfered with task performance. Significantly fewer items

were listed in the crowded ($M = 11.05$) than in the uncrowded condition ($M = 17.95$), $F(1,76) = 35.3, p < .001$. That is, crowded subjects attempted to find significantly fewer items than uncrowded subjects.

Subjects' shopping efficiency was also affected by crowding. The measure of efficiency used was the number of items *correctly* completed. The mean number of correct items for the crowded conditions was 8.43, as compared to 14.55 for the uncrowded conditions, $F(1,76) = 33.97, p < .01$.

Subjects in the crowded conditions also responded more negatively to all items on the questionnaire. They felt less satisfied with the supermarket, $F(1,76) = 5.56, p < .05$. They rated the items as more difficult to find, $F(1,76) = 20.0, p < .01$. Crowded subjects also were less comfortable, $F(1,76) = 18.6, p < .01$, and felt that others got in their way more, $F(1,76) = 33,49, p < .01$. They felt that they had a more difficult time deciding which items to choose, $F(1,76) = 41.68, p < .01$. They also experienced much more crowding, $F(1,76) = 125.17, p < .001$. The means for these measures are shown in Table 1.

Information

It was hypothesized that the negative effects of crowding outlined above could be attenuated by giving subjects information about the psychological effects of being in crowded situations. The predicted amelioration of negative emotional and behavioral consequences of crowding by the provision of this information was also obtained. Unexpectedly, this information seems to have had a beneficial influence even in the uncrowded condition. In the informed

Table 1 Mean Scores for Questionnaire Measures and Number of Items Completed as a Function of Density and Information

Measure	High density		Low density	
	Uninformed	Informed	Uninformed	Informed
Satisfaction with store	4.80	5.60	5.80	6.45
Ease in finding items	3.45	4.15	5.00	6.05
Customers in way[a]	3.10	4.50	5.20	6.80
Ease in decision making	3.45	4.10	5.10	6.75
Comfort[b]	3.10	5.45	5.20	6.45
Crowding[c]	2.70	3.50	6.05	6.90
Number of items attempted	8.50	13.60	14.95	19.95
Number of correctly completed items	6.81	3.66	2.61	3.09

[a] Lower score indicates more obstruction.
[b] Lower score indicates greater discomfort.
[c] Lower score indicates more perceived crowding.

conditions, ratings were significantly higher on five of the six questionnaire measures. These were as follows: ease of finding items, $F(1,76) = 5.14$, $p < .05$, the extent to which other customers interfered, $F(1,76) = 15.5$, $p < .01$, ease of decision making, $F(1,76) = 11.91$, $p < .01$, comfort, $F(1,76) = 25.02$, $p < .01$, and perceptions of crowding, $F(1,76) = 7.98$, $p < .01$.

The information provided also affected subjects' performance. Those in the informed conditions attempted more items on the shopping list, $F(1,76) = 22.01$, $p < .01$, and completed more items correctly (M informed = 13.25, M uninformed = 9.21), $F(1,76) = 18.54$, $p < .01$. No interactions between density and information were significant.

The means for the informed versus the uninformed conditions for each of these measures also appear in Table 1. As can be gleaned from the table, the order of the means for the four conditions for almost every measure taken, be it cognitive, affective, or behavioral, is the same. The least effective group was the uninformed/crowded, followed by the informed/crowded, uninformed/uncrowded, and finally informed/uncrowded group. A series of selected contrasts (McNemar, 1969) was performed to determine whether the experimental intervention reduced the high-density, informed subjects' responses to the same level as subjects in the low-density, uninformed condition. The absence of any significant differences on all seven measures indicated that, indeed, the subjects exhibited similar performances, attitudes, and feelings in both conditions. However, the same series of comparisons between the high- and low-density uninformed conditions revealed significant differences ($p < .01$) on all measures except satisfaction with the store and ease in finding items.

Before discussing these results, it is important to consider, first, an alternative, and indeed viable, interpretation to the one suggested by the findings as we have described them. Since subjects self-selected themselves into the crowded or uncrowded conditions, that is, chose the time of day to do their food shopping, it could have been that differences between the two groups of subjects, which are perhaps orthogonal to crowding, account for the above results. In order to assess this, subjects who shopped in the morning were compared to subjects who shopped in the afternoon within each condition. No differences were found between the two groups on either the behavioral or affective measures. Further, the subjects in all conditions were of comparable age; and self-report of habitual shopping patterns did not differ among the groups.

DISCUSSION

The findings of this study strongly indicate that high-density conditions may be aversive and that the aversiveness may be ameliorated by certain kinds of information. Unexpectedly, the information we provided for subjects increased their positive affect and task efficiency in the low-density conditions as well. The conclusions to be drawn from this study are as follows: (a) crowding can interfere with cognitive efficiency as well as with comfort and ease of behavior and (b) information about one's possible reactions to a situation works to the benefit of the person in that situation. Together these conclusions suggest that not only does crowding interfere with behavioral and cognitive control, but that even at noninterfering density levels, increased cognitive control is desirable.

The mechanism by which information improves cognitive efficiency and affect is not entirely clear. The most plausible explanation would seem to be that, having such information, people are more able (a) to select appropriate behavioral and cognitive strategies and (b) to feel and behave more confidently. This explanation is in keeping with other work suggesting that (a) the problematic aspect of high density has to do with information overload and behavioral constraint which combine to create difficulties for decision making and behavioral coordination (Saegert, 1973; Saegert et al., 1975) and (b) that, overall, a sense of control increases a person's feeling of confidence even when the salient events in question are not actually being controlled (Langer, 1975; Langer & Roth, 1975). Evidence already exists to support the notion that anticipation of crowding does result in behavioral and attitudinal adjustments, even when crowding is not actually experienced (Baum & Greenberg, 1975; Baum & Koman, 1976). The present study indicates that such anticipatory adjustments in fact allow the person to cope more successfully when actually in high-density situations. At this time we have no way of knowing if low-density subjects also were coping more effectively; although overall the stores were not crowded, it is possible that particularly congested areas were in fact encountered. For both groups, the impact of an increased sense of control cannot be separated from that of behavioral and cognitive adjustments.

One important implication of our findings is that information about possible reactions to an environment may not only make a person feel better, but may actually increase the attention available for tasks. This process could operate in a number of different ways.

As has been suggested, the person could perform more efficiently because of having selected more useful behavioral and information-processing strategies on the basis of the information received. However, the effect also could be the result of freeing the person from searching for explanations for his or her own feelings in the situation.

Probably the most significant implication of this study has to do with the critical role understanding seems to play in one's relationship with the environment. Clearly, for these subjects the greater their potential cognitive and behavioral control of the environment, the more effectively they behaved and the better they felt. Quite possibly, the sense of control was as significant as actual control; in fact, the requirement of controlling actions in such situations might even be negative, if more effort were necessary. Nonetheless, knowledge of one's potential relationships with the environment, which then allows the individual to choose courses of action, seems beneficial. Perhaps, as Proshansky, Ittelson, and Rivlin (1970) suggested, freedom of choice is really the critical issue in density-related phenomena. Both actual behavioral options and information about one's self and the environment contribute to such freedom.

It could be argued that the facilitative and relaxing effects of the information on subjects' task and affective responses reflect a reduction in test anxiety. This interpretation would imply that the findings of this study would generalize only to situations in which people were required to perform tasks that create some anxiety about performance. While this explanation is possible, the ecological validity of the task as well as the fact that subjects were tested in their habitual shopping environments, make it less plausible than it might be in a laboratory study.

Reference Notes

1. McCarty, D., & Saegert, S. *High-rise living, crowding and personal control.* Paper presented at the meeting of the Eastern Psychological Association, New York, April 1976.
2. Meichenbaum, D. H. *Cognitive factors in behavior modification: Modifying what clients say to themselves.* Paper presented at the meeting of the Association for the Advancement of Behavior Therapy, Washington, D.C., 1971.

References

Aiello, J. R., Epstein, Y. M., & Karlin, R. A. The effects of crowding on electrodermal activity. *Sociological Symposium,* 1975, Fall, 32-40.

Baum, A., & Greenberg, C. I. Waiting for a crowd: The behavioral and perceptual effects of anticipated crowding. *Journal of Personality and Social Psychology,* 1975, *32,* 671-679.

Baum, A., Harpin, R. L., & Valins, S. The role of group phenomena in the experience of crowding. *Environment and Behavior,* 1975, *7,* 185-198.

Baum, A., & Koman, S. Differential reponse to anticipated crowding: Psychological effects of social and spatial density. *Journal of Personality and Social Psychology,* 1976, *34,* 526-536.

Baum, A., Reiss, M., & O'Hara, J. Architectural variates of reaction to spatial invasion. *Environment & Behavior,* 1974, *6,* 91-101.

Bickman, L., et al. Dormitory density and helping behavior. *Environment and Behavior,* 1973, *5,* 465-490.

Bowers, K. Pain, anxiety and perceived control. *Journal of Consulting and Clinical Psychology,* 1968, *32,* 596-602.

Calhoun, J. B. Population density and social pathology. *Scientific American,* 1962, *206,* 139-148.

Calvert-Boyanowsky, I., & Leventhal, H. The role of information in attenuating behavioral responses to stress: A reinterpretation of the misattribution phenomenon. *Journal of Personality and Social Psychology,* 1975, *32,* 214-221.

Christian, J. J. Social subordination, population density and mammalian evolution. *Science,* 1970, *168,* 84-94.

Cohen, S. Environmental load and the allocation of attention. In A. Baum & S. Valins (Eds.), *Advances in environmental psychology.* Hillsdale, N.J.: Erlbaum, in press.

Corah, N. L., & Boffa, J. Perceived control, self-observation and response to aversive behavior. *Journal of Personality and Social Psychology,* 1970, *16,* 1-4.

D'Atri, D. Psychophysiological responses to crowding. *Environment and Behavior,* 1975, *7,* 237-252.

Davis, D. E. Physiological effects of continued crowding. In A. H. Esser (Ed.), *Behavior and Environment.* New York: Plenum Press, 1971.

Ellis, A. *Reason and emotion in psychotherapy.* New York: Lyle-Stuart, 1962.

Epstein, Y. M., & Karlin, R. A. Effects of acute experimental crowding. *Journal of Applied Social Psychology,* 1974, *5,* 34-53.

Freedman, J. L. *Crowding and behavior.* New York: Viking Press, 1975.

Freedman, J. L., Klevansky, S., & Ehrlich, P. R. The effects of crowding on human task performance. *Journal of Applied Social Psychology,* 1971, *1,* 7-25.

Glass, D. C., & Singer, J. E. *Urban stress.* New York: Academic Press, 1972.

Griffitt, W., & Veitch, R. Hot and crowded: Influences of population density and temperature on interpersonal affective behavior. *Journal of Personality and Social Psychology,* 1971, *17,* 92-98.

Langer, E. J. The illusion of control. *Journal of Personality and Social Psychology,* 1975, *32,* 311-328.

Langer, E. J., Janis, I., & Wolfer, J. A. Reduction of psychological stress in surgical patients. *Journal of Experimental Social Psychology,* 1975, *11,* 155-165.

Langer, E. J., & Roth, J. Heads I win, tails it's chance: The illusion of control as a function of sequence of outcomes in a purely chance task. *Journal of Personality and Social Psychology,* 1975, *32,* 951-955.

McCain, G., Cox, M., & Paulus, P. Illness complaints and crowding in prisons. *Environment and Behavior, 1976, 8,* 283-290.

McNemar, Q. *Psychological statistics.* New York: Wiley, 1969.

Milgram, S. The experience of living in cities. *Science,* 1970, *167,* 1,461-1,468.

Paulus, P., Annis, A. B., Seta, J. J., Schkade, J. K., & Mathews, R. W. Density does affect task performance. *Journal of Personality and Social Psychology,* 1976, *34,* 248-253.

Proshansky, H. M., Ittelson, W. H., & Rivlin, L. G. Freedom of choice and behavior in a physical setting. In H. Proshansky, W. Ittelson, & L. G. Rivlin (Eds.), *Environmental psychology: Man and his physical setting.* New York: Holt, Rinehart & Winston, 1970.

Rodin, J. Density, perceived choice and responses to controllable and uncontrollable outcomes. *Journal of Experimental Social Psychology,* 1976, *12,* 564-578.

Ross, L. D., Rodin, J., & Zimbardo, P. Toward an attribution therapy: The reduction of fear through induced cognitive emotional misattribution. *Journal of Personality and Social Psychology,* 1969, *12,* 279-288.

Saegert, S. Crowding: Cognitive overload and behavioral constraint. In W. Preiser (Ed.), *Environmental design research* (Vol. 2). Stroudsburg, Pa.: Dowden, Hutchinson and Ross, 1973.

Saegert, S. The effects of spatial and social density on arousal, mood and social orientation. Unpublished doctoral dissertation, University of Michigan, 1974. (Available from University Microfilms, Ann Arbor, Michigan)

Saegert, S. High density environments: Their personal and social consequences. In A. Baum & Y. Epstein (Eds.), *Human resources to crowding.* Hillsdale, N.J.: Erlbaum, in press.

Saegert, S., Mackintosh, E., & West, S. Two studies of crowding in urban public spaces. *Environment and Behavior,* 1975, *7,* 159-184.

Sherrod, D. Crowding, perceived control and behavioral after effects. *Journal of Applied Social Psychology,* 1974, *4,* 171-186.

Staub, E., & Kellet, O. S. Increasing pain tolerance by information about aversive stimuli. *Journal of Personality and Social Psychology,* 1972, *21,* 198-203.

Stokols, D., Rall, M., Pinner, B., & Schopler, J. Physical, social, and personal determinants of the perception of crowding. *Environment and Behavior,* 1973, *5,* 87-115.

Storms, M. D., & Nisbett, R. E. Insomnia and the attribution process. *Journal of Personality and Social Psychology,* 1970, *16,* 319-328.

Sundstrom, E. An experimental study of crowding, effects of room size, intrusion and goal blocking on nonverbal behavior, self-disclosure and self-reported stress. *Journal of Personality and Social Psychology,* 1975, *32,* 645-655.

Valins, S., & Baum, A. Residential group size, social interaction and crowding. *Environment and Behavior,* 1973, *5,* 421-439.

We would like to thank Cynthia Weinman and also Robert Redfield and Michele Rosenblatt for their careful execution of this research. In addition, we are grateful to Judy Rodin, Helen Newman, Reuben Baron, and Andrew Baum for having read and commented on an earlier draft of the manuscript.

Requests for reprints should be sent to Ellen Langer, Social-Personality Program, Graduate School and University Center, City University of New York, 33 West 42nd Street, New York, New York 10036.

Energy and Conservation

Reducing Air Conditioning Waste by Signalling it is Cool Outside[1]

Lawrence J. Becker   *Princeton University*
Clive Seligman

Abstract

This experiment looked at the effects on residential energy consumption of providing homeowners with (1) a signalling device that indicated a conservation opportunity and (2) information feedback about their rate of energy use. The signalling device operated when the outside temperature was below 68°F and the air conditioner was on. Homeowners were told that the signalling device indicated when they could cool their house effectively by opening the windows and turning off their air conditioner. Forty households were randomly assigned to one of four conditions: signalling device only, feedback only, both, neither. The results showed a significant 15.7% decrease in energy use for those households with the signalling devices. Neither the feedback nor interaction effect was significant. The advantages and disadvantages of having people in the control cycle were discussed.

Feedback or knowledge of results has long been known to be an effective aid to improved performance on a variety of tasks (Ammons, 1956; Bilodeau & Bilodeau, 1961). Recent research indicates that giving homeowners information feedback about their rate of residential electricity use is effective in reducing their consumption. Seligman and Darley (1977) found that homeowners who were given energy consumption feedback several times a week for approximately one

"Reducing Air Conditioning Waste by Signalling it is Cool Outside" by Lawrence J. Becker and Clive Seligman is reprinted from *Personality and Social Psychology Bulletin* Vol. 4, No. 3 (July 1978) pp. 412–415 by permission of The Society for Personality and Social Psychology and Lawrence J. Becker.

month used 10.5% less electricity than a control group. Becker (in press) demonstrated that a combined feedback and goal setting procedure led to a 13.0% reduction in residential electricity consumption compared to a control group. Groups that received neither feedback nor set a goal to save at least 20% of their energy use did not differ significantly from the control condition.

Feedback is a way of providing information to homeowners that informs them whether they are consuming too much energy. Presumably, homeowners whose feedback indicates wasteful consumption take corrective actions to reduce their energy use. Feedback is thus a signal that some energy control action is required. In the above studies, subjects were explicitly told that their best energy saving action was thermostat control. Therefore, waste-indicating feedback meant, to those homeowners, that they should raise the thermostat setting to reduce their air conditioning consumption. But there are also other ways to highlight the importance of thermostat control and to signal when it should be exercised.

One way that might help people living in air conditioned homes to reduce their electricity use during the summer is a signalling device that tells them when they can maintain their comfort without air conditioning by taking advantage of cooler outside temperatures. As the sun goes down the outside temperature drops. Sometimes, usually in the early and later periods of the day, the outside temperature actually drops below the temperature inside the house, even with the air conditioner on. It is at these times that it may be possible to maintain a house at a comfortable temperature without air conditioning simply by opening the windows.

To take advantage of "free" air conditioning by cooler outside temperatures requires that people in air conditioned homes be sensitive to outside temperatures. One of the rules for the proper use of an air conditioner is to keep doors and windows shut when an air conditioner is operating. Ironically, this reduces the residents' awareness of outside temperature. To the extent that unawareness of cool outside weather leads to wasteful air conditioning, a signalling device to increase such awareness should be an effective conservation tool.

The purpose of the present study was to look at the effects on summer electricity use of both a consumption feedback procedure and a cool-weather signalling device.

METHOD

Subjects. The study was conducted in a planned unit development in central New Jersey. A list was compiled of homeowners who live in three bedroom townhouses that are identical in floor plan, construction material, air conditioning system, and position in the interior of a row. Families on this list were called at random and asked if they would be willing to participate in an energy study. During the phone call, we said that we were interested in testing whether a signalling device we had designed would be helpful to people in reducing their energy consumption. Homeowners were told that we were drawing up a list of people who were interested, but since we were having trouble with our suppliers we were not sure how many of the people we contacted would finally get a test device. Homeowners were further told that if we did not have enough signalling devices we would choose people at random to receive them. Homeowners who agreed were told that we would get back to them in a few days. Forty homeowners agreed to participate and they were randomly assigned to one of four conditions: signalling device only, feedback information only, signalling device plus feedback, or neither (control). At the second phone call, subjects were informed as to whether they would receive a signalling device (or were given the appropriate apology) and in half the cases also were asked whether we could give them feedback information about their electricity use. All subjects agreed to participate in their assigned condition.

Signalling Device. The signalling device consisted of a 3.8-watt light bulb mounted in a 2½″ × 3½″ × ¾″ piece of maple-stained wood and covered in blue plexiglass. It was mounted on the side of the wall

phone where it could be seen from the kitchen and adjoining family room. The device was connected both to the air conditioner and to a thermostat we installed on the outside wall of the house. When the air conditioner was on *and* when the outside temperature was below 68° F, the blue light would blink repeatedly. The only way the homeowner could stop the blue light from blinking was to shut off the air conditioner. When the outside temperature was 68° F or higher, the blue light was off regardless of whether the air conditioner was on or off.

Feedback. Feedback was given for one month every Monday, Wednesday, and Friday. It was calculated by subtracting actual consumption for the most recent meter-reading period from predicted consumption for that period, then dividing the difference by predicted consumption. Predicted consumption for each house was determined by multiplying the cooling degree-hours[2] in the current feedback period by a house's consumption per cooling degree-hour index, which was determined from the ten weeks immediately preceding the start of the feedback. Feedback was marked on a 6″ × 9″ chart that fitted into a plastic pocket which was taped to the patio door of the family room. The feedback was displayed as "% conserved" or "% wasted" by marking the appropriate point on the chart and drawing a line between that point and the preceding one. This provided subjects with a record of their conservation performance over time that was visible from inside the house.

Procedure. All electric meters were read by a research assistant on August 10, 1977. Between August 10 and August 15 all signalling devices were installed and all feedback charts put up. From August 15 to September 12 feedback was given. Electric meters in all groups were read every Monday, Wednesday, and Friday.

RESULTS

The twelve meter-reading periods between August 15 and September 12 were divided into two sets based on whether the outside temperature dropped below 68° F, the point at which the signalling device could become operative.

Consider the six meter-reading periods during which the outside temperature fell below 68° F. An analysis of covariance (using pretreatment consumption as the covariate) revealed a significant effect due to the signalling device, $F(1,35) = 4.64$, $p < .04$. Homeowners with the signalling device used 15.7% less electricity than those without (see Table 1). Surprisingly, there was no significant feedback effect. Nor was there a significant interaction. During the meter-reading periods when the outside temperature did not drop below 68°F, no significant effects were found.

DISCUSSION

The results demonstrated that the signalling device was effective in alerting homeowners to a savings opportunity of which they apparently took advantage. The payback period for the device based on the savings achieved in this study would be about two years. State-sensing information systems, such as our signalling device, seem promising sources of energy consumption savings because they focus people's attention on specific conservation actions and do so exactly when these actions are appropriate. Indeed it is not hard to envision an energy control panel, perhaps situated somewhere in the kitchen, that provides homeowners with various detailed information about the house's energy performance and also indicates which energy conserving action to take.

Interestingly, removing the residents from the control cycle by eliminating the signal and, instead, connecting the device directly to the air conditioner would not necessarily make the system more effective. Admittedly, since people might not always heed the signal, there would be a gain if the device automatically turned off the air conditioner as soon as the outside temperature fell below 68°F. However, since there is a lag in time between a change in outdoor temperature and a corresponding change in indoor temperature, there would be a loss if the device automatically switched the air conditioner back on as soon as the outside temperature climbed over 68°F. Obviously, the longer the air conditioner remains off, the greater the savings; therefore it should be left to the residents to remember to turn on the air conditioner

again. Another advantage of signalling conservation opportunities rather than automating the system is that consumption is made more salient. This may increase people's general awareness of their consumption which may in turn lead them to conserve energy in additional ways not specifically indicated by the device.

In view of the positive conservation results of feedback in the Seligman and Darley (1977) and Becker (in press) studies, the failure of the feedback manipulation in the present study requires explanation. Interviews conducted after the experiment revealed that most residents thought the feedback scores jumped around too much to be believable. They reported seeing little relationship between their conservation actions and the feedback scores. Consequently, the feedback was ignored. The credibility of the feedback was not an issue in the two successful studies cited above. The main differences between the feedback given in the different experiments were in the methods of computation and display. In the previous experiments, predicted consumption used in the computation of feedback either was based on a regression model relating consumption to weather or used a control group correction for changes in weather. In this study, predicted consumption was based on pretreatment consumption per cooling degree-hour. Use of this index simplified calculations but, unfortunately, yielded less accurate feedback scores. In the Seligman and Darley (1977) study, feedback was not displayed over time, only for each feedback period. Thus swings in feedback over time were less salient. In the Becker (in press) study, feedback was displayed over time on a chart, but each feedback score was based on the whole period since the experiment began. Therefore, the feedback, being averaged over longer times, was actually smoother than it would have been if individual feedback periods were used. It appears that in the present experiment both the method of computation and the way it was displayed served to exaggerate the swings in feedback making it less credible. This result, of course, underscores the importance of providing credible feedback.

Footnotes

[1] This research was supported by DOE contract No. EY-76-5-02-2789. We would like to thank John Darley, Gautam Dutt, Dave Harrje, and Frank Sinden for advice and Roy Crosby, Ken Gadsby, Ray Kang, and Herb Mertz for technical assistance. Requests for reprints should be sent to Larry Becker, Psychology Department, Princeton University, Princeton, NJ 08540.

Table 1 Mean Daily Electric Consumption (KWH)

| | Signalling Device | |
	Yes	No
Feedback	18.30 (2.96)	20.61 (5.69)
No Feedback	18.24 (4.50)	22.76 (6.02)

Note: Means are adjusted by removing the effect of the covariate. Standard deviations are given in parentheses.

[2]Cooling degree-hours are the number of degrees that the average temperature in an hour exceeds 65°F. For example, if the average temperature in an hour is 75°F, then the cooling degree-hours equal 10 (75°–65°). To get the cooling degree-hours for any period, sum the cooling degree-hours over the hours in that period.

References

Ammons, R. B. Effects of knowledge of performance: A study and tentative theoretical formulation. *Journal of General Psychology,* 1956, *54,* 279-299.

Becker, L. J. The joint effect of feedback and goal setting on performance: A field study of residential energy conservation. *Journal of Applied Psychology,* in press.

Bilodeau, E. A. & Bilodeau, I. Motor skills learning. *Annual Review of Psychology,* 1961, *12,* 243-280.

Seligman, C. & Darley, J. M. Feedback as a means of decreasing residential energy consumption. *Journal of Applied Psychology,* 1977, *67,* 363-368.

Energy Demand Behavior in a Master-Metered Apartment Complex: An Experimental Analysis

James M. Walker   *Department of Economics, Texas A & M University*

Abstract

In a master-metered apartment complex, electricity use is metered at a single point for all tenants so that tenants do not pay energy bills based on their individual use. This article reports the results of an experiment with such a complex. The experiment demonstrates the successful development of an alternative method for making tenants liable for their own energy use. The experiment was conducted in a 176-unit master-metered apartment complex with a resident population of approximately 325. A similar complex served as a control. Tenants, whose apartments were checked at random, were paid cash rewards for meeting a specified energy conservation checklist. A comparison of samples, designed to monitor electricity consumption behavior during preexperimental and experimental periods, showed statistically significant changes in behavior between the two periods. Comparing electricity use in the experimental complex with electricity use in the control supported a hypothesis of significant reductions in electricity use by the experimental complex.

A research question that arises from the "energy crisis" concerns the use of electricity in master-metered apartment complexes and office buildings (in which electricity use is metered at a single point for all tenants) compared with electricity use in individually metered apartments. Comparisons of electricity use between master-metered and individually metered apartments in 10 large cities have shown that master-metered buildings use about 35% more electricity than individually metered buildings (Midwest Research Institute, Note 1). Estimates of this nature may be biased upward because differences between building units may obtain from self-selection biases such as household and business decisions to rent a master-metered unit instead of renting an individually metered unit. But, self-selection bias notwithstanding, once the tenant and the lessor have agreed on a fixed rent, one would predict higher use levels in master-metered units, since the cost to a tenant of each additional unit of electricity used is zero for the agreed rental period.

A standard solution for decreasing the quantity of

electricity consumed in master-metered buildings is to replace the master-meter with individual meters. When retrofitting simply requires the installation of individual meters, the rapidly increasing cost of electricity and the relatively low cost of individual meters (between $100 and $150) has made retrofitting a practical alternative. The result is more buildings being given individual meters. However, in many cases in which separate units share major electricity-using devices such as space heating and cooling equipment, metering individual tenants would require replacing this equipment with individually controlled units, causing increased conversion costs that might not be economically feasible. Under these circumstances an alternative method might still be found for reducing the quantity of electricity used, provided that the cost of each additional unit of electricity used by a tenant is positive and that these costs can be individualized so that the tenant recognizes that his or her own energy using behavior determines his or her costs. Unfortunately, it is not known whether feasible procedures exist for implementing such a plan, or under which conditions these procedures would prove cost effective. Researchers in the area of energy conservation (e.g., Cook & McClelland, Note 2) have experimented with various forms of rebates to tenants. But these researchers have focused on experimental designs in which subjects were divided into groups and rebates paid to the groups as a whole. Cook and McClelland (Note 2) reported significant reductions in electricity use for the rebate group during the first 2-week contest period. However, savings attributed to this group declined over time until by the sixth contest period, none of the rebate groups used significantly less energy.

When tenants earn rebates as a group, the individual tenant is inclined to perceive his or her own energy use as having little impact on the consumption of the group. Thus, tenants can be expected to show less response to group rebates.

The present experiment used monetary rebates to produce energy-conserving behaviors, but the rebates were awarded differently than in previous studies. Each tenant could receive a rebate if he or she made adjustments known to reduce the energy use of his or her unit. Specifically, occupants were given cash awards of $5 if on inspection, their windows were found closed and the thermostat was set to a lower than normal setting on a cold day or a higher than normal setting on a hot day. The research tested whether the announcement of the prize would increase the percentage of people exhibiting energy-conserving behaviors and whether that increase would be detectable as an energy consumption decrease for the experimental apartment complex when compared to a control complex.

METHOD

Subjects

The experiment took place in an all-electric, master-metered apartment complex in College Station, Texas, comprised of efficiency, one-bedroom, and two-bedroom apartments. This complex was chosen because it is typical of the apartment complexes in the College Station community and because the apartment owners were willing to supply the money for the rebates. Tenants were predominantly college students, and less than 2% had children. There were 176 apartment units in the complex with a resident population of approximately 325 people. Another all-electric complex in the area, similar in size and resident characteristics, served as a control unit. Occupancy rates in both complexes were approximately constant throughout the experimental period.

Tenants in the experimental complex were informed by letters distributed to each apartment that they were not *required* to participate. Tenants in the control apartment complex received no information concerning the experiment since their involvement was only in terms of having the master meter for the control complex read weekly by the experimental personnel.

Procedure

The experiment consisted of two parts: (a) a 4-week period beginning in early September 1976, when air conditioning is an important component of energy demand and (b) a 6-week period beginning in February 1977, when space heating comprises a substantial part of total electricity use. Both experimental periods coincided with the university in full session.

Tenants of the experimental complex received a $5 cash payment if their apartments satisfied the following criteria: (a) All windows and doors in the apartment had to be closed except when the cooling or heating unit was in the off position; (b) when the cooling unit was on, the thermostat had to be set at 74°F (23.3°C) or above; and (c) when the heating unit was on, the thermostat had to be set at 69°F (20.6°C) or below.

Apartments were checked randomly between 9:00 a.m. and 8:00 p.m. on any day to see if these criteria were met. Apartments were only checked when someone was at home to let the inspector in; tenants had the right to refuse entry at any time and to ask to be permanently excluded from the program. (Tenants in fewer than 2% of the apartments asked not to be included in the study.) The inspector was virtually never refused entry.

Apartments were checked each week until 10 tenants whose apartments met the criteria established in the checklist were found. The apartment check was conducted on three days that were chosen randomly along with the time of the inspection. On the first day, apartments were checked until four were found that met the checklist and on the next 2 days until three were found. Apartments to be checked were chosen by randomly drawing individual tenant's names so that all tenants had an equal chance of earning the $5. A tenant who won was not eligible to win again during the same week but was eligible during the succeeding weeks. Because tenants' names were drawn randomly, a single apartment could have more than one winner in a week. If the tenant whose name had been drawn was at home, and if his or her apartment satisfied the checklist, the $5 cash payment was made on the spot. If the tenant whose name had been drawn was not at home but one of his or her roommates was at home to let the inspector in, a note was left to inform the winner that the money could be picked up at the manager's office. Winners could share winnings as they desired.

Letters describing these procedures were distributed to each apartment several days before the beginning of each phase of the experiment. The letters explained that the study was being sponsored by the owners of the apartment in hope of reducing utility bills. By informing the manager or the student checking apartments, tenants could elect not to participate. The letters emphasized, however, that satisfying the checklist criteria was an easy way to win cash. The number of payment weeks was indicated for each phase of the program, although no indication was given in the first experimental period that there was to be a second one. The term *experiment* was never used in communications with subjects; instead, "energy conservation program" was used. Signs strategically placed in the complex noted the checklist criteria and emphasized the money that tenants could earn.

We wanted the energy checklist criteria to be easy for tenants to understand and to comply with as well as easy for us to enforce. We also wanted the criteria to be consistent with tenants' rights to privacy and to result in statistically significant reductions in energy use if a high percentage of tenants complied with it.

It was very helpful to this study that information existed about the relationship between electricity use and criteria that could be monitored individually, such as those in our checklist. Engineering research indicates that approximately 80% of total household consumption of electricity is used for space heating and cooling. Limiting the checklist to this demand source greatly simplified matters. The air conditioning thermostat criteria of 74°F (23.3°C) was based on two considerations: (a) Samples taken in the summer prior to the experiment showed an average thermostat setting of 71°F (21.7°C), and (b) engineering literature indicates that each increase of 1°F (.56°C) in thermostat setting results in about a 3% reduction in use. From these considerations and an earlier estimate of the variance in weekly energy use between the experimental and control apartments, it was determined that a 74°F (23.3°C) thermostat setting would be adequate to give significant experimental effects. Finally, one thermostat criterion was used because increasing payments for increasingly higher valued thermostat settings would have complicated the checklist and, given our budget constraint, would have involved lower payments for the minimally sufficient setting of 74°F (23.3°C) and/or reductions in the number of weekly payments. Using data from a sample taken during the winter prior to the second experimental period and using considerations similar to a and b above, the criterion for the heating thermostat was established.

An obvious problem was that tenants could readjust the thermostat when our inspector announced himself. To guard against this, the inspector used a thermometer that accurately read room temperature within a matter of seconds. In addition, both types of activities would be costly for tenants relative to the potential returns. Another problem was that tenants could satisfy the criteria during checking times and violate them outside the inspection periods. Circumstances militated against this behavior because of the bother in remembering to change the thermostat and because the criteria did not push temperatures outside the normal comfort zone.

Analysis

Because of these potential monitoring problems, analysis of the experiment is presented in two parts. First, the percentage of apartments meeting the checklist criteria during the experiment is compared to those meeting them prior to the experiment. The data for preexperimental periods were drawn in samples collected immediately prior to each phase at the same time as mean thermostat settings were determined. Statistically significant differences in these data would tend to support the hypothesis that experimental conditions effectively altered behavior, a necessary condition to attribute any reductions in energy use between the experimental and control complex to the experimental intervention.

Second, electricity consumption during the experimental period is compared for the experimental complex relative to the control. This analysis tests whether the experimental contingencies were effective in altering electricity use. The initial approach to comparing the electricity use of the two complexes is to transform the data on weekly use to percentage change in use during the experiment relative to a preexperimental base. In the first phase of the experiment, the week immediately preceding the experimental period served as the base. For the second phase of the experiment, the first 2 full weeks of school for the spring semester during which the experiment took place served as the base. The lengths of both base periods were limited (a) by the constraint that the university be in session for the apartment complexes to be fully occupied and (b) by changing weather conditions if the experiment were delayed. Once the weekly data are transformed into percentage change relative to base, the weekly percentage change of the experimental complex is statistically compared to the change for the control. This method allows for normalization of differences in absolute use levels between the two complexes and controls for changes in factors such as weather.

An alternative approach for comparing changes in electricity use of the experimental complex relative to that of the control is also tested. In comparing weekly electricity use relative to a base, a potential bias in the results is the possibility of recording an abnormal base use for either the experimental complex or the control complex. This could lead to a misinterpretation of the data and could suggest a reduction in relative use of the experimental complex even though no reduction took place (Campbell & Stanley, 1966). To guard against this misinterpretation, an extended baseline was recorded. The baseline was in the form of weekly readings of electricity use for the two complexes going back to November of the previous year. The tenant population was not exactly the same during the entire period, but there was a large degree of overlap; new tenants probably had similar energy habits since they were virtually all college students. Weekly electricity use records were gathered on the experimental and control complexes beginning in November preceding the experiment and continuing through the experimental periods, excluding vacation periods and summer months when occupancy rates in the two complexes varied. The weekly difference in electricity use of the two complexes is then modeled using the following least squares multiple regression model:

$$\text{Diff}_t = a_1 + a_2 \text{DD}_t + a_3 \text{Dum}_t + e_t \tag{1}$$

where Diff_t is the difference in weekly energy use of the two complexes, DD_t is a proxy variable for weather change measured by summing the absolute value of (average daily temperature minus 65°F [18.3°C]) over all days of the week, Dum_t is a dummy variable with a value of 0 for nonexperimental weeks and a value of 1 for the experimental weeks, and e_t is a random error term. The factor of primary importance in testing this model is whether the coefficient a_3 is negative and significantly different from 0. If this is the case, it supports the hypothesis of a reduction in energy use of the experimental complex relative to the control complex during the experimental period.

RESULTS

Table 1 presents data concerning the percentage of apartments meeting the checklist criteria during the two phases of the experiment and the measurements obtained from samples drawn prior to each phase. Using the normal approximation to the binomial distribution, we can test the null hypothesis of no difference between the experimental and nonexperimental periods (Ostle & Mensing, 1975, pp. 133-134). The null hypothesis was rejected in both cases, with $p < .012$ in Phase 1 and $p < .0001$ in Phase 2.

Figure 1 illustrates the weekly variation of the difference in percentage change in electricity use, relative to base, of the experimental complex compared to the control complex. More specifically, for each week, the following measurement is given:

$$[(\text{Use}_{Et} - B_E)/B_E] \\ - [(\text{Use}_{Ct} - B_C)/B_C] \tag{2}$$

Table 1 Percentage of Subjects Meeting Checklist

Item	Phase 1		Phase 2	
	Preexperimental	Experimental	Preexperimental	Experimental
Sample size	32	59	21	82
% meeting checklist[a]	.4375	.6779	.1429	.7317

[a] Difference between preexperimental percentage meeting checklist and experimental percentage meeting checklist: for Phase 1, $Z = 2.236$, $p < .012$; for Phase 2, $Z = 4.939$, $p < .0001$.

where Use_{Et} is the electricity use of the experimental complex in Week t, B_E is the base use for the experimental complex, Use_{Ct} is the electricity use of the control complex in Week t, and B_C is the base use for the control.

A one-tailed statistical test was used in testing hypotheses concerning these data, since the experimental contingencies are hypothesized to either increase the percentage of subjects meeting the checklist or to have no effect. Analysis of the data shows a statistically significant reduction of 8.6% by the experimental complex compared to the control complex during the first phase of the experiment, $t(6) = 4.33$, $p < .01$. During the second experimental period there was an average reduction of 2.2% in electricity use for the experimental complex relative to the control complex, which is not statistically significant, $t(10) = 1.36$. However, it was discovered that the management of the control complex had sent

Fig. 1. Difference Between Experimental Complex and Control in Percentage Change in Weekly Use Relative to Base.

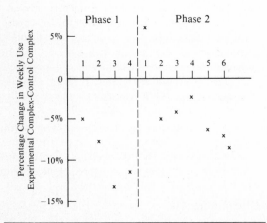

letters to each tenant at the beginning of the first experimental week, asking the tenants whether they would rather pay higher rent due to increased utility costs or have a rental plan in which tenants pay their own utility bills. Conceivably this letter had the short-term effect of inducing the control complex tenants to reduce their energy use. It can also be argued that after the first week, participation in the experimental complex increased as tenants heard about rebates being made. This argument is supported by earlier findings that show a positive correlation between subject response and reception of payments (Battalio, Kagel, Winkler, & Winett, in press) and by results from the first weeks of Phase 1. Omitting the first week, the average difference in electricity use for Phase 2 resulted in a mean significant reduction by the experimental complex of 3.4% when compared to control, $t(8) = 5.23$, $p < .01$.

Table 2 shows the multiple regression results for the second approach used to test the hypothesis of a reduction in electricity use by the experimental complex relative to the control complex. The coefficient for the degree day variable (DD_t) was not significantly different from zero ($p < .50$, two-tailed test). But the coefficient for the dummy variable (Dum_t), used to distinguish between experimental and nonexperimental periods, was negative and statistically significant, $t(20) = 2.45$, $p < .015$, one-tailed test.

DISCUSSION

Of first concern in the experimental analysis was the hypothesis that the experimental contingencies would alter behavior in the experimental complex so that a higher percentage of tenants would be satisfying checklist criteria compared to preexperimental samples. This hypothesis is strongly supported by the findings of both phases of the experiment. Because the method of analysis used to test this hypothesis compares tenants against themselves before and after intervention, there is the possibility that noncontrolled factors (e.g., a national appeal to lower thermostat settings just before the experiment began) influenced the above results. Even though such artifacts cannot be ruled out, the fact that the results of Phase 2 support the results of Phase 1 greatly reduces the chances that artifacts influenced the above results.

Given results that support a hypothesis of changed energy use behavior in the desired direction, the next question of concern is whether the behavior changes resulted in significant reductions in electricity use of the experimental complex compared to the control complex. Using two different approaches for comparing electricity use of the two apartment complexes, the hypothesis that the electricity use of the experimental complex is reduced relative to the control complex is supported in both cases. With regard to the higher savings found during Phase 1 relative to Phase 2, the following hypothesis should be considered: Because the experimental criteria involved air conditioning or heating, the effectiveness of the experimental conditions was dependent on the outside temperature during experimental weeks. Examination of data gathered during the first experimental period shows temperatures conducive to cooling (i.e., afternoon temperatures primarily in the range of 85°F [29.4°C] to 95°F [35°C] and average weekly degree days equal to 95.5°F [35.3°C]). But, in contrast to the first period, the second experimental period was accompanied by milder days not conducive to large amounts of heating or cooling (i.e., afternoon temperatures primarily in the range of 60°F [15.6°C] to 75°F [23.9°C] and average weekly degree days equal to 64.4°F [18°C]).

Also important to the conclusions of this experiment was the finding that in the weeks following intervention, particularly in the second week, significant lags were found in energy use differences between the two complexes in returning to their preexperi-

mental levels. Comparable behavior has been reported in other energy experiments in single-family residences (Battalio et al., in press) and is consistent with concepts of habit formation in application of consumer demand theory (Phlips, 1974). To further test whether a lagged effect existed, thermostat settings were checked in the experimental and control complexes 5 weeks after all experimentation. (During this period the weather was conducive to air conditioner use.) The sample results showed an average thermostat setting in the experimental complex that was 1.7°F (.94°C) higher, $t(33) = 1.89$, $p < .05$, one-tailed test, than the average setting of the control apartments. In contrast, three preexperimental samples of comparable size taken during the summer and during the week before the experiment showed no significant difference in average thermostat settings or apartment temperatures for the two apartment complexes, $N_1 = 15$, $t(14) = .22$; $N_2 = 23$, $t(22) = .32$; $N_3 = 25$, $t(24) = .38$. The persistence of the changes in electricity use patterns some five weeks following the termination of the experimental procedures seems to indicate that the results reported are not simply short-run responses but indicate what one is likely to find in a long-term application. If shown to be consistent, this type of result would be expected to increase the savings from the experimental procedures and to increase the magnitude of potential rebates.

Finally, several points should be made about the implementation and cost effectiveness of this experiment. First, the procedures were easy to administer. The inspector had no difficulty in checking apartments and was not treated as a nuisance by the tenants. It would have been helpful if postexperimental data had been collected with regard to differences in attitudes of tenants who had and had not received rebates. This type of data is not available for this particular experiment but should be considered in future studies.

Table 2 Comparison of Preexperimental to Experimental Differences in Weekly Energy Use: Results of Ordinary Least Squares Estimation

Dependent variable	Intercept	DD_t	DUM_t	R^2	Durbin-Watson
Weekly difference in kilowatt hour use (Experimental complex–control complex)	2276.50	17.02	−3083.4*	.22	1.41[a]
t ratio		.754	2.448		

[a] With the sample size of 23, we do not reject the hypothesis of no correlation between residual terms.
* Significant at .015 level (one-tailed test).

The cost effectiveness of the program depends on the costs of distributing information to tenants and monitoring checklists, the size of payments, and savings due to reduced energy use. The average experimental reduction in energy use relative to control was approximately 4.9%. On an average monthly use of 250,000 kwh, and with the price of each additional kwh equal to $.026, this yields a savings of $320 a month, as opposed to payments to tenants totaling $200 per month. Thus, the study showed a surplus that could finance the operating expenses of such a plan. These expenses vary among apartments, but the primary expense is the man-hours needed for inspection. A rough estimate for our experiment is approximately 6 hours a week. Because little training is necessary to inspect apartments, the cost of these man-hours is about $30 per week ($120 per month). Thus, even after allowing for expenses for inspection, an $80 surplus remains.

It is interesting to note that although the 4.9% reduction in electricity use seems small compared to the estimated potential savings of 35% cited earlier (MRI, Note 1), the potential savings reported for the study in Houston, a city with a climate similar to that of College Station, is only about 10% to 15%. This difference between the Houston and the MRI studies can be explained in part by the composition of the apartments surveyed; the Houston apartments used electricity for space heating and cooling whereas in some areas electricity is used primarily for purposes other than heating or cooling. This suggests that the effects of incentives designed to reduce energy use may vary between uses and with climatic factors, a result that is supported by other research (Battalio et al., in press). For this reason and others, such as tenant characteristics and peculiarities of procedures inherent in any experimental design, we caution against hasty generalization of the results reported here.

Reference Notes

1. Midwest Research Institute. *Energy Conservation Implications of Master Metering* (Final Rep., Vol. 1, MRI Project 4008-E) Kansas City, Missouri, October 1975.
2. Cook, S. W., & McClelland, L. *Motivating occupants of master metered buildings to conserve energy.* Unpublished manuscript, Institute of Behavioral Science, University of Colorado, June 1977.

References

Battalio, R. C., Kagel, J. H., Winkler, R. C., & Winett, R. A. Residential electricity demand: An experimental study. *Review of Economics and Statistics,* 1978, in press.

Campbell, D. T., & Stanley, J. C. *Experimental and quasi-experimental designs for research.* Chicago: Rand McNally, 1966.

Ostle, B., & Mensing, R. W. *Statistics in research* (3rd ed.). Iowa State University Press, 1975.

Phlips, L. *Applied consumption analysis.* New York: American Elsevier, 1974.

I would like to thank R. C. Battalio and J. H. Kagel for their assistance in this project. I am also grateful to an anonymous reviewer for several helpful comments.

This research was supported in part by a grant from the National Science Foundation.

Requests for reprints should be sent to James M. Walker, Department of Economics, University of Arizona, Tucson, Arizona 85721.

9

Program Evaluation and Evaluation Research

Although no one would say that we have definitely reached the condition of having an experimenting society, clearly we are getting closer to that state. With increasing frequency, social scientists are called on to help develop and assess social change; more and more social decisions are based on social science information.

The heart of this new orientation involves the application of experimental and quantitative methods to social data. Of these methods, program evaluation and evaluation research are the most typical analytical approaches which relate social sciences to social processes as they occur in society.

There are only slight differences between the terms program evaluation and evaluation research. Generally, the former is used to refer to assessment of the outcome effectiveness of a fairly specific social action program. Evaluation research has a somewhat broader connotation, referring to the analysis of changes induced by broad-ranging alterations in societal arrangements such as formal laws, government regulations, and economic changes. The similarities in these approaches are more important than the differences. Both are characterized by an interest in determining how some change in a social variable or process affects other social variables or processes, including individual behavior. The central features of this type of research are similar to those of laboratory research: (1) selection of appropriate measures in such ways as to insure adequate assessment of experimental and control conditions, (2) objectivity, and (3) quantifiable measurement when possible.

Evaluation in society represents a new set of challenges to researchers. Often the data comes from archival sources such as crime statistics, divorce records, public health records, and census tract information. Since the manipulations of program variables are often systemwide and everyone receives the treatment, it often is difficult to locate and assess appropriate control conditions and retrieving data for hypothesis testing often is difficult. Also, with this type of approach, the hypotheses are formulated and tested after the program already is in effect.

Of course there are a number of advantages and strengths of this type of research too. Since in most cases the program has already been instituted before the investigator is called in, the impact of the program can be investigated very broadly; often programs have an impact not directly expected, so the investigator can search broadly throughout the society to find unexpected influences, those not necessarily planned on in the initial development and implementation of the program. Serendipitous findings often are critical to the change, or elimination, of programs. Another advantage of this type of research is its close and intimate connection with real ongoing social processes; laboratory research often distorts ordinary social conditions in order to obtain necessary control and rigor, whereas natural experimentation relates directly to society. Finally, large samples of people are usually involved in program change, and thus the problems of representativeness and translation into natural conditions are not as pressing as they are in laboratory research with small samples which often are not typical of the larger societal context. Since the great majority of evaluation studies so far published relate to government-induced changes in laws, procedures, and policies concerning various segments of society, that type of research comprises the evaluation section of *Experimenting in Society*. The studies selected for this section were chosen because they involve relatively specific analyses, they delimit variables, and feature clear discussions of the methods used and the results obtained.

The first research section concerns health. The first article in this section studies nutritional characteristics of infants and mothers. The research demonstrates that a government-sponsored nutrition-enhancement project can have important beneficial affects on infants' physical and cognitive growth. Conversely, the other study reprinted here shows that people's health can be damaged by crowding in prisons. It shows that prison mortality rates are significantly increased in more crowded prisons. Both evaluations have implications for governmental policies which affect the development and maintenance of the health of individuals. The application of appropriate scientific methodology has clarified the nature of the policies and their impact on individuals.

The next section of the book concerns the family. The research in this section shows how marital stability is influenced by welfare programs. Even though the original plan for public welfare and economic aid was to help families in distress, the results of the first study show that divorce rates are significantly increased by welfare payments. The other study in this section shows that making divorce easier through no-fault divorce laws does not necessarily lead to general increases in divorce rates.

The final set of readings concerns one of society's most important contemporary problems, crime and criminal justice. This section contains two good examples of explicit program evaluation: One a careful scientific analysis of projects implemented to change criminal behavior and one used to reduce traffic fatalities. The first study shows that a Jamaican anticrime policy barring the sale and possession of guns was followed by a reduction in homicide rates. The investigators went beyond a superficial analysis of the data, however, and conclude that the reduction probably was not due to a reduced number of guns. Similarly, the other study shows that automobile-crash fatality rates may be increased when driver-education courses are provided for youth below the regular driving age of eighteen years.

These evaluation studies are useful examples of the impact of evaluation research. Although studies can analyze programs for the effects they are intended to have, they also are useful for detecting unintended influences, impacts which reach beyond the initial concepts behind the programs and have consequences, sometimes undesirable ones, that otherwise might not have been seen. The scientific approach is well suited to provide information on society and how it operates. The readings in this section are representative of the wide range of areas in which social scientists reveal the complex workings of the social arrangements we have developed.

HEALTH

Overpopulation and poverty often combine in many areas of the world to produce unfavorable living conditions. One of the major consequences of these conditions is malnutrition, and in the early stages of a child's development, this can have serious long-term consequences. Cognitive development as well as physical development can be hindered. Obviously, the mental ability of a country's citizens is critical to its future, so investigating the relationship between the nutritional health of mothers and their children and the children's later cognitive development would be very important to a government. The evaluation research project reported by Freeman, Klein, Kagan, and Yarbrough ("Relations between nutrition and cognition in rural Guatemala") demonstrates such a relationship.

The investigators were involved in assessing the impact of a nutrition-improvement program conducted by the Guatemalan government. The project extended over a number of years, so longitudinal data were available for assessing the impact of the program across several levels of birthyears. Fortunately, the investigators were able to develop a useful experimental design because two rural villages received enhanced nutritional treatment for their residents while two other villages which also were available for assessment did not.

The experiment sought to determine if nutritional enhancement in the form of daily high-protein food supplements would have a favorable impact on young children. The variables chosen to reflect that impact were wide-ranging: Cognitive factors such as language, memory, and perceptual ability revealed the impact on mental ability, and physical ability was assessed by measuring growth in height and head circumference. Since the role of economic and social factors might be just as powerful as nutrition, measures of these also were obtained. This multimeasure approach represents an impressive method of analysis but did not disturb the project's operation in the natural environment of the villages.

The results show a pattern of significant relationships between the nutrition and health measures: Children whose mothers had the nutritional supplement grew more and had higher scores on cognitive development measures than those not having the supplement. The economic and social variables also related significantly to the cognitive and physical measures, but more detailed additional analyses showed that the contribution of the nutrition factor was somewhat greater.

This data is very important. The protein supplement treatment is a relatively simple procedure for governments to implement. The cognitive and physical growth of children is of critical importance to a society concerned about its future. Of course before governments can be expected to undertake implementation of large-scale social programs they should undertake evaluation of smaller-range projects to carefully determine their impact. Program evaluation techniques are excellent assessors of the impact of those projects.

Paulus, McCain, and Cox ("Death rates, psychiatric commitments, blood pressure, and perceived crowding as a function of institutional crowding") investigate another facet of health and social conditions. Pursuing the notion that high density living can cause harmful effects (based on laboratory animal research), they asess the well-being of prisoners living in prisons of low, medium, and high density. They obtained measures of medical facts, prisoners' subjective perceptions of crowdedness, and measures of psychiatric well-being. The investigators note that prisons force continual and close contact between people while at the same time strongly limiting their privacy and freedom; that combination might be expected to have some measurable effects on psychological and physical well-being.

The results are quite consistent in showing that more crowded prisons have more negative effects on the prisoners than less crowded ones. Death rates were higher when prisons were more crowded; circulatory system diseases were involved in those higher morality figures. Also, there is a significant correlation between prison population size and the frequency of commitments to psychiatric centers. By using density measures (number of prisoners per square foot in cells), the investigators also found that blood pressure measures were higher in higher density conditions as were the prisoners' perception of the crowdedness of their living conditions.

Taken as a whole, the data shows a compelling picture of an unintended consequence of crowded prisons. This study brings into question the ability of prisons to carry out their rehabilitation functions; the very living conditions of prisons may be working against rehabilitation efforts. Remedy for such a problem would seem to lie in political and social changes outside the prisons, and that would require a willingness on society's part to actively use scientific information such as that gained in this study.

THE FAMILY

Government programs to aid citizens vary, but the intent of all of them is the same: To improve the welfare of citizens and thus to strengthen social relationships and to provide stability for the country. It is only recently, however, that social scientists have become involved in efforts to analyze systematically the impact of those social programs. Their role may ultimately turn out to be critical, for often such programs are subjects of controversy. Doubts about the wisdom of direct government influence on matters of individual welfare have been expressed by some organized groups while, of course, other groups are supportive. Social scientists can play a role in reducing conflicts by developing adequate assessment of the programs and detecting the intended and unintended impacts those programs have. We hope that accurate information can be used creatively to resolve differences and to orient helping for maximum effectiveness.

The study by Bahr ("The effects of welfare on marital stability and remarriage") is an example of evaluation research which assesses the impact of organized government programs. It is concerned with determining the impact of the program, Aid to the Families with Dependent Children (AFDC). Since that program is intended to provide economic aid to families in distress, it might be expected it would result in stabilized families. Bahr chose to analyze some measures of family stability such as rates of divorce, separation, and remarriage. He compares the rates from a nationwide sample of families receiving AFDC with those from a comparable sample of families not receiving aid. Age and race factors have been shown to be related to family stability, so these data were assessed too.

Although one might expect AFDC to help marital stability, it is possible that, under certain conditions, welfare payments may in fact discourage marriage: The money received by a single woman with children could be higher than that received by two working parents if both were paid at the minimum level. Clearly, then, an empirical issue was involved in Bahr's study.

The results show a significant tendency for white welfare recipients to have rates of separation and divorce at least twice as high as those not receiving welfare and there was a slight but non-significant tendency for this to be true of black families. The result was quite stable, as Bahr tested it separately for different age and income groups and across time periods and still found the effect to hold. Remarriage rates show that both blacks and whites not receiving welfare remarry at a rate three times higher than those receiving it, confirming the instability pattern from another perspective.

Although welfare might be thought to be destructive because it discourages stability, the idea that stability is the goal is valueladen. Contemporary society is changing rapidly, and new forms of family relationships are evolving. At the same time, data such as this is useful for hinting at society-wide social dynamics. Such data are not available from small-scale laboratory research. Often subtle and even unintended consequences of the forces set in motion by social policy changes can be detected with program evaluation techniques. And often such research opens up more questions than it answers, and that is where scientific, and we hope social, progress can begin.

Another view of the impact of laws on families concerns no-fault divorce laws. Recently, there has been a change in these laws so couples can divorce with no legal blame being attached to either one. This has had the effect of making divorce easier, at least in the economic and legal sense. Common sense (often at fault itself) would seem to suggest that divorce rates would increase after the introduction of such a law. The question might arise as to which social groups would be most affected by such changes; the poor might be affected more than higher income groups, younger people might be affected more than older people. In one sense, these could be seen as rather esoteric academic questions of interest only to researchers, but governmental policy has wide ranging effects, often undetected, so the knowledge of what happens after such a change is of critical importance at all levels.

Mazur-Hart and Berman ("Changing from fault to no-fault divorce: An interrupted time series analysis") seek to assess the impact of a change to no-fault laws in one state where very complete records were available: Nebraska. Since the law change was applied statewide, there were no control groups to whom the law did not apply. But a particular type of evaluation technique is available called time series analysis. This is used to analyze relationships in trends across time periods, assessing pre- and post-changes particularly well.

The results show that the trends for divorce are upward across the entire time span of the data records Mazur-Hart and Berman analyze. However, there is no differential rate of change: Divorce rates before and after the law were relatively constant, so the law was shown not to have a detectable influence on the overall trend line for divorce. Other variables assessed such as age, income, and economic level, did show some impact on the rates of change.

The concept of fault has been a central pivot in divorce laws: One person had to be seen as at fault even though marriage involves two people whose behavior is highly interdependent. By removing the concept of fault the process has been opened up. This study is able to use sophisticated statistical analyses of naturally occurring records to trace the impact of such a change. A great deal of useful and revealing information is often contained in state government record files, but often it is not fully used. This study shows the power and usefulness of applying evaluation research to a significant social issue by tracing already available records.

CRIMINAL JUSTICE

Social change is a complicated process, and one very difficult for social psychologists to analyze. Changes are often either too slow or too sudden for scientists to develop and apply assessment techniques in any satisfactory way. Sometimes, however, there are instances where governments consciously make planned, quick changes in policies; an alert investigator can obtain data before and after the changes and thus assess their impact. Such an event occurred in the report by Diener and Crandall reprinted here ("An evaluation of the Jamaican anticrime program").

As the investigators report, the island of Jamaica had experienced a very high and rapidly increasing rate of high violence crimes, most of them involving guns. As a massive and concentrated attack on the problem, the government passed laws strictly forbidding the sale, ownership, or even possession of guns. In addition, the government instituted other changes: Removal of guns from television shows, widespread public education campaigns, and even the painting of offenders with red paint.

Since these changes were instituted across the entire society, the investigators did not have control groups available for whom the changes did not apply. However, they did have crime statistics for the period before and after the change, so trend comparisons were possible. They compared records of the one year before the change against the one year following it, and the first post-change year against the trend across the entire ten-year period before the change. The data itself was available in archival records of government crime statistics.

The results show a significant increment in violent crime before the implementation of the change and significant reductions after it. Although homicides not involving guns increased even after the change, gun-related homicides decreased.

The authors note that only five hundred handguns actually were turned in by the citizens during the program's duration. They argue that it was unlikely that the removal of these relatively few handguns account for the results. The majority of personal guns was still in circulation, more guns could be imported readily, and criminals probably are not the people most likely to turn in their guns. Given this, the investigators argue that the total effect of all the government programs and all the intermixed parts was most likely responsible for the reduced crime rate.

It is rare that social scientists have a sudden manipulation of social variables available to them such as that involved here. Analyzing such a change is difficult; in this case, it is impossible to determine if the most effective element of the change was the law itself, the public campaigns, the treatment of the individual offenders, or something else. In spite of the complications, such situations are full of opportunities for understanding more clearly how social processes operate, so the study represents an excellent first step in obtaining that understanding.

As noted above, some social changes are more evolutionary in that they appear gradually and become slowly but steadily pervasive throughout a culture. Many of these tend to become institutionalized. When investigators later return to review these changes after the fact, oftentimes surprising and unexpected effects can be detected, ones not intended in the original change. Such is the case with the following study by Robertson and Zador on school driver education ("Driver education and fatal crash involvement of teenaged drivers").

Almost every American high school offers driver education courses, as do many private for profit firms. The assumption is that the courses are educational and increase driver safety. Robertson and Zador attempt to determine the effectiveness of such courses by analyzing data from a nationwide sample of twenty-seven states.

The investigators determined the ages at which people took driver education courses, the number of people obtaining drivers licenses, and an outcome measure: Actual death rates from car crashes. The investigators assumed that obtaining a driver's license (having had, or not having had, a prior driver education course) is likely to enhance the probability that one actually will drive. Since everyone can drive at age eighteen or beyond, the important question is: What happens to people who are not yet eighteen but who do or do not obtain driver's licenses and who have or have not had the experience of a driver education course?

The investigators obtained national data on the proportion of sixteen to seventeen- and eighteen- to nineteen-year-olds who had taken driver education, the proportion of the same age groups who were licensed, the proportion of those groups who were in the general population, the proportions who were drivers and, finally, the crash death rates for those age groups.

The data shows that taking a driver education course significantly increases the frequency with which sixteen- to seventeen-year-olds obtained licenses. That does not hold true for eighteen- to nineteen-year-olds for whom licenses are available without driver education courses. One analysis shows there is no relationship between driver education and fatal crash involvement. What is significant, however, is the relationship between licensing and death rates: Licensed drivers are more likely to be involved in crashes. Licensing itself is related to driving. So driver education per se does not lead to a lower death rate than no driver education, but it does lead to increased rates of obtaining driver's licenses, especially for the sixteen- to seventeen-year-olds. That resultant increase in driving itself leads to a higher death rate than the comparable same age group not having driver education. So driver education tends to encourage youths to drive but does not lower their death rates when they do drive. The investigators transformed their proportion data to actual raw frequencies and estimated that a minimum of two thousand fatal crashes would be avoided if sixteen- to seventeen-year-old drivers were prevented from driving, regardless of whether or not they had had driver education. Such courses increase exposure to risk and hazard with no corresponding increase in safety.

Needless to say, society has invested a good deal of its resources in public, private, and commercial driver education courses. The findings of this study imply that some thought should be given to which people should be allowed to take driver education courses. Changing any social program is difficult, even though facts, such as those generated by this study, can be used to justify change. Whether or not they should be used is a decision that ought to be faced. The use of scientific analyses for understanding how our society operates is much more than an exercise in technical analysis; it gives us guidance as to how we should arrange our society.

Health

Relations between Nutrition and Cognition In Rural Guatemala

Howard E. Freeman
Robert E. Klein
Jerome Kagan
Charles Yarbrough

Abstract

The nutritional status of three and four year old children, as measured by height and head circumference, is related to cognitive performance in four rural Guatemalan villages. The relationships persist when social factors are taken into account.

Families in two of the villages participate in a voluntary, high protein-calorie supplementation program. In the other two villages, the families receive a vitamin and mineral supplement with about one-third of the calories. Although the longitudinal study still is ongoing, there is some evidence that the children who receive the higher calorie supplement (or whose mothers received it during pregnancy and lactation) are most likely to score high in cognitive performance. The results support other animal and human studies that report an association between nutrition and cognitive development. The findings, while not diminishing social environmental explanations of differences in cognitive function, suggest the worth of nutrition intervention programs in rural areas of lesser-developed countries. (Am. J. Public Health 67:233–239, 1977)

During the 1960s, a number of investigators studying children in various regions of the world reported an association between severe protein-calorie malnutrition and intellectual functioning.[1-5] Laboratory studies with animals in the 1960s and early 1970s also provided important findings of the profound effects of malnutrition on neurological development[6,7] and on learning patterns and other individual behaviors.[8,9] The demonstration of a linkage between severe protein-calorie malnourishment and cognitive performance of children, bolstered by the animal studies, received widespread attention since an estimated three percent of the world's children experience one or more episodes of severe malnutrition before five years of age.[10]

In relation to the incidence of mild and moderate protein-calorie malnutrition, however, severe nutritional deficiencies are relatively unique events. It is estimated that fully one-half of the children in lesser developed nations are suffering from mild-to-moderate protein-calorie malnutrition,[11] as well as varying but critical numbers of children in low-income families in industrialized countries.[12] The finding that severe nutritional deficiencies of children appear to limit their mental development, when extrapolated to moderately and mildly malnourished children, has resulted in one of the important scientific and policy debates of the past decade. In part, the controversy centers around accepting a causal relationship on the basis of epidemiological data between measures of nutritional status and psychological test scores.[2,13] In part, it is the result of the efforts of well-intentioned policy makers and humanitarians who marshal all possible evidence to justify large-scale nutrition interventions.

The presumed causal link between malnutrition and intellectual development is challenged by the findings of numerous investigations of the influence of the social environment on the child's cognitive functioning. Evans and associates, for example, found that malnourished South African children and their

"Relations between Nutrition and Cognition in Rural Guatemala" by Howard E. Freeman, Robert E. Klein, Jerome Kagan, and Charles Yarbrough from *American Journal of Public Health,* Vol. 67, No. 3, March 1977, pp. 233–239. Reprinted by permission of American Public Health Association and Howard E. Freeman.

healthier siblings *both* attain similar scores on cognitive tests.[5] The widely-known Coleman report as well as less ambitious but more rigorous investigations provide support for an association between aspects of the child's social environment and cognitive development.[14] Economically advantaged children obtain larger values on the anthropometric indicators commonly used to measure nutritional status. Thus, many have suggested the covariation between economic and nutritional indices accounts for the relation between mild malnutrition and poor cognitive functioning.[15]

The intentioned and unintentioned efforts of scientists and policy makers to downgrade the influence of either nutrition or the social milieu is understandable in terms of both the disciplinary orientations of investigators—biological and medical on the one hand, and social and psychological on the other—and the passions that come into play among policy makers competing for limited funds, particularly those provided by industrialized countries to less developed ones.

By the mid-1960s, there was a widely acknowledged need to develop and implement investigations that took into account *both* nutritional and social determinants of cognitive development. The need to study both nutritional and social factors involves complex issues of conceptualization, design, and analysis. The number of variables that must be quantified and introduced into any reasonable design requires respectable sample sizes, extensive data collection and collation, and complex data analysis. Further, the immature state of the nutritional and behavioral sciences does not allow complete solutions to the major problems of method, including the operationalization and measurement of the several sets of key variables (see Klein, et al., for an expanded discussion of this point[15]).

The data reported here came from a long-term longitudinal investigation of nutrition and mental development being undertaken in Guatemala by the Institute of Nutrition of Central America and Panama (INCAP) and begun in 1968 (see McKay, et al. and Mora, et al. for discussions of related ongoing projects[16, 17]). The INCAP investigation, although still in its data collection phase, has resulted in a large number of papers on various substantive and methodological aspects of the project (see Klein, et al., for a recent review[18]). In a 1972 paper,[15] early data were reported that bear directly on the contributions of nutritional and social factors to cognitive functioning. The results of this analysis suggested that both

domains of measures are related to cognitive development, and that the relative importance of nutritional and social factors depended on the particular cognitive dimension selected as the criterion variable; further, that the sex of the children must be taken into account. There were major sex differences in the amount of variance accounted for by the different social and nutritional measures included as independent variables. Given the limited robustness of the findings, the sample size at that time, and the inevitable methodological weaknesses of a complex field study, we were forced to conclude that, while the results hint at the importance of nutritional as well as social factors, the findings were insufficient to advocate wide-scale social action programs that are predicated on nutritional status being related to cognitive functioning.

In this paper, we summarize a considerably larger body of data from the INCAP study on the contributions of nutritional and social factors to cognitive development. It is still a progress report since much of the longitudinal analysis awaits some two additional years of data collection. But the information at hand allows for a more definite examination of the competing viewpoints.

THE INCAP STUDY

The study population consists of children from four small, Spanish-speaking Guatemalan villages. The families in them are poor with average incomes less than $300 per year, most cannot read or write, live without indoor sanitary facilities, and drink water contaminated with enteric bacteria. Corn and beans are the major diet and animal protein is less than 12 percent of total protein intake.[19] Height and weight of both adults and children are strikingly low in comparison with standards for children in developed countries.

Study Design

The study can most properly be described as a quasi-experiment. In two of the villages, pregnant and lactating mothers and children are offered a protein-calorie supplement (11 gms. of protein per 180 ml. of supplement). In two other villages, a supplement that contains no protein is provided. The second supplement, a "Kool-aid" type drink, contains one-third of the calories of the protein-calorie supplement (59 total calories compared with 163 per 180 ml.).* Both preparations contain the vitamins, minerals, and fluorides possibly limited in the home diets. Attendance at the twice-daily supplementation program is voluntary, there are no restrictions on how much can be ingested, and a wide range of intake is observed in each village.

The supplementation of two of the four villages with a high-calorie diet, however, provides a study group that includes sufficient children and lactating mothers with an adequate calorie intake, even in families with minimal economic resources. The intervention is necessary because the proportion of poor families in rural Guatemalan villages with malnourished children is so large that it is not possible to examine thoroughly the relations between social-environmental variables, measures of nutritional status, and cognitive functioning. As reported elsewhere, the physical growth of young children in the set of villages receiving the high-calorie supplement is significantly higher than in the set receiving the low-calorie one.[20] In addition, preventive and curative medical care is provided in all villages by a physician-supervised resident nurse. Appropriate referrals are made to regional hospitals in cases of serious illness. Severe malnutrition is treated upon discovery in all four villages.

The Study Group

The longitudinal study group at the time of this report consisted of 1,083 children, 671 born alive since the field work started in 1969, and 412 alive and under three years of age when data collection commenced. The study group reported on here consists of those children from the 1,083 in the longitudinal panel who are old enough so that data are available at either age three (N = 573), age four (N = 536), or both ages. This point requires some amplification. When data are presented by age, the age designation refers to the information collected at a particular time-point; in other words, information reported for age three and then for age four includes many of the same children in the two analyses, but the data differ by time-point collected. The study group sizes are as follows:

3-year-old males	300
3-year-old females	273
4-year-old males	278
4-year-old females	258

*The protein-calorie supplement will be referred to as the "high-calorie" supplement or diet in this paper.

Exact study group sizes for each analysis presented vary somewhat because of missing data. In general, the tables contain about 95 percent of the subjects reported above.

VARIABLES

The project has collected an unusually large corpus of data on health status and medical treatment, food consumption, nutritional supplementation, physical growth, and social environmental factors. Because of the pressure to implement the field study, early data collection included many measures later discarded as either irrelevant or unreliable. In this paper, selected measures from three domains of variables are employed.

1. Dependent Variables

The cognitive measures come from a specially designed "preschool" battery. As in the previous report,[15] we use three variables selected from this battery.

Language Facility.   The score is based on the child's ability to name and recognize pictures of common objects and to note and state the relations among orally presented verbal concepts.

Short-term Memory for Numbers.   The child's score is based on his recall of increasingly long strings of numbers read to him at the rate of one per second.

Perceptual Analysis.   The child's score is based on his ability to locate hidden figures embedded in a complex picture or to detect which of several similar variations of an illustrated object was identical with a standard.

Test-retest reliabilities differ somewhat by age but are in the generally accepted range of .7 to .8 when the scores are obtained one month apart. Consistent with current thinking about cognitive performance, particularly the utility of Western-oriented tests to underdeveloped populations,[21] the general strategy has been to develop a set of measures that "sample" a domain of separate cognitive processes. For heuristic purposes, however, it also seemed useful to develop a single score reflecting the overall cognitive performance for each child. Since the earlier paper was published, a number of efforts based on theoretical considerations and factor analytic studies have been undertaken to develop a composite measure. The one that seems to satisfy both theoretical and psychometric requirements consists of 12 tests that represent the child's ability to memorize, recognize, perceive, infer, and verbalize. This measure, labeled *cognitive composite,* is included as a fourth dependent variable in the analysis. The test-retest reliability when the cognitive composite battery was administered the second time after one month was .88 for three-year-old children.

2. Social Environmental Measures

These measures were developed from first administering a large number of items, inspecting intercorrelations between items, and identifying scales that correlate with psychological test scores. Reliability of the measures in many cases was found to be too low to continue their use. Although the villages are relatively "flat" in stratification, nevertheless there is evidence of structural and life-style variation. It was decided to continue using three measures and to obtain family data repeatedly on them. The measures are the following:

Quality of house: Rating based on the type of construction, interior design and condition of dwelling. (Test-retest reliability = .80.)

Mother's dress: Rating based on whether or not the mother possessed particular items of commercially manufactured clothing. (Test-retest reliability = .65.)

Task instruction: Rating based on family members' reports of teaching the child to perform household tasks and to travel to a nearby town. (Test-retest reliability = .50.)

The first measure, quality of house, is conceived as a social-economic stratification measure. The second, mother's dress, reflects modernity as well as income. The third, task instruction, is viewed as an indicator of the parents' efforts to provide adult modeling and purposeful learning opportunities. Reliability of the two stratification measures is reasonably high, particularly the quality of house measure. The task instruction measure's reliability is border-line. Reliability of measures is increased by pooling the scores, usually three in number, that are obtained in repeated annual interviews. In part of the analysis, these three variables are combined. The composite measure is referred to as the *social factor index.* The test-retest reliability of the social factor index is .85.

3. Nutritional Data

The child's head circumference and total height are used as indices of nutritional status. Both variables presumably reflect the child's history of protein-calorie intake, although genetic background and illness experience also influence head size and height. Height is generally the best indicator of extended nutritional deficiency; head circumference is most sensitive to malnourishment before the age of two years.[20] Extensive field trials conducted as part of the INCAP program argue for the utility of anthropometric measures as indicators of nutritional status.[20] In villages in which children receive an annual intake of more than 20 liters of the high-calorie food supplement, children's physical growth velocities are similar to those recorded for children in the U.S. In villages receiving the low-calorie supplement, these velocities are significantly lower. In part of the analysis, these two measures (height and head circumference) are combined. The composite is referred to as the *nutrition index.*

4. Supplementation Data

Children and their mothers receive and drink the supplements under supervision and the amount is recorded for each visit. In this study, two separate measures are used. The first is the total caloric intake of mothers during their pregnancy and the period of their lactation. The second is the total calories consumed by the mothers and by the child directly.

In the two villages receiving the high-calorie supplement, the mothers of the children tested at three years of age, during pregnancy and lactation, ingested approximately twice as many calories as mothers in the villages receiving the vitamin-mineral supplement (67,000 calories compared with 32,000). The mothers of the four-year-old children averaged 53,000 and 24,000 calories respectively. The children themselves at three years of age had consumed an average of 97,000 calories in the two high-calorie supplement villages compared with 15,000 calories in the two low-calorie supplement villages; at four years of age the comparable figures were 121,000 and 31,000 calories respectively.

RESULTS

A multiple-regression analysis was employed. For each of the four cognitive measures, separate analyses were undertaken by age and sex with the data pooled for the four villages. A large number of repeated analyses were performed for three reasons. First, in order to estimate the independent and joint effects of variables reflecting the different domains of measures, the variables were "forced" into the analyses in different orders, e.g., the social factor measures first and then the nutritional measures. Second, analyses were undertaken with the individual measures and with the composite indices. The indices greatly reduce the number of variables, advantageous in conserving degrees of freedom and in simplifying the interpretation and presentation of findings. The measures in the composite indices are not highly correlated, however, and thus the amount of variance explained may be reduced. Third, analyses were undertaken with and without taking into account the interaction effects between variables. There were no interaction effects deemed useful to include in the data presented since the variance explained by them was small and outweighed by the loss of degrees of freedom. A further refinement was to adjust the correlations for the estimated reliability of these measures. Again, this procedure does not modify the results.

Nutrition and Cognitive Performance

In Table 1, the zero-order correlations of the two measures of nutritional status, the composite nutrition index, and the test-scores are presented. The R^2 values between these two variables and the psychological scores also are included.

In most cases, the correlations are statistically significant at the .05 or lower level. There are considerable variations in the magnitude of the correlations, by both psychological score and by age-

sex group. Values are consistently lower for boys at age three than for the other groups, possibly related to age-sex maturation differences.

The variations in the correlations of height and head circumference to the test scores is difficult to explain. Both are conventional measures that reflect nutritional status. Perhaps age-sex maturation patterns account for the differences. In any event, consistent with epidemiological studies of nutritional status and intellectual development, and the findings reported in our previous paper, there is a reasonably clear association between nutritional status and cognitive measures.

Social Factors and Cognitive Performance

Social-environmental factors, as well as nutritional status, are related to cognitive scores. In Table 2, the zero-order correlations are reported for the three individual measures—quality of house, mother's dress, and task instruction—and for the social factor index. In addition, the R^2 values are presented when the three individual measures are regressed on the test scores.

The social variables are significantly related to the psychological scores at the $p < .05$ level or lower in a number of instances. Only a few of the correlations between quality of house measure and the test scores are statistically significant. This social measure was a much better predictor of cognitive scores in the data reported on earlier.[15] The general direction of the correlations, however, is consistent enough to argue for a link between social-environmental differences and psychological performance. The relationship is most clear for the language measure.

Table 1 Correlations between Nutritional Status and Cognitive Scores

Nutritional Measures	Cognitive Measures															
	Language				Memory				Perception				Cognitive Composite			
	3 yrs.		4 yrs.		3 yrs.		4 yrs.		3 yrs.		4 yrs.		3 yrs.		4 yrs.	
	M	F	M	F	M	F	M	F	M	F	M	F	M	F	M	F
Nutritional Index	.20**	.34**	.29**	.30**	.05	.31**	.06	.14*	.14*	.25**	.09	.14*	.17**	.39**	.26**	.30**
Height	.24**	.26**	.29**	.27**	.11	.28**	.14*	.18*	.13*	.19*	.11	.14*	.20**	.30**	.28**	.29**
Head Circumference	.10	.31**	.19**	.25**	-.01	.26**	-.04	.09	.11	.24**	.05	.11	.09	.36**	.15*	.09
Multiple R	.06**	.12**	.09**	.10**	.02*	.10**	.02*	.03**	.02*	.07**	.01	.02*	.04**	.16**	.08**	.08**

* P < .05
** P < .01

Table 2   Correlations between Social Measures and Cognitive Scores

Social Measures	Cognitive Measures															
	Language				Memory				Perception				Cognitive Composite			
	3 yrs.		4 yrs.		3 yrs.		4 yrs.		3 yrs.		4 yrs.		3 yrs.		4 yrs.	
	M	F	M	F	M	F	M	F	M	F	M	F	M	F	M	F
Social Factor Index	.22**	.12*	.21**	.25**	.15*	.08	.10	.10	.16**	.04	.08	.08	.23**	.10	.18**	.23**
House Quality	.08	.11	.06	.23**	.04	−.01	.05	.15*	.02	.02	−.06	.05	.05	.04	.04	.19**
Mother's Dress	.18**	.07	.22**	.19**	.15*	.06	.11	.10	.12*	.00	.16*	.07	.18**	.06	.22**	.19**
Task Instruction	.20**	.05	.19**	.12*	.12*	.05	.10	−.06	.18**	.01	.10	.03	.22**	.03	.16*	.10
Multiple R^2	.06**	.01*	.07**	.07	.03	.00	.02	.04*	.04*	.00	.04*	.00	.07*	.00	.06*	.06*

* $P < .05$
** $P < .01$

Independent and Joint Contributions of Nutrition and Social Factors

As reported in studies primarily focused on *either* nutrition *or* social-environmental factors as explanatory variables, the INCAP data suggest that both domains of variables are related to psychological test performance. The issue is whether any general statement can be made about the unique contributions of nutritional status and social factors to mental development. Put another way, do the nutrition measures predict cognitive functioning after all the variance attributed to the social variables has been acknowledged, and vice-versa?

Multiple regressions were undertaken in which the social variables were forced in first, followed by the nutritional terms and the interactions between these measures. Likewise, in other regressions, the measures and the height × head circumference interaction were forced in first, followed by the social variables. The analysis was undertaken by the composite indices as well as by the separate variables.

In Table 3, we show the proportion of variance explained when the composite nutrition and social factor indices are regressed on the psychological measures. The total amount of variance explained tends to be somewhat lower when the composite indices are used instead of the separate variables. The results are substantially the same, however, and the use of the indices economizes on degrees of freedom.

In one-half of the regressions, the amount of variance explained by the nutrition index is statistically significant even when the social factor effects are first taken into account. When the procedure is reversed, the social factor index sometimes continues to explain a significant amount of variance, but primarily in the case of the language measure. The amount of variance explained by the social factor index is generally less than the nutritional measures.

These findings are consistent with the results reported in the earlier report. Further, there are differences by both age-sex group and cognitive domain. The earlier analysis was undertaken with the first 342 cases in the study, data were available for the memory and perception tests on slightly more than 200 children. Here, the size of the study group—over 500 children—and scores at two age-points provide strong evidence for the contribution of nutrition measures to cognitive performance, especially to language.

Impact of Supplementation

The data previously discussed make a substantial case for the view that inadequate nutrition is associated with lower cognitive performance. Statements of a causal nature, however, are risky from epidemiological data. Fortunately, the nutrition intervention is far enough along to use its results as supporting evidence of the identified relationships. In Table 4, the findings on supplementation and cognitive performance are shown. The variable labeled supplementation is the sum of calories consumed during pregnancy and the lactation of the tested child by the mother, added to the calories consumed by the child up until each testing point. The analysis was also undertaken using only calories consumed by the mother during pregnancy and lactation. Results are the same and this variable is not shown. As discussed elsewhere,[18] the INCAP results suggest that adequate nutrition of pregnant and lactating mothers, rather than the direct supplementation of children after weaning, may be the more important determinant of differences in young children's cognitive performance. Supplementation of young children, however, may be beneficial in terms of current and future health status and physical growth.

The data have their weaknesses. Ideally, it would be desirable to have measures of home diet-intake as well. Although home nutrition surveys are regularly undertaken, they are not precise enough by family members for use here. They do provide evidence that the interventions are "true supplementations" and do not substitute for food normally eaten by the children. Also, since over one-half of the children were born before the study started, many mothers in the study group were not exposed to the intervention while pregnant and lactating, and some one-quarter of the children were similarly unexposed to supplementation during early life.

Nevertheless, the results are encouraging from an intervention standpoint. Out of the 16 estimates of variance explained that are presented in the first line of Table 4, four are significant at the .05 level and five others are greater than zero. In all cases, the values are accounted for by direct relationships between nutritional status and test scores. The social factor index, however, is negatively related to the supplementation measure, although not always significantly. The direction of the relationships between the social factor index and the supplementation measure suggests that the "needier" children are benefiting most from the supplementation program. Removing the variance explained by the social factor index first, in some cases, raises the amount of variance explained by supplementation. With the social factor index removed first, 11 out of 16 times there are direct relationships between the amount of supplement ingested and cognitive test scores. These direct relationships account for all of the values greater than zero that are shown in the second line of Table 4.

In this analysis, the composite social and nutritional indices were employed to preserve degrees of freedom. Results are similar when the individual nutrition and social measures are employed. Although the amount of variance explained by the supplement is small, the findings lend support for the causal character of the relationship between nutrition and cognitive development.

Limitations of the Study

A number of criticisms can be addressed at this analysis. We are aware of the validity problems surrounding the variables selected. Even though there

Table 3 Proportion of Variance Explained by Nutrition and Social Factor Measures

	Cognitive Measures															
	Language				Memory				Perception				Cognitive Composite			
Factors	3 yrs.		4 yrs.		3 yrs.		4 yrs.		3 yrs.		4 yrs.		3 yrs.		4 yrs.	
	M	F	M	F	M	F	M	F	M	F	M	F	M	F	M	F
Nutrition Index Alone	.04**	.12**	.08**	.09**	.00	.09**	.00	.02*	.02*	.06**	.01	.02*	.03**	.15**	.07**	.09**
Social Factor Index Alone	.05**	.02*	.05**	.06**	.02*	.01	.01	.01	.03**	.00	.01	.01	.05**	.01	.03**	.05**
Nutrition and Social Indices Combined	.07**	.12**	.11**	.12**	.02*	.10**	.01	.03*	.04**	.06**	.01	.02	.06**	.15**	.08**	.11**
Nutrition Index with Social Factor Index First Removed	.02*	.11**	.06**	.06**	.00	.03*	.00	.02	.01	.00	.00	.00	.02	.05**	.05**	.06**
Social Factor Index with Nutrition Index First Removed	.03**	.00	.03**	.04**	.02	.00	.01	.01	.02*	.00	.00	.00	.03**	.00	.01	.02*

* $P < .05$
** $P < .01$

Table 4   Amount of Variance Explained by Supplementation, Social Factors, and Nutrition

	Cognitive Measures															
	Language				Memory				Perception				Cognitive Composite			
Factors	3 yrs.		4 yrs.		3 yrs.		4 yrs.		3 yrs.		4 yrs.		3 yrs.		4 yrs.	
	M	F	M	F	M	F	M	F	M	F	M	F	M	F	M	F
Supplementation only	.02*	.01	.02*	.02*	.00	.03*	.00	.00	.01	.00	.00	.00	.00	.01	.01	.01
Supplementation with Social Factor Index Removed	.03**	.01	.03*	.03*	.00	.03*	.00	.00	.01	.00	.00	.01	.01	.01	.01	.01

* P < .05
** P < .01

were strenuous efforts to develop reliable variables, some unreliability remains in both the social and psychological measures. As noted, however, adjusting the correlation coefficients by the estimated reliability of these measures does not substantially change the findings. We recognize that many of the measures are metrically inelegant and we have not met all the statistical assumptions required for some of the analyses performed. Additional indices of either nutrition and growth of social characteristics could have been included and may have modified the findings. Moreover, the two nutrition variables are not sensitive indices of the severity, duration, or age at onset of nutritional insult. The nutritional heterogeneity of the groups may account for some of the irregularities of the findings. Finally, the association may not be sustained as children approach adulthood. Rather, nutritional condition may simply postpone cognitive development temporarily.

Nevertheless, the analysis suggests that supplementation of pregnant and lactating mothers and young children is related to the latters' pre-school cognitive performance, and it is reasonable to suggest that the relationship is causal. The amount of variance explained by the nutrition measures is not always substantial, but consistent with the magnitudes of findings of most social-epidemiological investigations. Indeed, it is a fair assertion that given more reliable measures, and ones with better metric properties, the variance explained might be larger. Further, although we present only the results for three psychological variables and a composite score, the findings are generally consistent when other cognitive test measures are used as the dependent variables.

Finally, it is puzzling that the effect of nutrition is greater for a nondynamic cognitive variable like size of vocabulary than it is for memory, which requires

focused attention and cognitive strategies. Indeed, supplementation or the nutritional index, with social class removed, made a minimal contribution to memory or perceptual analysis. A child's vocabulary knowledge is the cognitive variable that consistently shows the highest correlation with social class of family—across cultures and time. It is also the best single correlate of the total IQ on intelligence tests which sample a variety of cognitive talents. Hence, the fact that vocabulary correlates best with nutrition indicates that vocabulary is either an extremely sensitive index of the quality of cognitive functioning or that social-cultural differences not captured by our social factor index, but nevertheless linked to cognitive performance, accounts for the high vocabulary score for the physically larger children.

IMPLICATIONS

The findings presented strongly suggest that calorie intake affects cognitive development as well as physical growth and general health status. There are a number of plausible explanations for the results. Either a lack of adequate total calories or a deficiency of protein may impede the development of the neurological system. Another hypothesis is that the poorly nourished child, pre- and post-partum, has insufficient energy to take advantage of opportunities for social contacts and learning. Finally, it may be that adults and older children treat the larger child as a more mature individual, which leads to increased social learning opportunities. Clearly, the state of knowledge, as Evans and associates have noted,[5] in neither the nutritional nor the social sciences is sufficient to suggest a single, primary explanation.

It bears emphasis that the findings do not diminish

social environmental explanations of difference in cognitive functioning. The generally persistent correlations between the social factor variables and cognitive functioning support the reasonableness of various views on the consequences of deficient family milieux. Moreover, the fairly systematic findings on the amounts of variance explained by nutritional and social measures from one cognitive dimension to the next suggest that the social and nutritional inputs into a child's life have different magnitudes of importance in determining performance on various cognitive dimensions.

At the same time, it is important to note that at least in rural Guatemala nutrition intervention programs are relatively easy to implement in comparison to most other social action efforts. In terms of the human and economic resources required for broad-scale, sustained social milieu interventions, and the political and cultural barriers to their rapid implementation, there is sound reason to stress nutrition intervention efforts in the formulation of social and community development policies for rural Guatemala and perhaps for other lesser-developed countries as well.

References

1. Cabak, V., and Najdanvic, R. Effect of undernutrition in early life on physical and mental development. Archives of Disease in Childhood 40:532-534, 1965.
2. Cravioto, J., DeLicardie, E. R., and Birch, H. G. Nutrition, growth and neurointegrative development: An experimental and ecologic study. Pediatrics 38:319-372, 1966.
3. Monckeberg, F. Effects of Early Marasmic Malnutrition on Subsequent Physical and Psychological Development. In Malnutrition, Learning and Behavior, edited by Scrimshaw, N. S., and Gordon, J. E., pp. 269-278, M.I.T. Press, Cambridge, 1968.
4. Stoch, M. B., and Smythe, P. M. Undernutrition During Infancy and Subsequent Brain Growth in Intellectual Development. In Malnutrition, Learning and Behavior, edited by Scrimshaw, N. S., and Gordon, J. E. M.I.T. Press, Boston, pp. 278-289, 1968.
5. Evans, D. E., Moodie, A. D., and Hansen, J. D. L. Kwashiorkor and intellectual development. S. A. Medical Journal 45:1413-1426, 1971.
6. Chase, H. P., Lindsley, W. F. B., and O'Brian, D. Undernutrition and cerebellar development. Nature 221:554-555, 1969.
7. Dobbing, J. Effects of Experimental Undernutrition on the Development of the Nervous System. In Malnutrition, Learning and Behavior, edited by Scrimshaw, N. S., and Gordon, J. E. M.I.T. Press, Boston, pp. 181-203, 1968.
8. Barnes, R. H., Moore, A. U., and Pond, W. G. Behavioral abnormalities in young adult pigs caused by malnutrition in early life. J. Nutrition 100:149-155, 1970.
9. Dobbing, J., and Smart, J. L. Clincis in Development Medicine. Heinemann Radical Publications, London, 1972.
10. Behar, M. Prevalence of Malnutrition among Preschool Children in Developing Countries. In Malnutrition, Learning and Behavior, edited by Scrimshaw, N. S., and Gordon, J. E. M.I.T. Press, Boston, p. 30, 1968.
11. Jelliffe, D. B. The Assessment of Nutritional Status of the Community. World Health Organization, Geneva, 1966.
12. U.S. Department of Health, Education, and Welfare, National Center for Health Statistics, Height and Weight of Children: Socioeconomic Status, Vital and Health Statistics, Series 11, No. 119, DHEW Publication No. (HSM) 73-1601, 1972.
13. Birch, H. G. Malnutrition, learning and intelligence. Am. J. Public Health 62:773-784, 1972.
14. Hertzig, M. E., Birch, H. G., Thomas, A., and Mendez, O. A. Class and Ethnic Differences in the Responsiveness of Preschool Children to Cognitive Demands. Monographs of SRCD 33:(Serial No. 117), 1968.
15. Klein, R. E., Freeman, H. E., Kagan, J., Yarbrough, C., and Habicht, J-P. Is big smart? The relation of growth to cognition. J. Health and Social Behavior 13:219-225, 1972.
16. McKay, H. E., McKay, A. C., and Sinisterra, L. Behavioral Effects of Nutritional Recuperation and Programmed Stimulation of Moderately Malnourished Preschool Age Children. Paper presented at the Meeting of the American Association for the Advancement of Science Symposium, 1969.
17. Mora, J. O., Amezquita, A., Castro, L., and associates. Nutrition and social factors related to intellectual performance. World Review of Nutrition and Dietetics 19:205-236, 1974.
18. Klein, R. E., Lester, B. M., Yarbrough, C., and Habicht, J. P. On Malnutrition and Mental Development; Some Preliminary Findings. In Nutrition, edited by Chavez, A., Bourges, H., and Basta, S., Vol. 2, pp. 315-321. S. Karger Basel, Switzerland, 1975.
19. Mejia-Pivaral, V. Characteristicas Economicas y Socioculturales de Cuatro Aldeas Ladinas de Guatemala. Guatemala Indigena, Vol. VII, No. 3. Instituto Indigenista National, Guatemala, 1972.
20. Yarbrough, C., Habicht, J-P., Martorell, R., and Klein, R. E. Physical Anthropology and Mild to Moderate Malnutrition: A Definition of the Problem. Wenner-Gren Foundation/Fels Research Institute, NY, 1974.
21. Berry, J. W., and Dasen, P. R. Culture and Cognition: Readings in Cross-Cultural Psychology. Methuen and Co. Ltd., London, 1974.

Acknowledgements

The data for this study are drawn from the Guatemalan growth and development project by Contract N01-HD-5-0640 of the National Institute of Child Health and Human Development, N.I.H. This investigation is part of a program of collaborative research and Uniform Measures of Social Competence by H. E. Freeman, J. Kagan, R. E. Klein, and A. K. Romney and is supported by the National Science Foundation (Grant GS-33047) and the Grant Foundation.

Address reprint requests to Howard E. Freeman, Department of Sociology, University of California at Los Angeles, Los Angeles, CA 90024. Authors Klein and Yarbrough are with the Institute of Nutrition of Central America and Panama (INCAP): author Kagan is with Harvard University. This paper, submitted to the Journal December 29, 1975, was revised and accepted for publication October 28, 1976.

Death Rates, Psychiatric Commitments, Blood Pressure, and Perceived Crowding as a Function of Institutional Crowding

Paul B. Paulus
Garvin McCain
Verne C. Cox

Abstract

The effects of crowding were examined in a prison system. Emphasis was directed toward three factors—social density (number of individuals in sleeping quarters), spatial density (space per person), and overall institutional population level. Archival data indicated that in prisons higher population years yielded higher death rates and higher rates of psychiatric commitments. Blood pressure measures were analyzed for inmates living in three types of housing that differed in degree of spatial and social density. Blood pressure was higher in more crowded housing. The degree of perceived crowding was more strongly related to space per person than number of occupants per housing unit.

The classic studies of Calhoun (1962) on crowding effects in animals generated considerable concern about the possible psychological consequences of crowding in humans. However, there is relatively little research regarding human reactions to long-term, intense, and inescapable crowding. Many crowding studies have been short-term laboratory studies or demographic analyses of large units such as census tracts or cities. In both of these approaches spatial and social density conditions differ substantially from the intense crowding employed by Calhoun in his animal studies. Several demographic studies have found evidence that living in socially dense environments is related to increased crime, impaired mental and physical health, and elevated death rates (Galle, Gove, & McPherson, 1972; Herzog, Levy, & Verdonk, 1977; Levy & Herzog, 1974; Golson, Note 1). However, Freedman, Heshka, and Levy (1975) found no evidence for such a relationship in a study of New York City. In any case, it is difficult to derive causal inferences from these studies since there exist many factors which may be confounded with crowding.

Some laboratory studies with humans have also found evidence that crowding can be aversive (Paulus, Annis, Seta, et al., 1976), while others have obtained no effects or sex-related effects (Epstein & Karlin, 1975; Freedman, Buchanan, & Price, 1972; Freedman, Klevansky, & Ehrlich, 1971; Ross, Layton, Erickson, & Schopler, 1973). While these types of studies have important implications for short-term crowded situations, the brief and relatively benign characteristics of the laboratory setting limit the generalization of these findings to long-term living situations.

An alternative approach has involved field studies of the effects of different kinds of housing environments. In these studies individuals often have limited control over their housing assignment. In one series of studies the effects of crowding in college dormitories were examined (Baron, Mandel, Adams, & Griffen, 1976; Baum & Valins, 1977; Aiello & Epstein, Note 2). Evidence from these studies indicates that crowding in dormitories produces negative reactions and social withdrawal even though the living conditions in these environments allow substantial freedom of movement to other environments and the densities are moderate and do not approximate those found in some of the animal studies.

Because of the above considerations, as well as the reasons given below, we have employed prisons as sites for our crowding research. In some ways, prisons provide an ideal environment for such research. Prisons range from small institutions of 100 inmates or less to very large institutions of 2,500 or more. In some cases inmates are kept in their living units all day, while in others they are required to be there only for sleeping. Within individual prisons, housing types range all the way from one-man cells with personal keys to open dorms of 120 men or more. The fact that the inmates have essentially no choice regarding the type and duration of their housing assignment and are often living among potentially hostile individuals led us to expect that they might find crowding particularly aversive. The intensity of the physical crowding in some prisons might be seen as approaching the levels employed in the animal studies. We felt that if crowding were to have any effects, they would be evident in prisons. The great variety of housing conditions in prisons allows one to determine the importance of a wide variety of components of crowding (e.g., size of the institution, number of inmates in a living unit, and the amount of space per inmate in a living unit). Another characteristic of prisons is that one can find institutions in which housing is randomly assigned or in which an assignment policy can be examined as a possible source of bias. For example, in some cases inmates

who have been in the prison the longest are assigned to certain units. One then can take length of stay in prison into account statistically in evaluating the effects of different types of housing conditions. Additional factors such as relative uniformity of diet, health care, and daily period of time in housing units increase the utility of prisons as research sites.

While it is true that there are many sources of stress in penal institutions, often it can be determined whether degree of crowding is an additional source of stress. We believe that studies of the effects of intense crowding can provide information regarding how humans might respond to situations analogous to those which yield pathology in animal studies. Such studies may also identify variables that may be operating in a less obvious fashion at the lesser degrees of crowding that are more commonly experienced in contemporary societies.

Recently we had an opportunity to examine a large state prison system. This system consisted primarily of 10 units ranging in population from 245 to 2400 in 1977. The units varied from minimum security to maximum security institutions. We had several aims in this study. One purpose was to obtain additional data on the effects of different types of housing in prisons. Our past research has shown that inmates living in dorms have more negative affect, higher levels of palmar sweating, and higher illness rates than inmates living in one- or two-man cells. Similarly, D'Atri (1975) and D'Atri & Ostfeld (1975) found that dorm inmates have higher blood pressure than those in one- or two-man units. To date, little evidence exists as to the effect of variations in number of occupants in intermediate size housing units such as housing units containing less than ten people. Consequently, we examined the effect of living in two-, three-, and six-man cells on blood pressure and ratings of crowding to determine whether such variations were sufficient to produce differences in stress levels. A second aim of the study was to determine the impact of the overall population density of the institution on physiological and mental functioning of inmates. The various demographic studies cited earlier (e.g., Levy & Herzog, 1974) suggest that overall institutional density, as well as density of particular housing units, may be a source of stress. We examined archival data from official reports on the variations in population of the various institutions in the system over a period of years and the corresponding variations in death and psychiatric commitment rates.

ARCHIVAL STUDIES
OF INSTITUTIONAL DENSITY

Psychiatric Unit Death Rates

Some data on death rates and populations were obtained from an examination of the official reports of a small psychiatric unit (normal rated capacity 600). Housing is presently in single cells with a two-tier arrangement. The data reported were taken from yearly reports and covered the odd-numbered years between 1953 and 1969. The reports for the even-numbered years were not available. Data after 1969 were not employed due to very substantial changes in policies and procedures. Total average yearly population in this unit ranged from a low of 369 to a high of 630. Examination of yearly reports indicated that the inmate population over 45 years of age averaged about 22% of the total population. This contrasts with about 6% in the general prison population. The number of deaths (range 1 to 17) were converted to rates per hundred (.27 to 2.83). Figure 1 shows the relation between death rates and total population which yielded a significant correlation ($r = .81$, $df = 8$, $p < .01$). The total yearly population rose and fell over time and hence other simple time-related factors do not appear tenable as explanations of this relationship. The data were also analyzed by comparing the lowest total population ranges (369-498) with the highest (546-630). The proportion of deaths was significantly higher in the higher population years ($\chi^2 = 7.74$, $df = 1$, $p < .01$). The possibility was also checked that yearly fluctuations in the percentage of older inmates might account for these results. However, we found no relationship between percentage of inmates over 45 and total population (Spearman rho $= 0.00$).

Mortality Survey

A statewide prison mortality survey covering the years 1969-1976 yielded, for men over 45, significantly higher death rates during the high population periods ($\chi^2 = 13.36$, $df = 1$, $p < .01$) as compared to low population periods. Death rates ranged from 1.2 to 5.3 per 100. We also considered only deaths attributed to diseases of the circulatory system and found a significant difference ($\chi^2 = 4.16$, $df = 1$, $p < .05$) in death rates when high and low population years were compared. Analysis of three other categories of causes of death (International Classification of Diseases, Eighth Revision, Adapted for Use in the United States) gave significant differences between high and low population years. In classification 140-239 (Neoplasms) there was a significantly higher death rate associated with higher population levels for inmates ($\chi^2 = 5.03$, $df = 1$, $p < .03$). In classification

Fig. 1.   Total Population and Death Rates per 100 Inmates for a Psychiatric Prison.

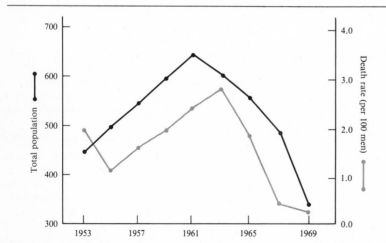

780-796 (symptoms and ill-defined conditions) there was also a significantly higher death rate associated with higher population levels for inmates over 45 ($\chi^2 =$ 4.91, $df = 1$, $p < .05$). In classification E800-E999 (accidents, poisoning, and violence—external cause) there was a significant difference with higher death rates related to lower population levels for inmates under 45 ($\chi^2 = 4.65$, $df = 1$, $p < .05$). In categories 780-796, 140-239, and E800-E999 there were a relatively small number of deaths and these were concentrated in a few years. In addition, categories E800-E999 and 780-796 cover a substantial number of possible causes of death. Some of the causes are quite vague; others (e.g., accidents) may have no relation to crowding. We do not believe any conclusions can be drawn regarding deaths in these categories because of the limitations mentioned above.

Psychiatric Commitments

Data were available from commitments to the psychiatric center from the years 1953-1972 from two major institutions (population ranges approximately 820-1,200 and 2,750-3,950). Since, as earlier indicated, there were major policy changes in the commitment procedures in 1970, only the data from 1953-1969 were used for analysis. Data from 1961 were incomplete and consequently were excluded. The data are shown

in 2-year blocks in Figure 2. The rate of commitment to the psychiatric center showed a strong positive correlation with the total population at these two institutions ($r = .701$, $df = 15$, $p < .01$). A comparison of the combined highest (4,500-5,100) levels of population with the lowest (3,700-4,400) levels of population also yielded a highly significant difference ($\chi^2 = 58.96$, $df = 1$, $p < .001$).

STUDY OF HOUSING DENSITY

A large (population approximately 2,400) maximum security prison was selected as the site for measurement of perceived crowding and blood pressure. We examined inmates living in the three most common types of housing: two-man cells with 29 square feet per inmate (2/29, $n = 37$), three-man cells with 19 square feet per inmate (3/19, $n = 38$), and six-man cells with 19 square feet (6/19, $n = 41$). After deducting the space covered by the bunks, toilet, and washbasin, there was approximately 10 square feet of free floor space per person in the 3/19 and 6/19 cells. Lighting in the 3/19 cells was typically furnished by a single light placed near the ceiling in the back of the cell. Spacing of the bunks in the 3/19 condition was such that inmates were unable to sit upright on the bunks. Inmates were assigned to cells based on prison job classification. There were no differences in body weight or race

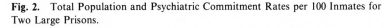

Fig. 2. Total Population and Psychiatric Commitment Rates per 100 Inmates for Two Large Prisons.

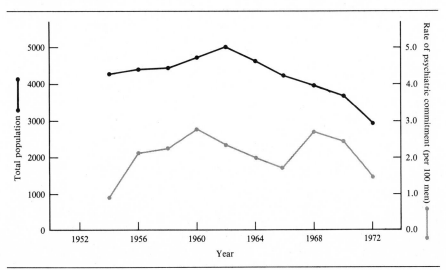

composition among the three housing groups. However, inmates were younger in the more crowded units ($F = 5.67$, $df = 2/113$, $p < .005$). Consequently, the data were analyzed using analyses of covariance with age as a covariate.

Perceived Crowding

Inmates were given a questionnaire on which they could indicate by a mark the degree to which they felt crowded. The following categories were used: uncrowded, moderately crowded, crowded, or very crowded. In general, inmates in the three types of housing perceived their housing conditions as crowded, but the inmates in the 3/19 and 6/19 units reported significantly higher degrees of perceived crowding as compared to inmates living in 2/29 cells ($F = 28.67$, $df = 2/110$, $p < .001$). Correlation analyses of perceived crowding scores of inmates in these as well as in other housing indicated that perceived crowding was strongly related to spatial density (square feet per man) with social density (number of inmates in cell) partialed out ($r = .48$, $df = 144$, $p < .01$). A similar correlation between perceived crowding and social density with spatial density partialed out was statistically significant but relatively weak ($r = .15$, $df = 144$, $p < .05$).

Blood Pressure

Blood pressures were obtained from inmates in the 2/29, 3/19, and 6/19 cells. An analysis of covariance with age as a covariate indicated significant differences in systolic blood pressures ($F = 3.16$, $df = 1/112$, $p < .05$) in the 3/19 and 6/19 conditions as compared to inmates housed in the 2/29 conditions. A Newman-Keuls analysis indicated the 6/19 and 3/19 groups were significantly different from the 2/29 group and not different from each other. The adjusted mean systolic values for the housing conditions were 2/29 = 126.5, 3/19 = 132.7, 6/19 = 133.9. The same analysis for diastolic pressure yielded no significant differences.

DISCUSSION

The results presented here indicate that the overall density of population level of an environment may have important consequences for the health of the inhabitants. As the population density of the prisons increased, the death rates and psychiatric commitment rates also increased. We interpret these results as indicating that high levels of social density within an institution may increase levels of stress and, in turn, lead to physical and psychological impairment. There may, of course, have been other factors which contributed to our findings. For example, higher death rates in crowded institutions may reflect poorer quality of medical service when institutions become overcrowded, since medical staffs may not increase proportionately with increases in population. We are not able to determine whether this is indeed the case, but our past research and that of others provides some support for our interpretation of the data as stress-related. We have found that high social density in living units can increase the incidence of illness complaints and palmar sweating (McCain, Cox, & Paulus, 1976; Cox, Paulus, McCain, & Schkade, Note 3). D'Atri (1975) and D'Atri & Ostfeld (1975) have found increased blood pressure under socially dense conditions. Evidence also exists that psychological stress can impair immunological mechanisms (Stein, Schiani, & Camerino, 1976). There are also data from nonhuman subjects showing increased death rates associated with crowding. For example, Myers, Hale, Mykytowycz, & Hughes (1971) found such a relationship with rabbits. Interestingly enough, they found that even in animals who were no longer crowded, the increased mortality associated with crowding continued.

Levy and Herzog (1974) and Herzog, Levy, & Verdonk (1977) have found a relation between either crowding or density and death rates in surveys conducted in a number of areas in the Netherlands. In these studies crowding was defined in terms of number of occupants per dwelling unit, while density was defined as the number of persons residing in a standard areal unit. They reported density had a significant independent effect upon age-adjusted death rate and male deaths of cardiovascular origin. They also found a relationship between density and general and mental hospital admissions. In a study concentrated on Rotterdam (Herzog, Levy, & Verdonk, 1977), a relationship was found between death rates and crowding. They found that a 1% increase in persons per room produced about a 1.2% increase in death rates. The Rotterdam study differs from the Levy and Herzog study since crowding rather than density was a critical factor. This is possibly due to the sites used. In the Levy and Herzog study 125 economic geographical regions were used. The populations of these units included, but were not confined to, major metropolitan centers. The Rotterdam study was concentrated on a single heavily populated metropolitan center. The findings of Levy and his coworkers regarding crowding, deaths, and psychiatric commitments are thus consistent with our own findings. The data from the present study appear more closely related to the Levy and Herzog study, although there may be some confounding of their density and crowding factors in the present study.

Measures obtained directly from inmates in our study provided further evidence from negative effects from crowding. The higher blood pressure and perceived crowding exhibited by inmates in the 3/19 and 6/19 cells relative to the 2/29 cells suggests that even relatively small variations in social and/or spatial density can increase stress reactions. These findings are consistent with the findings of the college dormitory studies that increasing the number of students in a room from two to three produces increased stress-related reactions (Aiello & Epstein, Note 2). The perceived crowding data indicated that inmates were responding primarily to spatial density and not social density. This result differs from our previous findings that social density was a more important factor than spatial density (Paulus, McCain, Cox, & Chandler, 1975). In our earlier study spatial density levels were not as high as those in the present study, so it is possible that when spatial density is at moderate levels social density is the primary factor, whereas spatial density becomes the more potent factor when it reaches high levels. It is also possible that the relatively small range of social density levels employed in this study limited the magnitude of the effects generated by this variable. Future research will be required to determine the parametric features of this relationship.

It is becoming increasingly clear that a number of factors are involved in producing the effects from what is generally described as "crowding." The number of individuals in a housing unit, the number of individuals in an area, the number of square feet per individual all seem to be a part of the complex influences. Other factors such as privacy, the composition and stability of the population, architectural features, and other elements as yet unknown may also contribute to the experience of "crowding."

In sum, we believe that the most reasonable interpretation of the present results and those cited is that long-term, intense, inescapable crowding can produce high levels of stress which can lead to physical and psychological impairment.

Reference Notes

1. Golson, H. *Crowding, social structure, and pathology in cities.* Unpublished doctoral dissertation, Georgia State University, 1976.
2. Aiello, J. R., & Epstein, Y. M. Effects of residential social density on human behavior: A longitudinal field experiment. In J. Aiello & A. Baum (Eds.), *Residential crowding and design.* New York: Plenum Press, in press.
3. Cox, V. C., Paulus, P. B., McCain, G., & Schkade, J. K. Field research on the effects of crowding in prisons and on offshore drilling platforms. In J. Aiello & A. Baum (Eds.), *Residential crowding and design.* New York: Plenum Press, in press.

References

Baron, R. M., Mandel, D. R., Adams, C. A., & Griffen, L. M. Effects of social density in university residential environments. *Journal of Personality and Social Psychology,* 1976, *34,* 434-446.

Baum, A., & Valins, S. *Architecture and social behavior: Psychological studies in social density.* Hillsdale, N.J.: Erlbaum, 1977.

Calhoun, J. B. Population density and social pathology. *Science,* 1962, *206,* 139-148.

D'Atri, D. A. Psychophysiological responses to crowding. *Environment and Behavior,* 1975, *7,* 237-251.

D'Atri, D. A., & Ostfeld, A. Crowding: Its effects on the elevation of blood pressure in a prison setting. *Preventive Medicine,* 1975, *4,* 550-566.

Epstein, Y., & Karlin, R. A. Effects of acute experimental crowding. *Journal of Applied Social Psychology,* 1975, *5,* 34-53.

Freedman, J. L., Buchanan, R. W., & Price, J. Crowding and human aggressiveness. *Journal of Experimental Social Psychology,* 1972, *8,* 528-548.

Freedman, J. L., Heshka, S., & Levy, A. Population density and pathology: Is there a relationship? *Journal of Experimental Social Psychology,* 1975, *11,* 539-552.

Freedman, J. L., Klevansky, S., & Ehrlich, P. I. The effect of crowding on human task performance. *Journal of Applied Social Psychology,* 1971, *1,* 7-26.

Galle, O. R., Gove, W. R., & McPherson, J. M. Population density and pathology: What are the relationships for man? *Science,* 1972, *176,* 23-30.

Herzog, A., Levy, L., & Verdonk, A. Some ecological factors associated with health and social adaptation in the city of Rotterdam. *Urban Ecology,* 1977, *2,* 205-234.

Levy, L., & Herzog, A. N. Effects of population density and crowding on health and social adaptation in the Netherlands. *Journal of Health and Social Behavior,* 1974, *15,* 228-240.

McCain, G., Cox, V. C., & Paulus, P. B. The relationship between illness complaints and degree of crowding in a prison environment. *Environment and Behavior,* 1976, *8,* 283-290.

Myers, K., Hale, C., Mykytowycz, R., & Hughes, R. The effects of varying density and space on sociality and health in animals. In A. H. Esser (Ed.), *Behavior and environment: The use of space by animals and men.* New York: Plenum Press, 1971.

Paulus, P. B., Annis, A. B., Seta, J. J., et al. Density does affect task performance. *Journal of Personality and Social Psychology,* 1976, *34,* 248-253.

Paulus, P. B., Cox, V. C., McCain, G., & Chandler, J. Some effects of crowding in a prison environment. *Journal of Applied Social Psychology,* 1975, *5,* 86-91.

Ross, M., Layton, B., Erickson, B., & Schopler, J. Affect, facial regard, and reactions to crowding. *Journal of Personality and Social Psychology,* 1973, *28,* 69-76.

Stein, M., Schiani, R., & Camerino, M. The influence of brain and behavior on the immune system. *Science,* 1976, *191,* 435-440.

Drs. Paulus, McCain, and Cox are professors in the Department of Psychology, University of Texas at Arlington. Requests for reprints should be addressed to Dr. Paul B. Paulus, Psychology Department, University of Texas at Arlington, Arlington, Texas 76019. The assistance of Ben Judd and Robert Matthews in this research is appreciated.

The Family

The Effects of Welfare on Marital Stability and Remarriage[1]

Stephen J. Bahr[2]   *Brigham Young University*

Abstract

The purpose of this study was to estimate the effects of welfare on marital dissolution and remarriage. The data were from a sample of 4,322 females age 30-44 from the National Longitudinal Surveys. It was found that those who received AFDC, food stamps, or other public assistance dissolved their marriages more frequently than those not receiving welfare. This finding held among low-income whites but not among low-income blacks. By controlling for other relevant variables, it was revealed that the relationship between welfare and marital dissolution decreased somewhat as duration of marriage increased. The remarriage rate of divorced females was three times greater among non-AFDC than AFDC recipients. This occurred among both low-income blacks and low-income whites. However, as age increased, the relationship between AFDC and remarriage decreased.

Welfare programs in the United States were designed to strengthen family life. The goal was humanitarian, to provide cash payments to needy families and individuals to alleviate their economic deprivation. It is ironic that these programs are now being labeled by some as "family-smashing devices" that aggravate the very problems they are supposed to resolve (Caplow, 1975:135, 1976; Greenfield and Falk, 1973). Critics contend that welfare programs encourage marital dissolution and discourage remarriage. The purpose of this research was to estimate the effects of welfare payments on marital dissolution and remarriage.

The fact that humans avoid painful, costly experiences and are attracted to activities and relationships that are pleasurable and rewarding is a truism as old as civilization (Homans, 1961; Simpson, 1972; Thibaut and Kelley, 1959). Levinger (1965, 197ο) has applied this basic concept to marital dissolution and maintains that marriages are held together by the perceived rewards of the relationship, the perceived costs of dissolution, and the perceived rewards of alternative relationships. If the effects of Aid to Families with Dependent Children (AFDC) and other welfare programs are examined from this perspective, dissolving the marriage could be a rational alternative for some low-income families because it increases their incomes. For example, Ross and Sawhill (1975:97) noted that, "if children in families are in economic need they will be eligible for assistance in virtually every case except where they are living with both natural parents." If a two-parent family qualifies for welfare, the benefits are less than for a female-headed family. In a study of 10 major U.S. cities, it was found that, "in every city, without exception, the female-headed family nets more income and benefits than the larger husband-wife family if both have a member who works full time at the minimum wage" (Ross and Sawhill, 1975:100). Thus, for low-income families, AFDC increases the economic rewards of an alternative to the existing marriage. It follows that AFDC might increase the rate of marital dissolution among low-income families. Whether this actually occurs or not would depend on the perceptions of the individuals involved, including the value of the income from AFDC compared to the rewards and costs of the current marriage and the costs involved in dissolving the marriage.

Honig (1974, 1976) compared the proportion of female-headed families to the average size of AFDC payments in major U.S. cities. She found that, among both whites and nonwhites, the proportion of female-headed families increased as the average size of the AFDC payment increased. In a similar study, Moles (1976) reported that, in 1970, states with higher welfare payments also had a higher proportion of separated mothers. His analysis using 1960 data revealed no such relationship (Moles, 1976). However, Moles found that changes in AFDC payments from 1960 to 1970 were positively correlated with changes during the same time period in the proportion of separated mothers. On the other hand, analyses by Cutright and Scanzoni (1973) and Minarik and Goldfarb (1976) revealed that the level of AFDC payment in a state was not related to the proportion of children living in female-headed families. Ross and Sawhill (1975:115-118) found that the relative size of welfare benefits available (computed as average AFDC grant in the state plus average food stamp bonus value in the county divided by the full-time

earnings of men in the city's low-income area) was correlated with the proportion of families headed by women among nonwhites but not among whites. They also found that whether or not a city had an unemployed parent program which allowed intact families to receive welfare benefits was not significantly associated with female headship. A limitation of all these studies was that only gross comparisons by state or area level of AFDC were used. Thus, it was not possible to determine if a family's receipt of AFDC was or was not related to its dissolution.

Two recent studies have produced data relevant to this problem. Greenfield and Falk (1973) examined the dissolution rate of a sample of 559 two-parent families from Monmouth County, New Jersey, that were affected by a change in the state's Working Poor Law. The new law dropped about 19,000 families from AFDC rolls and required them to reapply under the new Working Poor Law. Under the new law the amount received by a two-parent family was substantially less than that provided by AFDC to a family of the same size in which the husband had deserted or separated from his family. The number of families who began receiving AFDC benefits due to separation or desertion during the 13 months before the change in the law was compared to the number who separated or deserted during the 13 months after the change in the law. Greenfield and Falk (1973:29) found that separation and desertion were almost twice as frequent after the new law went into effect (6.4 percent to 11.6 percent). Furthermore, the rate of marital break-up was highest in the month immediately following the change in the law.

The second study was an analysis of the Seattle-Denver Income Maintenance Experiment by Hannan *et al.* (1977). It was found that women on income maintenance had a substantially higher rate of marital instability than a control group. The authors concluded that the income maintenance provided females with economic support that was independent of their marital status, as well as less stigmatizing and demanding for the recipient than welfare.

Overall, the evidence suggests that welfare programs probably increase marital dissolution, although the data are not entirely consistent and the magnitude of this effect is debatable. Ross and Sawhill (1975) concluded that the effect of welfare on marital dissolution is probably relatively small. On the other hand, Caplow (1976) contends that AFDC is a family-smashing device that has a substantial effect on family break-up. The present study was designed to overcome some of the limitations of existing research. Longitudinal data were used to determine whether intact families that were recipients of welfare dissolved their marriages more frequently than comparable families not receiving public assistance.

Another possible effect of welfare programs is the delay of remarriage. Females may choose to remain single if their welfare income may be affected by marriage, particularly if there is uncertainty about the ability of the prospective husband to earn an adequate income. This has implications for welfare programs, since inducements to remain single are likely to increase the number of female-headed families and thereby increase the number of families on welfare. Two studies were located which reported data relevant to this question. Ross and Sawhill (1975:119-120) found that females not receiving welfare who headed families remarried at a rate of 12 percent over a four-year period. The comparable rate for women receiving welfare was only 5 percent. The second study was an analysis by Hannan *et al.* (1977) of the Seattle-Denver Income Maintenance Experiment. They reported that income maintenance slightly increased the remarriage rates of blacks but had no effect on the remarriage rates of whites. The receipt of AFDC payments did not affect remarriage of either group in their sample. These two studies are contradictory and indicate the need for additional research on this topic.

SAMPLE AND MEASUREMENTS

The data for this analysis were collected as part of the National Longitudinal Survey of Labor Market Experience conducted by the Center for Human Resource Research at Ohio State University. A multistage sampling procedure was used to identify a national probability sample representing every state in the United States and the District of Columbia. Four different age-sex groups were sampled: males age 45-49, males age 14-24, females age 30-44, and females age 14-24. These four groups were sampled because transitions regarding labor-force participation typically occur during these age spans. To provide reliable data for blacks, households in predominantly black enumeration districts were oversampled. In each group, approximately 5,000 individuals were interviewed: 1,500 blacks and 3,500 whites. For the present study, only the data from the 5,083 females age 30-44 were analyzed. Each of these females was interviewed in 1967, 1969, 1971, 1972, and 1974. Eighty-five

percent of these females (4,322) could be followed for the entire seven-year period.

The first dependent variable in the present analysis was marital stability, a dichotomous variable. A marriage was defined as unstable if separation or divorce had occurred. This was measured by following married individuals over time to determine the proportion who became separated or divorced.

The second dependent variable was remarriage. An individual who was divorced at one interview and married by the next was classified as remarried.

Three different types of welfare payments were analyzed in this study. Each family was asked whether or not they received: (1) AFDC payments; (2) government food stamps; or (3) other welfare or public assistance. Information on age, race, education, earnings, duration of marriage, and previous marital status was also obtained and these variables were used as controls in the analysis.

FINDINGS ON MARITAL STABILITY

In 1967, 2.8 percent (104) of the married respondents were receiving some type of welfare. Almost 7 percent of these separated or divorced within the next two years, while 2.4 percent of those not receiving welfare separated or divorced during this period. By 1974, 9.6 percent of those not on welfare in 1967 had dissolved their marriages compared to 23.3 percent of those receiving welfare in 1967. Comparisons by type of welfare are shown in Table 1. Since the effects of the three different types of welfare were similar, they were combined into a single welfare category.

Previous research has shown that the stability of marriages is affected by income and race (Cutright, 1971; Ross and Sawhill, 1975). Since welfare recipients earn less than those not receiving welfare, these findings could be due to income differences in the families. The effects of welfare on marital dissolution might also vary by race as blacks have faced economic discrimination and are overrepresented among the poor. Therefore, the effects of welfare were examined while controlling for income and race, as shown in Table 2. Among low-income whites, marital dissolution was substantially higher among welfare recipients than among those not on welfare, while receipt of welfare was not related to the marital dissolution of low-income blacks.

To estimate more precisely the effects of welfare, we computed the proportion of married females who

Table 1. Percentage Separated or Divorced by Welfare Status

| | Type of Welfare Received in 1967 | | | | |
	None	AFDC	Other Welfare	Food Stamps	Any Welfare*
Percentage of Marriages	2.4	6.0	7.7*	8.3*	6.7*
Dissolved by 1969 N***	(3581)	(50)	(39)	(24)	(104)
Percentage of Marriages	9.6	20.5*	24.2*	26.3*	23.3*
Dissolved by 1974 N***	(3153)	(44)	(33)	(19)	(90)

*Significantly larger than the nonwelfare group, $p < .05$.

**If a family received any AFDC, food stamps, or other public assistance they were placed in this welfare category.

***This is the base on which the percentage was computed. For example, 2.4 percent of the 3,581 families not on welfare dissolved their marriages.

separated or divorced between each interview. This produced findings for four time periods: 1967-1969, 1969-1971, 1971-1972, and 1972-1974. The results of the four time periods were added together to obtain an overall estimate of the effects of welfare on low-income families.[3] Blacks on welfare dissolved their marriages more frequently than blacks not receiving welfare (5.5 percent compared to 3.6 percent), although this difference was not statistically significant ($.05 < p < .10$). White welfare recipients dissolved their marriages three times more frequently than those not on welfare (7.6 percent compared to 2.4 percent; $p < .001$ by a one-tailed difference in proportions test; see Blalock, 1960:176-178).

Since AFDC has been a frequently criticized welfare program, the effects of AFDC were examined separately. Among low-income blacks, 4.4 percent of those receiving AFDC dissolved their marriages within two years, compared to 4.0 percent for those not receiving AFDC. The comparable percentages for whites were 6.1 and 2.6. This difference was statistically significant for whites ($p < .05$) but not for blacks.

The effects of welfare on marital instability might also be influenced by age, age at marriage, education, duration of marriage, and first marriage. It was inappropriate to control for these variables using multiple-regression analysis because welfare status and marital instability were dichotomous and highly skewed. Small cell sizes precluded controlling for these variables simultaneously using cross-classifications. Therefore, each of these variables was controlled one at a time using first-order crosstabulations. For this analysis, the panel was divided into four time periods (1967-1969; 1969-1971; 1971-1972; 1972-1974) and the proportion of married individuals that separated or divorced during each period was computed for welfare recipients and those not receiving welfare. The results for each of the four time periods were summed to obtain an overall comparison that is shown in Table 3. It was found that current age of wife, age of wife at marriage, duration of current marriage, first marriage (whether or not it was the respondent's first marriage), education of husband, or education of wife did not change in the relationship

Table 2. Percentage Separated or Divorced by Welfare Status and Race of Low-Income Families: Entire Panel**

| | | Received Welfare in 1967 | |
	Race	No	Yes
Husband's Earnings Less than $4000	Black	17.0 (271)	17.1 (41)
	White	8.7 (542)	22.7* (22)
Husband-Wife Earnings Less than $6000	Black	16.5 (255)	18.4 (38)
	White	11.6 (335)	21.7* (23)

*Welfare group significantly larger than nonwelfare group, $p < .05$.

**This is the proportion of married couples in 1967 that separated or divorced during the period from 1967 to 1974. The number of parentheses is the total base on which the percentage was computed. For example, 17 percent of the 271 poor blacks not receiving welfare in 1967 separated or divorced by 1974. A family that reported receiving AFDC, foodstamps, or other public assistance was placed in the "yes" category of welfare.

Table 3. Percentage Separated or Divorced by Welfare and Selected Control Variables**

		Received Welfare	
Control Variable	Categories	No	Yes
Age	30-34	3.1 (4245)	9.4* (191)
	35-39	2.2 (4318)	4.8* (189)
	40-44	1.8 (4761)	4.7* (214)
Age at Marriage	18 or Less	2.9 (4844)	6.9* (332)
	19 or More	2.0 (8260)	5.8* (240)
Duration of Current Marriage	0-5 Years	6.1 (443)	19.4* (31)
	6 Years or More	2.2 (12841)	5.5* (563)
Education of Husband	0-11 Years	2.4 (4950)	5.5* (397)
	12 or More Years	1.9 (7312)	6.2* (97)
Education of Wife	1-11 Years	2.9 (4763)	6.3* (443)
	12 or More Years	2.1 (8504)	6.1* (147)
First Marriage	No	5.2 (1821)	11.3* (142)
	Yes	1.8 (11463)	4.6* (452)

*Welfare group significantly larger than the nonwelfare group, $p < .05$.

**These were the total number of females who were married and living with their spouse at the beginning of each of the four time periods (1967-1969; 1969-1971; 1971-1972; 1972-1974). Those who reported receiving AFDC, food stamps, or other public assistance at the beginning of a time period were classified as welfare families. All individuals were interviewed at the end of each time period, and the proportion that became separated or divorced during the period were classified as maritally unstable. The results of each of the time periods were added together to obtain the figures presented above. This procedure inflated the sample sizes, since a married person that stayed married would be counted four times. Nevertheless, this procedure appears legitimate since each married person was at risk of divorce during each time period.

between receipt of welfare and marital instability. In every first-order tabulation, those who received welfare dissolved their marriages more frequently than those not on welfare, and all the differences were statistically significant ($p < .05$). However, the difference between welfare and nonwelfare families was somewhat smaller among those who had been married longer.[4]

In summary, receipt of welfare was associated with higher levels of marital dissolution among low-income whites but not among low-income blacks. Other relevant variables did not alter this relationship except that duration of marriage reduced its magnitude somewhat.

FINDINGS ON REMARRIAGE

To estimate the effects of welfare on remarriage the data were again divided into four periods (1967-1969; 1969-1971; 1971-1972; 1972-1974). The number of divorced females that became married by the end of

each period were computed for welfare receipients and those not receiving welfare. Since remarriage may be affected by race and income (Norton and Glick, 1976:9), these two variables were controlled. The results of the four time periods were summed to obtain an overall estimate of the effects of welfare on remarriage.

It was found that those low-income females who received AFDC remarried within the next two years at a significantly lower rate than those who did not receive AFDC. Among both blacks and whites, the remarriage rate was about three times more frequent among non-AFDC recipients than among those who were receiving AFDC (see Table 4). When AFDC, food stamps, and other public assistance were combined into one welfare category, significant differences occurred among whites but not blacks.

In addition to income and race, the findings could be influenced by age. It is known that the remarriage of divorced females is less likely as age increases (Carter and Glick, 1976:46). Tabulations controlling for age are presented in Table 5. Within every age

Table 4. Percentage of Remarriage by Welfare Status and Race of Low-Income,** Divorced Females***

Race	Received AFDC		Received Any Welfare	
	No	Yes	No	Yes
Black	11.3 (124)	3.9* (76)	8.3 (109)	8.8 (91)
White	14.6 (239)	4.1* (73)	15.1 (218)	5.3* (94)

*Welfare group significantly smaller than nonwelfare group, $p < .05$.

**Low-income females were those who earned less than $4000 at the beginning of each period.

***The panel was divided into four periods, 1967-1969, 1969-1971, 1971-1972, 1972-1973. The number of divorced females who were married by the end of each period was computed by AFDC and non-AFDC females, and for welfare and nonwelfare females. Receipt of welfare (AFDC and other) was measured at the beginning of each period. The comparisons for each time period was summed to obtain an overall proportion of remarriage for each category.

category, those who received some type of welfare had a lower remarriage rate than those not on welfare. However, as age increased, the difference between the remarriage rate of welfare recipients and those not on welfare decreased. It was also found that AFDC had a greater effect on remarriage than did welfare in general.

SUMMARY AND DISCUSSION

The purpose of this study was to estimate the effects of welfare on marital dissolution and remarriage. The data were from the National Longitudinal Survey of females age 30 to 44. It was found that low-income whites who received AFDC, food stamps, or other public assistance dissolved their marriages more frequently than those not receiving any welfare. This finding did not hold among low-income blacks. Controls for other relevant variables revealed that the positive correlation between receipt of welfare and

marital dissolution decreased somewhat as duration of marriage increased.

The remarriage rate of divorced females was three times greater among non-AFDC than AFDC recipients. This relationship occurred among both low-income blacks and low-income whites but decreased in magnitude as age increased.

The data were consistent with the hypothesis that welfare contributes to (is a cause of) marital dissolution. However, other plausible explanations of the data exist. It could be that some uncontrolled variable encourages receipt of welfare *and* marital dissolution. Perhaps individuals with certain social or psychological characteristics are more prone to accept welfare and to dissolve their marriages. For example, a person who has a low self-concept, lacks communication skills, or feels powerless might more readily accept welfare and give up on a marriage than would other individuals. Hypotheses such as these need to be examined in future research.

It is possible that welfare does not encourage

Table 5. Percentage Remarried by Welfare Status and Age of Divorced Females***

Age	Received AFDC		Received Any Welfare	
	No	Yes	No	Yes
30-34	14.3 (265)	3.9** (51)	14.2 (254)	6.5* (62)
35-39	12.9 (233)	6.7 (60)	14.1 (227)	9.1 (66)
40-44	9.0 (312)	5.2 (58)	8.9 (291)	6.3 (79)

*$.05 < p < .10$.

**$p < .05$.

***The panel was divided into four periods, 1967-1969, 1969-1971, 1971-1972, 1972-1973. The number of divorced females who were married by the end of each period was computed for AFDC and non-AFDC females, and for welfare and nonwelfare females. Receipt of welfare (AFDC and other) was measured at the beginning of each period. The comparisons for each time period were summed to obtain an overall proportion of remarriage for each category.

marital dissolution but that it provides an economic alternative to the existing marriage if the marriage is unsatisfactory. The availability of welfare may lessen the economic costs of divorce. Couples who are married and on welfare may have fewer economic bonds and constraints against separation since the welfare income is not tied to their economic cooperation.

The data were also consistent with the hypothesis that AFDC discourages remarriage, particularly among relatively young females. Again, there could be uncontrolled variables that are related to a propensity to receive welfare and to remain single. The present findings were similar to those of Ross and Sawhill (1975:119-120) which increases the confidence that may be placed in them, since Ross and Sawhill controlled for income, residential location, number of children, age, education, race, marital status, and length of time as a female head.

One of the interesting findings of this study is that welfare was related to marital break-up among low-income whites but not among low-income blacks. Perhaps this is because welfare is defined differently among blacks than whites. Since blacks have faced economic discrimination and have been over-represented among the poor for years, receipt of welfare may be perceived as a legitimate alternative for families having economic problems. On the other hand, whites might view welfare as having more disgrace and stigma and as an indication that the father is not performing his role as family provider. Receipt of welfare may add to the strain that already exists and, therefore, could contribute to marital break-up. Research which replicates this black-white difference and explores the reasons underlying it would be useful.

With the passage of time, the costs of marital dissolution probably increase because of the larger investment in the marriage, the lower probability of remarriage, children and, simply, inertia. This may explain why the relationship between receipt of welfare and marital dissolution decreased somewhat as duration of marriage increased. Similarly, since opportunities for remarriage decrease with age, fewer females may be influenced by welfare considerations in their decisions to remarry. With limited choices it may be too "costly" to let welfare payments deter one from getting married.

The policy implications of these findings depend on the way economic factors affect marriages. If welfare programs actually encourage divorce and discourage remarriage, then it may be appropriate to label them as family-smashing devices. On the other hand, if they provide an alternative to an unsatisfactory marriage, that is another matter. Many females may remain in a very unsatisfactory marriage simply because they have no viable alternative. Welfare may provide them with an alternative to a negative, hopeless marital relationship. If this is the case, welfare programs would increase separation and divorce by relieving marital misery, yet it would not be appropriate to define them as family-smashing devices that encourage marital dissolution. Research is needed which distinguishes the extent to which welfare programs and other economic factors encourage dissolution and/or relieve unsatisfactory marriages.

Footnotes

[1] This research was supported by Public Health Service Grant No. 1 RO1 MH 27560-01, awarded by the National Institute of Mental Health. I am grateful to Darwin Thomas, Geoffrey Leigh, and Richard Galligan for comments on an earlier draft of this paper.

[2] Department of Child Development and Family Relations and Family Research Institute, Brigham Young University, Provo, Utah 84602.

[3] These were females who were married and living with their spouses at the beginning of each time period and whose husbands earned less than $4,000 that year. Those who reported receiving AFDC, food stamps, or other public assistance at the beginning of each period were classified as welfare families. All individuals were interviewed again at the end of the period. Marital instability was defined as the proportion that had become separated or divorced during the period. The results of each of the four times periods were summed to obtain the figures reported here.

[4] Since duration of marriage may be associated with first marriage, duration of marriage was also examined separately for first marriages and other marriages. In both cases, duration of marriage was dichotomized at about the median. Among first marriages with a duration of 16 years or less, the percentage of dissolution was 7.3 among welfare families compared to 2.5 for nonwelfare families ($p < 05$). The comparable percentages for first marriages with a duration of 17 years or more were 2.9 and 1.4 ($p < .05$). Among other marriages with a duration of 10 years or less, the percentage of dissolution was 18.0 for welfare families and 6.2 for nonwelfare families ($p < .05$). The comparable percentages for other marriages with a duration of 11 years or more were 7.6 and 3.3, respectively ($p < .05$). Thus, the basic relationships did not change using this different categorization of duration of marriage.

References

Blalock, Hubert M., Jr.
   1960   Social Statistics. New York:McGraw-Hill.

Caplow, Theodore
1975 Toward Social Hope, New York: Basic Books.
1976 "The loco parent: Federal policy and family life." Brigham Young University Law Review: 709-714.

Carter, Hugh, and Paul C. Glick
1976 Marriage and Divorce: A Social and Economic Study (Rev. ed.). Cambridge, Massachusetts: Harvard University Press.

Cutright, Phillips
1971 "Income and family events: Marital stability." Journal of Marriage and the Family 33 (May): 291-306.

Cutright, Phillips, and John Scanzoni
1973 "Income supplements and the American family." Pp. 54-89 in Studies in Public Welfare, Paper No. 12 (Part I), The Family, Poverty, and Welfare Programs: Factors Influencing Family Instability. Washington, D.C.: U.S. Government Printing Office.

Greenfield, Lawrence, and Mark Falk
1973 "Welfare grant reductions and family breakup among the working poor." Public Welfare 31 (Fall): 26-31.

Hannan, Michael T., Nancy Brandon Tuma, and Lyle P. Groenveld
1977 "Income and marital events: Evidence from an income-maintenance experiment." American Journal of Sociology 82 (May): 1186-1211.

Homans, George C.
1961 Social Behavior: Its Elementary Forms. New York: Harcourt, Brace, and World.

Honig, Marjorie
1974 "AFDC income, recipient rates, and family dis-

solution." Journal of Human Resources 9 (Summer): 303-322.
1976 "A reply." Journal of Human Resources 11 (Spring): 250-260.

Levinger, George
1965 "Marital cohesiveness and dissolution: An integrative review." Journal of Marriage and the Family 27 (February): 19-28.
1976 "A social psychological perspective on marital dissolution." Journal of Social Issues 32 (Winter): 21-47.

Minarik, Joseph J., and Robert S. Goldfarb
1976 "AFDC income, recipient rates, and family dissolution: A comment." Journal of Human Resources 11 (Spring): 243-250.

Moles, Oliver C.
1976 "Marital dissolution and public assistance payments: Variations among American states." Journal of Social Issues 32 (Winter): 87-101.

Norton, Arthur J., and Paul C. Glick
1976 "Marital instability: Past, present, and future." Journal of Social Issues 32 (Winter): 5-20.

Ross, Heather L., and Isabel v. Sawhill
1975 Time of Transition: The Growth of Families Headed by Women. Washington, D.C.: The Urban Institute.

Simpson, Richard L.
1972 Theories of Social Exchange. Morristown, New Jersey: General Learning Press.

Thibaut, John W., and Harold H. Kelley
1959 The Social Psychology of Groups. New York: John Wiley.

Changing from Fault to No-Fault Divorce:
An Interrupted Time Series Analysis

Stanley F. Mazur-Hart[1]   *Saginaw Valley State College*
John J. Berman   *University of Nebraska-Lincoln*

Abstract

The removal of fault as a criterion for the distribution of justice in domestic relations represents a major innovation in jurisprudence. Such innovations provide opportunities to evaluate the effects of legal changes on behavior. This research investigated the effects of no-fault divorce on divorce behavior in Nebraska. An interrupted time series quasiexperimental design was employed to test the hypothesis that no-fault divorce leads to an increase in the number of divorces granted. Results showed that the new law had no reliable effect on the overall divorce rate. Separate analyses were performed for urban and rural counties, black and white couples, marriages of various lengths, and people of various ages. No effects of the law were found in most of these analyses. However, no-fault divorce did appear to have significantly increased the number of divorces among blacks, among people over 50 years old, and among couples married longer than 25 years, although in the latter two cases the effect seemed short-lived. The implications of this study for the current debate surrounding no-fault divorce are discussed.

The difficulties that state legislatures face in reformulating divorce laws have been complicated by the central position of the concept of fault in the legal system. Traditionally, divorce has been viewed as one party accusing the other of failure to meet the obligations of the marital contract. Only the innocent party can bring the divorce action; and final settlements are usually made at the expense of the

"Changing from Fault to No-Fault Divorce" by Stanley F. Mazur-Hart and John J. Berman, *Journal of Applied Social Psychology*, 1977, Vol. 7, No. 4, pp. 300-312. Reprinted by permission of V. H. Winston & Sons, 7961 Eastern Ave., Silver Spring, MD 20910.

guilty party. Although fault may be a useful principle when applied to other legal areas (e.g., criminal proceedings), it has been attacked as unrealistic when applied to domestic relations. First, it is argued that there is no clear-cut behavioral manifestation of fault in many divorce cases. Second, even if fault does exist, it is generally unfair to blame only one partner in a dyad where few behaviors on the part of either spouse are independent of the other. In response to these arguments, several states have initiated reforms of their domestic relations laws. The State of Nebraska Unicameral passed no-fault divorce legislation in 1972. This legal change represents a naturally occurring manipulation whereby the effects of no-fault versus fault divorce laws can be evaluated.

Despite the radical change to no-fault divorce in Nebraska and elsewhere, systematic assessments of this change are noticeably lacking. Mace (1950) has reported on England's sharp upturn in divorce rates following that country's liberalization of divorce laws. Doroghi (1955) found that the number of divorces in Russia increased once marital dissolution was made a matter of mutual consent. Similarly, critics of no-fault divorce in the United States maintain that divorce rates are increasing rapidly in those jurisdictions which have adopted no-fault divorce laws. For example, one California judge has noted that in the 5 years since the introduction of no-fault divorce in that state, dissolutions of marriage jumped 25% ("5 Years of 'No-Fault Divorce'," 1975). However, it remains to be determined whether this phenomenon should be attributed to the inception of the no-fault divorce law.

The lack of research on this topic may be due to the difficulty in applying a design which would allow adequate manipulation of the data so that meaningful interpretations could be offered. Campbell (1969) pointed out that when a political unit initiates a reform which is put into effect across the entire unit, no group is available as a control and the only base of comparison is the record of observations taken in previous months or years. In those situations, Campbell and Stanley (1966) have recommended using the interrupted time series quasiexperimental design. Such a design was employed in the present research to test the effects of Nebraska's no-fault divorce law on the frequency of divorces. Specifically, the main goal of this study was to evaluate the primary criticism voiced against the introduction of no-fault divorce laws, namely, no-fault divorce will increase overall divorce rates (Brody, 1970). In addition, separate analyses were conducted on subgroups of Nebraska's population because there was reason to suspect that certain subgroups might be affected more than others by this change in the divorce law. In general, the people who ought be be affected most by the new law are those who are interested in a divorce but are reluctant to go through with it because of anticipated negative consequences of the traditional legal procedure.

In an investigation of the relationship between divorce rate and various demographic variables, Cannon (1947) found that the strongest correlate of the divorce rate was the urban-rural differential. Later, Cannon and Gingles (1956) attributed this higher divorce rate in urban areas to a reduction of the importance of traditional values—a reduction which they felt was directly related to urbanization. These authors can be interpreted as concluding that rural people believe in the indissolubility of marriage to a greater extent than urban people. If this is so, then rural people should be less affected by changes in divorce procedures than urban people, simply because rural people are less approving of divorce in any form.

Schmitt (1969) identified a U-shaped distribution relating age of marrieds to incidence of divorce, with the lowest divorce rates among couples between the ages of 30 and 50. A reason for the low divorce rate in this group is their responsibility for minor children. Since the introduction of no-fault divorce does not affect the source of this group's reluctance to seek divorces, the new laws should not increase the frequency of divorces among members of this age category.

One reason for adopting no-fault divorce was to reduce the number of divorces by desertion, sometimes termed poor man's divorce. Lawmakers expected that the no-fault law would make divorces not only easier to obtain but perhaps less expensive. If the change to no-fault divorce had this effect, then the new law should produce a greater increase in divorces

among the poor than among the rich. The available records in Nebraska did not contain an index of socioeconomic status. They did, however, indicate race which is highly correlated with socioeconomic status. Thus, in order to test any differential effects of the no-fault divorce law on rich and poor, the divorce rates for minority and majority couples were analyzed separately.

METHOD

The observations in these time series were the number of divorces per month over a 6-year period from January 1969 through December 1974. A shorter time period (e.g., divorces per week) was not used as the unit of analysis because Nebraska records divorces by the month in which they occur, not by the week or day. A longer time period (e.g., divorces per 3 months) was not used because it would have produced too few observations on each side of the interruption for analyses to be interpretable. The interruption in the time series was the enactment of Nebraska's no-fault divorce law on July 6, 1972. Because the law was enacted during the month of July, it was impossible to classify that month as either before or after the interruption; consequently, July 1972 was dropped from the series. In addition, an extremely high number of divorces was granted during June 1972. Because such outliers lead to incorrect identification of statistical models, Glass, Willson, and Gottman (1975) recommend excluding them from analyses. Thus, June 1972 was also dropped from the series. The analyses in this study were composed of 41 observations (months) before the interruption and 29 after it. The number of observations pre- and post-intervention were, therefore, well beyond the minimum of 25 suggested by Glass et al.

The data for these time series were collected from official records, which are maintained by the state's Department of Health as mandated by Nebraska statutes. At the time of final divorce decree, the lawyer(s) involved in the proceeding must complete a Report of Divorce Form, which is filed with the district court where the divorce has taken place and then sent to the Bureau of Vital Statistics. The data used in this research were obtained from this source.

Past work on divorce has sometimes used a ratio of divorces to population size rather than raw frequencies of divorce (e.g., Rheinstein, 1972). Such a ratio index is particularly useful in studies encompassing many years during which the marriageable and, hence, divorceable population may fluctuate greatly. But this study encompasses a 6-year span, and the population size of Nebraska has been relatively stable since peaking in the mid-1950s (Eastman, 1973). Furthermore, there is no completely accurate means of calculating movement in and out of Nebraska's divorceable population. In light of these factors, raw frequencies of divorce were used here.

Webb, Campbell, Schwartz, and Sechrest (1966) have been justifiably concerned with the limitations of archival research. One serious limitation involves the use of sampled data. In order to avoid such a problem, this study analyzed all the Nebraska divorce decrees granted between 1969 and 1974, inclusive. The total number of divorces for that 6-year period was 25,520. Since all cases were used rather than only a subset of them, statements about the effects of no-fault divorce throughout the state could be made more accurately. Webb et al. (1966) also warn researchers that a change in record-keeping procedures can pose a threat to the internal validity of a study. It is important to note, therefore, that a check on the record-keeping techniques at Nebraska's Bureau of Vital Statistics showed that there were no significant changes during the years studied here.

After the monthly frequencies for divorces in Nebraska were tabulated, the data were separated into divorces occurring in urban and rural counties. An urban county was one which contained either a city greater than 50,000 in population or the immediate suburbs of such a city. By these criteria 3 counties were classified as urban, and the remaining 90 counties were classified as rural. Next, males and females were separately grouped into three categories on the basis of age on last birthday prior to the divorce decree. The three age categories were: 29 years and younger, 30 through 50 years of age, and 51 years and older. The frequencies of divorces per month were then tabulated for each of the six groups and arranged into time series. A similar way of looking at this aspect of the data is to analyze divorces by length of marriage at the time of divorce. Thus, the length of each marriage at the time of divorce was calculated, and each case was put into one of the following six groups: married 1-5 years, married 6-10 years, married 11-15 years, married 16-20 years, married 21-25 years, and married 26 years or longer. The divorce records were also divided on the basis of the race of the couple. Initially several minority groups were to be separately analyzed. But the number of minorities other than

blacks is very small in Nebraska, and the frequencies of divorces per month in those groups were too few for meaningful statistical analyses. As a result, only cases where both spouses were either black or white were used for this particular study.

Time Series Analyses

The data were analyzed according to procedures outlined by Glass et al. (1975) and Kepka (1972). Special statistical procedures are required in order to analyze time series data because the observations are frequently correlated with each other. This dependency among observations violates the assumption of independence of errors, which is a necessary condition for making accurate probability statements about the effects of interest. The goal of these statistical procedures is to identify the nature of the dependency and to correct for it. The procedures can be divided into three parts: model identification, parameter estimation, and the testing of intervention effects.

In model identification, one attempts to determine whether there is any dependency among the observations and, if so, which of several statistical models best describes that dependency. To accomplish this, the pattern of autocorrelations and partial autocorrelations are inspected. It has been demonstrated that certain patterns indicate that certain models will best describe the observations in the series. Once the autocorrelations and partial autocorrelations have been inspected and a model chosen, that model is fitted to the data; and the residuals from the fit are tested to determine if any dependency remains. If the test shows that there is dependency, the wrong model has been used and another must be tried. If the test shows no dependence among the residuals, the correct model has been used and one can proceed to parameter estimation and the testing of intervention effects. These last two steps involve transforming the model which was chosen into a form of the general linear model so that standard techniques of parameter estimation and significance testing can be used.

Despite the complexities, the statistical models for testing the intervention effects in the interrupted time series quasiexperimental design have been developed (see Glass et al., 1975, for the most readable presentation); and the necessary computer programs for these analyses are available (Bower, Padia, & Glass, 1974). The method is useful for investigating the effects of new social programs, modifications in old programs, behavioral interventions, or legal changes, where the dependent variables of interest have been collected in a consistent manner for a period of time before and after the innovation.

RESULTS

The first step in analyzing the data was to inspect the autocorrelations and partial autocorrelations of each series. No dependencies in the observations were found and the classical multiple regression model was chosen as the best fit to the data. This model was used for each series, and the residuals were then tested for dependencies. The tests showed no dependencies, indicating that the classical multiple regression model was appropriate. If the tests on the residuals of any of the series had indicated dependence, the data from those series would have had to be fitted to one of the autoregressive integrated moving average (ARIMA) models discussed by Glass et al. as a means to remove the dependency among observations.

The most common types of effects investigated in the interrupted time series quasiexperimental design are changes in the level of the series (i.e., the series shifts up or down by a constant) and/or in the slope

(i.e., the series changes direction) at the point of the interruption. Thus, the multiple regression equation fitted to each series was:

$$Y = a + b_1 X_1 + b_2 X_2 + b_3 X_3 + \epsilon$$

where Y = number of divorces per month, a = overall level of the series, b_1 = a coefficient representing change in the level of the series, X_1 = a dummy variable coded to discriminate between months which were pre- and post-intervention, b_2 = a coefficient representing the overall slope of the series, X_2 = a dummy variable coded to discriminate each month of the series, b_3 = a coefficient representing change in slope of the series, X_3 = a dummy variable coded to discriminate post-intervention months from each other and from pre-intervention months, and ϵ = error.

Figure 1 shows a plot of the total number of divorces in Nebraska per month over the 6 years studied here. The partial regression coefficients showed that the overall slope of this series increased significantly, $F(1,66) = 30.9, p < .001$; but there was no significant change in level or in slope after the intervention, $F(1,66) = .1$ and .4, respectively. This indicated that during the period of time studied divorces did systematically increase but that the

Fig. 1. Number of Divorces per Month in Nebraska, 1969–1974.

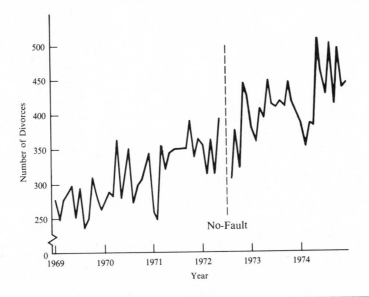

intervention of no-fault divorce had no discernable effects on that increase.

Separate analyses were performed on the data from urban and rural counties. In each case a significant overall slope was found: for urban counties, $F(1,66) = 11.71, p < .001$; for rural counties, $F(1,66) = 34.47, p < .001$. But in neither case was there a significant change in level: for urban counties, $F(1,66) = 1.2$; for rural counties, $F(1,66) = .8$. Nor was there a significant change in slope: for urban counties, $F(1,66) = .7$; for rural counties, $F(1,66) = .1$. Thus, divorces systematically increased for both types of county, but no effects of the new law were apparent.

Separate analyses were performed for three age groups of husbands and wives. The pattern of results found above was also found for both husbands and wives who were under 30 years old and between 30 and 50 years old. That is, for all four of these groups there was a significant overall increase in divorces ($p < .001$), but no evidence of any changes in level or changes in slope at the time of the interruption. However, the pattern of results was different for husbands and wives over 50 years of age. Each of these groups showed a significant overall slope: for husbands over 50, $F(1,66) = 4.4, p < .05$; for wives over 50, $F(1,66) = 4.8, p < .05$. Each group also

showed a lack of significance for change in slope: for husbands over 50, $F(1,66) = .5$; for wives over 50, $F(1,66) = 2.7$. However, both of these groups showed a significant increase in the level of the series after the inception of no-fault divorce: for husbands over 50, $F(1,66) = 4.3, p < .05$; for wives over 50, $F(1,66) = 4.4, p < .05$. Figure 2 presents the number of divorces per month for husbands and wives over 50 years of age at the time of divorce.

Another way these data were grouped was by length of the marriage at the time of the divorce. Separate analyses were performed on marriages lasting 1-5 years, 6-10 years, 11-15 years, 16-20 years, 21-25 years, and 26 years or longer. Analyses for the first five of these six groups (i.e., up through 20-25 years of marriage) resulted in the typical pattern found in this research, namely, a significant overall increasing slope ($p < .001$) but no significant change in level or change in slope at the point of interruption.[2] The analysis for those married 26 years or longer, however, showed a significant overall slope: $F(1,66) = 10.4, p < .005$; a near significant increase in level: $F(1,66) = 3.8, p < .06$; and a significant change in slope: $F(1,66) = 4.5, p < .05$. The sign of the partial regression coefficient for change in slope was negative, indicating that the

Fig. 2.   Number of Divorces per Month in Nebraska for Husbands and Wives over 50 Years of Age, 1969-1974.

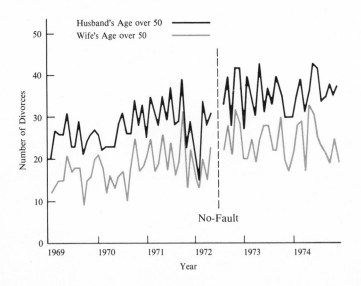

direction of the post-intervention series was downward. The number of divorces per month for couples married 26 years or longer are shown in Figure 3.

Divorces among white couples and black couples were analyzed separately. Among white couples there was the significant overall slope, $F(1,66) = 32.4$, $p < .001$, but no significant change in level or slope, $F(1,66) = .1$ and $.2$, respectively. Divorces among black couples showed somewhat similar results in that the overall slope approached significance, $F(1,66) = 2.9$, $p < .1$; and the change in slope was not significant, $F(1,66) = 1.3$. However, the data from black couples did show a significant change in level of the series, $F(1,66) = 4.7$, $p < .05$. It appears, therefore, that the change in the law did not affect white couples but did affect black couples. Figure 4 shows the data from black couples.

DISCUSSION

Contrary to opinions of some opponents of no-fault divorce, the results of this study showed that the inception of the law was not associated with any increase in the overall number of divorces granted in the state of Nebraska. The data showed that divorce is indeed increasing systematically in the state, but the increase seems totally unrelated to the no-fault divorce law.

There had been reason to expect that the law would affect couples in urban counties more than couples in rural counties. Contrary to expectation, the no-fault divorce law did not differentially affect divorce rates in either urban or rural counties. An overall increase in divorces did occur in both types of counties across the time period studied here, but that increase was not related to the inception of no-fault divorce law.

Analyses of the data for age groups of husbands and wives at the time of divorce also produced results contrary to expectation. It has been predicted that the change in the law would increase the number of divorces among spouses under 30 and over 50 years of age, but not among spouses between 30 and 50. In fact, only the husbands and wives over 50 years of age showed a statistically significant increase in divorces with the inception of no-fault divorce. In addition, the analyses by length of marriage at the time of divorce showed that marriages lasting longer than 25 years demonstrated a significant increase in divorce with the enactment of the new law.

The most reasonable explanation for this pattern of results seems to be that the longer a marriage lasts the

Fig. 3.   Number of Divorces per Month in Nebraska for Couples Married 26 Years or Longer at Time of Divorce, 1969-1974.

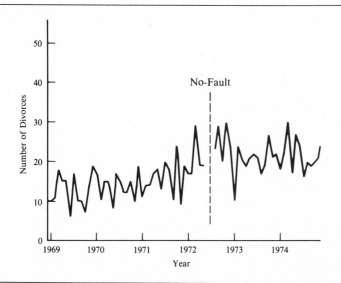

Fig. 4.   Number of Divorces per Month in Nebraska for Black Couples, 1969-1974.

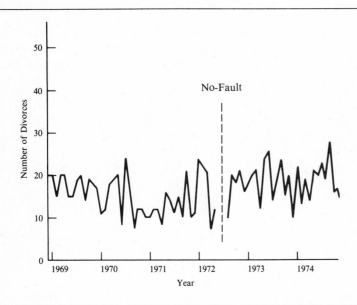

greater are the costs involved in getting a divorce and a significant portion of those costs has been reduced by the no-fault divorce law. Actually there are at least two types of costs that may have been reduced by the change in the law. The first is the emotional cost of establishing fault. In other words, it could be that for older couples the emotional cost of having to establish fault under the former law was too high a price to pay for getting a divorce. Once this price was lessened, however, the balance was tipped for these older people in the direction of proceeding with divorce. A second cost that may have been present under the former law and that may have been reduced by no-fault divorce was the financial one which many husbands in long-term marriages had to pay in order to get a divorce. In the past, the wife was generally favored in the financial distribution after a final divorce decree. Some jurisdictions even specified that the following criteria had to be considered in dividing property and deciding issues of alimony: length of marriage, employability of the wife, and marriageability of the wife (Brody, 1970). Women with no career and a long marriage gained the most whenever involved in divorce proceedings under these fault concepts. Many believe that under no-fault divorce the favors extended to the wife have been removed ("Axing Alimony," 1974). Thus, the new law may equalize the burden by removing benefits

previously given the wife. Husbands who previously could not afford the costs of divorce may now more readily file and obtain decrees.

The results of this study showed the effects of no-fault divorce among older and longer married couples to be short-lived. Evidence for this is the statistically significant change in slope of the number of divorces for couples married 26 years or longer. In other words, Figure 3 shows that the introduction of no-fault divorce did actually lead to an increase in the number of divorces among couples married 26 years or longer. However, that change in level was accompanied by a change in slope from positive to negative. Thus, although no-fault divorce did temporarily increase the number of divorces among older and longer married individuals, this increase has reversed; and the number of divorces seems to be returning to its preintervention level. This can be interpreted as indicating that there was a backlog of older and longer married people for whom the inception of no-fault divorce changed the cost-benefit ratio sufficiently for them to seek divorces. It should be noted that this effect of no-fault divorce is similar among older and longer married individuals because of the necessary connection between age and length of marriage.

The separate analyses for white and black couples showed that among white couples divorces have increased over time, but no statistically significant changes in the level or slope as a function of the no-fault divorce intervention were found. On the other hand, among black couples the level of divorces did significantly increase as a function of the new law; and this increase shows no signs of disappearing. It had been expected that black couples would be more affected by the change in the law than white couples. The reason for this was that one intended effect of no-fault divorce was to make divorce less expensive and, therefore, more available to people of low socioeconomic status. If race is highly correlated with socioeconomic status in Nebraska—and there is good reason to believe that it is ("Statistical Abstract of the United States," 1975)—then these data suggest that this objective of the law has been met.

Campbell and Stanley (1966) pointed out that the most serious threat to the internal validity of the interrupted time series quasiexperiment is history, i.e., the possibility that not the intervention but some simultaneous event produced an obtained shift in the series. A review of the divorce literature revealed that two major factors are most likely to account for sudden and dramatic shifts in divorce rates: a sudden economic change and the termination of a major war (Davis, 1950). Various economic indicators for Nebraska were inspected, and none of them showed any dramatic changes around the time of the inception of no-fault divorce. Troops were returning from Vietnam about the time of the change in the divorce law; but the Vietnam withdrawal was a gradual process conducted over several years, rather than an abrupt one. Moreover, when the end of a war affects divorce rates, the youngest age groups show an effect, not the older groups as was found in this study. In short, a consideration of possible alternatives produced no rival hypotheses which could better account for the changes that occurred in some of the interrupted time series of divorces in Nebraska. Thus, the enactment of no-fault divorce apparently provides the best explanation for the changes which did occur.

An analysis of divorce rates in one state certainly does not make a definitive case for or against no-fault divorce. Future studies should compare divorce rates in jurisdictions similar to Nebraska during the same time period examined in this study. Other states which have introduced no-fault divorce would provide interesting comparisons.

Another avenue for future research is a consideration of alimony and property settlements as a function of no-fault divorce. Feminist groups maintain that the financial segment of divorce proceedings is the single most important phase of a divorce. They note that no-fault divorce frequently calls for a 50-50 distribution of wealth between two people who are not socially or economically equal, before or after the decree. Feminists argue that women's work is usually not rewarded appropriately and that no-fault divorce completely strips women of all economic security ("NOW Votes for Changed Family Law," 1976). This so-called unilateral aspect of no-fault divorce law clearly needs further research that includes an analysis of male and female roles vis-a-vis earning power.

Footnotes

[1] Requests for reprints should be sent to Stanley F. Mazur-Hart, Department of Psychology, Saginaw Valley State College, University Center, Michigan 48710.

[2] The one exception to the pattern was the lack of significance for the overall slope among those couples married 16-20 years at the time of divorce.

References

Axing alimony: Some courts, citing women's liberation, go easy on husbands. *Wall Street Journal,* May 29, 1974, p. 1.

Bower, C. P., Padia, W. L., & Glass, G. V. *TMS = Two Fortran programs for analysis of time series experiments.* Boulder, Colorado: Laboratory of Educational Research, University of Colorado, 1974.

Brody, S. A. California's divorce reform: Its sociological implications. *Pacific Law Journal,* 1970, *1,* 223-232.

Campbell, D. T. Reforms as experiments. *American Psychologist,* 1969, *24,* 409-429.

Campbell, D. T., & Stanley, J. C. *Experimental and quasi-experimental designs for research.* Chicago: Rand McNally, 1966.

Cannon, K. L. Marriage and divorce in Iowa 1940-1947. *Marriage and Family Living,* 1947, *9,* 81-83; 98.

Cannon, K. L., & Gingles, R. Social factors related to divorce rates for urban counties in Nebraska. *Rural Sociology,* 1956, *21,* 34-40.

Davis, K. Statistical perspective on marriage and divorce. *Annals of the American Academy of Political and Social Sciences,* 1950, *272,* 9-21.

Doroghi, E. *Grounds for divorce in European countries.* New York: Research Division of the New School for Social Research, 1955.

Eastman, M. L. *Statistical report of the Bureau of Vital Statistics.* Lincoln, Nebraska: State Department of Health, 1973.

5 years of "no fault divorce" hike California breakups 25%. *The Lincoln Star,* March 12, 1975, p. 11.

Glass, G. V., Willson, V. L., & Gottman, J. M. *Design and analysis of time-series experiments.* Boulder, Colorado: Colorado Associated University Press, 1975.

Kepka, E. J. *Model representation and the threat of instability in the interrupted time series quasi-experiment.* Unpublished doctoral dissertation, Northwestern University, 1972.

Mace, D. R. Family life in Britain since the first World War. *Annals of the American Academy of Political and Social Sciences,* 1950, *272,* 179-180.

NOW votes for changed family law. *Sunday Journal and Star,* January 11, 1976, p. 4D.

Rheinstein, M. *Marriage stability, divorce, and the law.* Chicago: University of Chicago Press, 1972.

Schmitt, R. C. Age and race differences in divorce in Hawaii. *Journal of Marriage and the Family,* 1969, *31,* 48-50.

Statistical Abstract of the United States (House Document No. 94-267) Washington, D.C.: U.S. Government Printing Office, 1975.

Webb, E. J., Campbell, D. T., Schwartz, R. D., & Sechrest, L. *Unobtrusive measures: Nonreactive research in the social sciences.* Chicago: Rand McNally, 1966.

Criminal Justice

An Evaluation of the Jamaican Anticrime Program

Edward Diener   *University of Illinois at Champaign-Urbana*
Rick Crandall[1]   *Texas Christian University*

Abstract

A sweeping anticrime package was implemented in Jamaica in 1974. This program included severe penalties for possession of illegal guns, censorship of gun scenes from television and the movies, and greatly broadened police powers. The impact of this anticrime package on crime was assessed using quasiexperimental time-series designs with both months and years as the units of analysis. In a one year period there was a 14% reduction in homicides ($p < .05$), a 32% reduction in rapes ($p < .01$), a 25% reduction in robberies ($p < .05$), and a 37% reduction in nonfatal shootings ($p < .01$). Data from the second year following the implementation of the anticrime package were not available. The data from the first year suggest that strict anticrime measures can reduce crime.

As the problem of crime has grown in recent years, government officials have increasingly sought ways to reduce it. This study presents the results of a quasiexperiment based on a time-series analysis of crime rates in Jamaica before and after a strict anticrime package was instituted. On April 1, 1974, Jamaica instituted two sweeping laws: the Gun Court Act and the Suppression of Crime Act. Police permits were required for gun ownership and the permits were very difficult to obtain. Punishment for possession of an illegal firearm was intended to be immediate and severe in an announced "war with crime." The specific provisions were:

1. All guns were outlawed except licensed firearms of permit holders and military and police weapons.
2. Indefinite detention (up to life imprisonment) was mandated for those found guilty of gun crimes or illegal gun possession.
3. Searches without warrants were authorized and "raids" were made of homes in certain high crime areas (shanty-towns) to confiscate contraband firearms.
4. Curfews in high crime areas and increased patrols were instituted.
5. A separate pretrial prison for accused gun offenders was used.
6. A specially designed court and prison was constructed for those found guilty of illegal firearm possession.

"An Evaluation of the Jamaican Anticrime Program" by Edward Diener and Rick Crandall, *Journal of Applied Social Psychology,* 1979, Vol. 9, No. 2, pp. 135-146. Reprinted by permission of V. H. Winston & Sons, 7961 Eastern Ave., Silver Spring, MD 20910

7. Gun segments were censored from television and movies (*Daily Gleaner,* 1974).

It's estimated that there were about 25,000 private licensed guns in circulation held by 12 to 15,000 owners from before the laws were implemented (Note 1). More details about the program and the debate leading to the implementation of the laws are presented in Gendreau & Surridge (1978).

There are both similarities and differences between Jamaica and other countries which might try similar programs. Jamaica is an English speaking former colony of Britain, with a self-governing constitutional government. The island is predominately agricultural, but the one major metropolitan area, Kingston, has about 500,000 inhabitants (McFarlane, 1973). Jamaica's population of approximately 2,000,000 persons is mixed racially and religiously (although predominantly Christian) and there is free public education. The major sources of income in Jamaica are agriculture, bauxite mining, and tourism. As in the U.S., there seems to be a "subculture of violence" composed largely of people from "ghetto" (shantytown) areas. A very high percentage of Jamaica's crime occurs within Kingston's slums, but the crime also spills over into Kingston's more prosperous areas. Jamaica's crime rate has been growing at a rapid rate since her independence in 1962, and the homicide rate is currently about 10 per 100,000 people, compared to about 9.3 within the U.S. (Zimring, 1975).

Much of the past research on suppression of crime has focused on the impact of gun control measures. In the majority of these studies, the strictness of gun control laws in many areas (e.g., states) has been correlated with crime rates in those areas. The results of these studies have been mixed, with a tendency to find that gun control reduces crime (e.g., Bakal, 1966; Geisel, Roll, & Wettick, 1969; Hofstadter, 1970; Krug, 1968; Murray, 1975; Zimring, 1968, 1972, 1975). The Jamaican gun acts were part of a more comprehensive social experiment in which an attempt was made to greatly reduce illegally held guns, including both hand guns and long guns. The new prison in downtown Jamaica for firearm offenders looks like a concentration camp, in keeping with the theme, "Jamaican war with crime" (*Time,* 1974). The gun offender prison was painted red and was meant to be a highly visible reminder of the fate of gun offenders. The behavioral scientists who designed the laws and the prison and court procedures were attempting to eliminate the "hero worship" and excitement associated with violence. In order to do this, they censored all firearm segments from television programs (which are largely imported from the United States) and they dealt harshly with those convicted of gun crimes. The reason that the Jamaican data are of such interest is because the Jamaican anticrime program is a broad package of laws which covers the entire country.

METHOD

Jamaican crime statistics for 1964 through 1971 were obtained from the Statistical Yearbook of Jamaica (McFarland, 1973), from the Jamaican Director of Statistics (1972-1974) for 1972, and from the Jamaican Ministry of National Security and Justice for 1973 to 1975 (Note 2). Crime statistics were thus available for an 11-year period. Jamaica uses a crime year beginning April 1 of one year and extending to March 31 of the following year. The statistics available from 1965-1972 were for entire years, whereas monthly figures were available for 1973-1974 and 1974-1975. The gun laws went into effect on April 1, 1974, so monthly crime data are available for the preceding and following year. A time-series analysis was completed, comparing crime trends before and after the gun laws. The data for several crime categories were analyzed, including homicide, rape, robbery, and shooting.

RESULTS

The effects of the new laws can be analyzed both as a change from the previous year and as a change from the trend over the previous 10 years. Table 1 shows data for all 11 years for homicides and rapes. The data reveal that both crimes increased in frequency over the 11-year period. Homicides increased an average of 15% per year prior to the gun laws, while rapes increased at approximately 9% per year. The 1974-1975 crime data show a marked decline for both homicides and rapes. The 1974 homicide rate represents a 14.2% reduction in homicides from the previous year. When the 1974-1975 crime data is predicted based upon a linear regression least squares extension of the previous 10 years, it is predicted that 220 homicides should have occurred in 1974. The actual homicide count of 199 suggests that, based upon long-term trends, the gun laws saved about 21 lives, and confidence interval estimation from the predicted value shows that this decrease could have occurred by chance less than 5 times in 100. The

Table 1 Number of Homicides and Rapes, 1964-1975.

Year	Homicides	Rapes
1964-65	81	312
1965-66	65	331
1966-67	111	351
1967-68	104	377
1968-69	110	352
1969-70	153	429
1970-71	152	553
1971-72	145	544
1972-73	188	571
1973-74	232	641
1974-75	199	447

Note. 1964-1971 data are from Statistical Yearbook (McFarlane, 1973); 1972-1975 data are from the Director of Statistics and the Ministry of National Security and Justice. Gun laws were in effect from the beginning of the 1974 crime year (which began April 1, 1974). Homicides exclude manslaughter.

estimated number of lives saved, based upon the 1973-74 data as a baseline, is as many as 68, but such a figure could be misleading since 1973-74 appeared to be atypically high in homicides.

The linear regression prediction of rapes for 1974-1975 is 653, indicating that the actual figure of 447 was a reduction of 206 rapes below what would have occurred had past trends continued (confidence interval estimation, $p < .01$). This 1974 rape figure represents a 32% reduction in rapes from the previous year. Based upon long-range trends, it appears that the gun laws and anticrime program substantially decreased both homicides and rapes.

More detailed data are available for reporting years 1973-1974 and 1974-1975. Available crime data from April, 1973 to March, 1974, and from April, 1974 to March, 1975 are shown in Table 2. These data were available monthly on firearm and nonfirearm crimes. For purposes of simplicity and compactness, the data are presented by yearly quarters. The monthly crime data were examined with a time-series analysis. This is preferable to more traditional analyses primarily because it takes into account interdependence and trends in the points over time (Bower, Padia, & Glass, 1974; Glass, Willson, & Gottman, 1975; Gottman & Glass, 1978). As it turned out, six of the seven crime categories were identified by the time-series analyses as containing independent points which were then analyzed by traditional t-tests.

It can be seen in Table 2 that firearm homicides decreased substantially ($t(22) = 3.6, p < .002$), whereas nonfirearm homicides actually increased, but not

significantly ($t(22) = 1.5, p < .15$). The nonfirearm homicide increase could represent persons switching from firearms to other lethal means (e.g., Zimring, 1968), or could be due to general trends in homicide increase over the years.

Rapes in both gun and nongun categories fell from 1973-1974 to 1974-1975. Nonfirearm related rapes decreased significantly ($t(22) = 3.64, p < .002$). The gun related rape data showed some interdependence among points (Model 0, 0, 1) and so were analyzed using the time-series program. The analysis revealed that the change in firearm related rapes was nonsignificant ($t(22) = .11$). The percentage of rapes in which guns were used as a threat prior to the gun laws was quite low (about 12%), so we would not expect that the number of rapes would be substantially influenced by the availability of firearms. Yet the incidence of nonfirearm rapes dropped precipitously.

Robberies committed with firearms decreased about 31% from 1973-1974 to 1974-1975, a significant drop ($t(22) = 3.07, p < .01$), and robberies decreased 25% overall. Unlike the pattern for homicides, there was a slight (but nonsignificant) decrease in nongun robberies ($t(22) = .73$, n.s.). Robbery is usually not a crime of impulse or passion. It may be that in a planned crime such as robbery, reducing gun use does not lead to a large-scale substitution of other weapons. There was also a significant decrease in nonfatal shootings ($t(22) = 3.44, p < .01$). Since April 1, 1974, approximately 500 guns have been voluntarily surrendered or confiscated by the police (Criminal Investigation Department, Note 3).

DISCUSSION

The data show that there were overall declines for all categories of crime available for analysis. During the first year after enactment of the law there was a 14% reduction in homicides, a 32% reduction in rapes, a 25% reduction in robberies, and a 37% reduction in nonfatal shootings. Both the monthly and long-term yearly data show the significant decreases in crime. It appears that the anticrime measures adopted in Jamaica led to a substantial decrease in crime. Firearm homicides were reduced substantially, as well as the percentage of homicides committed with firearms. There was some increase in homicide by other methods, but overall there was a reduction in killings. In addition to homicides, there were large decreases in rapes, robbery, and shootings, even when nonfirearm categories are considered. In fact, the impact of the anticrime measures was greatest on crimes other than homicide, where both gun and nongun crimes dropped.

Given the large decreases in crime, the logical question is what components of the anticrime package were responsible for reducing crime? Was the decrease due to fear generated by the severe punishments for gun crimes, to a reduced number of firearms, or to increased police surveillance and curfews? There are indications that fear of gun use and police tactics were heavily responsible for the decrease. It is possible that the decreased number of guns had a relatively small impact. Note first that 500 or so guns were taken out of circulation, which probably does not represent a large proportion of the illegal guns in the country. It is our conjecture that a majority of the illegal guns in Jamaica before the ban were still in circulation a year later. If there were several thousand illegal guns in the hands of potential criminals, most would have remained in circulation, since many guns which were voluntarily surrendered were probably turned in by law-abiding citizens. The 500 firearms in the possession of the police, plus those which have broken and so become unusable, could easily have been replaced by smuggled imports, so it is possible that there was no absolute reduction in guns. Of course, any argument based on the number of guns in Jamaica is bound to be somewhat speculative because nobody really knows the number of illegal guns in circulation. Probably many illegal guns were hidden or buried for possible future use or the day when gun laws become less strict.

Had a decrease in the number of guns produced the reduction in crime, the pattern of crime decrease probably would have been the opposite of what occurred. If guns are taken out of circulation, then there should be fewer firearms as time progresses because all those guns turned in earlier will be gone plus those confiscated in the latest period. As time progressed, additional firearms would be taken out of circulation incrementally, with a concomitant greater decrease in crime over time. Since the decrease in crime was largest initially, it is probable that the reduced number of guns in circulation was not the

Table 2   1974 and 1975 Crime Data Reported by Quarters

Crime	April 1973—March 1974					April 1974—March 1975				
	Spring	Summer	Fall	Winter	Total	Spring	Summer	Fall	Winter	Total
Homicides (excluding manslaughter)										
Firearm involved	39	35	21	29	124	8	8	18	21	55
Nonfirearm	31	36	19	22	108	30	48	32	34	144
Total	70	71	40	51	232	38	56	50	55	199
Percent of homicides in which firearms used	56%	49%	53%	67%	53%	21%	14%	36%	38%	28%
Rapes										
Firearm involved	14	40	16	5	75	7	23	20	17	67
Nonfirearm	164	158	119	125	566	57	113	110	100	380
Total	178	198	135	130	641	64	136	130	117	447
Percent of rapes in which firearms used	8%	20%	12%	4%	12%	11%	17%	15%	15%	15%
Robbery										
Firearm involved	457	373	589	472	1891	272	407	351	280	1310
Nonfirearm	419	500	308	99	1326	139	242	405	321	1107
Total	876	873	897	571	3217	411	649	756	601	2417
Percent of robberies in which firearms used	52%	43%	66%	83%	59%	66%	63%	46%	47%	54%
Nonfatal shootings	229	235	227	188	879	69	156	207	124	556

major factor in suppressing crime. Last, it may be noted that 500 is a small number compared to the numbers of firearm crimes after the gun laws (shown in Table 2). Unless single firearms were involved in large numbers of crimes, the number of gun crimes suggests that there were a large number of illegal guns in circulation after the gun laws. Ultimately, an analysis of the number of illegal guns still in circulation must be somewhat conjectural. It is possible that the 500 guns collected represented a significant number, enough to substantially reduce crime. However, it is our belief, based on the number of guns confiscated and the pattern of crime decrease in the months following the laws, that the decrease in number of guns was not the major cause of the lowered crime rate.

The "get tough" law-and-order message of the gun laws may have reduced crime at least partly through fear of apprehension and lengthy imprisonment. Crime seemed to drop precipitously in all categories during the first quarter after the law went into effect. This quick drop and suggestive rise to earlier levels indicate that fear was at least partly responsible for producing the decrease. Initially, the new laws were widely publicized and fear among criminals of "indefinite detention" was probably quite high. However, as time went by, the people probably became habituated to the laws and hence less fearful. Also criminals learned that many or most crimes still went unpunished, and so the initial fear of the laws probably waned. Related to the psychological fear-inducing impact of the program is another potential effect: the reduction in all crime because of the failure of the populace to really understand the law and perceive its different aspects. In other words, the people may have perceived a global crackdown on crime and concomitant harsh sentences, and thus been more fearful of committing either firearm or nonfirearm crimes.

The homicide statistics also indicate a fear effect because there was a decrease in gun homicides but an *increase* in nongun homicides. Since increased penalties were attached only to gun crimes, it appears that people switched to a method which would bring a less severe punishment if they were apprehended. The increase in nongun firearms should be interpreted cautiously since it was not a statistically significant rise. However, the rise was substantial—a 33% increase over the previous year. It does appear that this rise was due to a switchover effect (not simply to a general rise in crime), since it is the only category

where crime increased and the rise represented a much larger increase than occurred in homicides in previous years. A shift to other weapons for assault agrees with findings of both Zimring (1968) and Geisel et al. (1969) within the U.S. that people will substitute other weapons when guns are less available. However, a shift to assault by other weapons does not offset the decrease in firearm homicides since other weapons are statistically less likely to kill than guns (Zimring, 1968). Thus, based upon patterns in other countries and the size of the increase in nonfirearm homicides, it appears that some switchover to attacks with other weapons probably occurred. However, an interpretation of the nonfirearm homicide increase in terms of a general rise in crime cannot be totally ruled out, but it does appear unlikely since this is the only one of the nongun categories which increased.

The rape data indicate that increased patrols and curfews also deterred crime. Since rape may be a more impulsive crime, it seems likely that the immediate possibility for apprehension or lessened opportunity (because of curfews) would be more likely to reduce the crime than a long-range fear of prison. Probably more convincing is the fact that nongun-related rapes dropped at least as much as those involving firearms. This means that fear of severe punishment probably was not primarily responsible for the decrease, because rapes committed without firearms were subject to the same penalties before and after the gun statutes. Thus, the evidence suggests that rapes were reduced most by police procedures, not by the gun laws per se or fear of greater penalties. In fact, the precipitous drop in rapes suggests most clearly that the anticrime package was more than just an elaborate antigun program (which was the public focus of the program).

The pattern of data for robbery also suggests that enforcement levels were at least partly responsible for decreases in this category. There were decreases for robbery with and without guns, indicating that neither illegal gun confiscation nor fear of the gun laws was solely responsible for the decrease. The decrease in nongun robberies suggests a police enforcement effect similar to that for rape. Alternate interpretations of the nongun crime decreases are that the Jamaican war on crime stimulated a strong national sentiment against crime which served to reduce lawlessness or that people perceived the anticrime program as a total crackdown on crime and thus were more fearful of carrying out all types of criminal activity.

In summary, the anticrime package certainly

reduced crime but the reasons for the reduction cannot be stated unequivocally. The anticrime measures introduced in Jamaica represent a comprehensive social experiment in combating crime, and as such, the impact of the individual components of the program cannot be pinpointed. Indeed, the impact of the laws could have resulted from an interaction of the measures more than from specific factors. Yet the analysis above suggests that some factors decreased crime more than others. The relatively small number of guns collected indicates that a reduction in the number of firearms was not solely responsible for the impact. The nonincremental nature of the crime decrease also suggests that the number of guns in circulation was not the major factor in crime reduction. The impact of fear is suggested by the switch to other weapons for homicides since other weapons did not carry as severe penalties. A fear effect is also suggested by the very precipitous drop in crime when the laws first went into effect. Last, the trends indicate an effect for police enforcement levels. Both robberies and rapes dropped substantially in nongun categories which can more logically be attributed to enforcement than to fear, since no new penalties were initiated for nongun crimes. The reader is referred to Gendreau and Surridge (1978) for a discussion from the perspective of insiders who were involved in the creation and implementation of the anticrime program. Their approach is complementary to the present analysis. There are several major differences in our studies. Their conclusions about the effectiveness of the program are somewhat more optimistic than ours, their emphasis is more on the gun control aspects, they present less data and do not use time-series analyses, they emphasize the historical and political climate, and they do not discuss the possible separate effects of different aspects of the program such as fear and the reduction in the number of illegal firearms.

The figures for the fall and winter quarters of 1974-1975 raise the question of whether the effect of the program was quite short-lived. However, data in most categories indicate that the laws were still reducing crime in the third and fourth quarters after passage, showing that the impact of the law did not totally dissipate. The apparent trend toward declining effectiveness of the laws may only be a short-term trend due to chance variations. It may be that if the strict measures were kept in effect their impact would grow over the years. This could occur if people were gradually impressed with the futility of opposing the new laws. Effective police activity could also result in the gradual confiscation of more guns and arrest of an increasing percent of the criminal element.

Only long-term crime data could clarify what the ultimate effects of the measures would be. Unfortunately, crime data for the second year following the new program have not been available after repeated inquiries to the Jamaican government. During this period there were major political conflicts, falling tourism, and negative publicity about Jamaican crime. The Jamaican government now seems hesitant to publicize anything about crime in Jamaica since this could further decrease tourism. It appears that the long-term effects of his major social experiment may never be known. (See also Gendreau and Surridge (1978) for a discussion of these changes.)

There is often a question about the accuracy of crime statistics (Doleschal & Wilkins, 1972) and if these are not fairly accurate, doubt is cast on the conclusions of the current report. A comparison of Jamaican crime statistics as reported by Interpol (International Criminal Police Organization, 1965, 1967, 1969) and by the Statistical Handbook of Jamaica (1973) reveals a few discrepancies. The data from the two sources are identical in most cases, which casts doubts on the possibility that the crime categories are simply defined differently in the two sources. With so much importance attached to the new programs within Jamaica, deliberate distortion of recent reporting is possible, although this seems unlikely in light of the often complex and not uniformly predictable results. That is, the rather complex trends in the Jamaican data suggest that the statistics were not simply manufactured to impress the public. Personal correspondence with the Jamaican Criminal Investigation Department (Note 3) and one of the psychologists involved in the program (Note 4) indicate that they believe the crime statistics are accurate.

Of course, generalizing from Jamaica to other countries such as the United States can only be done cautiously; the differences between the two countries are too obvious to list. But there are a number of similarities between Jamaica and the U.S.: The homicide rates are roughly similar; both countries are English speaking, capitalistic, and have constitutional governments and an English system of law; both have subcultures of poverty and these subcultures are predominantly responsible for violent crime; crime rates are high and on the rise in both locations; and the majority of crime occurs in the city in both locales. As always, one must be cautious in generalizing from one geographical area to another, but the U.S. and Jamaica are not as dissimilar as one might imagine, based solely on their relative size and wealth.

These data demonstrate that even strict anticrime measures will not eliminate crime, nor reduce crime so that it is no longer a serious concern. While a 14% reduction in homicides and larger reductions in other crime (25% to 37%) represents a substantial reduction in crime, the present data indicate that there will still be a large number of crimes after strict measures are enacted. In other words, a ban on most guns and concurrent enforcement measures can reduce crime, but not eliminate it. It is important to note that crime levels were still substantial after the anticrime measures were in effect, indicating that crime reduction is a multifaceted process that cannot be attained solely by strict law-and-order legislation.

Footnote
[1] Requests for reprints should be sent to Dr. Rick Crandall, Institute of Behavioral Research, Texas Christian University, Ft. Worth, Texas 76129. Thanks to P. Suedfeld, F. E. Surridge, F. E. Zimring and anonymous reviewers for comments on earlier drafts.

Reference Notes
1. C. T. Surridge. Comments on an evaluation of the Jamaican anticrime program.
2. Ministry of National Security and Justice, Headquarters House, P.O. Box 467, Kingston, Jamaica.
3. Personal correspondence, The Jamaican Constabulary, Criminal Investigation Department, P.O. Box 462, Kingston, Jamaica.
4. P. Gendreau, Ontario Ministry of Correctional Services, P.O. Box 100, Burritt's Rapids, Ontario, Canada.

References

Bakal, C. *The right to bear arms.* New York: McGraw-Hill, 1966.

Bower, C. P., Padia, W. L., & Glass, G. V. TMS: Two Fortran IV programs for the analysis of time-series experiments. Boulder, Col.: Laboratory of Educational Research, 1974.

Daily Gleaner, March-May, 1974, Kingston, Jamaica.

Director of Statistics, Department of Statistics, *Volume of Crime, 1972-1974.* 9 Swallowfield Road, Kingston, Jamaica.

Doleschal, E., & Wilkins, L. T. *Criminal statistics crime and delinquency topics: A monograph series.* Washington, D.C.: U.S. Government Printing Office, 1972. DHEW Publication Number (HSM) 72-9094.

Geisel, M. S., Roll, R., & Wettick, R.S. The effectiveness of state and local regulation of handguns: A statistical analysis. *Duke Law Journal,* 1969, *19,* 647-676.

Gendreau, P., & Surridge, C. T. Controlling gun crimes: The Jamaican experience. *International Journal of Criminology & Penology,* 1978, *6,* 43-60.

Glass, G. V., Willson, V. l., & Gottman, J. M. *Design and analysis of time series experiments.* Boulder, Col.: Colorado Associated University Press, 1975.

Gottman, J. M., & Glass, G. V. Analysis of interrupted time-series experiments. In T. R. Kratochwill (Ed.), *Strategies to evaluate change in single subject research.* New York: Academic Press, 1978.

Hofstadter, R. America as a gun culture. *American Heritage,* 1972, *21,* 4-11, 82-85.

International Criminal Police Organization: Interpol. *International crime statistics: 1965-1966, 1967-1968, 1969-1970* (3 volumes). St. Cloud, France: Interpol.

Krug, A. S. The true facts on firearm legislation: Three statistical studies. *Congressional Record,* January 30, 1968, H. 570.

McFarlane, C. P. (Ed.). *Statistical yearbook of Jamaica.* Kingston: Printing Unit, Department of Statistics, 1973.

Ministry of National Security and Justice, *Gun crimes reported to the police, 1973-1975.* Headquarters House, Kingston, Jamaica.

Murray, D. R. Handguns, gun control laws and firearm violence. *Social Problems,* 1975, *23,* 81-92.

Time, Stalag in Kingston. *Time,* 1974, *104,* 55.

Zimring, F. E. Is gun control likely to reduce violent killings? *University of Chicago Law Review,* 1968, *35,* 721-739.

Zimring, F. E. Getting serious about guns. *The Nation,* 1972, *214,* 457-461.

Zimring, F. E. Firearms and federal law: The gun control act of 1968. *Journal of Legal Studies,* 1975, *4,* 133-198.

Driver Education and Fatal Crash Involvement of Teenaged Drivers

Leon S. Robertson, PhD
Paul L. Zador, PhD

Abstract

Fatal crash involvement of teenagers per licensed driver and per population in 27 states was related to the proportions of teenagers who received high school driver education. Among 16-17 year olds, driver education was associated with a great increase in the number of licensed drivers, without a decrease in the fatal crash involvement per 10,000 licensed drivers. About 80 percent of the 16-17 year olds who took high school driver education obtained licenses that they would not otherwise have obtained until age 18 or thereafter. The net effect is much higher death involvement rates per 10,000 population, on average, in states with greater proportions of 16-17 year olds receiving high school driver education. The data suggest that most teenagers would obtain licenses when they are 18-19 years old, irrespective of high school driver education, and indicate that differences among the states in fatal crash involvement rates per 10,000 licensed 18-19 year old drivers were not significantly related to either high school driver education or delayed licensure. (Am. J. Public Health 68:959-965, 1978.)

Teenagers in the United States often learn to operate motor vehicles in high school driver education courses. The number of students enrolled in these courses increased from about one million in the 1961-62 school year to 2.5 million in the 1972-73 school year.[1] Nonetheless, the effects of driver education on

"Driver Education and Fatal Crash Involvement of Teenaged Drivers" by Leon S. Robertson and Paul L. Zador from *American Journal of Public Health,* October, 1978, Vol. 68, No. 10, pp 959–965. Reprinted by permission of American Public Health Association and Leon S. Robertson.

involvement in motor vehicle crashes remains a matter of dispute.

Proponents of driver education believe that such courses reduce the involvement in motor vehicle crashes of drivers who have had the course relative to other drivers.[1] Early studies compared crash records of drivers who had driver education with drivers who had not and found lower average crash rates in the former group.[2]

However, later studies found that factors other than driver education may have accounted for the differences. No controlled experiment of the effects of driver education has been done in U.S. high schools, but a number of studies found that, on average, students who chose to take driver education differed from those who did not. Those who took the course tended to have higher IQs, more intellectual interests, less aggressive or impulsive personalities, and— perhaps most important—they subsequently drove fewer miles per year than those who were licensed without having taken the course.[3-4]

In 1968, a committee advising the Secretary of the U.S. Department of Health, Education, and Welfare stated: "no one has yet produced clear proof that driver education, at least as presently constituted, has a significant favorable effect upon driver attitudes, motivations, performance or other achievements."[5] The following year, a review of driver education by the Highway Research Board of the National Academy of Sciences/National Academy of Engineering concluded "at the present time it is impossible to draw valid scientific inferences regarding the impact of driver education on subsequent driver behavior and performance, particularly as measured by accidents and traffic law violations."[6] A 1975 report to the Congress prepared by the National Highway Traffic Safety Administration drew similar conclusions.[7]

In the same year, the results of a large-scale, English experimental-control study of driver education given to selected students in their sixth form (16-17 year olds) were reported. Its author concluded that "we have, as yet, no evidence at all that driver education has been successful in reducing the accident rate per mile." However, she also reported that the total crash involvement per person among the group that had driver education was higher than among the untrained group because members of the trained group more often obtained driver's licenses. The author concluded that the driver education "accelerated the decision to learn to drive in the short term."[8]

If driver education increases the number of drivers without reducing the crash incidence per driver, the total effect of driver education on crashes would be adverse. Driver education can only be considered an effective loss reduction measure if it reduces the crashes per driver and that reduction is large enough to more than offset any increase in crashes because of increased numbers of persons obtaining licenses and driving earlier than they would otherwise. Because of concern that the pattern observed in the British experiment may be occurring in the United States, particularly with respect to severe crashes, the present study was undertaken.

DATA SOURCES AND METHODS

Participation in driver education courses in public and private high schools is not reported annually. However, reports from many states had been obtained systematically and published by the Insurance Institute for Highway Safety for the school years 1966-67 and 1967-68 as well as for a number of prior years.[9] In addition, the National Safety Council had continued that data collection and publication for the school years 1969-70, 1970-71, and 1972-73.[1] Neither organization had collected or published data for 1968-69 or 1971-72.

Some crashes are not reported to police or insurance companies. Therefore, only involvement in fatal crashes, which are quite accurately reported to official agencies, was considered. Data on fatal crash involvement were obtained from reports of state police or motor vehicle administrations for each calendar year. States where these reports do not include the specific age distributions of drivers involved in fatal crashes were not used in the analysis.

The age distribution of licensed drivers in the states was obtained from an annual report compiled by the Federal Highway Administration.[10] However, the data on licensure prior to 1967 were not used since consultation with the Federal Highway Administra-

tion raised questions concerning the reliability of licensure data from some states prior to 1967. Age distributions of state populations were extrapolated from census data.[11]

Thus, data were available to relate the fatal crash involvement of 16-17 year olds per licensed driver and per population in the calendar years 1967, 1968, 1970, 1971 and 1973 to driver education in the preceding and overlapping school years in many states and for some of these years in a majority of states. States were eliminated from the study if data were not available for 16-17 year olds on any one of the variables of interest—fatal crash involvement, licensure, and high school driver education—in at least two consecutive study years. In total, 103 years of experience with driver education among 16-17 year olds in 27 states were studied. The states and years in which data were available are presented in Table 1.

The effects of high school driver education on fatal crash rates and licensure were considered separately for 16-17 year olds and 18-19 year olds. High school driver education of 18-19 year olds was estimated by the number of people who were enrolled in a given state when those 18-19 years old would have been 16-17 years old.* Since driver education enrollment was not available in the 1968-69 school year, fatal crash data for 18-19 year olds in the 1971 calendar year could not be related to the proportion of 18-19 year olds with driver education in that year and, therefore, data for that year were not used.

Some states require driver education for licensure of persons less than 18 years of age, but most of these states allow exemptions or commercial driving training so that seldom have all licensed drivers under age 18 in a state had high school driver education. In most cases, these states raised their minimum age for licensure to 18 for persons who had not had driver education, but with exemptions. The years in which state laws required driver education for at least some licensees less than 18 years old are also indicated in Table 1.

The possible effect on fatal crash rates of factors other than driver education and licensure was controlled by introducing a composite variable—all motor vehicle deaths in a given state per 10,000 licensed drivers in the state in each year considered. The data were analyzed using an analysis of covariance that took into account the differences in law requiring driver education to be licensed among states, possible fluctuations in time, and the composite total motor vehicle death rate per 10,000 licensed drivers to control for factors contributing to interstate

Table 1 Twenty-seven States and Years
Included in the Study

State	1967	1968	1970	1971*	1973
Arizona			X	X	X
Arkansas			X	X	X
Connecticut	Y	Y	Y	Y	Y
Delaware			Y	Y	Y
Illinois	X	X	X	Y	Y
Indiana	X	X			
Iowa	Y	Y	Y	Y	Y
Kansas			X	X	X	X
Kentucky	X	X	X	X	X
Maine	Y	Y	Y	Y	Y
Maryland	Y	Y	Y	Y	Y
Massachusetts	X	X	X		
Michigan	Y	Y	Y		
Mississippi		X	X	X	X
Missouri	X	X	X		
Montana	X	X	X	X	X
Nevada			X	X	
New Jersey	X	X	X	X	
New York	Y	Y	Y	Y	Y
North Carolina	Y	Y	Y	Y	Y
Ohio	X	X			
Oregon				X	X
Pennsylvania	Y	Y	Y	Y	Y
South Carolina			X	X	X
Virginia	X	X	Y	Y	Y
Washington	Y	Y	Y	Y	Y
Wisconsin			Y	Y	

X Data available and no law requiring driver education to be licensed.

Y Laws require driver education to be licensed at age 16 or 17 with exemptions.

* Data were unavailable for 18-19 year olds in 1971.

variations in fatal crash rates not associated with driver education and licensure of teenagers. The particular method used allows for the missing data in those states for which data were not available in every year.[12]

ANALYSIS

Involvement Per Licensed Drivers. Averages and ranges of values of the principal variables are presented in Appendix 1. The relationships between high school driver education and the fatal crash involvement rate per 10,000 licensed drivers was estimated separately for the 16-17 year old population and the 18-19 year old population. In each age group, parameters were estimated for the equation:

(1) $y_{it} = a + b + c_t + \alpha f_{it} + \gamma u_{it} + r_{it}$

where y_{it} = fatal crash involvement per 10,000 licensed 16-17 year old drivers in state i in year t

a = constant

b = effect of requiring high school driver education for licenses

c_t = effect of fluctuations in time

f_{it} = number of students completing high school driver education in state i in year t per number of licensed drivers

u_{it} = all motor vehicle deaths per 10,000 licensed drivers in state i in year t

r_{it} = residual variation

In the analysis for 18-19 year olds, y_{it} and f_{it} each involved the approprite 18-19 years old rather than 16-17 year olds. If α is no more or less than zero than would be expected from random fluctuation, there is no association between driver education and the fatal crash involvement rate per 10,000 licensed drivers. But, if the effect of driver education, α, is significantly negative, driver education is associated with reductions in the fatal crash involvement per licensed driver. If it is significantly positive, driver education is associated with increases in the fatal crash involvement rate.

Table 2 presents the coefficients fitted to equation 1 and measures of the effects of laws requiring driver education. The table also shows the 95 percent confidence interval for each coefficient and the results of statistical tests for random fluctuation. Among 16-17 year olds, there was no statistically significant relationship between the proportion who took high school driver education and the involvement rate in fatal crashes. Both the estimates of effect of the laws requiring driver education and the estimated coefficients for the effect of the proportion of licensed drivers who took the course are well within the range that would be expected from random fluctuations in sampling. Among 18-19 year olds, similar results are also found. Polynomials of time are not presented in this and subsequent tables because they were not significantly related to any of the factors involved, indicating that it is very unlikely that the results were due to consistent secular variations among the states. The highly significant coefficients for all motor vehicle deaths per 10,000 licensed drivers of all ages indicate that the fatal crash involvement rate per 10,000 licensed 16-19 year old drivers in each state is strongly related to the total fatal crash rate per 10,000 licensed drivers.

Table 2 Relationship between High School Driver Education and Fatal Crash Involvement per 10,000 Licensed Drivers Controlling for Laws Requiring Driver Education and other Factors

16-17 Years Old	Sum of Squares		df	F	p
Effect of Law	16.3		1	2.27	n.s.
Residual	667.3		95		
Total	683.6		96		
		Covariate Effects		t*	p
Proportion of 16-17 year old licensed drivers with driver education (α)		2.2 ± 1.2		1.82	n.s.
All deaths per 10,000 licensed drivers (γ)		1.4 ± 0.2		7.64	<0.001

*df = 95, two-tailed test

18-19 Year Olds	Sum of Squares		df	F	p
Effect of Law	3.7		1	0.61	n.s.
Residual	308.0		71		
Total	305.3		72		
		Covariate Effects		t*	p
Proportion of 18-19 year old licensed drivers with driver education (α)		-0.4 ± 0.9		0.45	n.s.
All deaths per 10,000 licensed drivers		1.7 ± 0.2		9.63	<0.001

*df = 71, two-tailed test

Licensure. The lack of significant relationship between driver education and the fatal crash involvement rate per licensed driver does not necessarily mean that driver education is unrelated to the number of fatal crashes. To measure the possible relationships between driver education and licensure, the parameters of the following equation were estimated:

(2) $v_{it} = a + b + c_t + \beta d_{it} + r_{it}$

where v_{it} = proportion of population age group licensed without high school driver education

d_{it} = proportion of the population age group who had high school driver education

and a, b, c_t and r_{it} are the same as in equation 1.

If $\beta = -1$, the people who had licenses who had had driver education can plausibly be assumed to be the same as those who would have obtained licenses without driver education. In other words, the availability of driver education would not increase the number of licensed drivers. To the degree that β is greater than -1, driver education is associated with increased numbers of licensed drivers.

The estimated coefficients for equation 2 are presented in Table 3. Among 16-17 year olds, the coefficient for the proportion of that aged population with driver education is -0.2, only 20 percent of -1. In other words, there is a reduction of only two 16-17 year olds licensed without high school driver education for every increase of ten 16-17 year olds licensed with high school driver education. This indicates that as much as 80 percent of 16-17 year olds who took high school drivers education obtained licenses that they would not otherwise have obtained until they were at least 18 years old. The coefficient for 18-19 years olds is -0.8, much nearer to -1, indicating that 80 percent of those who had high school driver education would have been licensed when they were 18-19 irrespective of whether they had high school driver education.

The laws that required driver education to be licensed also had some effect, that is, the average proportion of 16-17 year olds licensed without driver education was smaller in states with such laws than in those without them (0.16 and 0.24 respectively). The relationships between the proportion of the population licensed without driver education and the proportions of the population age group with driver education, however, were not affected by the laws. Separate analyses of the data for the states with and without such laws produced coefficients that were essentially the same.

One assumption implicit in equation 2 is that all of the people who take high school driver education also obtained driver licenses. However, one study found only 70 percent licensed within two years after completing the course.[14] This difference is compensated for, at least in part, by the fact that in the present study too few 16-17 year olds were counted as licensed with driver education because those licensed at 16 years of age would be in the 16-17 year old age group at least part of the subsequent year. A sensitivity analysis of the effect of these two possibilities on the estimated effect of driver education on licensure indicated that each offsets the other.

Involvement Per Population.　Since it is very clear from the data that driver education is associated with increased licensure but not with fatal crash involve-

ment per 10,000 licensed drivers, the relationship between driver education and the fatal crash involvement rate per 10,000 population should be adverse.

To determine whether this was so, the relationship between driver education and fatal crash involvement per 10,000 population was estimated in the equation:

$$(3) \quad z_{it} = a + b + c_t + \delta d_{it} + \theta v_{it} + \gamma u_{it} + r_{it}$$

where z_{it} = fatal crash involvement per 10,000 population in the age group

　　d_{it} = proportion of the population age group with driver education

　　v_{it} = proportion of the population age group licensed without driver education

and a, b, c_t u_{it+} and r_{it} are the same as in equation (1).

The estimated effects of laws requiring driver education, and the coefficients for equation 3 are presented in Table 4. Among 16-17 year olds and among 18-19 year olds, the coefficient relating driver education per population and motor vehicle deaths per 10,000 population was about the same magnitude as the coefficient for those licensed without driver education. Thus, given increases in the proportion of

Table 3　Relationship between the Proportion of the Population with High School Driver Education and the Proportion of the Population Licensed Without Driver Education Controlling for Laws Requiring Driver Education

16-17 Years Old	Sum of Squares		df	F	p
Effect of Law	0.1		1	5.17	<0.05
Residual	1.3		97		
Total	1.4		98		
		Covariate Effects		t*	p
Proportion of the population with driver education		-0.2 ± 0.1		2.00	<0.05

*df = 97, two-tailed test

18-19 Year Olds	Sum of Squares		df	F	p
Effect of Law	0.0		1	0.09	n.s.
Residual	1.7		72		
Total	1.7		73		
		Covariate Effects		t*	p
Proportion of the population with driver education		-0.8 ± 0.1		9.48	<0.001

*df = 72, two-tailed test

Table 4 Relationship between High School Driver Education, Licensure without Driver Education and Fatal Crash Involvement per 10,000 Population Controlling for Laws Requiring Driver Education for Licensure and other Factors

16-17 Years Old	Sum of Squares	df	F	p
Effect of Law	0.2	1	0.17	n.s.
Residual	127.7	94		
Total	127.9	95		
	Covariate Effects		t*	p
Proportion with driver education (δ)	5.6 ± 1.1		5.21	<0.001
Proportion licensed without driver education (θ)	5.9 ± 1.0		6.02	<0.001
All deaths per 10,000 licensed drivers (γ)	0.6 ± 0.1		8.10	<0.001

*df = 93, two-tailed test

18-19 Year Olds	Sum of Squares	df	F	p
Effect of Law	0.35	1	0.16	n.s.
Residual	153.30	70		
Total	153.65	71		
	Covariate Effects		t*	p
Proportion with driver education (δ)	7.0 ± 1.2		6.02	<0.001
Proportion licensed without driver education (θ)	6.4 ± 1.1		5.62	<0.001
All deaths per 10,000 licensed drivers (γ)	1.2 ± 0.1		9.62	<0.001

*df = 70, two-tailed test

the population licensed with driver education are associated with increases in the fatal crash involvement per 10,000 population to about the same extent as changes in the proportion licensed without driver education. These relationships are in addition to the effects of the composite variable, motor vehicle deaths per 10,000 drivers, which adjusts for other factors that affect interstate variations in death rates.

Delayed Licensure.   Although high school driver education is associated with the proportion of the population licensed and the population motor vehicle death rates among 16-17 year olds, but not with changes in motor vehicle deaths per 10,000 such drivers, the possibility that those who delay licensure are more involved after their subsequent licensure because of inexperience must be considered. If newly licensed 18-19 year olds have higher fatal crash involvement than those licensed at a younger age, the states that have a higher proportion of 18-19 year olds that were licensed at age 16-17 should have lower fatal crash involvement of 18-19 year olds than those with lower proportions that were licensed at age 16-17.

To examine this, the possible relationships between delayed licensure and fatal crash involvement per 10,000 licensed 18-19 year old drivers were estimated in the equation:

(4) $g_{it} = a + \rho h_{it} + \gamma u_{it} + r_{it}$

where g_{it} = fatal crash involvement per 10,000 licensed 18-19 year old drivers in state i at time t

h_{it} = proportion of licensed 18-19 year olds that were licensed at age 16-17

and a, u_{it}, and r_{it} are the same as in equation 1.

In Table 5, the coefficients for equation 4 are presented. The relationship between the proportion of licensed 18-19 year olds who were licensed at age 16-17 and the fatal crash involvement per 10,000 18-19 year old licensed drivers is well within the bounds expected from random fluctuations in sampling. There is no evidence that delayed licensure was associated with increased fatal crash involvement of 18-19 year olds.

In additional analyses, regression coefficients were estimated separately for the states with and without laws requiring driver education to be licensed. The coefficients indicate parallel relationships among driver education, licensure, and motor vehicle death involvement per licensed driver and per population in states both with and without such laws. The basic conclusions of the study were supported by the results of these analyses.

DISCUSSION

This study finds that high school driver education is associated with substantial increases in the number of drivers licensed among persons 16-17 years old, but is not associated with reductions in the fatal crash involvement rate per licensed driver of that age. The net result is that high school driver education is associated with substantial increase in death involvement per 10,000 population, particularly in the 16-17 year old population. These results are consistent with those found regarding total crash involvement in the large-scale, controlled experiment in England referred to earlier.[8] Based on these two studies, it seems reasonable to conclude that the relationship between driver education and licensure is causal. Both the data and straightforward logic indicate that when more people are trained to do something, more of them do it.

The data from the 27 states analyzed in this report indicate that most teenagers who had high school driver education would not have obtained licenses until they were 18 or 19 if the education had not been available. In addition, the fatal crash rate per 10,000 licensed drivers among 18-19 year olds was unaffected by driver education. Delay of licensure from age 16-17 to age 18-19 also had no effect on fatal crash rate per 10,000 18-19 year old licensed drivers.

In 1975, some 4,000 drivers under 18 years of age were involved in fatal crashes in the United States.[13] In each of about one-half of those crashes, only one vehicle was involved. Either the occupants of that vehicle or pedestrians were killed. Thus, removing drivers under age 18 from the roads would prevent at least 2,000 fatal crashes per year in the United States. Where other vehicles and their drivers were involved,

many of the multiple-vehicle fatal crashes would also not have occurred if the involved teenager had not been driving. For this reason, the estimate of 2,000 fatal crashes that would be prevented if persons under age 18 were not driving is a conservative, minimum estimate.

If the age at which people are first allowed to drive were raised to age 18, the effect of high school driver education in early licensure would be removed. However, the results of the analyses presented in this paper also suggests that such education per se would not thereby be of benefit in reducing fatal crash involvement of those who received the education. It may be that there are sufficient societal reasons to justify allowing people as young as age 16 to operate motor vehicles but the burden of competent proof must rest on those who take this position. Moreover, society must understand the consequences of such a decision, one of which is that large number of such teenage drivers would continue to be involved in motor vehicle crashes fatal to themselves and others.

Although there is no apparent aggregate effect of high school driver education on the fatal crash involvement per licensed drivers among states, it is possible that some programs have small effects, positive or negative, that are not detectable by aggregated statistics. However, since high school driver education would have to reduce fatal crash involvement per licensed driver at least 60 percent merely to offset its effect of increasing licensure among 16 and 17 year olds, it is doubtful that any such program could produce a net reduction in fatal crash involvement unless the minimum licensing age were 18. Studies of commercial schools of driving training[14] and of practice driving on multiple-range driving courses[15] have found resultant crash rates similar to those of students who learned to drive in high school driver education courses. There is no competent research evidence that "advanced" driver education has any effect on crash involvement.

Table 5 Relationship between Licensure at Age 16-17 and Fatal Crash Involvement at Age 18-19

	Effect	t*	p
Proportion of 18-19 year olds licensed at 16-17 (α)	0.9 ± 2.6	0.35	n.s.
All deaths per 10,000 licensed drivers (γ)	1.5 ± 0.2	6.90	<0.001

*df = 33, two-tailed test

Proposals to increase motorcyclist education in high schools, if implemented, would likely worsen the present situation substantially. Motorcycles and mopeds (small motorcycles with pedals) have death rates per vehicle substantially in excess of those of cars.[16] If motorcyclist education in high schools increased the use of these vehicles without reducing fatal crash involvement to the substantial extent necessary to offset the effect of increased licensure, as driver education has done, death rates would soar.

There is also some evidence that motorcycle training may increase crashes and injuries. An English study found a greater average of crashes per mile among persons who had formal motorcyclist education compared with motorcyclists who had learned to ride by other means.[17] In addition, a comparison of motorcylists who had medically treated injuries with a sample of owners of registered cycles in a California county found a greater proportion who acknowledged training in the injured group.[18]

It should be emphasized that the conclusions of the present study apply to fatal motor vehicle crashes. Since the characteristics of motor vehicle crashes involving serious injury are generally similar to those of fatal crashes, it seems likely that these crashes are similarly affected. Run-of-the-mill crashes involving only property damage or minor injuries tend to have quite different characteristics, however, and therefore it is not safe to assume that the conclusions apply to such crashes. Nevertheless, the English study of driver education[8] that found similar results did include all crashes.

It is obvious that no one should operate a motor vehicle on public roads without first learning to drive. Most of the basic skills involved in vehicle operation are usually learned easily but the role of attitudes, peer pressures, and physical and emotional maturity as factors in crash involvements are not well understood. The lack of effect of presently used driver education programs should not deter the search for ways to help young people cope with motor vehicle while at the same time minimimizing damage to themselves and society as a whole.

As with any preventive measure to reduce pathology, programs aimed at such improvement should be demonstrated to be effective in scientifically well-designed experiment before they are adopted for widespread use. Clearly, if driver education is to be expected to reduce the fatal crash involvement of young drivers, it must be thoroughly researched to determine whether improvements are possible, and the best ways to implement them. Any educational or other program that has the potential for increasing exposure to hazards should be evaluated on the basis of total reduction of injury, not just injury per exposure as is commonly done. Programs that increase confidence that risk has been reduced, when in fact it has not, are worse than no programs at all.

References

1. National Safety Council, Driver Education Status Report, Chicago, 1971-72, 1974.
2. Allgaier, E.: Driver Education Reduces Accidents and Violations (no. 3782). American Automobile Association, Washington, DC, 1964.
3. Conger, JJ, Miller, WC, and Rainey, RV: Effects of driver education: the role of motivation, intelligence, social class, and exposure. Traffic Safety Research Review 10:67-71, 1966.
4. McGuire, FL and Kersh RC: An Evaluation of Driver Education. University of California Press, Berkeley, 1969.
5. Moynihan, DP, et al: Report of the Secretary's Advisory Committee on Traffic Safety, U.S. Government Printing Office, Washington, DC, 1968.
6. Harman, HH, et al: Evaluation of Driver Education and Training Programs. National Academy of Sciences/National Academy of Engineering, Washington, DC, 1969.
7. National Highway Traffic Safety Administration, The Driver Education Evaluation Program (DEEP) Study: A Report to the Congress, U.S. Department of Transportation, Washington, DC, 1975.
8. Shaoul, J: The Use of Accidents and Traffic Offenses as Criteria for Evaluating Courses in Driver Education. The University of Salford, England, 1975.
9. Insurance Institute for Highway Safety, Annual Driver Education Achievement Program, Washington, DC, 1967-1968.
10. Federal Highway Administration, Driver Licenses. U.S. Department of Transportation, Washington, DC, 1967-73.
11. U.S. Bureau of the Census, 1970 Census of the Population: General Population Characteristics. U.S. Government Printing Office, Washington, DC, 1972.
12. Dixon, WJ: Biomedical Computer Programs. University of California Press, Berkeley, 637-651, 1973.
13. National Highway Traffic Safety Administration, Fatal Accident Reporting System: 1975 Annual Report, U.S. Department of Transportation, Washington, DC, 1975.
14. Jones, MH: California Training Evaluation Study. California State Department of Motor Vehicles, Sacramento, 1973.
15. Council, FM, Roper, RB, and Sadof, MG: An Evaluation of North Carolina's Multi-vehicle Range Program in Driver Education: A Comparison of Range and Non-range Students. North Carolina Highway Safety Research Center, Chapel Hill, 1975.

16. European Conference of Ministers of Transport, Report By the Committee of Deputies on Road Safety Problems Concerning Two-Wheeled Vehicles, Paris, 1974.
17. Raymond, S and Tatum, S: An Evaluation of the Effectiveness of the RAC/ACU Motor Cycle Training Scheme—Final Report. The University of Salford, England, 1977.
18. Kraus, JF, Riggins, RS, and Franti, CE: Some epidemiologic features of motorcycle collision injuries. I. Introduction, methods and factors associated with incidence. Am J Epidemiology 102:74-97, 1975.

*e.g., the proportion of 18-19 year old licensed drivers in 1973 who had high school driver education was estimated by the number of students who had such education in 1970 and 1971 divided by the number of 18-19 year old licensed drivers in 1973.

From the Insurance Institute for Highway Safety, Watergate Six Hundred, Washington, DC 20037. Address reprint requests to Dr. Robertson. This paper, submitted to the Journal October 21, 1977, was revised and accepted for publication May 15, 1978.

Appendix 1. Averages and Ranges of Values of Principal Variables

	16-17 Year Olds		18-19 Year Olds	
	Average	Range	Average	Range
Fatal crash involvement per 10,000 licensed drivers	9.9	4.2-24.0	10.5	4.1-19.5
Proportion of licensed drivers with high school driver education	0.63	0.16-1.00	0.69	0.11-1.00
Fatal crash involvement per 10,000 population	4.9	1.6-11.2	8.1	3.3-17.1
Proportion of population with high school driver education	0.31	0.07-0.59	0.54	0.07-0.98

Index

Vincent, J. E., 117-18, 159-68
Violence
  assesssment of, and television,
    25-26
  effects of gun control laws on,
    272-74, 306-12
Voluntary participation, 42

Walder, P., 202, 203, 209-19, 223
Walker, J. M., 207, 208, 260-66
Walker, M. R., 59, 102-11
Walker, N. N., 219
Walster, E., 114, 122-31, 133, 216
Walster, G. W., 216
Walters, R. H., 140
We and they, correlation of, with
  winning and losing, 60, 102-11
Webb, E. J., 169, 300
Weber, S. J., 26
Weick, K. E., 1
Weiner, J., 229
Welch, C. E., 79
Welfare programs, effect of, on
  marital stability, 268, 271, 290-97
Welsh, G. S., 129

West, S. G., 10, 36-37, 250, 251, 254
Wettick, R. S., 307, 310
Weurth, J., 219
Wheeler, D., 117-18, 159-68
Wheeler, L., 140
White, G. M., 140
White, R. W., 98, 101
Whitney, G., 10
Wicklund, R. A., 229
Wilke, H., 160
Wilkins, L. T., 311
Williams, J. P., 86
Willis, F. N., 242
Willson, V. I., 308
Wilson, D. W., 40, 41
Wilson, V. L., 299, 300, 301
Winer, B. J., 179, 244
Winett, R. A., 264
Winkler, R. C., 264
Winning and losing, correlation of,
  with use of we and they, 60,
  102-11
Winters, I. C., 173
Wirth, L., 211
Wispe, L. G., 148, 210, 211, 217

Witmer, J. E., 204-5, 235-41
Wolfer, J. A., 56, 71, 77-84, 251
Wolosin, M. A., 183
Wolosin, R. J., 183
Woods, K., 183, 184
Woodworth, R. S., 98
Worchel, P., 132
Worchel, S., 229
Word, C. O., 93
Working poor law, 291
Wright, B. A., 140
Wrong number technique, and
  helping behavior, 116, 142-51
Wylie, R. C., 99, 240

Yarbrough, C., 269, 275-84

Zador, P. L., 273, 313-21
Zajonc, R. B., 183
Zander, A., 85
Zanna, M. P., 57, 92-97
Zero-based budgeting, 35
Zero sum, 121
Zimbardo, P. G., 71, 72, 211, 251, 252
Zimring, F. E., 307, 310